AMERICA'S
TEST KITCHEN

ALSO BY THE EDITORS AT AMERICA'S TEST KITCHEN

The Complete Mediterranean Cookbook

What Good Cooks Know

Cook's Science

Bread Illustrated

Master of the Grill

Kitchen Hacks

100 Recipes: The Absolute Best Ways to Make the True Essentials

The Best of America's Test Kitchen (2007–2017 Editions)

The Complete America's Test Kitchen TV Show Cookbook 2001–2017

The New Family Cookbook

The Complete Vegetarian Cookbook

The America's Test Kitchen Cooking School Cookbook

The Cook's Illustrated Meat Book

The Cook's Illustrated Baking Book

The Cook's Illustrated Cookbook

The Science of Good Cooking

The New Best Recipe

Soups, Stews, and Chilis

The America's Test Kitchen Quick Family Cookbook

The America's Test Kitchen Healthy Family Cookbook

The America's Test Kitchen Family Baking Book

THE COOK'S ILLUSTRATED ALL-TIME BEST SERIES

All-Time Best Appetizers

All-Time Best Soups

THE AMERICA'S TEST KITCHEN LIBRARY SERIES

Naturally Sweet

Foolproof Preserving

Paleo Perfected

The How Can It Be Gluten-Free Cookbook: Volume 2

The How Can It Be Gluten-Free Cookbook

The Best Mexican Recipes

The Make-Ahead Cook

Healthy Slow Cooker Revolution

Slow Cooker Revolution Volume 2: The Easy-Prep Edition

Slow Cooker Revolution

The Six-Ingredient Solution

Pressure Cooker Perfection

The America's Test Kitchen D.I.Y. Cookbook

Pasta Revolution

THE COOK'S COUNTRY SERIES

Cook It in Cast Iron

Cook's Country Eats Local

The Complete Cook's Country TV Show Cookbook

FOR A FULL LISTING OF ALL OUR BOOKS:

CooksIllustrated.com

AmericasTestKitchen.com

PRAISE FOR OTHER AMERICA'S TEST KITCHEN TITLES

"Ideal as a reference for the bookshelf and as a book to curl up and get lost in, this volume will be turned to time and again for definitive instruction on just about any food-related matter."
PUBLISHERS WEEKLY ON *THE SCIENCE OF GOOD COOKING*

"A one-volume kitchen seminar, addressing in one smart chapter after another the sometimes surprising whys behind a cook's best practices . . . You get the myth, the theory, the science and the proof, all rigorously interrogated as only America's Test Kitchen can do."
NPR ON *THE SCIENCE OF GOOD COOKING*

"A wonderfully comprehensive guide for budding chefs . . . Throughout are the helpful tips and exacting illustrations that make ATK a peerless source for culinary wisdom."
PUBLISHERS WEEKLY ON *THE COOK'S ILLUSTRATED COOKBOOK*

"The perfect kitchen home companion . . . The practical side of things is very much on display . . . cook-friendly and kitchen-oriented, illuminating the process of preparing food instead of mystifying it."
THE WALL STREET JOURNAL ON *THE COOK'S ILLUSTRATED COOKBOOK*

"If this were the only cookbook you owned, you would cook well, be everyone's favorite host, have a well-run kitchen, and eat happily every day."
THECITYCOOK.COM ON *THE AMERICA'S TEST KITCHEN MENU COOKBOOK*

"America's Test Kitchen spent two years reimagining cooking for the 21st century. The result is an exhaustive collection offering a fresh approach to quick cooking."
THE DETROIT NEWS ON *THE AMERICA'S TEST KITCHEN QUICK FAMILY COOKBOOK*

"This comprehensive collection of 800-plus family and global favorites helps put healthy eating in an everyday context, from meatloaf to Indian curry with chicken."
COOKING LIGHT ON *THE AMERICA'S TEST KITCHEN HEALTHY FAMILY COOKBOOK*

"There are pasta books . . . and then there's this pasta book. Flip your carbohydrate dreams upside down and strain them through this sieve of revolutionary, creative, and also traditional recipes."
SAN FRANCISCO BOOK REVIEW ON *PASTA REVOLUTION*

"This book upgrades slow cooking for discriminating, 21st-century palates—that is indeed revolutionary."
THE DALLAS MORNING NEWS ON *SLOW COOKER REVOLUTION*

"Forget about marketing hype, designer labels, and pretentious entrées: This is an unblinking, unbedazzled guide to the Beardian good-cooking ideal."
THE WALL STREET JOURNAL ON *THE BEST OF AMERICA'S TEST KITCHEN 2009*

"Expert bakers and novices scared of baking's requisite exactitude can all learn something from this hefty, all-purpose home baking volume."
PUBLISHERS WEEKLY ON *THE AMERICA'S TEST KITCHEN FAMILY BAKING BOOK*

"Scrupulously tested regional and heirloom recipes."
THE NEW YORK TIMES ON *THE COOK'S COUNTRY COOKBOOK*

"If you're hankering for old-fashioned pleasures, look no further."
PEOPLE MAGAZINE ON *AMERICA'S BEST LOST RECIPES*

"This tome definitely raises the bar for all-in-one, basic, must-have cookbooks. . . . Kimball and his company have scored another hit."
THE OREGONIAN ON *THE AMERICA'S TEST KITCHEN FAMILY COOKBOOK*

"A foolproof, go-to resource for everyday cooking."
PUBLISHERS WEEKLY ON *THE AMERICA'S TEST KITCHEN FAMILY COOKBOOK*

"These dishes taste as luxurious as their full-fat siblings. Even desserts are terrific."
PUBLISHERS WEEKLY ON *THE BEST LIGHT RECIPE*

"Further proof that practice makes perfect, if not transcendent. . . . If an intermediate cook follows the directions exactly, the results will be better than takeout or Mom's."
THE NEW YORK TIMES ON *THE NEW BEST RECIPE*

"The best instructional book on baking this reviewer has seen."
THE LIBRARY JOURNAL (STARRED REVIEW) ON *BAKING ILLUSTRATED*

THE COMPLETE
COOKING FOR TWO
COOKBOOK

650 RECIPES FOR **EVERYTHING** YOU'LL EVER WANT TO MAKE

BY THE EDITORS AT
AMERICA'S TEST KITCHEN

AMERICA'S TEST KITCHEN

17 Station Street, Brookline, MA 02445

The complete cooking for two cookbook : 650 recipes for everything you'll ever want to make / by the editors at America's Test Kitchen.

pages cm

Includes index.

ISBN 978-1-936493-83-8

1. Cooking for two. I. America's Test Kitchen (Firm) II. America's test kitchen (Television program)

TX652.C654 2014

641.5'612--dc23

2013043996

Manufactured in the United States of America

10 9 8 7

DISTRIBUTED BY

Penguin Random House Publisher Services

tel: 800-733-3000

PICTURED OPPOSITE TITLE PAGE: Free-Form Summer Fruit Tartlets (page 376)

PICTURED ON BACK COVER: Classic Lasagna (page 231), Warm Chocolate Fudge Cakes (page 403), Grilled Coriander-Rubbed Pork Tenderloin with Herbs (page 260), Chicken Pot Pie (page 122), and Banana Bread (page 354)

EDITORIAL DIRECTOR: Jack Bishop

EDITORIAL DIRECTOR, BOOKS: Elizabeth Carduff

EXECUTIVE EDITOR: Lori Galvin

EXECUTIVE FOOD EDITOR: Julia Collin Davison

SENIOR EDITORS: Suzannah McFerran and Dan Zuccarello

ASSOCIATE EDITOR: Alyssa King

ASSISTANT EDITOR: Melissa Herrick

TEST COOKS: Danielle DeSiato-Hallman, Sara Mayer, Ashley Moore, Stephanie Pixley, and Meaghen Walsh

ASSISTANT TEST COOK: Lainey Seyler

DESIGN DIRECTOR: Amy Klee

ART DIRECTOR: Greg Galvan

ASSOCIATE ART DIRECTOR: Taylor Argenzio

ASSOCIATE ART DIRECTOR, PHOTOGRAPHY: Steve Klise

DESIGNER: Jen Kanavos Hoffman

STAFF PHOTOGRAPHER: Daniel J. van Ackere

ADDITIONAL PHOTOGRAPHY BY: Keller + Keller and Carl Tremblay

FOOD STYLING: Catrine Kelty and Marie Piraino

PHOTOSHOOT KITCHEN TEAM:

ASSOCIATE EDITOR: Chris O'Connor

TEST COOK: Daniel Cellucci

ASSISTANT TEST COOK: Cecelia Jenkins

PRODUCTION DIRECTOR: Guy Rochford

SENIOR PRODUCTION MANAGER: Jessica Quirk

SENIOR PROJECT MANAGER: Alice Carpenter

PRODUCTION AND TRAFFIC COORDINATORS: Brittany Allen and Brit Dresser

WORKFLOW AND DIGITAL ASSET MANAGER: Andrew Mannone

SENIOR COLOR AND IMAGING SPECIALIST: Lauren Pettapiece

PRODUCTION AND IMAGING SPECIALISTS: Heather Dube and Lauren Robbins

COPYEDITOR: Cheryl Redmond

PROOFREADER: Christine Corcoran Cox

INDEXER: Elizabeth Parson

Contents

Welcome to America's Test Kitchen

This book has been tested, written, and edited by the folks at America's Test Kitchen, a very real 2,500-square-foot kitchen located just outside of Boston. It is the home of *Cook's Illustrated* magazine and *Cook's Country* magazine and is the Monday-through-Friday destination for more than 60 test cooks, editors, and cookware specialists. Our mission is to test recipes over and over again until we understand how and why they work and until we arrive at the "best" version.

We start the process of testing a recipe with a complete lack of preconceptions, which means that we accept no claim, no technique, and no recipe at face value. We simply assemble as many variations as possible, test a half-dozen of the most promising, and taste the results blind. We then construct our own recipe and continue to test it, varying ingredients, techniques, and cooking times until we reach a consensus. As we like to say in the test kitchen, "We make the mistakes so you don't have to." The result, we hope, is the best version of a particular recipe, but we realize that only you can be the final judge of our success (or failure). We use the same rigorous approach when we test equipment and taste ingredients.

All of this would not be possible without a belief that good cooking, much like good music, is based on a foundation of objective technique. Some people like spicy foods and others don't, but there is a right way to sauté, there is a best way to cook a pot roast, and there are measurable scientific principles involved in producing perfectly beaten, stable egg whites. Our ultimate goal is to investigate the fundamental principles of cooking to give you the techniques, tools, and ingredients you need to become a better cook. It is as simple as that.

To see what goes on behind the scenes at America's Test Kitchen, check out our social media channels for kitchen snapshots, exclusive content, video tips, and much more. You can watch us work (in our actual test kitchen) by tuning in to *America's Test Kitchen* or *Cook's Country from America's Test Kitchen* on public television or on our websites. Listen in to *America's Test Kitchen Radio* (ATKradio.com) on public radio to hear insights that illuminate the truth about real home cooking. Want to hone your cooking skills or finally learn how to bake—with an America's Test Kitchen test cook? Enroll in one of our online cooking classes. If the big questions about the hows and whys of food science are your passion, join our Cook's Science experts for a deep dive. However you choose to visit us, we welcome you into our kitchen, where you can stand by our side as we test our way to the best recipes in America.

FACEBOOK.COM/AMERICASTESTKITCHEN

TWITTER.COM/TESTKITCHEN

YOUTUBE.COM/AMERICASTESTKITCHEN

INSTAGRAM.COM/TESTKITCHEN

PINTEREST.COM/TESTKITCHEN

AMERICASTESTKITCHEN.TUMBLR.COM

GOOGLE.COM/+AMERICASTESTKITCHEN

Preface

A friend of mine in Vermont, Doug, cooks for two—himself and his 12-year-old daughter. He is not used to cooking every day and always worries about having too many leftovers, especially large cuts of meat. But he also wants good and interesting food, not just the usual standbys—spaghetti sauce 12 ways! And even he, as the cook in the house, realizes that Kraft Mac & Cheese is not a viable option.

For years, the test kitchen didn't take this subset of cooking seriously—after all, it seemed like an easy adaptation of most any recipe. But, after receiving literally hundreds of requests, we went into the kitchen and discovered that "cooking for two" is a lot more complicated than dividing by two. Truth be told, it is a whole new way of cooking.

Here are a few of our test kitchen solutions. Beef stew for two is based on steak tips, not chuck roast. Lasagna can be made in a loaf pan. A soufflé works nicely in a skillet, which also makes it easier. We found a new way to scale back our chocolate chip cookie recipe without losing an ounce of flavor. And mini Bundt pans are perfect for Rich Chocolate Bundt Cakes.

But our new cooking-for-two cookbook is not just about scaling back the classic American repertoire. We also include 150 Fast recipes (Teriyaki-Glazed Steak Tips, Pork Tacos with Mango Salsa, Pasta with Tomato and Almond Pesto...) and 100 Light recipes (Farmhouse Vegetable and Barley Soup, Thai Chicken with Basil, Berry Gratins...).

We also perfected "use-it-up" recipes for difficult leftover ingredients such as cabbage, canned tomatoes, eggplant, buttermilk, and fresh herbs. We investigated the world of cookware to find smaller-scale tools that really help and don't just take up more space. We also tested the best way to store ingredients so that you don't have to use everything all at once—did you ever think about freezing bacon in individual strips? Do you know the best techniques for prolonging the life of fresh herbs and berries? We also went shopping with an eye toward maximum efficiency—broth concentrates are better than canned stocks (just use a teaspoon at a time—the jar keeps for months in the fridge), and boxed wines keep for weeks thanks to their airtight plastic liner.

I know a lot of folks who think about weekday cooking differently than cooking for company. The former is a chore; the latter is a form of entertainment. After 50 years in the kitchen, I no longer make that distinction. Every time I step in the kitchen I expect to learn something, to have some fun, and to turn out something that is a lot more interesting than fuel. Every meal, every dish should have an element of surprise and wonder about it, even if one is cooking for two.

A book preface is always a bit of a sales pitch, although one usually reads a preface after, not before, purchasing a book. However, having spent many decades in and around Vermont, I can assure you that I'm not particularly prone to salesmanship. That reminds me of the story of the waiter at a Vermont church supper. It was summertime, and a lady from the city was staying in Thetford. She had finished the main course and the young waiter—he was just a local teenager—asked if she would like some dessert. She said that she might and inquired what was available. "Pie," said the young man, "apple and mince." She asked what he recommended. He replied, with good native practice and caution, "I don't."

Now I do recommend this volume for anyone who cooks for two, even if only occasionally. It's a good book, it has well-tested recipes, and you will not find them "foolish." (Charlie Bentley, the farmer I used to work for as a kid, used to say that a horse was foolish if it misbehaved. Vermonters don't have much patience with tomfoolery—they are too busy getting chores done.) What I mean by that is that the recipes are sensible—they are workhorse recipes that are practical and taste good. (I plan to give the first copy of this book to my neighbor Doug and then invite myself over for supper to see how things are going!)

Speaking of Charlie Bentley, he fell off of a hay wagon a few years ago. My daughter Caroline asked him if it hurt any. He replied, "The falling didn't hurt; it was the stopping."

Enjoy the book, the recipes, and the cooking.

Cordially,

CHRISTOPHER KIMBALL
Founder,
Cook's Illustrated and *Cook's Country*

The Basics of Cooking for Two

Introduction

The test kitchen has spent more than 20 years developing bulletproof recipes for dishes like meatloaf, lasagna, mashed potatoes, and chocolate cake. Like most recipes, ours typically serve four, six, and sometimes more. But we've realized that households change over time or through circumstance. Our readers started to echo this sentiment—whether they were single parents, empty nesters, or newlyweds, they wanted recipes for the dishes we'd been developing for years, but they wanted them scaled to serve just two.

We understood this challenge; many of our own test cooks cook for two at home. While occasional leftovers can be convenient, eating macaroni and cheese three nights in a row gets tiresome. And even in a household of four, a standard cheesecake often hits the trash before the last slice is eaten. This book is designed to be an all-purpose cookbook for today's smaller households. We included a wide range of recipes—everything you might want to eat during the course of the year. With a clear goal in mind—scale down our favorite recipes to serve two—we headed into the test kitchen to start revamping.

But once we got cooking, we discovered that our mission wasn't going to be so easy. Often there are amounts that don't divide evenly (one egg, for example). And even if you cut a recipe down perfectly, the cooking times and temperatures require adjustment—a small roast cooks faster than a larger one. Sometimes, an entire dish needs to be re-engineered from the ground up. Just how do you make a lasagna for two? You certainly can't use the standard 13 by 9-inch baking dish.

In short, we discovered there are different rules and approaches when cooking for two. And because we have vetted every recipe in our test kitchen, they are just as reliable as our standard recipes—no need to scale recipes yourself and hope they work.

Because households of two can be as time-pressed as larger households, we also looked for new approaches to complicated recipes. We've included streamlined recipes like a Weeknight Beef Stew (page 46) that relies on quick-cooking sirloin steak tips and an Easy Skillet Cheese Pizza (page 94) made in a 12-inch skillet—no preheated baking stone required. More than 150 of the recipes in the book (labeled "Fast" throughout) can be on the table half an hour after you walk into the kitchen. For traditionalists, we also developed a classic, slow-simmered beef stew and from-scratch parlor-style pizza for those occasions when you want to make the ultimate versions. And we've developed a host of healthier recipes (labeled "Light" throughout the book).

This book doesn't just include recipes—we also share what we've learned when cooking for two. For example, waste doesn't just happen with leftovers, it starts with shopping for the ingredients themselves. Proper storage of ingredients is also paramount since a smaller household may take longer to make it through a block of cheese or a box of brown sugar. In the following pages, we share our shopping strategies, storage recommendations, and how best to outfit your kitchen. No, you don't need all new equipment, but there are some specialty items we recommend that will make cooking for two easier. Above all, we aimed to make cooking for two foolproof.

How to Shop Smarter

Grocery stores are designed to entice shoppers to buy more, with buy-one-get-one sales, lower prices for bigger quantities, and everything packaged in "family-size" portions. It can seem impossible to shop for two without a lot of waste, but we've found there are a few simple ways to buy just what you need.

GET CREATIVE IN THE PRODUCE SECTION: Produce is often the most difficult thing to buy for two. Stores sell carrots by the bunch, lettuce by the head, and grapes and cherries in bags of 2 pounds or more. You may have better luck in the organic section, where produce is often sold loose by the pound. (Local farmers' markets are good for this, too.) Many grocery stores have a salad bar—perfect if you need just half a cup of chopped pepper or a handful of lettuce. Frozen fruits and vegetables are also very useful when cooking for two. Individually quick-frozen produce is often as good or better than what you can get fresh—frozen peas and blueberries are two good examples.

TAKE A NUMBER AT THE MEAT COUNTER: If you can buy your meat at a local butcher shop or if your supermarket has a meat counter, go for it. With everything packaged and priced to order, you can purchase just what you need, whether it's ½ pound of ground beef or two chicken breasts. And don't hesitate to buy frozen shrimp; most "fresh" shrimp already has been frozen and defrosted, so it's best to buy it frozen. You can defrost just what you need in minutes under cold running water.

SHOP THE BULK BINS FOR DRY GOODS: Buying prepackaged foods like flour, nuts, rice, and grains is almost always more expensive than buying just what you need from a bulk bin. If your supermarket doesn't have a bulk section, check out a natural foods store.

PAY MORE PER POUND: It's hard to turn down a good deal, and it can seem silly to buy a small package of meat when you could get twice as much for less per pound. However, the alternative is spending more money, buying more than you need, and likely throwing it away when it spoils before you can eat it all. Instead, look for six eggs instead of a dozen, a 4-ounce container of sour cream, or a package of just two pork chops. You'll pay more per pound or ounce, but spend less overall—and what you buy won't end up in the garbage.

LOOK FOR INDIVIDUALLY WRAPPED OPTIONS: Many items are available in single-serving packages that make it easy to use just a small amount and keep the rest sealed. Single-serving containers of yogurt, applesauce, sliced fruit, precooked rice, and even milk and juice can help you scale back on food waste.

BE THOUGHTFUL WHEN BUYING IN BULK: If you do want to shop in bulk to take advantage of lower prices, choose items that will keep well long term. Frozen vegetables and fruits, dried pasta, beans, and rice are all good to buy in bulk. Meat is often significantly cheaper in bulk, so although there will be a slight loss in quality, it can be worth buying in bulk and freezing. Most cuts can be kept frozen for several months; simply buy a large package and separate it into individual portions before freezing. For more information on freezing meat, see pages 6 and 140.

INGENIOUS INGREDIENTS FOR TWO

When you cook for two, you know the frustration of recipes calling for just half a cup of chicken broth or a tablespoon of red wine. Luckily, there are a few handy ingredients that make it easy to use smaller amounts and avoid waste.

BOUILLON AND BROTH CONCENTRATES: Dehydrated and concentrated forms of chicken and beef broth, these shelf-stable products are cost-effective (because you're not paying for the water) and last for up to two years once opened. Simply mix with water to make just as much broth as you need. We particularly like **Better than Bouillon Chicken Base**, which costs just $5.99 for a jar that makes 38 cups of broth.

BOXED WINE: Once opened, bottles of wine are rarely usable for more than a week. But boxed wine has an airtight inner bag that prevents exposure to oxygen even after the box is opened, so the wine lasts up to one month. Or, for easy substitutions for wine, see page 8.

NO-PREP AROMATICS: Most savory recipes call for onion or garlic. To save time on shopping and prep, we've found easy alternatives to both. An equal amount of store-bought frozen chopped onions can be used in place of fresh chopped onions in any recipe. You can also chop extra onion and freeze it in a zipper-lock bag to have on hand. And if you don't have fresh garlic on hand, you can swap ¾ teaspoon granulated garlic for 1 teaspoon fresh minced garlic.

SHALLOTS: Onions add great aromatic flavor to recipes, but a single onion is often too much for a recipe for two. To avoid forgotten onion halves going bad at the back of your fridge, you can swap them for shallots, another allium that offers a similar flavor in a much smaller package—a single shallot will yield just a few tablespoons when minced.

DRIED HERBS: Fresh herbs have a very short shelf life, and when a recipe calls for a single sprig, the rest of the bunch can easily go to waste. Luckily, as long as the herbs are cooked, you can substitute long-lasting dried herbs; this works especially well with sage, rosemary, and thyme. Just use one-third the amount called for. You can also dry your own fresh herbs to keep them from going bad; see page 13 for our recipe for Easy Dried Herbs.

How to Store Smarter

Despite your best intentions at the supermarket and in the kitchen, there are some ingredients that you might end up tossing out because they've gone bad before you've had time to finish them. In the test kitchen, we've developed useful strategies to help preserve the freshness of these pesky ingredients.

BACON: Recipes for two rarely call for more than a few slices of bacon; luckily, it freezes very well. But wrestling just one or two slices from a solid block of frozen bacon is a chore. Instead, simply roll up one or two slices into a tight cylinder, place the cylinders in a zipper-lock bag, and freeze them. Then you can easily pull out a few slices as needed.

BERRIES: Because they are prone to mold, wash berries before storing. Swish them in a solution of 3 parts water and 1 part vinegar, rinse, then dry thoroughly in a paper towel–lined salad spinner. Store in a loosely covered, paper towel–lined container.

BREAD: Crusty bread, like a rustic Italian loaf, will last a few days simply stored cut side down on the counter. Do not store it in plastic (the moisture encourages mold) or in the refrigerator, where bread stales faster than at room temperature. For longer storage, wrap the bread tightly in aluminum foil, place it in a zipper-lock bag, and store in the freezer for up to one month. To serve, bake the frozen foil-wrapped loaf directly on the rack of a 450-degree oven until warm and crisp, 10 to 30 minutes.

BUTTER: When stored in the fridge, even when wrapped, butter can pick up odors and turn rancid within just a few weeks. When you buy a pound of butter, store it in the freezer for up to four months and transfer it to the fridge one stick at a time as needed.

CHEESE: We find that cheeses are best wrapped in parchment paper and then in aluminum foil and refrigerated. The paper allows the cheese to breathe, and the foil keeps out off-flavors from the refrigerator and prevents the cheese from drying out.

CHILES: Fresh chiles like jalapeños and serranos quickly lose their flavor and crispness when left loose in the crisper drawer, but they will keep for several weeks halved then stored in a brine of 1 tablespoon salt per cup of water; rinse before using.

CHOCOLATE: Because cocoa butter easily picks up off-flavors from other foods, chocolate should never be stored in the refrigerator or freezer. To extend its shelf life, wrap it tightly in plastic wrap and store it in a cool, dry place. When exposed to rapid changes in temperature or humidity, it can develop a discolored surface. This condition, known as bloom, is only cosmetic—bloomed chocolate is safe to eat and cook with.

ROLL AND FREEZE: Roll up one or two slices of bacon at a time into tight cylinder, place cylinders in zipper-lock bag, and freeze.

SPIN AND STORE: Wash greens and dry thoroughly in salad spinner, then store directly in spinner between layers of paper towels, or lightly roll in paper towels and store in partially open zipper-lock bag; transfer to refrigerator.

PORTION AND FREEZE: Place portions of meat at separate locations inside zipper-lock freezer bag. Flatten out bag, forcing air out, so that meat portions do not touch. Fold bag over in center and freeze. (See more about freezing meat on page 6.)

STAND 'EM UP: To prolong freshness, stand scallions, chives, and leeks in 1 inch of water in tall container covered loosely with zipper-lock bag and refrigerate. (See more about storing alliums on page 7.)

PUT A LABEL ON IT: Label each spice jar with the date opened. Replace ground spices after one year and whole spices after two years. (See more about storing spices on page 7.)

Different types of produce have different storage requirements; some need to be placed in the coldest part of the refrigerator, some need humidity, and some don't need to be chilled at all. Storing your produce under the appropriate conditions is the key to prolonging its shelf life.

IN THE FRONT OF THE FRIDGE

These items are sensitive to chilling injury and should be placed in the front of the fridge, where the temperatures tend to be higher.

Berries	Corn on the Cob	Peas
Citrus	Melons	

IN THE CRISPER

These items do best in the humid environment of the crisper.

Artichokes	Cauliflower	Green Beans	Radishes
Asparagus	Celery	Leafy Greens	Scallions
Beets	Chiles	Leeks	Summer Squash
Broccoli	Cucumbers	Lettuce	
Cabbage	Eggplant	Mushrooms	Turnips
Carrots	Fresh Herbs	Peppers	Zucchini

CHILL ANYWHERE

These items are not prone to chilling injury and can be stored anywhere in the fridge (including its coldest zones), provided the temperature doesn't freeze them.

Apples	Cherries	Grapes

ON THE COUNTER

Some produce is sensitive to chilling injury, making it subject to dehydration, internal browning, and/or internal and external pitting if stored in the refrigerator.

Apricots	Kiwis*	Papayas	Pineapple
Avocados*	Mangos	Peaches	Plums
Bananas*	Nectarines	Pears	Tomatoes

*Once they've reached their peak ripeness, these fruits can be stored in the refrigerator to prevent overripening, but some discoloration may occur.

IN THE PANTRY

The following produce should be kept at cool room temperature and away from light to prevent sprouting (in the case of potatoes) and to prolong shelf life.

Garlic	Potatoes	Sweet Potatoes
Onions	Shallots	Winter Squash

EGGS: Properly stored eggs will last up to three months, but both the yolks and the whites become looser and their flavor will begin to fade over time. Store eggs in the back of the refrigerator (the coldest area) and keep them in the carton, which holds in moisture and protects the eggs from odors.

FLOUR: All-purpose flour is one ingredient that is useful to purchase in larger amounts. To keep our flour fresh, we store it in a wide-mouth container, which also makes it easy to dip in a measuring cup and level off the excess back into the container. All-purpose flour can be stored in the pantry for up to a year, but whole-grain flours like whole-wheat and rye are more perishable and should be stored in the freezer.

FRESH HERBS: Because they're highly perishable and sold in large bunches, herbs are one of the hardest things to avoid throwing out. To get the most life out of herbs, gently rinse and dry them (a salad spinner works well), wrap them in a damp paper towel, and place in a partially open zipper-lock bag in the crisper drawer. Basil, however, should be handled differently. Don't rinse it before you need to use it; the added moisture will decrease its shelf life. Simply wrap it in clean paper towels, place it in a partially open zipper-lock bag, and refrigerate.

GARLIC: Store heads of garlic in a cool, dark place with plenty of air circulation to prevent spoiling and sprouting. Store cut garlic in oil in the refrigerator for no more than four days.

GINGER: When wrapped in plastic or foil, ginger will grow mold where the condensation is trapped, so it's best to simply toss it into the refrigerator unwrapped.

GREENS: Delicate greens spoil quickly if not stored properly. Wash greens and dry thoroughly in a salad spinner, then store directly in the spinner between layers of paper towels, or lightly roll in paper towels and store in a zipper-lock bag left slightly open. If prewashed, store in the original plastic container or bag.

LEAVENERS: Keep baking powder and baking soda in the pantry and replace them every six months. Keep yeast in the refrigerator or freezer to slow its deterioration. And because yeast is a living organism, observe the expiration date.

MEAT: Raw or cooked meat should be refrigerated well wrapped and will keep for two to three days. To freeze meat in small batches for long-term storage, place two pieces of meat (such as chicken breasts, small steaks, or portions of ground meat) at different locations inside a large zipper-lock freezer bag. Flatten out the bag, forcing the air out, so that the meat portions do not touch. Then fold the bag over in the center and freeze it.

MUSHROOMS: Thanks to their high moisture content, raw mushrooms are very perishable. To maximize air circulation without drying out mushrooms, store them wrapped in plastic in their original packaging or in a partially open zipper-lock bag.

OILS: To prevent rancidity, store cooking oils in a cool, dark pantry. Unopened olive oil lasts for one year; once opened, it will last for about three months. Toasted sesame oil and nut oils, like peanut oil, should be stored in the refrigerator.

ONIONS AND OTHER ALLIUMS: Onions and shallots should be stored in a cool place away from light. Don't store onions in the refrigerator; their odor can permeate other foods. Delicate scallions, chives, and leeks do belong in the refrigerator; store them in a glass of water covered loosely with a zipper-lock bag. To store part of a chopped or sliced onion, refrigerate in a zipper-lock bag and rinse before using to remove residual odor.

POTATOES: If not stored correctly, potatoes will germinate and grow. To avoid this, keep them in a cool, dark place. Store them in a paper (not plastic) bag and keep them away from onions, which give off gases that will hasten sprouting.

SPICES: Keep spices in a cool, dark pantry to prolong their freshness. To keep track of your spices' freshness, it's helpful to label each jar with the date opened; whole spices are good for about two years and ground spices for one year.

SWEETENERS: Store brown sugar in an airtight container; a terra-cotta Brown Sugar Bear will help keep it soft. Keep molasses and honey in the pantry (they will crystallize in the refrigerator). Maple syrup should be refrigerated, as it is susceptible to mold. Syrup also can be kept in the freezer (it will not freeze solid because of its high sugar concentration).

TOMATOES: Because they're sensitive to chilling injury and will turn mealy in the refrigerator, tomatoes should be stored on the counter; place them stem side down to prolong their shelf life. Cut tomatoes can be stored tightly wrapped at room temperature for a few days.

10 THINGS YOU DIDN'T KNOW YOU COULD FREEZE

When it's not possible to use leftover ingredients immediately, we turn to the freezer for longer-term storage. You'll be surprised at some of the things you can keep frozen.

FOOD	PREP FOR FREEZER	STORAGE AND USE
Bananas	Peel bananas and freeze in zipper-lock freezer bag.	Defrost and use to make banana bread or muffins, or drop into blender while still frozen for fruit smoothies.
Butter	Stored in the refrigerator, butter can pick up off-flavors. Instead, freeze butter in its wrapper.	Transfer to refrigerator 1 stick at a time as needed. To quickly soften frozen butter, cut into small pieces or place in zipper-lock bag and pound to desired consistency with rolling pin.
Buttermilk	Place some small paper cups on tray and fill each with ½ cup buttermilk; place tray in freezer.	Once buttermilk is frozen, wrap each cup in plastic wrap and store in large zipper-lock freezer bag. Defrost in refrigerator before use.
Canned chipotle chiles in adobo	Spoon out chiles, each with a couple teaspoons of adobo sauce, onto different areas of baking sheet lined with parchment paper and freeze.	Transfer frozen chiles to zipper-lock freezer bag for long-term storage.
Cheese	Wrap hard and semifirm cheeses like Parmesan, cheddar, and Brie tightly in plastic wrap, seal in zipper-lock bag, and freeze.	Store in freezer for up to 2 months. Defrost in refrigerator before using.
Citrus zest	Remove zest from entire fruit. Deposit grated zest in ½-teaspoon piles on plate and freeze.	Once piles are frozen, place them in zipper-lock freezer bag and return them to freezer.
Egg whites	Pour leftover egg whites (never yolks) into each well of ice cube tray and freeze.	Use paring knife or small spatula to remove each frozen egg white cube and defrost in small bowl in refrigerator as needed.
Herbs	Place 2 tablespoons chopped fresh rosemary, sage, parsley, or thyme and water to cover (about 1 tablespoon) in each well of ice cube tray and freeze.	Once cubes are frozen, transfer to zipper-lock freezer bag and store. Add cubes directly to sauces, soups, or stews.
Nuts	Due to their high fat content, nuts go rancid quickly unless frozen. Freeze nuts in zipper-lock freezer bag.	Frozen nuts stay fresh for months. No need to defrost before using; frozen nuts can be chopped just as easily as fresh.
Wine	Measure 1 tablespoon wine into each well of ice cube tray and freeze.	Use paring knife or small spatula to remove each frozen wine cube and add as desired to pan sauces.

Emergency Substitutions

When you're shopping for just two, it's often impractical to stock half-and-half as well as heavy cream or both light and dark brown sugar, and no one wants to run out to the market for just one ingredient. But often a simple substitution can save you the hassle. Here is a list of common ingredients frequently called for in recipes and their recommended substitutes.

TO REPLACE	AMOUNT	SUBSTITUTE				
Whole Milk	½ cup	5 tablespoons skim milk + 3 tablespoons half-and-half ⅓ cup 1 percent low-fat milk + ⅙ cup half-and-half ⅜ cup 2 percent low-fat milk + 2 tablespoons half-and-half 7 tablespoons skim milk + 1 tablespoon heavy cream				
Half-and-Half	½ cup	⅜ cup whole milk + 2 tablespoons heavy cream ⅓ cup skim or low-fat milk + ⅙ cup heavy cream				
Heavy Cream	½ cup	½ cup evaporated milk **Not suitable for whipping or baking, but fine for soups and sauces.**				
Eggs		LARGE	JUMBO	EXTRA-LARGE	MEDIUM	For half of an egg, whisk the yolk and white together and use half of the liquid.
		1	1	1	1	
		2	1½	2	2	
		3	2½	2½	3½	
		4	3	3½	4½	
		5	4	4	6	
		6	5	5	7	
Buttermilk	½ cup	⅜ cup plain whole-milk or low-fat yogurt + 2 tablespoons whole milk ½ cup whole milk + 1½ teaspoons lemon juice or distilled white vinegar **Not suitable for raw applications, such as a buttermilk dressing.**				
Sour Cream	½ cup	½ cup plain whole-milk yogurt **Nonfat and low-fat yogurts are too lean to replace sour cream.**				
Plain Yogurt	½ cup	½ cup sour cream				
Cake Flour	1 cup	⅞ cup all-purpose flour + 2 tablespoons cornstarch				
Bread Flour	1 cup	1 cup all-purpose flour **Bread and pizza crusts may bake up with slightly less chew.**				
Baking Powder	1 teaspoon	¼ teaspoon baking soda + ½ teaspoon cream of tartar (use right away)				
Light Brown Sugar	½ cup	½ cup granulated sugar + 1½ teaspoons molasses		Pulse the molasses in a food processor along with the sugar or simply add it along with the other wet ingredients.		
Dark Brown Sugar	½ cup	½ cup granulated sugar + 1 tablespoon molasses				
Confectioners' Sugar	½ cup	½ cup granulated sugar + ½ teaspoon cornstarch, ground in a blender (not a food processor) **Works well for dusting over cakes, less so in frostings and glazes.**				
Fresh Herbs	1 tablespoon	1 teaspoon dried herbs				
Wine	¼ cup	¼ cup broth + ½ teaspoon wine vinegar (added just before serving) ¼ cup broth + ½ teaspoon lemon juice (added just before serving) **Vermouth makes an acceptable substitute for white wine.**				
Unsweetened Chocolate	1 ounce	3 tablespoons cocoa powder + 1 tablespoon vegetable oil 1½ ounces bittersweet or semisweet chocolate (remove 1 tablespoon sugar from the recipe)				
Bittersweet or Semisweet Chocolate	1 ounce	⅔ ounce unsweetened chocolate + 2 teaspoons sugar **Works well with fudgy brownies. Do not use in a custard or cake.**				

Putting Leftover Ingredients to Work

When cooking in smaller quantities, it's unavoidable that you'll end up with some leftover ingredients. Whether it's half a butternut squash or part of a can of beans or tomatoes, these odds and ends tend to languish in the refrigerator until they have to be thrown away. Our solution? Quick, simple recipes that make it easy to put these ingredients to work.

Bread

A family of two would have to eat sandwiches for days to use up an entire loaf of bread or a whole baguette. Bread can be frozen for up to one month, or you can try our recipes for decadent chocolate bread pudding, berry gratin, or easy garlicky croutons.

Garlic Croutons

MAKES 2 CUPS **FAST**

Heat oven to 350 degrees. Toss 4 slices hearty white sandwich bread, cut into ½-inch pieces, with 2 tablespoons melted unsalted butter and 1 minced garlic clove. Season with salt and pepper. Spread onto rimmed baking sheet and bake until golden brown and crisp, 15 to 20 minutes, stirring occasionally.

Summer Berry Gratin

SERVES 2

Heat oven to 450 degrees. Pulse 2 slices hearty white sandwich bread, 2 tablespoons brown sugar, 2 tablespoons softened unsalted butter, and pinch ground cinnamon in food processor to coarse crumbs, about 10 pulses. Gently toss 1½ cups blackberries, blueberries, raspberries, and/or quartered strawberries with 1 teaspoon granulated sugar, ¼ teaspoon vanilla extract, and pinch salt, then spread into 7¼ by 5¼-inch baking dish. Sprinkle crumb mixture evenly over fruit and bake until crumbs are deep golden brown and fruit is hot, 15 to 20 minutes, rotating dish halfway through baking. Let cool slightly before serving.

Individual Chocolate Bread Puddings

SERVES 2

Heat oven to 325 degrees. Whisk 1 large egg and 3 tablespoons sugar together in large bowl. Whisk in 1 cup half-and-half and ½ teaspoon vanilla. Stir in 2 ounces chopped bittersweet chocolate and 2½ cups ½-inch cubes baguette. Cover and soak for 20 minutes, stirring often. Portion mixture into 2 large greased, ovensafe coffee cups (or ramekins) and bake until puddings are set, 25 to 30 minutes. Let cool slightly before serving.

Buttermilk

Buttermilk is generally only sold by the quart, so when recipes call for a small amount you're stuck with lots of leftovers. You can refrigerate it for up to three weeks (with some flavor loss) or freeze it for up to two months, but we prefer to put it to work.

Very Berry Smoothie

SERVES 2 **FAST** LIGHT

For the nutritional information for this recipe, see page 412.

Process 1½ cups buttermilk, 1½ cups frozen berries, 1 peeled and chopped banana, 1 tablespoon sugar, and pinch salt on low speed in blender until berries are chopped, about 10 seconds. Increase speed to high and continue to process until smooth, 20 to 40 seconds. Season with more sugar and adjust consistency with water as needed. Serve.

Ranch Dressing

MAKES 1 CUP **FAST**

Whisk ⅔ cup sour cream, ¼ cup buttermilk, 2 tablespoons minced fresh cilantro (or dill, tarragon, or parsley), 1 tablespoon minced shallot, 2 teaspoons white wine vinegar, ½ teaspoon granulated garlic, ¼ teaspoon salt, and ¼ teaspoon pepper together until smooth. Season with sugar to taste.

Muffin Tin Doughnuts

MAKES 4 DOUGHNUTS

Heat oven to 400 degrees. Whisk 1¼ cups cake flour, ⅓ cup sugar, 1¼ teaspoons baking powder, ¼ teaspoon salt, and pinch nutmeg together in large bowl. In separate bowl, whisk ⅓ cup buttermilk, 3 tablespoons melted unsalted butter, and 1 large egg together. Stir buttermilk mixture into flour mixture until combined. Scoop batter into 4 greased wells of muffin tin and bake until lightly browned and toothpick inserted in center comes out clean, 15 to 18 minutes. Mix ½ cup sugar and ½ teaspoon ground cinnamon together in small bowl. Brush warm donuts with 2 tablespoons melted unsalted butter, then roll in cinnamon sugar to coat. Serve.

Butternut Squash

Once chopped, a single butternut squash can yield up to 8 or 9 cups—far too much for just two people. And since it can't be eaten raw like some vegetables, using it up isn't as easy as tossing it into a salad. Luckily, our recipes for leftover butternut squash are so good, you might not want to wait to have leftovers.

Roasted Butternut Squash Salad

SERVES 2

Heat oven to 425 degrees. Toss 1 pound butternut squash, peeled, seeded, and cut into 1-inch pieces (2½ cups), with 1 tablespoon extra-virgin olive oil and ¼ teaspoon salt; spread onto rimmed baking sheet. Roast until squash is spotty brown and tender, 30 to 35 minutes, stirring occasionally. Toss roasted squash with 4 ounces arugula, ¼ cup dried cranberries, 1 tablespoon extra-virgin olive oil, and 2 tablespoons cider vinegar. Season with salt and pepper to taste and serve.

Butternut Squash Breakfast Hash

SERVES 2   FAST

Microwave 1 pound butternut squash, peeled, seeded, and cut into ½-inch pieces (2½ cups), and 1 cup water in covered bowl until tender, 5 to 8 minutes; drain. Cook 2 slices chopped bacon in 12-inch nonstick skillet over medium-high heat until crisp, about 5 minutes; transfer to paper towel–lined plate. Add 1 chopped onion and 1 teaspoon paprika to fat left in skillet and cook over medium heat until softened, about 5 minutes. Add squash and cook, stirring often, until lightly browned, about 10 minutes. Sprinkle with bacon, season with salt and pepper to taste, and serve.

Cabbage

Inexpensive, healthy, and delicious, cabbage is a great addition to any recipe. But what do you do with leftovers? How about making creamy coleslaw, roasting it, or pickling it for kimchi?

Creamy New York Deli Coleslaw

SERVES 2

Toss 4½ cups shredded green cabbage (½ small head) and 1 peeled and grated carrot with ½ teaspoon salt in colander and let drain for 1 hour; rinse and pat dry with paper towels. In large bowl, whisk ¼ cup mayonnaise, 2 tablespoons minced shallot, 1 tablespoon distilled white vinegar, ½ teaspoon Dijon mustard, and ½ teaspoon sugar together. Stir in cabbage and season with salt and pepper to taste. Cover and refrigerate until chilled, at least 30 minutes, before serving.

Roasted Cabbage Wedges

SERVES 2   FAST

Place rimmed baking sheet on upper-middle rack and heat oven to 450 degrees. Combine ½ teaspoon sugar, ½ teaspoon pepper, and ¼ teaspoon salt in small bowl. Cut ½ small head green or napa cabbage through core into quarters. Brush with 2 tablespoons vegetable oil and sprinkle with sugar mixture. Place cabbage wedges on hot baking sheet, flat side down, and roast until tender and browned at edges, 15 to 20 minutes, flipping wedges halfway through roasting. Drizzle with 1 teaspoon balsamic vinegar and serve.

Quick Kimchi

MAKES 2 CUPS   FAST   LIGHT

For the nutritional information for this recipe, see page 412.

Toss 4 cups coarsely chopped napa cabbage (½ small head) with ¼ cup water and microwave until slightly softened, about 3 minutes. Drain cabbage and let cool slightly, about 5 minutes. Toss drained cabbage with 2 thinly sliced scallions, 1 tablespoon rice vinegar, 1 tablespoon Asian chili-garlic sauce, 1½ teaspoons sugar, and 1 teaspoon fish sauce. Season with salt to taste.

Canned Beans

Canned beans are particularly convenient when cooking for two because they're quick-cooking and don't require lengthy soaking times. And there's no need to toss the leftovers when you use just part of a can; here are our favorite recipes for using the rest.

Crispy Spiced Chickpeas

MAKES ⅔ CUP   FAST

Combine ¼ teaspoon smoked paprika, ⅛ teaspoon sugar, ⅛ teaspoon salt, and pinch pepper in medium bowl. Heat ¼ cup vegetable oil in 8-inch skillet over medium-high heat until just smoking. Carefully add ¾ cup rinsed and dried canned chickpeas to hot oil and cook until crisp throughout and dark brown, 10 to 15 minutes. Using slotted spoon, transfer hot chickpeas to bowl with spices and toss to coat. Let cool slightly before serving.

Kidney Bean Salad

SERVES 2   LIGHT

For the nutritional information for this recipe, see page 412.

Toss ¾ cup rinsed canned kidney beans (or cannellini beans), 1 peeled and thinly sliced small carrot, 1 thinly sliced celery rib, 1 thinly sliced small shallot, 1 tablespoon white wine vinegar, 1 tablespoon extra-virgin olive oil, 1 tablespoon chopped fresh parsley, and ¼ teaspoon salt in bowl and let marinate for 30 minutes. Season with salt and pepper to taste and serve.

Refried Beans

MAKES 1 CUP **FAST**

Process ¾ cup rinsed canned pinto beans (or red kidney beans or black beans) and ¼ cup chicken broth in food processor until smooth, about 30 seconds. Heat 2 tablespoons olive oil in 10-inch nonstick skillet over medium heat until shimmering. Add ¼ cup finely chopped onion and cook until softened, 2 to 4 minutes. Stir in 1 minced garlic clove and ⅛ teaspoon ground cumin and cook until fragrant, about 30 seconds. Stir in processed beans and cook until thickened, 3 to 5 minutes. Season with salt and pepper to taste and serve.

Garlicky Sautéed White Beans with Tomatoes

SERVES 2 **FAST**

Cook 2 thinly sliced garlic cloves with 2 tablespoons olive oil in 8-inch skillet over medium-low heat until fragrant and lightly golden, about 3 minutes. Stir in ¾ cup rinsed canned cannellini beans (or small white beans), 1 chopped tomato, and ¼ teaspoon salt. Increase heat to medium-high and cook, stirring often, until tomatoes are softened and beans are heated through, about 3 minutes. Off heat, stir in 1 tablespoon chopped fresh basil (or parsley, cilantro, chives, dill, or scallions). Season with salt and pepper to taste and serve.

Canned Tomatoes

Because canned tomatoes are of consistent quality year-round, we reach for them often in recipes. But not every recipe uses an entire can. Here's how to avoid letting them go to waste.

Quick Tomato Salsa

MAKES ½ CUP **FAST** **LIGHT**

For the nutritional information for this recipe, see page 412.

Pulse ½ cup drained canned diced tomatoes, 1 tablespoon minced shallot, 1 tablespoon minced fresh cilantro, and pinch cayenne pepper in food processor until roughly chopped, about 8 pulses. Transfer to fine-mesh strainer and let drain for 1 minute. Transfer to serving bowl and stir in 1 teaspoon lime juice. Season with salt and pepper to taste.

Spicy Chipotle Barbecue Sauce

MAKES ABOUT ¾ CUP

Melt 1 tablespoon unsalted butter in medium saucepan over medium heat. Add 1 minced shallot and ½ teaspoon chili powder and cook until shallot is softened, about 2 minutes. Stir in ½ cup drained canned diced tomatoes and cook until softened and dry, about 1 minute. Add ¼ cup ketchup, ¼ cup chicken broth, 2 tablespoons brown sugar, 2 teaspoons white vinegar, and ½ teaspoon minced canned chipotle chile in adobo sauce. Bring to simmer and cook until thickened, about 20 minutes. Process sauce in blender until smooth, about 30 seconds, adjusting consistency with extra broth as needed. Season with salt, pepper, vinegar, and chipotle to taste.

Easy Tomato Chutney

MAKES ¾ CUP **LIGHT**

For the nutritional information for this recipe, see page 412.

Combine ¾ cup canned diced tomatoes with their juice, ¾ cup water, 1 minced shallot, 2 tablespoons sugar, 2 tablespoons cider vinegar, 1 tablespoon golden raisins, ⅛ teaspoon salt, and pinch cayenne together in medium saucepan. Bring to simmer over medium-low heat and cook, stirring occasionally, until thickened and reduced to about ¾ cup, 45 to 50 minutes. Using potato masher, mash any large pieces of tomato. Let cool to room temperature.

Mexican Beer and Tomato Cocktail (Chavela)

SERVES 2 **FAST**

Mexico's answer to the bloody Mary, this refreshing cocktail swaps the usual vodka for lighter beer for a drink perfect for barbecues and brunch.

Process ¾ cup canned diced tomatoes with their juice, 1½ tablespoons lime juice, 1 tablespoon hot sauce, 1 teaspoon Worcestershire sauce, and ⅛ teaspoon salt in blender until smooth, about 30 seconds; pour evenly into 2 pint glasses or large beer mugs. Divide 12 ounces Mexican lager between 2 glasses. Garnish with celery sticks and serve.

Celery

Celery is usually sold in bunches, yet most recipes call for just a few stalks. These easy recipes will make sure the rest doesn't get forgotten in the crisper drawer.

Cream of Celery Soup

SERVES 2

Melt 1 tablespoon unsalted butter in large saucepan over medium-low heat. Add 4 chopped celery ribs, 1 small russet potato, peeled and chopped fine, 1 small chopped onion, ½ tablespoon sugar, ½ teaspoon dried sage, and pinch salt. Cover and cook until celery and onion are softened, about 15 minutes. Stir in 1½ cups chicken broth and simmer, uncovered, until potato is tender, 10 to 15 minutes. Process soup in blender until smooth, about 2 minutes, then return to clean saucepan. Stir in 3 tablespoons heavy cream (or half-and-half) and return to brief simmer. Season with salt and pepper to taste and serve.

Celery Salad with Red Onion and Orange

SERVES 2 **FAST**

Cut away peel and pith from 1 orange, cut orange into 8 wedges, then slice wedges crosswise into ½-inch-thick pieces. Toss 4 celery ribs, sliced thin on bias, orange pieces, 3 tablespoons finely chopped red onion, 2 tablespoons extra-virgin olive oil, 1 tablespoon cider vinegar, and 1 teaspoon honey together in bowl. Season with salt and pepper to taste and let salad sit for 15 minutes before serving.

Coconut Milk

Rich coconut milk is worth putting to use when you're left with part of a can. To make it easy, we came up with recipes for a decadent rice pudding, classic piña coladas, and creamy kulfi.

Coconut Rice Pudding

SERVES 2

Bring 1 cup water to boil in small saucepan. Stir in ½ cup long-grain or medium-grain rice and ⅛ teaspoon salt. Cover and simmer over low heat, stirring often, until water is almost fully absorbed, 10 to 15 minutes. Stir in 1 cup unsweetened coconut milk, 1½ cups milk, ⅓ cup sugar, ½ teaspoon vanilla extract, and ¼ teaspoon ground cinnamon. Simmer, stirring often, until spoon is able to stand up in pudding, 35 to 40 minutes. Serve warm or chilled.

Piña Coladas

SERVES 2 **FAST**

Process ¾ cup unsweetened coconut milk, ¼ cup dark rum, 2 cups pineapple chunks, 1 cup ice, 3 tablespoons sugar, and 2 teaspoons lime juice in blender on low speed until mixture is coarsely pureed, about 10 seconds. Increase speed to high and continue to process until mixture is completely smooth, 20 to 40 seconds. Season with more sugar and lime juice to taste and serve.

Easy Coconut Kulfi

SERVES 2

Kulfi is a cardamom-spiced frozen dessert similar to ice cream. The vodka is crucial to the kulfi's texture; do not omit it.

Whisk ¾ cup coconut milk (or light coconut milk), ¾ cup heavy cream (or half-and-half), ⅓ cup corn syrup, 1 tablespoon vodka, ¼ teaspoon lime zest, ¼ teaspoon ground cardamom, and ⅛ teaspoon salt in large bowl. Cover with plastic wrap and freeze until mixture begins to freeze around edges, 1½ to 2 hours. Vigorously stir mixture until smooth and slightly frothy. Transfer to 2-cup container with tight-fitting lid and freeze until firm, 4 to 5 hours, before serving.

Eggplant

Because it requires cooking, eggplant can be a tricky vegetable to use up. And recipes for two rarely call for a whole eggplant. Here are some tasty ideas for what to do with the other half.

Simple Ratatouille

SERVES 2

Heat 2 tablespoons extra-virgin olive oil in 12-inch nonstick skillet over medium-high heat until shimmering. Add 8 ounces eggplant, cut into ¾-inch pieces (2 cups), and ⅛ teaspoon salt and cook until eggplant is browned, 5 to 7 minutes. Stir in 1 tablespoon extra-virgin olive oil and ½ chopped onion and cook until onion is softened, 5 to 7 minutes. Stir in 2 minced garlic cloves and cook until fragrant, about 30 seconds. Stir in 1 large chopped tomato and ¾ cup chicken broth and simmer until vegetables are softened and liquid has thickened slightly, 10 to 15 minutes. Season with salt and pepper to taste. Sprinkle with Parmesan cheese and drizzle with more olive oil. Serve.

Easy Eggplant Dip

MAKES ⅔ CUP

Combine 8 ounces eggplant, peeled and cut into ¾-inch pieces (2 cups), 2 tablespoons extra-virgin olive oil, and ¼ teaspoon salt in 10-inch nonstick skillet. Cover and cook over medium heat, stirring often, until eggplant is lightly browned, very soft, and beginning to break down, about 10 minutes. Pulse cooked eggplant, 2 teaspoons lemon juice, and ⅛ teaspoon ground cumin in food processor until coarsely pureed, about 5 pulses. Transfer mixture to bowl and stir in 2 tablespoons plain Greek yogurt (or sour cream); season with salt and pepper to taste. Cover and refrigerate until chilled, about 30 minutes. Serve with bread or crackers.

Feta

Feta is often sold in large tubs and can spoil very quickly. While it's great crumbled over a salad or Mediterranean-inspired pasta dish, we came up with a few more creative ideas for putting this tangy cheese to work.

Spicy Whipped Feta

MAKES ½ CUP　FAST

Process ½ cup crumbled feta cheese, 1 tablespoon extra-virgin olive oil, 1 tablespoon water, 1 teaspoon lemon juice, ½ teaspoon paprika (or smoked paprika), and ⅛ teaspoon cayenne pepper together in food processor until smooth, about 20 seconds. Transfer mixture to serving bowl and drizzle with more olive oil. Serve with bread or crackers.

Watermelon and Feta Salad with Mint

SERVES 2　FAST　LIGHT

For the nutritional information for this recipe, see page 412.

Trim and discard rind from 12 ounces thinly sliced watermelon. Arrange watermelon on plate and sprinkle with ½ cup crumbled feta cheese and 1½ tablespoons chopped fresh mint. Serve.

Creamy Feta Dressing

MAKES 1¼ CUPS　FAST

Whisk ¾ cup crumbled feta, ¼ cup whole milk, ⅓ cup mayonnaise, 1 tablespoon lemon juice, ¼ teaspoon pepper, ¼ teaspoon granulated garlic, and ¼ teaspoon ground coriander together in bowl. Season with salt and pepper to taste.

Fresh Herbs

Highly perishable and most often sold in large bunches, fresh herbs are one of the hardest things to use up before they spoil. So we've found a few easy ways to preserve their fresh flavor.

Easy Dried Herbs　FAST

Lay sprigs of sage, rosemary, thyme, oregano, mint, or marjoram in single layer between 2 paper towels and microwave until dry and brittle, 1 to 3 minutes. Crumble herbs, discarding any tough stems, and store in airtight container for up to 3 months.

Always-Fresh Herb Ice Cubes

Place 1 tablespoon chopped fresh parsley, sage, rosemary, or thyme in ice cube tray, cover with water, and freeze. Place frozen cubes in zipper-lock freezer bag until needed for sauces, soups, or stews. Cubes can be stored indefinitely.

Lemon and Herb Compound Butter

MAKES 5 TABLESPOONS

This butter is delicious spread on toast or served over steaks, fish fillets, mashed potatoes, roasted vegetables, or pasta.

Using fork, beat 2 teaspoons minced fresh thyme (or rosemary, sage, oregano, mint, or marjoram), 4 tablespoons softened unsalted butter, 1 teaspoon lemon juice, ½ teaspoon lemon zest, and ½ teaspoon salt in small bowl until combined. Place butter mixture in center of sheet of plastic wrap and roll into thick cylinder, twisting ends of plastic shut. Refrigerate until firm, about 30 minutes. Butter can be kept refrigerated for several days or frozen for up to 1 month.

Ricotta Cheese

Creamy, delicious ricotta cheese is great in baked pasta dishes, but it's not a cheese you can easily eat out of hand. These easy recipes will ensure your leftover ricotta doesn't go to waste.

Herbed Ricotta Spread

MAKES ½ CUP

Line fine-mesh strainer with triple layer of coffee filters and place over bowl. Spoon ½ cup ricotta cheese (whole-milk or part-skim) into strainer, cover and let drain for 1 hour. Transfer drained ricotta to serving bowl and stir in 1 tablespoon minced fresh basil (or parsley, tarragon, cilantro, or dill), 1 tablespoon extra-virgin olive oil, 1 minced garlic clove, ½ teaspoon lemon juice, and ¼ teaspoon grated lemon zest. Season with salt and pepper to taste. Serve with crackers or toasted bread.

Lemon-Herb Ricotta Fritters

MAKES 6 FRITTERS　FAST

Combine 1 cup ricotta cheese (whole-milk or part-skim), ⅓ cup panko bread crumbs (or plain dried bread crumbs), ¼ cup grated Parmesan cheese, 2 tablespoons chopped fresh basil (or parsley, cilantro, tarragon, or chives), 1 egg yolk, ½ teaspoon salt, ¼ teaspoon pepper, and ⅛ teaspoon grated lemon zest in bowl. Using wet hands, shape mixture into six ½-inch-thick patties. Heat ¼ cup olive oil in 12-inch nonstick skillet over medium-high heat until shimmering. Fry patties until golden and crisp on both sides, 4 to 5 minutes, gently flipping halfway through cooking. Serve with green salad or freshly sliced tomato.

Sweet Ricotta Cheese Dip

MAKES ABOUT ¾ CUP　FAST

Process ¾ cup ricotta cheese (whole-milk or part-skim), 3 tablespoons confectioners' sugar, ½ teaspoon vanilla extract, and ¼ teaspoon grated lemon zest together in food processor until smooth, about 1 minute, scraping down sides of bowl as needed. Serve with cinnamon-sugar pita chips, biscotti, or toast, or spoon into bowl with fresh berries.

Handy Equipment for Two

Scaling down recipes often requires inventive use of standard kitchen essentials, like using a loaf pan to make a perfectly sized lasagna for two. And some for-two recipes require different-size cooking equipment, from smaller skillets and saucepans to specialty-size pie plates and more. Fortunately, these items are inexpensive and widely available in stores and online. Here's a list of the equipment we reach for when scaling recipes down to size.

SMALL SKILLETS: A 12-inch skillet is usually our favorite kitchen workhorse; we use it to cook everything from steaks to stir-fries and pasta to scrambled eggs. But once we started scaling down recipes, we found that many recipes required a scaled-down skillet as well—try to make just enough pan sauce for two steaks in a large skillet and it will overreduce and burn. So we recommend buying 10-inch and 8-inch skillets in addition to standard 12-inch skillets. We use both traditional and nonstick 10-inch skillets for sautés and stir-fries throughout the book, and an 8-inch skillet is essential for baking a small strata or soufflé.

SMALL, MEDIUM, AND LARGE SAUCEPANS: When cooking for two, we frequently reach for a saucepan instead of a larger pot. For braises, we use large (4-quart) saucepans in lieu of a large Dutch oven (most hold as much as 7 or 8 quarts). We use medium (2- to 3-quart) saucepans for soups and stews and small (1- to 2-quart) saucepans for melting just a little butter or chocolate or for making sauces. We recommend you have at least one saucepan in each size.

SMALL BAKING DISHES: Small baking dishes come in handy for scaled-down gratins and baked desserts. We use a 4-cup 8½ by 5½-inch baking dish for our Cauliflower Gratin (page 301) and our Potato Gratin (page 305); for a petite Tiramisù (page 404), we reach for a smaller 3-cup rectangular baking dish measuring approximately 7¼ by 5¼ inches, although dishes of comparable size work, too. Look for gratin dishes with straight sides no higher than 2 inches; taller sides inhibit browning.

MULTIPLE LOAF PANS: We use both traditional loaf pans and mini loaf pans (which measure approximately 5½ by 3 inches) in the for-two kitchen. We've found that standard loaf pans are the perfect size for baking small casseroles, lasagna, brownies, and bar cookies. Mini loaf pans are ideal for scaled-down baked goods such as quick breads and pound cake.

LOTS OF RAMEKINS: Ramekins, in various sizes, are handy for making scaled-down desserts. We use 5- to 12-ounce ramekins for making individual servings of desserts such as Individual Blueberry Crumbles (page 367), Warm Chocolate Fudge Cakes (page 403), and Crème Brûlée (page 409). We also use 12-ounce ramekins to make elegant individual Chicken Pot Pies (page 122).

SMALL CAKE PANS: With 6-inch round cake pans, you can make a perfectly sized coffee cake (like our Cinnamon Streusel Coffee Cake on page 353) or a mini Fluffy Yellow Layer Cake (page 398) just right for two.

SMALL PIE PLATES: We rely on 6-inch pie plates to make perfectly portioned pies for two. A small pie plate also makes it easy to scale down our Classic Cheese Quiche (page 338).

SMALL TART PANS: When you want to make individual tarts (sweet or savory), two 4-inch tart pans with removeable bottoms hold just the right amount of crust and filling.

SPRINGFORM PANS: Small 4½-inch springform pans are essential for making New York Cheesecakes (page 405) that don't feed a crowd. We also rely on this pan for delicate cakes like our Almond Cakes (page 395) and our Rustic Peach Cakes (page 396).

SMALL BUNDT PANS: Bundt pans make beautiful cakes, but a standard pan holds 12 cups and makes a cake large enough for a party. We've found that mini 1-cup Bundt pans are ideal for making two elegant single-serving cakes, like Bold and Spicy Gingerbread Cakes (page 395) or Summer Berry Snack Cakes (page 390).

A SMALL SLOW COOKER: For our slow-cooker suppers for two, we found a 4-quart oval slow cooker easier to maneuver and clean and less space-hogging than the standard 6- to 7-quart slow cookers (but the recipes in this book will work equally well with either size).

Kitchen Essentials Everyone Needs

In addition to the specialty items useful when cooking for two, here are all the knives, tools, measuring equipment, and more that are essential to foolproof cooking. You'll find everything you need for a well-stocked kitchen, as well as what to look for when shopping and exactly which brand is our test kitchen favorite. Our ratings are based on years of rigorously testing thousands of products to find out which brands and models work best and why. And because we accept no support from product manufacturers, you can trust our ratings. Prices in this chart are based on shopping at online retailers and will vary.

KNIVES AND MORE	ITEM	WHAT TO LOOK FOR	TEST KITCHEN FAVORITES
	Chef's Knife	• High-carbon stainless-steel knife • Thin, curved 8-inch blade • Lightweight • Comfortable grip and nonslip handle	**Victorinox Fibrox 8-Inch Chef's Knife** (formerly Victorinox Forschner) $29.99
	Paring Knife	• 3- to 3½-inch blade • Thin, slightly curved blade with pointed tip • Comfortable grip	**Wüsthof Classic with PEtec 3½-Inch Paring Knife** (model #4066) $39.95 BEST BUY: **Victorinox Fibrox 3¼-inch Paring Knife** $8.95
	Serrated Knife	• 10- to 12-inch blade • Somewhat flexible, slightly curved blade • Pointed serrations that are uniformly spaced and moderately sized	**Wüsthof Classic 10-Inch Bread Knife** $109.95 BEST BUY: **Victorinox Fibrox 10¼-Inch Bread Knife** $24.95
	Slicing Knife	• Tapered 12-inch blade for slicing large cuts of meat • Oval scallops (called a Granton edge) carved into blade • Fairly rigid blade with rounded tip	**Victorinox Fibrox 12-Inch Granton Edge Slicing Knife** $39.95
	Cutting Board	• Roomy work surface at least 20 by 15 inches • Teak board for minimal maintenance • Durable edge-grain construction (wood grain runs parallel to surface of board)	**Proteak Edge Grain Teak Cutting Board** $84.99 BEST BUY: **OXO Good Grips Carving and Cutting Board** $24.99
	Knife Sharpener	• Diamond sharpening material for electric sharpeners • Easy to use and comfortable • Clear instructions	ELECTRIC: **Chef'sChoice Model 130 Professional Sharpening Station** $149.95 MANUAL: **AccuSharp Knife and Tool Sharpener** $10.95

POTS AND PANS	ITEM	WHAT TO LOOK FOR	TEST KITCHEN FAVORITES
	Traditional Skillets	• Stainless-steel interior and fully clad for even heat distribution • 12-inch diameter and flared sides • Comfortable, ovensafe handle • Cooking surface of at least 9 inches • Good to have smaller (8- or 10-inch) skillets too	**All-Clad Stainless 12-Inch Frypan** $154.99
	Nonstick Skillets	• Dark, nonstick surface • 12- or 12½-inch diameter, thick bottom • Comfortable, ovensafe handle • Cooking surface of at least 9 inches • Good to have smaller (8- or 10-inch) skillets too	**T-Fal Professional Total Non-Stick 12½-Inch Fry Pan** $34.99
	Dutch Oven	• Enameled cast iron or stainless steel • Capacity of at least 6 quarts • Diameter of at least 9 inches • Tight-fitting lid • Wide, sturdy handles	**Le Creuset 7¼-Quart Round French Oven** $304.95 **All-Clad Stainless 8-Quart Stockpot** $294.95 BEST BUY: **Tramontina 6.5-Quart Cast Iron Dutch Oven** $49
	Saucepans	• Good to have in several sizes: large (4-quart), medium (2- to 3-quart), and small (1-quart) • Tight-fitting lids • Pans with rounded corners that a whisk can reach into • Long, comfortable handles that are angled for even weight distribution	LARGE: **All-Clad Stainless 4-Quart Saucepan** $179.95 BEST BUY: **Cuisinart MultiClad Unlimited 4-Quart Saucepan** $69.99 SMALL: **Calphalon Contemporary Nonstick 2½-Quart Shallow Saucepan** $39.95
	Rimmed Baking Sheets	• Light-colored surface (heats and browns evenly) • Thick and sturdy • Dimensions of 18 by 13 inches • Good to have at least two	**Wear-Ever 13-Gauge Half Size Heavy Duty Sheet Pan by Vollrath** (formerly Lincoln Foodservice) $13
	Roasting Pan	• At least 15 by 11 inches • Stainless-steel interior with aluminum core for even heat distribution • Upright handles for easy gripping • Light interior for better food monitoring	**Calphalon Contemporary Stainless Roasting Pan with V-Rack** $129.99

HANDY TOOLS	ITEM	WHAT TO LOOK FOR	TEST KITCHEN FAVORITES
	Tongs	• Scalloped edges • Slightly concave pincers • 12 inches in length (to keep your hand far from heat) • Open and close easily	**OXO Good Grips 12-Inch Locking Tongs** $12.95
	Wooden Spoon	• Slim yet broad bowl • Stain-resistant bamboo • Comfortable handle	**SCI Bamboo Wood Cooking Spoon** $2.40
	Slotted Spoon	• Deep bowl • Long handle • Enough holes for quick draining	**OXO Good Grips Nylon Slotted Spoon** $6.99
	All-Around Spatulas	• Head about 3 inches wide and 5½ inches long • 11 inches in length (tip to handle) • Long, vertical slots • Useful to have a metal spatula to use with traditional cookware and plastic for nonstick cookware	METAL: **Wüsthof Gourmet Fish Spatula** $34.95 PLASTIC: **Matfer Bourgeat Pelton Spatula** $11.95
	Rubber Spatula	• Wide, stiff blade with thin edge that's flexible enough to conform to curve of mixing bowl • Heatproof	**Rubbermaid Professional 13½-Inch High Heat Scraper** $18.99
	All-Purpose Whisk	• At least 10 wires • Wires of moderate thickness • Comfortable rubber handle • Balanced, lightweight feel	**OXO Good Grips 11-Inch Whisk** $9.99
	Garlic Press	• Large capacity to hold multiple garlic cloves • Curved plastic handles • Long handle and short distance between pivot point and plunger	**Kuhn Rikon Easy-Squeeze Garlic Press** $20 BEST BUY: **Trudeau Garlic Press** $11.99
	Pepper Mill	• Easy-to-adjust, clearly marked grind settings • Efficient, comfortable grinding mechanism • Generous capacity	**Cole and Mason Derwent Gourmet Precision Pepper Mill** $40
	Ladle	• Stainless steel • Hook handle • Pouring rim to prevent dripping • Handle 9 to 10 inches in length	**Rösle Ladle with Pouring Rim** $29.95
	Can Opener	• Intuitive and easy to attach • Smooth turning motions • Magnet for no-touch lid disposal • Comfortable handle	**OXO Good Grips Magnetic Locking Can Opener** $21.99

HANDY TOOLS	ITEM	WHAT TO LOOK FOR	TEST KITCHEN FAVORITES
	Vegetable Peeler	• Sharp carbon steel blade • 1-inch space between blade and peeler to prevent jamming • Lightweight and comfortable	**Kuhn Rikon Original 4-Inch Swiss Peeler** $3.50
	Grater	• Paddle-style grater • Sharp, extra-large holes and generous grating plane • Rubber-lined feet for stability • Comfortable handle	**Rösle Coarse Grater** $35
	Rolling Pin	• Moderate weight (1 to 1½ pounds) • 19-inch straight barrel • Slightly textured wooden surface to grip dough for easy rolling	**J.K. Adams Plain Maple Rolling Dowel** $13.95
	Mixing Bowls	• Good to have both stainless steel and glass (for mixing, microwaving, and holding prepped ingredients) • Sets of 6 to 9 nesting bowls ranging in capacity from about 1¼ ounces to 4 quarts (for glass) and 2 cups to 8 quarts (for stainless steel)	**Little difference among various brands**
	Oven Mitt	• Form-fitting and not overly bulky for easy maneuvering • Machine washable • Flexible, heat-resistant material	**Kool-Tek 15-Inch Oven Mitt by KatchAll** $44.95 **BEST BUY: OrkaPlus Silicone Oven Mitt with Cotton Lining** $14.95
	Colander	• 4- to 7-quart capacity • Metal ring attached to the bottom for stability • Many holes for quick draining • Small holes so pasta doesn't slip through	**RSVP International Endurance Precision Pierced 5-Quart Colander** $32.95
	Fine-Mesh Strainer	• At least 6 inches in diameter (measured from inside edge to inside edge) • Sturdy construction	**CIA Masters Collection 6¾-Inch Fine Mesh Strainer** $27.50
	Potato Masher	• Solid mashing disk with small holes • Comfortable grip	**WMF Profi Plus Stainless Steel Potato Masher** $19
	Salad Spinner	• Solid bottom for washing greens in bowl • Ergonomic and easy-to-operate hand pump	**OXO Good Grips Salad Spinner** $29.99

MEASURING EQUIPMENT	ITEM	WHAT TO LOOK FOR	TEST KITCHEN FAVORITES
	Dry Measuring Cups	• Stainless-steel cups (hefty and durable) • Measurement markings that are visible even once cup is full • Evenly weighted and stable • Long handles that are level with rim of cup	**Amco Basic Ingredient 4-Piece Measuring Cup Set** $11.50
	Liquid Measuring Cups	• Crisp, unambiguous markings that include ¼- and ⅓-cup measurements • Heatproof, sturdy cup with handle • Good to have in a variety of sizes (1, 2, and 4 cups)	**Pyrex 2-Cup Measuring Cup** $5.99
	Measuring Spoons	• Long, comfortable handles • Rim of bowl flush with handle (makes it easy to "dip" into dry ingredients and "sweep" across top for accurate measuring) • Slim design	**Cuisipro Stainless Steel Measuring Spoon Set** $9.95
	Kitchen Ruler	• Easy-to-clean stainless steel • 18 inches in length • Large, easy-to-read markings	**Empire 18-Inch Stainless Steel Ruler** $8.49

THERMOMETERS AND TIMERS	ITEM	WHAT TO LOOK FOR	TEST KITCHEN FAVORITES
	Instant-Read Thermometer	• Digital model with automatic shut-off • Quick-response readings in 10 seconds or less • Wide temperature range (-40 to 450 degrees) • Long stem that can reach interior of large cuts of meat • Water resistant	**ThermoWorks Splash-Proof Super-Fast Thermapen** $89 **BEST BUYS: ThermoWorks Super-Fast Pocket Thermometer** $19 **CDN ProAccurate Quick-Read Thermometer** $19.99
	Oven Thermometer	• Clearly marked numbers for easy readability • Hang model or stable base • Large temperature range (up to 600 degrees)	**Cooper-Atkins Oven Thermometer** (model #24HP) $6
	Kitchen Timer	• Lengthy time range (1 second to at least 10 hours) • Ability to count up after alarm goes off • Easy to use and read	**Polder 3-in-1 Clock, Timer, and Stopwatch** (model #898-95) $12

ESSENTIAL BAKEWARE	ITEM	WHAT TO LOOK FOR	TEST KITCHEN FAVORITES
	Glass Baking Dish	• Dimensions of 13 by 9 inches • Large enough to hold casseroles and large crisps and cobblers • Handles	**Pyrex Bakeware 9 x 13-Inch Baking Dish** $12.99
	Metal Baking Pan	• Dimensions of 13 by 9 inches • Straight sides and sharp rectangular corners • Nonstick coating for even browning and easy release of cakes and bar cookies	**Williams-Sonoma Goldtouch Nonstick Rectangular Cake Pan, 9" x 13"** $32.95
	Square Baking Pans	• Straight sides • Light gold or dark nonstick surface for even browning and easy release of cakes • Good to have both 9-inch and 8-inch square pans	**Williams-Sonoma Nonstick Goldtouch Square Cake Pan** $26, 8-inch $27, 9-inch **BEST BUY: Chicago Metallic Gourmetware 8-Inch Nonstick Square Cake Pan** $6.99
	Round Cake Pans	• Straight sides • Nonstick coating for even browning and easy release of cakes • Good to have two 9-inch and two 8-inch round pans	**Chicago Metallic Professional Lifetime 9-Inch Nonstick Round Cake Pan** $12.99
	Pie Plates	• Glass promotes even browning and allows progress to be monitored • ½-inch rim to shape decorative crusts • Shallow angled sides prevent crusts from slumping • Good to have two	**Pyrex Bakeware 9-Inch Pie Plate** $2.99
	Loaf Pans	• Light gold or dark nonstick surface for even browning and easy release • Good to have several	**Williams-Sonoma 8½ x 4½-Inch Nonstick Goldtouch Loaf Pan** $21 **BEST BUY: Baker's Secret 9 x 5-Inch Nonstick Loaf Pan** $5
	Muffin Tin	• Nonstick surface for even browning and easy release • Wide, extended rims and raised lip for easy handling • Cup capacity of ½ cup	**Wilton Avanti Everglide Metal-Safe Nonstick 12-Cup Muffin Pan** $13.99
	Cooling Rack	• Grid-style rack with tightly woven, heavy-gauge bars • Should fit inside standard 18 by 13-inch rimmed baking sheet • Dishwasher-safe	**CIA Bakeware 12 x 17-Inch Cooling Rack** $15.95 **BEST BUY: Libertyware Half-Size Sheet Pan Grate** $5.25

SMALL APPLIANCES	ITEM	WHAT TO LOOK FOR	TEST KITCHEN FAVORITES
	Food Processor	• 14-cup capacity • Sharp and sturdy blades • Wide feed tube • Should come with basic blades and discs: steel blade, dough blade, shredding and slicing disc	**Cuisinart Custom 14-Cup Food Processor** $199
	Hand-Held Mixer	• Lightweight model • Slim wire beaters without central post • Digital display • Separate ejector buttons (not part of speed dial) • Variety of speeds	**Cuisinart Power Advantage 7-Speed Hand Mixer** $49.95
	Blender	• Large blades that reach close to edge and bottom of jar • Powerful motor (at least 700 watts) • Automatic shut-off to keep motor from overheating • Clear jar to monitor progress	**Breville BBL605XL Hemisphere Control Blender** $200
	Slow Cooker	• At least 6-quart capacity (4-quart capacity for small slow cookers) • Insert handles • Clear lid to see progress of food • Dishwasher-safe insert • Intuitive control panel with programmable timer and warming mode	LARGE: **Crock-Pot Touchscreen Slow Cooker** $129.99 SMALL: **Cuisinart 4-Quart Cook Central 3-in-1 Multicooker** $129.95

KITCHEN SUPPLIES	ITEM	WHAT TO LOOK FOR	TEST KITCHEN FAVORITES
	Parchment Paper	• Sturdy paper for heavy doughs • Easy release of baked goods • At least 14 inches wide	**Reynolds Parchment Paper** $3.69
	Plastic Wrap	• Clings tightly and resticks well • Packaging with sharp teeth that aren't exposed (to avoid snags on clothing and skin) • Adhesive pad to hold cut end of wrap	**Glad Cling Wrap Clear Plastic** $2.59
	Aluminum Foil	• At least 14 inches wide • Packaging with sharp teeth to cut cleanly	**Little difference among various brands**

Faster, Easier Ingredient Prep

Whether you're cooking for two or 10, you'll end up prepping the same handful of ingredients again and again. Learning the best and fastest technique for chopping an onion or cutting up broccoli will save you lots of time in the kitchen. Here are the most efficient ways to prepare frequently used ingredients.

Holding a Knife

Much like holding a baseball bat, the way you hold a knife can make a difference in terms of control and force. And don't forget about the other hand—it should hold the food securely in place while you cut. Holding the food steady can make a difference in terms of safety.

Control Grip

For more control, choke up on the handle and actually grip the blade of the knife between your thumb and forefinger.

Force Grip

Holding the knife back on the handle allows you to use more force, and is helpful when cutting through hard foods or bone.

Protecting Your Fingertips

To keep your fingertips from getting nicked by the blade, use the "bear claw" grip by tucking your fingertips back away from the knife and letting your knuckles rest against the side of the blade. Reposition your hand as needed with every slice.

How to Prep Fresh Herbs

1. To mince fresh herbs, place your hand on handle of chef's knife and rest fingers of your other hand lightly on top of knife blade. Use up-and-down rocking motion to evenly mince herbs, pivoting knife as you chop.

2. For thyme or rosemary with thin, pliable stems, chop stems and leaves together, discarding tough bottom portions. If stems are thicker, hold sprig upright by top of stem, then run your thumb and forefinger down stem to release leaves and smaller offshoots. The tender tips can be left intact and chopped along with the leaves once the woodier stems have been sheared clean and discarded.

3. To shred (or chiffonade) basil, stack several clean leaves on top of one another. Roll them up, then slice roll crosswise into shreds.

How to Chop an Onion

1. Halve onion through root end, then peel onion and trim top. Make several horizontal cuts from 1 end of onion to other, but don't cut all way through root end.

2. Make several vertical cuts. Again, be sure to cut up to but not through root end.

3. Rotate onion so that root end is in back, behind your hand, and slice onion thin across previous cuts. As you slice, onion will fall apart into chopped pieces.

How to Mince Garlic

1. Trim off root end of garlic clove, then crush clove gently between side of chef's knife and cutting board to loosen papery skin. Paper skin will fall away from garlic.

2. Using two-handed chopping motion, run knife over garlic repeatedly to mince it.

3. Mincing garlic to a paste helps to distribute it evenly. Sprinkle minced garlic with pinch of salt, then scrape blade of knife back and forth over garlic until it forms sticky paste.

How to Prep Ginger

1. To quickly peel knob of ginger, hold it firmly against cutting board and use edge of teaspoon to scrape away thin, brown skin.

2. To grate ginger, peel just small section of large piece of ginger then grate peeled portion using rasp-style grater, using unpeeled ginger as handle to keep your fingers safely away from grater.

3. For smashed coins of ginger, slice peeled knob of ginger crosswise into coins, then use corner of heavy pan (or mallet) to gently smash ginger and release its flavor.

How to Cut Up a Bell Pepper

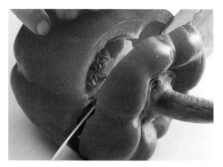

1. Slice off top and bottom of pepper and remove seeds and stem.

2. Slice down through side of pepper.

3. Lay pepper flat, trim away remaining ribs and seeds, then cut into pieces or strips as desired.

How to Cut Up a Carrot

1. Using chef's knife, cut peeled carrot in half widthwise, separating thick root end from thin tapered end.

2. Halve carrot pieces lengthwise, and if necessary, halve thicker pieces yet again until they are all roughly the same thickness.

3. Continue to cut carrots crosswise into similar-size pieces as desired.

How to Chop a Tomato

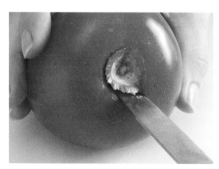

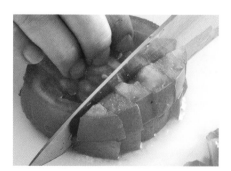

1. Remove core of tomato using paring knife.

2. Slice tomato crosswise.

3. Stack several slices of tomato, then slice both crosswise and widthwise into pieces as desired.

How to Cut Up Broccoli

1. Place head of broccoli upside down on cutting board and cut off florets.

2. Slice larger florets into bite-size pieces by slicing them through stem.

3. Cut away tough outer peel and square off stalks using chef's knife, then slice stalks into pieces.

How to Prep Leeks

1. Trim and discard root and dark green leaves.

2. Cut trimmed leek in half lengthwise, then slice it crosswise.

3. Submerge cut leeks in bowl of water and rinse thoroughly to remove dirt and sand. Drain.

How to Prep Mushrooms

1. Mushrooms should be rinsed under cold water just before being cooked. Don't wash mushrooms that will be eaten raw; brush dirt away with soft pastry brush or cloth.

2. For mushrooms with tender stems, such as white button mushrooms and cremini, stems can be trimmed, then prepped and cooked alongside caps. For mushrooms with tough, woody stems, such as shiitakes and portobellos, stems should be removed.

3. When cooking portobello mushrooms in soups and stews, you may want to remove the gills on the underside of the cap or your dish will taste and look muddy. Use soupspoon to scrape gills off underside of mushroom cap.

Soups and Chowders

▪ FAST (Start to finish in about 30 minutes)

▪ LIGHT (See page 412 for nutritional information)

Opposite: Sausage and Tortellini Florentine Soup; Creamless Creamy Tomato Soup; Escarole, Sausage, Orzo Soup

Hearty Chicken Noodle Soup

SERVES 2

✓ **WHY THIS RECIPE WORKS:** We wanted to streamline chicken noodle soup and make it quick enough to prepare for two any night of the week—without losing any of its soul-satisfying flavor. While homemade stock was out, we found that we could get great results from store-bought chicken broth with just a couple of extra steps. Adding sautéed aromatics lent our broth a welcome depth and complexity, while creating a simple roux contributed a nutty flavor and also thickened the broth slightly, giving our soup a long-simmered consistency. A bone-in chicken breast gave our broth more flavor than a boneless one did, and quick-cooking egg noodles turned our soup into a hearty one-dish meal. Be careful not to overcook the chicken in step 3 or it will taste dry.

 1   (12-ounce) bone-in split chicken breast, trimmed
     Salt and pepper
 2   teaspoons vegetable oil
 1   small onion, chopped fine
 1   celery rib, minced
 1   carrot, peeled and cut into ½-inch pieces
 1   teaspoon minced fresh thyme or
     ¼ teaspoon dried
 1   tablespoon all-purpose flour
 3   cups chicken broth
 1   bay leaf
 ½   cup wide egg noodles
 1   tablespoon minced fresh parsley

1. Pat chicken dry with paper towels and season with salt and pepper. Heat oil in medium saucepan over medium-high heat until just smoking. Brown chicken, skin side down, until golden, about 6 minutes; transfer to plate. Pour off all but 1 tablespoon fat from saucepan.

2. Add onion, celery, and carrot to fat left in saucepan and cook over medium heat until softened, about 5 minutes. Stir in thyme and cook until fragrant, about 30 seconds. Stir in flour and cook for 1 minute. Slowly whisk in broth, scraping up any browned bits.

3. Add browned chicken with any accumulated juices and bay leaf. Bring to simmer and cook until chicken registers 160 degrees, 20 to 22 minutes, flipping chicken halfway through cooking. Transfer chicken to cutting board, let cool slightly, then shred into bite-size pieces using 2 forks, discarding skin and bones.

4. Discard bay leaf. Return soup to simmer, stir in noodles, and cook until vegetables and noodles are tender, about 8 minutes. Off heat, stir in shredded chicken and let sit until heated through, about 2 minutes. Stir in parsley and season with salt and pepper to taste. Serve.

VARIATIONS
Hearty Chicken Noodle Soup with Leeks, Fennel, and Orzo
Substitute ½ leek, white and light green parts only, halved and sliced ¼ inch thick, for onion; ½ fennel bulb, cored and chopped, for celery; and ¼ cup orzo for egg noodles.

Hearty Chicken Noodle Soup with Tomatoes, Zucchini, and Shells
Omit carrot. Substitute ½ cup medium shells for egg noodles and simmer for 5 minutes. Stir in 1 zucchini, cut into ½-inch pieces, and 1 tomato, cored and chopped, and continue to simmer until pasta and zucchini are tender, about 5 minutes. Stir in shredded chicken and proceed with recipe.

Thai Chicken and Coconut Soup

SERVES 2

✓ **WHY THIS RECIPE WORKS:** We wanted to find a way to create an authentic-tasting Thai chicken soup without the time-consuming prep work and laundry list of hard-to-find ingredients. We found our solution in one single ingredient: red curry paste. Because Thai curry paste contains most of the ingredients we wanted to use in one jar, we were able to add big flavor and depth to our soup in record time. A combination of coconut milk and chicken broth provided richness and clear chicken flavor, while fish sauce, sugar, and lime juice added the proper salty, sweet, and sour notes. Although we prefer the deeper, richer flavor of regular coconut milk, light coconut milk can be substituted. Be careful not to overcook the chicken in step 3 or it will taste dry.

Shredding Chicken

Hold 1 fork in each hand, with tines facing down. Insert tines into meat and gently pull forks away from each other, breaking meat into bite-size pieces or large chunks.

1 (8-ounce) boneless, skinless chicken breast, trimmed
   Salt and pepper
1 tablespoon vegetable oil
1 shallot, minced
2 cups chicken broth
1 cup canned coconut milk
1 tablespoon fish sauce
1 teaspoon sugar
3 ounces white or cremini mushrooms, trimmed and
   sliced thin
3 ounces snow peas, strings removed, cut in half on bias
1 tablespoon lime juice
1 teaspoon Thai red curry paste
¼ cup minced fresh cilantro

1. Pat chicken dry with paper towels and season with salt and pepper. Heat oil in medium saucepan over medium-high heat until just smoking. Brown chicken lightly, 2 to 3 minutes per side; transfer to plate.

2. Add shallot to fat left in saucepan and cook over medium heat until softened, about 3 minutes. Stir in broth, coconut milk, 1 teaspoon fish sauce, and sugar, scraping up any browned bits.

3. Add browned chicken and any accumulated juices, bring to simmer, and cook until it registers 160 degrees, about 10 minutes, flipping chicken halfway through cooking. Transfer chicken to cutting board, let cool slightly, then shred into bite-size pieces using 2 forks.

4. Return soup to simmer, stir in mushrooms and snow peas, and cook until just tender, about 3 minutes. Whisk lime juice, curry paste, and remaining 2 teaspoons fish sauce together in bowl. Off heat, stir lime juice mixture and shredded chicken into soup and let sit until heated through, about 2 minutes. Season with salt and pepper to taste. Sprinkle individual portions with cilantro before serving.

Beef and Barley Soup

SERVES 2

✓ **WHY THIS RECIPE WORKS:** Beef and barley soup is not one that improves as it sits—the barley swells and turns gummy, making for a stodgy soup. To avoid leftovers, we needed a pot of soup for two, and we wanted it to be quick. Using store-bought broth saved us time, while blade steak—readily available in smaller portions—offered beefy flavor and tender, juicy meat without hours of simmering. Giving the meat a head start and adding the barley later ensured that the grains remained pleasantly chewy and

Caramelized vegetables plus a double dose of thyme and garlic give this easy beef and barley soup rich, satisfying flavor.

didn't overcook. Finally, for maximum flavor, we gave the vegetables time to caramelize, doubled the amount of thyme and garlic, and added some tomato paste and soy sauce for rich, beefy flavor. For more information on trimming blade steak, see page 30.

1 (8-ounce) beef blade steak, trimmed and cut into
   ½-inch pieces
   Salt and pepper
1 tablespoon vegetable oil
6 ounces cremini mushrooms, trimmed and sliced thin
2 carrots, peeled and cut into ½-inch pieces
1 small onion, chopped fine
2 tablespoons tomato paste
3 garlic cloves, minced
2 teaspoons minced fresh thyme or ½ teaspoon dried
2 cups beef broth
2 cups chicken broth
4 teaspoons soy sauce
½ cup quick-cooking barley
2 tablespoons chopped fresh parsley

1. Pat beef dry with paper towels and season with salt and pepper. Heat oil in medium saucepan over medium-high heat until just smoking. Brown beef on all sides, 5 to 7 minutes; transfer to bowl.

2. Add mushrooms, carrots, and onion to fat left in saucepan and cook over medium heat until any mushroom juice has evaporated and vegetables begin to brown, 6 to 8 minutes. Stir in tomato paste, garlic, and thyme and cook until fragrant, about 30 seconds.

3. Stir in beef broth, chicken broth, and soy sauce, scraping up any browned bits. Stir in browned beef and any accumulated juices, bring to simmer, and cook for 15 minutes.

4. Stir in barley and simmer until barley and beef are tender, 10 to 15 minutes. Stir in parsley and season with salt and pepper to taste. Serve.

Trimming Blade Steak

1. Halve each steak lengthwise, leaving gristle on 1 half.

2. Cut away gristle from half to which it is still attached.

Escarole, Sausage, and Orzo Soup

SERVES 2

✓ **WHY THIS RECIPE WORKS:** For a quick yet satisfying weeknight meal, we combined tender bites of sausage, delicate pasta, and hearty greens for a warming Italian-inspired soup. We browned the sausage to create a flavorful fond on the bottom of the pot then added onion and garlic. Red pepper flakes infused our soup with a subtle heat. Cooking orzo pasta right in the broth streamlined our dish, and the starch from the pasta gave the broth body and substance. Chopped escarole contributed a pleasant, mildly bitter flavor. Chicken sausage is available in a wide variety of flavors; feel free to choose one that you think will pair well with the other flavors in this dish.

1 tablespoon olive oil
6 ounces cooked chicken sausage, sliced ½ inch thick
1 small onion, chopped fine
1 garlic clove, minced

⅛ teaspoon red pepper flakes
3 cups chicken broth
2 ounces escarole, trimmed and chopped coarse (2 cups)
¼ cup orzo
¼ cup grated Parmesan cheese
1 tablespoon minced fresh parsley
   Salt and pepper

1. Heat 2 teaspoons oil in medium saucepan over medium-high heat until shimmering. Add sausage and cook until browned, about 5 minutes; transfer to bowl.

2. Heat remaining 1 teaspoon oil in now-empty saucepan over medium heat until shimmering. Add onion and cook until softened and lightly browned, 5 to 7 minutes. Stir in garlic and pepper flakes and cook until fragrant, about 30 seconds.

3. Stir in broth, scraping up any browned bits. Stir in browned sausage, escarole, and orzo. Bring to simmer and cook until orzo is tender, 10 to 12 minutes. Off heat, stir in Parmesan and parsley and season with salt and pepper to taste. Serve.

Potato and Leek Soup with Kielbasa

SERVES 2

✓ **WHY THIS RECIPE WORKS:** Potato-leek soup should be hearty and satisfying, with the flavor of the leeks holding its own instead of fading quietly into the background. For intense flavor, we cooked a full pound of leeks in a covered pot until they were meltingly tender and offered concentrated onion flavor. Cutting the leeks and potatoes into substantial pieces contributed a satisfying texture; this also helped the potatoes remain intact instead of disintegrating into the soup. Adding slices of kielbasa turned our soup into a meal, offering big, meaty bites in every spoonful.

1 tablespoon unsalted butter
4 ounces kielbasa sausage, sliced ½ inch thick
1 pound leeks, white and light green parts only, halved lengthwise, sliced 1 inch thick, and washed thoroughly
¼ teaspoon minced fresh thyme or pinch dried
1 tablespoon all-purpose flour
3 cups chicken broth
1 red potato (6 ounces), unpeeled, cut into ¾-inch pieces
   Salt and pepper

1. Melt butter in medium saucepan over medium-high heat. Add kielbasa and cook until browned, about 5 minutes; transfer to bowl.

2. Add leeks to fat left in saucepan, cover, and cook over medium heat, stirring occasionally, until leeks are tender but not mushy, about 15 minutes. Stir in thyme and cook until fragrant, about 30 seconds. Stir in flour and cook for 1 minute.

3. Slowly whisk in broth, scraping up any browned bits. Stir in browned kielbasa and potato, bring to simmer, and cook until potato is tender, about 15 minutes. Season with salt and pepper to taste and serve.

Preparing Leeks

1. Trim and discard root and dark green leaves, then cut trimmed leek in half lengthwise.

2. Slice leek crosswise as directed. Wash cut leeks thoroughly to remove dirt and sand.

Mushroom-Miso Soup with Shrimp and Udon

SERVES 2 · LIGHT

✔ **WHY THIS RECIPE WORKS:** We wanted a deeply flavorful soup inspired by Japanese cuisine without a lengthy ingredient list. The first step was finding a substitute for homemade dashi, a traditional soup base made of bonito flakes and seaweed. Store-bought vegetable broth worked well, providing vegetal notes and a subtle sweetness. To up the broth's savory depth, we added thinly sliced shiitakes; white miso provided complexity and a hint of nuttiness. Finished with chewy udon noodles, tender shrimp, and fresh spinach, this soup offers serious depth of flavor in a short amount of time. Don't be tempted to salt the noodle cooking water in step 1 or the soup may taste too salty. For the nutritional information for this recipe, see page 412.

- 4 ounces dried udon noodles
- 2 teaspoons vegetable oil
- 2 garlic cloves, minced
- 1 teaspoon grated fresh ginger
- 2 cups vegetable broth
- 1¼ cups water
- 4 ounces shiitake mushrooms, stemmed and sliced thin

Doctoring vegetable broth with white miso and shiitakes gives this Asian-inspired soup authentic flavor without any fuss.

- ¼ cup white miso
- 6 ounces extra-large shrimp (21 to 25 per pound), peeled, deveined, tails removed, and cut into ½-inch pieces
- 2 ounces (2 cups) baby spinach
- 1 teaspoon sesame oil, plus extra for seasoning
  Salt and pepper
- 2 scallions, sliced thin

1. Bring 2 quarts water to boil in large saucepan. Add noodles and cook, stirring often, until al dente. Drain noodles and rinse under warm water to remove excess starch. Drain noodles well, then portion into individual serving bowls.

2. Meanwhile, heat vegetable oil in medium saucepan over medium heat until shimmering. Add garlic and ginger and cook until fragrant, about 1 minute. Stir in broth, 1 cup water, and mushrooms. Bring to simmer and cook until flavors meld and mushrooms are tender, about 10 minutes.

3. Whisk miso and remaining ¼ cup water together in bowl. Off heat, stir miso mixture, shrimp, and spinach into soup, cover, and let sit until shrimp are opaque throughout and spinach is wilted, about 2 minutes. Stir in sesame oil and season with salt, pepper, and extra sesame oil to taste. Ladle soup into prepared bowls and sprinkle with scallions before serving.

Provençal Vegetable Soup with Pistou

SERVES 2 `LIGHT`

✔ WHY THIS RECIPE WORKS: Provençal vegetable soup is light and flavorful, featuring seasonal vegetables, white beans, and a dollop of garlicky pistou, the French equivalent of pesto. Since the delicate flavor of a homemade vegetable stock would be obscured by the flavors of the vegetables and the pistou, we were able to save time by using store-bought broth. Leek, green beans, and zucchini made for a balanced summer lineup. Just one tomato added color and brightness, and canned white beans contributed some substance to our soup and required zero prep. We didn't want to drag out the food processor for such a small amount of pistou, so instead we simply combined the oil, garlic, basil, and Parmesan in a bowl for easy prep (and cleanup). For the nutritional information for this recipe, see page 412.

4 teaspoons extra-virgin olive oil
1 carrot, peeled and cut into ¼-inch pieces
½ leek, white and light green parts only, sliced ½ inch thick and washed thoroughly
Salt and pepper
3 garlic cloves, minced
1½ cups vegetable broth
1½ cups water
3 ounces green beans, trimmed and cut into ½-inch lengths
1 small zucchini, quartered lengthwise and sliced ¼ inch thick
¾ cup canned cannellini or navy beans, rinsed
1 plum tomato, cored and chopped
2 tablespoons chopped fresh basil
2 tablespoons grated Parmesan cheese

1. Heat 1 tablespoon oil in medium saucepan over medium heat until shimmering. Add carrot, leek, and ¼ teaspoon salt and cook until softened, about 5 minutes. Stir in two-thirds of garlic and cook until fragrant, about 30 seconds.

2. Stir in broth and water and bring to simmer. Stir in green beans and simmer until bright green but still crunchy, about 5 minutes. Stir in zucchini, beans, and tomato and continue to simmer until vegetables are tender, about 3 minutes.

3. Combine remaining 1 teaspoon oil, remaining garlic, basil, and Parmesan in bowl and season with pepper to taste. Season soup with salt and pepper to taste. Top individual portions with basil mixture before serving.

Farmhouse Vegetable and Barley Soup

SERVES 2 `LIGHT`

✔ WHY THIS RECIPE WORKS: Most recipes for hearty winter vegetable soups are neither quick nor easy. For a satisfying soup for two that wouldn't take the better part of a day to make, we started with canned vegetable broth. To boost its flavor, we added soy sauce and just one dried porcini mushroom. These ingredients gave the soup plenty of savory, meaty flavor. To make the soup seriously satisfying, we added barley to the hearty combination of carrot, parsnip, potato, leek, and cabbage. A pat of butter, some thyme, and lemon juice added richness and brightened the flavors. We prefer an acidic, unoaked white wine such as Sauvignon Blanc for this recipe. Garnish the soup with crumbled cheddar cheese or herbed croutons, if desired. For the nutritional information for this recipe, see page 412.

2 parsley stems plus 1 tablespoon minced fresh parsley
2 sprigs fresh thyme plus ½ teaspoon chopped
1 dried porcini mushroom, rinsed
1 bay leaf
2 tablespoons unsalted butter
1 leek, white and light green parts only, halved lengthwise, sliced ½ inch thick, and washed thoroughly
1 small carrot, peeled and cut into ½-inch pieces
1 small parsnip, peeled and cut into ½-inch pieces
2 tablespoons dry white wine
¾ teaspoon soy sauce
Salt and pepper
2 cups water
1½ cups vegetable broth
3 tablespoons pearl barley
1 small garlic clove, peeled and smashed
1 small Yukon Gold potato (6 ounces), peeled and cut into ½-inch pieces
½ cup chopped green cabbage
¼ cup frozen peas
1 teaspoon lemon juice

1. Bundle parsley stems, thyme sprigs, mushroom, and bay leaf in cheesecloth and tie with kitchen twine to secure. Melt 1 tablespoon butter in medium saucepan over medium heat. Add leek, carrot, parsnip, wine, soy sauce, and ½ teaspoon salt. Cook, stirring occasionally, until liquid has evaporated and leek is softened, about 5 minutes.

2. Add herb and mushroom bundle, water, broth, barley, and garlic and bring to simmer. Reduce heat to medium-low, partially cover, and simmer for 15 minutes.

3. Stir in potato and cabbage and simmer, stirring occasionally, until barley, potato, and cabbage are tender, about 15 minutes.

4. Off heat, discard bundle. Stir in peas and let sit until heated through, about 2 minutes. Stir in minced parsley and chopped thyme, remaining 1 tablespoon butter, and lemon juice. Season with salt and pepper to taste. Serve.

NOTES FROM THE TEST KITCHEN

Soup Making

While the world of soup is diverse, there are some underlying principles that apply to most recipes, whether you're cooking for two or 10.

SAUTÉ AROMATICS: The first step in making many soups is sautéing aromatic vegetables such as onion and garlic. Sautéing not only softens their texture so that there is no unwelcome crunch in the soup, it also tames any harsh flavors and develops more complex flavors in the process.

START WITH GOOD BROTH: If you're not inclined to pack your freezer with homemade stock, packaged broth is a convenient option for soup making. But differences among packaged broths are quite significant—some are pretty flavorful, while others taste like salty dishwater. Shop carefully. See page 41 for more information about buying broth.

CUT VEGETABLES TO THE RIGHT SIZE: Most soups call for chunks of vegetables. Haphazardly cut vegetables will cook unevenly—some pieces will be underdone and crunchy while others will be soft and mushy. Cutting the vegetables to the size specified in the recipe ensures that the pieces will all be perfectly cooked.

STAGGER THE ADDITION OF VEGETABLES: When a soup contains a variety of vegetables, their addition to the pot must often be staggered to account for their varying cooking times. Hardy vegetables like potatoes and winter squash can withstand much more cooking than delicate asparagus or spinach.

SIMMER, DON'T BOIL: A simmer is a restrained version of a boil; fewer bubbles break the surface, and they do so with less vigor. Simmering heats food through more gently and more evenly than boiling; boiling can cause vegetables such as potatoes to break apart or fray at the edges, and it can toughen meat, too.

SEASON JUST BEFORE SERVING: In general, we add salt, pepper, and other seasonings—such as delicate herbs and lemon juice—after cooking, just before serving. The saltiness of the stock and ingredients such as canned tomatoes and beans can vary greatly, so it's always best to taste and adjust seasonings once the soup is complete, just before ladling it into bowls for serving.

Tortellini Florentine Soup
SERVES 2

✓ **WHY THIS RECIPE WORKS:** Tomato and tortellini soup can be the perfect comfort food on a cold winter day; we wanted a streamlined version that wouldn't take hours to prepare. Fortunately, store-bought tortellini offers both good flavor and tender texture in a fraction of the time of homemade. Since canned tomatoes can require a long simmer to get rid of their tinny taste, we turned to a rather unusual ingredient: V8 juice, which lent our soup a surprisingly rich, fresh tomato flavor. To boost its flavor, we rendered a little pancetta, then added an onion, some tomato paste to deepen the tomato flavor, brown sugar for balance, and garlic to boost the savory qualities. For a hearty dose of fresh leafy greens, we stirred in a couple of fistfuls of baby spinach.

> 1 tablespoon olive oil, plus extra for drizzling
> 1 ounce pancetta, chopped fine
> 1 small onion, chopped fine
> 1 teaspoon tomato paste
> 1 teaspoon packed brown sugar
> 2 garlic cloves, minced
> 2 cups chicken broth
> 1½ cups V8 juice
> 3 ounces dried cheese tortellini
> 3 ounces (3 cups) baby spinach
> Salt and pepper
> Grated Parmesan cheese

1. Heat oil in medium saucepan over medium-high heat until shimmering. Add pancetta and cook until fat is rendered, about 2 minutes. Stir in onion, tomato paste, and sugar and cook until onion is softened, about 5 minutes. Stir in garlic and cook until fragrant, about 30 seconds.

2. Stir in broth and V8 juice, scraping up any browned bits. Stir in tortellini, bring to simmer, and cook until tender, 12 to 15 minutes. Off heat, stir in spinach and let sit until wilted, about 2 minutes. Season with salt and pepper to taste. Drizzle individual portions with extra oil and serve with Parmesan.

VARIATION

Sausage and Tortellini Florentine Soup
Substitute 6 ounces hot or sweet Italian sausage for pancetta and cook until browned, about 5 minutes. Before adding spinach, transfer sausage to cutting board, let cool slightly, then slice into ½-inch-thick pieces. Stir sausage pieces into soup with spinach and proceed with recipe.

Pureeing Soup

The texture of a pureed soup should be as smooth and creamy as possible. With this in mind, we tried pureeing several soups with a food processor, a hand-held immersion blender, and a regular countertop blender. It pays to use the right appliance to produce a silky, smooth soup. And because pureeing hot soup can be dangerous, follow our safety tips.

BLENDER IS BEST: A standard blender turns out the smoothest pureed soups. The blade on the blender does an excellent job with soups because it pulls ingredients down from the top of the container. No stray bits go untouched by the blade. And as long as plenty of headroom is left at the top of the blender, there is no leakage.

IMMERSION BLENDER LEAVES BITS BEHIND: The immersion blender has appeal because it can be brought to the pot, eliminating the need to ladle hot ingredients from one vessel to another. However, we found that this kind of blender can leave unblended bits of food behind.

PROCESS WITH CAUTION: The food processor does a decent job of pureeing, but some small bits of vegetables can get trapped under the blade and remain unchopped. Even more troubling is the tendency of a food processor to leak hot liquid. Fill the workbowl more than halfway and you are likely to see liquid running down the side of the food processor base.

WAIT BEFORE BLENDING, AND BLEND IN BATCHES: When blending hot soup, follow a couple of precautions. Wait 5 minutes for moderate cooling, and never fill the blender jar more than halfway full; otherwise, the soup can explode out the top.

KEEP LID SECURE: Don't expect the lid on a blender to stay in place. Hold the lid securely with a folded kitchen towel to keep it in place and to protect your hand from hot steam.

Creamy Butternut Squash Soup

SERVES 2

✔ **WHY THIS RECIPE WORKS:** For a butternut squash soup with intense squash flavor, we started by browning the squash—and because we only needed a relatively small amount, we found that we could do this on the stovetop, which was faster than roasting the squash in the oven. Some onion and a little brown sugar emphasized the sweet, caramelized notes of the squash, greatly intensifying its flavor. Chicken broth gave our soup a savory depth, while a couple of tablespoons of half-and-half provided some richness and creamy texture. A little sage and minced fresh parsley provided just the right herbal notes. Serve with crumbled blue cheese and toasted, chopped walnuts.

1 tablespoon vegetable oil
1 pound butternut squash, peeled, seeded, and cut into 1-inch pieces (3 cups)
1 small onion, chopped
1 tablespoon packed brown sugar, plus extra for seasoning
1 garlic clove, minced
¼ teaspoon minced fresh sage or pinch dried
2 cups chicken broth, plus extra as needed
2 tablespoons half-and-half
1 tablespoon minced fresh parsley
Salt and pepper

1. Heat oil in medium saucepan over medium heat until shimmering. Add squash, onion, and sugar and cook until vegetables are softened and lightly browned, about 10 minutes. Stir in garlic and sage and cook until fragrant, about 30 seconds.

Preparing Butternut Squash

1. Peel squash then, using chef's knife, trim off top and bottom and cut in half where narrow neck and wide, curved bottom meet.

2. Cut neck of squash into 1-inch planks. Cut planks into 1-inch pieces.

3. Cut base of squash in half lengthwise and scoop out and discard seeds and fibers.

4. Slice each half of base into 1-inch-wide lengths. Cut lengths into 1-inch pieces.

2. Stir in broth, scraping up any browned bits. Bring to simmer and cook until squash is tender, about 20 minutes.

3. Process soup in blender until smooth, about 2 minutes. Return soup to clean saucepan, stir in half-and-half, and bring to brief simmer. Adjust soup consistency with extra broth as needed. Stir in parsley and season with salt, pepper, and extra sugar to taste. Serve.

VARIATION

Creamy Butternut Squash Soup with Coconut and Chai

Omit garlic and sage and reduce broth to 1 cup. Add 1 chai-flavored tea bag and 1 cup canned coconut milk with broth; remove tea bag before processing soup. Substitute 1 scallion, sliced thin, for parsley.

Creamy Curried Cauliflower Soup

SERVES 2   LIGHT

✔ **WHY THIS RECIPE WORKS:** We combined two ingredients popular in Indian cuisine—curry and cauliflower—in this boldly flavored soup. Coconut milk is often used in Indian cooking for its richness and sweetness, but regular coconut milk overpowered the delicate flavor of the cauliflower. Switching to the light variety worked better; it still provided a nice creaminess and subtle coconut notes, but the flavors of the curry and cauliflower were now front and center. Fresh ginger added spicy warmth to our soup, while a small chopped onion contributed a sweet aromatic presence. A sprinkling of cilantro at the end provided a burst of color and freshness. For the nutritional information for this recipe, see page 412.

Cutting Cauliflower

1. Pull off any leaves, then cut out core of cauliflower using paring knife.

2. Separate florets from inner stem using tip of paring knife. Cut larger florets into smaller pieces by slicing them through stem.

2   teaspoons vegetable oil
1   small onion, chopped
1   teaspoon grated fresh ginger
1   teaspoon curry powder
2   cups chicken broth, plus extra as needed
½   head cauliflower (1 pound), cored and cut into 1-inch florets
    Salt and pepper
¾   cup canned light coconut milk
1   tablespoon minced fresh cilantro

1. Heat oil in medium saucepan over medium heat until shimmering. Add onion and cook until softened and lightly browned, 5 to 7 minutes. Stir in ginger and curry powder and cook until fragrant, about 30 seconds.

2. Stir in broth, scraping up any browned bits. Stir in cauliflower and ¼ teaspoon salt, bring to simmer, and cook until cauliflower is tender, 15 to 20 minutes.

3. Process soup in blender until smooth, about 2 minutes. Return soup to clean saucepan, stir in coconut milk, and bring to brief simmer. Adjust soup consistency with extra broth as needed. Stir in cilantro and season with salt and pepper to taste. Serve.

Creamless Creamy Tomato Soup

SERVES 2   FAST

✔ **WHY THIS RECIPE WORKS:** While the cream in most tomato soups tempers the acidity of the tomatoes, it also dulls their flavor. We discovered we could achieve a creamy texture without cream by adding bread to our tomato soup. When simmered with the tomatoes and then blended, the bread broke down and disappeared into the soup, adding body and taming the tartness of the tomatoes while still allowing the tomato flavor to shine through. A little brown sugar heightened the sweet tomato flavor, as did a splash of brandy. As for the tomatoes, canned offered consistently better flavor all year round than the fresh offerings at the supermarket.

2   tablespoons extra-virgin olive oil, plus extra for drizzling
1   small onion, chopped
2   garlic cloves, minced
1   (28-ounce) can whole peeled tomatoes
2   slices hearty white sandwich bread, crusts removed, torn into 1-inch pieces
2   teaspoons packed brown sugar, plus extra for seasoning
½   cup chicken broth, plus extra as needed
1   tablespoon brandy (optional)
    Salt and pepper
2   tablespoons minced fresh chives

1. Heat 1 tablespoon oil in medium saucepan over medium heat until shimmering. Add onion and cook until softened, about 5 minutes. Stir in garlic and cook until fragrant, about 30 seconds. Stir in tomatoes and their juice and mash with potato masher until no pieces are larger than 2 inches.

2. Stir in bread and sugar, bring to simmer, and cook until bread is saturated and starts to break down, about 5 minutes. Process soup in blender with remaining 1 tablespoon oil until smooth, about 2 minutes. Return soup to clean saucepan.

3. Stir in broth and brandy, if using, and bring to brief simmer. Adjust soup consistency with extra broth as needed. Season with salt, pepper, and extra sugar to taste. Sprinkle individual portions with chives and drizzle with extra oil before serving.

Chilled Fresh Tomato Soup

SERVES 2 · LIGHT

✔ **WHY THIS RECIPE WORKS:** To create a chilled tomato soup for two that offered complex flavor, we used a combination of fresh and roasted tomatoes, which gave us a bright, tangy freshness as well as a deep, sweet flavor. We also used a small amount of tomato paste and lightly roasted garlic and shallot to boost the soup's flavor. Cream is a common inclusion, but to keep our chilled tomato soup light and bright-tasting, we opted for a mere drizzle of olive oil, which added body and richness without weighing the soup down. In-season, locally grown tomatoes and high-quality extra-virgin olive oil are ideal for this recipe. For the nutritional information for this recipe, see page 412.

A combination of fresh and roasted tomatoes emulsified with olive oil makes this summer soup both bright and richly flavored.

2	pounds tomatoes, cored
1	shallot, sliced thin
2	garlic cloves, unpeeled
2	teaspoons tomato paste
⅛	teaspoon smoked paprika (optional)
	Pinch cayenne pepper
	Salt and pepper
1	tablespoon extra-virgin olive oil
1	teaspoon sherry vinegar, plus extra for seasoning
1	tablespoon chopped fresh basil or mint

1. Adjust oven rack to middle position and heat oven to 375 degrees. Line rimmed baking sheet with aluminum foil and lightly spray with vegetable oil spray.

2. Cut 1 pound tomatoes in half horizontally and arrange cut side up on prepared sheet. Arrange shallot and garlic in single layer over 1 area of sheet. Roast for 15 minutes, then remove shallot and garlic. Return sheet to oven and continue to roast tomatoes until softened but not browned, 10 to 15 minutes. Let cool to room temperature, about 30 minutes.

3. Peel garlic cloves and place in blender with roasted shallot and roasted tomatoes. Cut remaining 1 pound tomatoes into eighths and add to blender along with tomato paste, paprika, if using, cayenne, and ½ teaspoon salt. Process until smooth, about 30 seconds. With blender running, slowly add oil until incorporated.

4. Pour puree through fine-mesh strainer into nonreactive bowl, pressing on solids to extract as much liquid as possible; discard solids. Stir in vinegar. Cover and refrigerate until well chilled and flavors meld, at least 4 hours or up to 24 hours.

5. To serve, stir soup to recombine and season with salt and extra vinegar to taste. Ladle soup into individual chilled serving bowls and sprinkle with basil. Season with pepper to taste. Serve immediately.

Gazpacho

SERVES 2 `LIGHT`

✔ **WHY THIS RECIPE WORKS:** While a bowl of chilled gazpacho is incredibly appealing on a hot summer day, chopping piles of vegetables is not, making this popular Spanish soup an ideal recipe to scale down. Since we wanted our soup chunky, we skipped the blender and food processor in favor of hand chopping the vegetables—but with just one tomato, half a bell pepper, and half a cucumber, our prep work was kept to a minimum. Shallot provided an aromatic note that was sweet, not harsh, and marinating the vegetables briefly in sherry vinegar ensured our soup was seasoned throughout. A cup of tomato juice along with a few ice cubes gave our soup just the right consistency and guaranteed it was thoroughly chilled. Cutting the vegetables into small (¼-inch) pieces is important for the texture of this soup; don't hesitate to pull out a ruler when prepping the vegetables. For the nutritional information for this recipe, see page 412.

1   large tomato, cored, seeded, and cut into ¼-inch pieces
½   red bell pepper, cut into ¼-inch pieces
½   cucumber, halved lengthwise, seeded, and cut into
    ¼-inch pieces
1   shallot, minced
2   tablespoons sherry vinegar
1   small garlic clove, minced
    Salt and pepper
1   cup low-sodium tomato juice
¼   teaspoon hot sauce (optional)
3   ice cubes
2   teaspoons extra-virgin olive oil
2   tablespoons minced fresh parsley or cilantro

1. Combine tomato, bell pepper, cucumber, shallot, vinegar, garlic, ¼ teaspoon salt, and ¼ teaspoon pepper in medium bowl and let sit for 5 minutes. Stir in tomato juice, hot sauce, if using, and ice cubes. Cover and refrigerate until well chilled and flavors meld, at least 4 hours or up to 24 hours.

2. To serve, discard any unmelted ice cubes. Stir soup to recombine and season with salt and pepper to taste. Ladle soup into individual chilled serving bowls, drizzle with oil, and sprinkle with parsley.

VARIATION
Gazpacho with Shrimp
For the nutritional information for this recipe, see page 412.

Add 8 ounces cooked and peeled small shrimp (51 to 60 per pound), chilled, to soup before seasoning with salt and pepper in step 2.

A brief marinade in bright sherry vinegar seasons the vegetables throughout for our light and refreshing gazpacho.

Seeding Raw Tomatoes

A. FOR ROUND TOMATOES:
Halve tomato through equator. Gently squeeze each half and shake out seeds and gelatinous material. Use your finger to scoop out any remaining seeds.

B. FOR PLUM TOMATOES:
Halve tomato through core end. Scoop out seeds and gelatinous material with your finger.

To streamline classic *pasta e fagioli*, we enrich canned beans and tomatoes with bacon and aromatics for long-simmered flavor.

Pasta e Fagioli

SERVES 2

✔ **WHY THIS RECIPE WORKS:** *Pasta e fagioli* is a hearty Italian soup composed of pasta and beans with a thick tomato base—we sought to create a perfect weeknight version made from pantry staples. Bacon, onion, and celery gave us a flavorful base on which to build our soup. Allowing canned, diced tomatoes to cook down with the aromatics before adding chicken broth and water helped reduce the tomato juice and concentrate its flavor. We also added the beans before the broth to infuse them with the flavor of the bacon and vegetables. Ditalini was the perfect bite-size pasta to round out our hearty, satisfying soup for two. Serve with grated Parmesan cheese and drizzle with extra-virgin olive oil.

2 slices bacon, chopped fine
1 small onion, chopped fine
1 celery rib, minced
 Salt and pepper
1 garlic clove, minced

1 teaspoon minced fresh oregano or ¼ teaspoon dried
 Pinch red pepper flakes
1 (14.5-ounce) can diced tomatoes
¾ cup canned cannellini beans, rinsed
1 cup chicken broth
1 cup water
⅔ cup small pasta, such as ditalini, tubettini, or mini elbows

1. Cook bacon in medium saucepan over medium heat until crisp, 5 to 7 minutes. Add onion, celery, and pinch salt and cook until softened and lightly browned, 5 to 7 minutes. Stir in garlic, oregano, and pepper flakes and cook until fragrant, about 30 seconds.

2. Stir in tomatoes and their juice, scraping up any browned bits. Stir in beans, bring to simmer, and cook until mixture has thickened slightly, about 5 minutes. Stir in broth, water, and ¼ teaspoon salt and bring to boil. Stir in pasta and cook until al dente, 8 to 12 minutes. Season with salt and pepper to taste and serve.

Tuscan White Bean Soup

SERVES 2   **FAST**

✔ **WHY THIS RECIPE WORKS:** With just a handful of ingredients, Tuscan white bean soup embodies the straightforward simplicity that Italian cooking is known for. But while the ingredient list is simple, it typically relies on a lengthy simmering time to build robust flavor. To cut back on cooking time without sacrificing flavor, we started with a potent base of bacon, carrot, onion, and dried rosemary. Allowing canned white beans to simmer for just 5 minutes with the broth gave them a significant flavor boost, and a last-minute addition of spinach brought some extra heartiness to our dish. We prefer the texture of cannellini beans in this soup; however, small white beans can be substituted. Serve with grated Parmesan cheese and drizzle with extra-virgin olive oil.

2 slices bacon, chopped fine
1 small onion, chopped fine
1 carrot, peeled and chopped fine
 Salt and pepper
1 garlic clove, minced
¼ teaspoon dried rosemary, crumbled
1¾ cups chicken broth
¼ cup water
1 (15-ounce) can cannellini beans, rinsed
5 ounces frozen spinach, thawed and squeezed dry

A potent base of bacon, carrot, onion, and rosemary gives this white bean soup robust flavor—without hours of simmering.

1. Cook bacon in medium saucepan over medium heat until crisp, 5 to 7 minutes. Add onion, carrot, and pinch salt and cook until softened and lightly browned, 5 to 7 minutes. Stir in garlic and rosemary and cook until fragrant, about 30 seconds.

2. Stir in broth, water, beans, spinach, and ½ teaspoon salt. Bring to simmer and cook until soup has thickened slightly, about 5 minutes. Season with salt and pepper to taste and serve.

U.S. Senate Navy Bean Soup

SERVES 2 LIGHT

✔ **WHY THIS RECIPE WORKS:** Navy bean soup is an American classic that combines hearty beans and a thick, creamy broth flavored with a ham hock. To scale it down for two, we replaced the ham hock with a single slice of smoky bacon and diced ham steak. We sautéed the bacon until crisp, then caramelized the diced ham in the bacon fat for rich, meaty bites of ham throughout the soup. Canned beans kept the recipe simple; after just 15 minutes of simmering in our rich broth, they were tender and full of flavor. To thicken the

broth, we simply mashed some of the beans right in the pot. Because ham steak can be quite salty, be careful when seasoning the soup with additional salt. You can get small ham steaks sliced to order at the deli counter. For the nutritional information for this recipe, see page 412.

> 1 slice bacon, chopped fine
> 4 ounces ham steak, patted dry and cut into ½-inch pieces
> 1 small onion, chopped fine
> 1 carrot, peeled and cut into ½-inch pieces
> 1 small celery rib, minced
> 2 garlic cloves, minced
> ½ teaspoon minced fresh thyme or ⅛ teaspoon dried
>   Salt and pepper
> 1 (15-ounce) can navy beans, rinsed
> 1 cup water
> ¾ cup chicken broth
> 1 bay leaf
> ¼ teaspoon red wine vinegar
>   Hot sauce

1. Cook bacon in medium saucepan over medium heat until crisp, 5 to 7 minutes. Using slotted spoon, transfer bacon to paper towel–lined plate. Add ham to fat left in saucepan and cook over medium heat until browned, 3 to 5 minutes.

2. Stir in onion, carrot, and celery and cook until softened, about 5 minutes. Stir in garlic, thyme, and ⅛ teaspoon pepper and cook until fragrant, about 30 seconds. Stir in beans, water, broth, bay leaf, and vinegar and bring to simmer. Reduce heat to medium-low, partially cover, and simmer until carrot is tender and beans are fully flavored, about 15 minutes.

3. Off heat, discard bay leaf. Use back of spoon to press about one-quarter of beans against side of pot to thicken soup. Season with salt and pepper to taste. Top individual portions with bacon pieces and serve with hot sauce.

Lentil Soup

SERVES 2

✔ **WHY THIS RECIPE WORKS:** We wanted our scaled-down lentil soup to have just the right consistency (one that was neither too brothy nor overly thick) and a deep, well-rounded flavor. Selecting the right lentils was key, and the earthy flavor and firm texture of *lentilles du Puy* won out over other varieties, which tended to disintegrate when simmered. Sweating the lentils in a covered pan with the aromatics (along with some tomatoes and salt for an additional flavor boost) prior to adding the liquid helped the lentils remain intact.

Gently sweating the lentils with flavorful aromatics gives our lentil soup rich flavor and helps keep the delicate lentils intact.

Pureeing a few cups of the soup created a substantial, creamy base. Bacon infused our soup with smoky flavor and offered a welcome textural contrast, while parsley and a splash of balsamic vinegar provided a bright finish. Although we prefer lentilles du Puy (also called French green lentils) for this recipe, it will work with any type of lentil except red or yellow. Note that cooking times may vary depending on the type of lentils you use.

    2   slices bacon, chopped fine
    1   small onion, chopped fine
    1   carrot, peeled and cut into ¼-inch pieces
    1   tomato, cored, seeded, and chopped fine
    1   garlic clove, minced
    ¼   teaspoon minced fresh thyme or pinch dried
    ½   cup dried lentils, picked over and rinsed
        Salt and pepper
    2   cups chicken broth
    1   cup water
    1   bay leaf
    1   tablespoon minced fresh parsley
    1   teaspoon balsamic vinegar

1. Cook bacon in medium saucepan over medium heat until crisp, 5 to 7 minutes. Add onion and carrot and cook until softened, about 5 minutes. Stir in tomato, garlic, and thyme and cook until fragrant, about 30 seconds. Stir in lentils and ½ teaspoon salt. Reduce heat to medium-low, cover, and cook until lentils have darkened, 5 to 8 minutes.

2. Stir in broth, water, and bay leaf, scraping up any browned bits. Bring to simmer, partially cover, and cook until lentils are tender but still hold their shape, 35 to 45 minutes.

3. Process 1½ cups of soup in blender until smooth, about 2 minutes. Return processed soup to saucepan and stir to combine. Season with salt and pepper to taste. Sprinkle individual portions with parsley and drizzle with vinegar before serving.

VARIATION

Curried Lentil Soup

Omit bacon. Heat 1 tablespoon vegetable oil in medium saucepan over medium heat until shimmering. Add onion and carrot and proceed with recipe. Add ¾ teaspoon curry powder and ½ teaspoon garam masala with tomato, garlic, and thyme. Substitute 1 tablespoon minced fresh cilantro for parsley.

Moroccan-Style Chickpea Soup

SERVES 2   LIGHT

✔ **WHY THIS RECIPE WORKS:** Knowing that the unique, complex flavors of a Moroccan-style chickpea soup would be a welcome addition to our for-two repertoire, we set about translating this recipe into an accessible weeknight meal. Canned chickpeas and store-bought vegetable broth, along with some onion, provided a streamlined-yet-flavorful base. Tomato paste lent a long-simmered depth to our soup, and cooking it briefly with garlic, paprika, garam masala, and cumin allowed all the flavors to bloom. Some chopped tomato and zucchini contributed freshness and textural interest, and a sprinkling of fresh cilantro was the perfect finishing touch to this simple, flavorful one-pot meal. For the nutritional information for this recipe, see page 412.

    1   tablespoon unsalted butter
    1   small onion, chopped fine
        Salt and pepper
    2   teaspoons tomato paste
    2   garlic cloves, minced
    ½   teaspoon paprika
    ½   teaspoon garam masala
    ¼   teaspoon ground cumin
    2   cups vegetable broth
    1   cup canned chickpeas, rinsed

1 tomato, cored, seeded, and chopped fine
1 small zucchini, cut into ½-inch pieces
1 tablespoon minced fresh cilantro

1. Melt butter in medium saucepan over medium heat. Add onion and ¼ teaspoon salt and cook until softened, about 5 minutes. Stir in tomato paste, garlic, paprika, garam masala, and cumin, and cook until fragrant, about 30 seconds.

2. Stir in broth and chickpeas, bring to simmer, and cook for 10 minutes. Stir in tomato and zucchini and continue to simmer until zucchini is tender, about 10 minutes. Stir in cilantro and season with salt and pepper to taste. Serve.

NOTES FROM THE TEST KITCHEN

Buying Broth

Nothing compares with the flavor of homemade stock, but few of us ever have time to make it from scratch. Fortunately, we've found a few good stand-ins at the supermarket that will deliver richly flavored yet speedy soups, stews, and more.

CHICKEN BROTH
In search of the best-tasting chicken broth, we discovered a few things that made a big difference in quality. First, look for a sodium content between 400 and 700 milligrams per serving. Too-salty broth can easily ruin a dish, but not enough salt can leave a dish tasting bland. Also, look for a mass-produced broth. Several broths had rancid off-flavors caused by fat oxidation; the worst offenders were made by smaller companies. Last, look for a short ingredient list that includes vegetables like carrots, celery, and onions. Our pick? **Swanson Chicken Broth**, which tastes rich and meaty thanks to its relatively high percentage of meat-based protein.

BEEF BROTH
Historically we've found beef broths short on beefy flavor, but our winning beef broth, **Rachael Ray Stock-in-a-Box All-Natural Beef Flavored Stock**, has a short ingredient list that starts with concentrated beef stock, which means this stock has more fresh, real meat than its competitors. Also, it managed to taste really beefy without a slew of processed additives.

BOUILLION AND BROTH CONCENTRATES
Dehydrated forms of chicken and beef broth, these shelf-stable products are cost-effective (because you're not paying for the water) and last for up to two years once opened, so they're particularly great for small households. Simply mix with water to make just as much broth as you need. We particularly like **Better than Bouillon Chicken Base**, which costs just $5.99 for a jar that makes 38 cups of broth.

VEGETABLE BROTH
For vegetarian dishes or dishes that would be overwhelmed by the flavor of chicken broth, we turn to vegetable broth. We sometimes use a mix of chicken and vegetable broths, as vegetable broth can be too sweet when used alone. In search of the best vegetable broth, we tested 10 brands and found that our favorites listed vegetable content first on the ingredients list and included a hefty amount of salt. Our winner? **Swanson Vegetarian Vegetable Broth**.

Corn Chowder
SERVES 2

✔ **WHY THIS RECIPE WORKS:** For a corn chowder loaded with fresh corn flavor, we grated the corn cobs after removing the kernels and then scraped off their pulp; adding the grated corn and pulp to our chowder gave it a thick, lush, smooth texture and dramatically improved its flavor. Adding the corn kernels toward the end of cooking helped them retain their fresh-from-the-cob flavor. Finely chopped bacon contributed a smoky backbone. Some chicken broth improved the flavor of our chowder, while a small amount of heavy cream provided just enough richness. A red potato, garlic, and onion added substance and just the right aromatic notes, and a sprinkling of fresh parsley was the perfect finishing touch. In-season sweet corn is ideal for this recipe; do not substitute frozen corn.

3 ears corn, husks and silk removed
2 slices bacon, chopped coarse
1 small onion, chopped fine
1 garlic clove, minced
¼ teaspoon minced fresh thyme or pinch dried
1 tablespoon all-purpose flour
2 cups chicken broth
1 red potato (6 ounces), unpeeled, cut into ½-inch pieces
¼ cup heavy cream
1 tablespoon minced fresh parsley
Salt and pepper

1. Cut kernels from 1 ear of corn into bowl. In separate bowl, grate remaining 2 ears corn over large holes of box grater. Using back of butter knife, scrape any remaining pulp from cobs into bowl with grated corn.

2. Cook bacon in medium saucepan over medium heat until crisp, 5 to 7 minutes. Add onion and cook until softened, about 5 minutes. Stir in garlic and thyme and cook until fragrant, about 30 seconds. Stir in flour and cook for 1 minute.

3. Slowly whisk in broth, scraping up any browned bits and smoothing out any lumps. Stir in potato and grated corn mixture, bring to simmer, and cook until potato is tender, about 15 minutes.

4. Stir in cream and remaining corn kernels and simmer until corn kernels are tender yet still slightly crunchy, about 5 minutes. Stir in parsley and season with salt and pepper to taste. Serve.

VARIATIONS
Maryland-Style Corn Chowder with Crabmeat
For a hearty crab presence, double the amount of crabmeat.
    Add 1½ teaspoons Old Bay seasoning with garlic and thyme. Substitute 1 tablespoon minced fresh chives for parsley and

add 4 ounces lump crabmeat, picked over for shells, to soup before seasoning with salt and pepper.

Southwestern-Style Corn Chowder with Chorizo and Chiles

For more heat, include the jalapeño seeds and ribs.

Substitute 4 ounces chorizo sausage, cut into ½-inch pieces, for bacon and cook until browned, about 3 minutes. Add 1 minced jalapeño chile with onion. Substitute 1 tablespoon minced fresh cilantro for parsley.

Chicken Chowder

SERVES 2

✔ **WHY THIS RECIPE WORKS:** Rustic, hearty, and made with readily accessible ingredients, chicken chowder makes a great one-pot meal. Cooking just one slice of bacon then sautéing the aromatics in the rendered fat provided a flavorful base, while stirring in a spoonful of flour contributed thickening power. Poaching a single chicken breast (just the right amount for two servings) right in the broth kept the meat moist. After poaching we shredded the meat before stirring it back into our chowder. A medium-starch Yukon Gold potato contributed earthy flavor, and the pieces retained their shape in the chowder. Carrot and red bell pepper offered sweetness and a light crunch, while cream stirred in at the end finished our chicken chowder with a silky richness. Be careful not to overcook the chicken in step 3 or it will taste dry.

- 1 **slice bacon, chopped fine**
- 1 **large shallot, minced**
- 1 **garlic clove, minced**
- ¼ **teaspoon minced fresh thyme or pinch dried**
- 1 **tablespoon all-purpose flour**
- 2 **cups chicken broth**
- 1 **Yukon Gold potato (8 ounces), peeled and cut into ½-inch pieces**
- 1 **small carrot, peeled and sliced ¼ inch thick**
- 1 **(8-ounce) boneless, skinless chicken breast, trimmed**
- ½ **red bell pepper, cut into ½-inch pieces**
- ¼ **cup heavy cream**
- 2 **teaspoons minced fresh parsley**
  Salt and pepper

1. Cook bacon in medium saucepan over medium heat until crisp, 5 to 7 minutes. Using slotted spoon, transfer half of bacon to paper towel–lined plate.

This satisfying chicken chowder boasts a rich, creamy broth, tender chicken, sweet carrot, and hearty bites of potato.

2. Add shallot to bacon and fat left in saucepan and cook until softened, about 3 minutes. Stir in garlic and thyme and cook until fragrant, about 30 seconds. Stir in flour and cook for 1 minute.

3. Slowly whisk in broth, scraping up any browned bits and smoothing out any lumps. Stir in potato and carrot. Add chicken, bring to simmer, and cook until it registers 160 degrees, 10 to 15 minutes, flipping chicken halfway through cooking. Transfer chicken to cutting board, let cool slightly, then shred into bite-size pieces using 2 forks.

4. Return chowder to simmer, stir in bell pepper, and cook until vegetables are tender, 10 to 15 minutes. Off heat, stir in shredded chicken and cream and let sit until heated through, about 2 minutes. Stir in parsley and season with salt and pepper to taste. Sprinkle individual portions with reserved bacon before serving.

VARIATION

Cajun Chicken Chowder with Corn

Omit carrot. Add 1 minced small celery rib to saucepan with shallot and ½ teaspoon Cajun seasoning with garlic and thyme. Add ¼ cup frozen corn with bell pepper.

New England Clam Chowder

SERVES 2

✓ **WHY THIS RECIPE WORKS:** Many people are intimidated by the thought of preparing clam chowder at home—clams can be expensive and a challenge to cook, and the dairy in chowder has a tendency to curdle. We wanted to make clam chowder accessible to the for-two kitchen, and we started with the clams. Cherrystones offered good value and flavor, and we found that if we steamed them they did not toughen up, so long as we removed them from the pot as soon as they opened. A combination of homemade clam broth and chicken broth provided a base that was balanced and not overly salty. Creamy Yukon Gold potatoes held their shape as the chowder simmered for hearty bites of potato throughout. Bacon provided a smoky note that completed our scaled down chowder. Serve with oyster crackers.

    1   cup water
    2   pounds medium hard-shell clams, such as cherrystones, scrubbed
    2   slices bacon, chopped fine
    1   small onion, chopped fine
    1   celery rib, minced
    ¼   teaspoon minced fresh thyme or pinch dried
    2½ tablespoons all-purpose flour
    1½ cups chicken broth
    1   Yukon Gold potato (8 ounces), peeled and cut into ½-inch pieces
    ⅓   cup heavy cream
    1   tablespoon minced fresh parsley
        Salt and pepper

1. Bring water to boil in medium saucepan. Add clams, cover, and cook for 5 minutes. Stir clams thoroughly, cover, and continue to cook until they just begin to open, 2 to 5 minutes. As clams open, transfer them to bowl and let cool slightly. Discard any unopened clams.

2. Measure out and reserve 1 cup of clam steaming liquid, avoiding any gritty sediment that has settled on bottom of saucepan. Using paring knife, remove clam meat from shells and chop coarse.

3. In clean saucepan, cook bacon over medium heat until crisp, 5 to 7 minutes. Add onion and celery and cook until softened, about 5 minutes. Stir in thyme and cook until fragrant, about 30 seconds. Stir in flour and cook for 1 minute.

4. Slowly whisk in broth and reserved clam steaming liquid, scraping up any browned bits and smoothing out any lumps. Stir in potatoes, bring to simmer, and cook until potatoes are tender, 20 to 25 minutes. Off heat, stir in chopped clams and cream and let sit until heated through, about 2 minutes. Stir in parsley and season with salt and pepper to taste. Serve.

VARIATION

Pantry Clam Chowder
Omit water and fresh clams and skip steps 1 and 2. Substitute 1 (8-ounce) bottle clam juice for clam steaming liquid and 2 (6.5-ounce) cans minced clams, drained, for chopped clams.

Removing Clam Meat from the Shell

1. Steam clams until they just open, as seen on right, rather than completely open, as shown on left.

2. Carefully use paring knife to open clam shell completely.

3. Once open, discard top shell and use knife to cut clam from bottom shell.

CHAPTER 2

Stews, Curries, and Chilis

■ FAST (Start to finish in about 30 minutes)

■ LIGHT (See page 413 for nutritional information)

Opposite: Italian Vegetable Stew; Turkey Chili; Classic Beef Stew

Weeknight Beef Stew

SERVES 2

✓ **WHY THIS RECIPE WORKS:** Beef stews typically require a lengthy simmering time and a large cut of meat and make enough to feed a crowd; we wanted a hearty, richly flavored beef stew that would cook in a fraction of the time and provide just enough for two. Instead of the usual chuck-eye roast, we chose steak tips, which don't require long-cooking. To mimic the flavor of a slow-cooked stew, we seared the beef in two batches to develop more fond and added tomato paste, a small amount of anchovy, and soy sauce for meaty flavor and savory depth. Steak tips, also known as flap meat, are sold as whole steak, cubes, and strips; look for either whole steak tips or strips that are easy to cut into small pieces for this recipe.

12	ounces sirloin steak tips, trimmed and cut into ½-inch pieces
	Salt and pepper
4	teaspoons vegetable oil
1	small onion, chopped fine
1	carrot, peeled and sliced ¼ inch thick
2	garlic cloves, minced
1	teaspoon tomato paste
½	anchovy fillet, rinsed and minced
½	teaspoon minced fresh thyme or ⅛ teaspoon dried
1	tablespoon all-purpose flour
3	tablespoons dry red wine
1½	cups beef broth
1	small Yukon Gold potato (6 ounces), peeled and cut into ½-inch pieces
¼	cup frozen peas
1	teaspoon soy sauce

1. Pat beef dry with paper towels and season with salt and pepper. Heat 2 teaspoons oil in medium saucepan over medium-high heat until just smoking. Brown half of beef on all sides, 5 to 7 minutes; transfer to bowl. Repeat with remaining 2 teaspoons oil and remaining beef; transfer to bowl.

2. Add onion and carrot to fat left in saucepan and cook over medium heat until softened, about 5 minutes. Stir in garlic, tomato paste, anchovy, and thyme and cook until fragrant, about 30 seconds. Stir in flour and cook for 1 minute.

3. Slowly whisk in wine, scraping up any browned bits and smoothing out any lumps. Stir in broth and potato and bring to simmer. Reduce heat to medium-low, cover, and simmer until vegetables are tender, 15 to 20 minutes.

4. Stir in browned beef and any accumulated juices, peas, and soy sauce and simmer until stew is heated through, about 2 minutes. Season with salt and pepper to taste and serve.

Classic Beef Stew

SERVES 2

✓ **WHY THIS RECIPE WORKS:** We wanted a recipe for an ultimate beef stew that would keep the cooking process simple without compromising the stew's deep, complex flavor. To start, we swapped out the usual chuck roast for boneless beef short ribs—which have outstanding beefy flavor and become supremely tender after a slow simmer—and browned them to develop a flavorful fond with which we could build the rest of our stew. A little flour added to the sautéed aromatics helped thicken our stew, while some *umami*-rich tomato paste and beef broth enhanced the meatiness of the ribs. Traditional carrots, potato, and peas worked well here, and cutting the carrots and potatoes into substantial pieces ensured they didn't overcook. You will need a medium ovensafe saucepan for this recipe.

1	pound boneless beef short ribs, trimmed and cut into 1½-inch pieces
	Salt and pepper
1	tablespoon vegetable oil
1	small onion, chopped fine
2	garlic cloves, minced
1	teaspoon tomato paste
½	teaspoon minced fresh thyme or ⅛ teaspoon dried
1	tablespoon all-purpose flour
¼	cup dry red wine
1½	cups beef broth
1	bay leaf
1	Yukon Gold potato (8 ounces), cut into ¾-inch pieces
2	carrots, peeled and sliced ¾ inch thick
¼	cup frozen peas
1	tablespoon minced fresh parsley

1. Adjust oven rack to middle position and heat oven to 300 degrees. Pat beef dry with paper towels and season with salt and pepper. Heat oil in medium ovensafe saucepan over medium-high heat until just smoking. Brown beef on all sides, about 8 minutes; transfer to bowl.

2. Add onion to fat left in saucepan and cook over medium heat until softened, about 5 minutes. Stir in garlic, tomato paste, and thyme and cook until fragrant, about 30 seconds. Stir in flour and cook for 1 minute.

3. Slowly whisk in wine, scraping up any browned bits and smoothing out any lumps. Stir in broth, bay leaf, and browned beef with any accumulated juices and bring to simmer. Cover, transfer saucepan to oven, and cook for 1 hour.

4. Stir in potato and carrots and continue to cook in oven, covered, until beef and vegetables are tender, 1½ to 2 hours.

5. Discard bay leaf. Using large spoon, skim excess fat from surface of stew. Stir in peas and let sit until heated through, about 2 minutes. Stir in parsley and season with salt and pepper to taste. Serve.

VARIATION

Provençal-Style Beef Stew

Omit potato and peas. Increase amount of garlic to 3 cloves, tomato paste to 2 teaspoons, and carrots to 4. Stir in 2 (2-inch) strips orange zest, ¼ ounce dried porcini mushrooms, rinsed and minced, and 1 rinsed anchovy fillet with garlic, tomato paste, and thyme. Stir in 1 (14.5-ounce) can diced tomatoes, drained, and ¼ cup coarsely chopped pitted kalamata olives with broth, bay leaf, and browned beef.

Trimming Short Ribs

Short ribs can be very fatty, so it's important to trim them well to avoid a greasy stew. Using sharp knife, trim away large piece of fat on top and, if necessary, any fat on bottom of each rib.

A slow-cooked *sofrito* of onion, spices, and herbs gives this Spanish-inspired beef stew a deep, complex flavor base.

Catalan-Style Beef Stew with Mushrooms

SERVES 2

✔ **WHY THIS RECIPE WORKS:** For a complexly flavored Spanish-style beef stew, we started with a *sofrito*, a slow-cooked mixture of onion, spices, and herbs. Salt and sugar helped the onion to caramelize, then we added a grated plum tomato and cooked it until the mixture was thick and jamlike. Boneless beef short ribs were easy to buy in small amounts and became ultratender after a slow simmer. A broth of water and white wine allowed the rich flavors of the meat and the sofrito to shine. A traditional *picada*, a mixture of toasted bread, almonds, garlic, and parsley, brightened the stew's flavor and thickened the broth. You will need a medium ovensafe saucepan for this recipe. Serve with potatoes or rice.

STEW

 1 tablespoon olive oil
 1 onion, chopped fine
 ¼ teaspoon sugar
 Salt and pepper
 1 plum tomato, halved lengthwise, pulp grated on large holes of box grater, and skin discarded
 ½ teaspoon smoked paprika
 1 bay leaf
 ¾ cup water
 ½ cup dry white wine
 8 ounces white mushrooms, trimmed and quartered
 1 sprig fresh thyme
 Pinch ground cinnamon
 1½ pounds boneless beef short ribs, trimmed and cut into 1½-inch pieces

PICADA

 2 tablespoons whole blanched almonds
 2 teaspoons olive oil
 ½ slice hearty white sandwich bread, crust removed, torn into 1-inch pieces
 1 garlic clove, peeled
 1½ tablespoons minced fresh parsley
 ¼ teaspoon sherry vinegar

1. FOR THE STEW: Adjust oven rack to middle position and heat oven to 300 degrees. Heat oil in medium ovensafe saucepan over medium-low heat until shimmering. Add onion, sugar, and ¼ teaspoon salt and cook, stirring often, until onion is deeply caramelized, 25 to 30 minutes. Stir in tomato, paprika, and bay leaf and cook, stirring often, until mixture is darkened and thick, 5 to 10 minutes.

2. Stir in water, wine, mushrooms, thyme sprig, and cinnamon, scraping up any browned bits. Season beef with salt and pepper, add to stew mixture, and bring to simmer. Transfer saucepan to oven and cook, uncovered, for 1 hour.

3. Stir stew to redistribute meat and continue to cook in oven, uncovered, until beef is tender, 1½ to 2 hours.

4. FOR THE PICADA: Meanwhile, combine almonds and oil in bowl and microwave until nuts are light golden, 45 to 60 seconds. Stir in bread and continue to microwave until bread is golden, 60 to 90 seconds; transfer to food processor. Add garlic and process until mixture is finely ground, about 20 seconds, scraping down sides of bowl as needed. Transfer mixture to bowl and stir in parsley.

5. Discard bay leaf and thyme sprig from stew. Stir in picada and vinegar and season with salt and pepper to taste. Serve.

Brazilian-Style Pork and Black Bean Stew

SERVES 2

✔ **WHY THIS RECIPE WORKS:** *Feijoada* is a hearty Brazilian stew featuring creamy black beans and smoky, tender pork. We wanted to scale down the yield while preserving its bold, potent flavors. Just one can of black beans provided a good base and saved us the long soaking time dried beans require. Smoky linguiça sausage and meaty country-style ribs (which, unlike other ribs, can be purchased individually) gave us the most pork flavor with the least amount of prep. For rich flavor without hours of simmering, we browned the ribs and added plenty of aromatics and vegetables—garlic, onion, bell pepper, jalapeño, and a tomato. A little flour and mashing some of the beans helped thicken our stew to the proper consistency. Finally, we topped our dish with a salsa for a fresh, bright contrast to the rich stew. To make this dish spicier, add the chile seeds. Serve with rice.

- 1 small green bell pepper, stemmed, seeded, and chopped fine
- 1 small tomato, cored, seeded, and chopped fine
- 1 small onion, chopped fine
- 1 jalapeño chile, stemmed, seeded, and minced
- 2 tablespoons vegetable oil
- 1 tablespoon white wine vinegar
- 1 tablespoon minced fresh cilantro
  Salt and pepper
- 12 ounces boneless country-style pork ribs, trimmed and cut into 1½-inch pieces
- 2 garlic cloves, minced
- 2 tablespoons all-purpose flour
- 2 cups chicken broth
- 1 (15-ounce) can black beans, rinsed
- 4 ounces linguiça sausage, cut into ½-inch pieces

1. Combine 2 tablespoons bell pepper, 2 tablespoons tomato, 2 tablespoons onion, 1 tablespoon jalapeño, 1 teaspoon oil, vinegar, cilantro, ⅛ teaspoon salt, and pinch pepper in bowl; set aside.

2. Pat pork dry with paper towels and season with salt and pepper. Heat 1 tablespoon oil in medium saucepan over medium-high heat until just smoking. Brown pork lightly on all sides, about 6 minutes; transfer to bowl.

3. Heat remaining 2 teaspoons oil in now-empty saucepan over medium heat until shimmering. Add remaining bell pepper, remaining onion, and remaining jalapeño and cook until softened, about 5 minutes. Stir in garlic and remaining tomato and cook until fragrant, about 30 seconds. Stir in flour and cook for 1 minute.

4. Slowly whisk in broth, scraping up any browned bits and smoothing out any lumps. Stir in browned pork and any accumulated juices, beans, and linguiça and bring to simmer. Reduce heat to medium-low, cover, and simmer until pork is tender, about 30 minutes.

5. Using back of wooden spoon, mash some of beans against side of pan to thicken stew. Season with salt and pepper to taste. Serve with salsa.

Seeding Chiles

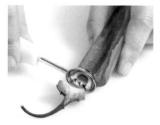

1. Cut chile in half lengthwise to expose core, then gently scrape out seeds and ribs using melon baller (or teaspoon).

2. Use sharp edge of melon baller to cut off stem.

Pork Vindaloo

SERVES 2

✔ **WHY THIS RECIPE WORKS:** Spices are the cornerstone of pork vindaloo, an Indian stew of Portuguese origin that combines elements of hot, sweet, and tangy into one boldly flavored dish. We found that just one ingredient, garam masala—a warm blend of spices typically including cumin, cardamom, cloves, and cinnamon, among others—gave our vindaloo its distinct flavor without cluttering our ingredient list. Tomatoes, mustard seeds, and chicken broth, along with some aromatic onion and garlic, provided a good base. For the pork, we chose country-style ribs, which have more flavor than pork tenderloin and are easier to get in small portions than the more traditional pork butt. Red wine vinegar contributed the classic tanginess, and some chopped fresh cilantro provided a burst of color and a distinct herbal note. Serve with rice.

12	ounces boneless country-style pork ribs, trimmed and cut into 1½-inch pieces
	Salt and pepper
2	tablespoons vegetable oil
1	small onion, chopped fine
2	garlic cloves, minced
2	teaspoons mustard seeds
1	teaspoon garam masala
1	teaspoon hot paprika
2	tablespoons all-purpose flour
2	cups chicken broth
1	(14.5-ounce) can diced tomatoes, drained
2	tablespoons minced fresh cilantro
1	tablespoon red wine vinegar

1. Pat pork dry with paper towels and season with salt and pepper. Heat 1 tablespoon oil in medium saucepan over medium-high heat until just smoking. Brown pork lightly on all sides, about 6 minutes; transfer to bowl.

2. Heat remaining 1 tablespoon oil in now-empty saucepan over medium heat until shimmering. Add onion, garlic, mustard seeds, garam masala, paprika, and ½ teaspoon salt. Cook, stirring often, until onion is softened and spices are fragrant, about 5 minutes. Stir in flour and cook for 1 minute.

3. Slowly whisk in broth, scraping up any browned bits and smoothing out any lumps. Stir in browned pork with any accumulated juices and tomatoes and bring to simmer. Reduce heat to medium-low, cover, and simmer until pork is tender, about 30 minutes. Stir in cilantro and vinegar and season with salt and pepper to taste. Serve.

Chicken Tagine

SERVES 2 `LIGHT`

✔ **WHY THIS RECIPE WORKS:** Tagines, a North African dish, are exotically spiced, assertively flavored stews traditionally slow-cooked in earthenware vessels. We wanted to streamline the ingredient list and time involved in making a tagine while retaining its authentic flavor. Convenient chicken breasts cooked at a gentle, slow simmer were an ideal choice for the meat. Garam masala and paprika packed plenty of flavor and color without a laundry list of ingredients. Chicken broth provided a good base, and a little flour helped the sauce thicken to just the right consistency. Canned diced tomatoes, chickpeas, and dried apricots rounded out our tagine, providing just the right mix of acidity and sweetness, as well as pleasantly contrasting textures. Be careful not to overcook the chicken in step 2 or it will taste dry. Serve with rice. For the nutritional information for this recipe, see page 413.

1	tablespoon vegetable oil
1	small onion, chopped fine
2	garlic cloves, minced
1	teaspoon garam masala
1	teaspoon paprika
	Salt and pepper
1	tablespoon all-purpose flour
2	cups chicken broth
1	(14.5-ounce) can diced tomatoes, drained
1	(14-ounce) can chickpeas, rinsed
½	cup dried apricots, quartered
1	(8-ounce) boneless, skinless chicken breast, trimmed
1	tablespoon minced fresh cilantro

1. Heat oil in medium saucepan over medium heat until shimmering. Add onion, garlic, garam masala, paprika, and ¼ teaspoon salt. Cook, stirring often, until onion is softened and spices are fragrant, about 5 minutes. Stir in flour and cook for 1 minute.

2. Slowly whisk in broth, scraping up any browned bits and smoothing out any lumps. Stir in tomatoes, chickpeas, and apricots. Season chicken with salt and pepper, add to stew mixture, and bring to simmer. Reduce heat to medium-low, cover, and simmer until chicken registers 160 degrees, 10 to 15 minutes, flipping chicken halfway through cooking. Transfer chicken to cutting board, let cool slightly, then shred into bite-size pieces using 2 forks.

3. Off heat, stir in shredded chicken and let sit until heated through, about 2 minutes. Stir in cilantro and season with salt and pepper to taste. Serve.

Shrimp and Sausage Gumbo

SERVES 2

✔ WHY THIS RECIPE WORKS: Traditional gumbo relies on hours of preparation and cooking to develop its signature flavor and thick, satisfying texture; we hoped to replicate that slow-cooked richness in a fraction of the time. Cooking the flour and oil over medium heat—rather than the typical low heat—was a simple change that gave us a roasted, nutty roux in short order. Onion, bell pepper, celery, and garlic provided the aromatic base, while just a teaspoon of Cajun seasoning gave us complex, authentic flavor with just one ingredient. Garlicky andouille sausage and quick-cooking shrimp were simple to prepare and rounded out our gumbo to make it an ideal one-pot meal for two.

- ¼ cup all-purpose flour
- 3 tablespoons vegetable oil
- 8 ounces andouille sausage, halved lengthwise and sliced ½ inch thick
- 1 small onion, chopped fine
- 1 red bell pepper, stemmed, seeded, and cut into ½-inch pieces
- 1 celery rib, minced
- 2 garlic cloves, minced
- 1 teaspoon Cajun seasoning
- ½ teaspoon minced fresh thyme or ⅛ teaspoon dried
- 1 (8-ounce) bottle clam juice
- ½ cup water
- 8 ounces extra-large shrimp (21 to 25 per pound), peeled, deveined, and tails removed
- 2 scallions, sliced thin

1. Whisk flour and oil together in medium saucepan until smooth. Cook over medium heat, whisking occasionally, until mixture is deep brown and fragrant, about 15 minutes.

2. Add andouille, onion, bell pepper, and celery, and cook until vegetables are softened and lightly browned, about 10 minutes. Stir in garlic, Cajun seasoning, and thyme and cook until fragrant, about 30 seconds.

3. Slowly whisk in clam juice and water, scraping up any browned bits and smoothing out any lumps. Bring to simmer and cook until vegetables are tender and mixture has thickened, about 10 minutes. Stir in shrimp and continue to simmer until opaque throughout, about 3 minutes. Stir in scallions and season with salt and pepper to taste. Serve.

NOTES FROM THE TEST KITCHEN

Guidelines for Using Dried Herbs

Dried herbs are more convenient than fresh because they don't spoil and need no more prep than a twist of a lid. But they can add a dusty quality to dishes, especially when added at the end. Here are the tricks we've found for using them successfully.

WHEN DRIED HERBS SHINE AND HOW TO SUBSTITUTE: Only some dried herbs give good results, mainly in recipes with longer cooking times (20 minutes or more) and a good amount of moisture. Chili is one dish that is better made with dried oregano than with fresh. Dried rosemary, sage, marjoram, and thyme also fare reasonably well in certain applications; the flavor compounds in these herbs are relatively stable at high temperature, so they maintain their flavor through the drying process. To replace fresh herbs with dried, use one-third the amount, and add them early in the cooking process so they have time to soften.

WHEN FRESH IS BEST: Those herbs that we consider delicate (basil, chives, and parsley) lose most of their flavor when dried; we prefer fresh forms of these herbs. Two herbs, tarragon and dill, fall into a middle category: They do add flavor in their dried form, but it is more muted than that provided by other dried herbs.

SMART STORAGE: Like spices, dried herbs should be stored in a cool, dark, dry place, not near the stove where heat, light, and moisture will shorten their shelf life. However, even when properly stored, dried herbs lose their potency six to 12 months after opening, so it's important to replace them frequently. You can test dried herbs for freshness by rubbing them between your fingers—if they don't release a bright fragrance, buy a new jar.

Mediterranean-Style Fish Stew

SERVES 2

✔ WHY THIS RECIPE WORKS: Since fish is naturally quick cooking, we thought a Mediterranean-inspired fish stew would make an easy yet elegant weeknight meal for two. To build an intensely flavorful base in a short amount of time, we sautéed a generous amount of onion and fennel in fruity extra-virgin olive oil. A few ounces of smoky chorizo sausage contributed hearty flavor and spicy complexity. White wine, diced tomatoes, and a bottle of clam juice gave the broth brightness, a welcome acidity, and just the right amount of brininess. The fish (we liked substantial pieces of cod) needed just a few minutes of simmering in our highly flavorful broth to cook through. Serve with crusty bread or rice.

- 1 tablespoon extra-virgin olive oil, plus extra for serving
- 4 ounces chorizo sausage, cut into ½-inch pieces
- 1 small onion, chopped fine
- ½ fennel bulb, stalks discarded, bulb cored and sliced thin
- 2 garlic cloves, minced

We combine delicate cod with spicy chorizo, fennel, and diced tomatoes for an elegant fish stew with bold, fresh flavors.

⅓ cup dry white wine
1 (14.5-ounce) can diced tomatoes
1 (8-ounce) bottle clam juice
12 ounces skinless cod fillets, 1 to 1½ inches thick, cut into 2-inch pieces
   Salt and pepper
1 tablespoon minced fresh parsley

1. Heat oil in medium saucepan over medium heat until shimmering. Add chorizo, onion, and fennel and cook until vegetables are softened, about 8 minutes. Stir in garlic and cook until fragrant, about 30 seconds. Stir in wine, scraping up any browned bits. Stir in tomatoes with their juice and clam juice, bring to simmer, and cook until flavors meld, about 10 minutes.

2. Season cod with salt and pepper. Nestle cod into stew mixture, spoon some of sauce over fish, and bring to simmer. Reduce heat to medium-low, cover, and simmer until fish flakes apart when gently prodded with paring knife and registers 140 degrees, about 5 minutes. Gently stir in parsley and season with salt and pepper to taste. Drizzle individual portions with extra oil before serving.

Italian Vegetable Stew

SERVES 2

✔ **WHY THIS RECIPE WORKS:** Italy's answer to ratatouille, *giambotta* is a dish that turns a bounty of summer vegetables into a fresh, satisfying stew. But given that the mix of vegetables typically includes zucchini, tomatoes, and eggplant, it's no surprise that the result is often a watery, flavorless dish. Browning the eggplant helped rid it of excess moisture and contributed rich flavor. Similarly, we found that sautéing canned tomatoes drove off excess moisture and developed good caramelization; the addition of a little tomato paste further concentrated the tomato flavor. Just one potato (we liked buttery Yukon Gold) added plenty of starch and heft to this dish; giving it a jump start in the microwave ensured it was tender at the same time as the other vegetables. Finished with a sprinkling of fresh basil, grated Pecorino Romano, and a drizzle of oil, this is a stew we can enjoy any time of year. Do not peel the eggplant, as the skin helps hold it together during cooking.

3 tablespoons extra-virgin olive oil, plus extra for serving
½ eggplant (8 ounces), cut into 1-inch pieces
1 Yukon Gold potato (8 ounces), peeled and cut into ½-inch pieces
1 (14.5-ounce) can whole peeled tomatoes, drained with juice reserved
3 garlic cloves, minced
1 teaspoon tomato paste
¼ teaspoon minced fresh oregano or pinch dried
   Salt and pepper
3 cups vegetable broth
1 small zucchini, halved lengthwise, seeded, and cut into 1-inch pieces
2 tablespoons chopped fresh basil
¼ cup grated Pecorino Romano cheese

Seeding Zucchini

Cut zucchini in half lengthwise, then run small spoon inside each zucchini half to scoop out seeds.

1. Heat 2 tablespoons oil in medium saucepan over medium-high heat until shimmering. Brown eggplant lightly on all sides, 5 to 7 minutes; transfer to bowl. Meanwhile, microwave potato and 1 teaspoon oil in covered bowl until softened, about 5 minutes.

2. Heat remaining 2 teaspoons oil in now-empty saucepan over medium heat until shimmering. Add tomatoes, garlic, tomato paste, oregano, ¼ teaspoon salt, and ¼ teaspoon pepper and cook until mixture is dry and beginning to brown, 11 to 13 minutes.

3. Stir in broth and reserved tomato juice, scraping up any browned bits. Stir in browned eggplant, softened potato, and zucchini and bring to simmer. Reduce heat to medium-low, partially cover, and simmer until vegetables are tender and stew has thickened, 25 to 35 minutes. Gently stir in basil and season with salt and pepper to taste. Sprinkle individual portions with Pecorino and drizzle with extra oil before serving.

Quinoa and Vegetable Stew

SERVES 2   `LIGHT`

✔ **WHY THIS RECIPE WORKS:** Looking to add a hearty vegetarian meal to our for-two repertoire, we decided to develop a recipe for a quinoa and vegetable stew. A staple in Peru, quinoa stew typically includes a good mix of vegetables, with potatoes and corn at the forefront. We found that red potatoes most closely resembled the flavor and texture of native Peruvian potatoes. While there was no exact substitute for the chewy, nutty Andean corn, sweet locally grown corn worked just fine. Paprika was similar in color and flavor to hard-to-find annatto powder, and cumin and coriander rounded out the spice profile for rich, balanced flavor. Adding the spices with the aromatics prevented them from burning and allowed time for their flavors to develop. Simmering the quinoa for a few extra minutes allowed it to release additional starch, thickening our stew to just the right consistency. This stew tends to thicken as it sits; add additional warm vegetable broth as needed before serving to loosen. Be sure to rinse the quinoa to remove its bitter coating (known as saponin). Serve with lime wedges, diced avocado, and crumbled *queso fresco* cheese. For the nutritional information for this recipe, see page 413.

- 1   **tablespoon vegetable oil**
- 1   **small onion, chopped**
- ½   **red bell pepper, cut into ½-inch pieces**
- 2   **garlic cloves, minced**
- 1   **teaspoon paprika**
- ¾   **teaspoon ground coriander**

This warmly spiced dish combines hearty quinoa with potatoes, corn, and red bell pepper for a satisfying vegetarian stew.

- ½   **teaspoon ground cumin**
- ½   **cup water**
- 2   **cups vegetable broth**
- 1   **red potato (6 ounces), unpeeled, cut into ½-inch pieces**
- ⅓   **cup quinoa, rinsed**
- ⅓   **cup fresh or frozen corn**
    Salt and pepper
- 3   **tablespoons minced fresh cilantro**

1. Heat oil in medium saucepan over medium heat until shimmering. Add onion, bell pepper, garlic, paprika, coriander,

Preparing Fresh Corn

To remove kernels from ear of corn, stand cob upright inside bowl, then slice down along sides of cob using sharp knife.

and cumin. Cook, stirring often, until vegetables are softened and spices are fragrant, about 5 minutes. Stir in water, scraping up any browned bits. Stir in broth and potato, bring to simmer, and cook for 10 minutes.

2. Stir in quinoa and simmer for 8 minutes. Stir in corn and continue to simmer until vegetables and quinoa are just tender, 6 to 8 minutes. Season with salt and pepper to taste. Sprinkle individual portions with cilantro before serving.

Indian-Style Chicken Curry with Cauliflower and Peas

SERVES 2

✅ **WHY THIS RECIPE WORKS:** For a streamlined version of chicken curry that we could make in a skillet in less than an hour, we focused first on the cornerstone of a good curry—the spices. After extensive testing, we discovered that store-bought curry powder and garam masala provided all the flavor and complexity we wanted—no need for a long list of hard-to-find exotic spices. Blooming them briefly in oil turned these already bold ingredients into flavor powerhouses. Onion, along with equal amounts of ginger and garlic, provided the aromatic base, while a little tomato paste offered sweet depth. Boneless chicken breasts cooked quickly, and cauliflower and peas—a classic pairing in curries—added heartiness and a burst of color to our curry. Coconut milk contributed a creamy, savory richness. Be careful not to overcook the chicken in step 2 or it will taste dry. Serve with rice.

1 tablespoon vegetable oil
1 small onion, chopped fine
1 tablespoon curry powder
2 teaspoons grated fresh ginger
2 teaspoons tomato paste
2 garlic cloves, minced
½ teaspoon garam masala
  Salt and pepper
1 tablespoon all-purpose flour
1½ cups chicken broth
1½ cups cauliflower florets, cut into 1-inch pieces
12 ounces boneless, skinless chicken breasts, trimmed
½ cup canned coconut milk
¼ cup frozen peas
2 tablespoons minced fresh cilantro

1. Heat oil in medium saucepan over medium heat until shimmering. Add onion, curry powder, ginger, tomato paste, garlic, garam masala, and ¼ teaspoon salt. Cook, stirring

All About Spices

Just one or two spices can elevate an everyday dish to the next level. But a jar of spices doesn't stay good forever; spices can go rancid or stale, and all too often home cooks reach for old bottles of spices that essentially have turned into expensive dust. Here are a few tips to help you get the most from your spice rack.

BUYING SPICES: Because grinding releases the compounds that give a spice its flavor and aroma, it's best to buy spices whole and grind them just before using; the longer a spice sits, the more its flavor will fade. That said, there's no denying the convenience of preground spices. If you buy spices preground, try to buy them in small quantities, preferably from places (like spice shops) more likely to have high turnover.

STORING SPICES PROPERLY: Don't store spices and herbs on the counter close to the stove because heat, as well as light and moisture, shortens their shelf life. Keep them in a cool, dark, dry place in well-sealed containers.

CHECKING FOR FRESHNESS: Grind or finely grate a small amount of whole spices and take a whiff. If the spice releases a lively aroma, it's still good to go. If the aroma and color have faded, it's time to restock. It's helpful to label each spice with the date opened; whole spices are generally good for two years and ground spices for one year.

SPICE RACK ESSENTIALS: From arrowroot to mountain pepper to sumac to za'atar, there are hundreds of spices out there to choose from, but in the test kitchen there are only a few we believe are a must in every pantry. We have found we go through chili powder, cinnamon, paprika, and peppercorns fairly quickly; all others we recommend buying on a need-to-use basis.

BLOOMING SPICES BUILDS FLAVOR: In the test kitchen, we often like to bloom spices, a technique that removes any raw flavor or dustiness from spices and intensifies their flavor. To bloom spices, cook them briefly on the stovetop or in the microwave in a little oil or butter. As they dissolve, their flavorful essential oils are released from a solid state into solution form, where they mix and interact, producing a more complex flavor. Just be careful to avoid burning them.

GETTING A GOOD GRIND: Freshly ground spices have superior aroma and vibrancy, and because whole spices have a longer shelf life than preground, grinding your own will help you get more out of the spices you buy. We recommend buying a designated blade-type coffee grinder for grinding spices. Our favorite, the **Krups Fast-Touch Coffee Mill**, $19.99, produced an exceptionally fine grind of all spices. We found that it easily ground amounts anywhere from 1 teaspoon to ¼ cup.

often, until onion is softened and spices are fragrant, about 5 minutes. Stir in flour and cook for 1 minute.

2. Slowly whisk in broth, scraping up any browned bits and smoothing out any lumps. Stir in cauliflower. Season chicken with salt and pepper, add to curry mixture, and bring to simmer. Reduce heat to medium-low, cover, and simmer until chicken registers 160 degrees, 10 to 15 minutes, flipping chicken halfway through cooking. Transfer chicken to cutting board, let cool slightly, then shred into bite-size pieces using 2 forks.

3. Return stew to simmer, stir in shredded chicken, coconut milk, and peas and cook until heated through, about 2 minutes. Stir in cilantro and season with salt and pepper to taste. Serve.

VARIATION

Indian-Style Chicken Curry with Chickpeas and Green Beans

Omit peas. Substitute 1 (14-ounce) can chickpeas, rinsed, and 3 ounces green beans, trimmed and cut into 1-inch lengths, for cauliflower.

Indian-Style Vegetable Curry with Sweet Potato and Eggplant
SERVES 2

✔ **WHY THIS RECIPE WORKS:** For a vegetable curry that would be every bit as flavorful and satisfying as a meat-based one, we started by sautéing onion with a potent blend of curry powder, ginger, tomato paste, garlic, and garam masala—cooking the aromatics and spices together allowed time for their flavors to fully develop. Eggplant, sweet potato, and green beans added heft and substance to our curry, and cooking the vegetables, covered, for a full 10 minutes before adding the liquid components created a fond that resulted in deep, complex flavor. Vegetable broth provided a clean backdrop for the spices and vegetables, and coconut milk unified the sauce. A sprinkling of fresh cilantro provided the perfect finishing touch. Do not peel the eggplant as the skin helps hold it together during cooking. Serve with rice.

1 tablespoon vegetable oil
1 small onion, chopped fine
1 tablespoon curry powder
2 teaspoons grated fresh ginger
2 teaspoons tomato paste
2 garlic cloves, minced
½ teaspoon garam masala
   Salt and pepper

½ eggplant (8 ounces), cut into 1-inch pieces
½ sweet potato (6 ounces), peeled and cut into ½-inch pieces
3 ounces green beans, trimmed and cut into 1-inch lengths
1½ cups vegetable broth
½ cup canned coconut milk
2 tablespoons minced fresh cilantro

1. Heat oil in medium saucepan over medium heat until shimmering. Add onion, curry powder, ginger, tomato paste, garlic, garam masala, and ¼ teaspoon salt. Cook, stirring often, until onion is softened and spices are fragrant, about 5 minutes.

2. Stir in eggplant, potato, and green beans. Reduce heat to medium-low, cover, and cook until vegetables are softened, about 10 minutes. Stir in broth, scraping up any browned bits. Bring to simmer, cover, and cook until vegetables are tender, about 10 minutes.

3. Stir in coconut milk and let sit until heated through, about 2 minutes. Stir in cilantro and season with salt and pepper to taste. Serve.

Thai-Style Red Curry with Beef and Eggplant
SERVES 2

✔ **WHY THIS RECIPE WORKS:** To create a quick, Thai-style beef curry for two, we started with the meat. We chose sirloin steak tips for their deep, beefy flavor and substantial texture. Jarred red curry paste eliminated much of the prep work, and coconut milk contributed a creamy richness. A combination of fish sauce, brown sugar, and lime juice provided the proper salty, sweet, and sour elements. The addition of hearty eggplant complemented the beef. Steak tips, also known as flap meat, are sold as whole steak, cubes, and strips; look for either whole steak tips or strips that are easy to cut into small pieces for this recipe. To make the beef easier to slice, freeze it for 15 minutes. Depending on the freshness and spice level of your curry paste, you may need to add more or less to taste. If you can't find Thai basil leaves, regular basil will work fine. Serve with rice.

5 teaspoons vegetable oil
½ eggplant (8 ounces), cut into ½-inch pieces
2 teaspoons Thai red curry paste, plus extra for seasoning
¾ cup canned coconut milk
1 tablespoon fish sauce
2 teaspoons packed brown sugar

¾ cup chicken broth

½ teaspoon cornstarch

8 ounces sirloin steak tips, trimmed, cut into strips (if necessary), and sliced thin against grain

¼ cup fresh Thai basil leaves

2 teaspoons lime juice

Salt and pepper

1. Heat 1 tablespoon oil in 12-inch nonstick skillet over medium-high heat until shimmering. Brown eggplant lightly on all sides, 5 to 7 minutes; transfer to bowl.

2. Heat remaining 2 teaspoons oil in now-empty skillet over medium-high heat until shimmering. Add curry paste and cook until fragrant, about 30 seconds. Whisk in coconut milk, fish sauce, and sugar. Whisk broth and cornstarch together in bowl, then whisk mixture into skillet. Bring to simmer and cook until sauce is slightly thickened, 5 to 8 minutes. Season with extra curry paste to taste.

3. Stir in beef and simmer until strips separate and turn firm, about 5 minutes. Stir in browned eggplant and continue to simmer until beef and eggplant are tender and sauce has thickened, about 8 minutes. Off heat, stir in basil and lime juice and season with salt and pepper to taste. Serve.

Thai-Style Red Curry with Shrimp, Bell Pepper, and Snap Peas

SERVES 2 `FAST`

☑ **WHY THIS RECIPE WORKS:** For a streamlined Thai red curry dish that was scaled down in size but not in flavor, we eliminated homemade curry paste and went with the jarred variety; it contains many of the hard-to-find ingredients required for homemade, and we found that just a small amount packed a punch. A little chicken broth cut through the richness of the coconut milk, while easy-to-find Thai staples such as fish sauce, brown sugar, lime juice, and basil offered welcome complexity. Blooming the curry paste in oil allowed its flavor to fully develop, and stirring in a little extra toward the end of cooking guaranteed deep flavor. Quick-cooking shrimp, red bell pepper, and snap peas paired well with our flavorful sauce. Depending on the freshness and spice level of your curry paste, you may need to add more or less to taste; season the sauce before you add the shrimp to make sure they do not overcook. If you can't find Thai basil leaves, regular basil will work fine. Serve with rice.

For an easy but flavorful sauce for our shrimp stir-fry, we combine store-bought red curry paste, coconut milk, and chicken broth.

2 teaspoons vegetable oil

2 teaspoons Thai red curry paste, plus extra for seasoning

¾ cup canned coconut milk

1 tablespoon fish sauce

2 teaspoons packed brown sugar

¼ cup chicken broth

½ teaspoon cornstarch

1 red bell pepper, stemmed, seeded, and cut into ¼-inch-wide strips

4 ounces sugar snap peas, strings removed, cut in half on bias

8 ounces extra-large shrimp (21 to 25 per pound), peeled, deveined, and tails removed

¼ cup fresh Thai basil leaves

2 teaspoons lime juice

Salt and pepper

1. Heat oil in 10-inch nonstick skillet over medium-high heat until shimmering. Add curry paste and cook until fragrant, about 30 seconds. Whisk in coconut milk, fish sauce, and sugar. Whisk broth and cornstarch together in bowl, then whisk mixture into skillet and bring to simmer.

2. Stir in bell pepper and snap peas and simmer until vegetables are crisp-tender and sauce has thickened slightly, 5 to 8 minutes. Season with extra curry paste to taste.

3. Stir in shrimp and simmer until opaque throughout, 3 to 5 minutes. Off heat, stir in basil and lime juice and season with salt and pepper to taste. Serve.

VARIATION
Thai-Style Red Curry with Shrimp, Asparagus, and Carrots
Substitute 8 ounces asparagus, trimmed and cut on bias into 2-inch lengths, for bell pepper and 2 carrots, peeled and cut into 2-inch-long matchsticks, for snap peas.

Prepping Bell Pepper

1. Slice off top and bottom of pepper and remove seeds and stem. Slice down through side of pepper.

2. Lay pepper flat on cutting board and cut into strips or pieces as directed.

Thai-Style Green Curry with Tofu, Snap Peas, and Mushrooms
SERVES 2

✔ WHY THIS RECIPE WORKS: We wanted a recipe for a flavorful Thai curry easy enough for a weeknight dinner. Jarred Thai green curry paste gave our dish authentic flavor without the laborious task of preparing it from scratch. Brown sugar tempered the spiciness of the curry paste, lime juice provided a sour element, and salty fish sauce balanced the other flavors. The subtle flavor of tofu was an ideal complement to the richly flavored curry sauce; cooking the tofu until golden gave it a crisp crust that contrasted nicely with its tender interior. Snap peas and shiitake mushrooms required little prep and cooked quickly, making them ideal additions to this simple weeknight curry. We prefer the texture of firm tofu here. Extra-firm tofu will also work, but it will be drier. Depending on the freshness

and spice level of your curry paste, you may need to add more or less to taste. If you can't find Thai basil leaves, regular basil will work fine. Serve with rice.

7   **ounces firm tofu**
    Salt and pepper
5   **teaspoons vegetable oil**
2   **teaspoons Thai green curry paste, plus extra for seasoning**
¾   **cup canned coconut milk**
1   **tablespoon fish sauce**
2   **teaspoons packed brown sugar**
1   **cup chicken broth**
½   **teaspoon cornstarch**
4   **ounces sugar snap peas, strings removed, cut in half on bias**
4   **ounces shiitake mushrooms, stemmed and sliced thin**
¼   **cup fresh Thai basil leaves**
2   **teaspoons lime juice**

1. Slice tofu crosswise into 1-inch-thick slabs. Spread tofu out over paper towel–lined plate and let drain for 15 minutes.

2. Gently pat tofu dry with paper towels and season with salt and pepper. Heat 1 tablespoon oil in 10-inch nonstick skillet over medium-high heat until just smoking. Add tofu and cook until golden and crisp on all sides, about 5 minutes; transfer to clean paper towel–lined plate.

3. Heat remaining 2 teaspoons oil in now-empty skillet over medium-high heat until shimmering. Add curry paste and cook until fragrant, about 30 seconds. Whisk in coconut milk, fish sauce, and sugar. Whisk broth and cornstarch together in bowl, then whisk mixture into skillet and bring to simmer.

4. Stir in snap peas and mushrooms and simmer until vegetables are crisp-tender and sauce has thickened slightly, 5 to 8 minutes. Season with extra curry paste to taste.

5. Stir in browned tofu and simmer until heated through, 3 to 5 minutes. Off heat, stir in basil and lime juice and season with salt and pepper to taste. Serve.

Trimming Snow and Snap Peas

Using paring knife and your thumb, snip off tip of pea and pull along flat side of pod to remove string at same time.

Classic Beef Chili

SERVES 2

✓ **WHY THIS RECIPE WORKS:** Recipes for chili are typically geared toward a crowd, so we knew that creating a scaled-down version for two would require a careful balancing act. Starting with the spices, we determined that 1½ tablespoons of chili powder was just right; although this seemed like a modest amount, even for two servings, we found that if we used any more it simply overwhelmed the other layers of flavor in our chili. Cumin, coriander, red pepper flakes, oregano, and cayenne rounded out our spices, and we found that adding them early—along with the aromatics—helped develop their flavors fully. Twelve ounces of beef and ¾ cup of canned beans provided just the right meat-to-bean ratio. The juice from a can of diced tomatoes and a little tomato sauce was all the liquid we needed, creating a chili that was thick, rich, and utterly satisfying. Serve with your favorite chili garnishes.

- 1 **tablespoon vegetable oil**
- 1 **small onion, chopped fine**
- ½ **red, green, or yellow bell pepper, cut into ½-inch pieces**
- 1½ **tablespoons chili powder**
- 3 **garlic cloves, minced**
- 1 **teaspoon ground cumin**
- ¾ **teaspoon ground coriander**
- ¼ **teaspoon red pepper flakes**
- ¼ **teaspoon dried oregano**
  Salt and pepper
- ⅛ **teaspoon cayenne pepper**
- 12 **ounces 85 percent lean ground beef**
- 1 **(14.5-ounce) can diced tomatoes**
- 1 **(8-ounce) can tomato sauce**
- ¾ **cup canned kidney or pinto beans, rinsed**

1. Heat oil in medium saucepan over medium heat until shimmering. Add onion, bell pepper, chili powder, garlic, cumin, coriander, pepper flakes, oregano, ¼ teaspoon salt, and cayenne. Cook, stirring often, until vegetables begin to soften and spices are fragrant, 3 to 5 minutes.

2. Add ground beef and cook, breaking up meat with wooden spoon, until no longer pink and just beginning to brown, 3 to 5 minutes. Stir in tomatoes and their juice, tomato sauce, and beans and bring to simmer. Cover, reduce heat to medium-low, and simmer, stirring occasionally, for 45 minutes.

3. Uncover and continue to simmer, stirring occasionally, until beef is tender and chili is slightly thickened, about 15 minutes. (If chili begins to stick to bottom of pot, stir in ¼ cup water.) Season with salt and pepper to taste and serve.

VARIATIONS

Beef Chili with Bacon

Cook 4 slices bacon, cut into ¼-inch pieces, in medium saucepan over medium heat until crisp, 5 to 7 minutes. Omit oil and add vegetables and spices to saucepan with bacon and bacon fat; proceed with recipe.

Beef Chili with Chipotle, Black Beans, and Corn

Omit red pepper flakes and cayenne pepper. Add 1 teaspoon minced canned chipotle chile in adobo sauce with vegetables and spices. Substitute ¾ cup rinsed canned black beans for kidney beans. After chili is thickened in step 3, stir in ½ cup frozen corn and let sit until heated through, about 2 minutes. Stir in 1 to 2 teaspoons more minced chipotle to taste before serving.

Beef Chili with Moroccan Spices and Chickpeas

Omit chili powder and red pepper flakes. Add 1 teaspoon paprika, 1 teaspoon ground ginger, and ⅛ teaspoon ground cinnamon with vegetables and spices. Substitute ¾ cup rinsed canned chickpeas for kidney beans and add ¼ cup raisins, if desired, with tomatoes and chickpeas. Stir in ¼ teaspoon grated lemon zest plus 1 teaspoon juice before serving.

Texas Chili

SERVES 2

✓ **WHY THIS RECIPE WORKS:** We wanted a chili that would be hearty, with satisfying chunks of meat, and spicy, but not overwhelmingly hot. We'd typically choose a chuck-eye roast for this type of chili, but since we didn't need that much meat for our scaled-down version, we found that boneless beef short ribs worked just as well, offering plenty of meaty flavor in every bite. Some kidney beans provided additional heft. A full 2 tablespoons of chili powder and some minced chipotle chile contributed plenty of smoky heat. One can of diced tomatoes pureed with a corn tortilla (a readily available substitute for authentic masa harina) helped thicken the chili to just the right consistency. You will need a medium ovensafe saucepan for this recipe. Serve with your favorite chili garnishes.

1 (14.5-ounce) can diced tomatoes
1 (6-inch) corn tortilla, chopped coarse
1½ pounds boneless beef short ribs, trimmed and cut into
   1½-inch pieces
   Salt and pepper
1 tablespoon vegetable oil
1 small onion, chopped fine
2 tablespoons chili powder
2 teaspoons ground cumin
2 garlic cloves, minced
2 teaspoons minced canned chipotle chile in adobo sauce
1 (15-ounce) can kidney beans, rinsed

1. Adjust oven rack to middle position and heat oven to 300 degrees. Process tomatoes with their juice and tortilla pieces in food processor until smooth, about 30 seconds.

2. Pat beef dry with paper towels and season with salt and pepper. Heat oil in medium ovensafe saucepan over medium-high heat until just smoking. Brown beef on all sides, about 8 minutes; transfer to bowl.

3. Add onion, chili powder, cumin, garlic, and chipotle to fat left in saucepan. Cook over medium heat, stirring often, until onion is softened and spices are fragrant, about 5 minutes. Stir in tomato mixture, scraping up any browned bits. Stir in beans and browned beef with any accumulated juices and bring to simmer. Cover, transfer saucepan to oven, and cook until beef is tender, 2½ to 3 hours.

4. Using large spoon, skim excess fat from surface of stew. Season with salt and pepper to taste. Serve.

Five-Alarm Chili

SERVES 2

✔ **WHY THIS RECIPE WORKS:** For a seriously hot five-alarm chili, we combined fresh jalapeños, canned chipotle chiles, dried ancho chiles, cayenne, and chili powder for complex, multilayered flavor. Ground beef and creamy pinto beans bulked up the chili, and fresh tomatoes added brightness. To round out the chili and give it some body, we turned to a few unusual additions: A splash of light-bodied beer gave our chili malty depth and a little bitterness, and crushed corn tortilla chips thickened it and added a subtle background of corn flavor. Dried ancho chiles can be found in the international aisle of most supermarkets. Light-bodied American lagers, such as Budweiser, work best in this recipe. Serve with your favorite chili garnishes.

Five-Alarm Chili gets its fiery heat, complex flavor, and colloquial name from a tasty combination of fresh, smoked, and dried chiles.

½ ounce dried ancho chiles, stemmed, seeded, and
   torn into 1-inch pieces
1⅓ cups water
4 plum tomatoes, cored and halved lengthwise
3 tablespoons crushed corn tortilla chips
1 tablespoon minced canned chipotle chile in
   adobo sauce
4 teaspoons vegetable oil
12 ounces 85 percent lean ground beef
   Salt and pepper
1 onion, chopped fine
½ jalapeño chile, stemmed, seeds reserved,
   and minced
2 garlic cloves, minced
1½ teaspoons ground cumin
1½ teaspoons chili powder
½ teaspoon sugar
⅛ teaspoon cayenne pepper
⅓ cup beer
¾ cup canned pinto beans, rinsed

1. Combine anchos and ⅓ cup water in bowl and microwave until softened, about 2 minutes. Drain and discard liquid. Process anchos, remaining 1 cup water, tomatoes, tortilla chips, and chipotle in blender until smooth, about 1 minute; set aside.

2. Heat 2 teaspoons oil in medium saucepan over medium-high heat until just smoking. Add ground beef, ¼ teaspoon salt, and ⅛ teaspoon pepper and cook, breaking up meat with wooden spoon, until all liquid has evaporated and beef begins to sizzle, 5 to 7 minutes. Drain in colander; set aside.

3. Heat remaining 2 teaspoons oil in now-empty saucepan over medium-high heat until shimmering. Add onion, jalapeño, and reserved seeds and cook until onion is softened and lightly browned, 5 to 7 minutes. Stir in garlic, cumin, chili powder, sugar, and cayenne and cook until fragrant, about 30 seconds. Stir in beer and bring to simmer. Stir in ancho-tomato mixture, cooked beef, and beans and bring to simmer. Cover, reduce heat to medium-low, and simmer, stirring occasionally, until thickened, about 30 minutes. Season with salt to taste and serve.

Turkey Chili

SERVES 2

✔ **WHY THIS RECIPE WORKS:** For a no-fuss turkey chili that would rival its beef counterpart, we found that the type of turkey we used and the point at which we added it to the chili were key. Ground turkey that was 93 percent lean remained moist and had enough fat to flavor our chili. Adding half of the meat to the cooked vegetables in the beginning allowed time for its flavor to infuse the chili, while adding the other half after the chili had simmered for 30 minutes ensured that some of the meat remained in larger pieces. A can of diced tomatoes and a small amount of tomato sauce provided enough liquid without making our chili too thin. Be sure to use ground turkey, not ground turkey breast (also labeled 99 percent fat free), in this recipe. Serve with your favorite chili garnishes.

1	**tablespoon vegetable oil**
1	**small onion, chopped fine**
½	**red, green, or yellow bell pepper, cut into ½-inch pieces**
1½	**tablespoons chili powder**
3	**garlic cloves, minced**

All About Chile Peppers

Chiles get their heat from a group of chemical compounds called capsaicinoids, the best known being capsaicin. Capsaicin in a chile is concentrated mostly in the inner whitish pith (called ribs), with progressively smaller amounts in the seeds and flesh. If you like a lot of heat, you can use the entire chile when cooking. If you prefer a milder dish, remove the ribs and seeds. Here are the chiles we reach for most in the test kitchen.

JALAPEÑO

Perhaps the best-known chile, jalapeños are moderately hot and have a bright, grassy flavor similar to a green bell pepper. They can be dark green or scarlet red.

CHIPOTLE

Smoky, sweet, and moderately spicy, chipotle chiles are jalapeños that have been smoked over aromatic wood and dried. They are sold as is or canned in adobo, a tangy tomato-and-herb sauce. We recommend using canned chipotles; they can be added straight to a dish and they last indefinitely when frozen.

POBLANO

These chiles are very dark green in color—sometimes nearly black. When ripe, they turn a reddish-brown. We love poblanos for their fruity, subtly spicy flavor. Thanks to their large size, they are also ideal for stuffing. Poblanos can be found in Latin markets and many supermarkets. Their peak season is summer and early fall. When dried, they are known as ancho chiles and have a rich, earthy flavor.

ANAHEIM

With their acidic, lemony flavor, mild spiciness, and crisp texture, these popular chiles can be eaten raw, roasted, or fried; they are also frequently stuffed or used in salsa. Anaheim chiles are medium green in color and have a long, tapered shape. When dried, they are called New Mexico or Colorado chiles.

SERRANO

Similar in appearance to jalapeños but with a slightly more slender shape and brazen heat, these chiles have a fresh, clean, fruity flavor. They are good both raw in salsa and cooked in chilis and curries.

HABANERO

These small, lantern-shaped chiles pack intense heat. They have a floral, fruity flavor that makes them—when used sparingly—a great addition to marinades, salsas, and cooked dishes. They range from light green to orange to red in color.

THAI

These tiny, multicolored chiles look ornamental, but they mean business. They have a flavor similar to that of black peppercorns and a bold, lingering heat. They are best when used sparingly in cooked dishes. The bird chile is the dried form.

1	teaspoon ground cumin
¾	teaspoon ground coriander
¼	teaspoon red pepper flakes
¼	teaspoon dried oregano
	Salt and pepper
⅛	teaspoon cayenne pepper
12	ounces ground turkey
1	(14.5-ounce) can diced tomatoes
1	(8-ounce) can tomato sauce
¾	cup canned kidney or pinto beans, rinsed

1. Heat oil in medium saucepan over medium heat until shimmering. Add onion, bell pepper, chili powder, garlic, cumin, coriander, pepper flakes, oregano, ¼ teaspoon salt, and cayenne. Cook, stirring often, until vegetables begin to soften and spices are fragrant, 3 to 5 minutes.

2. Add 6 ounces ground turkey and cook, breaking up meat with wooden spoon, until no longer pink and just beginning to brown, 3 to 5 minutes. Stir in tomatoes and their juice, tomato sauce, and beans and bring to simmer. Cover, reduce heat to medium-low, and simmer, stirring occasionally, for 30 minutes.

3. Pat remaining 6 ounces ground turkey together into ball, then pinch off teaspoon-size pieces and stir into chili. Simmer, uncovered, stirring occasionally, until turkey is tender and chili is slightly thickened, about 30 minutes. (If chili begins to stick to bottom of pot, stir in ¼ cup water.) Season with salt and pepper to taste and serve.

VARIATION
Tequila and Lime Turkey Chili
Add 1 tablespoon tequila with tomatoes and beans in step 2. Stir in 1 tablespoon more tequila and 1 teaspoon grated lime zest plus 2 teaspoons juice before serving.

Crumbling Ground Turkey

To give ground turkey an appealing crumbled texture similar to ground beef (ground turkey naturally has a stringy appearance), pack remaining half of turkey together into ball, then pinch off teaspoon-size pieces of meat and stir them into simmering chili.

A puree of hominy and chicken broth plus a little toasted flour gives this white chicken chili a thick, velvety texture.

White Chicken Chili
SERVES 2 **LIGHT**

✓ **WHY THIS RECIPE WORKS:** To achieve the right consistency for our white chicken chili, we utilized two thickeners: flour and pureed hominy. Cooking the flour briefly with the aromatics and spices—poblano chiles, onion, garlic, cumin, and coriander—allowed it to not only thicken the chili, but also build depth of flavor. And pureeing a portion of the hominy with some chicken broth gave our chili a luxuriously thick texture. Adding store-bought tomatillo salsa—a zesty combination of green tomatoes, chiles, and cilantro that is also known as salsa verde—was a quick and easy way to boost the flavor of our chili at the end. Both white hominy and yellow hominy will work in this chili; however, we prefer the deeper flavor of white hominy here. To make this dish spicier, add the chile seeds. Be careful not to overcook the chicken in step 3 or it will taste dry. Serve with your favorite chili garnishes. For the nutritional information for this recipe, see page 413.

The Importance of Rinsing Beans

Canned beans are made by pressure-cooking dried beans directly in the can with water, salt, and preservatives. As the beans cook, starches and proteins leach into the liquid, thickening it. We generally call for canned beans to be rinsed to remove this starchy liquid, but is the extra step really necessary? To find out, we used canned beans in two recipes: chickpeas in hummus and red kidney beans in a simple beef chili.

Tasters found no difference in the chili; there are so many bold flavors and contrasting textures in this dish that rinsing the beans didn't matter. However, they detected notable differences in the hummus. Most tasters thought the version with rinsed beans was brighter in flavor and less pasty than the version with unrinsed beans. So while rinsing the beans may not be necessary for a robust dish like chili, the thick, salty bean liquid does have the potential to throw a simpler recipe off-kilter. And since rinsing beans only takes a few seconds, we recommend doing so.

- 1 (15-ounce) can white or yellow hominy, rinsed
- 2 cups chicken broth
- 1 tablespoon vegetable oil
- 2 poblano chiles, stemmed, seeded, and chopped
- 1 small onion, chopped fine
- 2 garlic cloves, minced
- 1 teaspoon ground cumin
- 1 teaspoon ground coriander
- 1 tablespoon all-purpose flour
- 12 ounces boneless, skinless chicken breasts, trimmed
  Salt and pepper
- ½ cup jarred tomatillo salsa (salsa verde)
- 2 tablespoons minced fresh cilantro

1. Process 1 cup hominy and ½ cup broth in blender until smooth, about 10 seconds.

2. Heat oil in medium saucepan over medium heat until shimmering. Add poblanos, onion, garlic, cumin, and coriander. Cook, stirring often, until vegetables are softened and spices are fragrant, about 5 minutes. Stir in flour and cook for 1 minute.

3. Slowly whisk in remaining 1½ cups broth, scraping up any browned bits and smoothing out any lumps. Stir in pureed hominy mixture and remaining ½ cup hominy. Season chicken with salt and pepper, add to chili mixture, and bring to simmer. Cover, reduce heat to medium-low, and simmer until chicken registers 160 degrees, 10 to 15 minutes, flipping chicken halfway through cooking. Transfer chicken to cutting board, let cool slightly, then shred into bite-size pieces using 2 forks.

4. Return chili to simmer, stir in shredded chicken and tomatillo salsa, and cook until heated through, about 2 minutes. Stir in cilantro and season with salt and pepper to taste. Serve.

Vegetarian Chili

SERVES 2 LIGHT

WHY THIS RECIPE WORKS: Vegetarian chili is often little more than a mishmash of beans and vegetables. To create a true chili—not a bean and vegetable stew—we found it best to keep our ingredient list relatively simple: just one bell pepper and one type of bean were all we needed. Onion, garlic, chili powder, and cumin provided a solid base of flavor, while some minced chipotle chile contributed a subtle warmth and smokiness. Crushed tomatoes gave our chili a hearty, thick consistency. Finally, crumbled tempeh filled out our vegetarian chili, giving it a substantial texture. Any type of tempeh will work well here. To make this dish spicier, add the larger amount of chipotle. Serve with your favorite chili garnishes. For the nutritional information for this recipe, see page 413.

- 1 tablespoon vegetable oil
- 1 small red, green, or yellow bell pepper, stemmed, seeded, and cut into ½-inch pieces
- 1 small onion, chopped fine
- 1 tablespoon chili powder
- 2 garlic cloves, minced
- 1–2 teaspoons minced canned chipotle chile in adobo sauce
- 1 teaspoon ground cumin
  Salt and pepper
- 1 cup water
- 1 (28-ounce) can crushed tomatoes
- 1 (15-ounce) can kidney, black, or pinto beans, rinsed
- 1 (8-ounce) package tempeh, crumbled
- 2 tablespoons minced fresh cilantro

1. Heat oil in medium saucepan over medium heat until shimmering. Add bell pepper, onion, chili powder, garlic, chipotle, cumin, and ½ teaspoon salt. Cook, stirring often, until vegetables are softened and spices are fragrant, about 5 minutes.

2. Stir in water, scraping up any browned bits. Stir in tomatoes, beans, and tempeh and bring to simmer. Cover, reduce heat to medium-low, and simmer, stirring occasionally, for 30 minutes.

3. Uncover and continue to simmer, stirring occasionally, until vegetables and tempeh are tender and chili is slightly thickened, about 15 minutes. (If chili begins to stick to bottom of pot, stir in ¼ cup water.) Stir in cilantro and season with salt to taste. Serve.

CHAPTER 3

Side Salads and Dinner Salads

◼ FAST (Start to finish in about 30 minutes)

◼ LIGHT (See page 413 for nutritional information)

Opposite: Classic Caesar Salad; Wilted Spinach Salad with Radishes, Feta, and Pistachios; Tortellini Salad with Bell Pepper, Pine Nuts, and Basil

Foolproof Vinaigrette

MAKES ABOUT ¼ CUP, ENOUGH TO DRESS 8 TO 10 CUPS
LIGHTLY PACKED GREENS **FAST**

✔ **WHY THIS RECIPE WORKS:** Vinaigrettes often seem a little slipshod—harsh and bristling in one bite, dull and oily in the next—plus they tend to separate soon after being prepared. To get the best flavor, we found that top-notch ingredients were crucial. And for a well-balanced vinaigrette that wouldn't separate, we carefully whisked fruity extra-virgin olive oil and vinegar together with a little mayonnaise, which acts as an emulsifier. Some minced shallot and Dijon mustard rounded out the flavors in our classic vinaigrette. This vinaigrette works with nearly any type of green. Red wine, white wine, or Champagne vinegar will work in this recipe; however, it is important to use high-quality ingredients. For a hint of garlic flavor, rub the inside of the salad bowl with a cut clove of garlic before adding the lettuce and dressing. Placing the oil in a small measuring cup will make it easy to pour in a steady stream.

1	tablespoon wine vinegar
1½	teaspoons minced shallot
½	teaspoon mayonnaise
½	teaspoon Dijon mustard
⅛	teaspoon salt
	Pepper
3	tablespoons extra-virgin olive oil

1. Whisk vinegar, shallot, mayonnaise, mustard, salt, and pepper to taste together in small bowl until mixture is milky in appearance and no lumps of mayonnaise remain.

2. Whisking constantly, drizzle oil into vinegar mixture in slow, steady stream. If pools of oil gather on surface as you whisk, stop adding oil and whisk mixture well to combine, then resume whisking in oil in slow stream. Vinaigrette should be glossy and lightly thickened, with no pools of oil on its surface. (Vinaigrette can be refrigerated for up to 2 weeks.)

VARIATIONS

Foolproof Lemon Vinaigrette

This vinaigrette is best for dressing mild greens.

Omit shallot. Substitute lemon juice for vinegar and add ¼ teaspoon finely grated lemon zest and pinch of sugar with salt and pepper.

Foolproof Balsamic-Mustard Vinaigrette

This vinaigrette is best for dressing assertive greens.

Substitute balsamic vinegar for wine vinegar, increase amount of mustard to 2 teaspoons, and add ½ teaspoon chopped fresh thyme with salt and pepper.

Foolproof Walnut Vinaigrette

This vinaigrette will work well with mild or assertive greens.

Substitute 1½ tablespoons roasted walnut oil and 1½ tablespoons regular olive oil for the extra-virgin olive oil.

Foolproof Herb Vinaigrette

This vinaigrette will work well with mild or assertive greens.

Add 1 tablespoon minced fresh parsley or chives and ½ teaspoon minced fresh thyme, tarragon, marjoram, or oregano to vinaigrette just before use.

Classic Caesar Salad

SERVES 2

✔ **WHY THIS RECIPE WORKS:** For our Caesar salad, we wanted crisp-tender romaine lettuce with a creamy dressing and crunchy, garlicky croutons strewn throughout. We cut the extra-virgin olive oil in the dressing with vegetable oil, which gave it a mellower flavor, and we used an egg yolk instead of a whole egg to add richness. For a robust but not aggressive garlic flavor, we grated a small garlic clove into a paste and steeped it in lemon juice. Adding Parmesan to the dressing and sprinkling more on top before serving provided a double layer of cheese flavor. We preferred chewy, crisp ciabatta bread for our croutons; we sprinkled them with a little water before frying them in a skillet to ensure that the interiors stayed moist and chewy while the exteriors crisped. For a flavor boost, we tossed the croutons with a mixture of garlic, olive oil, and Parmesan. You will need one small ciabatta roll for this recipe. You can substitute 2 tablespoons Egg Beaters for the egg yolk.

CROUTONS

2	tablespoons extra-virgin olive oil
1	small garlic clove, minced to paste
2	ounces ciabatta bread, cut into ¾-inch pieces (1½ cups)
1	tablespoon water
	Pinch salt
2	teaspoons grated Parmesan cheese

SALAD

1½	teaspoons lemon juice, plus extra for seasoning
1	small garlic clove, minced to paste
1	large egg yolk
2	anchovy fillets, rinsed, patted dry, and mashed to fine paste
⅛	teaspoon Worcestershire sauce
2½	tablespoons vegetable oil

2½ teaspoons extra-virgin olive oil
⅓ cup grated Parmesan cheese
   Salt and pepper
1 small romaine lettuce heart (4½ ounces), torn into
   bite-size pieces

1. FOR THE CROUTONS: Combine 1 tablespoon oil and garlic in small bowl; set aside. Place bread pieces in separate bowl and sprinkle with water and salt. Toss, squeezing gently until bread absorbs water. Heat remaining 1 tablespoon oil in 10-inch nonstick skillet over medium-high heat until shimmering. Add soaked bread cubes and cook, stirring frequently, until browned and crisp, 7 to 10 minutes.

2. Off heat, clear center of skillet, add oil-garlic mixture, and let heat until fragrant, about 10 seconds. Stir mixture into croutons, sprinkle with Parmesan, and toss to coat. Transfer croutons to bowl and let cool while finishing salad.

3. FOR THE SALAD: Whisk lemon juice and garlic together in large bowl and let sit for 10 minutes.

4. Whisk egg yolk, anchovies, and Worcestershire into lemon-garlic mixture. Whisking constantly, drizzle vegetable oil and olive oil into bowl in slow, steady stream until fully emulsified. Whisk in 3 tablespoons Parmesan and season with pepper to taste.

5. Add lettuce and croutons to dressing and gently toss to coat. Season with extra lemon juice, salt, and pepper to taste. Sprinkle with remaining Parmesan and serve immediately.

Greek Chopped Salad

SERVES 2 **FAST**

✔ **WHY THIS RECIPE WORKS:** Most Greek salads consist of iceberg lettuce, chunks of green pepper, and a few pale wedges of tomato, all sparsely dotted with olives and cubes of feta. We wanted a salad with crisp ingredients and bold flavors all blended together with a bright-tasting dressing infused with fresh herbs. We made a simple dressing with olive oil, red wine vinegar, and a little garlic, then tossed it over cucumbers, tomatoes, chickpeas, olives, shallot, and fresh parsley. Salting the cucumber and tomato and letting them drain kept their excess moisture from watering down the salad. Marinating the vegetables in the vinaigrette allowed the flavors to meld before we added in crisp romaine lettuce, briny olives, and salty feta cheese. If cherry tomatoes are unavailable, substitute grape tomatoes; cut the grape tomatoes in half along the equator rather than quartering them. Don't skimp on the draining time in step 1 or the salad will taste watery.

Storing and Preparing Salad Greens

HOW TO STORE SALAD GREENS: For crisp lettuce, such as iceberg and romaine, core the lettuce, wrap it in moist paper towels, and refrigerate in a partially open plastic produce bag or zipper-lock bag.

For leafy greens, such as arugula, baby spinach, and mesclun, store in the original plastic container or bag if prewashed. If not prewashed, wash and dry thoroughly in a salad spinner and store directly in the spinner between layers of paper towels, or lightly roll in paper towels and store in a zipper-lock bag left slightly open.

For tender lettuce such as Boston, Bibb, and butterhead lettuce, if the lettuce comes with the roots attached, leave the lettuce portion attached to the roots and store in the original plastic container, plastic produce bag, or a zipper-lock bag left slightly open. If the lettuce is without roots, wrap it in moist paper towels and refrigerate in a plastic produce bag or a zipper-lock bag left slightly open.

HOW TO WASH AND DRY SALAD GREENS: Nothing ruins a salad faster than biting into gritty leaves, and trying to dress a salad while the greens are still wet is a losing battle—the dressing will slide off and the water from the greens will dilute the dressing. To wash salad greens, fill a sink or salad spinner bowl with cool water, add the cut greens, and gently swish them around. Let the grit settle to bottom of sink or bowl, then lift the greens out and drain the water. Repeat until the greens no longer release any dirt. Dry the greens in a salad spinner, stopping several times to dump out excess moisture from the bottom of the spinner. Keep spinning the greens until no more moisture accumulates in the spinner.

Putting Together a Perfect Salad

PAIRING LEAFY GREENS WITH VINAIGRETTES: Vinaigrettes are always the best choice for dressing leafy greens; heavier, creamier dressings should be reserved for use on sturdy lettuce such as romaine or iceberg. Most salad greens fall into one of two categories: mellow or assertive. Mellow-flavored lettuces like Boston, Bibb, mâche, mesclun, red and green leaf, red oak, and flat-leaf spinach are easily overpowered and are best complemented by a simple dressing such as a classic red wine vinaigrette. Assertive or spicy greens such as arugula, escarole, chicory, Belgian endive, radicchio, frisée, and watercress can easily stand up to strong flavors like mustard, shallots, and balsamic vinegar and can also be paired with a slightly sweet or creamy vinaigrette.

HOW TO DRESS A SALAD: Once you have made your vinaigrette, getting a properly dressed salad requires a few simple steps. You never want to dump a set amount of dressing over greens at one time and assume they will be perfectly coated. Once you have overdressed your salad, there is no going back, so lightly drizzling and tossing the salad with tongs a couple of times, tasting as you go, is best. Generally, ¼ cup vinaigrette dresses 8 to 10 cups of lightly packed greens, enough for 4 to 6 side salads or 2 to 3 dinner salads. For the freshest salad, make sure to dress your greens just before serving. Also, for just a hint of garlic flavor, you can rub the inside of the salad bowl with half a clove of peeled garlic before adding the lettuce.

Our Greek salad features lots of bold Mediterranean flavors: olives, chickpeas, and feta tossed with tomatoes, cucumber, and romaine.

½ cucumber, peeled, halved lengthwise, seeded, and
   cut into ½-inch pieces
4 ounces cherry tomatoes, quartered
   Salt and pepper
1 tablespoon extra-virgin olive oil
1 tablespoon red wine vinegar
1 small garlic clove, minced
¾ cup canned chickpeas, rinsed
¼ cup minced fresh parsley
1 shallot, minced
2 tablespoons chopped pitted kalamata olives
½ romaine lettuce heart (3 ounces), torn into
   bite-size pieces
1 ounce feta cheese, crumbled (¼ cup)

1. Toss cucumber, tomatoes, and ¼ teaspoon salt together and let drain in colander for 15 minutes.

2. Whisk oil, vinegar, and garlic together in large bowl. Add drained cucumber and tomatoes, chickpeas, parsley, shallot, and olives and toss to combine. Let sit until flavors meld, about 5 minutes. Add lettuce and feta and gently toss to combine. Season with salt and pepper to taste and serve.

Wilted Spinach Salad with Radishes, Feta, and Pistachios

SERVES 2 FAST

✔ **WHY THIS RECIPE WORKS:** We wanted a foolproof recipe for a wilted spinach salad that would provide a nice alternative to basic greens. We experimented with various types of spinach and found that flat-leaf and baby spinach became soft and mushy, but hardier curly-leaf spinach stood up to the heat. To make the dressing, we began by heating 2 tablespoons of fruity extra-virgin olive oil in a Dutch oven along with some minced shallot. For bright citrus flavor, we also simmered a strip of lemon zest in the oil, then we added fresh lemon juice before tossing in the spinach. Peppery sliced radishes, crumbled feta, and toasted pistachios rounded out our updated spinach salad. Be sure to cook the spinach just until it begins to wilt; any longer and the leaves will overcook and clump.

2 tablespoons crumbled feta cheese
2 tablespoons extra-virgin olive oil
1 (2-inch) strip lemon zest plus 2 teaspoons juice
1 small shallot, minced
1 teaspoon sugar
5 ounces curly-leaf spinach, stemmed and torn into
   bite-size pieces
3 radishes, trimmed and sliced thin
2 tablespoons chopped toasted shelled pistachios
   Salt and pepper

1. Place feta on plate and freeze until slightly firm, about 15 minutes.

2. Heat oil, lemon zest, shallot, and sugar in Dutch oven over medium-low heat until shallot is softened, 2 to 4 minutes. Discard lemon zest and stir in lemon juice. Add spinach, cover, and cook until spinach is just beginning to wilt, about 30 seconds.

3. Transfer spinach and hot dressing to large bowl. Add chilled feta, radishes, and pistachios, and gently toss to combine. Season with salt and pepper to taste and serve.

Stemming Curly-Leaf Spinach

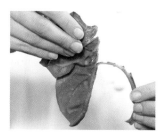

Hold each leaf with 1 hand and use other hand to pull down and remove stem.

Wilted Spinach Salad with Cherries, Goat Cheese, and Almonds

Substitute 2 tablespoons crumbled goat cheese for feta cheese, 1 (2-inch) strip grapefruit zest for lemon zest, 2 teaspoons grapefruit juice for lemon juice, 2 tablespoons dried cherries for radishes, and 2 tablespoons chopped toasted sliced almonds for pistachios.

Roasted Beet Salad with Goat Cheese and Pistachios

SERVES 2

✓ **WHY THIS RECIPE WORKS:** With a sweet, earthy flavor, juicy texture, and ruby-red hue, beets are a real showstopper. To make them the star of a simple yet elegant salad, we had to find the easiest way to prepare them. Boiling and steaming diluted their flavor, but when wrapped in foil and roasted, the beets were juicy and tender with a concentrated sweetness. Peeling was easier when the beets were still warm—the skins slid off effortlessly. We also tossed the sliced beets with the dressing while still warm, allowing them to absorb maximum flavor. Crumbled goat cheese, peppery arugula, and toasted pistachios rounded out the dish. When buying beets, look for bunches that have the most uniformly sized beets so that they will roast in the same amount of time. If the beets are different sizes, remove the smaller ones from the oven as they become tender. You can use either golden or red beets or a mix of the two in this recipe.

1 **pound beets, trimmed**
2 **tablespoons extra-virgin olive oil**
5 **teaspoons sherry vinegar**
  Salt and pepper
1 **cup baby arugula**
1 **ounce goat cheese, crumbled (¼ cup)**
2 **tablespoons chopped toasted shelled pistachios**

1. Adjust oven rack to middle position and heat oven to 400 degrees. Wrap beets individually in aluminum foil and place on rimmed baking sheet. Roast beets until skewer inserted into center meets little resistance, 45 minutes to 1 hour.

2. Remove beets from oven and carefully remove foil (watch for steam). When beets are cool enough to handle, rub off skins with paper towels or clean dish towel and cut into ½-inch-thick wedges; if large, cut wedges in half crosswise.

3. Meanwhile, whisk oil, vinegar, ¼ teaspoon salt, and ¼ teaspoon pepper together in large bowl. Add sliced beets, toss to coat, and let cool to room temperature, about 20 minutes.

Tossing cooked beets with a simple sherry vinegar dressing while they're still warm allows them to absorb the dressing's flavor.

4. Add arugula to beets and gently toss to coat. Season with salt and pepper to taste. Sprinkle with goat cheese and pistachios and serve.

VARIATION
Roasted Beet Salad with Blood Orange and Almonds

Reduce amount of sherry vinegar to 4 teaspoons. Substitute ½ cup shaved ricotta salata for goat cheese and 2 tablespoons toasted sliced almonds for pistachios. Cut away peel and pith from 1 blood orange. Quarter orange, then slice crosswise into ½-inch-thick pieces; add blood orange pieces with arugula.

Removing Beet Skins

To easily skin beets without straining your hands, cradle roasted beet in your hands in several layers of paper towels or clean dish towel, then gently rub off skin.

For a refreshing cucumber salad, we drain the sliced cucumbers and add a concentrated dressing to keep the flavors bright.

Cucumber Salad with Olives, Oregano, and Almonds

SERVES 2 **FAST** **LIGHT**

✓ **WHY THIS RECIPE WORKS:** Cucumbers can make a cool, crisp salad—but not if they're soggy from their own moisture and swimming in a watery dressing. For a cucumber salad with good crunch, we drained the sliced cucumbers on paper towels while we prepared the dressing. Then, to prevent the dressing from getting watered down, we made a concentrated version with 2½ tablespoons of vinegar and just 1 teaspoon of olive oil. To keep the vinegar from tasting harsh, we simmered it for a few minutes. When tossed with the cucumbers, this potent mixture retained its bright flavor. Briny kalamata olives, a thinly sliced shallot, and some toasted almonds added more flavor and crunch and nicely complemented the cool cucumber. The texture of this salad depends upon thinly sliced cucumbers and shallots. Be sure to slice the vegetables ⅛ to 3⁄16 inch thick. This salad is best served within 1 hour of being dressed. For the nutritional information for this recipe, see page 413.

2 small cucumbers, peeled, halved lengthwise, seeded, and sliced thin
2½ tablespoons white wine vinegar
1 teaspoon extra-virgin olive oil
1 teaspoon sugar
¾ teaspoon lemon juice
Salt and pepper
2 tablespoons chopped pitted kalamata olives
1 small shallot, sliced thin
½ teaspoon minced fresh oregano
1½ tablespoons coarsely chopped toasted sliced almonds

1. Line baking sheet with paper towels and evenly spread cucumber slices on sheet. Refrigerate while preparing dressing.

2. Bring vinegar to simmer in small saucepan and cook until reduced to 1 tablespoon, 3 to 5 minutes. Transfer to large bowl and let cool to room temperature, about 5 minutes. Whisk in oil, sugar, lemon juice, ½ teaspoon salt, and pinch pepper until well combined.

3. Add chilled cucumbers, olives, shallot, and oregano to dressing and toss to combine. Let sit for 5 minutes, then toss to redistribute dressing. Season with salt and pepper to taste and sprinkle with almonds. Serve.

VARIATIONS

Cucumber Salad with Chile, Mint, and Peanuts

For the nutritional information for this recipe, see page 413.

Omit pepper, olives, and shallot. Substitute 1 teaspoon vegetable oil for olive oil and increase amount of sugar to 1¼ teaspoons. Substitute ¾ teaspoon lime juice for lemon juice and add 1½ teaspoons fish sauce and 1 seeded and minced Thai chile to dressing in step 2. Substitute 2 tablespoons minced fresh mint for oregano and 2 tablespoons coarsely chopped toasted peanuts for almonds.

Cucumber Salad with Jalapeño, Cilantro, and Pepitas

For the nutritional information for this recipe, see page 413.

Omit pepper, olives, and shallot. Substitute ¾ teaspoon lime juice for lemon juice and add 1 teaspoon grated lime zest and ½ seeded and minced jalapeño chile to dressing in step 2. Substitute ½ cup minced fresh cilantro for oregano and 1½ tablespoons toasted pepitas for almonds.

Cucumber Salad with Ginger, Sesame, and Scallions

For the nutritional information for this recipe, see page 413.

Omit pepper, olives, and shallot. Substitute 1 teaspoon toasted sesame oil for olive oil and increase amount of sugar to 1¼ teaspoons. Substitute ¾ teaspoon lime juice for lemon juice and add 1 teaspoon grated fresh ginger to dressing in step 2. Substitute 2 thinly sliced scallions for oregano and 1½ tablespoons toasted sesame seeds for almonds.

Broccoli Salad

SERVES 2

✔ **WHY THIS RECIPE WORKS:** Most recipes for this potluck favorite make enough for a crowd, but we thought its short ingredient list made it a great option for two. Rather than leaving the broccoli raw, we found that cooking it briefly in boiling water improved both its flavor and texture and kept it bright green. Adding the hardier stems to the cooking water first ensured that they were crisp-tender at the same time as the quick-cooking florets. Drying the broccoli in a salad spinner prevented the dressing—a tangy mayo-and-vinegar mixture—from getting watered down. Crisp bacon, toasted walnuts, and raisins brought crunch and a salty-sweet balance to this salad. When prepping the broccoli, keep the stems and florets separate. If you don't own a salad spinner, lay the broccoli on a clean dish towel to dry in step 3.

2 slices bacon, chopped fine
3 tablespoons golden raisins
½ bunch broccoli (12 ounces), florets cut into 1-inch pieces, stalks peeled and sliced ¼ inch thick
¼ cup mayonnaise
1½ teaspoons balsamic vinegar
Salt and pepper
3 tablespoons coarsely chopped toasted walnuts
1 small shallot, minced

1. Cook bacon in 8-inch skillet over medium heat until crisp, 5 to 7 minutes. Using slotted spoon, transfer bacon to paper towel–lined plate.

2. Bring 2 quarts water to boil in large saucepan. Remove ¼ cup boiling water and combine with raisins in small bowl. Let sit, covered, for 5 minutes, then drain.

3. Meanwhile, fill large bowl halfway with ice and water. Add broccoli stalks to boiling water and cook for 1 minute. Add florets and cook until slightly tender, about 1 minute. Drain broccoli and immediately transfer to bowl of ice water to stop cooking; let sit until fully chilled, about 2 minutes. Drain and transfer broccoli to salad spinner and spin dry.

4. Whisk mayonnaise, vinegar, ¼ teaspoon salt, and ⅛ teaspoon pepper together in large bowl. Add broccoli, raisins, walnuts, and shallot and toss to combine. Season with salt and pepper to taste. Sprinkle with crisp bacon and serve.

Cherry Tomato Salad with Basil and Fresh Mozzarella

SERVES 2

✔ **WHY THIS RECIPE WORKS:** Cherry tomatoes can make a great salad, but the liquid they exude can make a soggy mess. To get rid of some of their juice without throwing away flavor, we salted and drained the tomatoes then used a salad spinner to separate the tomato jelly from the flesh. We reduced the liquid to a flavorful concentrate (adding shallot, olive oil, and vinegar) and reunited it with the tomatoes. Some fresh mozzarella and chopped basil rounded out this great all-season salad. If cherry tomatoes are unavailable, substitute grape tomatoes; cut the grape tomatoes in half along the equator rather than quartering them. Don't skimp on the tomato sitting time in step 1, or the salad will taste watery.

6 ounces cherry tomatoes, quartered
½ teaspoon sugar
Salt and pepper
1 small shallot, minced
1 teaspoon balsamic vinegar
2 teaspoons extra-virgin olive oil
2 ounces fresh mozzarella, cut into ½-inch pieces and patted dry with paper towels (½ cup)
¼ cup chopped fresh basil

1. Toss tomatoes, sugar, and ¼ teaspoon salt together in large bowl; let sit for 30 minutes.

2. Transfer tomatoes to salad spinner and spin until most of seeds and excess liquid have been removed, 45 to 60 seconds, stirring frequently to redistribute tomatoes. Return tomatoes to now-empty bowl and set aside. Strain tomato liquid through fine-mesh strainer, pressing on solids to extract as much liquid as possible. Reserve 2 tablespoons liquid; discard extra liquid and tomato solids.

3. Bring reserved tomato liquid, shallot, and vinegar to simmer in small saucepan and cook until reduced to 1 tablespoon, 2 to 3 minutes. Transfer mixture to small bowl; let cool to room temperature, about 5 minutes. Whisk in oil until combined.

4. Add dressing, mozzarella, and basil to tomatoes and toss to combine. Season with salt and pepper to taste and serve.

VARIATION

Cherry Tomato Salad with Tarragon and Blue Cheese

Toasted chopped pecans or walnuts are a nice addition here.

Substitute 1 teaspoon cider vinegar for balsamic vinegar,

¼ cup crumbled blue cheese for mozzarella, and 2 teaspoons chopped fresh tarragon for basil. Whisk 2 teaspoons honey and 1 teaspoon Dijon mustard into tomato liquid with oil in step 3.

Italian Bread Salad (Panzanella)

SERVES 2

✔ **WHY THIS RECIPE WORKS:** When the rustic Italian bread salad *panzanella* is done well, the sweet juice of tomatoes mixes with a bright-tasting vinaigrette, moistening chunks of thick-crusted bread until they're soft and just a little chewy—but the line between lightly moistened and soggy is very thin. Toasting fresh bread in the oven, rather than using the traditional day-old bread, was a good start. The bread lost enough moisture in the oven to absorb the dressing without getting waterlogged. A 10-minute soak in a simple red wine vinaigrette yielded perfectly moistened, nutty-tasting bread ready to be tossed with the tomatoes, which we salted to intensify their flavor. A thinly sliced cucumber and shallot for crunch and bite plus a handful of chopped fresh basil perfected our salad. In-season, locally grown tomatoes and high-quality extra-virgin olive oil are ideal for this recipe.

- 3 ounces rustic Italian or French bread, cut into 1-inch pieces (2 cups)
- ¼ cup extra-virgin olive oil
  Salt and pepper
- 2 tomatoes, cored, seeded, and cut into 1-inch pieces
- 1 tablespoon red wine vinegar
- ½ cucumber, peeled, halved lengthwise, seeded, and sliced thin
- 2 tablespoons chopped fresh basil
- 1 small shallot, sliced thin

1. Adjust oven rack to middle position and heat oven to 400 degrees. Toss bread pieces with 1 tablespoon oil and ⅛ teaspoon salt. Spread bread over rimmed baking sheet and bake until light golden brown, 10 to 12 minutes, tossing occasionally. Let cool to room temperature, about 15 minutes.

2. Meanwhile, toss tomatoes and ⅛ teaspoon salt together, transfer to colander set over large bowl, and let drain for 15 minutes.

3. Whisk remaining 3 tablespoons oil, vinegar, and ⅛ teaspoon pepper into drained tomato juices. Add cooled bread, toss to coat, and let sit for 10 minutes, tossing occasionally.

4. Add drained tomatoes, cucumber, basil, and shallot to bread and toss to combine. Season with salt and pepper to taste and serve immediately.

VARIATIONS

Italian Bread Salad with Garlic and Capers
Whisk 1 minced small garlic clove, 1 rinsed and minced anchovy fillet, and 2 teaspoons rinsed capers into drained tomato juices in step 3.

Italian Bread Salad with Olives and Feta
Add 2 tablespoons chopped pitted kalamata olives and 3 tablespoons crumbled feta cheese to salad in step 4.

NOTES FROM THE TEST KITCHEN

Buying and Storing Fresh Tomatoes

Buying tomatoes at the height of summer won't guarantee juicy, flavorful fruit, but keeping these guidelines in mind will help.

CHOOSE LOCALLY GROWN TOMATOES: If at all possible, this is the best way to ensure a flavorful tomato. The shorter the distance a tomato has to travel, the riper it can be when it's picked. And commercial tomatoes are engineered to be sturdier, with thicker walls and less of the flavorful jelly and seeds.

LOOKS AREN'T EVERYTHING: When selecting tomatoes, oddly shaped tomatoes are fine, and even cracked skin is OK. Avoid tomatoes that are overly soft or leaking juice. Choose tomatoes that smell fruity and feel heavy. And consider trying heirloom tomatoes; grown from naturally pollinated plants and seeds, they are some of the best local tomatoes you can find.

BUY SUPERMARKET TOMATOES ON THE VINE: If supermarket tomatoes are your only option, look for tomatoes sold on the vine. Although this does not mean that they were fully ripened on the vine, they are better than regular supermarket tomatoes, which are picked when still green and blasted with ethylene gas to develop texture and color.

STORING TOMATOES: Once you've brought your tomatoes home, proper storage is important to preserve their fresh flavor and texture for as long as possible. Here are the rules we follow in the test kitchen:

- Never refrigerate tomatoes; the cold damages enzymes that produce flavor compounds, and it ruins their texture, turning the flesh mealy. Even when cut, tomatoes should be kept at room temperature (wrap them tightly in plastic wrap).
- If the vine is still attached, leave it on and store the tomatoes stem end up. Tomatoes off the vine should be stored stem side down at room temperature. We have found that this prevents moisture from escaping and bacteria from entering, and thus prolongs shelf life.
- To quickly ripen hard, unripened tomatoes, store them in a paper bag with a banana or apple, both of which emit ethylene gas, which hastens ripening.

Fennel, Apple, and Chicken Chopped Salad

SERVES 2 `LIGHT`

✓ **WHY THIS RECIPE WORKS:** Great chopped salads are lively mixes of lettuce, vegetables, fruit, nuts, and cheeses, offering a variety of tastes, textures, and visual appeal. Unfortunately, they're more often random collections of leftovers from the crisper drawer doused with a watery, bland dressing. To make a cohesive version that was light and flavorful, we chose a mix of cucumber, fennel, apple, romaine, and chicken. First we salted the cucumber to remove its excess moisture. To keep the lean chicken breast tender, we browned it on just one side then poached it. A minced shallot cut the sweetness of the apples nicely, and some creamy goat cheese added richness. For the dressing, an assertive, vinegar-heavy ratio delivered a welcome acidic kick. Fuji and Gala apples are widely available year-round, but Jonagold, Pink Lady, Jonathan, and Macoun can be substituted. Avoid Granny Smith apples here; they are too tart. Don't skimp on the cucumber draining time, or the salad will taste watery. For the nutritional information for this recipe, see page 413.

A complementary combination of apple, anise-flavored fennel, crisp cucumber, and tender chicken transforms chopped salad.

½ cucumber, peeled, halved lengthwise, seeded, and sliced ½ inch thick
  Salt and pepper
1 (8-ounce) boneless, skinless chicken breast, trimmed
1 tablespoon extra-virgin olive oil
1 ounce goat cheese, crumbled (¼ cup)
2 tablespoons cider vinegar
2 tablespoons minced fresh tarragon
1 Fuji or Gala apple, cored, quartered, and sliced crosswise ¼ inch thick
1 small fennel bulb, stalks discarded, bulb halved, cored, and sliced ¼ inch thick
1 large shallot, minced
½ romaine lettuce heart (3 ounces), torn into bite-size pieces

Preparing Fennel

1. After cutting off stalks and feathery fronds, cut thin slice from base of fennel bulb and remove any tough or blemished layers.

2. Cut bulb in half vertically through base, then use small knife to remove pyramid-shaped core.

3. Cut or slice each half as directed.

1. Toss cucumber and ¼ teaspoon salt together and let drain in colander for 15 minutes.

2. Meanwhile, pat chicken dry with paper towels and season with salt and pepper. Heat 1 teaspoon oil in 8-inch nonstick skillet over medium-high heat until just smoking. Lay chicken in skillet and cook until well browned on first side, 5 to 7 minutes.

3. Flip chicken, add ½ cup water, and reduce heat to medium-low. Cover and continue to cook until chicken registers 160 degrees, 5 to 7 minutes. Transfer chicken to cutting board, let cool slightly, then cut into 1-inch pieces.

4. Whisk goat cheese, vinegar, tarragon, and remaining 2 teaspoons oil together in large bowl until smooth. Add drained cucumber, cut chicken, apple, fennel, and shallot and toss to combine. Let sit until flavors meld, about 5 minutes. Add lettuce and gently toss to coat. Season with salt and pepper to taste and serve.

Chinese Chicken Salad

SERVES 2   LIGHT

✔ **WHY THIS RECIPE WORKS:** To give this stale chain restaurant standby a fresh makeover, we cut back on the oil in the dressing and bumped up the flavor with rice vinegar, fresh ginger, soy sauce, hoisin sauce, and toasted sesame oil. Using a hybrid cooking method—first browning, then poaching—delivered moist, tender chicken that boasted rich, browned flavor. Thinly sliced cabbage, shredded carrot, sliced red bell pepper, and bean sprouts provided a good mix of textures and flavors and rounded out our salad. Rather than finish the dish with nuts, we opted for a handful of chow mein noodles, which contributed a big crunch factor. Chow mein noodles can be found in most supermarkets with other Asian ingredients; La Choy is the most widely available brand. For the nutritional information for this recipe, see page 413.

1   (8-ounce) boneless, skinless chicken breast, trimmed
    Salt and pepper
1   tablespoon vegetable oil
½   small head napa cabbage, cored and shredded (4 cups)
1   small carrot, peeled and shredded
½   small red bell pepper, cut into ¼-inch-wide strips
1   ounce (½ cup) bean sprouts
¼   cup chow mein noodles
1   scallion, sliced thin on bias
2   teaspoons minced fresh cilantro

We freshened up Chinese chicken salad with poached chicken, bean sprouts, and a bright ginger, soy sauce, and hoisin dressing.

3½   tablespoons rice vinegar
2½   tablespoons hoisin sauce
2½   teaspoons soy sauce
1½   teaspoons grated fresh ginger
½   teaspoon toasted sesame oil

1. Pat chicken dry with paper towels and season with salt and pepper. Heat 1 teaspoon vegetable oil in 8-inch nonstick skillet over medium-high heat until just smoking. Lay chicken in skillet and cook until well browned on first side, 5 to 7 minutes.

2. Flip chicken, add ½ cup water, and reduce heat to medium-low. Cover and continue to cook until chicken registers 160 degrees, 5 to 7 minutes. Transfer chicken to cutting board, let cool slightly, then shred into bite-size pieces using 2 forks.

3. Combine shredded chicken, cabbage, carrot, bell pepper, bean sprouts, chow mein noodles, scallion, and cilantro in large bowl. In separate bowl, whisk remaining 2 teaspoons vegetable oil, vinegar, hoisin, soy sauce, ginger, and sesame oil together. Drizzle dressing over salad and toss to coat. Season with salt and pepper to taste. Serve.

Chopped Cobb Salad

SERVES 2

✓ **WHY THIS RECIPE WORKS:** To make a simple chopped Cobb salad, we needed to get the most out of a few ingredients. First, for perfect hard-cooked eggs, we added eggs to a pot of water, brought it to a boil, then let the eggs cook through gently off heat. Moving the cooked eggs to a bowl of ice water kept them from overcooking. We sautéed four slices of chopped bacon until crisp, then cubed a raw chicken breast and sautéed it in the rendered bacon fat for maximum browning and flavor. To get blue cheese flavor in every bite, we pureed half of the cheese right into the vinaigrette. For the best flavor and creamy texture, we carefully selected avocados that yielded slightly when squeezed but weren't mushy or bruised. If cherry tomatoes are unavailable, substitute grape tomatoes; cut the grape tomatoes in half along the equator rather than quartering them.

2 **large eggs**
    Salt and pepper
4 **slices bacon, chopped fine**
1 **(8-ounce) boneless, skinless chicken breast, trimmed and cut into 1-inch pieces**
2 **ounces blue cheese, crumbled (½ cup)**
2 **tablespoons extra-virgin olive oil**
1 **tablespoon red wine vinegar**
6 **ounces cherry tomatoes, quartered**
1 **romaine lettuce heart (6 ounces), torn into bite-size pieces**
½ **avocado, cut into ½-inch pieces**

1. Bring 2 quarts water, eggs, and 1 tablespoon salt to boil in medium saucepan over high heat. As soon as water reaches boil, remove saucepan from heat, cover, and let sit for 10 minutes.

All About Avocados

The flesh of this rich fruit has a creamy, buttery texture and a delicate flavor. Here are our tips for buying and storing avocados.

BUYING AVOCADOS: Although there are many varieties of avocado, in the United States, small, rough-skinned Hass avocados are the most common, and we prefer them in the test kitchen. When ripe, their skin turns from green to dark purply black, and the fruit yields to a gentle squeeze. However, when selecting avocados, keep in mind that a soft avocado may be a bruised fruit rather than a ripe one. A good test is to try to flick the small stem off the avocado. If it comes off easily and you can see green underneath it, the avocado is ripe. If you see brown underneath after prying it off, the avocado is not usable. If it does not come off easily, the avocado is still unripe. Because these fruits ripen off the tree, that's not a problem; you just have to plan ahead when buying them and allow time for them to ripen.

RIPENING AND STORING AVOCADOS: At room temperature, rock-hard avocados generally ripen within two days, but they may ripen unevenly. Once ripe, they will last two days on average if kept at room temperature. Avocados may take up to four days to ripen in the refrigerator, but they will ripen more evenly. Ripe avocados last about five days when refrigerated, though some discoloration may occur. Store them toward the front of the refrigerator, on the middle to bottom shelves, where temperatures are more moderate. Avocado flesh does not freeze well; as the water in the fruit crystallizes, it destroys the avocado's creamy texture, leaving it mushy and watery when defrosted.

KEEPING LEFTOVER AVOCADO GREEN: Avocado flesh turns brown very quickly once it is exposed to air. To minimize the effect, it's best to prepare avocados at the last moment whenever possible. However, if you only need to use half of an avocado, you can store the leftover half by rubbing 1 tablespoon of olive oil on all of the exposed avocado flesh, allowing the excess oil to drip into a shallow bowl, then placing the avocado half cut side down in the center of the oil puddle, creating a "seal." Store the avocado in the refrigerator.

Pitting and Dicing an Avocado

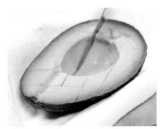
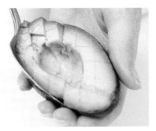

1. Slice avocado in half around pit, then lodge edge of knife blade into pit and twist to remove.

2. Don't pull pit off with your hand. Instead, use large wooden spoon to pry pit safely off knife.

3. Using dish towel to hold avocado steady, make ½-inch crosshatch incisions in flesh of each avocado half, cutting down to but not through skin.

4. Separate diced flesh from skin with soupspoon inserted between skin and flesh, gently scooping out avocado pieces.

Meanwhile, fill large bowl halfway with ice and water. Transfer eggs to bowl of ice water to stop cooking and let sit until fully chilled, about 10 minutes. Peel and quarter eggs.

2. Cook bacon in 10-inch nonstick skillet over medium heat until crisp, 5 to 7 minutes. Using slotted spoon, transfer bacon to paper towel–lined plate. Pour off all but 1 tablespoon fat from skillet.

3. Pat chicken dry with paper towels and season with salt and pepper. Return skillet to stovetop and heat fat left in skillet over medium-high heat until just smoking. Cook chicken until well browned on all sides and registers 160 degrees, 2 to 4 minutes; transfer to plate and let cool slightly.

NOTES FROM THE TEST KITCHEN

All About Vinegars

Of course we use vinegars in salad dressings, but we also use them to perk up sauces, stews, soups, and bean dishes. Here are the vinegars we recommend stocking at home.

DISTILLED WHITE VINEGAR
Made from grain alcohol, white vinegar has no added flavor and is therefore the harshest—and yet most pure—vinegar. We use it most often to make pickles and, diluted with water, as a cleaning agent for kitchen surfaces and hard-skinned fruits and vegetables.

CIDER VINEGAR
This vinegar has a bite and fruity sweetness that work perfectly in bread-and-butter pickles, barbecue sauce, and coleslaw. Unfiltered varieties of cider vinegar typically have the most apple flavor.

RED WINE VINEGAR
Use this slightly sweet, sharp vinegar for bold vinaigrettes and rich sauces—it works particularly well with potent flavors. We prefer red wine vinegars made from a blend of wine grapes and Concord grapes (typically used in grape juice) because the latter add a welcome hint of sweetness.

WHITE WINE VINEGAR
This vinegar's refined, fruity bite makes it the perfect complement to light vinaigrettes and buttery sauces. We use white wine vinegar in dishes like potato salad and hollandaise sauce, where the color of red wine vinegar would detract from the presentation.

RICE VINEGAR
Also referred to as rice wine vinegar, this vinegar is made from steamed rice. Since rice vinegar has lower acidity than other vinegars, we use it to add gentle balance to Asian-influenced marinades and dressings. Avoid cooking with seasoned rice vinegar, as it can taste overly sweet.

BALSAMIC VINEGAR
Traditional Italian balsamic vinegars are highly concentrated, aged for years to develop complex flavor—and pricey. They're best saved to drizzle over finished dishes. For vinaigrettes and glazes and to finish soups and sauces, we use less-expensive commercial balsamic vinegars, which are younger wine vinegars with sugar and coloring added. **Lucini Gran Riserva Balsamico** is our favorite.

4. Process ¼ cup blue cheese, oil, and vinegar in food processor until well combined and smooth, about 15 seconds, scraping down sides of bowl as needed. Transfer dressing to large bowl. Add chicken, tomatoes, and remaining ¼ cup blue cheese and toss to combine. Add lettuce and gently toss to coat. Season with salt and pepper to taste. Divide salad among individual plates or transfer to serving platter. Top with quartered eggs, crisp bacon, and avocado. Serve.

Steak, Mushroom, and Blue Cheese Salad

SERVES 2 **FAST**

✔ **WHY THIS RECIPE WORKS:** For a flavorful dinner salad, we wanted to marry juicy steak, meaty mushrooms, and blue cheese. We first cooked the steak until just medium rare, then we used the flavorful fond left in the skillet to cook the mushrooms. Sautéing them with a tablespoon of vinaigrette, rather than the usual oil, gave them a bright, tangy flavor that nicely balanced their earthiness. To complement the salad's main components, we made a simple vinaigrette with oil, vinegar, shallot, and mustard. We tossed the vinaigrette with tender baby spinach and briny capers, then topped the greens with the mushrooms, steak, and blue cheese. We prefer the steak cooked to medium-rare, but if you prefer it more or less done, see our guidelines on page 155.

1 **(8-ounce) boneless strip steak, ¾ inch thick, trimmed**
  Salt and pepper
¼ **cup extra-virgin olive oil**
2 **tablespoons red wine vinegar**
1 **small shallot, minced**
1½ **teaspoons Dijon mustard**
8 **ounces white or cremini mushrooms, trimmed and quartered**
4 **ounces (4 cups) baby spinach**
1 **tablespoon capers, rinsed and minced**
1 **ounce blue cheese, crumbled (¼ cup)**

1. Pat steak dry with paper towels and season with salt and pepper. Heat 1 tablespoon oil in 10-inch skillet over medium-high heat until just smoking. Lay steak in skillet and cook until well browned on first side, 3 to 5 minutes. Flip steak, reduce heat to medium, and continue to cook until meat registers 120 to 125 degrees (for medium-rare), 1 to 4 minutes. Transfer steak to cutting board, tent loosely with aluminum foil, and let rest while finishing salad. Pour off fat from skillet but do not wipe clean.

2. Whisk remaining 3 tablespoons oil, vinegar, shallot, and mustard together in large bowl. Add mushrooms and 1 tablespoon vinaigrette to now-empty skillet and cook over medium heat until mushrooms are golden, 6 to 8 minutes; let cool slightly.

3. Add spinach and capers to remaining vinaigrette and gently toss to coat. Season with salt and pepper to taste. Divide spinach among individual plates or transfer to serving platter and top with mushrooms. Slice steak thin and arrange over salad. Sprinkle with blue cheese and serve.

Thai-Style Beef Salad

SERVES 2

✅ **WHY THIS RECIPE WORKS:** Traditionally, the steak for Thai-style beef salad is marinated for hours before cooking. We came up with a far quicker method: marinating the meat after cooking. We let the steak rest, sliced it, then tossed it with the tangy, Asian-inspired dressing. Meanwhile, we chopped onion, cucumber, and herbs and tossed them with cooked rice noodles and more of the dressing. The salty dressing pulled moisture from the vegetables, so we drained the excess liquid from the mixture before combining the steak, vegetables, and noodles on a bed of lettuce and drizzling the salad with the remaining dressing. A garnish of chopped peanuts provided the finishing touch. Do not substitute other types of noodles for the rice vermicelli here. We prefer the steak cooked to medium-rare, but if you prefer it more or less done, see our guidelines on page 155.

2	ounces dried rice vermicelli
1	(8-ounce) flank steak, trimmed
	Salt and pepper
3	tablespoons vegetable oil
3	tablespoons lime juice (2 limes)
3	tablespoons fish sauce
1	tablespoon packed brown sugar
1	small red onion, halved and sliced thin
½	cucumber, peeled, halved lengthwise, seeded, and sliced thin
2	teaspoons minced fresh cilantro
2	teaspoons minced fresh mint
½	head Bibb lettuce (4 ounces), leaves separated
2	tablespoons chopped dry-roasted peanuts

1. Bring 2 quarts water to boil in medium saucepan. Off heat, add noodles and let sit, stirring occasionally, until tender, about 10 minutes. Drain noodles, rinse with cold water, and drain again, leaving noodles slightly wet.

2. Meanwhile, pat steak dry with paper towels and season with salt and pepper. Heat 1 tablespoon oil in 10-inch skillet over medium-high heat until just smoking. Lay steak in skillet and cook until well browned on first side, 3 to 5 minutes. Flip steak, reduce heat to medium, and continue to cook until meat registers 120 to 125 degrees (for medium-rare), 3 to 5 minutes. Transfer steak to cutting board, tent loosely with aluminum foil, and let rest for 5 minutes.

3. Whisk remaining 2 tablespoons oil, lime juice, fish sauce, and sugar together in bowl until sugar dissolves. Slice steak in half lengthwise, then slice thin against grain. Toss sliced steak with 2 tablespoons dressing in separate bowl and let sit for 5 minutes. In third bowl, toss cooked noodles, onion, cucumber, cilantro, and mint with 3 tablespoons dressing and let sit for 5 minutes.

4. Divide lettuce leaves among individual plates or arrange on serving platter. Drain noodle mixture and arrange over lettuce. Drain steak and arrange over salad. Sprinkle with peanuts and drizzle with remaining dressing.

Turkey Taco Salad

SERVES 2

✅ **WHY THIS RECIPE WORKS:** We wanted a recipe for a fresh, easy taco salad with spicy, saucy meat. To make crispy tortilla bowls, we skipped the deep-fryer and baked the tortillas on overturned soup bowls instead; this gave us a pair of golden, ultracrisp taco shells with a lot less fuss. Sautéed aromatics and tomato sauce and a hefty dose of chili powder added savory depth and heat to our ground turkey filling. For heartiness, we added beans to our salad along with cherry tomatoes and shredded romaine. Thanks to the saucy, boldly-flavored taco meat, a squeeze of tart lime juice was all the dressing our salad needed. Be sure to use ground turkey, not ground turkey breast (also labeled 99 percent fat free), in this recipe. If cherry tomatoes are unavailable, substitute grape tomatoes; cut the grape tomatoes in half along the equator rather than quartering them. You will need two ovensafe soup bowls for this recipe.

TURKEY

2	teaspoons vegetable oil
1	small onion, chopped fine
2	teaspoons chili powder
1	garlic clove, minced
6	ounces ground turkey
½	cup canned tomato sauce
¼	cup chicken broth

Topped with spicy, saucy turkey taco meat, this fresh salad is so flavorful, the only dressing it needs is a squeeze of lime juice.

1 teaspoon cider vinegar
½ teaspoon light brown sugar
Salt and pepper

SALAD
2 (10-inch) flour tortillas
Vegetable oil spray
1 romaine lettuce heart (6 ounces), shredded
¾ cup canned black beans, rinsed
4 ounces cherry tomatoes, quartered
1 scallion, sliced thin
2 tablespoons chopped fresh cilantro
1 tablespoon lime juice
Salt and pepper
1 ounce cheddar cheese, shredded (¼ cup)

1. FOR THE TURKEY: Heat oil in 10-inch nonstick skillet over medium-high heat until shimmering. Add onion and cook until softened, about 5 minutes. Stir in chili powder and garlic and cook until fragrant, about 30 seconds. Add ground turkey and cook, breaking up meat with wooden spoon, until almost cooked through but still slightly pink, about 2 minutes. Stir in tomato sauce, broth, vinegar, and sugar. Bring to

simmer and cook until slightly thickened, about 5 minutes; mixture will be saucy. Season with salt and pepper to taste.

2. FOR THE SALAD: Adjust oven rack to middle position and heat oven to 425 degrees. Arrange 2 ovensafe soup bowls upside down on rimmed baking sheet (or use 2 slightly flattened 3-inch aluminum foil balls). Place tortillas on plate, cover with damp paper towel, and microwave until warm and pliable, about 20 seconds.

3. Generously spray both sides of warm tortillas with oil spray. Drape tortillas over soup bowls, pressing tops flat and pinching sides to create 4-sided bowls. Bake until tortillas are golden and crisp, 8 to 10 minutes, rotating sheet halfway through baking. Let tortilla bowls cool upside down.

4. Toss lettuce, beans, tomatoes, scallion, and 1 tablespoon cilantro with lime juice in large bowl. Season with salt and pepper to taste. Place tortilla bowls on individual plates. Divide salad between bowls and top with turkey mixture. Sprinkle with cheddar and remaining 1 tablespoon cilantro. Serve.

Shaping Taco Bowls

Warm tortillas in microwave until pliable, then spray with vegetable oil spray. Arrange 2 ovensafe soup bowls upside down on baking sheet; drape tortillas on top. Press tops flat and pinch sides to create two 4-sided bowls and bake as directed.

Italian Chef's Salad

SERVES 2 **FAST**

✔ **WHY THIS RECIPE WORKS:** We put a new spin on this old classic by swapping out the usual deli ham for flavorful capicola (a nicely seasoned Italian salami) and adding sweet cherry peppers and anise-flavored fennel to the mix. Using the liquid from the peppers in our red wine vinaigrette helped balance the richness of the meat and cheese and ensured a hint of heat in every bite. Garlic and oregano rounded out the dressing. Although hard-cooked eggs are traditional in chef's salads, we found our version was so fresh and flavorful that we didn't miss the eggs when we left them out. When buying the capicola and provolone for this salad, ask the deli to slice each into ¼-inch-thick slabs so that you can easily cut them into ¼-inch strips. If cherry tomatoes are unavailable, substitute grape tomatoes; cut the grape tomatoes in half along the equator rather than quartering them.

3 tablespoons extra-virgin olive oil

2 tablespoons jarred sliced sweet cherry peppers, plus 1 teaspoon brine

2 tablespoons red wine vinegar

1 garlic clove, minced

¼ teaspoon minced fresh oregano or pinch dried

1 romaine lettuce heart (6 ounces), torn into bite-size pieces

½ fennel bulb, stalks discarded, cored, and sliced thin

6 ounces cherry tomatoes, quartered

Salt and pepper

2 (¼-inch-thick) slices capicola (4 ounces), cut into ¼-inch-thick strips

2 (¼-inch-thick) slices provolone cheese (4 ounces), cut into ¼-inch-thick strips

1. Whisk oil, pepper brine, vinegar, garlic, and oregano together in large bowl. Add lettuce, fennel, and tomatoes and gently toss to combine. Season with salt and pepper to taste.

2. Divide salad among individual plates or transfer to serving platter. Top with cherry peppers, capicola, and provolone. Serve.

Poached Shrimp Salad with Avocado and Grapefruit

SERVES 2 LIGHT

✔ **WHY THIS RECIPE WORKS:** Poached shrimp salad makes a great, naturally light meal, but too-lean versions often leave us wanting more. We wanted to develop a satisfying yet healthy salad featuring tender shrimp and a complementary mix of fresh fruit and vegetables. To poach the shrimp, we made a flavorful poaching liquid called a court-bouillon with cold water, lemon juice, sugar, salt, peppercorns, and a bay leaf, then brought the mixture to a gentle simmer over medium heat. Just 10 minutes on the stove plus a 2-minute rest off the heat gave us perfectly cooked, tender shrimp infused with the subtle flavor of the broth. A combination of tart ruby-red grapefruit, buttery avocado, and a bold dressing with ginger, honey, and Dijon mustard gave our shrimp salad a balance of sweet, tart, and tangy flavors. If your grapefruit tastes especially tart, add ¼ teaspoon more honey to the dressing. If you are short on grapefruit juice, substitute water. For the nutritional information for this recipe, see page 413.

SHRIMP

12 ounces extra-large shrimp (21 to 25 per pound), peeled, deveined, and tails removed

¼ cup lemon juice, spent halves reserved (2 lemons)

1 tablespoon sugar

1 teaspoon whole black peppercorns

1 teaspoon salt

1 bay leaf

SALAD AND VINAIGRETTE

½ red grapefruit

1 small shallot, minced

1 tablespoon lime juice

2 teaspoons extra-virgin olive oil

¾ teaspoon grated fresh ginger

¾ teaspoon honey

½ teaspoon Dijon mustard

Salt and pepper

½ avocado, cut into ½-inch pieces

1 ounce snow peas, strings removed, sliced thin on bias

1 tablespoon minced fresh mint

1 head Bibb lettuce (8 ounces), leaves separated

1. FOR THE SHRIMP: Combine shrimp, 2 cups cold water, lemon juice, reserved lemon halves, sugar, peppercorns, salt, and bay leaf in medium saucepan. Place saucepan over medium heat and cook shrimp, stirring several times, until opaque throughout, 8 to 10 minutes (water should be just bubbling around edge of pan and register 165 degrees). Off heat, cover saucepan and let shrimp sit in broth for 2 minutes.

2. Meanwhile, fill large bowl halfway with ice and water. Drain shrimp, discarding lemon half and spices. Immediately transfer shrimp to bowl of ice water to stop cooking and let

Segmenting Citrus Fruit

1. Slice off top and bottom of grapefruit or orange, then cut away peel and pith using paring knife.

2. Slice between membrane and 1 segment to center of fruit. Turn blade and slice along membrane on segment's other side to free segment. Repeat with remaining segments.

Sweet-tart grapefruit and creamy avocado plus a tangy ginger and mustard dressing perfectly complement the shrimp in this salad.

sit until fully chilled, about 5 minutes. Remove shrimp from ice water and pat dry with paper towels.

3. FOR THE SALAD AND VINAIGRETTE: Cut away peel and pith from grapefruit. Working over bowl, use paring knife to slice between membranes to release segments. Reserve 2 tablespoons juice; discard any extra.

4. Whisk reserved grapefruit juice, shallot, lime juice, oil, ginger, honey, mustard, ¼ teaspoon salt, and ⅛ teaspoon pepper together in large bowl. Add chilled shrimp, grapefruit segments, avocado, snow peas, and mint and gently toss to combine. Season with salt and pepper to taste. Divide lettuce leaves among individual plates or arrange on serving platter. Spoon shrimp mixture over lettuce and drizzle with any dressing left in bowl. Serve.

VARIATION

Poached Shrimp Salad with Avocado, Orange, and Arugula

For the nutritional information for this recipe, see page 413.

Substitute 1 whole orange for grapefruit and grapefruit juice and 3 ounces baby arugula for Bibb lettuce. Reduce amount of honey to ¼ teaspoon.

Seared Scallop Salad with Snap Peas and Radishes

SERVES 2 **FAST**

✔ WHY THIS RECIPE WORKS: For an elegant yet easy dinner salad, we wanted to combine tender seared sea scallops with fresh spring vegetables. Because the scallops would be the star of the dish, we needed to ensure they were perfectly cooked. Sandwiching the scallops between paper towels and letting them drain for 10 minutes before cooking rid them of excess moisture that would prevent them from developing a burnished crust in the skillet. Once they were ready to cook, we seasoned them with salt and pepper and seared them in a hot skillet for just a few minutes until their centers were just opaque and their exteriors were well browned and flavorful. For the salad, we tossed delicate mesclun greens, fresh sugar snap peas, and thinly sliced, peppery radishes with a simple vinaigrette and arranged the scallops on top. We recommend buying "dry" scallops, which don't have chemical additives and taste better than "wet." Dry scallops will look ivory or pinkish; wet scallops are bright white.

- 12 ounces large sea scallops, tendons removed
- 1 tablespoon red wine vinegar
- ½ teaspoon Dijon mustard
- 3 tablespoons extra-virgin olive oil
- 6 ounces sugar snap peas, strings removed, halved crosswise
- 4 ounces (4 cups) mesclun
- 4 radishes, trimmed and sliced thin
- 1 shallot, sliced thin
  Salt and pepper

1. Place scallops on large plate lined with clean dish towel. Place second clean dish towel on top of scallops and press gently on towel to blot liquid. Let scallops sit at room temperature for 10 minutes while towels absorb moisture.

2. Meanwhile, combine vinegar and mustard in large bowl. Whisking constantly, drizzle 2 tablespoons oil into vinegar mixture in slow, steady stream. Add snap peas, mesclun, radishes, and shallot and gently toss to coat. Season with salt and pepper to taste. Divide salad among individual plates or transfer to serving platter.

3. Season scallops with salt and pepper. Heat remaining 1 tablespoon oil in 12-inch nonstick skillet over high heat until just smoking. Add scallops in single layer, flat side down, and cook, without moving, until well browned, 1½ to 2 minutes. Flip scallops and continue to cook until sides of scallops are firm and centers are opaque, 30 to 90 seconds (remove smaller scallops as they finish cooking). Arrange scallops over salad. Serve.

Pasta Salad with Arugula and Sun-Dried Tomatoes

SERVES 2   **FAST**   **LIGHT**

✔ **WHY THIS RECIPE WORKS:** Developing a foolproof pasta salad recipe was tricky: While some acidity was needed to brighten the flavor of the salad, too much made the pasta mushy. We liked red wine vinegar for contributing a sharp flavor that wasn't too harsh. Just 1 tablespoon of olive oil was enough to coat the pasta while keeping the brightness of the vinegar at the forefront. A little shallot, Dijon, garlic, and red pepper flakes rounded out the flavors of our vinaigrette. Flavorful sun-dried tomatoes were an easy addition, and tender baby arugula and fresh parsley added color and freshness. Be sure to use oil-packed sun-dried tomatoes here because they have the soft, supple texture necessary for the salad. Cooking the penne until it is completely tender and leaving it slightly wet after rinsing are important for the texture of the finished salad. Other short, bite-size pasta such as fusilli, farfalle, or orecchiette can be substituted for the penne in this salad; however, their cup measurements may vary (see page 228). For the nutritional information for this recipe, see page 413.

4   ounces (1¼ cups) penne
    Salt and pepper
2   tablespoons minced oil-packed sun-dried tomatoes
1½ tablespoons red wine vinegar
1   tablespoon extra-virgin olive oil
1   small shallot, minced
1   teaspoon Dijon mustard
1   garlic clove, minced
    Pinch red pepper flakes
1   cup baby arugula
1   tablespoon chopped fresh parsley
1   ounce provolone cheese, shredded (¼ cup)

1. Bring 4 quarts water to boil in large pot. Add pasta and 1 tablespoon salt and cook, stirring often, until tender. Drain pasta, rinse with cold water, and drain again, leaving pasta slightly wet.

2. Meanwhile, whisk tomatoes, vinegar, oil, shallot, mustard, garlic, ⅛ teaspoon salt, and pepper flakes together in large bowl. Add pasta, arugula, and parsley and toss to combine. Stir in provolone and season with salt and pepper to taste. Serve.

Tortellini Salad with Bell Pepper, Pine Nuts, and Basil

SERVES 2

✔ **WHY THIS RECIPE WORKS:** For a super-easy pasta salad that would be welcome at any picnic, we paired convenient store-bought cheese tortellini with sweet red bell pepper and a simple yet bold dressing made of extra-virgin olive oil, lemon juice, and shallot. To give the salad a flavor reminiscent of pesto and some crunch, we added a handful of chopped basil and stirred in toasted pine nuts before serving. Cooking the tortellini until it is completely tender and leaving it slightly wet after rinsing are important for the texture of the finished salad. You can substitute one 9-ounce package of fresh cheese tortellini for the dried tortellini.

6   ounces dried cheese tortellini
    Salt and pepper
2   tablespoons extra-virgin olive oil
2   tablespoons lemon juice
1   small shallot, minced
1   small red bell pepper, stemmed, seeded, and cut into ¼-inch-wide strips
¼   cup coarsely chopped fresh basil
2   tablespoons pine nuts, toasted

1. Bring 4 quarts water to boil in large pot. Add tortellini and 1 tablespoon salt and cook, stirring often, until tender. Drain tortellini, rinse with cold water, and drain again, leaving tortellini slightly wet.

2. Meanwhile, whisk oil, lemon juice, shallot, ⅛ teaspoon salt, and ⅛ teaspoon pepper together in large bowl. Add tortellini, bell pepper, and basil and toss to combine. Let sit for 10 minutes. Stir in pine nuts and season with salt and pepper to taste. Serve.

Toasting Pine Nuts

Toast pine nuts in dry skillet over medium heat, shaking pan occasionally to prevent scorching, until slightly darkened in color, 3 to 5 minutes.

Classic Chicken Salad

SERVES 2

✔ **WHY THIS RECIPE WORKS:** There are many varieties of chicken salad, but there's no beating the classic version: tender cubes of moist chicken lightly bound with mayonnaise and freshened up with celery and aromatic flavors. For juicy and tender chicken, we added the chicken to a pot of water, heated the water to 170 degrees, then let the chicken finish cooking through gently off heat. Salting the water helped to season the chicken throughout. Then, while the chicken cooled, we simply mixed up a classic dressing with mayonnaise, lemon juice, mustard, celery, shallot, and fresh parsley or tarragon for a quintessential chicken salad. To ensure that the chicken cooks through, start with cold water in step 1 and don't use breasts that weigh more than 8 ounces or are thicker than 1 inch. Serve over mixed salad greens or in a sandwich.

- Salt and pepper
- 2 (6- to 8-ounce) boneless, skinless chicken breasts, trimmed
- ¼ cup mayonnaise
- 1 teaspoon lemon juice
- ½ teaspoon Dijon mustard
- 1 celery rib, minced
- 1 small shallot, minced
- 1 tablespoon minced fresh parsley or tarragon

1. Dissolve 1 tablespoon salt in 3 cups cold water in medium saucepan. Submerge chicken in water. Heat saucepan over medium heat until water registers 170 degrees. Off heat, cover saucepan and let sit until chicken registers 165 degrees, 15 to 17 minutes.

2. Transfer chicken to paper towel–lined plate and refrigerate until cool, about 30 minutes. Pat chilled chicken dry with paper towels and cut into ½-inch pieces.

3. Whisk mayonnaise, lemon juice, and mustard together in medium bowl. Add cut chicken, celery, shallot, and parsley and toss to combine. Season with salt and pepper to taste and serve.

Mediterranean Tuna Salad

SERVES 2 `FAST`

✔ **WHY THIS RECIPE WORKS:** For a twist on the usual tuna salad laden with mayonnaise, we made a fresh Mediterranean-style tuna salad. We swapped the mayonnaise for a vinaigrette made with olive oil, shallot, lemon juice, garlic, and mustard.

We sided with tradition for this classic chicken salad, focusing on perfectly poached chicken, mayo, and a simple blend of aromatics.

Letting the vinaigrette sit for 5 minutes before tossing it with the tuna and vegetables allowed the flavors to meld nicely. We started with high-quality canned tuna and added celery, sweet red bell pepper, and briny chopped kalamata olives for a light, fresh salad that didn't compromise on flavor. High-quality extra-virgin olive oil and canned tuna (solid white albacore packed in water) are crucial to the success of this recipe. Serve over mixed salad greens or in a sandwich.

- 1½ tablespoons extra-virgin olive oil
- 1 small shallot, minced
- 2 teaspoons lemon juice
- 1 small garlic clove, minced
- ¼ teaspoon Dijon mustard
- Salt and pepper
- 1 (5-ounce) can solid white tuna in water, drained thoroughly and flaked
- 1 celery rib, minced
- ½ red bell pepper, chopped fine
- 1 tablespoon chopped pitted kalamata olives
- 1 tablespoon minced fresh parsley

1. Whisk oil, shallot, lemon juice, garlic, mustard, ¼ teaspoon salt, and ⅛ teaspoon pepper together in medium bowl and let sit for 5 minutes.

2. Add tuna, celery, bell pepper, olives, and parsley to dressing and gently toss to combine. Season with salt and pepper to taste and serve.

VARIATION

Mediterranean Tuna Salad with Carrot, Radishes, and Cilantro

Substitute 3 minced radishes for celery, ½ peeled and shredded carrot for bell pepper, and 1 tablespoon minced fresh cilantro for parsley.

Classic Shrimp Salad

SERVES 2 **FAST**

✅ **WHY THIS RECIPE WORKS:** Great shrimp salad should have firm and tender shrimp and a perfect deli-style dressing that complements, but does not mask, the flavor of the shrimp and the other ingredients. We started by adding the shrimp to a cold court-bouillon (an aromatic mixture of water, lemon juice, parsley, sugar, salt, and peppercorns), then heated the liquid to just a near simmer. After several minutes, we took the shrimp off heat to finish cooking. We kept the traditional mayonnaise, but used just 2 tablespoons to allow the flavor of the shrimp to come through. We preferred milder minced shallot to onion and added minced celery for its subtle flavor and crunch. This recipe can also be prepared with large shrimp (26 to 30 per pound); the cooking time will be 1 to 2 minutes less. Serve over mixed salad greens or on a buttered and grilled bun.

    8 ounces extra-large shrimp (21 to 25 per pound), peeled,
       deveined, and tails removed
    4½ tablespoons lemon juice, spent halves reserved
       (2 lemons)
    4 sprigs fresh parsley or tarragon plus 1 teaspoon minced
    1 tablespoon sugar
    1 teaspoon whole black peppercorns
       Salt and pepper
    2 tablespoons mayonnaise
    1 small shallot, minced
    1 small celery rib, minced

1. Combine shrimp, 2 cups cold water, ¼ cup lemon juice, reserved lemon halves, parsley sprigs, sugar, peppercorns, and 1 teaspoon salt in medium saucepan. Place saucepan over

medium heat and cook shrimp, stirring several times, until opaque throughout, 8 to 10 minutes (water should be just bubbling around edge of pan and register 165 degrees). Off heat, cover saucepan and let shrimp sit in broth for 2 minutes.

2. Meanwhile, fill large bowl halfway with ice and water. Drain shrimp, discarding lemon halves, parsley stems, and peppercorns. Immediately transfer shrimp to bowl of ice water to stop cooking and let sit until fully chilled, about 5 minutes. Remove shrimp from ice water and pat dry with paper towels. Cut shrimp in half lengthwise, then cut each half into thirds.

3. Whisk mayonnaise, shallot, celery, minced parsley, and remaining ½ tablespoon lemon juice together in medium bowl. Add shrimp and toss to coat. Season with salt and pepper to taste and serve.

All-American Potato Salad

SERVES 2

✅ **WHY THIS RECIPE WORKS:** Potato salad is too often blanketed in a bland, mayonnaise-rich dressing. We wanted lightly dressed, flavorful, tender potatoes punctuated by crunchy bits of onion and celery. We found that seasoning the potatoes while still hot maximized flavor, so we tossed hot russets with white vinegar then added a judicious amount of mayonnaise. One small rib of celery and a minced shallot added just the right amount of crunch and onion flavor. Prep-free pickle relish added a subtle sweetness. Celery seeds reinforced the flavor of the fresh celery and provided an underlying complexity. Note that this recipe calls for celery seeds, not celery salt; if only celery salt is available, use half the amount and be careful when seasoning the salad with additional salt in step 3. Be careful not to overcook the potatoes or they will become mealy and break apart. If you find the potato salad a little dry for your liking, add up to 2 tablespoons more mayonnaise.

    1 pound russet potatoes, peeled and cut into ¾-inch pieces
       Salt and pepper
    1 tablespoon distilled white vinegar
    ¼ cup mayonnaise
    1 small celery rib, minced
    1½ tablespoons sweet pickle relish
    1 small shallot, minced
    1 tablespoon minced fresh parsley
    ½ teaspoon dry mustard
    ½ teaspoon celery seeds
    1 large hard-cooked egg, cut into ¼-inch pieces (optional)

1. Place potatoes and 1 tablespoon salt in medium saucepan and add water to cover by 1 inch. Bring to boil over medium-high heat, then reduce heat to medium and simmer, stirring once or twice, until potatoes are tender, about 8 minutes.

2. Drain potatoes and transfer to medium bowl. Add vinegar and, using rubber spatula, gently toss to coat. Let sit until potatoes are just warm, about 20 minutes.

3. Meanwhile, whisk mayonnaise, celery, pickle relish, shallot, parsley, mustard, and celery seeds together in small bowl. Gently fold dressing and egg, if using, into potatoes. Season with salt and pepper to taste. Cover and refrigerate until chilled, at least 1 hour or up to 1 day. Serve.

VARIATION

Garlicky Potato Salad with Tomatoes and Basil

Omit parsley and egg. Add 1 minced small garlic clove to dressing in step 3. Gently fold 2 tablespoons coarsely chopped basil and 3 ounces quartered cherry tomatoes into potatoes with dressing.

French Potato Salad

SERVES 2

✓ **WHY THIS RECIPE WORKS:** French potato salad should be pleasing to the eye and to the palate. The potatoes (small red potatoes are traditional) should be tender but not mushy, and the flavor of the vinaigrette should penetrate the potatoes, seasoning them throughout. To eliminate torn skins and broken slices, a common pitfall when boiling skin-on red potatoes, we sliced the potatoes before boiling them. Then, to evenly infuse the potatoes with the garlicky mustard vinaigrette, we added them to the vinaigrette while they were still warm and let them sit for 10 minutes. Gently folding in minced shallot and fresh herbs just before serving helped keep the potatoes intact. Use small red potatoes measuring 1 to 2 inches in diameter. For the best flavor, serve the salad warm.

12 **ounces small red potatoes, unpeeled, sliced ¼ inch thick**
    Salt and pepper
2   **tablespoons extra-virgin olive oil**
1   **tablespoon Champagne vinegar or white wine vinegar**
1   **garlic clove, minced**
1   **teaspoon Dijon mustard**
1   **small shallot, minced**
1   **tablespoon minced fresh parsley**
1   **tablespoon minced fresh tarragon**

We toss red potatoes with a simple vinaigrette, shallot, and fresh herbs for a French potato salad that looks as good as it tastes.

1. Place potatoes and 1 tablespoon salt in medium saucepan and add water to cover by 1 inch. Bring to boil over medium-high heat, then reduce heat to medium and simmer, stirring once or twice, until potatoes are tender, about 10 minutes. Drain potatoes, reserving 2 tablespoons potato cooking water.

2. Whisk reserved potato water, oil, vinegar, garlic, and mustard together in medium bowl. Add warm potatoes and gently toss to coat; let sit for 10 minutes.

3. Add shallot, parsley, and tarragon to potatoes and gently toss to combine. Season with salt and pepper to taste and serve immediately.

VARIATION

French Potato Salad with Radishes and Cornichons

Substitute 1 tablespoon minced red onion for shallot. Toss dressed potatoes with 2 thinly sliced radishes and 2 tablespoons thinly sliced cornichons in step 3.

Sweet and Tangy Coleslaw

SERVES 2 **FAST** **LIGHT**

WHY THIS RECIPE WORKS: For a bright, tangy coleslaw, we ditched the mayonnaise in favor of a light dressing of oil and cider vinegar. To keep the moisture of the cabbage from diluting the dressing, we lightly salted the cabbage and microwaved it, which pulled out its excess water, then quickly dried it in a salad spinner. Chilling the dressing helped to compensate for the warm cabbage. We replaced the usual domineering onion with grated carrot and chopped parsley and added celery seeds for a little zip to make a refreshing slaw that would go with almost anything. A brief chill in the fridge allowed its flavors to meld. If you don't have a salad spinner, use a colander to drain the cabbage and press out the residual liquid with a rubber spatula. For the nutritional information for this recipe, see page 413.

This fresh, tangy coleslaw features crunchy shredded carrot, fresh parsley, and a sweet, bright cider vinegar dressing.

  2 tablespoons cider vinegar, plus extra for seasoning
  1 tablespoon vegetable oil
     Pinch celery seeds
     Salt and pepper
  ½ small head green cabbage, halved, cored, and shredded (4 cups)
  2 tablespoons sugar, plus extra for seasoning
  1 small carrot, peeled and shredded
  1 tablespoon minced fresh parsley

1. Combine vinegar, oil, celery seeds, and pinch pepper in medium bowl. Place bowl in freezer until vinegar mixture is well chilled, at least 10 or up to 20 minutes.

2. While vinegar mixture chills, toss cabbage with sugar and ½ teaspoon salt in separate bowl. Cover and microwave until cabbage is partially wilted and reduced in volume by one-third, 45 to 90 seconds, stirring cabbage halfway through microwaving.

3. Transfer cabbage to salad spinner and spin until excess water is removed, 10 to 20 seconds. Add cabbage, carrot, and parsley to chilled vinegar and toss to combine. Season with extra vinegar, extra sugar, and salt to taste. Cover and refrigerate until chilled, at least 15 minutes or up to 1 day. Toss to redistribute dressing and serve.

VARIATIONS

Sweet and Tangy Coleslaw with Bell Pepper and Jalapeño

For the nutritional information for this recipe, see page 413.

Substitute 2 teaspoons lime juice for celery seeds, ½ thinly sliced small red bell pepper and ½ seeded and minced jalapeño chile for carrot, and 1 thinly sliced small scallion for parsley.

Sweet and Tangy Coleslaw with Apple and Tarragon

For the nutritional information for this recipe, see page 413.

Reduce amount of cider vinegar to 1 tablespoon. Substitute ¼ teaspoon Dijon mustard for celery seeds, ½ Granny Smith apple, cored and cut into 2-inch-long matchsticks, for carrot, and 1 teaspoon minced fresh tarragon for parsley.

Shredding Cabbage

1. Cut cabbage into quarters, then cut away hard piece of core attached to each quarter.

2. Flatten small stacks of leaves on cutting board and use chef's knife to cut each stack crosswise into ¼-inch-wide shreds.

CHAPTER 4

Burgers, Sandwiches, Pizza, and More

BURGERS

SANDWICHES

PIZZAS, CALZONES, AND STROMBOLI

■ FAST (Start to finish in about 30 minutes)

■ LIGHT (See page 413 for nutritional information)

Opposite: Easy Skillet Pizza with Ricotta, Bacon, and Scallions; Salmon Burgers with Tomato Chutney; Portobello Panini

Juicy Pub-Style Burgers

SERVES 2

✔ **WHY THIS RECIPE WORKS:** Few things are as satisfying as a thick, juicy pub-style burger. But avoiding the usual gray band of overcooked meat is a challenge. We wanted a patty that was well-seared, juicy, and evenly rosy from center to edge. Grinding our own meat in the food processor was a must for this ultimate burger, and sirloin steak tips were the right cut for the job. Cutting the meat into small ½-inch chunks before grinding and lightly packing the meat to form patties gave the burgers just enough structure to hold their shape in the skillet. A little melted butter improved their flavor and juiciness, but our biggest discovery came when we transferred the burgers from the stovetop to the oven to finish cooking—the stovetop provided intense heat for searing, while the oven's gentle ambient heat allowed for even cooking, thus eliminating the overcooked gray zone. Steak tips, also known as flap meat, are sold as whole steak, cubes, and strips; look for either whole steak tips or strips that are easy to cut into small pieces for this recipe. When stirring the butter and pepper into the ground meat and shaping the patties, take care not to overwork the meat, or the burgers will become dense. We prefer these burgers cooked to medium-rare, but if you prefer them more or less done, see our guidelines on page 155. Serve with your favorite burger toppings.

Grinding our own meat, adding a little melted butter, and finishing them in the oven make these the juiciest, meatiest burgers ever.

1 pound sirloin steak tips, trimmed and cut into ½-inch pieces

2 tablespoons unsalted butter, melted and cooled

Salt and pepper

1 teaspoon vegetable oil

¼ cup mayonnaise

2 teaspoons soy sauce

2 teaspoons minced fresh chives

1 teaspoon packed brown sugar

¾ teaspoon Worcestershire sauce

1 small garlic clove, minced

2 large hamburger buns, toasted and buttered

1. Place beef on rimmed baking sheet in single layer. Freeze beef until very firm and starting to harden around edges but still pliable, about 25 minutes.

2. Pulse half of beef in food processor until finely ground into 1/16-inch pieces, about 35 pulses, scraping down sides of bowl as needed to ensure that beef is evenly ground. Return ground beef to empty side of sheet. Repeat with remaining half of beef; return to sheet. Spread ground beef on sheet and inspect carefully, removing any long strands of gristle and large chunks of hard meat or fat.

3. Adjust oven rack to middle position and heat oven to 300 degrees. Drizzle melted butter over ground beef and add ½ teaspoon pepper. Gently toss with fork to combine, being careful not to overwork meat. Divide meat mixture into 2 lightly packed balls, and gently flatten each ball into ¾-inch-thick patty.

4. Season patties with salt and pepper. Heat oil in 10-inch skillet over high heat until just smoking. Using spatula, place burgers in skillet and cook without moving for 2 minutes. Flip burgers and continue to cook for 2 minutes. Transfer patties to clean, dry rimmed baking sheet and bake until burgers register 120 to 125 degrees (for medium-rare), 3 to 6 minutes. Transfer burgers to plate and let rest for 5 minutes.

5. Whisk mayonnaise, soy sauce, chives, sugar, Worcestershire, garlic, and ¼ teaspoon pepper together in bowl. Serve burgers on buns with sauce.

Juicy Pub-Style Burgers with Peppered Bacon and Aged Cheddar

While beef is in freezer, sprinkle ½ teaspoon coarsely ground pepper over 3 slices bacon. Cook bacon in 10-inch skillet over medium heat until crisp, about 10 minutes. Using slotted spoon, transfer bacon to paper towel–lined plate; cut bacon in half crosswise. Pour off all but 1 teaspoon fat from skillet; substitute bacon fat for vegetable oil. Proceed with recipe, topping each burger with ¼ cup shredded aged cheddar cheese before transferring to oven. Top burgers with sauce and bacon just before serving.

Juicy Pub-Style Burgers with Crispy Shallots and Blue Cheese

While beef is in freezer, heat ⅓ cup vegetable oil and 2 thinly sliced shallots in small saucepan over medium-high heat. Cook, stirring frequently, until shallots are golden, 6 to 8 minutes. Using slotted spoon, transfer shallots to paper towel–lined plate and season with salt to taste. Proceed with recipe, topping each burger with ¼ cup crumbled blue cheese before transferring to oven. Top burgers with sauce and crispy shallots just before serving.

Turkey Burgers

SERVES 2 FAST

✓ **WHY THIS RECIPE WORKS:** In theory, turkey burgers are an easy, healthy weeknight meal, but in practice they often turn out bland, dry, and boring. To keep our turkey burgers moist and tender, we mixed a panade—a paste of bread and milk—into the ground turkey. Pantry-friendly Worcestershire sauce and Dijon mustard gave the burgers a complex meaty flavor. To cook the burgers to a safe temperature without burning them or drying out the meat, we first seared the burgers to ensure they got nicely browned, then we partially covered the pan and turned the heat to low during the last few minutes of cooking to cook them gently through. Be sure to use ground turkey, not ground turkey breast (also labeled 99 percent fat free), in this recipe. Serve with your favorite burger toppings.

½ slice hearty white sandwich bread, crusts removed, torn into quarters
1 tablespoon whole milk
12 ounces ground turkey
1 teaspoon Worcestershire sauce

1 teaspoon Dijon mustard
¼ teaspoon salt
⅛ teaspoon pepper
1 tablespoon vegetable oil
2 hamburger buns

1. Mash bread and milk into paste with fork in large bowl. Using your hands, mix in ground turkey, Worcestershire, mustard, salt, and pepper until thoroughly combined. Divide meat mixture into 2 lightly packed balls, and gently flatten each ball into 1-inch-thick patty.

2. Heat oil in 10-inch nonstick skillet over medium heat until shimmering. Gently place burgers in skillet and cook until lightly browned and crusted on both sides, 3 to 4 minutes per side.

3. Reduce heat to low, partially cover, and cook until burgers register 160 degrees, 8 to 10 minutes, flipping burgers halfway through cooking. Serve burgers on buns.

Turkey Burgers with Olives and Feta

Omit Worcestershire and mustard. Mix 3 tablespoons chopped pitted kalamata olives, ¼ cup crumbled feta cheese, 1 small minced shallot, and 1 minced garlic clove into turkey mixture in step 1.

Shrimp Burgers

SERVES 2 LIGHT

✓ **WHY THIS RECIPE WORKS:** We loved the notion of a shrimp burger, one on par with a crab cake but made with shrimp that could be served on a toasted bun or on top of salad greens. Our early tests produced burgers that were dry, mushy, or rubbery, but with a few key steps we avoided these textural problems. We used a food processor to get a combination of textures—finely chopped pieces of shrimp to help bind the burger and larger, bite-size chunks. A minimal amount of bread crumbs were also necessary to bind the burgers. We found that packing the burgers firmly made them dense and rubbery, so we handled them gently when shaping. To help prevent them from falling apart during cooking, we allowed them to firm up in the refrigerator. Do not overprocess the shrimp in step 1 or the burgers will have a pasty texture. Serve with lettuce, sliced tomato, sliced red onion, and/or tartar sauce. For the nutritional information for this recipe, see page 413.

For perfectly tender shrimp burgers, we bound them minimally and handled them lightly to avoid dense, rubbery patties.

12 ounces extra-large shrimp (21 to 25 per pound), peeled, deveined, and tails removed
¼ cup panko bread crumbs
1½ tablespoons mayonnaise
1 scallion, sliced thin
1 tablespoon minced fresh parsley
½ teaspoon grated lemon zest
⅛ teaspoon salt
⅛ teaspoon pepper
   Pinch cayenne pepper
1 teaspoon vegetable oil
2 hamburger buns

1. Pulse shrimp in food processor until there is an even mix of finely minced and coarsely chopped pieces of shrimp, about 7 pulses, scraping down sides of bowl as needed.

2. Whisk panko, mayonnaise, scallion, parsley, lemon zest, salt, pepper, and cayenne together in large bowl. Gently fold in processed shrimp until just combined.

3. Scrape shrimp mixture onto small baking sheet. Divide mixture into 2 equal portions, gently flatten each portion into 1-inch-thick patty, and press shallow divot in center of each patty. Cover with plastic wrap and refrigerate for 15 minutes.

4. Heat oil in 10-inch nonstick skillet over medium heat until shimmering. Gently place burgers in skillet and cook until crisp and browned on both sides, about 4 minutes per side. Serve burgers on buns.

Salmon Burgers with Tomato Chutney
SERVES 2

✔ **WHY THIS RECIPE WORKS:** We love the meaty richness of salmon burgers and set out to make a juicy pan-seared salmon burger topped with a flavorful tomato chutney. Using the food processor ensured the salmon was chopped just right, and binding the patties with crunchy panko bread crumbs (and a little mayo) helped prevent a mushy texture. For fresh flavor, scallions, cilantro, and lemon juice did the trick. A chopped tomato cooked with Asian sweet chili sauce, ginger, and lemon juice created a sweet-and-sour chutney that served as a bright counterpoint to the salmon's richness. Be sure to use raw salmon here; do not substitute cooked salmon. Do not overprocess the salmon in step 1 or the burgers will have a pasty texture. Serve with your favorite burger toppings.

1 (12-ounce) skinless salmon fillet, cut into 1-inch pieces
¼ cup panko bread crumbs
¼ cup chopped fresh cilantro
4 scallions, sliced thin
4 teaspoons lemon juice
1 tablespoon mayonnaise
¼ teaspoon salt
⅛ teaspoon pepper
2 teaspoons vegetable oil
1 tablespoon grated fresh ginger
1 tomato, cored, seeded, and chopped
1½ tablespoons Asian sweet chili sauce
2 hamburger buns

1. Pulse salmon in food processor until there is an even mix of finely minced and coarsely chopped pieces of salmon, about 2 pulses, scraping down sides of bowl as needed.

2. Whisk panko, 3 tablespoons cilantro, 2 tablespoons scallions, 2 teaspoons lemon juice, mayonnaise, salt, and pepper together in large bowl. Gently fold in processed salmon until just combined.

3. Scrape salmon mixture onto small baking sheet. Divide mixture into 2 equal portions, gently flatten each portion into 1-inch-thick patty, and press shallow divot in center of each patty. Cover with plastic wrap and refrigerate for 15 minutes.

4. Meanwhile, heat 1 teaspoon oil in 10-inch nonstick skillet over medium-high heat until shimmering. Add ginger and remaining scallions and cook until fragrant, about 1 minute. Add tomato, chili sauce, and remaining 2 teaspoons lemon juice and cook until mixture is very thick, about 6 minutes. Stir in remaining 1 tablespoon cilantro and season with salt and pepper to taste. Transfer chutney to bowl and wipe skillet clean.

5. Heat remaining 1 teaspoon oil in now-empty skillet over medium heat until shimmering. Gently place burgers in skillet and cook until crisp and browned on both sides, about 4 minutes per side. Serve burgers on buns with tomato chutney.

Chopping Salmon and Shrimp for Burgers

To ensure seafood burgers hold together in the skillet without turning pasty and dense, process salmon or shrimp in food processor until there is an even mix of finely minced and coarsely chopped pieces.

Grilled Cheese Sandwiches

SERVES 2   **FAST**

✔ **WHY THIS RECIPE WORKS:** For a grown-up version of a classic grilled cheese sandwich, we wanted to keep the cheese front and center but round out its character with a few complementary flavors. We started with flavorful aged cheddar and processed it with a small amount of wine and Brie. These two additions helped the aged cheddar melt evenly without becoming greasy. A little minced shallot increased the sandwiches' complexity without detracting from the cheese, and we spiked the butter with a little Dijon mustard before buttering up the bread. Look for a cheddar aged for about one year (avoid cheddar aged for longer; it won't melt well). To quickly bring the cheddar to room temperature, microwave the pieces until warm, about 30 seconds. Be sure to remove the rind from the Brie before measuring; you will need to start with about 2 ounces. It is important to leave a ¼-inch border at the edge of the bread when spreading on the cheese mixture; otherwise, the cheese will ooze out of the sides while cooking.

Aged cheddar plus meltable Brie and a splash of white wine transform basic grilled cheese into a sophisticated treat.

3½ ounces aged cheddar cheese, cut into 12 equal pieces, room temperature
½ ounce rindless Brie cheese (1 tablespoon)
1 tablespoon dry white wine or vermouth
2 teaspoons minced shallot
1½ tablespoons unsalted butter, softened
½ teaspoon Dijon mustard
4 slices hearty white sandwich bread

1. Process cheddar, Brie, and wine in food processor until smooth paste is formed, 20 to 30 seconds, scraping down sides of bowl as needed. Add shallot and pulse to combine, 3 to 5 pulses. Combine butter and mustard in bowl.

2. Working on parchment paper–lined counter, spread mustard butter evenly over slices of bread. Flip 2 slices of bread over and spread cheese mixture evenly over slices, leaving ¼-inch border at edge. Top with remaining 2 slices of bread, buttered sides up.

3. Preheat 12-inch nonstick skillet over medium heat for 2 minutes. (Droplets of water should just sizzle when flicked onto pan.) Place sandwiches in skillet, reduce heat to medium-low, and cook until crisp and golden brown on both sides, 6 to 9 minutes per side, moving sandwiches to ensure even browning. Remove sandwiches from skillet and let sit for 3 minutes before serving.

VARIATIONS

Grilled Cheese Sandwiches with Asiago and Dates

Substitute 3½ ounces Asiago for cheddar, 2 teaspoons finely chopped pitted dates for shallot, and 4 slices oatmeal sandwich bread for white sandwich bread.

Grilled Cheese Sandwiches with Gruyère and Chives

Substitute 3½ ounces Gruyère for cheddar, 2 teaspoons minced fresh chives for shallot, and 4 slices rye sandwich bread for white sandwich bread.

Portobello Panini

SERVES 2

✔ **WHY THIS RECIPE WORKS:** Add fontina cheese, roasted red peppers, and garlic-rosemary mayonnaise to meaty portobellos and you are guaranteed an irresistible sandwich. To ensure the mushrooms would be tender, we precooked them in the grill pan before assembling and toasting the sandwiches. Using shredded fontina helped speed the melting process and guaranteed an even layer of gooey cheese. A nonstick grill pan and a Dutch oven mimicked the signature marks of a panini press. Don't substitute sandwich bread for the crusty Italian loaf. We like to use rustic, artisanal bread for this recipe; do not use a baguette, but rather look for a wide loaf that will yield big slices. We like the attractive grill marks that a grill pan gives the panini, but you can substitute a 12-inch nonstick skillet.

> 3 large portobello mushroom caps, halved
> 2 tablespoons extra-virgin olive oil
> ¼ teaspoon salt
> ⅛ teaspoon pepper
> 2 tablespoons mayonnaise
> 2 garlic cloves, minced
> 1 teaspoon minced fresh rosemary
> 4 (½-inch-thick) slices crusty bread
> 4 ounces fontina cheese, shredded (1 cup)
> ¼ cup jarred roasted red peppers, rinsed, patted dry, and sliced ½ inch thick

1. Preheat 12-inch nonstick grill pan over medium heat for 2 minutes. (Droplets of water should just sizzle when flicked onto pan.) Toss mushrooms, 1 tablespoon oil, salt, and pepper together. Place mushrooms, gill side up, in pan and weight with Dutch oven. Cook until mushrooms are well browned on both sides, about 5 minutes per side. Transfer mushrooms to plate and wipe pan clean.

2. Combine mayonnaise, garlic, and rosemary in bowl. Spread mayonnaise mixture evenly over 1 side of each slice of bread. Assemble 2 sandwiches by layering ingredients as follows between prepared bread (with mayonnaise mixture inside sandwich): half of fontina, cooked mushrooms, red peppers, and remaining fontina. Press gently on sandwiches to set.

3. Reheat now-empty pan over medium heat for 1 minute. Brush outside of sandwiches lightly with remaining 1 tablespoon oil. Place sandwiches in pan and weight with Dutch oven. Cook sandwiches until bread is golden brown and crisp on both sides and cheese is melted, about 4 minutes per side. Serve.

A Panini Press Alternative

To make panini without using a panini press, place sandwiches in heated 12-inch nonstick grill pan or skillet and weight sandwiches with Dutch oven. Cook until bread is golden and crisp on both sides and cheese is melted, flipping sandwiches halfway through cooking.

NOTES FROM THE TEST KITCHEN

All About Portobellos

Portobellos are the giants of the mushroom family, ranging from 4 to 6 inches in diameter. They are the mature form of cremini mushrooms, and due to the extra time they are allowed to mature, they have a particularly intense, meaty flavor. Available year-round, they have a steak-like texture and robust flavor that make them ideal for being sautéed, stir-fried, roasted, grilled, or stuffed.

BUYING PORTOBELLOS: If possible, buy loose mushrooms rather than prepackaged so you can inspect the quality of the mushrooms. Look for mushrooms with fully intact caps and dry gills. Wet, damaged gills are a sign of spoilage. The stems are woody and are often discarded, so you only need to buy mushrooms with stems if you plan to use them (such as in a soup, stock, or stuffing).

STORING PORTOBELLOS: Because they release moisture, which can encourage spoilage, portobellos need some air circulation to stay fresh. They are best stored in a partially opened zipper-lock bag, which maximizes air circulation without drying out the mushrooms.

PREPARING PORTOBELLOS: To clean portobellos, simply wipe them with a damp towel. Remove the woody stems before cooking and either discard or reserve them. If you are using the portobellos in a sauce, we recommend gently scraping out the black gills with a spoon before cooking to prevent a muddy-looking sauce.

Caprese Panini with Olive Tapenade

SERVES 2

✔ **WHY THIS RECIPE WORKS:** We wanted to translate the classic flavors of Caprese salad to crispy, toasty panini. We started by searing halved tomatoes in a grill pan until they were softened and browned. We spread slices of crusty bread with briny olive tapenade then layered the bread with the warm tomatoes, shredded mozzarella, and fresh basil leaves. We brushed the bread with oil and cooked the panini in the grill pan until the bread was toasted and crisp and the mozzarella was melted and gooey. To mimic a panini press, we weighed the panini down with a Dutch oven so that they cooked evenly and developed distinct grill marks. We like to use rustic, artisanal bread for this recipe; do not use a baguette, but rather look for a wide loaf that will yield big slices. We like the attractive grill marks that a grill pan gives the panini, but you can substitute a 12-inch nonstick skillet.

- 3 tomatoes, cored and halved
- 2 tablespoons extra-virgin olive oil
- ¼ teaspoon salt
- ⅛ teaspoon pepper
- 2 tablespoons olive tapenade
- 4 (½-inch-thick) slices crusty bread
- 4 ounces mozzarella cheese, shredded (1 cup)
- ¼ cup fresh basil leaves

1. Preheat 12-inch nonstick grill pan over medium heat for 2 minutes. (Droplets of water should just sizzle when flicked onto pan.) Toss tomatoes, 1 tablespoon oil, salt, and pepper together. Place tomatoes, cut side up, in pan and weight with Dutch oven. Cook until tomatoes are softened and browned on first side, about 5 minutes. Transfer tomatoes to plate and wipe pan clean.

2. Spread olive tapenade evenly over 1 side of each slice of bread. Assemble 2 sandwiches by layering ingredients as follows between prepared bread (with olive tapenade inside

Shredding Semisoft Cheese

Mozzarella and other semi-soft cheeses can stick to a coarse grater and cause a real mess. To keep the holes on the grater from becoming clogged, use vegetable oil spray to lightly coat the grater before shredding.

sandwich): half of mozzarella, cooked tomatoes, basil, and remaining mozzarella. Press gently on sandwiches to set.

3. Reheat now-empty pan over medium heat for 1 minute. Brush outside of sandwiches lightly with remaining 1 table-spoon oil. Place sandwiches in pan and weight with Dutch oven. Cook sandwiches until bread is golden brown and crisp on both sides and cheese is melted, about 4 minutes per side. Serve.

Greek-Style Lamb Pita Sandwiches

SERVES 2

✔ **WHY THIS RECIPE WORKS:** We wanted restaurant-style Greek gyros—slices of shaved, marinated lamb, tomato slices, crisp lettuce, and cooling cucumber-yogurt sauce stuffed inside a soft pita—that we could make at home. Rather than the traditional shaved slices of meat from a vertical rotisserie, we pan-fried ground lamb patties flavored with mint, onion, and minced garlic. To make the patties juicier, we added a panade (a paste of fresh bread crumbs and lemon juice), using pita for the bread crumbs. Cooking the patties in a hot oiled skillet ensured a crisp outside and juicy interior. Topped with the cucumber-yogurt sauce, these home-style gyros are a satisfying alternative to the real deal. You can substitute 85 percent lean ground beef for the lamb. If using pocketless pitas, do not cut the top 2 inches off the pitas as directed in step 2; instead, use a portion of a third pita to create the pieces. When cooking the patties, use a splatter screen to keep the mess to a minimum. Serve with sliced tomato, shredded lettuce, and feta cheese in addition to the yogurt sauce.

- ¼ cucumber, peeled, halved lengthwise, seeded, and chopped fine
  Salt and pepper
- 2 (8-inch) pita breads
- 1 small onion, chopped fine
- 4 teaspoons lemon juice
- 4 teaspoons minced fresh mint or dill
- 2 garlic cloves, minced
- 8 ounces ground lamb
- 2 teaspoons vegetable oil
- ½ cup plain Greek yogurt

1. Toss cucumber and ⅛ teaspoon salt together and let drain in colander for 30 minutes.

2. Meanwhile, trim 2 inches from each pita bread, then tear pita scraps into 1-inch pieces. (You should have about ⅓ cup pita pieces.)

These pan-fried ground lamb patties flavored with mint, onion, and minced garlic and tucked into a pita mimic a traditional Greek gyro.

3. Process pita pieces, onion, 2 teaspoons lemon juice, 2 teaspoons mint, half of garlic, ¼ teaspoon salt, and ⅛ teaspoon pepper in food processor to smooth paste, about 30 seconds, scraping down sides of bowl as needed. Transfer mixture to large bowl and mix in lamb with hands until thoroughly combined. Pinch off and roll meat mixture into 6 balls, then flatten into ½-inch-thick patties.

4. Heat oil in 12-inch nonstick skillet over medium-high heat until just smoking. Gently place patties in skillet and cook until well browned and crusted on first side, 3 to 4 minutes. Flip patties, reduce heat to medium, and continue to cook until well browned and crusted on the second side, about 5 minutes. Transfer patties to paper towel–lined plate and tent loosely with aluminum foil.

5. Combine yogurt, drained cucumber, remaining 2 teaspoons lemon juice, remaining 2 teaspoons mint, and remaining garlic in bowl and season with salt and pepper to taste. Microwave trimmed pitas until warmed, about 30 seconds. Nestle 3 patties inside each warm pita, drizzle with yogurt sauce, and serve.

Simple Spicy Shrimp and Herb Salad Wraps

SERVES 2 **FAST**

✔ **WHY THIS RECIPE WORKS:** For a one-of-a-kind sandwich wrap with fresh, bright flavors, we developed a quick shrimp salad recipe that along with shrimp boasted plenty of garden-fresh herbs and a creamy, piquant dressing. For the salad, we chopped convenient precooked shrimp and tossed it with red bell pepper and a simple dressing of mayonnaise, lemon juice, cayenne, paprika, and garlic. To brighten things up, we added a hefty amount of chopped cilantro and mint, folding half of the herb mixture into the shrimp salad, then topping the salad with the remaining herbs before wrapping it up in soft flour tortillas. Parsley is a good alternative to the cilantro in this recipe.

  1 **cup coarsely chopped fresh cilantro**
  ½ **cup coarsely chopped fresh mint**
  ¼ **cup mayonnaise**
  1 **garlic clove, minced**
  1 **teaspoon lemon juice**
  ¼ **teaspoon paprika**
  ¼ **teaspoon cayenne pepper**
    Salt and pepper
 12 **ounces cooked and peeled medium shrimp (41 to 50 per pound), cut into ½-inch pieces**
  1 **red bell pepper, stemmed, seeded, and cut into 2-inch-long matchsticks**
  2 **(10-inch) flour tortillas**

Assembling Shrimp and Herb Salad Wraps

1. Spread shrimp mixture on bottom half of each tortilla, leaving 2-inch border at bottom edge, then sprinkle half of reserved herb mixture on top.

2. Fold sides of tortilla over filling, then tightly roll bottom edge up over filling and continue to roll into wrap.

1. Combine cilantro and mint in bowl. In separate large bowl, whisk half of herb mixture, mayonnaise, garlic, lemon juice, paprika, cayenne, ¼ teaspoon salt, and ⅛ teaspoon pepper together. Add shrimp and bell pepper and toss to combine. Season with salt and pepper to taste.

2. Lay tortillas on clean counter and spread half of shrimp mixture evenly over bottom half of each tortilla, leaving 2-inch border at edge. Sprinkle remaining chopped herbs evenly over shrimp mixture. Working with 1 tortilla at a time, fold sides of tortilla over filling, then tightly roll bottom edge of tortilla up over filling and continue to roll into wrap. Cut each wrap in half on bias. Serve.

Basic Pizza Dough
MAKES 8 OUNCES DOUGH

✓ **WHY THIS RECIPE WORKS:** It's easy enough to buy pizza dough at the grocery store, but the standard 1-pound bags mean lots of leftovers when cooking for two. We wanted a recipe for a great-tasting pizza dough that would make just enough for a small pizza or couple of calzones. The first key was getting the right ratio of flour to water. High-protein bread flour ensured our dough baked up chewy with a crisp crust. A little olive oil added richness and made the dough easier to roll out. All-purpose flour can be substituted for the bread flour, but the resulting crust will be a little less chewy. If desired, you can slow down the dough's rising time by letting it rise in the refrigerator for 8 to 16 hours in step 2; let the refrigerated dough soften at room temperature for 30 minutes before using.

> 1   **cup (5½ ounces) bread flour, plus extra as needed**
> ¾   **teaspoon instant or rapid-rise yeast**
> ½   **teaspoon salt**
> 1½   **teaspoons olive oil**
> 7   **tablespoons warm water (110 degrees)**

1. Process flour, yeast, and salt in food processor until combined, about 2 seconds. With processor running, slowly add oil, then water, and process until dough forms sticky ball that clears sides of bowl, 1½ to 2 minutes. (If, after 1 minute, dough is sticky and clings to blade, add extra flour, 1 tablespoon at a time, as needed until it clears sides of bowl.)

Active Dry vs. Instant Yeast

ACTIVE DRY YEAST
Active dry yeast sold in packets or jars is most often called for in bread recipes. (However, we prefer instant yeast; see below.) To produce active dry yeast, fresh yeast is given heat treatment that kills the outermost cells. Therefore, to use active dry yeast, the granules must first be proofed, or dissolved in liquid, with some sugar to speed up the process. Proofing sloughs off the dead cells and renders the yeast active.

INSTANT (RAPID-RISE) YEAST
Instant, or rapid-rise, yeast is much like active dry yeast, but it has undergone a gentler drying process that has not destroyed the outer cells. Instant yeast does not require proofing and can be added directly to the dry ingredients when making bread—hence the name "instant." Our recipes call for instant yeast because it's easier to use. We have also found that when making basic breads, such as baguettes, that contain just flour, salt, water, and yeast, instant yeast yields a cleaner, purer flavor than active dry yeast because it doesn't contain any dead yeast cells. However, in breads that contain butter, sugar, and other flavorings, we find virtually no difference in flavor between instant and active dry yeasts.

HOW TO SUBSTITUTE TYPES OF YEAST: If you have active dry yeast on hand, you can use it in place of the instant yeast in our recipes. To substitute active dry for instant yeast, use 25 percent more active dry. For example, if the recipe calls for 1 teaspoon of instant yeast, use 1¼ teaspoons of active dry. And don't forget to proof the yeast—that is, dissolve it in a portion of the water called for in the recipe, heated to 110 degrees. If you have a recipe that calls for active dry yeast, you can use instant as long as you reduce the amount of yeast by 25 percent. You don't need to proof the instant yeast; just add it directly to the dry ingredients. When substituting one type of yeast for another, pay close attention to the dough as it rises; dough made with instant yeast may rise faster than dough made with active dry yeast.

HOW TO STORE YEAST: Store yeast in the refrigerator or freezer to slow deterioration. And because yeast is a living organism, the expiration date on the package should be observed.

2. Transfer dough to lightly floured counter and shape into tight ball. Place dough in large, lightly oiled bowl and cover tightly with greased plastic wrap. Let rise at room temperature until doubled in size, 1 to 1½ hours.

VARIATION
Whole-Wheat Pizza Dough
Substitute ½ cup whole-wheat flour for ½ cup of bread flour.

Our pizza crust quickly gets crisp and spotty brown in a skillet over high heat, then we finish it in the oven for a moist, chewy interior.

Easy Skillet Cheese Pizza

SERVES 2

✓ **WHY THIS RECIPE WORKS:** We wanted to come up with an easier, quicker way to make pizza at home. Our idea was to build the pizza in a skillet, give the crust a jump start with heat from the stovetop, then transfer it to the oven to cook through—no pizza stone required. We oiled the skillet to keep the dough from sticking and to encourage browning, then we added the dough and turned up the heat. A simple no-cook sauce of diced tomatoes, olive oil, and garlic and a combination of mozzarella and a little Parmesan were all the toppings this easy pizza needed. You can substitute 8 ounces of store-bought pizza dough for the dough in this recipe. Let the dough sit out at room temperature while preparing the remaining ingredients and heating the oven; otherwise, it will be difficult to stretch. Feel free to add simple toppings before baking, such as pepperoni, sautéed mushrooms, or browned sausage, but keep the toppings light or they may weigh down the thin crust and make it soggy.

3 tablespoons extra-virgin olive oil
½ cup canned diced tomatoes, drained with juice reserved
1 small garlic clove, minced
⅛ teaspoon salt
1 recipe Basic Pizza Dough (page 93), room temperature
4 ounces whole-milk mozzarella cheese, shredded (1 cup)
2 tablespoons grated Parmesan cheese

1. Adjust oven rack to upper-middle position and heat oven to 500 degrees. Grease 12-inch ovensafe skillet with 2 tablespoons oil.

2. Pulse tomatoes, garlic, salt, and remaining 1 tablespoon oil together in food processor until coarsely ground, about 12 pulses. Transfer mixture to liquid measuring cup and add reserved tomato juice until sauce measures ½ cup.

3. Place dough on lightly floured counter. Press and roll dough into 11-inch round. Transfer dough to prepared skillet; reshape as needed. Spread sauce over dough, leaving ½-inch border at edge. Sprinkle mozzarella and Parmesan evenly over sauce.

4. Set skillet over high heat and cook until outside edge of dough is set, pizza is lightly puffed, and bottom crust is spotty brown when gently lifted with spatula, about 3 minutes.

5. Transfer pizza to oven and bake until crust is brown and cheese is golden in spots, 7 to 10 minutes. Using potholders (skillet handle will be hot), remove skillet from oven and slide pizza onto cutting board. Let pizza cool for 5 minutes before slicing and serving.

VARIATIONS
Easy Skillet Pizza with Fontina, Arugula, and Prosciutto
Toss 1 cup baby arugula with 2 teaspoons extra-virgin olive oil and salt and pepper to taste in bowl. Omit Parmesan and substitute 1 cup shredded fontina for mozzarella. Immediately after baking, sprinkle 2 ounces thinly sliced prosciutto, cut into ½-inch strips, and dressed arugula over top of pizza.

Easy Skillet Pizza with Goat Cheese, Olives, and Spicy Garlic Oil
Mix 1 tablespoon olive oil, 1 minced small garlic clove, and ⅛ teaspoon red pepper flakes together in bowl. Brush garlic-oil mixture over top of pizza dough before adding sauce in step 3. Omit Parmesan and reduce amount of mozzarella to ¼ cup. Sprinkle ½ cup crumbled goat cheese and ¼ cup pitted and halved kalamata olives on top of mozzarella before baking.

Easy Skillet Pizza with Ricotta, Bacon, and Scallions
Cook 2 slices bacon, cut into ¼-inch pieces, in 8-inch skillet over medium heat until crisp, 5 to 7 minutes. Using slotted

spoon, transfer bacon to paper towel–lined plate. Mix ½ cup whole-milk ricotta, 1 thinly sliced scallion, ⅛ teaspoon salt, and pinch pepper together in bowl. Omit Parmesan and reduce amount of mozzarella to ¼ cup. Dollop ricotta mixture, 1 tablespoon at a time, on top of mozzarella, then sprinkle with bacon. Sprinkle pizza with 1 more sliced scallion before serving.

Ultimate Thin-Crust Pizza

SERVES 2

✔ **WHY THIS RECIPE WORKS:** With home ovens that reach only 500 degrees and dough that's impossible to stretch thin, even the savviest cooks can struggle to produce New York–style parlor-quality pizza. We were in pursuit of a New York–style pizza with a perfect crust—thin, crisp, and spottily charred on the exterior; tender yet chewy within. High-protein bread flour gave us a chewy, nicely tanned pizza crust, and the right ratio of flour, water, and yeast gave us dough that stretched and retained moisture as it baked. We kneaded the dough quickly in a food processor then let it proof in the refrigerator to develop its flavors. After we shaped and topped the pizza, it went onto a blazing hot baking stone to cook. Placing the stone near the top of the oven allowed the top of the pizza to brown as well as the bottom. If you don't have a peel or a stone, see Pizza 101 for alternatives. It is important to use ice water to prevent overheating the dough while in the food processor.

DOUGH

1½ cups (8¼ ounces) bread flour
1 teaspoon sugar
¼ teaspoon instant or rapid-rise yeast
⅔ cup ice water
1½ teaspoons vegetable oil
¾ teaspoon salt

SAUCE

½ cup canned whole peeled tomatoes, drained
1 teaspoon extra-virgin olive oil
1 small garlic clove, minced
¼ teaspoon red wine vinegar
¼ teaspoon dried oregano
⅛ teaspoon salt
⅛ teaspoon pepper

¼ cup grated Parmesan cheese
4 ounces whole-milk mozzarella cheese, shredded (1 cup)

Pizza 101

Making your own pizza should be fun, not stressful. Here are some of our favorite tips for easy, parlor-worthy pizza.

EASY CHEESE SHREDDING: Use a clean plastic bag (a large zipper-lock bag works best) to hold the grater and the cheese. By placing the bag around both, you can grate without getting your hands dirty, and you don't have to worry about rogue pieces flying off into your kitchen. The best part? Leftover shredded cheese is ready for storage, no transfer needed.

KEEP TOPPINGS ON HAND: Homemade pizza is like a blank canvas for the creative use of myriad toppings. The problem is that you don't always have that many topping options on hand. Try this simple solution. Whenever cooking something such as roasted red peppers, caramelized onions, or sausage, reserve some in a plastic container, label it, and freeze it. The next time you're making pizza, simply defrost and top away.

NO PEEL? NO STONE? NO PROBLEM: A baking stone is a terrific investment if you enjoy making bread and pizza, and a peel makes the process easier. But you can also make do with rimless or inverted baking sheets for both the stone and peel. To improvise a baking stone, preheat a baking sheet for 30 minutes. As for an improvised peel, simply cover a rimless or inverted baking sheet with parchment paper, shape and top the pizza on the parchment, and slide it directly onto the hot, preheated stone (or baking sheet).

CLEAN CUTTING GUARANTEED: If you use a knife to cut pizza, you risk pulling cheese in every direction. A pizza wheel negates this risk. In search of one large and sharp enough to glide through thick and thin crusts without dislodging toppings, we tested five types: three with stainless-steel blades, one with polycarbonate plastic, and one dual wheel. For overall comfort, extreme sharpness, and heft, one pizza wheel was named the test kitchen's favorite. The **OXO Good Grips 4-Inch Pizza Wheel** won points for its thumb guard, the large, soft handle that absorbed extra pressure, and its well-designed wheel, which was easy to clean and safe for nonstick surfaces.

TWO WAYS TO REHEAT: Reheated leftover pizza always pales in comparison with a freshly baked pie. The microwave turns it soggy, and just throwing it into a hot oven can dry it out. Here's a reheating method that really works: Place the cold slices on a rimmed baking sheet, cover the sheet tightly with aluminum foil, and place it on the lowest rack of a cold oven. Then set the oven temperature to 275 degrees and let the pizza warm for 25 to 30 minutes. This approach leaves the interior of the crust soft, the cheese melty, and the toppings and bottom hot and crisp but not dehydrated. However, for just a slice or two of pizza, heating the oven is impractical. Instead, pull out your skillet. Place a nonstick skillet over medium heat and add dried oregano. Place the pizza in the skillet and cook, covered, for about 5 minutes. The pizza will come out hot and crisp, with an irresistible aroma.

For the ultimate cheese pizza, we use high-protein bread flour, proof the dough, and elevate the oven rack for perfect results.

1. FOR THE DOUGH: Process flour, sugar, and yeast in food processor until combined, about 2 seconds. With processor running, slowly add water and process until dough is just combined and no dry flour remains, about 10 seconds. Let dough sit for 10 minutes.

2. Add oil and salt to dough and process until dough forms satiny, sticky ball that clears sides of bowl, about 30 seconds. Transfer dough to lightly oiled counter and knead briefly until smooth, about 1 minute. Shape dough into tight ball, place in large, lightly oiled bowl, and cover tightly with greased plastic wrap. Refrigerate for at least 24 hours or up to 3 days.

3. FOR THE SAUCE: Process all ingredients together in food processor until smooth, about 15 seconds, scraping down sides of bowl as needed. Transfer to bowl and refrigerate until ready to use.

4. One hour before baking, position oven rack 4½ inches from top of oven, set baking stone on rack, and heat oven to 500 degrees. Meanwhile, place dough on lightly oiled baking sheet, cover loosely with lightly greased plastic, and let sit at room temperature for 1 hour.

5. Coat dough generously with flour and place on well-floured counter. Using your fingertips, gently flatten into 8-inch disk, leaving 1 inch of outer edge slightly thicker than center. Using your hands, gently stretch disk into 12-inch round, working along edge and giving disk quarter-turns as you stretch.

6. Transfer dough to well-floured peel and stretch into 13-inch round. Spread tomato sauce over dough, leaving ¼-inch border around edge. Sprinkle Parmesan evenly over sauce, followed by mozzarella.

7. Carefully slide pizza onto stone and bake until crust is well browned and cheese is bubbly and beginning to brown, 10 to 12 minutes, rotating pizza halfway through baking. Transfer pizza to wire rack and let cool for 5 minutes. Slice and serve.

Shaping Thin-Crust Pizza

On well-floured counter, gently flatten dough into 8-inch disk, leaving outer edge slightly thicker. Continue to stretch into 12-inch round, working along edge and giving dough quarter turns. Transfer dough to well-floured peel and finish stretching into 13-inch round.

Shrimp and Artichoke Lavash Pizza

SERVES 2 **FAST**

✓ **WHY THIS RECIPE WORKS:** Using store-bought lavash, a Middle Eastern flatbread, rather than traditional pizza dough gave this crust a crisp, crackerlike texture, and since the lavash is ready-made, the whole meal came together in less than 30 minutes. To top the pizza, a combination of shrimp, artichoke hearts, garlic, and mozzarella and Parmesan cheeses made it a simple but sophisticated dinner. Lavash, a flatbread commonly used in Middle Eastern cooking, can be found near the tortillas in the supermarket. Because lavash can vary greatly in size, you may need to trim the bread.

Crisp, crackerlike store-bought lavash serves as an easy no-prep crust for this fresh, flavorful shrimp and artichoke pizza.

12 ounces medium shrimp (41 to 50 per pound), peeled, deveined, and tails removed
5 ounces frozen artichoke hearts, thawed, patted dry, and chopped
2 tablespoons extra-virgin olive oil
2 garlic cloves, minced
¼ teaspoon salt
⅛ teaspoon pepper
1 (11 by 8-inch) piece lavash bread
4 ounces mozzarella cheese, shredded (1 cup)
2 tablespoons grated Parmesan cheese

1. Adjust oven rack to middle position and heat oven to 425 degrees. Pat shrimp dry with paper towels. Combine shrimp, artichokes, 1 tablespoon oil, garlic, salt, and pepper in bowl.

2. Brush remaining 1 tablespoon oil over both sides of lavash. Arrange lavash on baking sheet and bake until browned and crisp, 5 to 7 minutes.

3. Sprinkle mozzarella and Parmesan evenly over lavash. Top with shrimp mixture and bake until shrimp are opaque throughout and cheese is melted, 6 to 8 minutes. Slice and serve.

Fresh vs. Supermarket Mozzarella

For such a mild-mannered cheese, mozzarella sure is popular. In 2006, it passed cheddar to become the leading cheese in the United States in per-capita consumption, with most supermarkets stocking two main varieties: fresh (usually packed in brine) and supermarket, or low-moisture (available either as a block or preshredded).

WHAT'S THE DIFFERENCE? Both varieties are made by stretching and pulling the curds by hand or machine, which aligns the proteins into long chains and gives the cheese its trademark elasticity. However, the final products differ considerably, particularly when it comes to water weight. According to federal standards, fresh mozzarella must have a moisture content between 52 percent and 60 percent by weight, which makes it highly perishable. Drier, firmer low-moisture mozzarella hovers between 45 percent and 52 percent and is remarkably shelf-stable—it can last in the fridge for weeks.

Low-Moisture Mozzarella   Fresh Mozzarella

WHEN TO USE FRESH: We prefer the sweet richness and tender bite of the fresh stuff for snacking, sandwiches, and Caprese salad but tend not to use it in cooked applications, since heat can destroy its delicate flavor and texture.

WHEN TO USE SUPERMARKET: For most baked dishes, we turn to the low-moisture kind. It offers mellow flavor that blends seamlessly with bolder ingredients and melts nicely in everything from lasagna to pizza. It's a staple in the test kitchen and in many of our home refrigerators. The test kitchen's top-rated supermarket mozzarella is block-style **Sorrento Whole Milk Mozzarella**. Its gooey creaminess and clean dairy flavor were exactly what we wanted on pizza. It was so good that we even found ourselves snacking on it straight out of the package.

HOW TO STORE MOZZARELLA: Storing supermarket mozzarella presents a conundrum: as it sits, it releases moisture. If this moisture evaporates too quickly, the cheese dries out. But if the moisture stays on the cheese's surface, it encourages mold. To find the best storage method, we tried wrapping mozzarella in various materials, refrigerated the samples for six weeks, and monitored them for mold and dryness. Those wrapped in plastic—whether cling wrap or zipper-lock bags—were the first to show mold. Those in waxed or parchment paper alone lost too much moisture and dried out. The best method: waxed or parchment paper loosely wrapped with aluminum foil. The paper wicks moisture away, while the foil cover traps enough water to keep the cheese from drying out. Fresh mozzarella does not store well and is best eaten within a day or two.

Spinach Calzone

SERVES 2

✔ **WHY THIS RECIPE WORKS:** With soggy fillings and bready crusts, bad calzones are a dime a dozen. We wanted to balance a crisp crust with plenty of chew and a healthy proportion of rich, creamy, flavorful filling. A combination of ricotta and mozzarella plus a little flavorful Parmesan cheese made for an indulgently cheesy filling. Frozen spinach was an easy addition; carefully squeezing it dry kept it from watering down the filling. We bumped up the flavor with garlic, oregano, and red pepper flakes and added an egg yolk to help bind everything together. Cutting vents in the dough let off some steam, and cooling the calzone on a wire rack prevented a soggy bottom. You can substitute 8 ounces of store-bought pizza dough for the dough in this recipe. Let the dough sit out at room temperature while preparing the remaining ingredients and heating the oven; otherwise, it will be difficult to stretch. Serve with your favorite tomato sauce.

    5   ounces frozen spinach, thawed and squeezed dry
    4   ounces (½ cup) whole-milk ricotta cheese
    2   ounces mozzarella cheese, shredded (½ cup)
    ¼   cup Parmesan cheese, grated
    1   tablespoon olive oil
    1   large egg yolk, plus 1 large egg, lightly beaten with
        2 tablespoons water
    1   garlic clove, minced
    ¼   teaspoon salt
        Pinch pepper
        Pinch dried oregano
        Pinch red pepper flakes (optional)
    1   recipe Basic Pizza Dough (page 93), room temperature

1. Adjust oven rack to lower-middle position and heat oven to 500 degrees. Cut one 9-inch-square piece of parchment paper. Combine spinach, ricotta, mozzarella, Parmesan, oil, egg yolk, garlic, salt, pepper, oregano, and pepper flakes, if using, in bowl.

2. Place dough on lightly floured counter. Press and roll dough into 9-inch round. Transfer dough to parchment square and reshape as needed.

3. Spread spinach filling evenly over bottom half of dough round, leaving 1-inch border at edge. Brush edge with some of egg wash. Fold top half of dough over bottom half, leaving ½-inch border of bottom layer uncovered. Press edges of dough together and crimp to seal.

4. With sharp knife, cut 5 steam vents, about 1½ inches long, in top layer of dough. Brush with remaining egg wash. Slide calzone (still on parchment) onto baking sheet, trimming parchment as needed to fit. Bake until golden brown, about 15 minutes, rotating sheet halfway through baking. Transfer calzone to wire rack and let cool for 5 minutes before slicing and serving.

VARIATIONS

Sausage and Broccoli Rabe Calzone

Omit spinach. Microwave 2 ounces Italian sausage, casings removed and broken into ½-inch pieces, with 4 ounces broccoli rabe, trimmed and cut into 1-inch pieces, and 1 tablespoon water in covered bowl until sausage is no longer pink and broccoli rabe is crisp-tender, about 4 minutes. Drain mixture well, let cool slightly, and add to ricotta mixture.

Meat Lover's Calzone

Omit spinach and salt. Arrange 2 ounces thinly sliced salami, 2 ounces thinly sliced capicola, and 1 ounce thinly sliced

Assembling Calzones

1. Place filling in center of bottom half of dough round. Spread or press filling in even layer over bottom half of dough round, leaving 1-inch border at edge.

2. Brush bottom edge with egg wash. Fold top half of dough over filling, leaving ½-inch border of bottom dough uncovered. Lightly press edges of dough together to seal, pressing out any air pockets.

3. Starting at 1 end of seam, place your index finger diagonally across edge and gently pull bottom layer of dough over tip of your finger; press into dough to seal.

4. Cut 5 steam vents, about 1½ inches long, across top of calzone. Cut through only top layer of dough.

pepperoni, all cut into quarters, between double layer of coffee filters on plate. Microwave until fat begins to render, about 30 seconds. Add microwaved meats and 1 tablespoon chopped fresh basil to ricotta mixture.

Salami, Capicola, and Provolone Stromboli

SERVES 2

✔ **WHY THIS RECIPE WORKS:** With a crisp, golden-brown exterior and a layered meat and cheese filling, stromboli makes a great casual dinner. We wanted a streamlined recipe that had a flavorful filling, a crispy crust, and a properly cooked interior. A combination of salami, capicola, and provolone cheese plus jarred roasted red peppers made an easy, no-prep filling with bold flavor. Patting the peppers dry kept their liquid from turning the stromboli soggy. You can substitute 8 ounces of store-bought pizza dough for the dough in this recipe. Let the dough sit out at room temperature while preparing the remaining ingredients and heating the oven; otherwise, it will be difficult to stretch. Serve with your favorite tomato sauce.

1   **recipe Basic Pizza Dough (page 93), room temperature**

2   **ounces thinly sliced deli salami**

2   **ounces thinly sliced deli capicola**

2   **ounces thinly sliced deli provolone cheese**

¼   **cup jarred roasted red peppers, rinsed, patted dry, and sliced thin**

¼   **cup grated Parmesan cheese**

1   **large egg, lightly beaten with 2 tablespoons water**

1   **teaspoon sesame seeds**

    Kosher salt (optional)

1. Adjust oven rack to middle position and heat oven to 400 degrees. Spray rimmed baking sheet with vegetable oil spray.

2. Place dough on lightly floured counter. Press and roll dough into 10 by 7½-inch rectangle, about ¼ inch thick, with long side facing you.

3. Lay salami, capicola, and provolone over dough, leaving ¾-inch border at edge. Top with red peppers and Parmesan. Brush edge with some of egg wash. Starting from long side, roll dough tightly into long cylinder, then pinch seam and ends to seal. Transfer stromboli to prepared baking sheet, seam side down.

4. Brush top of stromboli with remaining egg wash and sprinkle with sesame seeds and salt, if using. Cover loosely with greased aluminum foil and bake for 15 minutes. Remove foil and continue to bake until crust is golden, about 20 minutes, rotating sheet halfway through baking. Transfer stromboli to wire rack and let cool for 5 minutes before slicing and serving.

VARIATION

Ham and Cheddar Stromboli

Swiss cheese also works well here.

Omit Parmesan. Substitute 4 ounces thinly sliced deli ham for salami and capicola and 2 ounces thinly sliced deli cheddar for provolone. After laying ham on dough in step 3, spread with 1 tablespoon yellow mustard, then top with cheddar. Substitute 1 small dill pickle, cut into matchsticks and patted dry, for red peppers.

Assembling Stromboli

1. Place dough on lightly floured counter. Press and roll dough into 10 by 7½-inch rectangle, about ¼ inch thick, with long side facing you.

2. Arrange meat and provolone over dough, leaving ¾-inch border at edge. Top with red peppers and Parmesan, then brush edge with egg wash.

3. Starting from long side, roll dough tightly into long cylinder.

4. Pinch seam and ends of dough to seal them securely.

Chicken

■ FAST   (Start to finish in about 30 minutes)

■ LIGHT   (See page 413 for nutritional information)

Opposite: Parmesan and Basil–Stuffed Chicken with Roasted Carrots; Chicken Pot Pie; Weeknight Roast Chicken

Chicken Saltimbocca

SERVES 2

✅ **WHY THIS RECIPE WORKS:** Chicken saltimbocca—a spin on veal saltimbocca—sounds promising, but most versions take this dish too far from its roots. We wanted to give each of its three main elements—chicken, prosciutto, and sage—their due. Starting with already thin chicken cutlets made this recipe quick cooking, and flouring the chicken allowed it to brown evenly and prevented gummy, uncooked spots. Using thinly sliced prosciutto prevented its flavor from overwhelming the dish. A single fried sage leaf is the usual garnish, but we wanted more sage flavor, so we also sprinkled some minced fresh sage over the floured chicken before adding the prosciutto. Most supermarkets carry chicken cutlets, but if you can't find them (or they look ragged), simply buy two boneless, skinless chicken breasts and slice your own. Make sure to buy prosciutto that is thinly sliced, but not shaved. The prosciutto slices should be large enough to fully cover one side of each cutlet; if the slices are too large, simply cut them down to size. If you prefer not to make the garnish, leave out the four fresh sage leaves and skip step 2.

Prosciutto, sage, and a buttery white wine sauce dress up easy chicken breasts in this modern version of saltimbocca.

¼ cup plus ½ teaspoon all-purpose flour

4 (4-ounce) chicken cutlets, ¼ inch thick, trimmed

Salt and pepper

2 teaspoons minced fresh sage, plus 4 large fresh leaves

4 thin slices prosciutto (1½ ounces)

2 tablespoons olive oil, plus extra as needed

1 small shallot, minced

⅓ cup chicken broth

¼ cup dry vermouth or dry white wine

1 tablespoon unsalted butter, chilled

2 teaspoons minced fresh parsley

1 teaspoon lemon juice

1. Spread ¼ cup flour in shallow dish. Pat chicken dry with paper towels and season with pepper. Working with 1 cutlet at a time, dredge cutlets in flour. Sprinkle 1 side of each cutlet with minced sage, then top with 1 slice prosciutto and press firmly to help it adhere.

2. Heat oil in 12-inch skillet over medium-high heat until shimmering. Add sage leaves and cook until leaves begin to change color and are fragrant, 15 to 20 seconds. Using slotted spoon, transfer fried sage leaves to paper towel–lined plate.

3. Lay cutlets, prosciutto side down, in oil left in skillet and cook over medium-high heat until golden brown on first side, about 2 minutes. Flip cutlets and continue to cook until lightly browned on second side, about 1 minute; transfer to plate and tent loosely with aluminum foil.

4. Pour off all but 1 teaspoon oil from skillet (or add more oil if necessary). Add shallot and cook over medium heat until softened, about 2 minutes. Stir in remaining ½ teaspoon flour and cook for 1 minute. Whisk in broth and vermouth, scraping up any browned bits. Bring to simmer and cook until sauce is slightly thickened and reduced to ⅓ cup, 3 to 5 minutes.

5. Return cutlets to skillet, prosciutto side up, along with any accumulated juices, and simmer until heated through, about 30 seconds; transfer cutlets to serving platter. Off heat, whisk butter, parsley, and lemon juice into sauce and season with salt and pepper to taste. Pour sauce over cutlets, garnish with fried sage leaves, and serve.

Making Chicken Cutlets

You can buy packaged chicken cutlets at the supermarket. But if they look ragged or are uneven in thickness, you can easily make your own using two 8-ounce boneless, skinless chicken breasts.

1. If small strip of meat (tenderloin) is loosely attached to underside of breast, simply pull it off and reserve for another use.

2. Lay chicken smooth side up on cutting board. With your hand on top of chicken, carefully slice it in half horizontally to yield 2 pieces between ⅜ and ½ inch thick.

3. Lay each cutlet between 2 sheets of plastic wrap and pound with meat pounder or small skillet until roughly ¼ inch thick.

Sautéed Chicken Breasts with White Wine and Herb Pan Sauce

SERVES 2

✔ **WHY THIS RECIPE WORKS:** Nothing dresses up a simple sautéed chicken breast like a good pan sauce. We wanted an elegant, easy chicken dinner with a white wine and herb sauce. Pounding the breasts ensured even cooking, and dredging them in flour yielded a golden-brown crust and plenty of flavorful fond to use as a base for the sauce. We sautéed a minced shallot then deglazed the skillet with wine and chicken broth. A little flour thickened the sauce, then we finished it with a pat of butter and some fresh parsley. Since we were only cooking enough for two, we were able to cook everything in one batch in a 10-inch skillet, making this already simple dish even faster and easier.

¼ cup plus ½ teaspoon all-purpose flour
2 (6- to 8-ounce) boneless, skinless chicken breasts, trimmed and pounded if necessary
Salt and pepper
2 tablespoons vegetable oil
1 small shallot, minced
½ cup chicken broth
¼ cup dry white wine or dry vermouth
1 tablespoon unsalted butter, chilled
2 teaspoons minced fresh parsley or tarragon

1. Spread ¼ cup flour in shallow dish. Pat chicken dry with paper towels and season with salt and pepper. Working with 1 breast at a time, dredge breasts in flour.

2. Heat 1 tablespoon oil in 10-inch skillet over medium-high heat until just smoking. Lay chicken in skillet and cook until well browned on first side, 6 to 8 minutes. Flip chicken, reduce heat to medium, and continue to cook until chicken registers 160 degrees, 6 to 8 minutes; transfer to serving platter and tent loosely with aluminum foil.

3. Heat remaining 1 tablespoon oil in now-empty skillet over medium heat until shimmering. Add shallot and cook until softened, about 2 minutes. Stir in remaining ½ teaspoon flour and cook for 1 minute. Whisk in broth and wine, scraping up any browned bits. Bring to simmer and cook until sauce is slightly thickened, about 5 minutes. Stir in any accumulated chicken juices and simmer for 30 seconds. Off heat, whisk in butter and parsley and season with salt and pepper to taste. Pour sauce over chicken and serve.

VARIATION

Sautéed Chicken Breasts with Creamy Whole-Grain Mustard and Dill Pan Sauce

Omit ½ teaspoon flour and butter in step 3. Reduce amount of wine to 1 tablespoon. After sauce has thickened slightly in step 3, stir in 3 tablespoons heavy cream with accumulated chicken juices and simmer for 1 minute. Substitute 2 teaspoons minced fresh dill for parsley and stir in 1 tablespoon whole-grain mustard with dill.

Pounding Chicken Breasts

Packaged chicken breasts often contain breasts of varying sizes. To ensure they will cook through at the same rate, simply pound the thicker ends of the chicken breasts lightly until the breasts are all roughly the same thickness.

A surprising combination of fresh oranges and salty, creamy feta cheese gives sautéed chicken breasts a fresh spin.

Sautéed Chicken Breasts with Oranges and Feta

SERVES 2   FAST   LIGHT

✔ **WHY THIS RECIPE WORKS:** For a tasty chicken dinner with relatively little work, we used a few carefully chosen ingredients that added up to big flavor. We wanted to get chicken breasts with a flavorful browned crust and a moist, juicy interior, then dress them up with an interesting flavor combination. To get perfectly sautéed chicken, we used a high-low approach. We started with a smoking-hot pan for the first side of the breasts then turned down the heat to medium for the second side. While the second side slowly browned, the interior gently cooked through without drying out. While the chicken rested, we toasted minced garlic and whole fennel seeds in the same skillet, then added orange pieces and cooked them until softened for a sweet, fruity relish that nicely complemented the chicken. Salty feta and fresh scallions topped off the dish. Tangerines can be substituted for the oranges. For the nutritional information for this recipe, see page 413.

2   oranges
¼   cup all-purpose flour
2   (6- to 8-ounce) boneless, skinless chicken breasts, trimmed and pounded if necessary
    Salt and pepper
1   tablespoon vegetable oil
1   small garlic clove, minced
⅛   teaspoon fennel seeds
1   tablespoon water
2   tablespoons crumbled feta cheese
2   scallions, sliced thin

1. Cut away peel and pith from oranges. Quarter oranges, then slice crosswise into ½-inch-thick pieces. Spread flour in shallow dish. Pat chicken dry with paper towels and season with salt and pepper. Working with 1 breast at a time, dredge breasts in flour.

2. Heat oil in 10-inch skillet over medium-high heat until just smoking. Lay chicken in skillet and cook until well browned on first side, 6 to 8 minutes. Flip chicken, reduce heat to medium, and continue to cook until chicken registers 160 degrees, 6 to 8 minutes; transfer to serving platter and tent loosely with aluminum foil.

3. Add garlic and fennel seeds to now-empty skillet and cook over medium heat until fragrant, about 30 seconds. Stir in orange pieces and water, scraping up any browned bits, and cook until oranges are just softened, about 2 minutes. Stir in any accumulated chicken juices and season with salt and pepper to taste. Pour relish over chicken, sprinkle with feta and scallions, and serve.

Cutting Citrus into Pieces

1. Slice off top and bottom of orange or grapefruit, then cut away peel and pith using paring knife.

2. Quarter peeled fruit, then slice each quarter crosswise into ½-inch-thick pieces.

Chicken Marsala

SERVES 2

✓ **WHY THIS RECIPE WORKS:** Chicken Marsala is an Italian restaurant standby, and we wanted a home version that rivaled the one at our favorite restaurant—with juicy chicken, meaty mushrooms, and a well-balanced Marsala sauce. We began by testing cooking methods. We found that the classic method of sautéing the meat, removing it from the pan, and then building a sauce from the browned bits left in the pan proved best. We also liked the flavor of a chopped onion added in with the mushrooms. For the sauce, we liked sweet Marsala (rather than dry) for its depth of flavor and smooth finish. We finished our sauce with butter for silky richness and added a dash of fresh parsley.

¼ cup plus ½ teaspoon all-purpose flour

2 (6- to 8-ounce) boneless, skinless chicken breasts, trimmed and pounded if necessary

Salt and pepper

1 tablespoon vegetable oil

3 tablespoons unsalted butter, chilled

4 ounces white mushrooms, trimmed and sliced thin

1 small onion, chopped coarse

1 garlic clove, minced

½ cup sweet Marsala

¼ cup chicken broth

1 tablespoon minced fresh parsley

1. Spread ¼ cup flour in shallow dish. Pat chicken dry with paper towels and season with salt and pepper. Working with 1 breast at a time, dredge breasts in flour.

2. Heat oil in 10-inch skillet over medium-high heat until just smoking. Lay chicken in skillet and cook until well browned on first side, 6 to 8 minutes. Flip chicken, reduce heat to medium, and continue to cook until chicken registers 160 degrees, 6 to 8 minutes; transfer to plate and tent loosely with aluminum foil.

3. Melt 1 tablespoon butter in now-empty skillet over medium heat. Add mushrooms and onion and cook until mushrooms have released their liquid and vegetables are softened and lightly browned, 5 to 7 minutes. Stir in garlic and cook until fragrant, about 30 seconds; transfer mixture to bowl.

4. Add remaining ½ teaspoon flour to again-empty skillet and cook over medium heat for 1 minute. Whisk in Marsala and broth, scraping up any browned bits. Bring to simmer and cook until sauce is slightly thickened, about 5 minutes. Return chicken and any accumulated juices to skillet and simmer until heated through, about 1 minute; transfer chicken to serving platter. Off heat, whisk mushroom mixture, remaining 2 tablespoons butter, and parsley into sauce and season with salt and pepper to taste. Pour sauce over chicken and serve.

NOTES FROM THE TEST KITCHEN

Buying Chicken

Once considered a luxurious protein, chicken has become a cheap supermarket staple. But with wide availability comes a glut of choices. Here's what you need to know when buying chicken.

DECIPHERING LABELS: A lot of labeling doesn't (necessarily) mean much. Companies can exploit loopholes to qualify for "Natural/All-Natural," "Hormone-Free," and "Vegetarian Diet/Fed" labeling. "USDA Organic," however, isn't all hype: The chickens must eat organic feed without animal by-products, be raised without antibiotics, and have access to the outdoors.

PAY ATTENTION TO PROCESSING: Our tasting and research showed that processing is the major player in chicken's texture and flavor. We found brands labeled "water-chilled" (soaked in a water bath in which they absorb up to 14 percent of their weight in water—which you pay for since chicken is sold by the pound) or "enhanced" (injected with broth and flavoring) are unnaturally spongy and are best avoided. Labeling law says water gain must be shown on the product label, so these should be easily identifiable. When buying whole chickens or chicken parts, look for those that are labeled "air-chilled." Without the excess water weight, these brands are less spongy in texture (but still plenty juicy) and have more chicken flavor.

BONELESS, SKINLESS BREASTS AND CUTLETS: When buying boneless, skinless breasts, be aware that breasts of different sizes are often packaged together, which is a problem since they won't cook through at the same rate. Try to pick a package with breasts of similar size and pound them to an even thickness. You can buy cutlets ready to go at the grocery store, but we don't recommend it. These cutlets are usually ragged and of various sizes; it's better to cut your own cutlets from breasts (see page 103). Our favorite supermarket brand is **Bell & Evans Air Chilled Boneless, Skinless Chicken Breasts**, which are aged for 12 hours before being boned and are moist and tender with a clean chicken flavor.

WHOLE CHICKENS: Whole chickens come in various sizes. When cooking for two, we look for broilers or fryers, which are younger chickens that weigh 2½ to 4½ pounds; a 3- to 3½-pound bird yields a good amount of meat for two. To find the best widely available brand of chicken, we tasted eight brands, seasoned minimally and roasted. We found two favorites, both air-chilled: **Mary's Free Range Air Chilled Chicken** (also sold as Pitman's) and **Bell & Evans Air Chilled Premium Fresh Chicken**. Both brands boast moist meat and a concentrated savory flavor.

Chicken Piccata

SERVES 2

✓ **WHY THIS RECIPE WORKS:** Chicken piccata is a simple dish that should be easy to get right. But many recipes miss the mark with extraneous ingredients or paltry amounts of lemon juice and capers. We wanted properly cooked chicken and a streamlined sauce that would keep the star ingredients at the forefront. To ensure the chicken cooked evenly, we found it best to pound the breasts and then sauté them in one batch in a 10-inch skillet. For bold lemon flavor that wasn't harsh or overly acidic, we simmered strips of lemon zest in the sauce and added lemon juice at the end of cooking to keep its flavor bright. A generous 1 tablespoon of capers perfectly balanced the rich sauce.

¼ cup plus ½ teaspoon all-purpose flour
2 (6- to 8-ounce) boneless, skinless chicken breasts, trimmed and pounded if necessary
  Salt and pepper
2 tablespoons vegetable oil
1 small shallot, minced
1 garlic clove, minced
½ cup chicken broth
¼ cup dry white wine
2 (2-inch) strips lemon zest plus 1 tablespoon juice
1 tablespoon capers, rinsed
1 tablespoon unsalted butter, chilled
1 tablespoon minced fresh parsley

1. Spread ¼ cup flour in shallow dish. Pat chicken dry with paper towels and season with salt and pepper. Working with 1 breast at a time, dredge breasts in flour.

2. Heat 1 tablespoon oil in 10-inch skillet over medium-high heat until just smoking. Lay chicken in skillet and cook until well browned on first side, 6 to 8 minutes. Flip chicken, reduce heat to medium, and continue to cook until chicken registers 160 degrees, 6 to 8 minutes; transfer to serving platter and tent loosely with aluminum foil.

Making Zest Strips

Use vegetable peeler to remove long, wide strips of citrus zest from fruit. Try not to remove any white pith beneath zest, as it is bitter.

3. Heat remaining 1 tablespoon oil in now-empty skillet over medium heat until shimmering. Add shallot and cook until softened, about 2 minutes. Stir in garlic and cook until fragrant, about 30 seconds. Stir in remaining ½ teaspoon flour and cook for 1 minute. Whisk in broth, wine, lemon zest, and capers, scraping up any browned bits. Bring to simmer and cook until sauce is slightly thickened, about 5 minutes. Stir in any accumulated chicken juices and simmer for 30 seconds. Off heat, discard zest and whisk in butter, parsley, and lemon juice. Season with salt and pepper to taste. Pour sauce over chicken and serve.

Spa Chicken

SERVES 2 **LIGHT**

✓ **WHY THIS RECIPE WORKS:** Poaching promises moist, tender chicken every time. We wanted to take advantage of this easy technique to make a healthy and flavorful chicken dish. We started with boneless, skinless chicken breasts and added them to a small skillet with a cup of water. Next we added aromatic ingredients to make a poaching liquid that would infuse the chicken with flavor. Smashed garlic cloves, fresh thyme, and soy sauce lent the chicken breasts meaty, complex flavor as they simmered. A sprinkle of chives and a squeeze of lemon juice were all our tender, flavorful chicken needed. Do not let the poaching liquid boil or the chicken will be tough. For the nutritional information for this recipe, see page 413.

1 cup water
3 garlic cloves, peeled and smashed
3 sprigs fresh thyme
2 teaspoons soy sauce
2 (6- to 8-ounce) boneless, skinless chicken breasts, trimmed and pounded if necessary
  Salt and pepper
1 tablespoon minced fresh chives, parsley, or tarragon
  Lemon wedges

1. Combine water, garlic, thyme sprigs, and soy sauce in 10-inch skillet. Season chicken with salt and pepper, lay in skillet, and bring to simmer over medium-low heat, 10 to 15 minutes.

2. When water is simmering, flip chicken, cover, and continue to cook until chicken registers 160 degrees, 10 to 15 minutes.

3. Transfer chicken to cutting board, tent loosely with aluminum foil, and let rest for 5 minutes. Cut chicken into ½-inch-thick slices, sprinkle with chives, and serve with lemon wedges.

Spa Chicken with Apricot-Orange Chipotle Sauce

For the nutritional information for this recipe see page 413.

Omit chives and lemon wedges. Cut away peel and pith from ½ orange. Halve orange, then slice crosswise into ½-inch-thick pieces. While chicken simmers, heat 1 teaspoon oil in 8-inch nonstick skillet over medium heat until shimmering. Add 1 small minced shallot and cook until softened, about 2 minutes. Stir in 1 minced garlic clove and ¼ teaspoon minced chipotle chile and cook until fragrant, about 30 seconds. Stir in ½ cup orange juice and 2 tablespoons finely chopped apricots and simmer until apricots are plump and sauce has reduced to ⅓ cup, 3 to 5 minutes. Off heat, stir in orange pieces and 1 tablespoon minced fresh cilantro. Season with salt and pepper to taste. Serve chicken with sauce.

Spa Chicken with Caramelized Onion and Whole-Grain Mustard Sauce

For the nutritional information for this recipe see page 413.

Omit chives and lemon wedges. While chicken simmers, heat 2 teaspoons extra-virgin olive oil in 8-inch nonstick skillet over medium-high heat until shimmering. Add 1 small onion, halved and sliced thin, and 1 teaspoon brown sugar and cook until onion is softened, about 5 minutes. Reduce heat to medium-low and continue to cook, stirring often, until onion is dark golden and caramelized, 15 to 20 minutes. Stir in 1 small minced garlic clove and 1 teaspoon all-purpose flour and cook until fragrant, about 30 seconds. Whisk in ¾ cup broth and 1 tablespoon whole-grain mustard, scraping up any browned bits. Simmer until sauce has thickened and reduced to ½ cup, about 5 minutes. Off heat, stir in 1 teaspoon lemon juice. Season with salt and pepper to taste. Serve chicken with sauce.

Crispy Chicken Breasts

SERVES 2 · FAST

✔ **WHY THIS RECIPE WORKS:** For a foolproof recipe for this classic comfort food, we started with a standard flour, egg wash, and bread-crumb coating. We found that ultracrisp panko bread crumbs gave us the crunchiest coating. Pounding the chicken to an even thickness ensured that the chicken browned evenly. Cooking for two meant we could cook everything in one batch in a 10-inch skillet; thanks to the smaller vessel, just 6 tablespoons of oil was enough to get a crispy fried coating.

¼ cup all-purpose flour
1 large egg
1 cup panko bread crumbs

2 (6- to 8-ounce) boneless, skinless chicken breasts, trimmed and pounded if necessary
  Salt and pepper
6 tablespoons vegetable oil
  Lemon wedges

1. Spread flour in shallow dish. Beat egg in second shallow dish. Spread bread crumbs in third shallow dish. Pat chicken dry with paper towels and season with salt and pepper. Working with 1 breast at a time, dredge breasts in flour, dip in egg, then coat with bread crumbs, pressing gently to adhere.

2. Line large plate with triple layer of paper towels. Heat oil in 10-inch nonstick skillet over medium-high heat until shimmering. Lay chicken in skillet and cook until golden brown on both sides and chicken registers 160 degrees, 4 to 6 minutes per side. Drain chicken briefly on paper towel–lined plate. Serve with lemon wedges.

NOTES FROM THE TEST KITCHEN

Chicken Safety and Handling

It's important to follow some basic safety procedures when storing, handling, and cooking chicken.

REFRIGERATING: Keep chicken refrigerated until just before cooking. Bacteria thrive at temperatures between 40 and 140 degrees. This means leftovers should also be promptly refrigerated.

FREEZING AND THAWING: Chicken can be frozen in its original packaging or after repackaging. If you are freezing it for longer than two months, rewrap (or wrap over packaging) with foil or plastic wrap, or place inside a zipper-lock freezer bag. You can keep chicken frozen for several months, but after two months the texture and flavor will suffer. Don't thaw frozen chicken on the counter; this puts it at risk of growing bacteria. Thaw it in its packaging in the refrigerator overnight (in a container to catch its juices), or in the sink under cold running water. Count on one day of defrosting in the refrigerator for every 4 pounds of bird.

HANDLING RAW CHICKEN: When handling raw chicken, make sure to wash hands, knives, cutting boards, and counters (and anything else that has come into contact with the raw bird, its juices, or your hands) with hot, soapy water. Be careful not to let the chicken, its juices, or your unwashed hands touch foods that will be eaten raw. When seasoning raw chicken, touching the saltshaker or pepper mill can lead to cross-contamination. To avoid this, set aside the necessary salt and pepper before handling the chicken.

RINSING: The U.S. Department of Agriculture advises against washing chicken. Rinsing chicken will not remove or kill much bacteria, and the splashing of water around the sink can spread the bacteria found in raw chicken.

COOKING AND LEFTOVERS: Chicken should be cooked to an internal temperature of 160 degrees to ensure any bacteria have been killed (however, we prefer the flavor and texture of thigh meat cooked to 175 degrees). Leftover cooked chicken should be refrigerated and consumed within three days.

Chicken Parmesan

SERVES 2

WHY THIS RECIPE WORKS: Chicken Parmesan is a perennial favorite, but its multiple components can make it a time-consuming affair. We wanted to streamline this dish to make it feasible for two. We made a quick but flavorful tomato sauce by whirring together canned tomatoes in a food processor. Garlic sautéed in olive oil provided a rich backbone, and basil, sugar, and salt rounded it out. For the chicken, we coated breasts in flour, dipped them in an egg wash, then rolled them in a crumb coating of ultracrisp panko bread crumbs and freshly grated Parmesan cheese. Pan-frying the chicken produced an evenly browned crust that stayed crisp even when topped with a mix of mozzarella and fontina and broiled until the cheese turned gooey. Spooning the sauce over the cheese, not the chicken, also ensured a crisp crust. We saved the remaining sauce for tossing with a side of hot spaghetti.

SAUCE

- 1 (28-ounce) can whole peeled tomatoes, drained
- 2 tablespoons extra-virgin olive oil
- 2 garlic cloves, minced
- 2 tablespoons chopped fresh basil
- ¼ teaspoon sugar, plus extra as needed
- Salt

CHICKEN AND SPAGHETTI

- ¼ cup all-purpose flour
- 1 large egg
- ¾ cup panko bread crumbs
- ¼ cup grated Parmesan cheese
- 2 (6- to 8-ounce) boneless, skinless chicken breasts, trimmed and pounded if necessary
- Salt and pepper
- 6 tablespoons vegetable oil
- 1 ounce whole-milk mozzarella cheese, shredded (¼ cup)
- 1 ounce fontina cheese, shredded (¼ cup)
- 1 tablespoon chopped fresh basil
- 4 ounces spaghetti

1. FOR THE SAUCE: Pulse tomatoes in food processor until coarsely ground, 6 to 8 pulses. Cook oil and garlic in medium saucepan over medium heat, stirring often, until garlic is fragrant but not browned, about 2 minutes. Stir in pulsed tomatoes, bring to simmer, and cook until sauce is slightly thickened, 10 to 15 minutes. Off heat, stir in basil and sugar and season with salt and extra sugar to taste; cover to keep warm.

2. FOR THE CHICKEN AND SPAGHETTI: Adjust oven rack 4 inches from broiler element and heat broiler. Spread flour in

Adding Parmesan right into the crisp bread-crumb coating gives our classic chicken Parmesan exceptionally rich, cheesy flavor.

shallow dish. Beat egg in second shallow dish. Combine bread crumbs and Parmesan in third shallow dish. Pat chicken dry with paper towels and season with salt and pepper. Working with 1 breast at a time, dredge breasts in flour, dip in egg, then coat with bread-crumb mixture, pressing gently to adhere.

3. Line large plate with triple layer of paper towels. Heat oil in 10-inch nonstick skillet over medium-high heat until shimmering. Lay chicken in skillet and cook until golden brown on both sides and chicken registers 160 degrees, 4 to 6 minutes per side. Drain chicken briefly on paper towel–lined plate, then transfer to rimmed baking sheet.

4. Combine mozzarella and fontina in bowl. Sprinkle cheese mixture evenly over chicken, covering as much surface area as possible. Broil until cheese is melted and beginning to brown, 2 to 4 minutes. Transfer chicken to serving platter, top each breast with 2 tablespoons tomato sauce, and sprinkle with basil.

5. Meanwhile, bring 4 quarts water to boil in large pot. Add pasta and 1 tablespoon salt and cook, stirring often, until al dente. Reserve ½ cup cooking water, then drain pasta and return it to pot. Add remaining sauce to pasta and toss to combine. Season with salt and pepper to taste and add reserved cooking water as needed to adjust consistency. Serve chicken with pasta.

Chicken Tikka Masala

SERVES 2

✓ WHY THIS RECIPE WORKS: We wanted to re-create the classic Indian dish chicken tikka masala. To develop an approachable method for producing moist, tender chunks of chicken in a rich, warmly spiced tomato sauce, we began by coating the chicken in a yogurt mixture seasoned with garlic and ginger. Baking the chicken breasts was quick and worked well, but the additional char we achieved with the broiler was better and required no extra effort. Meanwhile, a traditional combination of garam masala, fresh ginger, and cilantro gave our masala sauce an authentic Indian taste. This dish tastes best when prepared with whole-milk yogurt, but low-fat yogurt can be substituted; do not use nonfat yogurt. Serve with rice.

CHICKEN

- ½ teaspoon salt
- ½ teaspoon garam masala
- ⅛ teaspoon cayenne pepper
- 2 (6- to 8-ounce) boneless, skinless chicken breasts, trimmed and pounded if necessary
- ½ cup plain whole-milk yogurt
- 1 tablespoon vegetable oil
- 2 garlic cloves, minced
- 2 teaspoons grated fresh ginger

SAUCE

- 1 (14.5-ounce) can whole tomatoes
- 2 tablespoons vegetable oil
- 1 small onion, chopped fine
- 1 small serrano chile, stemmed, seeded, and minced
- 1½ teaspoons tomato paste
- 1½ teaspoons garam masala
- 1 garlic clove, minced
- 1 teaspoon grated fresh ginger
- 1 teaspoon sugar
  Salt
- ⅓ cup plain whole-milk yogurt
- 2 tablespoons chopped fresh cilantro

1. FOR THE CHICKEN: Combine salt, garam masala, and cayenne in bowl. Pat chicken dry with paper towels and season thoroughly with spice mixture. Place chicken on plate, cover, and refrigerate for 30 minutes to 1 hour. Whisk yogurt, oil, garlic, and ginger together in medium bowl, cover, and refrigerate until needed.

A tomato sauce spiced with garam masala, ginger, and bright cilantro gives this Indian dish authentic flavor with minimal fuss.

2. FOR THE SAUCE: Process tomatoes and their juice in food processor until smooth, about 15 seconds. Heat oil in large saucepan over medium heat until shimmering. Add onion and cook until softened and lightly browned, 5 to 7 minutes. Stir in serrano, tomato paste, garam masala, garlic, and ginger and cook until fragrant, about 30 seconds. Stir in processed tomatoes, sugar, and ¼ teaspoon salt and bring to simmer. Reduce heat to low, cover, and simmer, stirring occasionally, until flavors meld, about 15 minutes. Off heat, stir in yogurt; cover to keep warm.

3. Meanwhile, adjust oven rack 6 inches from broiler element and heat broiler. Set wire rack in aluminum foil–lined rimmed baking sheet. Using tongs, dip chicken into yogurt mixture (chicken should be coated with thick layer of yogurt) and arrange on prepared wire rack. Discard excess yogurt mixture. Broil chicken until lightly charred in spots and chicken registers 160 degrees, 10 to 18 minutes, flipping chicken halfway through cooking.

4. Transfer chicken to cutting board, let rest for 5 minutes, then cut into 1-inch pieces. Stir chicken pieces into warm sauce (do not simmer chicken in sauce). Stir in cilantro, season with salt to taste, and serve.

Principles of Cooking Chicken

A number of cooking methods work well when preparing chicken. But whether you are roasting a whole chicken, grilling chicken parts, or sautéing cutlets, there are a few basic cooking principles that you should always keep in mind.

BRINE OR SALT TO INCREASE JUICINESS: Brining chicken in a saltwater solution boosts the flavor and juiciness of the meat. However, there's a drawback to brining skin-on chicken: Because it's soaking up liquid, achieving perfectly crisp skin is more difficult. In these cases, make sure to pat the skin as dry as possible prior to cooking. Alternatively, for some cuts you might opt to salt the chicken. See page 115 for more information about how brining and salting works and for details on salting and brining specific cuts of chicken.

COOK WHITE MEAT LESS THAN DARK MEAT: Dark meat (thighs and drumsticks) cooks more slowly than white breast meat. This is mainly due to the fact that dark meat is denser because it has more fat and proteins. To account for this difference when cooking a whole bird, we cook the bird thigh side down in a hot skillet to give the dark meat a head start. To prevent it from drying out while ensuring it is safe to eat, white meat should be cooked to an internal temperature of 160 degrees and dark meat should be cooked to 175 degrees. Having a good instant-read thermometer is essential for getting perfectly cooked chicken.

CRISP THE SKIN OR LOSE THE SKIN: For many of us, the crisp skin on a piece of chicken is the best part. On the flip side, flabby chicken or turkey skin isn't something anyone wants to eat (nor is it visually appealing). So either make sure the skin is crispy or remove it. The key to crisp skin is rendering all the fat that is between the skin and the meat. When cooking skin-on chicken pieces, we typically will brown the skin in a hot skillet and then finish cooking the chicken over a lower temperature or in the even heat of the oven (this has the added benefit of creating flavorful browned bits—fond—in the skillet, great for making a pan sauce). When roasting a whole bird, if you don't want to serve the skin you can still keep it on while roasting to protect the delicate breast meat from the heat, but discard it before serving. For stews and braises, if you don't crisp the skin and render the fat, you should typically discard the skin before cooking. If you don't, the fat will render into the stew or sauce, which will wind up being overly greasy.

LET IT REST: As chicken cooks, the juices are driven toward the center of the cut, so a resting period after cooking is essential to allow those juices time to redistribute evenly throughout. Logically, the larger the piece of chicken, the longer the resting time required. A whole chicken needs 10 to 20 minutes and bone-in chicken parts 5 to 10 minutes. Cuts like boneless breasts and thighs and cutlets are small enough that the juices will redistribute in just a few minutes, so they don't require a designated resting time.

Moroccan Chicken with Green Olives

SERVES 2　LIGHT

✔ **WHY THIS RECIPE WORKS:** Traditional North African tagines (aromatic braises of meat, vegetables, and fruits) are labor-intensive and use hard-to-find ingredients. We came up with a few timesaving tricks for this version made with chicken, lemon, and olives. We swapped out bone-in chicken thighs for quicker-cooking boneless thighs. Poaching the chicken in a flavorful broth infused it with flavor and ensured the chicken was tender. Instead of calling for a laundry list of spices, we used garam masala, an Indian spice mix, and gave it a further flavor boost with paprika. Coarsely chopped dried figs added a hint of sweetness. Look for large, pitted green olives at the olive bar in the supermarket. Pimento-stuffed olives can be substituted for the large green olives in a pinch. Serve with rice or couscous. For the nutritional information for this recipe, see page 413.

1　tablespoon olive oil
1　small onion, halved and sliced thin
1　(3-inch) strip lemon zest plus 1½ teaspoons juice
2　garlic cloves, minced
1　teaspoon garam masala
½　teaspoon paprika
½　cup chicken broth
¼　cup pitted large green olives, chopped coarse
¼　cup dried figs, stemmed and chopped coarse
4　(3-ounce) boneless, skinless chicken thighs, trimmed
　　Salt and pepper
1　tablespoon minced fresh cilantro

1. Heat oil in 10-inch skillet over medium heat until shimmering. Add onion and cook until softened, about 5 minutes. Stir in lemon zest, garlic, garam masala, and paprika and cook until fragrant, about 30 seconds. Stir in broth, olives, and figs, scraping up any browned bits.

2. Season chicken with salt and pepper, lay in skillet, and bring to simmer. Reduce heat to medium-low, cover, and simmer until chicken is very tender, about 15 minutes; transfer chicken to serving platter and tent loosely with aluminum foil.

3. Discard lemon zest. Continue to simmer sauce until slightly thickened, about 3 minutes. Stir in any accumulated chicken juices and simmer for 30 seconds. Stir in cilantro and lemon juice and season with salt and pepper to taste. Pour sauce over chicken and serve.

Chicken Mole

SERVES 2

✓ **WHY THIS RECIPE WORKS:** Mole sauce is a rich blend of chocolate, dried fruits, nuts, spices, and chiles. An authentic mole has complex layers of flavor and an extensive ingredient list, but we found that we could get surprising depth of flavor in much less time with a combination of chili powder, chipotle chiles, and peanut butter. Simmering the chiles, spices, and chocolate developed their flavors even more. Downsizing to a 10-inch skillet prevented the sauce from burning. For a smooth, velvety texture, we processed the sauce in a blender, then poured it over chicken breasts and baked them until they were tender and flavorful. Take care not to burn the spice and chocolate mixture in step 2; add a small splash of water or broth to the skillet if it begins to scorch. If using kosher chicken, do not brine. If brining the chicken, do not season with salt in step 3.

>   1 tablespoon vegetable oil
>   1 small onion, chopped fine
>   ½ ounce bittersweet, semisweet, or Mexican chocolate, chopped coarse
>   1 tablespoon chili powder
>   1 teaspoon minced canned chipotle chile in adobo sauce
>   ¼ teaspoon ground cinnamon
>   Pinch ground cloves
>   1 garlic clove, minced
> 1¼ cups chicken broth
>   1 tomato, cored, seeded, and chopped
>   2 tablespoons raisins
>   1 tablespoon peanut butter
>   1 tablespoon sesame seeds, toasted, plus extra for serving
>   Salt and pepper
>   Sugar
>   2 (12-ounce) bone-in split chicken breasts, skin removed, trimmed and brined if desired (see page 115)

1. Adjust oven rack to middle position and heat oven to 400 degrees. Heat oil in 10-inch skillet over medium heat until shimmering. Add onion and cook until softened, about 5 minutes.

2. Reduce heat to medium-low, stir in chocolate, chili powder, chipotle, cinnamon, and cloves; cook, stirring frequently, until spices are fragrant and chocolate is melted and bubbly, about 1 minute. Stir in garlic and cook until fragrant, about 30 seconds. Stir in broth, tomato, raisins, peanut butter, and sesame seeds. Bring to simmer and cook, stirring occasionally, until sauce is slightly thickened and reduced to about 1¾ cups, 10 to 15 minutes. Transfer sauce to blender and process until smooth, about 30 seconds. Season with salt, pepper, and sugar to taste.

3. Pat chicken dry with paper towels and season with salt and pepper. Place chicken, skinned side down, in 8-inch square baking dish and pour pureed sauce over top, turning chicken to coat evenly. Bake chicken for 20 minutes. Flip chicken skinned side up and continue to bake until chicken registers 160 degrees, 15 to 25 minutes. Let chicken rest in sauce for 5 minutes. Sprinkle with extra sesame seeds and serve.

Orange-Glazed Chicken

SERVES 2

✓ **WHY THIS RECIPE WORKS:** Bright, tangy orange-glazed chicken wins points for simplicity, but the recipes we tested produced painfully sweet glazes, soggy skin, and dry meat. To ensure crisp skin, we placed the chicken breasts in a skillet and weighed them down with a heavy saucepan. The extra weight pressed out the fat from under the skin, allowing the skin to crisp. To infuse the chicken with both moisture and orange flavor, we processed salt with grated orange zest and used it to brine the chicken before cooking. For a bright, citrusy glaze that wasn't too sweet, we reduced orange juice with a little sugar and a pinch of cayenne. The fat will render best if you pat the chicken thoroughly dry after removing it from the brine. Brining is crucial to the flavor of this dish; do not omit this step and do not use kosher chicken here. In step 2, weight the saucepan with a 28-ounce can or two 15-ounce cans.

>   ¼ cup salt
>   4 teaspoons grated orange zest plus ⅓ cup juice
>   2 (12-ounce) bone-in split chicken breasts, trimmed and halved crosswise
>   1 tablespoon vegetable oil
>   1 tablespoon sugar
>   ½ teaspoon cornstarch
>   Pinch cayenne pepper

1. Process salt and 3¾ teaspoons orange zest together in food processor until zest is finely ground, about 10 seconds. Dissolve orange salt in 1 quart cold water in large container. Submerge chicken in brine, cover, and refrigerate for 30 minutes to 1 hour. Remove chicken from brine and pat dry with paper towels.

2. Wrap bottom of large saucepan with aluminum foil, then place 1 large can or 2 smaller cans inside. Heat oil in 10-inch nonstick skillet over medium-high heat until just smoking. Lay chicken skin side down in skillet and weigh down with prepared saucepan. Cook chicken until skin is well browned and crisp, 10 to 15 minutes.

Adding orange zest to the brine and reducing fresh orange juice to a sweet, sticky glaze gives this dish bold, bright orange flavor.

3. Remove saucepan and flip chicken skin side up. Reduce heat to medium and continue to cook, without weight, until chicken registers 160 degrees, 5 to 10 minutes; transfer to plate. Pour off fat from skillet.

4. Meanwhile, whisk orange juice, sugar, cornstarch, cayenne, and remaining ¼ teaspoon orange zest together in bowl. Add orange juice mixture to now-empty skillet and bring to simmer over medium heat. Return chicken, skin side up, and any accumulated juices to skillet and simmer until glaze is thick and glossy, 2 to 3 minutes. Turn chicken to coat evenly with glaze. Serve.

Crisping Chicken Skin

For chicken skin that stays crisp even when glazed, set weighted saucepan (wrapped in aluminum foil for easy cleanup) on chicken as it browns in pan.

Teriyaki Chicken
SERVES 2

✔ **WHY THIS RECIPE WORKS:** For an easy and approachable chicken teriyaki recipe that would deliver juicy meat and crisp skin covered with a sweet and salty glaze, we needed to render as much fat as possible from the skin. We discovered that setting a weight on top of the chicken as it cooked (we used a saucepan and a couple of cans) helped to brown more surface area and pressed out most of the fat, for thin, ultracrisp skin. For the sauce, we found that simmering a quick mix of soy sauce, mirin, ginger, garlic, and sugar until thick and glossy made a bright, balanced teriyaki sauce that far surpassed any we could buy in a bottle. In step 1, weight the saucepan with a 28-ounce can or two 15-ounce cans. Serve with rice.

4   (5- to 7-ounce) bone-in chicken thighs, trimmed
    Pepper
1   teaspoon vegetable oil
¼   cup sugar
2   tablespoons soy sauce
1   tablespoon mirin, sweet sherry, or dry white wine
1   teaspoon grated fresh ginger
1   garlic clove, minced
¼   teaspoon cornstarch
    Pinch red pepper flakes

1. Wrap bottom of large saucepan with aluminum foil, then place 1 large can or 2 smaller cans inside. Pat chicken dry with paper towels and season with pepper. Heat oil in 10-inch nonstick skillet over medium-high heat until just smoking. Lay chicken skin side down in skillet and weigh down with prepared saucepan. Cook chicken until skin is well browned and crisp, 10 to 15 minutes.

2. Remove saucepan and flip chicken skin side up. Reduce heat to medium and continue to cook, without weight, until chicken registers 175 degrees, about 10 minutes; transfer to plate. Pour off fat from skillet.

3. Meanwhile, whisk sugar, soy sauce, mirin, ginger, garlic, cornstarch, and pepper flakes together in bowl. Add soy mixture to now-empty skillet and bring to simmer. Return chicken, skin side up, and any accumulated juices to skillet and simmer until sauce is thick and glossy, 2 to 3 minutes. Turn chicken to coat evenly with sauce. Serve.

Tandoori Chicken with Yogurt Sauce

SERVES 2

✔ **WHY THIS RECIPE WORKS:** Tandoori chicken traditionally calls for a 24-hour marinade and a 900-degree oven. We wanted to turn this Indian classic into an easy dish that we could make indoors. We skipped the marinade in favor of a simple salt-spice rub, then we dipped the chicken pieces in a spice-flavored yogurt. To mimic the extreme heat of a tandoor oven, we started the chicken in a moderate 325-degree oven then finished it under the broiler to lightly char the exterior. We prefer this dish made with whole-milk yogurt, but low-fat yogurt can be substituted. It is important to remove the chicken from the oven before switching to the broiler setting to allow the broiler element time to come up to temperature. Serve with rice and chutney.

CHICKEN

- 2 tablespoons vegetable oil
- 3 garlic cloves, minced
- 1 tablespoon grated fresh ginger
- 1½ teaspoons garam masala
- 1 teaspoon ground cumin
- 1 teaspoon chili powder
- ½ cup plain whole-milk yogurt
- 2 tablespoons lime juice
- 1 teaspoon salt
- 2 (12-ounce) bone-in split chicken breasts, skin removed, trimmed and halved crosswise

SAUCE

- ½ cup plain whole-milk yogurt
- 1 tablespoon minced fresh cilantro
- 1 tablespoon minced fresh mint
- 1 small garlic clove, minced
  Salt and pepper

1. FOR THE CHICKEN: Cook oil, garlic, ginger, garam masala, cumin, and chili powder in 8-inch nonstick skillet over medium heat until fragrant, 30 to 60 seconds; remove from heat. Whisk 1 tablespoon of garlic-spice mixture, yogurt, and 1 tablespoon lime juice together in medium bowl, cover, and refrigerate until needed.

2. In large bowl, combine remaining garlic-spice mixture, remaining 1 tablespoon lime juice, and salt. Score skinned side of each chicken piece twice with sharp knife. Add chicken to spice-salt mixture; rub mixture into chicken until all pieces are evenly coated. Cover and let sit at room temperature for 30 minutes.

3. Meanwhile, adjust oven rack to upper-middle position and heat oven to 325 degrees. Line rimmed baking sheet with aluminum foil and set wire rack in sheet. Using tongs,

For boldly flavored tandoori chicken, we coat bone-in breasts with creamy spiced yogurt then broil them until lightly charred.

dip chicken into yogurt mixture (chicken should be coated with thick layer of yogurt) and arrange skinned side down on prepared wire rack. Discard excess yogurt mixture. Bake until chicken registers 125 degrees, 15 to 25 minutes.

4. Remove chicken from oven, adjust oven rack 6 inches from broiler element, and heat broiler. Flip chicken skinned side up and broil until lightly charred in spots and chicken registers 160 degrees, 8 to 15 minutes. Transfer chicken to serving platter, tent loosely with foil, and let rest for 5 minutes.

5. FOR THE SAUCE: Combine all ingredients in small bowl and season with salt and pepper to taste. Serve chicken with yogurt sauce.

Scoring Tandoori Chicken

Score each piece of chicken with sharp knife, making 2 shallow cuts about 1 inch apart and ⅛ inch deep.

Weeknight Baked Chicken with Lemon and Thyme

SERVES 2

✔ **WHY THIS RECIPE WORKS:** Recipes for baked chicken parts often produce bland, dry meat and flabby skin. Attempts to cover up such disappointments with potent ingredients only make matters worse for this simple dish. We found that a few simple tricks (and a few ingredients) gave us superb baked chicken. We started with flavorful bone-in, skin-on chicken pieces to help insulate the meat and keep it juicy in the oven. We infused the chicken with flavor by spreading butter, flavored with lemon and thyme, under the skin of each piece before cooking. Then we brushed the chicken pieces with melted butter and baked them in a hot 450-degree oven to encourage crisp skin. Elevating the chicken on a broiler pan allowed the fat to render from the chicken quickly.

 2 **tablespoons butter, softened, plus 1 tablespoon melted**
 2 **teaspoons minced fresh thyme**
 ½ **teaspoon grated lemon zest**
    Salt and pepper
1½ **pounds bone-in chicken pieces (split breasts, drumsticks, and/or thighs), trimmed**

1. Adjust oven rack to upper-middle position and heat oven to 450 degrees. Line broiler-pan bottom with aluminum foil and top with slotted broiler pan top. Mix softened butter, thyme, lemon zest, ⅛ teaspoon salt, and ⅛ teaspoon pepper together in bowl.

2. Pat chicken dry with paper towels. Use your fingers to gently loosen center portion of skin covering each chicken piece; place softened herb butter evenly under skin, directly on meat in center of each piece. Arrange chicken, skin side up, on prepared broiler pan. Brush chicken with melted butter and season with salt and pepper.

3. Roast chicken until breasts register 160 degrees and drumsticks/thighs register 175 degrees, 30 to 50 minutes. Transfer chicken to cutting board and let rest for 5 minutes before serving.

VARIATIONS

Weeknight Baked Chicken with Ginger

Substitute 2 teaspoons grated fresh ginger for thyme and ½ teaspoon five-spice powder for lemon zest.

Jamaican Jerk Weeknight Baked Chicken

Substitute ½ teaspoon grated lime zest for lemon zest and ½ teaspoon Jamaican jerk seasoning for thyme, salt, and pepper. Add 1 minced garlic clove to softened butter mixture.

Pan-Roasted Chicken Breasts with Garlic and Sherry Sauce

SERVES 2

✔ **WHY THIS RECIPE WORKS:** Bone-in, skin-on chicken breasts offer more flavor than their boneless, skinless counterparts, but getting the skin to crisp without overcooking the delicate breast meat can be a challenge. For the best results, we turned to pan roasting, a restaurant technique in which food is browned in a skillet and then slid, skillet and all, into a hot oven to finish cooking. Brining the chicken helped the meat stay moist and flavorful, and patting the brined meat dry with paper towels ensured that the skin would sear, rather than steam. We browned the chicken on both sides on the stovetop before placing the skillet in the oven. Cooking the chicken at 450 degrees allowed the skin to crisp while the meat cooked through relatively quickly. Finally, we used the caramelized drippings, or fond, left in the pan to make a quick and flavorful sauce of garlic, sherry, and chicken broth. If using kosher chicken, do not brine. If brining the chicken, do not season with salt in step 1.

 2 **(12-ounce) bone-in split chicken breasts, trimmed and brined if desired (see page 115)**
    Salt and pepper
 2 **teaspoons vegetable oil**
 3 **garlic cloves, sliced thin**
 ½ **teaspoon all-purpose flour**
 ½ **cup chicken broth**
 ¼ **cup dry sherry**
 2 **sprigs fresh thyme**
 1 **tablespoon butter, chilled**
 ½ **teaspoon lemon juice**

1. Adjust oven rack to lowest position and heat oven to 450 degrees. Pat chicken dry with paper towels and season with salt and pepper.

2. Heat oil in 10-inch ovensafe skillet over medium-high heat until just smoking. Lay chicken skin side down in skillet and cook until well browned on first side, 6 to 8 minutes, reducing heat if pan begins to scorch. Flip chicken and continue to cook until lightly browned, about 3 minutes.

3. Flip chicken skin side down and transfer skillet to oven. Roast until chicken registers 160 degrees, 15 to 18 minutes.

4. Using potholders (skillet handle will be hot), remove skillet from oven. Transfer chicken to serving platter and tent loosely with aluminum foil.

5. Being careful of hot skillet handle, pour off all but 1 tablespoon fat from skillet, add garlic, and cook over medium heat until softened, about 2 minutes. Stir in flour and cook for 1 minute. Whisk in broth, sherry, and thyme sprigs, scraping up any browned bits. Bring to simmer and cook until slightly thickened, about 5 minutes. Stir in any accumulated chicken juices and simmer for 30 seconds. Off heat, remove thyme sprigs and whisk in butter and lemon juice. Season with salt and pepper to taste. Pour sauce over chicken and serve.

VARIATION

Pan-Roasted Chicken Breasts with Pomegranate and Balsamic Sauce

Reduce amount of chicken broth to ¼ cup. Substitute 1 minced small shallot for garlic, ½ cup pomegranate juice for sherry, and ½ teaspoon balsamic vinegar for lemon juice.

Trimming Split Chicken Breasts

Split chicken breasts are sold with a rib section still attached. To remove it, use kitchen shears to trim rib section from each breast, following vertical line of fat from tapered end of breast up to socket where wing was attached.

Weeknight Roast Chicken

SERVES 2

✔ **WHY THIS RECIPE WORKS:** To get a beautifully browned, perfectly roasted chicken for two on the table any night of the week, we skipped brining and turned to a hybrid roasting technique. We began by roasting a small chicken in a ripping-hot skillet. We started the chicken thigh side down to give the longer-cooking dark meat a head start, so that both thighs and breasts would cook through in sync. After the skin crisped, we turned the oven off to cook the breast meat through gently, which yielded flawless results every time. And while the chicken rested before carving, we simply moved the skillet to the stovetop to turn the flavorful pan juices into a tasty sauce.

Brining and Salting Chicken

We often rely on one of two methods to boost flavor and juiciness in delicate white meat chicken: brining or salting. Salting requires more time than brining, but it won't thwart the goal of crisp skin. Brining works faster and is best for lean cuts because it adds, rather than merely retains, moisture. Note that kosher chicken or "enhanced" chicken has already been treated with salt and should not be brined or salted.

HOW BRINING WORKS: Brining chicken involves soaking the raw chicken in a saltwater solution before cooking. The brining solution flows into the meat, distributing moisture and seasoning and protecting the meat from drying out. Brined meat retains more of its moisture as it cooks, resulting in juicier, more flavorful meat. We prefer to use table salt for brining since it dissolves quickly in the water.

CUT	WATER	TABLE SALT	TIME
2 (6- to 8-ounce) boneless, skinless chicken breasts	3 cups	1½ tablespoons	30 minutes to 1 hour
2 (12-ounce) bone-in chicken breasts	1 quart	¼ cup	30 minutes to 1 hour
1½ pounds bone-in chicken pieces	1 quart	¼ cup	30 minutes to 1 hour
1 (3- to 3½-pound) whole chicken	2 quarts	½ cup	1 hour
2 (1¼- to 1½-pound) Cornish game hens	2 quarts	½ cup	30 minutes to 1 hour

HOW SALTING WORKS: When salt is applied to raw chicken, juices inside are drawn to the surface. The salt then dissolves in the exuded liquid, forming a brine that is eventually reabsorbed by the chicken. The salt changes the structure of the muscle proteins, allowing them to hold on to more of their own natural juices. Kosher salt is best for salting because it's easier to distribute the salt evenly over the meat. We use Diamond Crystal Kosher Salt; if using Morton Kosher Salt, reduce the amounts listed by one-third.

SALTING BONE-IN CHICKEN PIECES: Apply ¾ teaspoon salt per pound of chicken evenly between skin and meat, leaving skin attached. Let rest in refrigerator on wire rack set in rimmed baking sheet for at least 6 hours or up to 24 hours. (Wrap with plastic wrap if salting for longer than 12 hours.)

SALTING A WHOLE CHICKEN: Apply 1 teaspoon salt per pound of chicken evenly inside cavity and under skin of breast and legs. Let rest in refrigerator on wire rack set in rimmed baking sheet for at least 6 hours or up to 24 hours. (Wrap with plastic wrap if salting for longer than 12 hours.)

CHICKEN

1 tablespoon kosher salt

½ teaspoon pepper

1 (3- to 3½-pound) whole chicken, giblets discarded

1 tablespoon olive oil

PAN SAUCE

1 shallot, minced

1 cup chicken broth

2 teaspoons Dijon mustard

2 tablespoons unsalted butter, chilled

2 teaspoons minced fresh tarragon

2 teaspoons lemon juice

Pepper

1. FOR THE CHICKEN: Adjust oven rack to middle position, place 12-inch ovensafe skillet on rack, and heat oven to 450 degrees. Combine salt and pepper in bowl. Pat chicken dry with paper towels. Rub entire surface with oil. Sprinkle evenly all over with salt mixture and rub in mixture with your hands to coat evenly. Tie legs together with kitchen twine and tuck wingtips behind back.

2. Transfer chicken, breast side up, to preheated skillet in oven. Roast chicken until breast registers 120 degrees and thighs register 135 degrees, 25 to 35 minutes. Turn off oven and leave chicken in oven until breast registers 160 degrees and thighs register 175 degrees, 25 to 35 minutes.

3. Using potholders (skillet handle will be hot), remove skillet from oven. Transfer chicken to carving board and let rest, uncovered, for 20 minutes.

4. FOR THE PAN SAUCE: Being careful of hot skillet handle, remove all but 1 tablespoon fat from skillet using large spoon, leaving any fond and jus in skillet. Place skillet over medium-high heat, add shallot, and cook until softened, about 2 minutes. Stir in broth and mustard, scraping up browned bits. Bring to simmer and cook until reduced to ¾ cup, about 3 minutes. Stir in any accumulated chicken juices and simmer for 30 seconds. Off heat, whisk in butter, tarragon, and lemon juice. Season with pepper to taste; cover to keep warm. Carve chicken and serve with pan sauce.

Honey-Roasted Cornish Game Hens
SERVES 2

✔ **WHY THIS RECIPE WORKS:** Inexpensive and quick-cooking, Cornish game hens are ideal when cooking for two. But these small birds have many of the same pitfalls as whole chickens: The white and dark meat cook at different rates, and it can be a challenge to brown and lightly crisp the skin before the meat dries out. We decided to roast our birds on a wire rack set in a rimmed baking sheet to allow the heat of the oven to circulate around them. Turning the birds once partway through cooking helped the meat to cook more evenly. We also increased the oven temperature at the same time to give the skin rich color without drying out the meat. A quick glaze of honey and cider vinegar gave the birds great flavor and glossy exteriors. If using kosher hens, do not brine. If brining the hens, omit the salt in step 1.

Carving a Whole Chicken

1. Cut chicken where leg meets breast.

2. Pull leg quarter away from carcass. Separate joint by gently pressing leg out to side and pushing up on joint. Cut through joint to remove leg quarter.

3. Cut through joint that connects drumstick to thigh. Repeat steps 1 through 3 on chicken's other side.

4. Cut down along side of breastbone, pulling breast meat away from breastbone as you cut. Remove wing from breast by cutting through wing joint. Slice breast crosswise into slices. Repeat with other side.

Salt and pepper

½ teaspoon paprika

2 (1¼- to 1½-pound) whole Cornish game hens, giblets discarded, brined if desired (see page 115)

5 tablespoons honey

5 teaspoons cider vinegar

2 teaspoons plus ½ cup water

1 teaspoon cornstarch

½ cup chicken broth

½ teaspoon minced fresh thyme

1 tablespoon unsalted butter, chilled

1. Adjust oven rack to middle position and heat oven to 400 degrees. Set wire rack in rimmed baking sheet. Combine ¾ teaspoon salt, ¼ teaspoon pepper, and paprika in bowl.

2. Pat hens dry with paper towels. Sprinkle evenly all over with salt mixture and rub in mixture with your hands to coat evenly. Tuck wingtips behind backs and lay hens breast side down on prepared wire rack. Roast hens until backs are golden brown, about 25 minutes.

3. Meanwhile, bring ¼ cup honey and 1 tablespoon vinegar to simmer in small saucepan over medium-high heat. Whisk together 2 teaspoons water and ½ teaspoon cornstarch in small bowl, then whisk into saucepan. Continue to simmer glaze until thickened, 1 to 2 minutes. Remove from heat and cover to keep warm.

4. Remove hens from oven and brush backs with one-third of glaze. Flip hens breast side up and brush with half of remaining glaze. Continue to roast for 15 minutes.

5. Remove hens from oven and increase oven temperature to 450 degrees. Pour remaining ½ cup water and broth into baking sheet. Brush hens with remaining glaze and continue to roast until glaze is spotty brown and breasts register 160 degrees and thighs register 175 degrees, 5 to 10 minutes. Transfer hens to serving platter and let rest, uncovered, for 10 minutes.

6. Pour liquid from baking sheet into now-empty saucepan and let settle for 5 minutes. Using large spoon, skim excess fat from surface of liquid. Stir in thyme and remaining 1 tablespoon honey, bring to simmer, and cook until sauce is reduced to ½ cup, 2 to 6 minutes.

7. Whisk together remaining 2 teaspoons vinegar and remaining ½ teaspoon cornstarch in bowl, then whisk into saucepan. Continue to simmer sauce until thickened, 1 to 2 minutes. Stir in any accumulated juices and simmer for 30 seconds. Off heat, whisk in butter and season with salt and pepper to taste. Serve hens with sauce.

For moist, seasoned chicken perfect for wrapping in soft tortillas, we poach the chicken breasts right in a flavorful marinade.

Chicken Soft Tacos

SERVES 2

✔ **WHY THIS RECIPE WORKS:** We like the convenience of boneless, skinless chicken breasts in chicken tacos, but the meat can easily turn out dry and rubbery. We wanted to get tender, shreddable meat infused with spicy flavor. We poached the chicken in a simple but flavorful combination of bright cilantro, sweet orange juice, and savory Worcestershire sauce. Once it was tender, we set it aside to rest while we reduced the poaching liquid to make a sauce. We then stirred in fresh cilantro and piquant yellow mustard, which nicely balanced the sweet sauce. Tossed in the sauce, dolloped with spicy chipotle sour cream, and wrapped in warm tortillas, our chicken filling was incredibly moist and laced with spice, heat, and tang. To make this dish more or less spicy, adjust the amount of chipotle chiles. Serve with your favorite taco toppings.

1 teaspoon vegetable oil

3 garlic cloves, minced

1 teaspoon minced canned chipotle chile in adobo sauce

½ cup minced fresh cilantro

½ cup orange juice

1 tablespoon Worcestershire sauce

2 (6- to 8-ounce) boneless, skinless chicken breasts, trimmed and pounded if necessary

1 teaspoon yellow mustard

Salt and pepper

½ cup sour cream

6 (6-inch) corn tortillas, warmed

1. Heat oil in 10-inch nonstick skillet over medium heat until shimmering. Stir in garlic and ½ teaspoon chipotle and cook until fragrant, about 30 seconds. Stir in 5 tablespoons cilantro, orange juice, and Worcestershire. Lay chicken in skillet and bring to simmer over medium-low heat, 10 to 15 minutes.

2. When water is simmering, flip chicken, cover, and continue to cook until chicken registers 160 degrees, 10 to 15 minutes.

3. Transfer chicken to cutting board, let cool slightly, then shred into bite-size pieces using 2 forks. Meanwhile, continue to simmer poaching liquid over medium heat until slightly thickened and reduced to ⅓ cup, about 2 minutes. Off heat, stir in mustard, 2 tablespoons cilantro, and shredded chicken and let sit until heated through, about 2 minutes. Season with salt and pepper to taste.

4. Combine sour cream, remaining ½ teaspoon chipotle, and remaining 1 tablespoon cilantro in bowl. Season with salt and pepper to taste. Serve chicken with warm tortillas and sour cream sauce.

Chicken Fajitas

SERVES 2

✓ **WHY THIS RECIPE WORKS:** Grilled chicken fajitas are a backyard favorite. We wanted to create full-of-flavor fajitas that we could enjoy year-round. First we cooked the chicken quickly in a skillet to give it a well-browned exterior while keeping the interior juicy. Then we tossed the chicken with a tangy marinade of lime juice, cilantro, and Worcestershire sauce, which mimicked the savory smokiness of the grill. While the chicken rested, we took advantage of the flavorful fond left in the skillet to sauté the peppers and onions. To make these fajitas spicy, add a sliced jalapeño along with the bell pepper. Serve with your favorite fajita toppings.

2 (6- to 8-ounce) boneless, skinless chicken breasts, trimmed and pounded if necessary

Salt and pepper

2 tablespoons vegetable oil

1 red, green, or yellow bell pepper, stemmed, seeded, and cut into ½-inch-wide strips

1 small red onion, halved and sliced thin

2 tablespoons water

1 teaspoon chili powder

2 tablespoons lime juice

1 tablespoon chopped fresh cilantro

1 teaspoon Worcestershire sauce

½ teaspoon brown sugar

6 (6-inch) flour tortillas, warmed

1. Pat chicken dry with paper towels and season with salt and pepper. Heat 1 tablespoon oil in 10-inch nonstick skillet over medium-high heat until just smoking. Lay chicken in skillet and cook until well browned on first side, 6 to 8 minutes. Flip chicken, reduce heat to medium, and continue to cook until chicken registers 160 degrees, 6 to 8 minutes. Transfer chicken to cutting board, tent loosely with aluminum foil, and let rest while preparing vegetables.

2. Add bell pepper, onion, water, chili powder, and ¼ teaspoon salt to now-empty skillet and cook over medium heat until vegetables are softened, 5 to 7 minutes; transfer to serving platter.

3. Meanwhile, whisk lime juice, cilantro, Worcestershire, brown sugar, ¼ teaspoon salt, and remaining 1 tablespoon oil together in large bowl. Cut chicken into ¼-inch-thick slices and toss with lime juice mixture. Arrange chicken on platter with vegetables and serve with warm tortillas.

Warming Tortillas

Warming the tortillas to soften them is crucial. If your tortillas are dry, pat each with a little water before warming them. Wrap warm tortillas in foil or a clean dish towel to keep them warm and soft.

Warm tortillas, one at a time, directly on cooking grate over medium gas flame until slightly charred around edges, about 30 seconds per side. Or warm, one at a time, in dry skillet over medium-high heat until softened and speckled brown, 20 to 30 seconds per side.

Thai Chicken with Basil

SERVES 2 `LIGHT`

✔ **WHY THIS RECIPE WORKS:** Capturing the flavors of this traditional Thai dish required not only the right ingredients but also learning a whole new way to stir-fry. Stir-frying at a low temperature (versus the usual high-heat method) allowed us to add aromatics and basil in the beginning so they infused the dish with flavor. Grinding the chicken in a food processor gave us coarse-textured meat that retained moisture during cooking. Oyster sauce and vinegar added rich but bright flavor. Stirring in more basil at the end added a fresh finish and bold basil flavor. For a mild version of the dish, remove the seeds and ribs from the chiles. If fresh Thai chiles are unavailable, substitute two serranos or one medium jalapeño. Serve with rice. For the nutritional information for this recipe, see page 413.

A double dose of basil (chopped leaves sautéed to start and whole leaves stirred in at the end) infuses this Thai dish with fresh flavor.

  1 cup fresh basil leaves
  2 green or red Thai chiles, stemmed
  1 garlic clove, peeled
2½ teaspoons fish sauce, plus extra for serving
1½ teaspoons oyster sauce
1½ teaspoons sugar, plus extra for serving
  ½ teaspoon distilled white vinegar, plus extra for serving
  1 (8-ounce) boneless, skinless chicken breast, trimmed and cut into 2-inch pieces
  1 shallot, sliced thin
  1 tablespoon vegetable oil
    Red pepper flakes

1. Pulse ½ cup basil, Thai chiles, and garlic in food processor until finely chopped, 10 to 12 pulses, scraping down sides of bowl as needed. Transfer 1½ teaspoons of basil mixture to small bowl and stir in 1½ teaspoons fish sauce, oyster sauce, sugar, and vinegar. Transfer remaining basil mixture to 10-inch nonstick skillet.

2. Without washing food processor bowl, pulse chicken and remaining 1 teaspoon fish sauce in food processor until meat is coarsely chopped, 6 to 8 pulses; transfer to medium bowl and refrigerate for 15 minutes.

3. Stir shallot and oil into basil mixture in skillet. Cook over medium-low heat, stirring constantly, until garlic and shallot are golden brown, 5 to 8 minutes. (Mixture should start to sizzle after about 1½ minutes; if it doesn't, adjust heat accordingly.)

4. Stir in chopped chicken and cook over medium heat, breaking up chicken with wooden spoon, until only traces of pink remain, 2 to 4 minutes. Add reserved basil–fish sauce mixture and cook, stirring constantly, until chicken is no longer pink, about 1 minute. Stir in remaining ½ cup basil leaves and cook, stirring constantly, until basil is wilted, 30 to 60 seconds. Serve immediately, passing extra fish sauce, sugar, vinegar, and pepper flakes separately.

Sweet-and-Sour Chicken with Pineapple and Red Onion

SERVES 2 `LIGHT`

✔ **WHY THIS RECIPE WORKS:** We wanted a sweet-and-sour chicken with all the flavor—but not the fat—of a Chinese restaurant version. We started by marinating the chicken in a fragrant mixture of red wine vinegar, orange juice, ketchup, and soy sauce, reserving some of the marinade to use as the sauce. We steamed the vegetables until softened then sautéed the marinated chicken in the same pan. Next, we cooked an aromatic mixture of ginger and garlic. Finally, we added the vegetables back in along with fresh pineapple and simmered everything until the sauce was thick and glossy. To make the chicken easier to slice, freeze it for 15 minutes. Serve with rice. For the nutritional information for this recipe, see page 413.

- 3 tablespoons red wine vinegar
- 3 tablespoons orange juice
- 3 tablespoons sugar
- 1½ tablespoons ketchup
- 1 tablespoon soy sauce
- 2 teaspoons cornstarch
- 12 ounces boneless, skinless chicken breasts, trimmed and sliced ¼ inch thick
- 2 teaspoons toasted sesame oil
- 2 garlic cloves, minced
- 2 teaspoons grated fresh ginger
- 1 small red onion, halved and sliced ½ inch thick
- ½ cup water
- 4 ounces snow peas, strings removed, halved crosswise
- 1 cup ½-inch pineapple pieces
- 2 scallions, sliced thin

1. Whisk vinegar, orange juice, sugar, ketchup, soy sauce, and cornstarch together in small bowl. Measure 1 tablespoon sauce into medium bowl, then stir in chicken and 1 teaspoon oil. Cover and marinate chicken in refrigerator for at least 10 minutes or up to 30 minutes. Meanwhile, in separate bowl, combine garlic, ginger, and remaining 1 teaspoon oil.

2. Cook onion and water, covered, in 12-inch nonstick skillet over high heat until water is boiling and onion begins to soften, about 5 minutes. Stir in snow peas and cook, uncovered, until water has evaporated and vegetables are crisp-tender, about 2 minutes; transfer to bowl.

3. Return now-empty skillet to high heat. Add chicken, break up any clumps, and cook until lightly browned on all sides, about 6 minutes. Push chicken to sides of skillet. Add garlic mixture to center and cook, mashing mixture into skillet, until fragrant, about 30 seconds. Stir garlic mixture into chicken.

4. Stir in pineapple and cooked vegetable mixture. Whisk sauce to recombine, then add to skillet. Cook, stirring constantly, until sauce is thickened, about 1 minute. Transfer to serving platter, sprinkle with scallions, and serve.

Slicing Chicken Breasts Thin

Slice breast across grain into ¼-inch-thick strips that are 1½ to 2 inches long. Cut center pieces in half so they are approximately same length as end pieces.

Sichuan Orange Chicken with Broccoli

SERVES 2 · LIGHT

✔ **WHY THIS RECIPE WORKS:** For sweet and spicy orange chicken with real orange flavor, we used both orange juice and orange zest. We added the zest and juice to our marinade along with sweet hoisin sauce, salty soy sauce, and spicy chili-garlic sauce. Red bell pepper and scallions provided flavor, color, and textural contrast to the tender chicken breasts, and steaming them in the skillet gave us the perfect crisp-tender texture. A smoking-hot skillet ensured that the marinated chicken cooked through without drying out. To make the chicken easier to slice, freeze it for 15 minutes. For a spicier dish, use the larger amount of chili-garlic sauce. Serve with rice. For the nutritional information for this recipe, see page 413.

- 2 tablespoons hoisin sauce
- 1 tablespoon soy sauce
- 2 teaspoons cornstarch
- 2–3 teaspoons Asian chili-garlic sauce
- 1 teaspoon grated orange zest plus ¼ cup juice
- 12 ounces boneless, skinless chicken breasts, trimmed and sliced ¼ inch thick
- 2 teaspoons toasted sesame oil
- 2 garlic cloves, minced
- 2 teaspoons grated fresh ginger
- 8 ounces broccoli florets, cut into 1-inch pieces
- 1 small red bell pepper, stemmed, seeded, and cut into 2-inch-long matchsticks
- ¼ cup water
- 1 scallion, sliced thin

1. Whisk hoisin, soy sauce, cornstarch, chili-garlic sauce, and orange zest and juice together in small bowl. Measure 1 tablespoon sauce into medium bowl, then stir in chicken and 1 teaspoon oil. Cover and marinate chicken in refrigerator for at least 10 minutes or up to 30 minutes. Meanwhile, in separate bowl, combine garlic, ginger, and remaining 1 teaspoon oil.

2. Cook broccoli, bell pepper, and water, covered, in 12-inch nonstick skillet over high heat until water is boiling and vegetables begin to soften, about 3 minutes. Uncover and continue to cook until water has evaporated and vegetables are crisp-tender, about 2 minutes; transfer to bowl.

3. Return now-empty skillet to high heat. Add chicken, break up any clumps, and cook until lightly browned on all sides, about 6 minutes. Push chicken to sides of skillet.

Add garlic mixture to center and cook, mashing mixture into skillet, until fragrant, about 30 seconds. Stir garlic mixture into chicken.

4. Stir in cooked vegetable mixture. Whisk sauce to recombine, then add to skillet. Cook, stirring constantly, until sauce is thickened, about 1 minute. Transfer to serving platter, sprinkle with scallion, and serve.

Chicken Vesuvio

SERVES 2

✔ WHY THIS RECIPE WORKS: Chicken Vesuvio is a dish born in Chicago's Italian restaurants. With crisp-skinned chicken, bronzed potatoes, and a rich garlic, herb, and wine sauce, it's a welcome diversion from the ordinary baked chicken dinner. First we dredged chicken breasts in flour and browned them in a skillet. Then we cooked the potatoes in the same skillet until golden brown before adding the aromatics and deglazing the skillet with broth and white wine. We added the chicken back in to simmer until cooked through before finishing the sauce with frozen peas, butter, and a squeeze of fresh lemon juice. For a spicier dish, stir in ⅛ teaspoon red pepper flakes with the garlic in step 3.

We make this classic Italian dish of moist, tender chicken, crisp potatoes, bright peas, and a rich sauce all in a single skillet.

¼ cup all-purpose flour

2 (6- to 8-ounce) boneless, skinless chicken breasts, trimmed and pounded if necessary

   Salt and pepper

5 teaspoons olive oil

12 ounces red potatoes, unpeeled, cut into 1-inch pieces

1 garlic clove, minced

1 teaspoon minced fresh oregano or ¼ teaspoon dried

½ teaspoon minced fresh rosemary or ⅛ teaspoon dried

1 cup chicken broth

¼ cup dry white wine

½ cup frozen peas, thawed

2 tablespoons unsalted butter, chilled

1 teaspoon lemon juice

1. Spread flour in shallow dish. Pat chicken dry with paper towels and season with salt and pepper. Working with 1 breast at a time, dredge breasts in flour.

2. Heat 1 tablespoon oil in 10-inch nonstick skillet over medium-high heat until just smoking. Brown chicken lightly, 3 to 4 minutes per side; transfer to plate and wipe skillet clean.

3. Heat remaining 2 teaspoons oil in now-empty skillet over medium-high heat until shimmering. Add potatoes and cook, stirring occasionally, until golden brown, about 7 minutes. Stir in garlic, oregano, rosemary, and ⅛ teaspoon salt and cook until fragrant, about 30 seconds. Stir in broth and wine, scraping up any browned bits.

4. Nestle browned chicken into potatoes, add any accumulated juices, and bring to simmer. Reduce heat to medium-low, cover, and simmer until chicken registers 160 degrees, 12 to 18 minutes, flipping chicken halfway through cooking; transfer chicken to serving platter and tent loosely with aluminum foil.

5. Increase heat to medium and continue to simmer potatoes and sauce, uncovered, until potatoes are tender and sauce is slightly thickened, 5 to 7 minutes. Using slotted spoon, transfer potatoes to platter with chicken. Off heat, stir peas, butter, and lemon juice into sauce and season with salt and pepper to taste. Pour sauce over chicken and potatoes and serve.

Cooking Oils

In the test kitchen, we use different cooking oils to suit the flavor and cooking temperature requirements of the recipe at hand. Here are the oils we commonly use. Aside from nut, peanut, and sesame oils, which belong in the refrigerator, keep cooking oils in a cool, dark pantry to prevent rancidity.

VEGETABLE OIL

Loosely speaking, a vegetable oil is made from any number of "vegetable" sources, including nuts, grains, beans, seeds, and olives. In the narrow confines of recipe writing, it usually refers to one of the more popular brands of cooking oil labeled "vegetable oil"; on inspection of the ingredient label, you'll usually find that these generic vegetable oils consist of soybean oil. These oils, and canola oil (a vegetable oil prepared from rapeseed), have high smoke points and almost no flavor; we use them for shallow frying, sautéing, stir-frying, and in dressings with strong flavors. With the exception of canola oil (which can give food an off-flavor when the oil is heated for a long time), these oils are also fine for deep frying.

OLIVE OIL

Also called "pure" olive oil, this product adds some—but not too much—fruity flavor to foods. Unlike extra-virgin olive oil, basic olive oil has been refined so it has a higher smoke point. We use it to brown meats, to start soups and stews, and in sauces and dressings with strong flavors. We especially like to use olive oil for dishes with Mediterranean flavors.

EXTRA-VIRGIN OLIVE OIL

Because extra-virgin olive oil's strong flavors dissipate when exposed to high heat, we use it in dishes that are cooked quickly. We also use it to dress vegetables and to drizzle over soups and grilled foods, and it's our choice in most vinaigrettes. It will lose freshness, even unopened, rather quickly. After 12 months, you can taste the difference, and after 18 months the oil should be replaced. Depending on the region, the harvest occurs between September and December, so a bottle labeled "2013" will be past its prime in 2015.

TOASTED SESAME OIL

The potent flavor of toasted sesame oil (sometimes labeled Asian sesame oil) fades quickly when exposed to heat, so we add this oil in the final moments of cooking. We use toasted sesame oil in Asian-inspired dishes, dressings, sauces, and marinades. It is highly perishable, so store it in the refrigerator.

PEANUT OIL

Refined peanut oil, such as **Planters**, is our first choice for deep frying. It has a neutral flavor and high smoke point, and it doesn't break down and impart off-flavors, even with prolonged heat (a problem we've had with other oils). Unrefined peanut oil, which has a nutty flavor that we like in stir-fries, is sold in small bottles for a hefty price.

Chicken Pot Pie

SERVES 2

✓ **WHY THIS RECIPE WORKS:** To simplify chicken pot pie for two, we opted to make two individual pies. Two 12-ounce ramekins were the perfect size vessels. A single boneless, skinless chicken breast was easy to work with and substantial enough for two pies when combined with the rest of the ingredients. Cooking the chicken right in the sauce enriched its flavor and cut down on dishes. A little soy sauce added complex, meaty flavor without a lengthy simmer. Parcooking the crusts on a baking sheet ensured they didn't collapse into the filling. We prefer the flavor and texture of homemade pie dough here; however, you can substitute 1 (9-inch) store-bought pie dough round. If using store-bought pie dough, parbake the crusts for only 7 minutes in step 1. You will need two ovensafe 12-ounce ramekins or bowls for this recipe.

1   recipe Classic Single-Crust Pie Dough (page 369)
2   tablespoons unsalted butter
2   carrots, peeled and sliced ¼ inch thick
1   small onion, chopped fine
1   small celery rib, sliced ¼ inch thick
     Salt and pepper
2   garlic cloves, minced
1   teaspoon minced fresh thyme
3   tablespoons all-purpose flour
1¾   cups chicken broth
⅓   cup heavy cream
½   teaspoon soy sauce
1   (8-ounce) boneless, skinless chicken breast, trimmed
¼   cup frozen peas
2   teaspoons minced fresh parsley
¼   teaspoon lemon juice

1. Adjust oven rack to middle position and heat oven to 450 degrees. Roll out dough on parchment paper to 12-inch round, about ¼ inch thick. Using 12-ounce ovensafe ramekin as guide, cut out 2 rounds of dough about ½ inch larger than diameter of ramekin. Fold under and crimp outer ½ inch of dough round, then cut 3 vents in center of each crust. Slide parchment paper with crusts onto rimmed baking sheet. Bake until crusts just begin to brown and no longer look raw, 10 to 12 minutes; set aside.

2. Meanwhile, melt butter in medium saucepan over medium heat. Add carrots, onion, celery, and ½ teaspoon salt and cook until vegetables are softened and browned, 8 to 10 minutes. Stir in garlic and thyme and cook until fragrant, about 30 seconds. Stir in flour and cook for 1 minute.

3. Slowly whisk in broth, cream, and soy sauce, scraping up any browned bits. Nestle chicken into sauce and bring to simmer. Cover, reduce heat to medium-low, and cook until chicken registers 160 degrees, 10 to 15 minutes. Transfer chicken to plate; let cool slightly. Using 2 forks, shred chicken into bite-size pieces.

4. Meanwhile, return pan with sauce to medium heat and simmer until thickened and sauce measures 2 cups, about 5 minutes. Off heat, return shredded chicken and accumulated juice to pan. Stir in peas, parsley, and lemon juice and season with salt and pepper to taste.

5. Divide filling between ramekins and place parbaked crusts on top of filling. Place pot pies on baking sheet and bake until crusts are deep golden brown and filling is bubbling, 10 to 15 minutes. Let pot pies cool for 10 minutes before serving.

Chicken and Couscous with Dried Fruit and Smoked Almonds

SERVES 2

✔ **WHY THIS RECIPE WORKS:** This easy yet elegant chicken and couscous dish relies on just one 10-inch skillet to cook the chicken, sauté the aromatics, and simmer the couscous. Cooking the chicken first meant we were able to capitalize on the flavorful browned bits, or fond, left behind to infuse the couscous with deep, savory flavor. And since couscous cooks so quickly, it came together in a flash while the chicken rested. For some crunch and more savory depth, we stirred in a handful of chopped smoked almonds. The smoky flavor contrasted nicely with the sweetness of the dried apricots and added an unexpected twist to this simple dinner. Be sure to use regular (or fine-grain) couscous; large-grain couscous, often labeled Israeli-style, takes much longer to cook and won't work in this recipe.

¼ cup all-purpose flour
2 (6- to 8-ounce) boneless, skinless chicken breasts, trimmed and pounded if necessary
Salt and pepper
2 tablespoons olive oil
1 shallot, minced
½ cup couscous
½ teaspoon garam masala
¾ cup chicken broth
¼ cup dried apricots, chopped coarse
2 tablespoons coarsely chopped smoked almonds
1 tablespoon minced fresh parsley

1. Spread flour in shallow dish. Pat chicken dry with paper towels and season with salt and pepper. Working with 1 breast at a time, dredge breasts in flour.

2. Heat 1 tablespoon oil in 10-inch skillet over medium-high heat until just smoking. Lay chicken in skillet and cook until well browned on first side, 6 to 8 minutes. Flip chicken, reduce heat to medium, and continue to cook until chicken registers 160 degrees, 6 to 8 minutes; transfer to serving platter and tent loosely with aluminum foil.

3. Heat remaining 1 tablespoon oil in now-empty skillet over medium heat until shimmering. Add shallot and ¼ teaspoon salt and cook until softened, about 2 minutes. Stir in couscous and garam masala and cook until fragrant, about 30 seconds. Stir in broth and apricots, scraping up any browned bits. Bring to brief simmer, then remove from heat, cover, and let sit until liquid is absorbed and grains are tender, about 3 minutes.

4. Uncover and fluff grains with fork. Stir in almonds and parsley and season with salt and pepper to taste. Serve chicken with couscous.

Chicken and Orzo with Spinach and Feta

SERVES 2

✔ **WHY THIS RECIPE WORKS:** To make this simple skillet chicken supper memorable, we wanted the side to be the star of the show. We chose orzo, a small pasta that's quick and easy to cook. To add deep, complex flavor, we toasted the orzo until golden brown, then simmered it in just the right amount of chicken broth until perfectly tender. To give the dish Mediterranean flair and vibrant flavor, we added garlic, oregano, and red pepper flakes and stirred in baby spinach, briny feta, and a squeeze of bright lemon juice just before serving.

¾ cup orzo
2 (6- to 8-ounce) boneless, skinless chicken breasts, trimmed and pounded if necessary
Salt and pepper
1 tablespoon olive oil
2 garlic cloves, minced
1 teaspoon minced fresh oregano or ¼ teaspoon dried
Pinch red pepper flakes
1¼ cups chicken broth, plus extra as needed
4 ounces (4 cups) baby spinach
2 ounces feta cheese, crumbled (½ cup)
1½ teaspoons lemon juice

1. Toast orzo in 10-inch nonstick skillet over medium-high heat until golden brown, 3 to 5 minutes; transfer to bowl.

2. Pat chicken dry with paper towels and season with salt and pepper. Heat 1 teaspoon oil in now-empty skillet over medium-high heat until just smoking. Brown chicken lightly, 3 to 4 minutes per side; transfer to plate.

3. Add remaining 2 teaspoons oil, garlic, oregano, and pepper flakes to now-empty skillet and cook until fragrant, about 30 seconds. Stir in broth and toasted orzo.

4. Nestle browned chicken into orzo, add any accumulated juices, and bring to simmer. Reduce heat to medium-low, cover, and simmer until chicken registers 160 degrees, 10 to 12 minutes, flipping chicken halfway through cooking. Transfer chicken to serving platter, brushing any orzo that sticks to chicken back into skillet; tent loosely with aluminum foil.

5. Continue to cook orzo until al dente and creamy, 2 to 5 minutes, stirring in additional broth, 1 tablespoon at a time, as needed to loosen consistency. Stir in spinach, 1 handful at a time, until wilted, about 2 minutes. Stir in feta and lemon juice and season with salt and pepper to taste. Serve chicken with orzo.

Chicken and Chorizo Paella

SERVES 2

✔ **WHY THIS RECIPE WORKS:** *Paella* is a fragrant Spanish rice dish usually loaded with meat, seafood, and vegetables. While delicious, it's quite a labor of love. We wanted to translate this classic into a streamlined weeknight version with all the flavor of the original. A combination of chorizo sausage and chicken breasts was hearty enough that we could forgo the seafood altogether. A rich *sofrito* of onion, garlic, and tomato gave our dish a deep flavor, and bright peas and briny olives added color and dimension. Just a pinch of pricey saffron was enough to give our paella authentic Spanish flavor. We like to use short-grain Valencia rice for this dish, but you can substitute Arborio rice if you cannot find Valencia. Do not substitute long-grain rice. Look for large, pitted green olives at the olive bar in the supermarket. Pimento-stuffed olives can be substituted for the large green olives in a pinch. To make the chicken easier to slice, freeze it for 15 minutes.

1½ **cups water**
½   **cup Valencia or Arborio rice**
    Salt and pepper
4   **teaspoons vegetable oil**
4   **ounces chorizo sausage, halved lengthwise and sliced ¼ inch thick**

With spicy chorizo and chicken, our streamlined version of classic Spanish paella captures all of the flavor in a fraction of the time.

1   **(8-ounce) boneless, skinless chicken breast, trimmed and sliced ¼ inch thick**
1   **small onion, chopped fine**
¾   **cup canned diced tomatoes, drained with juice reserved**
2   **garlic cloves, minced**
⅛   **teaspoon saffron threads, crumbled**
¼   **cup pitted large green olives, quartered**
¼   **cup frozen peas**

1. Combine 1 cup water, rice, and ⅛ teaspoon salt in bowl. Cover and microwave until rice is softened and most of liquid is absorbed, 6 to 8 minutes.

2. Meanwhile, heat 2 teaspoons oil in 10-inch nonstick skillet over medium-high heat until just smoking. Add chorizo and cook until lightly browned, about 2 minutes. Using slotted spoon, transfer chorizo to plate. Pat chicken dry with paper towels and season with salt and pepper. Add chicken to fat left in skillet, break up any clumps, and cook until lightly browned on all sides, about 4 minutes; transfer to plate with chorizo.

3. Heat remaining 2 teaspoons oil in now-empty skillet over medium heat until shimmering. Add onion and cook until softened, about 5 minutes. Stir in tomatoes and cook until beginning to soften and darken, 3 to 5 minutes. Stir in garlic and saffron and cook until fragrant, about 30 seconds. Stir in remaining ½ cup water and reserved tomato juice, scraping up any browned bits. Stir in parcooked rice, breaking up any large clumps, and bring to simmer. Reduce heat to medium-low, cover, and simmer until rice is tender and liquid is absorbed, 8 to 12 minutes.

4. Stir in browned chorizo and chicken and any accumulated juices, olives, and peas and increase heat to medium-high. Cook, uncovered, until bottom layer of rice is golden and crisp, about 5 minutes, rotating skillet halfway through cooking to ensure even browning. Season with salt and pepper to taste and serve.

Chicken and Rice

SERVES 2

✔ **WHY THIS RECIPE WORKS:** For the ultimate easy week-night dinner, we wanted to streamline classic chicken and rice. To get perfectly al dente rice without overcooking the chicken, we microwaved the rice to parcook it, then added it to the pot with the chicken to cook through gently in the even heat of the oven. We chose bone-in, skin-on chicken thighs for rich flavor and seared them to get nicely browned skin. For aromatics, we quickly sautéed onion, garlic, and a little fresh thyme. A sprinkling of parsley finished the dish. You will need a medium ovensafe saucepan for this recipe.

This classic dinner boasts juicy chicken with crisp browned skin alongside rice flavored with onion, garlic, and thyme.

1¼ cups chicken broth
½ cup long-grain white rice
    Salt and pepper
4 (5- to 7-ounce) bone-in chicken thighs, trimmed
1 teaspoon vegetable oil
1 small onion, chopped fine
2 garlic cloves, minced
¾ teaspoon minced fresh thyme or ⅛ teaspoon dried
¼ cup dry white wine
2 tablespoons chopped fresh parsley

1. Adjust oven rack to lower-middle position and heat oven to 350 degrees. Combine ¾ cup broth, rice, and ¼ teaspoon salt in bowl. Cover and microwave until rice is softened and most of liquid is absorbed, 6 to 8 minutes.

2. Meanwhile, pat chicken dry with paper towels and season with salt and pepper. Heat oil in medium ovensafe saucepan over medium-high heat until just smoking. Brown chicken well, about 5 minutes per side; transfer to plate.

3. Pour off all but 1 teaspoon fat from saucepan. Add onion and ¼ teaspoon salt and cook over medium-low heat until

softened and lightly browned, 5 to 7 minutes. Stir in garlic and thyme and cook until fragrant, about 30 seconds. Stir in remaining ½ cup broth and wine, scraping up any browned bits. Stir in parcooked rice, breaking up any large clumps, and bring to simmer. Place browned chicken skin side up on rice, cover, and bake until rice is cooked through and chicken registers 175 degrees, about 25 minutes.

4. Using potholders (saucepan handle will be hot), remove saucepan from oven. Transfer chicken to serving platter and tent chicken loosely with aluminum foil. Fluff rice with fork, cover, and let sit for 10 minutes. Stir in parsley and season with salt and pepper to taste. Serve chicken with rice.

VARIATIONS
Chicken and Rice with Five-Spice and Scallions
Substitute ¼ teaspoon five-spice powder for thyme and 2 thinly sliced scallions for parsley.

Chicken and Rice with Smoked Paprika and Cilantro
Substitute ¼ teaspoon smoked paprika for thyme and 2 tablespoons chopped fresh cilantro for parsley.

Braised Chicken Thighs with Potatoes, Fennel, and Tarragon

SERVES 2

✔ **WHY THIS RECIPE WORKS:** When done right, braised chicken thighs are the ultimate comfort food, with juicy meat surrounded by a rich pan sauce and tender vegetables. But most recipes make enough for a crowd; we wanted a simplified formula for braised chicken that could easily be made in a skillet. For the chicken, we chose bone-in thighs, which would retain more flavor and moisture over the extended cooking time thanks to their fat and connective tissue. We started by browning the thighs to develop a flavorful fond in the pan, then we removed the skin to prevent the final dish from being greasy. For the braising liquid, a combination of chicken broth and wine lent the dish acidity and depth of flavor. To make this dish a hearty meal, we added red potatoes, carrots, and onions, plus some sliced fennel and tarragon for a fresh finish.

4   (5- to 7-ounce) bone-in chicken thighs, trimmed
    Salt and pepper
2   teaspoons vegetable oil
8   ounces red potatoes, unpeeled, cut into ½-inch pieces
3   carrots, peeled and sliced ½ inch thick
1   small onion, chopped fine
1   garlic clove, minced
½   teaspoon minced fresh thyme or ⅛ teaspoon dried
1¼ cups chicken broth
¼   cup dry white wine
½   fennel bulb, stalks discarded, bulb cored and sliced thin
2   tablespoons minced fresh tarragon
1   teaspoon lemon juice

1. Pat chicken dry with paper towels and season with salt and pepper. Heat oil in 10-inch skillet over medium-high heat until just smoking. Brown chicken well, about 5 minutes per side. Transfer chicken to plate, let cool slightly, then remove skin.

2. Pour off all but 1 tablespoon fat from skillet. Add potatoes, carrots, onion, and ¼ teaspoon salt and cook over medium heat until onion is softened, about 5 minutes. Stir in garlic and thyme and cook until fragrant, about 30 seconds. Stir in broth and wine, scraping up any browned bits.

3. Nestle browned chicken into vegetables, add any accumulated juices, and bring to a simmer. Reduce heat to medium-low, cover, and simmer until chicken is very tender and almost falling off bone, about 1 hour, flipping chicken halfway through cooking. Transfer chicken to serving dish and tent loosely with aluminum foil.

4. Increase heat to medium, stir in fennel, and continue to simmer, uncovered, until vegetables are tender and sauce is slightly thickened, about 8 minutes. Stir in any accumulated chicken juices and simmer for 30 seconds. Off heat, stir in tarragon and lemon juice and season with salt and pepper to taste. Spoon vegetables and sauce over chicken and serve.

VARIATION

Braised Chicken Thighs with Potatoes, Carrots, Asparagus, and Dill

Substitute 4 ounces asparagus, trimmed and cut on bias into 2-inch lengths, for fennel and 2 tablespoons minced fresh dill for tarragon.

Removing Chicken Skin

Chicken skin is often slippery, making it a challenge to remove by hand, even when the chicken has been browned. To remove skin easily, use a paper towel to provide extra grip while pulling.

Chicken en Papillote with Zucchini and Tomatoes

SERVES 2   LIGHT

✔ **WHY THIS RECIPE WORKS:** Cooking *en papillote* allows meat to steam in its own juices, developing a delicate texture and intense, clean flavor. We wanted to update this French cooking method to make it simpler and faster. First we swapped the traditional intricately folded parchment for a simple aluminum foil packet. We knew that we needed the chicken and vegetables to cook through at the same rate, so dense vegetables like potatoes were out. We landed on a combination of zucchini and tomato and tossed them with a little olive oil, garlic, oregano, and red pepper flakes before adding them to the packet with the chicken. After just 25 minutes in the oven, the vegetables were tender and the chicken was exceptionally moist and flavorful. To prevent overcooking, open each packet promptly after baking. For the nutritional information for this recipe, see page 413.

2   (6- to 8-ounce) boneless, skinless chicken breasts, trimmed and pounded if necessary
    Salt and pepper
1   tablespoon extra-virgin olive oil

1 garlic clove, minced

1 teaspoon chopped fresh oregano

   Pinch red pepper flakes

2 plum tomatoes, cored, seeded, and chopped

1 zucchini, sliced ¼ inch thick

2 tablespoons chopped fresh basil

1. Adjust oven rack to middle position and heat oven to 450 degrees. Pat chicken dry with paper towels and season with salt and pepper.

2. Combine oil, garlic, oregano, pepper flakes, ⅛ teaspoon salt, and ⅛ teaspoon pepper in bowl. Toss half of oil mixture with tomatoes and toss remaining oil mixture separately with zucchini.

3. Cut two 14 by 12-inch rectangles of aluminum foil and lay them flat on counter. Shingle half of zucchini in center of each piece of foil. Place chicken breast on top of zucchini, then top with half of tomatoes. Tightly crimp foil into packets.

4. Set packets on rimmed baking sheet and bake until chicken registers 160 degrees, about 25 minutes.

5. Carefully open packets, allowing steam to escape away from you, and let cool briefly. Smooth out edges of foil and, using spatula, gently transfer chicken, vegetables, and any accumulated juices to individual plates. Sprinkle with basil and serve.

VARIATION

Chicken en Papillote with Artichokes, Lemon, and Tomatoes

For the nutritional information for this recipe, see page 413.

Substitute 1 teaspoon minced fresh thyme for oregano, 2 teaspoons grated lemon zest for red pepper flakes, and 9 ounces frozen artichoke hearts, thawed and patted dry, for zucchini. Add 1 thinly sliced shallot to artichoke and olive oil mixture in step 2.

Making Foil Packets

1. Assemble ingredients in center of 14 by 12-inch sheet of aluminum foil as directed in recipe.

2. Bring longer sides of foil up to meet over top and crimp edges to seal. Then, crimp open edges at either end of packets together to seal.

Cooking with Wine

Over the years, the test kitchen has developed hundreds of recipes with wine. Here's what we've found works best.

RED WINE

After testing more than 30 bottles of red wine, we divined a few guidelines about those that are best for cooking. Stick with blends like Côtes du Rhône or generically labeled "table" wines that use a combination of grapes to yield a balanced, fruity finish. If you prefer single-grape varietals, choose medium-bodied wines, such as Pinot Noir and Merlot. Avoid oaky wines like Cabernet Sauvignon, which turn bitter when cooked.

WHITE WINE

The best white wines for cooking are medium-bodied, unoaked varieties that aren't terribly sweet. We prefer clean, crisp, dry Sauvignon Blancs to sweet Rieslings or heavily oaked Chardonnays, which can dominate subtle flavors. We have found that only Sauvignon Blanc consistently boils down to a "clean" yet sufficiently acidic flavor that meshes nicely with a variety of ingredients in savory recipes.

VERMOUTH

Dry vermouth makes a good substitute for white wine in many sauces and other savory recipes, and because it has a shelf life of several months, it's a great option for small households. Vermouth adds herbaceous notes to any dish and is a bit more alcoholic than white wine. Replace white wine with an equal amount of vermouth.

COOKING WINE

We've learned that when it comes to wine, it's best not to cook with anything you would not drink. This includes "cooking wines" sold in many supermarkets. They taste horrible and include a lot of sodium, so if the wine is cooked down it can make your recipe unappetizingly salty. That said, there's no need to spend a fortune on wine destined for sauces or stews. We've tested good $10 bottles versus better-tasting $30 wines and found that any differences in the glass disappear in a cooked application.

NONALCOHOLIC SUBSTITUTIONS FOR WINES

Broth can work as an equal replacement in sauces and stews that call for small amounts of wine. The dish won't taste exactly the same, but the recipe will work. For every ½ cup broth used, you should also stir in ½ teaspoon red or white wine vinegar or lemon juice before serving, which will mimic some of the acidity otherwise provided by the wine.

Simple Chicken Bake with Fennel, Tomatoes, and Olives

SERVES 2

✔ **WHY THIS RECIPE WORKS:** To turn simple baked chicken breasts into an inspiring main course, we wanted to include a bold sauce and an imaginative mix of vegetables. We started by flavoring the chicken with a garlic, shallot, and herb marinade. We chose a mix of easy-prep Mediterranean vegetables: whole cherry tomatoes, thinly sliced fennel, and kalamata olives. We tossed the vegetables with some reserved marinade; as they cooked, the tomatoes released juice that combined with the marinade to make a tasty sauce. Some fresh basil and lemon juice at the end completed the dish. You can substitute boneless, skinless breasts here if desired; marinate the boneless chicken as directed, but reduce the baking time by 10 to 15 minutes. The marinade takes the place of a brine in this recipe, so there's no need to brine the chicken.

CHICKEN

- ⅓ cup extra-virgin olive oil
- 1 shallot, minced
- 2 tablespoons water
- 2 tablespoons chopped fresh basil
- 4 garlic cloves, minced
- ½ teaspoon salt
- ⅛ teaspoon pepper
- 2 (12-ounce) bone-in split chicken breasts, trimmed

VEGETABLES

- 1 fennel bulb, stalks discarded, bulb halved, cored, and sliced thin
- 6 ounces cherry tomatoes
- ¼ cup pitted kalamata olives
- ¼ teaspoon salt
- ⅛ teaspoon pepper
- 1 tablespoon lemon juice
- 2 tablespoons chopped fresh basil

1. FOR THE CHICKEN: Whisk oil, shallot, water, basil, garlic, salt, and pepper together in bowl until well combined. Measure out and reserve ¼ cup marinade. Pour remaining marinade into 1-gallon zipper-lock bag, add chicken, seal bag tightly, and toss to coat. Marinate chicken in refrigerator for at least 1 hour or up to 24 hours. (If marinating chicken for more than 1 hour, refrigerate ¼ cup reserved marinade as well; return it to room temperature before using.)

2. FOR THE VEGETABLES: Adjust oven rack to middle position and heat oven to 450 degrees. In large bowl, combine 1 tablespoon reserved marinade with fennel, tomatoes, olives,

salt, and pepper and toss to coat. Transfer vegetables to 8-inch square baking dish.

3. Remove chicken from marinade and lay skin side up on top of vegetables; discard any marinade left in bag. Bake until chicken registers 160 degrees, 35 to 45 minutes. Meanwhile, stir lemon juice into remaining 3 tablespoons reserved marinade.

4. Transfer chicken and vegetables to serving platter along with juices from baking dish. Pour lemon-marinade mixture over chicken and let rest for 5 minutes. Sprinkle with basil and serve.

Parmesan and Basil–Stuffed Chicken with Roasted Carrots

SERVES 2

✔ **WHY THIS RECIPE WORKS:** We wanted an elegant yet easy recipe for stuffed chicken breasts and roasted carrots. We started with a no-fuss cream cheese filling with basil and garlic. Rather than turn to a fussy preparation for stuffing the breasts, we simply spooned the filling under the skin of bone-in chicken breasts; the skin held the filling in place, and the meat emerged from the oven moist and juicy. Brushing the skin with melted butter and baking the breasts in a hot 450-degree oven ensured crisp, golden brown skin. For a simple side, we tossed carrots with melted butter and a little brown sugar and roasted them alongside the chicken. It is important to buy chicken breasts with the skin still attached and intact; otherwise, the stuffing will leak out. Be sure to spread the carrots in an even layer halfway through baking to ensure that they cook through and brown properly. If using kosher chicken, do not brine. If brining the chicken, do not season with salt in step 2.

- 1 ounce Parmesan cheese, grated (½ cup)
- 1 ounce cream cheese, softened
- 2 tablespoons chopped fresh basil
- 1 tablespoon extra-virgin olive oil
- 1 small garlic clove, minced
  Salt and pepper
- 2 (12-ounce) bone-in split chicken breasts, trimmed and brined if desired (see page 115)
- 1 tablespoon unsalted butter, melted
- 6 small carrots, peeled and sliced ½ inch thick on bias
- 1½ teaspoons packed dark brown sugar

1. Adjust oven rack to middle position and heat oven to 450 degrees. Line rimmed baking sheet with aluminum foil. Mix Parmesan, cream cheese, basil, oil, garlic, pinch salt, and pinch pepper together in bowl.

2. Pat chicken dry with paper towels and season with salt and pepper. Use your fingers to gently loosen center portion of skin covering each breast. Using spoon, place half of cheese mixture underneath skin over center of each breast. Gently press on skin to spread out cheese mixture.

3. Arrange chicken skin side up on 1 side of baking sheet. Brush chicken with half of melted butter. Toss carrots with remaining melted butter and sugar and season with salt and pepper. Mound carrots in pile on baking sheet, opposite chicken.

4. Bake until chicken registers 160 degrees and carrots are browned and tender, 30 to 35 minutes, rotating sheet and spreading out carrots into even layer halfway through baking. Let chicken and carrots rest on sheet for 5 minutes before serving.

VARIATION

Goat Cheese and Olive–Stuffed Chicken with Roasted Carrots

Omit Parmesan, basil, and olive oil. Add 1½ ounces softened goat cheese, 2 tablespoons finely chopped pitted kalamata olives, and 1 teaspoon minced fresh oregano to cream cheese mixture.

Stuffing Bone-In Chicken Breasts

1. Using fingers, gently loosen center portion of skin covering each breast, making pocket for filling.

2. Using spoon, place filling underneath loosened skin, over center of each breast. Gently press on skin to spread out filling.

Roasted Chicken Breasts with Red Potatoes and Brussels Sprouts

SERVES 2

✔ **WHY THIS RECIPE WORKS:** For the ultimate easy roast chicken and vegetable dinner, we used bone-in, skin-on chicken breasts for roasted chicken flavor in less time. We tossed red potatoes, Brussels sprouts, and carrots with garlic and thyme and brushed the chicken with melted butter mixed with thyme. We spread the vegetables on a sheet pan and topped them with the chicken breasts so that they basted in the chicken's drippings as it roasted. A hot 475-degree oven gave us crisp, well-browned chicken skin by the time the breast meat was cooked to perfection. Be sure to use a light-colored baking sheet; nonstick or other dark pans will cause the vegetables to burn. If using kosher chicken, do not brine. If brining the chicken, do not season with salt in step 2.

- 6 ounces Brussels sprouts, trimmed and halved if small or quartered if large
- 1 red potato (6 ounces), unpeeled, cut into 1-inch pieces
- 2 carrots, peeled and cut into 2-inch lengths, thick ends halved lengthwise
- 4 shallots, peeled and halved
- 3 garlic cloves, peeled
- 1 tablespoon vegetable oil
- 2 teaspoons minced fresh thyme
- ½ teaspoon sugar
- Salt and pepper
- 1 tablespoon unsalted butter, melted
- 2 (12-ounce) bone-in split chicken breasts, trimmed and brined if desired (see page 115)

1. Adjust oven rack to upper-middle position and heat oven to 475 degrees. Toss Brussels sprouts, potato, carrots, shallots, garlic, oil, 1 teaspoon thyme, sugar, ¼ teaspoon salt, and ⅛ teaspoon pepper together in medium bowl. Combine melted butter, remaining 1 teaspoon thyme, ¼ teaspoon salt, and pinch pepper in small bowl.

2. Pat chicken dry with paper towels and season with salt and pepper. Place vegetables in single layer on rimmed baking sheet, arranging Brussels sprouts in center and leaving 2-inch border between vegetables and sides of sheet. Place chicken skin side up on top of Brussels sprouts.

3. Brush chicken with herb butter and roast until chicken registers 160 degrees, about 35 minutes, rotating sheet halfway through cooking. Transfer chicken to serving platter, tent loosely with aluminum foil, and let rest for 5 minutes. If necessary, return vegetables to oven until well browned and tender, 5 to 10 minutes. Toss vegetables with pan juices and transfer to platter with chicken. Serve.

VARIATION

Roasted Chicken Breasts with Fennel and Parsnips

Substitute ½ fennel bulb, cored and sliced into ½-inch wedges, for Brussels sprouts, and 4 ounces parsnips, peeled and cut into 2-inch pieces, thick ends halved lengthwise, for carrots.

CHAPTER 6

Beef, Pork, and Lamb

■ FAST (Start to finish in about 30 minutes)

■ LIGHT (See pages 413–414 for nutritional information)

Opposite: Pot-Roasted Steaks with Root Vegetables; Sautéed Boneless Pork Chops with Port Wine and Cherry Sauce; Roast Rack of Lamb with Whiskey Sauce

Pan-Seared Rib-Eye Steaks with Sweet-Tart Red Wine Sauce

SERVES 2 | **FAST**

✔ **WHY THIS RECIPE WORKS:** For easy-to-prepare yet elegant pan-seared steaks, we selected rib eyes for their rich, beefy flavor. Patting the steaks dry before cooking removed excess moisture that would inhibit browning. Heating the oil over medium-high heat until just smoking ensured our steaks developed a crisp, caramelized crust, and reducing the heat to medium once we flipped them allowed the steaks to cook through without developing a tough exterior. The fond left behind in the skillet formed the base for our pan sauce, a classic red wine sauce featuring balsamic vinegar, Dijon mustard, and a touch of brown sugar for a balanced sweet yet tart flavor. Use a good-quality medium-bodied wine, such as a Côtes du Rhône or Pinot Noir. We prefer these steaks cooked to medium-rare, but if you prefer them more or less done, see our guidelines on page 155.

- 2 (8-ounce) boneless rib-eye steaks, ¾ inch thick, trimmed
  Salt and pepper
- 1 tablespoon vegetable oil
- 1 shallot, minced
- 1 teaspoon packed brown sugar
- ¼ cup dry red wine
- ¼ cup chicken broth
- 2 teaspoons balsamic vinegar
- ½ teaspoon Dijon mustard
- 1 bay leaf
- 2 tablespoons unsalted butter, chilled
- ½ teaspoon minced fresh thyme

1. Pat steaks dry with paper towels and season with salt and pepper. Heat oil in 12-inch skillet over medium-high heat until just smoking. Lay steaks in skillet and cook until well browned on first side, 3 to 5 minutes. Flip steaks, reduce heat to medium, and continue to cook until meat registers 120 to 125 degrees (for medium-rare), 1 to 4 minutes; transfer to plate and tent loosely with aluminum foil.

2. Add shallot and sugar to fat left in skillet and cook over medium heat until shallot is just softened and browned and sugar is melted, about 1 minute. Stir in wine, broth, vinegar, mustard, and bay leaf, scraping up any browned bits. Bring to simmer and cook until sauce is slightly thickened, 2 to 4 minutes. Stir in any accumulated meat juices and simmer for 30 seconds. Discard bay leaf. Off heat, whisk in butter and thyme and season with salt and pepper to taste. Serve steaks with sauce.

Steak au Poivre with Brandied Cream Sauce

SERVES 2

✔ **WHY THIS RECIPE WORKS:** At its best, steak *au poivre* features a slightly sweet, smooth sauce with hints of shallot and brandy that's a perfect counterpoint to the fiery pungency of the peppercorn crust. We started with beefy, well-marbled boneless strip steaks. For the pepper crust, cracked black peppercorns provided the right amount of sharp bite, intense flavor, and subtle smokiness. To tame the heat from the peppercorns, we opted to coat only one side of the steaks. Pressing on the steaks with a cake pan as they cooked allowed us to get a good sear, which produced the fond that was key to developing a rich foundation of flavor for the sauce. Reserving a small amount of the brandy to stir into the sauce at the end ensured that its flavor came through. Do not substitute finely ground pepper for the cracked peppercorns here. We prefer these steaks cooked to medium-rare, but if you prefer them more or less done, see our guidelines on page 155.

- 2 (8-ounce) boneless strip steaks, ¾ inch thick, trimmed
  Salt and pepper
- 4 teaspoons peppercorns, cracked
- 5 teaspoons vegetable oil
- 1 shallot, minced
- 1 teaspoon all-purpose flour
- ¾ cup chicken broth
- 3 tablespoons brandy
- 2 tablespoons heavy cream
- 2 tablespoons minced fresh chives
- 2 teaspoons lemon juice
- ½ teaspoon Dijon mustard

1. Pat steaks dry with paper towels and season with salt. Rub cracked peppercorns evenly over 1 side of each steak, and, using your fingers, press peppercorns into steaks to make them adhere.

Cracking Peppercorns

Spread peppercorns on cutting board, place skillet on top, and, pressing down firmly with both hands, use rocking motion to crack peppercorns beneath "heel" of skillet.

2. Heat 1 tablespoon oil in 12-inch skillet over medium-high heat until just smoking. Lay steaks peppered side up in skillet, firmly press down on steaks with bottom of cake pan, and cook until well browned on first side, 3 to 5 minutes. Flip steaks and reduce heat to medium. Firmly press down on steaks with bottom of cake pan and continue to cook until meat registers 120 to 125 degrees (for medium-rare), 1 to 4 minutes; transfer to plate and tent loosely with aluminum foil. Pour off fat from skillet and remove any stray peppercorns.

3. Heat remaining 2 teaspoons oil in now-empty skillet over medium heat until shimmering. Add shallot and cook until softened, about 2 minutes. Stir in flour and cook for 1 minute. Whisk in broth and 2 tablespoons brandy, scraping up any browned bits. Bring to simmer and cook until sauce is slightly thickened, 6 to 8 minutes. Stir in cream and any accumulated meat juices and simmer for 30 seconds. Off heat, whisk in remaining 1 tablespoon brandy, chives, lemon juice, and mustard. Season with salt and pepper to taste. Serve steaks with sauce.

Perfect Filets Mignons with Horseradish Sauce

SERVES 2

✔ **WHY THIS RECIPE WORKS:** We wanted to develop a recipe for restaurant-style filets mignons we could make at home. For a rich, browned crust with a tender interior, we pan-seared oiled filets in a hot skillet until they were well browned on both sides. We then moved the steaks to the oven to finish cooking—this prevented the fond from burning and allowed the steaks to cook through evenly to a perfect medium-rare. Extremely tender yet mild, filets mignons benefit from a rich sauce, so while the steaks rested we prepared a creamy horseradish sauce to accompany them by combining sour cream, horseradish, a little mayonnaise, garlic, and a squeeze of lemon juice. We prefer these steaks cooked to medium-rare, but if you prefer them more or less done, see our guidelines on page 155.

5 teaspoons vegetable oil
2 (8-ounce) center-cut filets mignons, 1½ to 2 inches thick
   Salt and pepper
½ cup sour cream
2 tablespoons prepared horseradish
1 tablespoon mayonnaise
2 teaspoons lemon juice
1 small garlic clove, minced

Key Steps to Pan-Searing Steaks

Though few foods are as perfect as a grilled steak, pan-searing in a skillet over high heat works particularly well with steaks that are ¾ to 1½ inches thick. Because the bone can prevent bone-in steaks from even contact with the pan, we prefer boneless steaks for pan-searing. Here are our other tips for great steak.

DRY THE STEAKS: Browning a steak adds dramatically to its flavor. To ensure proper browning, make sure the meat is dry before it goes into the pan by patting it thoroughly with paper towels. This is especially important with previously frozen meat, which often releases a great deal of water.

SEASON THE MEAT ALL OVER: Season both sides of the meat with salt and pepper. It's OK to season ahead of time, but since salt draws juices to the surface, make sure if you are going to let the meat sit more than a couple of minutes that you allow enough time for that liquid to then be reabsorbed (we have found that 40 minutes is sufficient). This will actually flavor the meat more deeply.

USE THE RIGHT SIZE SKILLET AND GET IT HOT: Choose a traditional (not nonstick) skillet large enough to allow at least ¼ inch of space between the steaks; any closer together and the meat will steam instead of browning. Heat 1 tablespoon vegetable oil over medium-high heat until just smoking, then add the steaks. If your pan isn't properly preheated, the steaks will overcook before developing a good crust.

ONLY FLIP THE STEAKS ONCE: Add the steaks and brown the first side well. Flip the steaks with tongs and cook until the meat registers 120 to 125 degrees (for medium-rare), 3 to 5 minutes longer. (See below for more on checking the temperature of steaks.) To ensure a good crust, don't move the steaks during cooking.

ALWAYS TAKE THE TEMPERATURE: To ensure a perfectly cooked steak, always use a thermometer to check for doneness. When taking the temperature of thin steaks (or pork chops), it's easy to insert the thermometer too far or not far enough. To avoid this, use tongs to hold the meat, then insert the thermometer sideways into the center, taking care not to hit any bones. You can also use this technique for pork tenderloin or rack of lamb; just lift the meat with a pair of tongs and insert the thermometer into the end, parallel to the meat. For more information on doneness temperatures, see page 155.

LET THE STEAKS REST: Transfer the steaks to a cutting board and let them rest, tented loosely with aluminum foil, for 5 minutes to allow the juices to redistribute. Note that the internal temperature will continue to climb about 5 degrees as the steaks rest.

1. Adjust oven rack to lower-middle position, place rimmed baking sheet on oven rack, and heat oven to 450 degrees. When oven reaches 450 degrees, heat 1 tablespoon oil in 10-inch skillet over high heat until just smoking.

2. Meanwhile, rub each side of steaks with ½ teaspoon oil and season with salt and pepper. Lay steaks in skillet and cook, without moving them, until well browned on both sides, about 3 minutes per side. Transfer steaks to hot sheet in oven and roast until meat registers 120 to 125 degrees (for medium-rare), about 4 minutes. Transfer steaks to plate, tent loosely with aluminum foil, and let rest for 5 minutes.

3. While steaks rest, combine sour cream, horseradish, mayonnaise, lemon juice, and garlic in bowl and season with salt and pepper to taste. Serve steaks with sauce.

Minute (Cubed) Steaks with Garlic-Parsley Butter

SERVES 2 **FAST**

✔ **WHY THIS RECIPE WORKS:** Minute, or cubed, steaks are cut from the relatively tough round and tenderized in a butcher's tenderizing machine. They can be a delicious, easy, and inexpensive dinner—but they can also be tough, chewy, and bland if they're not properly cooked. To eliminate any lingering toughness, we pounded the steaks to an even ¼-inch thickness. For an exceptionally crisp, browned crust, we dredged the steaks in flour and seared them in a hot skillet with plenty of oil. A simple herb butter flavored with garlic, parsley, and Worcestershire mixed with the steaks' juices to make a rich and flavorful sauce that belied their inexpensive price tag. Serve with mashed potatoes.

    1 tablespoon unsalted butter, softened
    2 teaspoons minced fresh parsley
    1 small garlic clove, minced
    ½ teaspoon Worcestershire sauce
      Salt and pepper
    2 (6-ounce) beef cubed steaks
    ½ cup all-purpose flour
    2 tablespoons vegetable oil

1. Combine butter, parsley, garlic, Worcestershire, and ⅛ teaspoon pepper in bowl; set aside.

2. Lay each steak between 2 sheets of plastic wrap and pound until roughly ¼ inch thick. Spread flour in shallow dish. Pat steaks dry with paper towels and season with salt and pepper. Working with 1 steak at a time, dredge steaks in flour.

3. Heat oil in 12-inch nonstick skillet over medium-high heat until just smoking. Lay steaks in skillet and cook until well browned on first side, about 3 minutes. Flip steaks and cook until well browned on second side, 1 to 2 minutes. Drain steaks briefly on paper towel–lined plate. Serve steaks with seasoned butter.

For a classic steak supper in under 30 minutes, we combine quick-cooking sirloin steak tips with a simple red wine pan sauce.

Steak Tips with Red Wine Pan Sauce

SERVES 2

✔ **WHY THIS RECIPE WORKS:** Sirloin steak tips have a rich, beefy flavor and satisfying texture, and since they're quick-cooking, they're a good option for an easy weeknight meal. A 10-inch skillet was just the right size for our scaled-down portion of meat, and cooking the tips over medium-high heat gave them a well-seared exterior and allowed them to cook through in just a matter of minutes. While the meat rested we prepared a simple yet flavorful red wine pan sauce, which we used to coat the steak tips just before serving. Steak tips, also known as flap meat, are sold as whole steak, cubes, and strips. To ensure evenly sized pieces, we prefer to purchase whole steak tips and cut them ourselves. Use a good-quality medium-bodied wine, such as a Côtes du Rhône or Pinot Noir. We prefer these steak tips cooked to medium-rare, but if you prefer them more or less done, see our guidelines on page 155. Note that the cooking times may change depending on the size of the steak tips.

1 pound sirloin steak tips, trimmed and cut into
    2-inch pieces
    Salt and pepper
1 tablespoon vegetable oil
2 tablespoons unsalted butter
1 small shallot, minced
¼ cup dry red wine
½ teaspoon brown sugar
½ cup beef broth
⅛ teaspoon minced fresh thyme

1. Pat beef dry with paper towels and season with salt and pepper. Heat oil in 10-inch skillet over medium-high heat until just smoking. Add beef and cook until well browned on all sides and meat registers 120 to 125 degrees (for medium-rare), 5 to 7 minutes; transfer to plate and tent loosely with aluminum foil.

2. Add 1 tablespoon butter to fat left in skillet and melt over medium heat. Add shallot and cook until softened, about 2 minutes. Stir in wine and sugar, scraping up any browned bits. Bring to simmer and cook until nearly evaporated, about 3 minutes. Stir in broth, bring to simmer, and cook until sauce is slightly thickened, about 3 minutes. Stir in any accumulated meat juices and simmer for 30 seconds. Off heat, whisk in remaining 1 tablespoon butter and thyme and season with salt and pepper to taste. Return browned steak tips to skillet and turn to coat with sauce. Serve.

Teriyaki-Glazed Steak Tips

SERVES 2   FAST

✔ **WHY THIS RECIPE WORKS:** We wanted to bring flavorful, juicy steak teriyaki to the table without having to head outside and fire up the grill. For the steak, we settled on steak tips, which have lots of beefy flavor and cook quickly. Next, we made a simple teriyaki glaze with soy sauce, sugar, mirin, ginger, and garlic. Red pepper flakes provided a subtle kick, while a little cornstarch helped thicken the glaze to nicely coat the beef. We found that using a skillet rather than a saucepan to reduce the glaze was quicker due to the larger surface area, giving us a perfectly glossy sweet glaze in record time. Steak tips, also known as flap meat, are sold as whole steak, cubes, and strips. To ensure evenly sized pieces, we prefer to purchase whole steak tips and cut them ourselves. We prefer these steak tips cooked to medium-rare, but if you prefer them more or less done, see our guidelines on page 155. Note that the cooking times may change depending on the size of the steak tips.

see our guidelines on page 155.

NOTES FROM THE TEST KITCHEN

Pan Sauces 101

THE FOUR-STEP PROCESS
A quick pan sauce can liven up a steak (or chicken breast or pork chop) with minimal work. Here are the basics.

BROWN THE MEAT: In a skillet large enough to avoid crowding, heat oil over medium-high heat until just smoking. Add the meat and cook until well browned on both sides and cooked to the desired doneness. Transfer the meat to a platter and tent with foil.

BROWN THE AROMATICS: Add minced aromatics, such as garlic, shallot, or oregano, to the skillet and cook until fragrant, about 30 seconds.

ADD THE LIQUID: Add the liquid (usually about ½ cup broth, wine, or juice for two servings) and use a wooden utensil to scrape up the bits left from browning the meat. Simmer until the liquid has reduced by about half. Pour in any accumulated juices from the resting meat.

FINISH THE SAUCE: Simmer the sauce until it has thickened slightly. For added richness, whisk in 1 to 2 tablespoons of butter. Season the sauce with salt and pepper and serve with the meat.

THE TOOLS

TRADITIONAL SKILLET: When making a pan sauce, always use a traditional—not a nonstick—skillet, since the latter won't develop a proper fond. Also make sure to use a skillet that is big enough, as crowded food won't brown properly. Our favorite traditional skillet is the **All-Clad Stainless Fry Pan.**

WOODEN UTENSIL: Because it is rigid, a wooden utensil works best for scraping up the fond while deglazing. Our favorite is the **Mario Batali 13-Inch Wooden Spoon**, a lightweight yet durable spoon with a comfortable handle and a broad bowl that will maximize the surface area covered when scraping browned bits.

WHISK: For maximum efficiency and easy maneuverability, use a medium-size "skinny" balloon whisk, one that is 10 to 12 inches long with flexible wires that can get into the rounded corners of the skillet. Our favorite is **Best Manufacturers Standard 12-Inch French Whip.**

1 pound sirloin steak tips, trimmed and cut into
    2-inch pieces
    Pepper
1 tablespoon vegetable oil
¼ cup sugar
2 tablespoons soy sauce
1 tablespoon mirin, sweet sherry, or dry white wine
1 teaspoon grated fresh ginger
1 garlic clove, minced
¼ teaspoon cornstarch
    Pinch red pepper flakes
2 scallions, sliced thin

1. Pat beef dry with paper towels and season with pepper. Heat oil in 10-inch skillet over medium-high heat until just smoking. Add beef and cook until well browned on all sides and meat registers 120 to 125 degrees (for medium-rare), 5 to 7 minutes; transfer to plate and tent loosely with aluminum foil. Pour off fat from skillet

2. Meanwhile, whisk sugar, soy sauce, mirin, ginger, garlic, cornstarch, and pepper flakes together in bowl. Add soy sauce mixture to now-empty skillet, bring to simmer, and cook, stirring occasionally, until sauce is thick and glossy, about 2 minutes. Stir in any accumulated meat juices and simmer for 30 seconds. Return browned steak tips to skillet and turn to coat with sauce. Sprinkle with scallions and serve.

New York Strip Steaks with Crispy Potatoes and Parsley Sauce

SERVES 2

✔ **WHY THIS RECIPE WORKS:** For a steak-and-potatoes recipe that was anything but ordinary, we started with boneless strip steaks and small red potatoes. Cooking everything in a single skillet cut down on cleanup, and the rendered fat from the steak lent the potatoes a rich, meaty flavor. But the potatoes took nearly 40 minutes to cook through on the stovetop—not the simple weeknight meal we had in mind. To speed up the process, we jump-started the potatoes in the microwave, then added them to the skillet for just 10 minutes to develop a crisp, golden-brown crust. A quick parsley sauce seasoned with garlic, vinegar, a dash of red pepper, and a little chopped red onion contributed vibrant flavor to our hearty meal. We prefer these steaks cooked to medium-rare, but if you prefer them more or less done, see our guidelines on page 155.

PARSLEY SAUCE

½   cup fresh parsley leaves
¼   cup extra-virgin olive oil
2   tablespoons chopped red onion
2   tablespoons red wine vinegar
1   tablespoon water
2   garlic cloves, minced
½   teaspoon salt
⅛   teaspoon red pepper flakes

STEAK AND POTATOES

12   ounces red potatoes, unpeeled, cut into 1-inch wedges
3   tablespoons vegetable oil
    Salt and pepper
2   (8-ounce) boneless strip steaks, ¾ inch thick, trimmed

1. FOR THE PARSLEY SAUCE: Process all ingredients in food processor until well combined, about 20 seconds, scraping down sides of bowl as needed. Transfer sauce to bowl and set aside.

2. FOR THE STEAK AND POTATOES: Toss potatoes with 1 tablespoon oil, ¼ teaspoon salt, and ⅛ teaspoon pepper in bowl. Cover and microwave until potatoes begin to soften, 5 to 7 minutes, stirring potatoes halfway through microwaving. Drain well.

3. Meanwhile, pat steaks dry with paper towels and season with salt and pepper. Heat 1 tablespoon oil in 12-inch nonstick skillet over medium-high heat until just smoking. Lay steaks in skillet and cook until well browned on first side, 3 to 5 minutes. Flip steaks, reduce heat to medium, and continue to cook until meat registers 120 to 125 degrees (for medium-rare), 1 to 4 minutes; transfer to plate and tent loosely with aluminum foil.

4. Add remaining 1 tablespoon oil to fat left in skillet and heat over medium heat until shimmering. Add drained potatoes and cook until golden brown and tender on all sides, about 10 minutes. Serve steaks with potatoes and sauce.

Preparing Red Potatoes

Because the skins will be in the final dish, it's important to scrub the potatoes well before cutting them into wedges to ensure there is no dirt or grit left behind.

Sirloin Steak with Boursin Mashed Potatoes

SERVES 2

✔ **WHY THIS RECIPE WORKS:** We wanted a steak-and-potatoes dinner that we could get on the table fast with a minimum number of ingredients—without sacrificing flavor. A one-pound boneless top sirloin steak was just the right size for two servings, and searing it over high heat then turning down the heat allowed the steak to develop a well-browned exterior without overcooking. For quick mashed potatoes to accompany our steak, we simply simmered potatoes until tender then stirred in warm milk and Boursin cheese, a garlic-and-herb flavored cheese that gave our potatoes a creamy texture and loads of flavor with just one ingredient. A sprinkling of fresh chives folded into the potatoes was the perfect finishing touch. We prefer this steak cooked to medium-rare, but if you prefer it more or less done, see our guidelines on page 155.

12 ounces russet potatoes, peeled and sliced ½ inch thick
1 tablespoon vegetable oil
1 (1-pound) boneless top sirloin steak, ¾ to 1 inch thick, trimmed
   Salt and pepper
¼ cup whole milk, warmed, plus extra as needed
½ (5.2-ounce) package Boursin Garlic and Fine Herbs cheese
1 tablespoon minced fresh chives

1. Cover potatoes by 1 inch of water in medium saucepan. Bring to boil over medium-high heat, then reduce to simmer and cook, stirring once or twice, until potatoes are tender, 16 to 18 minutes.

2. Meanwhile, heat oil in 10-inch skillet over medium-high heat until just smoking. Pat steak dry with paper towels and season with salt and pepper. Lay steak in skillet and cook until well browned on first side, 3 to 5 minutes. Flip steak, reduce heat to medium, and continue to cook until meat registers 120 to 125 degrees (for medium-rare), 5 to 7 minutes. Transfer steak to cutting board, tent loosely with aluminum foil, and let rest for 5 minutes.

3. While steak rests, drain potatoes and return to saucepan. Cook over low heat, stirring constantly, until potatoes are thoroughly dried, about 2 minutes. Off heat, mash potatoes with potato masher until smooth. Gently fold in warm milk and Boursin until incorporated. Adjust consistency with extra warm milk as needed. Stir in chives and season with salt and pepper to taste. Slice steak thin. Serve with potatoes.

Spice-Rubbed Flank Steak with Spicy Corn and Black Bean Salad
SERVES 2

WHY THIS RECIPE WORKS: We wanted a simple meal that would pair tender, well-seared steak with a light and easy side. We settled on flank steak and found that the proper cooking technique was key: Coating the steak with a spice rub before searing contributed bold flavor, and heating the oil in a heavy 10-inch skillet until just smoking ensured a substantial, well-browned crust. A roasted corn and black bean salad was the perfect accompaniment to our steak; after toasting the corn in the skillet, we added canned black beans, red bell pepper, jalapeño, a squeeze of lime juice, and a sprinkling of cilantro for a Southwestern-inspired meal we could enjoy any night of the week. Be sure to use fresh corn here; canned or frozen corn will not toast well. We prefer this steak cooked to medium-rare, but if you prefer it more or less done, see our guidelines on page 155.

This Southwestern dish features juicy, tender spice-rubbed flank steak topped with an easy roasted corn and black bean salad.

SALAD
1 teaspoon vegetable oil
1 ear corn, kernels cut from cob
¾ cup canned black beans, rinsed
1 red bell pepper, stemmed, seeded, and chopped fine
½ jalapeño chile, stemmed, seeded, and minced
2 tablespoons lime juice
2 tablespoons minced fresh cilantro
2 garlic cloves, minced
   Salt and pepper

STEAK
½ teaspoon chili powder
½ teaspoon ground cumin
¼ teaspoon granulated garlic
¼ teaspoon salt
¼ teaspoon pepper
1 (1-pound) flank steak, trimmed
1 tablespoon vegetable oil

1. FOR THE SALAD: Heat oil in 10-inch nonstick skillet over medium-high heat until shimmering. Add corn and cook, without stirring, until well browned and toasted, 5 to 7 minutes. Transfer corn to medium bowl and let cool slightly. Wipe skillet clean.

2. Stir black beans, bell pepper, jalapeño, lime juice, cilantro, and garlic into toasted corn and season with salt and pepper to taste. Cover and refrigerate until flavors meld, about 15 minutes.

3. FOR THE STEAK: Meanwhile, combine chili powder, cumin, granulated garlic, salt, and pepper in separate bowl.

Pat steak dry with paper towels, then rub spice mixture evenly over steak.

4. Heat oil in now-empty skillet over medium-high heat until just smoking. Lay steak in skillet and cook until well browned on first side, 3 to 5 minutes, reducing heat if spices begin to burn. Flip steak, reduce heat to medium, and continue to cook until meat registers 120 to 125 degrees (for medium-rare), 5 to 7 minutes. Transfer steak to cutting board, tent loosely with aluminum foil, and let rest for 5 minutes. Slice steak thin against grain. Serve with salad.

NOTES FROM THE TEST KITCHEN

The Best Steaks for Two

These are our favorite steaks to cook for two. These cuts can easily be purchased in sizes good for serving two. We've rated each steak on a scale from 1 to 4 stars for both tenderness and flavor.

RIB-EYE STEAK

Cut from the rib area just behind the shoulder, a rib-eye steak is essentially a boneless piece of prime rib. This pricey, fat-streaked steak is tender and juicy, with a pronounced beefiness. It is sometimes labeled Spencer steak or Delmonico steak. Grill, pan-sear, or broil.

TENDERNESS: ★★★

FLAVOR: ★★★★

STRIP STEAK

Available both boneless and bone-in, this moderately expensive steak is also called top loin, shell, sirloin strip, Kansas City strip, or New York strip. Cut from the shell muscle that runs along the middle of the steer's back, strip steaks are well marbled, with a tight grain, pleasantly chewy texture, and big, beefy flavor. Grill, pan-sear, or broil.

TENDERNESS: ★★★

FLAVOR: ★★★★

TENDERLOIN STEAK

Cut from the center of the back, the tenderloin is the most tender (and most expensive) cut of the cow. Depending on their thickness, tenderloin steaks may be labeled (from thickest to thinnest) Châteaubriand, filet mignon, or tournedo. Tenderloin steaks are buttery smooth and very tender, but have little flavor. Grill, pan-sear, or broil.

TENDERNESS: ★★★★

FLAVOR: ★

CUBED STEAK

This inexpensive steak is taken from the tough top or bottom round and tenderized (or cubed) by running it through a butcher's tenderizing machine once or twice. It boasts a lot of flavor and because it is very thin, it cooks quickly. Grill, pan-sear, or broil.

TENDERNESS: ★

FLAVOR: ★★

FLAP MEAT SIRLOIN STEAK

Sirloin steak tips, one of the most convenient cuts when cooking for two, are cut from this large (upward of 2½ pounds), rectangular steak from the area just before the hip. Though not particularly tender, flap meat has a distinct grain and a robust beefiness. Slice thin against the grain after cooking. Pan-sear.

TENDERNESS: ★★

FLAVOR: ★★★

TOP SIRLOIN STEAK

Cut from the hip, this steak is sometimes called New York sirloin or sirloin butt. Top sirloin is a large, inexpensive steak with decent tenderness and flavor, but do not confuse it with the superior strip steak. Slice thin against the grain after cooking. Grill or pan-sear.

TENDERNESS: ★★

FLAVOR: ★★

FLANK STEAK

Flank steak, also called jiffy steak, is a large, flat cut from the underside of the cow, with a distinct longitudinal grain. Flank steak is thin and cooks quickly. Although very flavorful, flank is slightly chewy. It should not be cooked past medium and should always be sliced thin across the grain. Grill, pan-sear, or slice thinly and stir-fry.

TENDERNESS: ★★

FLAVOR: ★★★

TOP BLADE STEAK

Top blade (or simply blade) steak is a small shoulder cut. While it is very tender and richly flavored, a line of gristle that runs through the center of the meat makes it a poor option for grilling or pan-frying and serving whole. Remove the gristle and slice the steak thin for stir-fries, cut into cubes for kebabs or stews, or braise until fork-tender.

TENDERNESS: ★★★

FLAVOR: ★★★

Pot-Roasted Steaks with Root Vegetables

SERVES 2

✔ **WHY THIS RECIPE WORKS:** For a hearty, warming winter meal, we wanted to braise steaks and root vegetables for a satisfying dinner. We set out to find a cut of meat that would be well suited to pot-roasting. Blade steak proved ideal, with a meaty flavor and plenty of collagen that broke down into gelatin when slow-cooked for a supremely tender texture. Searing the steaks first added flavor and color, and 1½ cups of liquid (we chose a combination of chicken broth and water) provided ample braising liquid. Onion, garlic, celery, and thyme added another layer of flavor, and the addition of potatoes turned our dish into a one-pot meal. Finally, we reduced the braising liquid at the end and finished it with a little red wine to create a flavorful sauce. The vegetables in the braising liquid do not get strained out before serving, so be mindful to cut them into fairly even pieces.

- 2 (6- to 8-ounce) beef blade steaks, ¾ to 1 inch thick
  Salt and pepper
- 2 tablespoons vegetable oil
- 4 ounces baby carrots
- 1 small onion, chopped fine
- 1 celery rib, chopped
- 2 garlic cloves, minced
- 1 teaspoon minced fresh thyme or ¼ teaspoon dried
- ½ teaspoon sugar
- 1 cup chicken broth
- ½ cup water
- 8 ounces red potatoes, unpeeled, cut into 1-inch pieces
- 2 tablespoons dry red wine
- 2 teaspoons chopped fresh parsley

1. Adjust oven rack to lower-middle position and heat oven to 350 degrees. Pat steaks dry with paper towels and season with salt and pepper. Heat 1 tablespoon oil in 12-inch ovensafe nonstick skillet over medium-high heat until just smoking. Lay steaks in skillet and cook until well browned on both sides, 3 to 5 minutes per side; transfer to plate.

2. Add remaining 1 tablespoon oil to fat left in skillet and heat over medium heat until shimmering. Add carrots, onion, and celery and cook until onion is softened, about 5 minutes. Stir in garlic, thyme, and sugar and cook until fragrant, about 30 seconds. Stir in broth and water, scraping up any browned bits, and bring to simmer.

3. Nestle potatoes and browned steaks into skillet along with any accumulated meat juices and bring to simmer.

Cover, transfer skillet to oven, and cook until steaks are fully tender and fork slips easily in and out of meat, about 1¼ hours, flipping steaks halfway through cooking.

4. Using potholders (skillet handle will be hot), remove skillet from oven. Transfer steaks to plate and tent loosely with aluminum foil.

5. Being careful of hot skillet handle, bring cooking liquid left in skillet to simmer over medium-high heat and cook until slightly thickened, 5 to 7 minutes. Stir in wine and any accumulated beef juices and continue to simmer for 1 minute. Off heat, stir in parsley and season with salt and pepper to taste. Serve steaks with vegetables and sauce.

Classic Pot Roast

SERVES 2

✔ **WHY THIS RECIPE WORKS:** There's not much more satisfying than a fall-apart tender, meaty pot roast on a cold night, but that doesn't mean we want to eat it every night for a week. We wanted a recipe for a scaled-down pot roast that would deliver all the hearty flavor and succulent texture of a full-size roast. After testing various cuts, we found that a 1½-pound chuck-eye roast was best suited to braising. Salting the roast and letting it rest for just an hour dramatically improved its flavor. A small amount of beef broth and red wine provided enough liquid for braising yet left the top of the roast exposed during cooking to encourage browning. Tomato paste contributed a savory depth, while shallot, carrot, celery, garlic, a bay leaf, and some thyme rounded out the flavors. To finish, we pureed the softened vegetables with the cooking liquid for a rich, full-bodied gravy. This might seem like a lot of meat for two servings, but it will cook down substantially in the oven.

- 1 (1½-pound) boneless beef chuck-eye roast, trimmed
  Salt and pepper
- 1 tablespoon unsalted butter
- 1 large shallot, halved and sliced thin
- 1 small carrot, peeled and cut into ½-inch pieces
- 1 celery rib, cut into ½-inch pieces
- 1 small garlic clove, minced
- ½ cup beef broth, plus extra as needed
- ¼ cup plus 1 tablespoon dry red wine
- 1 teaspoon tomato paste
- 1 bay leaf
- 1 sprig fresh thyme, plus ¼ teaspoon minced
- 1 teaspoon balsamic vinegar

1. Season roast with ½ teaspoon salt, place on wire rack set in rimmed baking sheet, and let sit at room temperature for 1 hour.

2. Adjust oven rack to lower-middle position and heat oven to 300 degrees. Melt butter in medium saucepan over medium heat. Add shallot and cook, stirring occasionally, until softened and beginning to brown, 3 to 5 minutes. Stir in carrot and celery and cook for 5 minutes. Stir in garlic and cook until fragrant, about 30 seconds. Stir in broth, ¼ cup wine, tomato paste, bay leaf, and thyme sprig, scraping up any browned bits, and bring to simmer.

3. Pat roast dry with paper towels and season with pepper. Tie 3 pieces of kitchen twine around roast to keep it from falling apart. Nestle roast on top of vegetables. Cover saucepan tightly with aluminum foil and cover with lid.

NOTES FROM THE TEST KITCHEN

Storing Meat Safely

Throwing away meat because it went bad before you had a chance to cook it is frustrating, particularly when you've spent a lot of money on a nice steak or cut of lamb. Proper storage is the best way to prolong its shelf life and prevent waste.

REFRIGERATING MEAT: Raw meat should be refrigerated well wrapped and never on shelves that are above other food. Check regularly to ensure your refrigerator's temperature is between 35 and 40 degrees. Raw or cooked meat will keep for two to three days in the refrigerator; raw ground meat and raw poultry will keep for two days. Smoked ham or bacon will keep for up to two weeks (see page 5 for information on freezing bacon).

FREEZING MEAT: In general, meat tastes best when it hasn't been frozen. The slow process of freezing that occurs in a home freezer (as compared with a commercial freezer) causes large ice crystals to form. The crystals rupture the cell walls of the meat, permitting the release of juices during cooking, resulting in drier meat. If you're going to freeze meat, wrap it well in plastic and then place the meat in a zipper-lock bag and squeeze out excess air. Label the bag with the contents and date and use the meat within a few months.

THAWING MEAT: All meat can be thawed safely on a plate or rimmed baking sheet in the refrigerator (and this is the only safe method for large cuts like whole chickens). Never thaw meat on the counter, where bacteria will rapidly multiply. According to the USDA, frozen food that is properly thawed is safe to refreeze. However, a second freeze-thaw cycle aggravates moisture loss, reducing the quality of the meat, so we don't recommend it.

QUICK THAW FOR SMALL CUTS: Flat cuts like chicken breasts, pork chops, or steaks will thaw more quickly when left on a metal surface rather than a wood or plastic one; metal can transfer ambient heat much more quickly. To thaw frozen wrapped steaks, chops, or ground meat (flattened to 1 inch thick before freezing), place in a skillet (heavy steel and cast-iron skillets work best) in a single layer. Flip the meat every half hour until it's thawed. Small cuts can also be sealed in zipper-lock bags and submerged in hot (140-degree) water—this method will safely thaw chicken breasts, steaks, and chops in under 15 minutes.

Transfer saucepan to oven and cook beef until fully tender and fork slips easily in and out of meat, 3½ to 4 hours, turning roast halfway through cooking.

4. Using potholders (saucepan handle will be hot), remove saucepan from oven. Transfer roast to carving board and tent loosely with foil. Strain braising liquid through fine-mesh strainer into liquid measuring cup. Discard bay leaf and thyme sprig, then transfer vegetables to blender.

5. Let braising liquid settle for 5 minutes, then remove fat from surface using large spoon. Add beef broth if needed to bring liquid amount to ¾ cup. Add liquid to blender with vegetables and process until smooth, about 1 minute. Being careful of hot saucepan handle, transfer sauce to now-empty saucepan and bring to simmer over medium heat. Off heat, stir in remaining 1 tablespoon wine, minced thyme, and vinegar and season with salt and pepper to taste.

6. Remove twine from roast and slice against grain into ½-inch-thick slices. Transfer meat to individual plates and spoon half of sauce over meat. Serve, passing remaining sauce separately.

Prime Rib for Two

SERVES 2

✔ **WHY THIS RECIPE WORKS:** When it comes to roast beef, prime rib is supreme. But even the smallest prime rib roast is too big for two, so we turned to bone-in rib steak. It's from the same juicy, tender rib section of the cow but is the perfect size for two. To get both the crusty, browned exterior and juicy, rosy interior of perfect prime rib, we seared the meat in a skillet, then moved it to a wire rack set in a rimmed baking sheet to cook through in a low oven. While the meat roasted, we used the skillet to make a quick jus with shallot, thyme, beef broth, and red wine. Finally, to approximate the big, rosy slices of prime rib, we sliced our rib steak on the bias. Be sure to brown the edges of the steak to render the fat. You can do this easily by using tongs to hold the steak on its side in the hot skillet. We prefer these steaks cooked to medium-rare, but if you prefer them more or less done, see our guidelines on page 155.

1 (1½-pound) bone-in rib-eye steak, 1¾ to 2 inches thick, trimmed
Salt and pepper
1 tablespoon vegetable oil
1 shallot, minced
1 teaspoon ketchup
1 teaspoon minced fresh thyme or ¼ teaspoon dried
½ cup beef broth
¼ cup dry red wine

1. Adjust oven rack to lowest position and heat oven to 200 degrees. Pat steak dry with paper towels and season with salt and pepper.

2. Heat oil in 12-inch skillet over medium-high heat until just smoking. Brown steak well on all sides, 10 to 12 minutes; transfer to wire rack set in rimmed baking sheet. Roast steak until meat registers 120 to 125 degrees (for medium-rare), 25 to 30 minutes. Transfer steak to cutting board, tent loosely with aluminum foil, and let rest for 5 to 10 minutes.

3. Meanwhile, pour off all but 2 teaspoons fat from skillet. Add shallot and cook over medium heat until softened, about 2 minutes. Stir in ketchup and thyme and cook until fragrant, about 30 seconds. Stir in broth and wine, scraping up any browned bits. Bring to simmer and cook until jus is reduced to ⅓ cup, about 10 minutes. Stir in any accumulated meat juices and simmer for 30 seconds. Cut steak neatly away from bone and slice into ½-inch-thick slices on bias. Serve steak with jus.

All-American Mini Meatloaves

SERVES 2

✔ **WHY THIS RECIPE WORKS:** For a scaled-down but full-flavored take on this comfort-food classic, we wanted to make single-serving individual meatloaves. We started with tender meatloaf mix; panko bread crumbs, milk, and an egg yolk helped to bind the mixture and added richness and moisture. Sautéed onion, garlic, Worcestershire sauce, mustard, and herbs mixed in with the meat gave us a flavorful loaf, and a classic sweet and tangy ketchup glaze pulled the flavors together. To keep things simple, we pressed the mixture into two free-form loaves by hand, browned them in a skillet, and cooked them through in the oven. Meatloaf mix is a combination of equal parts ground beef, pork, and veal and is available in most grocery stores. If you can't find meatloaf mix, substitute 8 ounces each of ground pork and 90 percent lean ground beef.

GLAZE

- ¼ cup ketchup
- 2 tablespoons packed light brown sugar
- 2 teaspoons cider vinegar

MEATLOAVES

- 4 teaspoons vegetable oil
- ⅓ cup finely chopped onion
- 1 small garlic clove, minced
- 1 teaspoon minced fresh thyme or ¼ teaspoon dried
- ½ cup panko bread crumbs

For meatloaf without endless leftovers, we brown mini meatloaves in a skillet then move them to the oven to cook through.

- ¼ cup minced fresh parsley
- 3 tablespoons whole milk
- 2 tablespoons Worcestershire sauce
- 1 large egg yolk
- 1 tablespoon Dijon mustard
- ¼ teaspoon salt
- ¼ teaspoon pepper
- 1 pound meatloaf mix

1. FOR THE GLAZE: Whisk all ingredients together in bowl.

2. FOR THE MEATLOAVES: Adjust oven rack to middle position and heat oven to 350 degrees. Heat 2 teaspoons oil in 10-inch ovensafe nonstick skillet over medium heat until shimmering. Add onion and cook until softened, about 5 minutes. Stir in garlic and thyme and cook until fragrant, about 30 seconds; transfer to large bowl. Wipe skillet clean.

3. Stir panko, parsley, milk, Worcestershire, egg yolk, mustard, salt, and pepper into onion mixture. Using hands, gently mix in meatloaf mix until thoroughly combined. Divide mixture into 2 equal portions and press each portion into small oval loaf.

4. Heat remaining 2 teaspoons oil in now-empty skillet over medium-high heat until just smoking. Gently place meatloaves in skillet and cook until well browned on first side, 2 to 3 minutes. Carefully flip meatloaves, neaten edges with 2 spatulas, and cook until lightly browned on second side, about 2 minutes.

5. Brush meatloaves with glaze and transfer skillet to oven. Bake until meatloaves register 160 degrees, 20 to 30 minutes. Transfer meatloaves to serving platter and let rest for 5 minutes before serving.

Beef and Broccoli Stir-Fry

SERVES 2 **FAST**

✔ **WHY THIS RECIPE WORKS:** For a streamlined beef and broccoli stir-fry that didn't require a laundry list of ingredients, we experimented with a wide variety of Asian condiments to find just a couple that would deliver the most bang for our buck. Oyster sauce gave us the perfect thick, clingy texture, and sweet chili sauce offered complex flavor with its sweet, spicy, and bright notes. Using toasted sesame oil—rather than vegetable oil—to sauté the beef and vegetables added a layer of nutty flavor and richness, and we also added some toasted sesame oil to the sauce to ensure its rich, nutty flavor shone through in the final dish. Thin flank steak cooked quickly and offered big beefy flavor, and a combination of broccoli, red bell pepper, and scallion contributed heft, color, and brightness. To make the beef easier to slice, freeze it for 15 minutes. Serve with rice.

½ cup water

¼ cup Asian sweet chili sauce

2 tablespoons oyster sauce

2 tablespoons toasted sesame oil

1 (12-ounce) flank steak, trimmed and sliced thin against grain

6 ounces broccoli florets, cut into 1-inch pieces

1 small red bell pepper, stemmed, seeded, and cut into 2-inch-long matchsticks

2 scallions, white parts minced, green parts sliced thin

1. Whisk ¼ cup water, chili sauce, oyster sauce, and 1 tablespoon oil together in small bowl. Measure 1 tablespoon sauce into medium bowl, then stir in beef and remaining 1 tablespoon oil. Cover and marinate beef in refrigerator for at least 10 minutes or up to 30 minutes.

2. Cook broccoli, bell pepper, and remaining ¼ cup water, covered, in 12-inch nonstick skillet over high heat until water is boiling and vegetables begin to soften, about 3 minutes.

We use sweet chili sauce, oyster sauce, and sesame oil to build deep flavor for an authentic-tasting stir-fry with few ingredients.

Uncover and continue to cook until water has evaporated and vegetables are crisp-tender, about 2 minutes; transfer to bowl.

3. Return now-empty skillet to high heat. Add beef, break up any clumps, and cook until lightly browned on all sides and liquid has evaporated, about 6 minutes. Push beef to sides of skillet. Add scallion whites and cook, mashing whites into skillet, until fragrant, 15 to 30 seconds. Stir scallion whites into beef.

4. Stir in cooked vegetables. Whisk sauce to recombine, then add to skillet. Cook, stirring constantly, until sauce is thickened, about 1 minute. Transfer to serving platter, sprinkle with scallion greens, and serve.

Beef and Kimchi Stir-Fry

SERVES 2 **FAST**

✔ **WHY THIS RECIPE WORKS:** A stir-fry is an ideal quick and easy weeknight meal for two. Our goal was to create a beef stir-fry with minimal ingredients but maximum flavor. Flank steak was ideal here; this lean cut has plenty of beefy flavor and is easy to slice thin. Since the key to a good stir-fry is plenty of intense heat, we cooked the beef over high heat, which gave it good caramelization. For the vegetable component we selected kimchi, a spicy Korean pickled vegetable condiment, for a prep-free way to add plenty of bold flavor. To balance the tangy spice of the kimchi, we added a little brown sugar for sweetness and some salty soy sauce. Sautéing the beef in toasted sesame oil contributed a subtle nutty complexity. You can find kimchi in the refrigerated section of Asian markets and in some well-stocked supermarkets. Cut large pieces of kimchi into bite-size pieces before stir-frying. To make the beef easier to slice, freeze it for 15 minutes. Serve with rice.

1½ cups medium-spicy or spicy cabbage kimchi, plus
    2 tablespoons kimchi liquid
¼   cup water
3   tablespoons soy sauce
2   tablespoons packed brown sugar
1   teaspoon cornstarch
1   tablespoon toasted sesame oil
1   (12-ounce) flank steak, trimmed and sliced
    thin against grain

1. Whisk 1 tablespoon kimchi liquid, water, soy sauce, sugar, and cornstarch together in bowl. Heat oil in 12-inch nonstick skillet over high heat until just smoking. Add beef, break up any clumps, and cook until lightly browned on all sides and liquid has evaporated, about 6 minutes.

2. Stir in kimchi and remaining 1 tablespoon kimchi liquid. Whisk sauce to recombine, then add to skillet. Cook, stirring constantly, until mixture is heated through and sauce is thickened, about 3 minutes. Serve.

Slicing Flank Steak Thin

1. To make it easier to slice steak thin, freeze it for 15 minutes. Slice partially frozen steak with grain into roughly 2-inch-wide pieces.

2. Slice each piece against grain into very thin slices.

Tips for Stir-Fry Success

The beauty of stir-frying is that you can do it quickly with just about anything in your fridge—but it's not a free-for-all. Here are some of our best tips and tricks for making great stir-fries.

CHOOSE THE RIGHT VEGETABLES: Choose relatively sturdy vegetables that can withstand high heat but that cook quickly. Some of our favorites include onions, bell peppers, broccoli, eggplant, and snow peas, to name a few. Remember that they'll cook best if the pieces are uniform in size and that a crisp-tender or al dente texture is desirable.

CHOOSE THE RIGHT PROTEINS: Good protein choices for stir-fries are cuts that are tender to start—more or less the same ones that do well cooked on a grill or seared in a hot pan on the stovetop—because stir-frying happens so quickly that it doesn't give tough muscles a chance to become tender. Flank steak, pork tenderloin, chicken breast, and shrimp are all good options. Freezing the meat for about 15 minutes can make it easier to slice thin. Tofu can also be stir-fried, but it should be cooked in several tablespoons of oil for the best results.

MARINATE THE MEAT: Salty liquids like soy sauce or fish sauce not only boost meat's savory flavor but also act as a brine, helping the meat retain moisture during cooking.

SWAP YOUR WOK FOR A SKILLET: The broad surface of a 10-inch nonstick skillet makes more contact with flat Western burners than a round-bottomed wok, making it a better choice for browning. Don't use a smaller pan.

DON'T CROWD THE PAN: Adding all the ingredients at once will cause the meat to steam rather than sear. Add the food to the pan in an even layer and leave space between pieces of meat so that they brown well.

ADD AROMATICS LATER: Waiting to add aromatics like ginger and garlic until after the protein and vegetables are cooked prevents them from scorching over the high heat.

DON'T STIR TOO MUCH: Nomenclature aside, it's best not to stir your stir-fry too much. Western-style burners have a relatively low heat output, so stirring food frequently during cooking will inhibit proper browning.

Beef Satay with Spicy Peanut Dipping Sauce
SERVES 2

✔ **WHY THIS RECIPE WORKS:** Slices of marinated beef woven onto skewers and briefly grilled are a Southeast Asian favorite known as *satay*. We thought beef satay would make a perfect casual dinner for two, so we set out to bring it indoors. Flank steak was easy to slice into long, thin strips and had great beefy flavor. Slicing the meat against the grain and pounding it thin kept it tender, while a marinade of brown sugar, fish sauce, and Sriracha guaranteed moist, full-flavored meat. The intense, direct heat of the broiler approximated that of a grill. Finally, we created a peanut dipping sauce with sweet, tart, and spicy elements, sprinkled with fresh cilantro and scallions for a bright finish. To make the beef easier to slice, freeze it for 15 minutes.

SATAY

1	(8-ounce) flank steak, trimmed
4	teaspoons packed brown sugar
1	teaspoon fish sauce
1	teaspoon Sriracha sauce
10–14	wooden skewers

DIPPING SAUCE

2	tablespoons creamy peanut butter
2	tablespoons hot tap water
1½	teaspoons lime juice
1½	teaspoons Sriracha sauce
1	teaspoon fish sauce
¾	teaspoon brown sugar
1	garlic clove, minced
1	tablespoon minced fresh cilantro
1	scallion, sliced thin

1. FOR THE SATAY: Slice steak in half with grain, then slice each piece against grain on bias into ¼-inch-thick slices. Lay pieces of meat in single layer between 2 sheets of plastic wrap and pound until roughly ⅛ inch thick.

2. Combine sugar, fish sauce, and Sriracha in medium bowl. Stir in beef, cover, and marinate in refrigerator for at least 30 minutes or up to 1 hour.

3. FOR THE DIPPING SAUCE: Meanwhile, whisk peanut butter, water, lime juice, Sriracha, fish sauce, sugar, and garlic

together in bowl until smooth. Sprinkle with cilantro and scallion; set aside.

4. Adjust oven rack 6 inches from broiler element and heat broiler. Pat beef dry with paper towels and weave onto wooden skewers, 1 piece per skewer. Lay skewers on aluminum foil–lined baking sheet and cover skewer ends with strip of foil. Broil until meat is browned, 6 to 9 minutes, flipping skewers halfway through cooking. Serve skewers with dipping sauce.

Steak Fajitas

SERVES 2 FAST

👌 **WHY THIS RECIPE WORKS:** For indoor steak fajitas we could make any time of year, we pan-seared steak over medium-high heat to mimic the caramelized exterior and crisp edges of grilled steak. Flank steak had great beefy flavor; slicing it against the grain kept it tender. Tossing it with a squeeze of lime juice after cooking added the bright tang and flavor of a marinade in a fraction of the time. Bell pepper and onion are traditional for fajitas; just one of each was plenty for our scaled-down recipe. Chili powder, cumin, and hot sauce added the smoky, spicy notes we wanted. To make these fajitas spicy, add a sliced jalapeño with the bell pepper. We prefer this steak cooked to medium-rare, but if you prefer it more or less done, see our guidelines on page 155. Serve with your favorite fajita toppings.

1	(12-ounce) flank steak, trimmed
	Salt and pepper
2	tablespoons vegetable oil
1	tablespoon lime juice
1	red, green, or yellow bell pepper, stemmed, seeded, and cut into ½-inch-wide strips

Making Beef Satay

1. To make it easier to slice beef thin, freeze it for 15 minutes. Slice steak in half with grain, then slice halves against grain on bias into ¼-inch-thick slices.

2. Lay pieces of meat in single layer between 2 sheets of plastic wrap and pound until roughly ⅛ inch thick.

3. After marinating steak pieces, weave them onto skewers, 1 piece per skewer, until each strip is secure.

4. Cover ends of skewers with aluminum foil to keep them from burning.

We pan-sear flank steak over high heat then toss it with fresh lime juice for easy indoor steak fajitas that taste as good as grilled.

1 small red onion, halved and sliced thin
2 tablespoons water
1 teaspoon chili powder
¼ teaspoon ground cumin
¼ teaspoon hot sauce
6 (6-inch) flour tortillas, warmed

1. Pat steak dry with paper towels and season with salt and pepper. Heat 1 tablespoon oil in 10-inch skillet over medium-high heat until just smoking. Lay steak in skillet and cook until well browned on first side, 3 to 5 minutes. Flip steak, reduce heat to medium, and continue to cook until meat registers 120 to 125 degrees (for medium-rare), 3 to 5 minutes; transfer to cutting board and drizzle with lime juice. Tent loosely with aluminum foil.

2. Heat remaining 1 tablespoon oil in now-empty skillet over medium heat until shimmering. Add bell pepper, onion, water, chili powder, cumin, hot sauce, and ¼ teaspoon salt. Cook, scraping up any browned bits, until vegetables are softened, 5 to 7 minutes; transfer to serving platter.

3. Slice steak thin against grain, arrange on platter with vegetables, and serve with warm tortillas.

Sautéed Pork Cutlets with Mustard-Cider Sauce

SERVES 2

✔ **WHY THIS RECIPE WORKS:** Pork cutlets offer everything a time-pressed cook could want in a weeknight meal: thrift, minimal preparation, and dinner on the table in minutes. But store-bought cutlets are often lean and unevenly portioned and end up dry, stringy, and unevenly cooked. To solve these problems, we decided to make our own cutlets from boneless country-style ribs. These ribs contain flavorful shoulder meat and little connective tissue and they are portioned into small pieces and available in small packages. After cutting the ribs into pieces and pounding them thin, our cutlets required just 4 minutes in a hot skillet for a deep brown crust and tender, juicy interior. A simple pan sauce featuring mustard, apple cider, and fresh herbs was the perfect finishing touch. Look for ribs that are 3 to 5 inches long. If your ribs are more than 5 inches long, cut them in half crosswise before slicing them lengthwise to ensure more evenly sized cutlets. If the pork is enhanced (injected with a salt solution), do not brine. If brining the pork, do not season with salt in step 1.

12 ounces boneless country-style pork ribs, trimmed and brined if desired (see page 150)
Salt and pepper
½ teaspoon sugar
1 tablespoon olive oil
1 tablespoon unsalted butter, cut into 2 pieces
1 shallot, minced
½ teaspoon all-purpose flour
¼ cup chicken broth
¼ cup apple cider
¼ teaspoon minced fresh sage, parsley, or thyme
2 teaspoons whole-grain mustard

1. Cut each rib lengthwise into 2 or 3 pieces about ⅜ inch wide. Lay each piece between 2 sheets of plastic wrap and pound until roughly ¼ inch thick. Pat cutlets dry with paper towels and season with salt and pepper. Sprinkle sugar evenly over each cutlet.

2. Heat oil in 12-inch skillet over medium-high heat until just smoking. Add 1 piece butter, let melt, then quickly add cutlets. Brown cutlets on both sides, about 2 minutes per side; transfer to plate and tent loosely with aluminum foil.

3. Add shallot to fat left in skillet and cook over medium heat until softened, about 2 minutes. Stir in flour and cook for 1 minute. Whisk in broth, cider, and sage, scraping up any browned bits. Bring to simmer and cook until sauce is slightly thickened, 2 to 3 minutes.

4. Return browned cutlets and any accumulated juices to skillet and simmer until heated through, about 30 seconds; transfer cutlets to serving platter. Off heat, whisk mustard and remaining 1 piece butter into sauce and season with salt and pepper to taste. Pour sauce over cutlets and serve.

VARIATION

Sautéed Pork Cutlets with Lemon-Caper Sauce
Substitute ¼ cup dry white wine for apple cider. Substitute 2 tablespoons rinsed capers, 1 teaspoon grated lemon zest, and 1 teaspoon lemon juice for mustard.

Cutting Country-Style Ribs into Cutlets

1. Slice each rib lengthwise to create 2 or 3 cutlets, each about ⅜ inch wide.

2. Lay each piece between 2 sheets of plastic wrap and pound until roughly ¼ inch thick.

Sautéed Boneless Pork Chops with Sage-Butter Sauce
SERVES 2

✔ **WHY THIS RECIPE WORKS:** For perfectly cooked, juicy pan-seared pork chops, we found that the thickness of the chops was key: A ¾-inch chop was thick enough to stay moist during cooking, but thin enough that we could cook it entirely on the stovetop. We also sautéed the chops over two different heat levels. First we seared them on one side over medium-high heat for a nicely browned exterior, then we flipped them over and turned the heat down to let them finish cooking through without drying out. To dress up our simple chops, we created two effortless yet impressive pan sauces—one a simple sage-butter sauce and the other a robust port wine and cherry sauce—with the browned bits left behind in the pan. If the pork is enhanced (injected with a salt solution), do not brine. If brining the pork, do not season with salt in step 1.

2 (6- to 8-ounce) boneless pork chops, ¾ to 1 inch thick, trimmed and brined if desired (see page 150)
  Salt and pepper
2 teaspoons vegetable oil
1 shallot, minced
2 tablespoons minced fresh sage or 2 teaspoons dried
2 garlic cloves, minced
½ cup chicken broth
¼ cup dry white wine
2 tablespoons unsalted butter, chilled

1. Cut 2 slits, about 2 inches apart, through outer layer of fat and silverskin on each chop. Pat chops dry with paper towels and season with salt and pepper.

2. Heat 1 teaspoon oil in 10-inch skillet over medium-high heat until just smoking. Lay chops in skillet and cook until well browned on first side, about 3 minutes. Flip chops, reduce heat to medium, and continue to cook until meat registers 145 degrees, 5 to 10 minutes; transfer to serving platter and tent loosely with aluminum foil.

3. Add remaining 1 teaspoon oil to fat left in skillet and heat over medium heat until shimmering. Add shallot and cook until softened, about 2 minutes. Stir in sage and garlic and cook until fragrant, about 30 seconds. Stir in broth and wine, scraping up any browned bits. Bring to simmer and cook until sauce is slightly thickened, about 5 minutes. Stir in any accumulated meat juices and simmer for 30 seconds. Off heat, whisk in butter and season with salt and pepper to taste. Pour sauce over chops and serve.

VARIATION

Sautéed Boneless Pork Chops with Port Wine and Cherry Sauce
Substitute ½ teaspoon minced fresh rosemary for sage and ¼ cup ruby port for wine. Add ¼ cup dried cherries to skillet with broth in step 3.

Preventing Curled Pork Chops

To prevent pork chops from curling while cooking, cut 2 slits, about 2 inches apart, through outer layer of fat and silverskin of each chop (this method works for both bone-in and boneless chops). This will ensure better browning and more even cooking.

A sweet maple-cider glaze seasoned with Dijon mustard and thyme is the perfect match for juicy sautéed pork chops.

Skillet-Glazed Pork Chops

SERVES 2 **FAST** **LIGHT**

✓ WHY THIS RECIPE WORKS: We wanted to complement convenient boneless pork chops with a sweet, glossy, flavorful glaze. First, for deeply browned, juicy chops, we started them over medium-high heat to get the dark crust and rich flavor that only searing can provide. Then we flipped the chops and turned the heat down so they could finish cooking through without drying out. For the glaze, a quick combination of maple syrup, cider vinegar, Dijon mustard, and thyme provided just the right balance of flavors, and briefly reducing it in the skillet gave it the perfect consistency for coating our chops. If the pork is enhanced (injected with a salt solution), do not brine. If brining the pork, do not season with salt in step 1. For the nutritional information for this recipe, see page 413.

2 (6- to 8-ounce) boneless pork chops, ¾ to 1 inch thick, trimmed and brined if desired (see page 150)
   Salt and pepper
1 teaspoon vegetable oil

3 tablespoons maple syrup
2 tablespoons cider vinegar
1½ teaspoons Dijon mustard
½ teaspoon minced fresh thyme or ⅛ teaspoon dried

1. Cut 2 slits, about 2 inches apart, through outer layer of fat and silverskin on each chop. Pat chops dry with paper towels and season with salt and pepper.

2. Heat oil in 10-inch skillet over medium-high heat until just smoking. Lay chops in skillet and cook until well browned on first side, about 3 minutes. Flip chops, reduce heat to medium, and continue to cook until meat registers 145 degrees, 5 to 10 minutes; transfer to plate and tent loosely with aluminum foil.

3. Meanwhile, whisk maple syrup, vinegar, mustard, and thyme together in bowl. Add maple syrup mixture to fat left in skillet, scraping up any browned bits. Bring to simmer over medium heat and cook until thick and syrupy, 2 to 4 minutes. Return browned chops and any accumulated juices to skillet and simmer, flipping chops frequently, until coated in glaze, 1 to 2 minutes. Serve.

Sautéed Boneless Pork Chops with Quick Apple-Ginger Chutney

SERVES 2 **LIGHT**

✓ WHY THIS RECIPE WORKS: To prevent lean boneless pork chops from turning out dry and flavorless, they're often accompanied by a rich butter sauce. We wanted an accompaniment that would pack plenty of flavor but would keep our pork chops light. Pork and apples are a classic pairing, so we created an apple chutney featuring freshly grated ginger and a touch of allspice for spicy warmth. The fond left in the pan from sautéing the pork chops gave the chutney a meaty backbone and depth of flavor. Once the apple was softened, we stirred in cider and a little sugar and thickened the chutney to the perfect consistency. We like the flavor of Granny Smith apples here; however, any type of apple will work fine. If the pork is enhanced (injected with a salt solution), do not brine. If brining the pork, do not season with salt in step 1. For the nutritional information for this recipe, see page 413.

2 (6- to 8-ounce) boneless pork chops, ¾ to 1 inch thick, trimmed and brined if desired (see page 150)
   Salt and pepper
2 teaspoons vegetable oil
1 Granny Smith apple, peeled, cored, and cut into ½-inch pieces
1 shallot, minced

1½ teaspoons grated fresh ginger

⅛ teaspoon ground allspice

½ cup apple cider

2 tablespoons packed light brown sugar

1. Cut 2 slits, about 2 inches apart, through outer layer of fat and silverskin on each chop. Pat chops dry with paper towels and season with salt and pepper.

2. Heat 1 teaspoon oil in 10-inch skillet over medium-high heat until just smoking. Lay chops in skillet and cook until well browned on first side, about 3 minutes. Flip chops, reduce heat to medium, and continue to cook until meat registers 145 degrees, 5 to 10 minutes; transfer to serving platter and tent loosely with aluminum foil.

3. Add remaining 1 teaspoon oil, apple, and shallot to fat left in skillet, cover, and cook over medium-low heat until apple is softened, 8 to 10 minutes. Uncover, stir in ginger and allspice, and cook until fragrant, about 30 seconds. Stir in cider, sugar, and any accumulated meat juices, scraping up any browned bits. Bring to simmer and cook until chutney is slightly thickened, about 2 minutes. Season with salt and pepper to taste. Spoon chutney over chops and serve.

Gently shaking the cutlets as they cook in hot oil gives our pork schnitzel a super-crisp crust with a distinctly crinkled appearance.

Pork Schnitzel

SERVES 2

✓ **WHY THIS RECIPE WORKS:** For tender pork schnitzel with a crisp but not greasy coating, we first considered the cut of pork. One small pork tenderloin was just the right size for two servings, and its tenderness and mild flavor are similar to those of veal (the traditional cutlet for schnitzel). Cutting the tenderloin crosswise at an angle and pounding the pieces gave us two oblong cutlets that fit perfectly in the pot. Cubing and microwaving bread before processing it gave us instant dry bread crumbs for a coating that cooked up extra crisp. Cooking the cutlets in plenty of oil and shaking the pot the entire time gave our schnitzel the characteristic puffed, crinkled appearance. If the pork is enhanced (injected with a salt solution), do not season with salt in step 2. The 2 cups of oil called for in this recipe may seem like a lot, but it's necessary to achieve an authentic crinkled, puffed texture on the finished cutlets. When properly cooked, the cutlets absorb very little oil. You will need at least a 6-quart Dutch oven for this recipe.

PORK

4 slices hearty white sandwich bread, crusts removed, cut into ¾-inch cubes (4 cups)

¼ cup all-purpose flour

2 large eggs

2 cups plus 1 tablespoon vegetable oil

1 (12-ounce) pork tenderloin, trimmed

Salt and pepper

GARNISHES

Lemon wedges

1 tablespoon minced fresh parsley

1 tablespoon capers, rinsed

1 large hard-cooked egg, yolk and white separated and passed separately through a fine-mesh strainer

1. Set wire rack in rimmed baking sheet. Place bread cubes in single layer on large plate and microwave until bread is dry and a few pieces start to brown lightly, 4 to 6 minutes, stirring halfway through microwaving. Process dry bread in food processor to very fine crumbs, about 45 seconds (you should have about ⅔ cup crumbs); transfer to shallow dish. Spread flour in second shallow dish. Beat eggs with 1 tablespoon oil in third shallow dish.

2. Cut tenderloin crosswise on angle into 2 pieces. Lay each piece between 2 sheets of plastic wrap and pound until roughly ⅛ to ¼ inch thick. Pat cutlets dry with paper towels and season with salt and pepper. Working with 1 cutlet at a time, dredge cutlets in flour, dip in egg mixture, then coat with bread crumbs, pressing gently to adhere. Transfer to prepared rack and let coating dry for 5 to 10 minutes.

3. Line large plate with triple layer of paper towels. Add remaining 2 cups oil to large Dutch oven until it measures about ½ inch deep and heat over medium-high heat to 375 degrees. Carefully lay cutlets in hot oil, without overlapping, and cook, shaking pot gently and continuously, until cutlets are wrinkled and light golden brown on both sides, 1 to 2 minutes per side. Transfer cutlets to paper towel–lined plate and blot well on both sides to absorb excess oil. Serve cutlets with garnishes.

Turning Tenderloin into Cutlets

1. Cut tenderloin crosswise on angle into 2 equal pieces.

2. Lay each piece between 2 sheets of plastic wrap and pound with meat pounder until roughly ⅛ to ¼ inch thick.

Crispy Cornflake Pork Chops

SERVES 2

✔ **WHY THIS RECIPE WORKS:** For pan-fried pork chops with a light, crisp coating that would stay put, it was time for a breading makeover. We opted for coating the cutlets with cornstarch instead of flour, which provided a lighter, crisper crust. Substituting cornflakes for bread crumbs ensured a craggy, crisp coating and gave the dish rich flavor. Replacing the usual egg with buttermilk gave us a wetter wash, and lightly scoring the pork then letting the breaded chops rest for just 10 minutes kept the coating from flaking off in the pan. You can substitute ½ cup store-bought cornflake crumbs for the whole cornflakes. If using crumbs, omit the processing step and mix the crumbs with the cornstarch, salt, and pepper. If the pork is enhanced (injected with a salt solution), do not brine. If brining the pork, do not season with salt in step 2. Don't let the pork chops drain on the paper towels for longer than 30 seconds, or the heat will steam the crust and make it soggy.

We use cornflakes in place of bread crumbs to make pan-fried pork chops with an especially crisp, craggy, and tasty crust.

½ cup cornstarch
½ cup buttermilk
1 tablespoon Dijon mustard
1 garlic clove, minced
1½ cups cornflakes
Salt and pepper
4 (3- to 4-ounce) boneless pork chops, ½ to ¾ inch thick, trimmed and brined if desired (see page 150)
⅓ cup vegetable oil
Lemon wedges

1. Set wire rack in rimmed backing sheet. Spread ¼ cup cornstarch in shallow dish. In second shallow dish, whisk buttermilk, mustard, and garlic together until combined. Process remaining ¼ cup cornstarch, cornflakes, ¼ teaspoon salt, and ¼ teaspoon pepper in food processor until cornflakes are finely ground, about 10 seconds; transfer mixture to third shallow dish.

2. Using sharp knife, cut 1/16-inch-deep slits on both sides of chops, spaced ½ inch apart, in crosshatch pattern. Pat chops dry with paper towels and season with salt and pepper. Working with 1 chop at a time, dredge chops in cornstarch, dip in buttermilk mixture, then coat with cornflake mixture, pressing gently to adhere. Gently pat off any excess coating from chops, then transfer to prepared rack and let sit for 10 minutes.

3. Line large plate with triple layer of paper towels. Heat oil in 12-inch nonstick skillet over medium-high heat until shimmering. Carefully lay chops in skillet and cook until golden brown and crisp on both sides and meat registers 145 degrees, 2 to 5 minutes per side. Drain chops briefly on paper towel–lined plate. Serve chops with lemon wedges.

NOTES FROM THE TEST KITCHEN

Brining Pork

Like chicken, lean cuts of pork benefit from brining, which seasons the meat and adds moisture to keep it from drying out as it cooks. Note that if you are buying pork that is enhanced (injected with a salt solution), it does not require brining; see below for more information. Here are our guidelines for brining cuts of pork. See page 115 for more information on how brining works.

CUT	WATER	TABLE SALT	TIME
12 ounces boneless country-style ribs	3 cups	1½ tablespoons	½ to 1 hour
Boneless pork chops	3 cups	1½ tablespoons	½ to 1 hour
Bone-in blade-cut pork chops	3 cups	1½ tablespoons	½ to 1 hour
Bone-in pork rib or center-cut chops	3 cups	1½ tablespoons	½ to 1 hour
1 (12-ounce) pork tenderloin	1½ quarts	3 tablespoons	½ to 1 hour

NATURAL VS. ENHANCED PORK: Because modern pork is so lean and therefore somewhat bland and prone to dryness if overcooked, many producers now inject their fresh pork products with a sodium solution. So-called enhanced pork is now the only option at many supermarkets, especially when buying lean cuts like the tenderloin. (To be sure, read the label; if the pork has been enhanced it will have an ingredient label.) Enhanced pork is injected with a solution of water, salt, sodium phosphates, sodium lactate, potassium lactate, sodium diacetate, and varying flavor agents, generally adding 7 to 15 percent extra weight. While enhanced pork does cook up juicier (it has been pumped full of water!), we find the texture almost spongy, and the flavor is often unpleasantly salty. We prefer the genuine pork flavor of natural pork and rely on brining to keep it juicy. Also, enhanced pork loses six times more moisture when frozen and thawed compared to natural pork—yet another reason to avoid enhanced pork. If you do buy enhanced pork, do not brine it.

VARIATIONS

Crispy Cornflake Pork Chops with Latin Spice Rub

Omit pepper and combine ¾ teaspoon ground cumin, ¾ teaspoon chili powder, ¼ teaspoon ground coriander, pinch ground cinnamon, and pinch red pepper flakes in small bowl. Coat pork chops with spice rub before breading.

Crispy Cornflake Pork Chops with Five-Spice Rub

Combine 1 teaspoon five-spice powder, pinch red pepper flakes, and pinch dried ginger in small bowl. Coat pork chops with spice rub before breading.

Helping the Coating Stick

Making shallow slits on both sides of chops, spaced ½ inch apart, in a crosshatch pattern releases juices and sticky meat proteins that dampen the cornstarch, helping the cornflake coating adhere.

Crispy Sesame Pork Chops with Wilted Napa Cabbage Salad

SERVES 2

✔ **WHY THIS RECIPE WORKS:** For simple pan-fried pork chops with an Asian-inspired twist, we coated our pork chops in crisp panko bread crumbs and sesame seeds, which added nutty flavor and even more crunch to the coating. Using a generous ⅓ cup of oil to fry the chops ensured that the coating came out crisp and golden brown. To round out the meal, we tossed together an easy gingery cabbage slaw. If the pork is enhanced (injected with a salt solution), do not brine. If brining the pork, do not season with salt in step 2. Don't let the pork chops drain on the paper towels for longer than 30 seconds, or the heat will steam the crust and make it soggy.

- ¼ cup all-purpose flour
- 1 large egg
- ⅔ cup panko bread crumbs
- ⅓ cup sesame seeds
- 4 (3- to 4-ounce) boneless pork chops, ½ to ¾ inch thick, trimmed and brined if desired (see page 150)

Salt and pepper

1½ tablespoons plus ⅓ cup vegetable oil

1½ teaspoons toasted sesame oil

1 garlic clove, minced

½ teaspoon grated fresh ginger

½ small head napa cabbage, cored and shredded (4 cups)

1 carrot, peeled and shredded

1 tablespoon rice vinegar, plus extra for seasoning

1. Set wire rack in rimmed backing sheet. Spread flour in shallow dish. Beat egg in second shallow dish. Combine panko and sesame seeds in third shallow dish.

2. Pat chops dry with paper towels and season with salt and pepper. Working with 1 chop at a time, dredge chops in flour, dip in egg, then coat with panko mixture, pressing gently to adhere; transfer to prepared rack.

3. Heat 1½ tablespoons vegetable oil and sesame oil in 12-inch nonstick skillet over medium heat until shimmering. Add garlic and ginger and cook until fragrant, about 30 seconds. Stir in cabbage and carrot and cook until just wilted, about 1 minute. Off heat, add rice vinegar and toss to combine. Transfer to serving bowl and season with salt, pepper, and extra vinegar to taste. Wipe skillet clean.

4. Line large plate with triple layer of paper towels. Heat remaining ⅓ cup vegetable oil in 12-inch nonstick skillet over medium-high heat until shimmering. Carefully lay chops in skillet and cook until golden brown and crisp on both sides and meat registers 145 degrees, 2 to 5 minutes per side. Drain chops briefly on paper towel–lined plate. Serve with cabbage salad.

Smothered Pork Chops

SERVES 2

✓ **WHY THIS RECIPE WORKS:** For tender smothered pork chops with plenty of flavor, bone-in blade-cut chops were our cut of choice—their higher fat content protected them from drying out during braising. A potent spice rub of onion powder, paprika, and cayenne gave us boldly seasoned meat. Sautéing the onion in butter until lightly browned before adding the other sauce components deepened its flavor. Because both the chops and the onion released a significant amount of liquid during braising, we thickened a small amount of the sauce with cornstarch to get the perfect velvety consistency. Be sure to use blade-cut pork chops, which are cut from the shoulder end of the loin and contain a significant amount of fat and connective tissue. If the pork is enhanced (injected with a salt solution), do not brine. If brining the pork, omit the salt in step 1.

Well-marbled bone-in blade-cut pork chops stay juicy when braised; once they're tender, we smother them with buttery sautéed onions.

½ teaspoon onion powder

¼ teaspoon paprika

Salt and pepper

⅛ teaspoon cayenne pepper

2 (8- to 10-ounce) bone-in blade-cut pork chops, ¾ to 1 inch thick, trimmed and brined if desired (see page 150)

1 tablespoon vegetable oil

1 tablespoon unsalted butter

1 onion, halved and sliced thin

1 garlic clove, minced

½ teaspoon minced fresh thyme or ⅛ teaspoon dried

½ cup plus 1 tablespoon beef broth

1 bay leaf

¾ teaspoon cornstarch

½ teaspoon cider vinegar

1. Adjust oven rack to middle position and heat oven to 300 degrees. Combine onion powder, paprika, ¼ teaspoon salt, ¼ teaspoon pepper, and cayenne in bowl. Cut 2 slits, about 2 inches apart, through outer layer of fat and silverskin on each chop. Pat chops dry with paper towels and rub evenly with spice mixture.

2. Heat oil in 10-inch ovensafe skillet over medium-high heat until just smoking. Brown chops well on both sides, 3 to 5 minutes per side; transfer to plate. Add butter to fat left in skillet and melt over medium heat. Add onion and cook until softened and well browned, 8 to 10 minutes. Stir in garlic and thyme and cook until fragrant, about 30 seconds. Stir in ½ cup broth and bay leaf, scraping up any browned bits, and bring to simmer.

3. Nestle browned chops into skillet along with any accumulated juices, cover, and transfer to oven. Cook until chops are fully tender and fork slips easily in and out of meat, about 1½ hours.

4. Using potholders (skillet handle will be hot), remove skillet from oven. Transfer chops to serving platter and tent loosely with aluminum foil. Strain braising liquid through fine-mesh strainer into liquid measuring cup. Discard bay leaf, then transfer onion to bowl.

5. Let braising liquid settle for 5 minutes, then remove fat from surface using large spoon. Being careful of hot skillet handle, return ⅓ cup defatted pan juices to now-empty skillet and bring to simmer. Whisk remaining 1 tablespoon broth and cornstarch together in small bowl, then whisk into skillet. Continue to simmer until sauce is thickened, about 30 seconds. Stir in onions and vinegar and season with salt and pepper to taste. Pour sauce over chops and serve.

Sautéed Pork Chops with Pears and Blue Cheese

SERVES 2

✓ **WHY THIS RECIPE WORKS:** Caramelized pears have a mild sweetness that is nicely balanced by the pungent flavor of blue cheese, and we looked to this pairing to give our sautéed pork chops sophisticated flavor in a snap. Bone-in chops stayed juicy and moist, and a dual heat approach to cooking them—searing one side over medium-high, then turning the heat down to cook the second side—allowed the chops to develop nice browning without overcooking. A simple pan sauce of chicken broth, butter, and balsamic vinegar complemented our dish without overwhelming the other flavors. Bosc pears, a firm, russet-colored variety, work great here. For the boldest flavor, use an assertive blue cheese such as Gorgonzola or Roquefort. If the pork is enhanced (injected with a salt solution), do not brine. If brining the pork, do not season with salt in step 1. Serve with polenta or a green salad.

An elegant combination of sautéed pears and tangy blue cheese dresses up these sautéed pork chops.

2 (8- to 10-ounce) bone-in pork rib or center-cut chops, ¾ to 1 inch thick, trimmed and brined if desired (see page 150)
　Salt and pepper
2 teaspoons vegetable oil
1 pear, halved, cored, and cut into ¾-inch wedges
½ teaspoon sugar
¾ cup chicken broth
2 tablespoons unsalted butter, chilled
2 teaspoons balsamic vinegar
1 ounce blue cheese, crumbled (¼ cup)

1. Cut 2 slits, about 2 inches apart, through outer layer of fat and silverskin on each chop. Pat chops dry with paper towels and season with salt and pepper.

2. Heat 1 teaspoon oil in 10-inch skillet over medium-high heat until just smoking. Lay chops in skillet and cook until well browned on first side, about 3 minutes. Flip chops, reduce heat to medium, and continue to cook until meat registers 145 degrees, 5 to 10 minutes; transfer to serving platter and tent loosely with aluminum foil.

3. Toss pear with sugar, ¼ teaspoon salt, and ⅛ teaspoon pepper in bowl. Heat remaining 1 teaspoon oil over medium-high heat until shimmering. Lay pear slices cut side down in skillet and cook until golden brown on both sides, 1 to 2 minutes per side. Stir in broth, scraping up any browned bits. Bring to simmer and cook until pears are softened, about 5 minutes. Transfer pears to platter with pork.

4. Stir any accumulated meat juices into sauce and simmer until slightly thickened, 1 to 2 minutes. Off heat, whisk in butter and vinegar and season with salt and pepper to taste. Pour sauce over chops and pear, sprinkle with blue cheese, and serve.

Pan-Seared Pork Chops with Dirty Rice

SERVES 2

✓ **WHY THIS RECIPE WORKS:** For a weeknight meal with a Southern spin, we combined quick and flavorful pan-seared pork chops with rich and earthy dirty rice. We went with bone-in rib chops, which are higher in fat than other types and therefore less prone to drying out. Browning the chops on just one side gave us the golden, crisp crust we sought while still ensuring juicy meat (and the side of the pork that was getting nestled into the rice lost its crispness anyway). Then we browned some spicy chorizo; sautéed celery, bell pepper, and onion; added the rice and chicken broth (which contributed more flavor to the rice than water); and simmered until the rice was tender. A sprinkling of scallions provided a fresh finish to our one-skillet meal. If you can't find chorizo sausage, use andouille or linguiça. If the pork is enhanced (injected with a salt solution), do not brine. If brining the pork, do not season with salt in step 1.

- 2 (12- to 14-ounce) bone-in pork rib or center-cut chops, 1½ inches thick, trimmed and brined if desired (see page 150)
  Salt and pepper
- 2 tablespoons vegetable oil
- 4 ounces chorizo, halved lengthwise and cut crosswise into ¼-inch pieces
- 1 small onion, chopped fine
- 1 celery rib, minced
- ½ red bell pepper, stemmed, seeded, and chopped fine
- ½ cup long-grain white rice, rinsed
- 2 garlic cloves, minced
- ½ teaspoon minced fresh thyme or ⅛ teaspoon dried
- ⅛ teaspoon cayenne pepper
- 1¾ cups chicken broth
- 2 scallions, sliced thin

1. Cut 2 slits, about 2 inches apart, through outer layer of fat and silverskin on each chop. Pat chops dry with paper towels and season with salt and pepper. Heat oil in 10-inch skillet over medium-high heat until just smoking. Lay chops in skillet and cook until well browned on one side, 4 to 6 minutes. Transfer chops to plate browned side up.

2. Pour off all but 1 tablespoon fat from skillet. Add chorizo and cook over medium heat until browned, 2 to 3 minutes. Stir in onion, celery, and bell pepper and cook until vegetables are softened, about 5 minutes. Stir in rice, garlic, thyme, and cayenne and cook until fragrant, about 30 seconds. Stir in broth, scraping up any browned bits.

3. Nestle chops into rice, browned side up, along with any accumulated juices, and bring to simmer. Reduce heat to medium-low, cover, and simmer until meat registers 145 degrees, 8 to 10 minutes. Transfer chops to serving platter, brushing any rice that sticks to chops back into skillet; tent loosely with aluminum foil.

4. Continue to cook rice, covered, stirring occasionally, until liquid has been absorbed and rice is tender, about 15 minutes. Off heat, gently fold in scallions and season with salt and pepper to taste. Serve chops with rice.

Bacon-Wrapped Pork Chops with Roasted Potatoes

SERVES 2

✓ **WHY THIS RECIPE WORKS:** Baked pork chops couldn't be easier, but the results are often disappointing—all that dry heat usually results in dry meat. We wanted tender and juicy baked chops paired with a flavorful side dish. To keep the chops from drying out, we wrapped them in bacon; the fat from the bacon melted as it cooked, basting our chops and adding a subtle smoky flavor as well as juiciness. Microwaving the bacon for a few minutes gave it a jump start and allowed some of the fat to render, then we finished the chops under the broiler to crisp the bacon. Cooking the pork chops on a baking sheet made it easy to roast some potatoes alongside. If you can't find red potatoes measuring less than 1 inch in diameter, you can substitute larger red potatoes cut into ¾-inch chunks. The bacon should completely cover the top of the pork chops. If your bacon is narrow, you may need three slices per chop. If the pork is enhanced (injected with a salt solution), do not brine. If brining the pork, do not season with salt in step 3.

12 ounces extra-small red potatoes, halved

2 tablespoons olive oil

Salt and pepper

4–6 slices bacon

2 (6- to 8-ounce) boneless pork chops, ¾ to 1 inch thick, trimmed and brined if desired (see page 150)

1 teaspoon ground fennel

1 tablespoon minced fresh parsley

1. Adjust oven rack to upper-middle position and heat oven to 375 degrees. Line rimmed baking sheet with aluminum foil. Toss potatoes with 1 tablespoon oil and season with salt and pepper. Lay potatoes cut side down on half of prepared sheet and roast until just tender, about 20 minutes.

2. Meanwhile, lay bacon on large plate and weigh it down with second plate. Microwave bacon until slightly shriveled but still pliable, 1 to 3 minutes. Transfer bacon to paper towel–lined plate and let cool slightly.

3. Pat chops dry with paper towels, rub evenly with fennel, and season with salt and pepper. Shingle 2 or 3 slices of bacon lengthwise over top of each pork chop so each chop is covered, tucking ends underneath to secure.

4. Remove potatoes from oven, arrange pork tucked side down on empty half of sheet, and roast until pork registers 135 degrees, 12 to 15 minutes.

5. Remove pork and potatoes from oven, adjust oven rack 6 inches from broiler element, and heat broiler. Broil pork and potatoes until bacon is crisp and browned and meat registers 145 degrees, 2 to 4 minutes. Transfer pork to large plate, tent loosely with aluminum foil, and let rest for 5 minutes.

6. While chops rest, whisk remaining 1 tablespoon oil and parsley together in large bowl. Add potatoes and toss to coat. Season with salt and pepper to taste. Serve chops with potatoes.

Preparing Bacon-Wrapped Pork Chops

1. Shingle 2 or 3 bacon slices lengthwise over top of pork, overlapping them slightly and making sure pork chop is covered by bacon.

2. Tuck ends of bacon slices underneath chop to secure them.

Maple-Glazed Pork Tenderloin

SERVES 2 **LIGHT**

✔ **WHY THIS RECIPE WORKS:** Maple-glazed pork tenderloin is a New England tradition—and since a tenderloin serves two perfectly, this was a natural dish to adapt for two. Searing the meat gave it a flavorful browned exterior and created a fond on which we could build our glaze. Maple syrup, mustard, cider vinegar, a little bourbon, and a pinch of cayenne provided a balanced glaze with sweet, smoky, tart, and spicy notes. A sugar-and-cornstarch coating created a rough exterior to which the glaze could adhere so that every bite had plenty of maple flavor. Don't be tempted to substitute imitation maple syrup—it will be too sweet. If the pork is enhanced (injected with a salt solution), do not brine. If brining the pork, omit the salt in step 2. Be sure to pat off the cornstarch mixture thoroughly in step 2, as any excess will leave gummy spots on the tenderloin. For the nutritional information for this recipe, see page 414.

⅓ cup plus 1 tablespoon maple syrup

2 tablespoons whole-grain mustard

1 tablespoon bourbon

2 teaspoons cider vinegar

Salt and pepper

Pinch cayenne pepper

1 tablespoon cornstarch

1 teaspoon sugar

1 (12-ounce) pork tenderloin, trimmed and brined if desired (see page 150)

2 teaspoons vegetable oil

1. Adjust oven rack to middle position and heat oven to 350 degrees. Stir ⅓ cup maple syrup, mustard, bourbon, vinegar, ¼ teaspoon salt, and cayenne together in small bowl.

2. Combine cornstarch, sugar, ¼ teaspoon salt, and ¼ teaspoon pepper in shallow dish. Pat tenderloin dry with paper towels, then roll in cornstarch mixture until evenly coated on all sides; thoroughly pat off excess cornstarch mixture.

3. Heat oil in 10-inch ovensafe nonstick skillet over medium-high heat until just smoking. Brown tenderloin well on all sides, 6 to 8 minutes; transfer to plate.

4. Pour off fat from skillet and return to medium heat. Add syrup mixture to now-empty skillet, bring to simmer, scraping up any browned bits, and cook until reduced to ⅓ cup, 30 seconds to 1 minute. Return browned tenderloin to skillet and turn to coat with glaze. Transfer skillet to oven and roast tenderloin until meat registers 145 degrees, 8 to 12 minutes.

5. Using potholders (skillet handle will be hot), remove skillet from oven. Transfer tenderloin to cutting board, tent loosely with aluminum foil, and let rest for 10 minutes.

Pork tenderloin—brushed with a maple glaze spiked with bourbon and mustard—makes a perfectly proportioned roast for two.

6. Meanwhile, being careful of hot skillet handle, transfer glaze left in skillet to small bowl and stir in remaining 1 tablespoon maple syrup. Brush tenderloin with 1 tablespoon glaze, then slice into ¼-inch-thick slices. Serve pork, passing remaining glaze separately.

VARIATIONS

Maple-Glazed Pork Tenderloin with Orange and Chipotle

For the nutritional information for this recipe, see page 414.

Substitute 1 teaspoon Dijon mustard for whole-grain mustard and 2 teaspoons minced chipotle chile for cayenne. Add 1 tablespoon orange marmalade to bowl along with maple syrup, mustard, bourbon, vinegar, and salt.

Maple-Glazed Pork Tenderloin with Smoked Paprika and Ginger

For the nutritional information for this recipe, see page 414.

Substitute 1 teaspoon Dijon mustard for whole-grain mustard, 1 tablespoon dry sherry for bourbon, and ¾ teaspoon grated fresh ginger and ½ teaspoon smoked paprika for cayenne.

NOTES FROM THE TEST KITCHEN

Taking the Temperature of Meat

Whether cooking a burger or roasting a pork tenderloin, you should always take the temperature of the area of the meat that will be the last to finish cooking, which is the thickest part or, in some cases, the center. Bones conduct heat, so if the meat you are cooking contains bone, make sure that the thermometer is not touching it. For roasts, take more than one reading to confirm you're at the right point of doneness.

Since the temperature of meat will continue to rise as it rests, an effect called carryover cooking, meat should be removed from the oven, grill, or pan when it's 5 to 10 degrees below the desired serving temperature. Carryover cooking doesn't apply to poultry and fish (they don't retain heat as well as the dense muscle structure in meat), so they should be cooked to the desired serving temperatures. The following temperatures should be used to determine when to stop the cooking process.

DESIRED DONENESS	COOK UNTIL IT REGISTERS
Beef/Lamb	
Rare	115 to 120 degrees (120 to 125 degrees after resting)
Medium-Rare	120 to 125 degrees (125 to 130 degrees after resting)
Medium	130 to 135 degrees (135 to 140 degrees after resting)
Medium-Well	140 to 145 degrees (145 to 150 degrees after resting)
Well-Done	150 to 155 degrees (155 to 160 degrees after resting)
Pork	
Medium	140 to 145 degrees (145 to 150 degrees after resting)
Well-Done	150 to 155 degrees (155 to 160 degrees after resting)

THE IMPORTANCE OF RESTING MEAT: You'll never see anyone in the test kitchen cut into meat straight from the oven; we always let it rest first. When exposed to heat, proteins undergo a radical transformation in which they uncoil then reconnect in haphazard structures. This process, called coagulation, is why proteins become firm and lose moisture as they cook. The longer the meat cooks, the tighter the proteins coagulate, driving liquid toward both the surface and the center of the meat, much like wringing a towel. If you cut the meat immediately after cooking, the liquid suspended between the interior proteins would simply pool on the carving board or plate. The best way to prevent this is to rest the roast. Allowing the protein molecules to relax after cooking slows the rate at which they continue to squeeze the liquid between their tight coils and increases their capacity to retain moisture. A short rest on the carving board will decrease the amount of liquid lost during carving by about 40 percent.

A warm spice rub of cocoa and chili powder contrasts nicely with a fresh mango and cilantro relish for a pork roast with bold flavor.

Spice-Rubbed Pork Tenderloin with Mango Relish

SERVES 2 LIGHT

✅ **WHY THIS RECIPE WORKS:** Lean pork tenderloin makes a great choice for a light and healthy meal. But its leanness also means it has a mild flavor and is quick to dry out; we aimed to solve both these problems without adding a lot of fat. Searing the pork on the stovetop and then finishing it in the oven was a good start—this allowed the tenderloin to develop a flavorful crust without drying out. A warm spice rub of cocoa powder, chili powder, and salt boosted the flavor of the pork. And for moisture and textural contrast, we added a bright mango relish flavored with cilantro, lime juice, and shallot, plus jalapeño for a little kick. We prefer fresh mango here, but you can substitute 1 cup frozen mango. If your mango is unripe, add sugar as needed in step 4. If the pork is enhanced (injected with a salt solution), do not brine. If brining the pork, omit the salt

in step 1. Note that the cocoa and chili powders will make the exterior of the pork look almost blackened. For the nutritional information for this recipe, see page 414.

- 2 **teaspoons chili powder**
- ½ **teaspoon unsweetened cocoa powder**
  Salt
- 1 **(12-ounce) pork tenderloin, trimmed and brined if desired (see page 150)**
- 2 **teaspoons vegetable oil**
- ½ **mango, peeled and cut into ½-inch pieces (1 cup)**
- 2 **tablespoons chopped fresh cilantro**
- 1 **tablespoon lime juice**
- 1 **small shallot, minced**
- 1 **teaspoon minced jalapeño chile, seeds and ribs removed**

1. Adjust oven rack to middle position and heat oven to 425 degrees. Combine chili powder, cocoa, and ¼ teaspoon salt in bowl. Pat tenderloin dry with paper towels and rub evenly with spice mixture.

2. Heat oil in 10-inch ovensafe nonstick skillet over medium-high heat until just smoking. Brown tenderloin well on all sides, 6 to 8 minutes, reducing heat if spices begin to burn. Transfer skillet to oven and roast tenderloin until meat registers 145 degrees, 12 to 15 minutes.

3. Using potholders (skillet handle will be hot), remove skillet from oven. Transfer tenderloin to cutting board, tent loosely with aluminum foil, and let rest for 10 minutes.

4. Meanwhile, combine mango, cilantro, lime juice, shallot, jalapeño, and ⅛ teaspoon salt in bowl. Slice tenderloin into ¼-inch-thick slices and serve with mango relish.

Trimming Pork Tenderloin

Silverskin is a swath of connective tissue located between the meat and the fat that covers its surface. Not only does this tissue have a tough, rubbery texture, but it contracts during cooking, forcing the meat to buckle and curl. This is a particular issue with long, thin pork tenderloin.

To remove silverskin from pork tenderloin, slip knife underneath it, angle knife slightly upward, and use gentle back-and-forth motion to cut it away from meat.

Artichokes, tomatoes, and fennel roast alongside a juicy herb-rubbed pork tenderloin in this satisfying one-dish dinner.

Herb-Rubbed Pork Tenderloin with Fennel and Artichokes

SERVES 2

✔ **WHY THIS RECIPE WORKS:** We wanted a light recipe for pork tenderloin inspired by the flavors of Provence. Since mild pork tenderloin benefits from bold seasoning, we opted to coat ours with a dry rub—some herbes de Provence (plus a little salt and pepper) hit the mark, and its potent flavor allowed us to skip the step of browning the tenderloin before putting it in the oven. To make this a one-dish meal, we added a flavorful combination of fennel, artichoke hearts, olives, and cherry tomatoes. Because the pork cooked quickly, we found the fennel needed a jump start in the microwave before being added to the baking dish with the other vegetables. If the pork is enhanced (injected with a salt solution), do not brine. If brining the pork, do not season with salt in step 1. To thaw frozen artichokes quickly, microwave them, covered, for 3 to 5 minutes, drain well in a colander, and thoroughly pat dry with paper towels.

1 (12-ounce) pork tenderloin, trimmed and brined if desired (see page 150)
1 teaspoon herbes de Provence
Salt and pepper
1 fennel bulb, stalks discarded, bulb halved, cored, and sliced ½ inch thick
5 ounces frozen artichoke hearts, thawed and patted dry
¼ cup pitted niçoise or kalamata olives, halved
1 tablespoon extra-virgin olive oil
6 ounces cherry tomatoes, halved
1 teaspoon grated lemon zest
1 tablespoon minced fresh parsley

1. Adjust oven rack to lower-middle position and heat oven to 450 degrees. Pat tenderloin dry with paper towels, rub evenly with herbes de Provence, and season with salt and pepper.

2. Combine fennel and 1 tablespoon water in medium bowl, cover, and microwave until fennel is softened, 2 to 3 minutes. Drain fennel well, then toss with artichokes, olives, and oil and season with salt and pepper.

3. Arrange vegetables in 8-inch square baking dish. Lay tenderloin on top of vegetables and roast until center of meat registers 145 degrees, 25 to 30 minutes, flipping tenderloin halfway through roasting. Transfer tenderloin to cutting board and tent loosely with aluminum foil.

4. Stir cherry tomatoes and lemon zest into vegetables and continue to roast until fennel is tender and tomatoes have softened, about 10 minutes. Stir parsley into vegetables and season with salt and pepper to taste. Slice tenderloin into ¼-inch-thick slices and serve with vegetables.

Smoky Indoor Ribs

SERVES 2

✔ **WHY THIS RECIPE WORKS:** Smoked ribs take as much as a day in a smoker to become fall-off-the-bone tender. This low-and-slow method is effective, but it isn't very convenient when cooking for two, so we sought to move our ribs indoors. We braised the ribs in the oven until the meat was tender, then brushed them with a simple barbecue sauce and roasted them until they had a crusty exterior like the "bark" of real barbecue. But the ribs were light on smoky flavor. Adding liquid smoke and espresso powder to both our braising liquid and our barbecue sauce and swapping regular paprika for smoked paprika solved the problem. Now our indoor ribs boasted intense depth and tasted as if they'd been in the smoker all day long. Look for liquid smoke that contains no salt or additional flavorings. Slicing the rack of ribs in half ensures that it fits perfectly in the baking dish.

Liquid smoke, smoked paprika, and instant espresso powder give these saucy baked pork ribs smoky flavor any time of year.

RIBS

- 1 **cup water**
- 1 **tablespoon instant espresso powder**
- 1 **tablespoon liquid smoke**
- 1½ **teaspoons salt**
- 1 **(2½- to 3-pound) rack pork spareribs, preferably St. Louis cut, trimmed, membrane removed, and rack cut in half**

BARBECUE SAUCE

- 2 **teaspoons vegetable oil**
- 1 **small onion, chopped fine**
  Salt and pepper
- 1½ **teaspoons smoked paprika**
- ¾ **cup chicken broth**
- ⅓ **cup cider vinegar**
- ⅓ **cup dark corn syrup**
- ⅓ **cup ketchup**
- ¼ **cup molasses**
- 1 **tablespoon brown mustard**
- 1½ **teaspoons hot sauce**
- 1½ **teaspoons instant espresso powder**
- ¼ **teaspoon liquid smoke**

1. FOR THE RIBS: Adjust oven rack to middle position and heat oven to 300 degrees. Bring water, espresso powder, liquid smoke, and salt to boil in small saucepan. Pour mixture into 13 by 9-inch baking dish. Place rib halves, meat side down, in liquid. Cover dish tightly with aluminum foil and bake for 1½ hours.

2. FOR THE BARBECUE SAUCE: Meanwhile, heat oil in medium saucepan over medium heat until shimmering. Add onion and ⅛ teaspoon salt and cook until softened, about 5 minutes. Stir in paprika and cook until fragrant, about 30 seconds. Stir in broth, vinegar, corn syrup, ketchup, molasses, mustard, hot sauce, and espresso powder. Bring to simmer and cook, stirring occasionally, until thickened and reduced to 1 cup, 20 to 25 minutes. Stir in liquid smoke and season with salt and pepper to taste. Let cool for 20 minutes. Reserve ¼ cup sauce for serving.

3. Set wire rack in aluminum foil–lined baking sheet. Remove ribs from baking dish and transfer, meat side up, to prepared rack; discard braising liquid. Brush both sides of ribs with sauce. Bake until tender and fork inserted into meat meets no resistance, about 1½ hours, brushing meat with sauce after 30 and 60 minutes of cooking. Tent ribs loosely with foil and let rest for 30 minutes. Slice meat between bones. Serve with reserved sauce.

Garlicky Pork with Eggplant

SERVES 2

✔ **WHY THIS RECIPE WORKS:** Takeout can be tempting, but sometimes we don't want to dial up dinner. Here, we wanted a pork and vegetable stir-fry in a tangy Southeast Asian–inspired sauce. Pork tenderloin is ideal for stir-fries—it's easy to slice thin, cooks quickly, and is the perfect amount for two servings—plus its mild flavor benefits from a bold stir-fry sauce. A simple sauce of brown sugar, fish sauce, soy sauce, and lime juice did the trick, and it also doubled as a marinade for the pork. Eggplant and onion provided heft and textural interest to our stir-fry, while a generous dose of garlic and black pepper provided a final punch of flavor. To make the pork easier to slice, freeze it for 15 minutes. Do not peel the eggplant, as the skin helps hold it together during cooking. Stir-fries cook quickly, so have everything prepped before you begin cooking. Serve with rice.

¼ cup chicken broth
3 tablespoons vegetable oil
1 tablespoon packed light brown sugar
2 teaspoons fish sauce
2 teaspoons soy sauce
1 teaspoon lime juice
1 (12-ounce) pork tenderloin, trimmed and sliced thin
½ teaspoon cornstarch
6 garlic cloves, minced
½ teaspoon pepper
½ eggplant (8 ounces), cut into ¾-inch pieces
1 small onion, halved and sliced ¼ inch thick
2 tablespoons coarsely chopped fresh cilantro

1. Whisk broth, 1 tablespoon oil, sugar, fish sauce, soy sauce, and lime juice together in small bowl. Measure 1 tablespoon sauce into medium bowl, then stir in pork, cornstarch, and 1 tablespoon oil. Cover and marinate pork in refrigerator for at least 10 minutes or up to 30 minutes. Meanwhile, in separate bowl, combine garlic, pepper, and 1 teaspoon oil.

2. Heat remaining 2 teaspoons oil in 12-inch nonstick skillet over high heat until just smoking. Add eggplant and onion, cover, and cook until vegetables are softened and lightly browned, about 3 minutes. Uncover and continue to cook until vegetables are tender, about 5 minutes; transfer to bowl.

3. Return now-empty skillet to high heat. Add pork, break up any clumps, and cook until no longer pink and liquid has evaporated, 4 to 6 minutes. Push pork to sides of skillet. Add garlic mixture to center and cook, mashing mixture into pan, until fragrant, about 1 minute. Stir garlic mixture into pork.

4. Stir in cooked vegetables. Whisk sauce to recombine, then add to skillet. Cook, stirring constantly, until sauce is thickened, about 1 minute. Transfer to serving platter, sprinkle with cilantro, and serve.

Slicing Pork for Stir-Fries

1. To make pork easier to slice, freeze it for 15 minutes. Slice partially frozen pork crosswise into ¼-inch-thick medallions.

2. Slice each medallion into ¼-inch-wide strips.

Stir-Fried Pork with Shiitakes and Snow Peas
SERVES 2

✔ **WHY THIS RECIPE WORKS:** For a super-easy pork stir-fry, we paired pork tenderloin with earthy mushrooms, sweet snow peas, and crisp bean sprouts for a pleasing contrast of textures and flavors. We knew our mild pork would benefit from a bold sauce; a combination of sweet hoisin sauce, salty soy sauce, tart rice vinegar, and spicy red pepper flakes added just the right complexity with a minimum of ingredients. Marinating the pork in some of the sauce and a little cornstarch ensured it was well seasoned and stayed tender when cooked over high heat. A little ginger and garlic rounded out the flavors of this simple yet satisfying one-dish meal. To make the pork easier to slice, freeze it for 15 minutes. Serve with rice.

½ cup water
3 tablespoons vegetable oil
2 tablespoons hoisin sauce
2 tablespoons soy sauce
1 teaspoon rice vinegar
¼ teaspoon red pepper flakes
1 (12-ounce) pork tenderloin, trimmed and sliced thin
½ teaspoon cornstarch
2 garlic cloves, minced
2 teaspoons grated fresh ginger
6 ounces shiitake mushrooms, stemmed and sliced thin
4 ounces snow peas, strings removed
4 ounces (2 cups) bean sprouts

1. Whisk ¼ cup water, 1 tablespoon oil, hoisin, soy sauce, vinegar, and pepper flakes together in small bowl. Measure 1 tablespoon sauce into medium bowl, then stir in pork, cornstarch, and 1 tablespoon oil. Cover and marinate pork in refrigerator for at least 10 minutes or up to 30 minutes. Meanwhile, in separate bowl, combine garlic, ginger, and remaining 1 tablespoon oil.

2. Cook mushrooms, snow peas, and remaining ¼ cup water, covered, in 12-inch nonstick skillet over high heat until water is boiling and vegetables begin to soften, about 3 minutes. Uncover and cook until water has evaporated and vegetables are crisp-tender, about 30 seconds; transfer to bowl.

3. Return now-empty skillet to high heat. Add pork, break up any clumps, and cook until no longer pink and liquid has evaporated, 4 to 6 minutes. Push pork to sides of skillet. Add garlic mixture to center of skillet and cook, mashing mixture into pan, until fragrant, 15 to 30 seconds. Stir garlic mixture into pork.

4. Stir in cooked vegetables and bean sprouts. Whisk sauce to recombine, then add to skillet. Cook, stirring constantly, until sauce is thickened, about 1 minute. Serve.

Pork Fajitas

SERVES 2 FAST

✓ **WHY THIS RECIPE WORKS:** Fajitas are by design a quick-cooking, all-in-one meal, making them the perfect choice for a busy evening. And while they are more traditionally made with chicken or beef, for something a little different, we decided to develop a recipe for juicy pork fajitas. Slicing pork tenderloin into thin pieces before cooking sped up the cooking process. A duo of bell pepper and red onion added just the right texture, color, and sweetness to our meal. A little chili powder, added to the skillet while the vegetables cooked, gave our dish a flavor boost. Once the vegetables were done, we set them aside and added the pork to the pan to cook for just a few minutes. Lime juice, cilantro, and cumin contributed brightness and complexity. To make the pork easier to slice, freeze it for 15 minutes. Serve with your favorite fajita toppings.

- 1 tablespoon lime juice
- 2 tablespoons minced fresh cilantro
- 2 tablespoons vegetable oil
- 1 red, green, or yellow bell pepper, stemmed, seeded, and cut into ½-inch-wide strips
- 1 small red onion, halved and sliced thin
- 1 teaspoon chili powder
  Salt and pepper
- 1 (12-ounce) pork tenderloin, trimmed, halved lengthwise and sliced crosswise ¼ inch thick
- ¼ teaspoon ground cumin
- 6 (6-inch) flour tortillas, warmed

1. Whisk lime juice, cilantro, and 2 teaspoons oil together in bowl.

2. Heat 1 tablespoon oil in 12-inch skillet over medium-high heat until shimmering. Add bell pepper, onion, chili powder, and ½ teaspoon salt and cook until vegetables are softened, 5 to 7 minutes; transfer to serving platter and tent loosely with aluminum foil.

3. Pat pork dry with paper towels and season with salt and pepper. Heat remaining 1 teaspoon oil in now-empty skillet over high heat until just smoking. Add pork, break up any clumps, and cook until no longer pink and liquid has evaporated, 4 to 6 minutes. Stir in cumin and cook until fragrant, about 30 seconds. Off heat, stir in lime juice mixture and season with salt and pepper to taste; transfer to platter with vegetables. Serve pork with warm tortillas.

We use chipotle chiles to give quick-cooking ground pork the smoky, long-cooked flavor of traditional Mexican *tacos al pastor*.

Pork Tacos with Mango Salsa

SERVES 2 FAST

✓ **WHY THIS RECIPE WORKS:** We wanted to capture the flavor of *tacos al pastor*—a Mexican taco filling of slow-cooked, chile-rubbed pork with chopped onion, cilantro, and lime—in a weeknight recipe. Since the traditional large cut of pork shoulder was out of the question for two, we aimed to infuse quick-cooking ground pork with smoky flavor. Chipotle chiles were exactly what we needed; they provided a slow-smoked flavor and a subtle, lingering heat. A generous dose of cilantro and lime juice gave our dish an authentic flavor profile. A little shredded Monterey Jack cheese melted into the pork created a cohesive filling. Spooned into warm corn tortillas and topped with a bright mango salsa, this was a dish we could easily enjoy any night of the week. We prefer fresh mangos here, but you can substitute 1½ cups frozen mango. If your mango is unripe, add sugar as needed in step 1.

1 pound mangos, peeled, pitted, and cut into ¼-inch pieces
¼ cup minced fresh cilantro
1 shallot, minced
4 teaspoons lime juice
  Salt and pepper
2 teaspoons vegetable oil
1 teaspoon minced canned chipotle chile in adobo sauce
12 ounces ground pork
1 ounce Monterey Jack cheese, shredded (¼ cup)
6 (6-inch) corn tortillas, warmed
  Lime wedges

1. Combine mangos, 2 tablespoons cilantro, half of shallot, 2 teaspoons lime juice, ⅛ teaspoon salt, and ⅛ teaspoon pepper in bowl; set aside.

2. Heat oil in 10-inch skillet over medium heat until shimmering. Add remaining shallot, chipotle, and ¼ teaspoon salt and cook until shallot is softened, about 2 minutes. Add pork and cook, breaking meat up with wooden spoon, until pork is no longer pink, about 5 minutes.

3. Off heat, stir in remaining 2 tablespoons cilantro, remaining 2 teaspoons lime juice, and Monterey Jack and season with salt and pepper to taste. Serve pork with warm tortillas, mango salsa, and lime wedges.

Cutting Mangos

1. After cutting thin slice from 1 end of mango, rest mango on trimmed bottom and cut off skin in thin strips, top to bottom.

2. Cut down along each side of flat pit to remove flesh.

3. Trim any remaining flesh off sides of pit. Once fruit is peeled and sliced, it can be chopped as desired.

Mediterranean-Style Braised Lamb Chops

SERVES 2

✔ **WHY THIS RECIPE WORKS:** When buying lamb, many people turn to the tried and true (and expensive) loin or rib chops. But overlooked shoulder chops deliver good flavor and are easy to prepare, making them an ideal choice for a simple weeknight braise. Since shoulder chops are not a tough cut of meat, we found that they didn't need to cook for very long—in just 30 minutes, we had extraordinarily tender chops. Rich lamb stands up well to bold flavors, so we created a Mediterranean-inspired braise with tomatoes, fragrant rosemary, briny olives, and a sprinkling of fresh parsley. Because they are generally leaner, round bone chops, also called arm chops, are preferable for this braise. If available, however, lean blade chops also braise nicely. Serve with polenta or rice.

2 (10-ounce) shoulder lamb chops, ¾ to 1 inch thick, trimmed
  Salt and pepper
1 tablespoon olive oil
1 small onion, chopped fine
2 garlic cloves, minced
2 teaspoons minced fresh rosemary or ½ teaspoon dried
¼ cup dry red wine
1 (14.5-ounce) can diced tomatoes
¼ cup pitted kalamata olives, chopped
2 tablespoons minced fresh parsley

1. Pat chops dry with paper towels and season with salt and pepper. Heat oil in 12-inch skillet over medium-high heat until just smoking. Brown chops well on both sides, 3 to 5 minutes per side; transfer to plate.

2. Pour off all but 1 tablespoon fat from skillet. Add onion and cook over medium heat until softened, about 5 minutes. Stir in garlic and rosemary and cook until fragrant, about 30 seconds. Stir in wine, scraping up any browned bits, and bring to simmer.

3. Stir in tomatoes and their juice and olives. Nestle browned chops into skillet along with any accumulated juices and bring to simmer. Reduce heat to medium-low, cover, and simmer until chops are fully tender and fork slips easily in and out of meat, 20 to 30 minutes. Transfer chops to serving platter and tent loosely with aluminum foil.

4. Continue to simmer sauce until thickened, 2 to 3 minutes. Stir in parsley and season with salt and pepper to taste. Pour sauce over chops and serve.

Pan-Roasted Lamb Chops with Mint Relish

SERVES 2

✔ **WHY THIS RECIPE WORKS:** Lamb chops, particularly rib or loin chops, are premium cuts of meat, so our goal was to develop a foolproof recipe that would guarantee perfectly cooked lamb every time. For chops with a crisp, well-browned exterior and a tender, rosy interior, we found that a two-step approach was key. We started by pan-searing the chops on the stovetop before moving them to the oven (425 degrees was just right) to finish cooking through gently. A quick, fresh mint relish seasoned with shallot, honey, and garlic was the perfect foil to the rich lamb. We prefer the milder taste and bigger size of domestic lamb chops. If using lamb from New Zealand or Australia, the chops will probably be smaller and cook more quickly. We prefer these chops cooked to medium-rare, but if you prefer them more or less done, see our guidelines on page 155.

MINT RELISH
- 2 tablespoons extra-virgin olive oil
- 1 tablespoon minced fresh parsley
- 1 tablespoon minced fresh mint
- 1 small shallot, minced
- 2 teaspoons red wine vinegar
- 2 teaspoons honey
- 1 garlic clove, minced
  Salt and pepper

LAMB
- 4 (6- to 8-ounce) lamb loin chops, 1½ inches thick, trimmed
  Salt and pepper
- 2 teaspoons vegetable oil

1. FOR THE MINT RELISH: Combine all ingredients in bowl and season with salt and pepper to taste. Let relish sit at room temperature while preparing lamb.

NOTES FROM THE TEST KITCHEN

Domestic vs. Imported Lamb

While almost all of the beef and pork sold in American markets are raised domestically, you can purchase imported as well as domestic lamb. Domestic lamb is distinguished by its larger size and milder flavor, while lamb imported from Australia and New Zealand features a far gamier taste. Imported lamb is pasture-fed on mixed grasses, while lamb raised in the United States begins on a diet of grass but finishes with grain. The switch to grain has a direct impact on the composition of the animal's fat, reducing the concentration of the fatty acids that give lamb its characteristic "lamby" flavor—and ultimately leading to sweeter-tasting meat.

A fresh mint relish with shallot, vinegar, and a little honey is the perfect complement to tender, juicy pan-seared lamb chops.

2. FOR THE LAMB: Adjust oven rack to middle position and heat oven to 425 degrees. Pat chops dry with paper towels and season with salt and pepper.

3. Heat oil in 10-inch ovensafe skillet over medium-high heat until just smoking. Brown chops well on both sides, 3 to 5 minutes per side. Transfer skillet to oven and roast chops until meat registers 120 to 125 degrees (for medium-rare), 6 to 8 minutes.

4. Using potholders (skillet handle will be hot), remove skillet from oven. Transfer chops to plate, tent loosely with aluminum foil, and let rest for 5 minutes. Serve chops with relish.

VARIATION
Pan-Roasted Lamb Chops with Apricot Chutney
Bring ¼ cup water, ¼ cup chopped dried apricots, 2 tablespoons minced shallot, 2 tablespoons packed brown sugar, 2 tablespoons cider vinegar, 1 (1-inch) piece ginger, peeled and sliced into ¼-inch-thick rounds, ½ minced jalapeño, and ⅛ teaspoon salt to simmer in small saucepan. Cook, stirring occasionally, until chutney is thickened, about 15 minutes. Discard ginger rounds and season with salt and pepper to taste. Substitute chutney for mint relish.

Roast Rack of Lamb with Whiskey Sauce

SERVES 2

✔ **WHY THIS RECIPE WORKS:** Roast rack of lamb for two? No problem. Most home cooks have little experience preparing this classic, whether for two or more, so we set out to create an approachable, foolproof recipe. Searing the rack of lamb in a skillet to get a good caramelized crust was key. We used tongs to sear it well on the sides and bottom before transferring the lamb to the oven. We roasted the rack on a rimmed baking sheet until it reached just the right temperature. A smoky, slightly sweet whiskey sauce was the perfect accompaniment to the rich flavor of the lamb. We prefer the milder taste and bigger size of domestic lamb. If using lamb from New Zealand or Australia, the rack will probably be smaller and cook more quickly. We like the smoky flavor of Scotch whiskey, but Irish or American whiskey can be substituted. Have the butcher french the racks for you; the ribs will need some cleaning up, but it will minimize your prep work. We prefer the lamb cooked to medium-rare, but if you prefer it more or less done, see our guidelines on page 155.

LAMB

- 1 (1¼- to 1½-pound) rack of lamb (8 to 9 ribs), frenched and trimmed
  Salt and pepper
- 1 teaspoon vegetable oil

WHISKEY SAUCE

- 1 shallot, minced
- 1 sprig fresh rosemary
- 1 garlic clove, minced
- ½ teaspoon all-purpose flour
- 5 tablespoons Scotch whiskey
- ¾ cup chicken broth
- 1 tablespoon chopped fresh parsley
- 1 tablespoon unsalted butter
- ½ teaspoon lemon juice
  Salt and pepper

1. FOR THE LAMB: Adjust oven rack to lower-middle position, place rimmed baking sheet on rack, and heat oven to 425 degrees.

2. Pat lamb dry with paper towels and season with salt and pepper. Heat oil in 10-inch skillet over medium-high heat until just smoking. Lay lamb in skillet meat side down and cook, without moving, until well browned, 3 to 5 minutes. Reduce heat to medium and, using tongs, hold rack upright in skillet to brown bottom, 2 to 3 minutes.

3. Transfer lamb meat side up to hot sheet in oven, setting skillet aside for sauce. Roast lamb until meat registers 120 to 125 degrees (for medium-rare), 12 to 15 minutes. Transfer lamb to carving board, tent loosely with aluminum foil, and let rest for 5 to 10 minutes.

4. FOR THE WHISKEY SAUCE: Meanwhile, pour off all but 1 teaspoon fat from skillet. Add shallot and rosemary sprig and cook over medium heat until shallot is softened, about 2 minutes. Stir in garlic and cook until fragrant, about 30 seconds. Stir in flour and cook for 1 minute.

5. Off heat, slowly stir in ¼ cup whiskey, scraping up any browned bits, and let sit until bubbling subsides, about 1 minute. Carefully return skillet to medium heat and simmer until whiskey has almost completely evaporated, 2 to 3 minutes. Stir in broth and continue to simmer, stirring occasionally, until sauce is slightly thickened and reduced to ⅓ cup, 3 to 5 minutes. Stir in any accumulated meat juices and simmer for 30 seconds.

6. Off heat, discard rosemary sprig. Whisk in remaining 1 tablespoon whiskey, parsley, butter, and lemon juice and season with salt and pepper to taste. Carve lamb, slicing between each rib into individual chops. Serve lamb with sauce.

Preparing Rack of Lamb

1. Using boning knife, scrape rib bones clean of any scraps of meat or fat.

2. Trim off outer layer of fat, thin flap of meat underneath it, and fat underneath that flap.

3. Remove silverskin by sliding boning knife between silverskin and flesh.

CHAPTER 7

Fish and Shellfish

■ FAST (Start to finish in about 30 minutes)

▣ LIGHT (See page 414 for nutritional information)

Opposite: Lemon-Steamed Sole with Green Pea Sauce; Pan-Seared Salmon with Braised Lentils and Swiss Chard; Pan-Seared Scallops

Fish Meunière

SERVES 2   **FAST**

✓ **WHY THIS RECIPE WORKS:** The best versions of fish meunière feature perfectly cooked fillets that are lightly crisp and golden brown on the outside, napped with a nutty browned butter sauce. For the fish, we liked sole or flounder; using ⅜-inch-thick fillets prevented them from overcooking. We seasoned the fish and let it sit for 5 minutes until beads of moisture appeared on the surface before dredging it with flour. This gave us a crisp, not heavy, coating. A nonstick skillet coated with a mixture of oil and butter prevented sticking. For the sauce, we browned butter in a traditional skillet (which allowed us to monitor the color of the butter) and brightened it with lemon. Try to purchase fillets that are similar in size; avoid those that weigh less than 5 ounces because they will cook too quickly.

¼ cup all-purpose flour

2 (5- to 6-ounce) boneless, skinless sole or flounder fillets, ⅜ inch thick

   Salt and pepper

2 tablespoons vegetable oil

3 tablespoons unsalted butter

2 teaspoons lemon juice

1½ teaspoons minced fresh parsley

   Lemon wedges

1. Adjust oven rack to lower-middle position, set 2 ovensafe dinner plates on rack, and heat oven to 200 degrees. Spread flour in shallow dish. Pat sole dry with paper towels and season generously with salt and pepper. Let sit until fillets are glistening with moisture, about 5 minutes. Working with 1 fillet at a time, dredge fillets in flour.

2. Heat oil in 12-inch nonstick skillet over high heat until shimmering, then add 1 tablespoon butter and swirl to coat skillet bottom. Lay fillets skinned side up in skillet. Immediately reduce heat to medium-high and cook, without moving fillets, until edges of fillets are opaque and bottom is golden brown, about 3 minutes. Using 2 spatulas, gently flip fillets and cook until fish flakes apart when gently prodded with paring knife, about 2 minutes. Transfer fillets, one to each heated dinner plate, keeping skinned side down; return plates to oven.

3. Melt remaining 2 tablespoons butter in 8-inch skillet over medium-high heat. Continue to cook, swirling skillet constantly, until butter is golden brown and has nutty aroma, about 2 minutes. Off heat, stir in lemon juice and season with salt and pepper to taste. Using potholders (plates will be hot), remove plates from oven. Spoon sauce over fillets and sprinkle with parsley. Serve immediately with lemon wedges.

Lemon-Steamed Sole with Green Pea Sauce

SERVES 2   **LIGHT**

✓ **WHY THIS RECIPE WORKS:** Steaming is not only healthy and quick, it also keeps food moist and flavors pure. We wanted to dress up simple steamed sole with a complementary sauce. The key to perfect steamed fish was to roll the thin fillets into tight cylinders; this protected them from overcooking and ensured that they cooked uniformly. To keep the fish from sticking to the steamer basket, we lined it with lemon slices and placed the rolled fillets on top—the lemon also imparted some bright flavor to the fish. For a vibrant sauce to accent the mild fish, we sautéed frozen peas with shallot, garlic, white wine, and chicken broth then pureed the mixture until smooth. Try to purchase fillets that are similar in size. Avoid using frozen fish in this recipe; it will be hard to roll. If necessary, reheat the sauce briefly over medium-low heat before serving. You will need a steamer basket for this recipe. For the nutritional information for this recipe, see page 414.

8 (¼-inch-thick) slices lemon

1 teaspoon extra-virgin olive oil

1 small shallot, minced

1 garlic clove, minced

⅓ cup chicken broth

2 tablespoons dry white wine

½ cup frozen peas

½ teaspoon lemon juice

   Salt and pepper

4 (3-ounce) boneless, skinless sole or flounder fillets, ⅛ to ¼ inch thick

1 tablespoon chopped fresh basil

1. Fit Dutch oven with steamer basket and add water to pot until it just touches bottom of basket. Line basket with 4 lemon slices, cover, and bring to boil.

2. Meanwhile, heat oil in small saucepan over medium heat until shimmering. Add shallot and cook until softened, about 2 minutes. Stir in garlic and cook until fragrant, about 30 seconds. Stir in broth and wine and bring to boil. Stir in peas and cook until tender, about 2 minutes. Transfer mixture to blender and process until completely smooth, about 30 seconds, scraping down sides of blender jar as needed. Return sauce to now-empty saucepan, stir in lemon juice, and season with salt and pepper to taste; cover to keep warm.

3. Pat sole dry with paper towels and season with salt and pepper. Arrange fillets skinned side up with tail end pointing away from you. Tightly roll fillets from thick end to thin end to form cylinders.

4. Reduce heat under Dutch oven so that water is at simmer. Lay fillets seam side down on top of each lemon slice and top with remaining 4 lemon slices. Cover and steam until fish flakes apart when gently prodded with paring knife, 4 to 6 minutes. Gently transfer fillets to individual plates, discarding lemon slices. Top fillets with sauce and sprinkle with basil. Serve.

NOTES FROM THE TEST KITCHEN

Buying and Storing Fish

WHAT TO LOOK FOR: The most important factor when buying fish is making sure the fish you buy is fresh. Always buy fish from a trusted source (preferably one with high volume to help ensure freshness). The store, and the fish in it, should smell like the sea, not fishy or sour. And all the fish should be on ice or be properly refrigerated. Fillets and steaks should look bright, shiny, and firm, not dull or mushy. Whole fish should have moist, taut skin, clear eyes, and bright red gills.

WHAT TO ASK FOR: It is always better to have your fishmonger slice steaks and fillets to order rather than buying precut pieces that may have been sitting around. Don't be afraid to be picky at the seafood counter; a ragged piece of cod or a tail-end of salmon will be difficult to cook properly. It is important to keep your fish cold, so if you have a long ride home, ask your fishmonger for a bag of ice.

BUYING FROZEN FISH: Thin fish fillets like flounder and sole are the best choice if you have to buy your fish frozen because thin fillets freeze quickly, minimizing moisture loss. Firm fillets like halibut, snapper, tilapia, and salmon are acceptable to buy frozen if they will be cooked beyond medium-rare, but at lower degrees of doneness they will have a dry, stringy texture. When buying frozen fish, make sure the fish is frozen solid, with no signs of freezer burn or excessive crystallization around the edges and no blood inside the packaging. The ingredients should include nothing but the name of the fish you are buying.

DEFROSTING FISH: To defrost fish in the refrigerator overnight, remove the fish from its packaging, place it in a single layer on a rimmed plate or dish (to catch released water), and cover it with plastic wrap. You can also do a "quick thaw" by leaving the vacuum-sealed bags under cool running tap water for 30 minutes. Do not use a microwave to defrost fish; it will alter the texture of the fish or, worse, partially cook it. Dry the fish thoroughly with paper towels before seasoning and cooking it.

HOW TO STORE IT: Because fish is so perishable, it's best to buy it the day it will be cooked. But if that's not possible, it's important to store it properly. As soon as you get home with your fish, unwrap it, pat it dry, put it in a zipper-lock bag, press out the air, and seal the bag. Then set the fish on a bed of ice in a bowl or other deep container (that can contain the water once the ice melts), and place the bowl in the back of the fridge, where it is coldest. If the ice melts before you use the fish, replenish it. The fish should keep for one day.

Steamed Sole and Vegetable Bundles with Tarragon

SERVES 2 `LIGHT`

WHY THIS RECIPE WORKS: For a light and easy supper with an elegant presentation, we steamed delicate bundles of vegetables wrapped in fillets of sole. A combination of asparagus, carrot, and red onion made a tasty and visually appealing filling. To ensure they were nicely crisp-tender, we steamed the vegetables on their own for 5 minutes before rolling them in the fish fillets. To flavor the mild fish and add some richness, we rubbed it with a compound butter made with tarragon, minced shallot, garlic, and lemon zest and juice. Propping up the bundles on lemon slices reinforced the citrus flavor and prevented them from sticking to the steamer basket. Avoid using frozen fish in this recipe; it will be hard to roll. If your asparagus spears are very thick, halve them lengthwise before using. You will need a steamer basket for this recipe. For the nutritional information for this recipe, see page 414.

8 ounces asparagus, trimmed and cut into
    2-inch lengths
1 carrot, peeled and cut into 2-inch-long matchsticks
½ red onion, sliced thin
1 tablespoon unsalted butter, softened
1 tablespoon chopped fresh tarragon
1 small shallot, minced
1 garlic clove, minced
¼ teaspoon grated lemon zest plus ½ teaspoon juice
    Salt and pepper
4 (3-ounce) boneless, skinless sole or flounder fillets,
    ⅛ to ¼ inch thick
8 (¼-inch-thick) slices lemon

Cutting Carrots into Matchsticks

1. Slice carrot on bias into 2-inch-long oval-shaped pieces.

2. Lay ovals flat on cutting board, then slice into 2-inch-long matchsticks, about ¼ inch thick.

1. Fit Dutch oven with steamer basket. Fill pot with water until it just touches bottom of basket and bring to boil. Add asparagus, carrot, and onion to basket, cover, and steam until just tender, about 5 minutes. Remove steamer basket and vegetables from pot, rinse vegetables with cool water, then pat dry. Cover pot to keep water warm.

2. Meanwhile, mix butter, 2 teaspoons tarragon, shallot, garlic, lemon zest and juice, ⅛ teaspoon salt, and pinch pepper together in bowl.

3. Pat sole dry with paper towels and season with salt and pepper. Arrange fillets skinned side up with tail end pointing away from you. Spread one-quarter of tarragon butter over each fillet. Divide vegetables among fillets, laying them across wider end of each piece of fish. Tightly roll fillets around vegetables from thick end to thin end to form tidy bundles.

4. Return steamer basket to pot with steaming water and line with 4 lemon slices. Lay fish bundles seam side down on top of each lemon slice. Sprinkle bundles with remaining 1 teaspoon tarragon and lay remaining 4 lemon slices on top.

5. Bring water in pot to boil. Cover and steam until fish flakes apart when gently prodded with paring knife, 5 to 7 minutes. Gently transfer bundles to individual plates; discard lemon slices. Serve.

NOTES FROM THE TEST KITCHEN

Judging the Doneness of Fish

Overcooking fish is a common cooking mistake. The trick to perfectly cooked fish—fish that is cooked all the way through, but not dried out and flavorless—is knowing when to remove it from the heat so that it is just slightly underdone, then allowing the residual heat to finish the cooking. The most accurate way to make sure that thicker fish fillets and steaks are properly cooked is to use an instant-read thermometer. Tuna is best when rare; it should register 110 degrees in the thickest part, with only the outer layer opaque and the rest of the fish translucent. Salmon is best cooked to medium-rare; it should register 125 degrees in the thickest part, with the center still translucent. White fish should register 135 to 140 degrees. However, a thermometer is not practical if you are cooking very thin fish fillets. In these cases, use a paring knife to peek inside; the fish should separate into neat flakes. The flesh should look opaque but still appear moist.

Rare	110 degrees (for tuna only)
Medium-Rare	125 degrees (for tuna or salmon)
Medium	135 to 140 degrees (for white-fleshed fish)

Skillet-Braised Cod Provençal

SERVES 2 　LIGHT

✔ **WHY THIS RECIPE WORKS:** For a fresh approach to cod, we set our sights on braised cod napped with a garlicky tomato sauce inspired by the sunny flavors of Provence. For the sauce, we started by sautéing shallot and garlic. Fresh tomato made a big impact here, providing great flavor and just the right amount of juice for a sauce that nicely coated the fish. White wine, kalamata olives, and fennel—all reminiscent of southern France—gave the sauce a bold, complex flavor. For this one-skillet dish, we braised the fish directly in the sauce. Keeping the heat low and the skillet covered were key to getting the delicate fish to turn out moist and silky. Try to purchase cod fillets that are similar in size so that they cook at the same rate. If the fillets are much thinner than 1 inch, simply fold them over to make them thicker. Halibut and haddock are good substitutes for the cod. Serve with crusty bread to soak up the extra sauce. For the nutritional information for this recipe, see page 414.

2　teaspoons extra-virgin olive oil, plus extra for serving
1　fennel bulb, stalks discarded, bulb halved, cored, and sliced thin
1　shallot, halved and sliced thin
　　Salt and pepper
4　garlic cloves, minced
½　teaspoon minced fresh thyme or ⅛ teaspoon dried
1　large tomato, cored and chopped
¼　cup pitted kalamata olives, chopped coarse
¼　cup dry white wine or dry vermouth
2　(6- to 8-ounce) skinless cod fillets, 1 to 1½ inches thick
1　tablespoon minced fresh parsley

1. Heat oil in 10-inch nonstick skillet over medium heat until shimmering. Add fennel, shallot, and ¼ teaspoon salt and cook until vegetables are softened, 5 to 7 minutes. Stir in garlic and thyme and cook until fragrant, about 30 seconds. Stir in tomato, olives, and wine and bring to simmer.

2. Season cod with salt and pepper. Nestle fillets into skillet, spoon some of sauce over fillets, and bring to simmer. Reduce heat to medium-low, cover, and simmer until fish flakes apart when gently prodded with paring knife and registers 140 degrees, 8 to 10 minutes.

3. Gently transfer fillets to individual plates. Off heat, stir parsley into sauce and season with salt and pepper to taste. Spoon sauce over fillets and serve, passing extra oil separately.

Mild cod gets a boost of flavor from a saucy mix of sautéed bell pepper, onion, diced tomatoes, garlic, and thyme.

2 teaspoons olive oil
1 red bell pepper, stemmed, seeded, and cut into ¼-inch-wide strips
1 small onion, halved and sliced thin
1 teaspoon paprika
    Salt and pepper
2 garlic cloves, minced
½ teaspoon minced fresh thyme or ⅛ teaspoon dried
½ cup canned diced tomatoes, drained
¼ cup dry white wine
2 (6- to 8-ounce) skinless cod fillets, 1 to 1½ inches thick
1 tablespoon chopped fresh basil
1 teaspoon balsamic or sherry vinegar

1. Heat oil in 10-inch nonstick skillet over medium heat until shimmering. Add bell pepper, onion, paprika, and ¼ teaspoon salt and cook until vegetables are softened and lightly browned, 8 to 10 minutes. Stir in garlic and thyme and cook until fragrant, about 30 seconds. Stir in tomatoes, wine, and ⅛ teaspoon pepper and bring to simmer.

2. Season cod with salt and pepper. Nestle fillets into skillet, spoon some of sauce over fillets, and bring to simmer. Reduce heat to medium-low, cover, and simmer until fish flakes apart when gently prodded with paring knife and registers 140 degrees, 8 to 10 minutes.

3. Gently transfer fillets to individual plates. Off heat, stir basil and vinegar into sauce and season with salt and pepper to taste. Spoon sauce over fillets and serve.

Braised Cod Peperonata

SERVES 2 `LIGHT`

✓ **WHY THIS RECIPE WORKS:** Following the success of our Provençal-style braised cod, we wanted to make an Italian-inspired version with *peperonata*, a flavorful condiment made from tomatoes, red bell pepper, onion, and garlic. We sautéed the bell pepper and onion until softened and browned, added garlic, thyme, and diced tomatoes, and brought everything to a simmer before nestling the fish into the sauce. The sauce infused the fish fillets with flavor as they braised and protected them from the heat so they stayed moist and tender. Chopped basil and a dash of balsamic vinegar added freshness and reinforced our Italian theme. Try to purchase cod fillets that are similar in size so that they cook at the same rate. If the fillets are much thinner than 1 inch, simply fold them over to make them thicker. Halibut and haddock are good substitutes for the cod. You can substitute smoked paprika for the sweet paprika. For the nutritional information for this recipe, see page 414.

Poached Cod with Miso, Shiitakes, and Edamame

SERVES 2 `LIGHT`

✓ **WHY THIS RECIPE WORKS:** Poaching in a seasoned broth is a great way to add flavor to white fish. We set out to give mild cod an Asian-inspired spin with this easy technique. We used low heat to cook the fish gently and covered the skillet so that the fish partially simmered and partially steamed. A combination of mirin, soy sauce, garlic, and ginger infused the fish with flavor. To round out the meal, we sautéed shiitake mushrooms then simmered shelled edamame with the fish. Finally, we stirred the mushrooms into the broth along with miso paste, toasted sesame oil, and added a sprinkling of fresh scallion. Try to purchase cod fillets that are similar in size so that they cook at the same rate. If the fillets are much thinner than 1 inch, simply fold them over to make them thicker. Halibut and haddock are good substitutes for the cod. You can substitute white, brown, barley, or brown rice miso for the red miso, but do not substitute "light" miso; its flavor is too mild. For the nutritional information for this recipe, see page 414.

2 teaspoons vegetable oil
4 ounces shiitake mushrooms, stemmed and sliced ¼ inch thick
1 cup shelled frozen edamame, thawed
⅔ cup water
2 teaspoons soy sauce
2 teaspoons mirin
2 garlic cloves, peeled and smashed
1 (1-inch) piece ginger, peeled and sliced into ¼-inch-thick rounds and smashed
2 (6- to 8-ounce) skinless cod fillets, 1 to 1½ inches thick
 Salt and pepper
2 teaspoons red miso paste
½ teaspoon toasted sesame oil
1 scallion, sliced thin

1. Heat vegetable oil in 10-inch skillet over medium heat until shimmering. Add mushrooms and cook until they have released their liquid and are lightly browned, 3 to 4 minutes; transfer to bowl.

2. Combine edamame, water, soy sauce, mirin, garlic, and ginger in now-empty skillet. Season cod with salt and pepper. Nestle fillets into skillet, spooning some of poaching liquid over fillets, and bring to simmer. Reduce heat to medium-low, cover, and simmer until fish flakes apart when gently prodded with paring knife and registers 140 degrees, 5 to 7 minutes.

3. Gently transfer fillets to individual shallow serving bowls. Discard garlic and ginger. Stir mushrooms, miso, and sesame oil into poaching liquid and let sit until heated through, about 1 minute. Using slotted spoon, transfer vegetables to bowls with fillets. Pour hot broth over fillets and sprinkle with scallion. Serve.

Folding Fillets

Because fish fillets can often differ in thickness, you may end up with a thin fillet or with fillets of fish with thinner tail ends. If fillets are thin or have thinner tail ends, simply fold them over to make them thicker.

Baked Sole Fillets with Herbs and Bread Crumbs

SERVES 2 LIGHT

✔ **WHY THIS RECIPE WORKS:** We wanted a fuss-free, foolproof sole recipe suitable for a weeknight yet elegant enough for a special occasion. We found that rolling the fillets into compact bundles eased the transport from baking dish to plate, and covering the baking dish with foil protected the delicate fish from the drying heat of the oven. To ramp up the sole's mild flavor, we brushed the fillets with Dijon mustard, seasoned them with fresh herbs and lemon zest, and drizzled them with melted butter and garlic. For texture, we topped the fillets with a mixture of herbs and panko bread crumbs browned in butter. Try to purchase sole fillets that are similar in size so that they cook at the same rate. Avoid using frozen fish in this recipe; it will be hard to roll. For the nutritional information for this recipe, see page 414.

2 tablespoons minced fresh chives
1 teaspoon minced fresh tarragon, basil, or dill
¼ teaspoon grated lemon zest
2 tablespoons unsalted butter
1 garlic clove, minced
2 (5- to 6-ounce) boneless, skinless sole or flounder fillets, ⅜ inch thick
 Salt and pepper
1 teaspoon Dijon mustard
⅓ cup panko bread crumbs
 Lemon wedges

1. Adjust oven rack to middle position and heat oven to 325 degrees. Combine chives and tarragon in small bowl. Measure out 1 teaspoon herb mixture and set aside. Stir lemon zest into remaining herb mixture.

2. Melt 1 tablespoon butter in 8-inch skillet over medium heat. Add half of garlic and cook, stirring often, until fragrant, about 1 minute. Remove skillet from heat.

3. Pat sole dry with paper towels and season with salt and pepper. Arrange fillets skinned side up with tail end pointing away from you. Spread ½ teaspoon mustard over each fillet, sprinkle each evenly with half of herb–lemon zest mixture, and drizzle each with 1 teaspoon garlic butter. Tightly roll fillets from thick end to thin end to form cylinders. Set fillets seam side down in 8-inch square baking dish. Drizzle remaining garlic butter over fillets, cover baking dish with aluminum foil, and bake for 25 minutes.

4. Meanwhile, wipe skillet clean. Melt remaining 1 tablespoon butter in now-empty skillet over medium heat. Add panko and cook, stirring often, until panko is deep golden brown, 5 to 8 minutes. Reduce heat to low, add remaining garlic, and cook, stirring constantly, until garlic is fragrant and evenly distributed throughout panko, about 1 minute. Transfer mixture to small bowl and season with salt and pepper to taste. Let cool slightly, then stir in reserved 1 teaspoon herb mixture.

5. Remove baking dish from oven. Baste fillets with melted garlic butter from baking dish and sprinkle with all but 1 tablespoon panko mixture. Continue to bake, uncovered, until fish flakes apart when gently prodded with paring knife, 6 to 10 minutes. Gently transfer fillets to individual plates and sprinkle with remaining 1 tablespoon panko mixture. Serve with lemon wedges.

Baked Fish with Crisp Bread Crumbs

SERVES 2

For a bread-crumb coating that's anything but bland, we toast the crumbs in butter with garlic, shallot, and thyme.

✔ WHY THIS RECIPE WORKS: Baked fish sounds like a great option for two: healthy and easy to prepare, with a crunchy, buttery crumb topping to complement the moist fish. To ensure that this easy weeknight meal lived up to its potential, we gently baked the fish in a low oven so there would be no chance of it overcooking. Elevating it on a wire rack allowed the air to circulate around it for even cooking and a crisp crust. To avoid bland bread crumbs, we sautéed crisp panko bread crumbs in butter with garlic, shallot, and thyme until golden brown. To keep the coating from falling off the fish, we used mayonnaise (flavored with lemon zest and pepper) to adhere them securely. Try to purchase cod fillets that are similar in size so that they cook at the same rate. If the fillets are much thinner than 1 inch, simply fold them over to make them thicker. Halibut and haddock are good substitutes for the cod.

2 tablespoons unsalted butter
1 small shallot, minced
  Salt and pepper
1 small garlic clove, minced
¾ teaspoon minced fresh thyme or ¼ teaspoon dried
½ cup panko bread crumbs
1½ tablespoons minced fresh parsley
2 tablespoons mayonnaise
¼ teaspoon grated lemon zest
2 (6- to 8-ounce) skinless cod fillets, 1 to 1½ inches thick

1. Adjust oven rack to middle position and heat oven to 300 degrees. Set wire rack in rimmed baking sheet and spray with vegetable oil spray.

2. Melt butter in 10-inch skillet over medium heat. Add shallot and ⅛ teaspoon salt and cook until shallot is softened, about 2 minutes. Stir in garlic and thyme and cook until fragrant, about 30 seconds. Stir in panko and ⅛ teaspoon pepper and cook, stirring often, until panko is deep golden brown, 5 to 8 minutes. Transfer panko to shallow dish, let cool slightly, then stir in parsley.

3. Whisk mayonnaise, lemon zest, and ⅛ teaspoon pepper together in bowl. Pat cod dry with paper towels and season with salt and pepper. Coat tops of fillets evenly with mayonnaise mixture. Working with 1 fillet at a time, dredge coated side in panko mixture, pressing gently to adhere. Place fillets panko side up on prepared rack and bake until fish flakes apart when gently prodded with paring knife and registers 140 degrees, 30 to 35 minutes, rotating sheet halfway through baking. Serve.

This one-dish dinner combines crispy, garlicky potato slices with flaky cod fillets lightly flavored with lemon and thyme.

Lemon-Herb Cod with Crispy Garlic Potatoes

SERVES 2

✔ **WHY THIS RECIPE WORKS:** We set out to develop a simple one-dish dinner of flaky cod and crispy roasted potatoes. For potatoes that would cook through quickly, we sliced russet potatoes thin, tossed them with oil and garlic, and shingled them into two piles in a greased baking dish. We roasted the potatoes until they were spotty brown and tender then added the cod fillets—topped with pieces of butter, sprigs of thyme, and slices of lemon—and slid it all back into the oven. After just 15 minutes more, we had a perfect dinner of moist, subtly flavored cod and crispy, garlicky potatoes. Try to purchase cod fillets that are similar in size so that they cook at the same rate. If the fillets are much thinner than 1 inch, simply fold them over to make them thicker. Halibut and haddock are good substitutes for the cod.

2 tablespoons olive oil
2 (8-ounce) russet potatoes, sliced ¼ inch thick (about 18 slices)
2 garlic cloves, minced
   Salt and pepper
2 (6- to 8-ounce) skinless cod fillets, 1 to 1½ inches thick
1 tablespoon unsalted butter, cut into ¼-inch pieces
2 sprigs fresh thyme
½ lemon, sliced thin

1. Adjust oven rack to lower-middle position and heat oven to 425 degrees. Brush 13 by 9-inch baking dish with 1 tablespoon oil.

2. Toss potatoes with remaining 1 tablespoon oil and garlic and season with salt and pepper. Shingle potatoes into baking dish in 2 rectangular piles measuring 4 by 6 inches. Roast potatoes until spotty brown and just tender, 30 to 35 minutes, rotating dish halfway through roasting.

3. Pat cod dry with paper towels and season with salt and pepper. Carefully place 1 fillet skinned side down on top of each potato pile. Top fillets with butter pieces, thyme sprigs, and lemon slices. Roast cod and potatoes until fish flakes apart when gently prodded with paring knife and registers 140 degrees, about 15 minutes.

4. Slide spatula underneath potatoes and fillets and gently transfer to individual plates. Serve.

Arranging Cod with Potatoes and Lemon

1. Shingle potato slices into 2 piles of 3 tight rows, each measuring about 4 by 6 inches. Gently push rows together so that potatoes are tidy and cohesive.

2. After parcooking potatoes, carefully place 1 cod fillet skinned side down on top of each set of potatoes. Top fish with butter pieces, thyme sprigs, and lemon slices and return to oven to finish cooking.

Baked Cod with Cherry Tomatoes and Artichokes

SERVES 2 **FAST** **LIGHT**

✔ **WHY THIS RECIPE WORKS:** Cooking mild cod together with a mixture of bright, fresh vegetables is an easy way to enhance its delicate flavor. We wanted a one-dish meal where the vegetables would lend flavor and moisture to the fish as they cooked down into a chunky sauce. Thick cod fillets lightly brushed with olive oil stayed moist in the oven. To complement the fish (and minimize prep), we chose cherry tomatoes and frozen artichoke hearts for the vegetables. We tossed them with minced shallot, olives, white wine, and olive oil before baking so they would emerge from the oven as a hearty and flavorful sauce. Try to purchase cod fillets that are similar in size so that they cook at the same rate. If the fillets are much thinner than 1 inch, simply fold them over to make them thicker. Halibut and haddock are good substitutes for the cod. To thaw the frozen artichokes quickly, microwave them on high, covered, for about 3 minutes. Be sure to pat the artichokes dry with paper towels before using. For the nutritional information for this recipe, see page 414.

6 ounces cherry tomatoes, quartered
5 ounces frozen artichoke hearts, thawed and patted dry
¼ cup pitted kalamata olives, chopped coarse
2 tablespoons dry white wine
1 shallot, minced
2 teaspoons extra-virgin olive oil
1 garlic clove, minced
½ teaspoon minced fresh thyme or ⅛ teaspoon dried
    Salt and pepper
2 (6- to 8-ounce) skinless cod fillets, 1 to 1½ inches thick
1 tablespoon chopped fresh basil
    Lemon wedges

1. Adjust oven rack to middle position and heat oven to 450 degrees. Toss tomatoes, artichokes, olives, wine, shallot, 1 teaspoon oil, garlic, thyme, ⅛ teaspoon salt, and ⅛ teaspoon pepper together in bowl; transfer to 8-inch square baking dish.

2. Pat cod dry with paper towels and nestle into tomato mixture. Brush tops of fillets with remaining 1 teaspoon oil and season with salt and pepper. Cover dish tightly with aluminum foil and bake for 10 minutes.

3. Remove foil and continue to bake until fish flakes apart when gently prodded with paring knife and registers 140 degrees, 5 to 10 minutes. Sprinkle with basil and serve with lemon wedges.

We pair mild snapper with a rich, roasted ratatouille of eggplant, zucchini, tomatoes, and shallots flavored with garlic and herbs.

Baked Snapper with Roasted Ratatouille

SERVES 2

✔ **WHY THIS RECIPE WORKS:** We wanted a simple, sophisticated seafood dish with the bright and sunny flavors of Mediterranean cuisine. *Ratatouille*, a Provençal dish that combines tomatoes, eggplant, and squash seasoned with garlic and herbs, fit the bill. We thought that the clean, mild flavor and firm texture of red snapper paired well with the roasted vegetables. To keep our dish weeknight-friendly, we wanted to cook all the vegetables together in one dish. Roasting them at 375 degrees proved best; it was hot enough to evaporate the vegetables' exuded liquid, keeping the dish from becoming waterlogged, but not so hot that the vegetables scorched. To give the fish its own distinct flavor, we marinated it in olive oil flavored with basil, lemon, and garlic while the vegetables roasted. Then we simply nestled the fillets into the vegetables for the final 10 minutes of roasting. You can substitute Arctic char, catfish, cod, grouper, or tilefish fillets for the snapper. Be sure to remove the fish from the marinade after 30 minutes.

1 (14.5-ounce) can diced tomatoes

1 zucchini or summer squash, cut into ½-inch pieces

½ eggplant (8 ounces), cut into ½-inch pieces

2 shallots, halved and sliced ¼ inch thick

¼ cup extra-virgin olive oil

4 garlic cloves, minced

½ teaspoon minced fresh thyme or ⅛ teaspoon dried
   Salt and pepper

1 tablespoon chopped fresh basil

1 teaspoon grated lemon zest

2 (6-ounce) skin-on snapper fillets, 1 to 1¼ inches thick

1½ teaspoons red wine vinegar
   Lemon wedges

1. Adjust oven rack to middle position and heat oven to 375 degrees. Combine tomatoes and their juice, zucchini, eggplant, shallots, 1 tablespoon oil, half of garlic, and thyme in bowl and season with salt and pepper.

2. Spread vegetable mixture in 8-inch square baking dish. Roast until vegetables are browned and softened, 50 to 60 minutes, stirring halfway through cooking.

3. Meanwhile, whisk remaining 3 tablespoons oil, remaining garlic, 2 teaspoons basil, and lemon zest together in bowl. Pat snapper dry with paper towels and season with salt and pepper. Add fillets to bowl and turn to coat. Cover and refrigerate for 30 minutes.

4. Remove fillets from marinade and gently nestle into roasted vegetables. Bake until fish flakes apart when gently prodded with paring knife and registers 140 degrees, about 10 minutes. Sprinkle with remaining 1 teaspoon basil and vinegar. Serve with lemon wedges.

Cutting Up Eggplant

Cutting up an awkwardly shaped vegetable like eggplant can be tricky. Here's how we do it.

1. To cut eggplant into tidy pieces, first cut eggplant crosswise into 1-inch-thick rounds.

2. Then cut each round into pieces as directed in recipe.

Pan-Roasted Thick-Cut Fish Fillets

SERVES 2   FAST

✓ WHY THIS RECIPE WORKS: Pan-roasted fish seems like a simple dish, but in practice it is usually only well executed by skilled chefs—attempts by home cooks often result in dry, overbaked fillets. We set out to develop a foolproof recipe for succulent, well-browned fillets. We quickly learned that we needed thick fillets; thinner pieces overcooked by the time they browned. To ensure the fillets didn't overcook, we seared them in a hot pan, flipped them, then moved the skillet to the oven to finish cooking. Seasoning the fillets with a little sugar accelerated browning, shortening the cooking time to prevent the fish from drying out. The fish emerged from the oven well browned, tender, and moist. Try to purchase cod fillets that are similar in size so that they cook at the same rate; if the fillets are thicker or thinner, be sure to adjust the cooking time as needed. Halibut and haddock are good substitutes for the cod. If your nonstick skillet isn't ovensafe, sear the cod as directed in step 2, then transfer it to a baking sheet and bake as directed in step 3.

2 (6- to 8-ounce) skinless cod fillets, 1 to 1½ inches thick
   Salt and pepper

¼ teaspoon sugar

2 teaspoons vegetable oil
   Lemon wedges

1. Adjust oven rack to middle position and heat oven to 425 degrees. Pat cod dry with paper towels and season with salt and pepper. Sprinkle ⅛ teaspoon sugar evenly over skinned side of each fillet.

2. Heat oil in 10-inch ovensafe nonstick skillet over high heat until just smoking. Place fillets in skillet, sugared sides down, and press down lightly to ensure even contact with skillet. Cook until browned on first side, 1 to 1½ minutes. Using 2 spatulas, gently flip fillets and transfer skillet to oven.

3. Roast fillets until fish flakes apart when gently prodded with paring knife and registers 140 degrees, 7 to 10 minutes. Serve immediately with lemon wedges.

VARIATIONS

Pan-Roasted Thick-Cut Fish Fillets with Green Olive, Almond, and Orange Relish

Pimento-stuffed olives can be substituted for the large green olives in a pinch.

Omit lemon wedges. Pulse ¼ cup pitted large green olives, ¼ cup toasted slivered almonds, 1 minced small garlic clove, and ½ teaspoon grated orange zest in food processor until nuts and olives are finely chopped, 10 to 12 pulses, scraping down sides of bowl as needed. Transfer mixture to medium bowl and stir in 2 tablespoons orange juice, 2 tablespoons extra-virgin olive oil, 2 tablespoons minced fresh mint, and 1 teaspoon white wine vinegar. Season with salt and pepper to taste. Cook fish as directed. Spoon relish over fillets before serving.

Pan-Roasted Thick-Cut Fish Fillets with Roasted Red Pepper, Hazelnut, and Thyme Relish

We prefer the flavor of smoked paprika in this recipe, but sweet paprika can be substituted.

Omit lemon wedges. Pulse ¼ cup jarred roasted red peppers, rinsed, patted dry, and coarsely chopped; ¼ cup toasted skinned hazelnuts; 1 minced small garlic clove; and ¼ teaspoon grated lemon zest in food processor until finely chopped, 10 to 12 pulses, scraping down sides of bowl as needed. Transfer mixture to medium bowl and stir in 2 tablespoons extra-virgin olive oil, 2 tablespoons minced fresh parsley, 2 teaspoons lemon juice, ½ teaspoon minced fresh thyme, and ⅛ teaspoon smoked paprika. Season with salt and pepper to taste. Cook fish as directed. Spoon relish over fillets before serving.

Moroccan Fish and Couscous Packets

SERVES 2

✔ **WHY THIS RECIPE WORKS:** Cooking fish *en papillote* is a French technique where fish and a side are artfully folded into a parchment paper packet to steam together in the oven, concentrating and marrying their flavors. We found that aluminum foil was easier to work with than parchment. White fish fillets worked best; oilier fishes like salmon or tuna ended up greasy and overwhelmingly pungent. For a simple side, we liked quick-cooking couscous, and we dressed it up with a zesty chermoula sauce—a flavorful Moroccan condiment of cilantro, ginger, garlic, lemon, and spices. Try to purchase cod fillets that are similar in size so that they cook at the same rate. If the fillets are much thinner than 1 inch, simply fold them over to make them thicker. Halibut and haddock are good substitutes for the cod. For an accurate measurement of boiling water, bring a full kettle of water to a boil then measure out the desired amount. For more information on making a foil packet, see page 127.

A simple foil packet gives us the moist texture and concentrated flavors of fish *en papillote* without the usual fussy preparation.

¼   cup minced fresh cilantro
2   tablespoons extra-virgin olive oil
1   tablespoon grated fresh ginger
2   teaspoons smoked paprika
2   garlic cloves, minced
2   teaspoons grated lemon zest plus 1 tablespoon juice
1   teaspoon ground cumin
⅛   teaspoon red pepper flakes
    Salt and pepper
    Brown sugar
¾   cup couscous
1   cup boiling water
2   (6- to 8-ounce) skinless cod fillets, 1 to 1½ inches thick
    Lemon wedges

1. Adjust oven rack to middle position and heat oven to 400 degrees. Combine 3 tablespoons cilantro, oil, ginger, paprika, garlic, 1½ teaspoons lemon zest and juice, cumin, and pepper flakes in small bowl. Season with salt, pepper, and sugar to taste.

2. Place couscous in medium bowl. Pour boiling water over couscous. Immediately cover with plastic wrap and let sit until liquid is absorbed and couscous is tender, about 5 minutes. Fluff couscous with fork, stir in remaining ½ teaspoon lemon zest, and season with salt and pepper to taste.

3. Pat cod dry with paper towels and season with salt and pepper. Cut two 14 by 12-inch rectangles of aluminum foil and lay them flat on counter. Divide couscous in half evenly, mound in center of each piece of foil, then place fillets on top. Spread 1 tablespoon of sauce over top of each fillet, then tightly crimp foil into packets.

4. Set packets on rimmed baking sheet and bake until fish flakes apart when gently prodded with paring knife and registers 140 degrees, 14 to 18 minutes. Carefully open packets, allowing steam to escape away from you. Sprinkle fillets with remaining 1 tablespoon cilantro and serve with remaining sauce and lemon wedges.

Thai-Style Fish and Creamy Coconut Rice Packets

SERVES 2

✔ **WHY THIS RECIPE WORKS:** For a Thai-inspired take on fish *en papillote*, we combined meaty halibut fillets and rice with a quick yet potent sauce made from coconut milk, green curry paste, lime zest, and a little cilantro, which we simply whisked together. The sauce did more than infuse the fish with flavor—it also provided a burst of color and transformed the rice into a rich, creamy accompaniment for our hearty halibut fillets. Try to purchase halibut fillets that are similar in size so that they cook at the same rate. If the fillets are much thinner than ¾ inch, simply fold them over to make them thicker. Cod and haddock are good substitutes for the halibut. You can use leftover rice or store-bought precooked rice here. For more information on making a foil packet, see page 127.

½ cup canned coconut milk
¼ cup minced fresh cilantro
4 teaspoons Thai green curry paste
1 teaspoon lime zest
2 (6- to 8-ounce) skinless halibut fillets, ¾ inch to 1 inch thick
  Salt and pepper
2 cups cooked rice
  Lime wedges

1. Adjust oven rack to middle position and heat oven to 400 degrees. Whisk coconut milk, 3 tablespoons cilantro, curry paste, and lime zest together in bowl.

2. Pat halibut dry with paper towels and season with salt and pepper. Cut two 14 by 12-inch rectangles of aluminum foil and lay them flat on counter. Mound 1 cup cooked rice in center of each piece of foil, then place fillets on top. Spoon coconut mixture over top of fillets, then tightly crimp foil into packets.

3. Set packets on rimmed baking sheet and bake until fish flakes apart when gently prodded with paring knife and registers 140 degrees, 18 to 20 minutes. Carefully open packets, allowing steam to escape away from you. Sprinkle fillets with remaining 1 tablespoon cilantro and serve with lime wedges.

Spiced Swordfish with Avocado-Grapefruit Salsa

SERVES 2 **FAST**

✔ **WHY THIS RECIPE WORKS:** For a quick but satisfying weeknight dinner, we started with meaty swordfish, a fish with an assertive flavor that fares well in robustly flavored dishes. One-inch-thick steaks made it easy to brown the fish nicely without overcooking. For bold flavor, we brushed the steaks with a chili powder and cayenne–spiced oil. To get a nice char and get dinner on the table fast, we took advantage of the intense heat of the broiler, which cooked the steaks in less than 10 minutes. A tangy grapefruit and avocado salsa gave the fish a burst of fresh flavor. Try to purchase swordfish steaks that are about 1 inch thick; if the steaks are thicker or thinner, be sure to adjust the cooking time as needed. Other firm-fleshed fish such as bluefish, red snapper, or grouper can be used in place of the swordfish. If you can find ruby red grapefruit, its color and tangy sweetness work well in this dish.

SALSA
½ grapefruit
½ avocado, cut into ½-inch pieces
1 small shallot, sliced thin
1 tablespoon minced fresh mint
1½ teaspoons lime juice
  Salt and pepper

SWORDFISH
1 tablespoon vegetable oil
1 teaspoon chili powder
  Pinch cayenne pepper
2 (6- to 8-ounce) skinless swordfish steaks, 1 inch thick
  Salt and pepper

A bright avocado and grapefruit salsa nicely balances rich, meaty swordfish spiced with chili powder and cayenne.

1. FOR THE SALSA: Cut away peel and pith from grapefruit. Cut into 4 wedges, then slice each wedge crosswise into ½-inch-thick pieces. Combine grapefruit, avocado, shallot, mint, and lime juice in bowl and season with salt and pepper to taste; set aside.

2. FOR THE SWORDFISH: Adjust oven rack 6 inches from broiler element and heat broiler. Line rimmed baking sheet with aluminum foil and spray with vegetable oil spray. Combine oil, chili powder, and cayenne in bowl. Pat swordfish dry with paper towels, brush with spiced oil, and season with salt and pepper. Lay steaks on prepared sheet and broil until fish flakes apart when gently prodded with paring knife and registers 140 degrees, 6 to 9 minutes. Serve with salsa.

Sesame-Crusted Tuna with Wasabi Dressing
SERVES 2 **FAST**

✓ **WHY THIS RECIPE WORKS:** In our opinion, pan-seared tuna should have a nice crust, a rare to medium-rare center, and simple, complementary flavors. We found that a coating of sesame seeds helped us accomplish all of these things in one fell swoop. Our simple sesame-seed crust minimized the time the fish needed to spend in the skillet and all but eliminated the risk of overcooking the interior. Once toasted, the sesame seeds also contributed great nutty flavor but were still mild enough that they didn't compete with the flavor of the fish. A creamy, spicy dressing of wasabi paste, mayonnaise, and lime juice was the perfect accent. We prefer the flavor and texture of yellowfin tuna here; however, any type of fresh tuna will work. Try to purchase tuna steaks that are about 1 inch thick; if the steaks are thicker or thinner, be sure to adjust the cooking time as needed.

DRESSING
2 tablespoons mayonnaise
1½ teaspoons lime juice
1½ teaspoons wasabi paste
Salt and pepper

TUNA
¼ cup sesame seeds
2 (6- to 8-ounce) tuna steaks, 1 inch thick
1½ tablespoons vegetable oil
Salt and pepper

1. FOR THE DRESSING: Whisk all ingredients together in bowl and season with salt and pepper to taste; set aside.

2. FOR THE TUNA: Spread sesame seeds in shallow dish. Pat tuna dry with paper towels, rub with 1½ teaspoons oil, and season with salt and pepper. Press both sides of each steak in sesame seeds to coat.

3. Heat remaining 1 tablespoon oil in 10-inch nonstick skillet over medium-high heat until just smoking. Lay steaks in skillet and cook until seeds are golden brown, about 2 minutes. Using 2 spatulas, gently flip steaks and continue to cook until seeds are just golden and fish registers 110 degrees (for rare), about 1½ minutes (steaks will be opaque at perimeters and translucent red at center when checked with tip of paring knife), or 125 degrees (for medium-rare), about 3 minutes (steaks will be opaque at perimeters and reddish pink at center). Transfer steaks to cutting board and immediately slice on bias. Serve with wasabi dressing.

VARIATION
Sesame-Crusted Tuna with Ginger-Soy Sauce
Whisk following ingredients together in bowl and substitute for dressing: 2 tablespoons soy sauce, 2 tablespoons water, 1 thinly sliced small scallion, 1 tablespoon rice vinegar, 1 tablespoon sugar, 1 teaspoon grated fresh ginger, 1 teaspoon toasted sesame oil, and pinch red pepper flakes.

Pan-seared salmon and sautéed asparagus drizzled with a bright fresh herb dressing make an elegant yet easy supper.

2   (6- to 8-ounce) skin-on salmon fillets, 1½ inches thick
    Salt and pepper
¼   cup olive oil
1   tablespoon unsalted butter
8   ounces thick asparagus, trimmed
4   teaspoons lemon juice
1   small shallot, minced
2   teaspoons minced fresh parsley, basil, or mint
½   teaspoon Dijon mustard

1. Pat salmon dry with paper towels and season with salt and pepper. Heat 2 teaspoons oil in 10-inch nonstick skillet over medium-high heat until just smoking. Lay fillets skin side up in skillet and cook until well browned on first side, about 5 minutes. Using tongs, gently flip fillets. Reduce heat to medium and continue to cook until center of fish is still translucent when checked with tip of paring knife and registers 125 degrees (for medium-rare), 3 to 5 minutes; transfer to serving platter and tent loosely with aluminum foil. Wipe skillet clean.

2. Add butter and 1 teaspoon oil to now-empty skillet and heat over medium heat until butter is melted. Add half of asparagus to skillet with tips pointed in one direction and add remaining spears with tips pointed in opposite direction. Sprinkle with ⅛ teaspoon salt and gently shake asparagus into even layer.

3. Cover and cook until spears are bright green and still crisp, about 5 minutes. Uncover, increase heat to high, and continue to cook until spears are tender and well browned on one side, 5 to 7 minutes, using tongs to move spears from center of pan to edge of pan to ensure all are browned.

4. Meanwhile, whisk remaining 3 tablespoons oil, lemon juice, shallot, parsley, and mustard together in small bowl and season with salt and pepper to taste. Transfer asparagus to platter with fillets, drizzle with dressing, and serve.

Salmon with Asparagus and Herb Dressing

SERVES 2

✔ **WHY THIS RECIPE WORKS:** Salmon is rich, buttery, and satisfying, and pan searing is a perfect way to take advantage of its high fat content to produce a flavorful caramelized crust. We wanted to pair salmon with a side of crisp, nicely browned asparagus spears for a simple skillet dinner. To ensure a good sear, we carefully patted the salmon dry then seared it over medium-high heat on one side before flipping it and reducing the heat to gently cook it through. For the asparagus, we chose thick spears; thinner spears were tough and overcooked by the time they browned. To pull the dish together, we whisked together a simple dressing of shallot, lemon juice, mustard, and fresh parsley (basil or mint were good as well). Try to purchase center-cut salmon fillets of similar size so that they cook at the same rate. This recipe works best with asparagus that is at least ½ inch thick near the base. Do not use pencil-thin asparagus; it will overcook.

Pan-Seared Salmon with Braised Lentils and Swiss Chard

SERVES 2

✔ **WHY THIS RECIPE WORKS:** We wanted to pair earthy braised lentils and Swiss chard with buttery pan-seared salmon for a hearty, satisfying meal for two. First, we braised the lentils in a skillet (to cut down on dishes) with onion, garlic, thyme, chicken broth, and the chard stems to infuse the lentils with flavor. Once they were tender, we removed them from the skillet and quickly pan-seared the salmon until it had a beautiful browned, caramelized crust and a moist, medium-rare interior. While the salmon rested, we rewarmed the lentils, stirring in the chard leaves until they were just wilted. Try to purchase center-cut salmon fillets of similar size so that they cook at the same rate. If you purchase skin-on fillets, follow the instructions on page 183 to remove the skin. Although we prefer *lentilles du Puy* (also called French green lentils) for this recipe, it will work with any type of lentil except red or yellow. Note that cooking times may vary depending on the type of lentils you use.

    2 tablespoons unsalted butter
    6 ounces Swiss chard, stems chopped, leaves cut into
       1-inch pieces
    ¼ cup finely chopped onion
    1 garlic clove, minced
    ¼ teaspoon minced fresh thyme or pinch dried
    2 cups chicken broth
    ½ cup brown lentils, picked over and rinsed
    ½ teaspoon lemon juice
       Salt and pepper
    2 (6- to 8-ounce) skinless salmon fillets, 1½ inches thick
    1 tablespoon vegetable oil
       Lemon wedges

1. Melt 1 tablespoon butter in 10-inch nonstick skillet over medium heat. Add chard stems and onion and cook until vegetables are softened, about 5 minutes. Stir in garlic and thyme and cook until fragrant, about 30 seconds. Stir in 1¾ cups broth, lentils, and lemon juice and bring to simmer. Reduce heat to low, cover, and simmer until lentils are tender, about 30 minutes. Season with salt and pepper to taste, transfer to bowl, and cover to keep warm.

2. Wipe skillet clean. Pat salmon dry with paper towels and season with salt and pepper. Heat oil in now-empty skillet over medium-high heat until just smoking. Lay fillets in skillet and cook until browned on first side, about 5 minutes. Using tongs, gently flip fillets and continue to cook until center of fish is still translucent when checked with tip of paring knife and registers 125 degrees (for medium-rare), 3 to 5 minutes; transfer to plate and tent loosely with aluminum foil.

3. Wipe skillet clean and return to medium-high heat. Add cooked lentil mixture and remaining ¼ cup broth to now-empty skillet and cook until hot, about 1 minute. Stir in chard leaves and remaining 1 tablespoon butter and cook, stirring constantly, until chard is wilted, 2 to 3 minutes. Serve fillets with lentils and lemon wedges.

Chili-Glazed Salmon with Bok Choy

SERVES 2   **FAST**

✔ **WHY THIS RECIPE WORKS:** To turn glazed salmon into a simple skillet meal, we wanted a foolproof way to get perfectly cooked fish with a crisp, well-browned crust alongside an easy vegetable side. Cooking the fillets in a nonstick skillet kept the browned crust on the fish, not stuck to the pan. We started our Asian-inspired glaze with sweet chili sauce; a little savory fish sauce and fresh ginger were all we needed to turn it into a boldly flavored glaze. A pinch of cornstarch helped to thicken the glaze so that it nicely coated the fish. Baby bok choy sautéed until lightly browned paired perfectly with the rich salmon. Try to purchase center-cut salmon fillets of similar size so that they cook at the same rate. Be sure to use sweet chili sauce here; hot chili sauce (such as chili-garlic sauce) will make the glaze too spicy and thin. If you purchase skin-on fillets, follow the instructions on page 183 to remove the skin.

    2   tablespoons Asian sweet chili sauce
    1   tablespoon fish sauce
    1½ teaspoons grated fresh ginger
    ¼   teaspoon cornstarch
    2   tablespoons vegetable oil
    2   heads baby bok choy (4 ounces each), halved
    2   (6- to 8-ounce) skinless salmon fillets, 1½ inches thick
        Salt and pepper
        Lime wedges

1. Whisk chili sauce, fish sauce, ginger, and cornstarch together in small bowl. Heat 1 tablespoon oil in 10-inch nonstick skillet over high heat until shimmering. Add bok choy cut side down to skillet and cook until lightly browned on both sides, 1 to 2 minutes per side; transfer to plate.

2. Pat salmon dry with paper towels and season with salt and pepper. Heat remaining 1 tablespoon oil in now-empty skillet over medium-high heat until just smoking. Lay fillets in skillet and cook until browned on first side, about 5 minutes. Using tongs, gently flip fillets and continue to cook until center of fish is still translucent when checked with tip of paring knife and registers 125 degrees (for medium-rare), 3 to 5 minutes. Holding fillets in place with spatula, carefully pour off any rendered fat in skillet. Off heat, add chili sauce mixture to skillet with salmon and gently flip fillets once or twice to coat. Transfer fillets to serving platter.

3. Add bok choy to skillet with glaze and toss until coated; transfer to platter with fillets. Serve with lime wedges.

Oven-Roasted Salmon with Fresh Tomato Relish

SERVES 2 | **FAST**

✓ **WHY THIS RECIPE WORKS:** Roasting a salmon fillet can create a beautiful bronzed, flavorful crust, but often the price is a dry, chalky interior. To get the best of both worlds, we developed a hybrid roasting method, preheating the oven to 500 degrees but turning down the heat to just 275 before placing the fish in the oven. The initial blast of high heat firmed the exterior and rendered some fat, then as the temperature dropped, the fish gently cooked through. Cutting several slits in the salmon skin helped the fat to render. A fresh tomato relish was the perfect accompaniment to the rich, roasted salmon. Try to purchase center-cut salmon fillets of similar size so that they cook at the same rate. It is important to keep the salmon skin on during cooking; if desired, remove it before serving.

RELISH
- 1 tomato, cored, seeded, and cut into ¼-inch pieces
- 1 tablespoon chopped fresh basil, parsley, or tarragon
- 2 teaspoons minced shallot
- 2 teaspoons extra-virgin olive oil
- 1 small garlic clove, minced
- ½ teaspoon red wine vinegar
   Salt and pepper

SALMON
- 2 (6- to 8-ounce) skin-on salmon fillets, 1½ inches thick
- 1 teaspoon olive oil
   Salt and pepper

1. FOR THE RELISH: Combine all ingredients in bowl and season with salt and pepper to taste; set aside.

2. FOR THE SALMON: Adjust oven rack to lowest position, place rimmed baking sheet on rack, and heat oven to 500 degrees. Using sharp knife, make 4 or 5 shallow slashes about 1 inch apart along skin side of each fillet, being careful not to cut into flesh. Pat fillets dry with paper towels, rub with oil, and season generously with salt and pepper.

3. Reduce oven temperature to 275 degrees and remove hot sheet. Carefully lay fillets skin side down on sheet and roast until center of fish is still translucent when checked with tip of paring knife and registers 125 degrees (for medium-rare), 9 to 13 minutes. Serve with relish.

VARIATIONS
Oven-Roasted Salmon with Spicy Cucumber Relish
A small jalapeño chile can be substituted for the serrano chile.

Combine ½ cucumber, peeled, halved lengthwise, seeded, and cut into ¼-inch pieces; 1 tablespoon chopped fresh mint; 1 minced small shallot; ½ minced serrano chile; 2 teaspoons lime juice; and 1 teaspoon extra-virgin olive oil in bowl. Season with salt and extra lime juice to taste. Substitute cucumber relish for tomato relish.

Oven-Roasted Salmon with Tangerine and Ginger Relish
If you are short on tangerine juice, substitute water.

Cut away peel and pith from 2 tangerines. Cut tangerines into 8 wedges, then slice each wedge crosswise into ½-inch-thick pieces. Place tangerine pieces in fine-mesh strainer set over medium bowl and let drain for 15 minutes; measure out and reserve 2 teaspoons drained juice. Whisk reserved tangerine juice, 1 thinly sliced scallion, 1 teaspoon grated fresh ginger, 1 teaspoon lemon juice, and 1 teaspoon extra-virgin olive oil together in medium bowl. Stir in drained tangerine pieces and season with salt and pepper to taste. Substitute tangerine relish for tomato relish.

NOTES FROM THE TEST KITCHEN

Buying Salmon

FRESH VS. FARMED: In season, we prefer the more pronounced flavor of wild-caught salmon to farmed Atlantic salmon (traditionally the main farm-raised variety in the Unites States). If you're going to spend the extra money for wild salmon, make sure it looks and smells fresh, and realize that high-quality salmon is available only from late spring through the end of summer.

CUTS OF SALMON: There are many ways to buy salmon. Our preference is to buy thick, center-cut fillets, which can be poached, steamed, pan-seared, roasted, or grilled. Cut from the head end or center, these fillets are the prime cut of the fish. They are thick enough to sear nicely without overcooking and are easy to skin (if desired). Buy the total amount you need in one piece and cut the individual fillets yourself. You will also see thin fillets at the market. Stay away from these. These are cut from the tail end, and they cook so fast that it is impossible to get a nice sear before the fish is overcooked—plus one end is very, very thin while the other is always much thicker.

SKIN-ON OR BONE-IN: For some recipes you will want to buy the salmon skin-on; for recipes that call for skinless salmon, you can easily remove it yourself (see page 183) or ask your fishmonger to do it for you. Bone-in steaks are an excellent choice for pan searing, grilling, or roasting, but they should not be poached. You may also see boneless steaks rolled and tied into a circular shape. These are as versatile as the bone-in steaks.

Miso-Glazed Salmon Fillets

SERVES 2 LIGHT

✓ **WHY THIS RECIPE WORKS:** *Misoyaki* has long been a staple of Japanese cuisine: An oil-rich fish like salmon is marinated in a combination of sugar and miso (a paste made from fermented soybeans) for up to three days. The fish is then grilled or broiled to produce a dark brown crust and a candylike coating with nutty, salty miso flavor. To translate this dish to the home kitchen, we marinated salmon fillets in a combination of white miso, sugar, sake, and freshly grated ginger for 5 hours. This gave us fish with a wonderful salty, sweet flavor brightened by the ginger. Then, to caramelize and brown the fish, we broiled the fillets; in under 10 minutes, we had juicy, moist fish with a beautiful browned crust. Scoring the skin before cooking helped the fat to render. Try to purchase center-cut salmon fillets of similar size so that they cook at the same rate. Although we prefer the flavor of white miso here, you can substitute brown, red, barley, or brown rice miso; do not substitute "light" miso. Note that the fish needs to marinate for a minimum of 5 hours. For the nutritional information for this recipe, see page 414.

- ¼ cup white miso
- 2 tablespoons sake
- 2 tablespoons sugar
- 1 teaspoon grated fresh ginger
- 2 (6- to 8-ounce) skin-on salmon fillets, 1½ inches thick

1. Whisk miso, sake, sugar, and ginger together in bowl until sugar and miso are dissolved (mixture will be quite thick). Using sharp knife, make 4 or 5 shallow slashes about 1 inch apart along skin side of each fillet, being careful not to cut into flesh. Place fillets in 1-gallon zipper-lock bag and pour marinade into bag. Seal bag, pressing out as much air as possible, and refrigerate for at least 5 hours or up to 24 hours, flipping bag occasionally to ensure that fillets marinate evenly. (Do not marinate for longer than 24 hours.)

Scoring Salmon Skin

To help the salmon's fat to render, we cut several slits in the skin before cooking. Using sharp or serrated knife, cut 4 or 5 shallow slashes, about 1 inch apart, through skin of each fillet of salmon, being careful not to cut into flesh.

2. Adjust oven rack 6 inches from broiler element and heat broiler. Line rimmed baking sheet with aluminum foil and spray with vegetable oil spray. Remove fillets from marinade and lay skin side down on prepared sheet. Spoon 1 tablespoon marinade over each fillet and smooth into even layer. Discard remaining marinade.

3. Broil salmon until nicely browned and center is still translucent when checked with tip of paring knife and registers 125 degrees (for medium-rare), 6 to 9 minutes. Serve.

Salmon Fillets with Soy-Mustard Glaze

SERVES 2 FAST

✓ **WHY THIS RECIPE WORKS:** Traditionally, glazed salmon is broiled, but reaching into a broiling-hot oven every minute to baste the fish is a hassle, and the fillets often burn if your timing isn't spot-on. We wanted an easier method that would still deliver a slightly crusty and flavor-packed glazed exterior. Reducing the oven temperature and gently baking the fish cooked the salmon perfectly. To rapidly caramelize the outside of the salmon, we sprinkled the fillets with sugar and quickly pan-seared each side before transferring them to the oven. To ensure the glaze stayed put, we rubbed the fish with a mixture of cornstarch, brown sugar, and salt before searing. Try to purchase center-cut salmon fillets of similar size so that they cook at the same rate. If your nonstick skillet isn't ovensafe, sear the salmon as directed in step 3, then transfer it to a rimmed baking sheet, glaze it, and bake as directed in step 4.

GLAZE

- 5 teaspoons packed brown sugar
- 1 tablespoon soy sauce
- 1 tablespoon mirin
- 1½ teaspoons whole-grain mustard
- 1½ teaspoons sherry vinegar
- 1½ teaspoons water
- ½ teaspoon cornstarch
  Pinch red pepper flakes

SALMON

- ½ teaspoon brown sugar
- ⅛ teaspoon cornstarch
  Salt and pepper
- 2 (6- to 8-ounce) skin-on salmon fillets, 1½ inches thick
- 1 teaspoon vegetable oil

1. **FOR THE GLAZE:** Whisk all ingredients together in small saucepan. Bring to simmer over medium-high heat and cook, stirring frequently, until thickened, about 1 minute. Remove from heat and cover.

2. **FOR THE SALMON:** Adjust oven rack to middle position and heat oven to 300 degrees. Combine sugar, cornstarch, ⅛ teaspoon salt, and ⅛ teaspoon pepper in bowl. Pat salmon dry with paper towels and rub sugar mixture evenly over flesh side of fillets.

3. Heat oil in 10-inch ovensafe nonstick skillet over medium-high heat until just smoking. Lay fillets flesh side down in skillet and cook until well browned, about 1 minute. Using tongs, gently flip fillets and cook on skin side for 1 minute.

4. Off heat, spoon glaze evenly over fillets. Transfer skillet to oven and roast until center of fish is still translucent when checked with tip of paring knife and registers 125 degrees (for medium-rare), 7 to 10 minutes. Serve.

VARIATIONS

Salmon Fillets with Pomegranate-Balsamic Glaze

Substitute following ingredients for glaze and cook as directed: 2 tablespoons pomegranate juice, 5 teaspoons packed brown sugar, 1 tablespoon balsamic vinegar, 1½ teaspoons whole-grain mustard, ½ teaspoon cornstarch, and pinch cayenne pepper.

Salmon Fillets with Asian Barbecue Glaze

Substitute following ingredients for glaze and cook as directed: 1 tablespoon ketchup, 1 tablespoon hoisin sauce, 1 tablespoon rice vinegar, 1 tablespoon packed brown sugar, 1½ teaspoons soy sauce, 1½ teaspoons toasted sesame oil, 1 teaspoon Asian chili-garlic sauce, and ½ teaspoon grated fresh ginger.

Broiled Salmon with Pineapple Salsa

SERVES 2   FAST   LIGHT

✓ **WHY THIS RECIPE WORKS:** We love salmon's naturally rich flavor, and when it's broiled, the textural contrast between the crisp, golden crust and the moist flesh underneath is unbeatable. We wanted to pair perfect broiled salmon with a fresh, complementary salsa. To give the salmon great flavor and a satisfying crust, we seasoned it with a spice rub of coriander, ginger, granulated garlic, salt, and pepper. A glaze of honey and brown sugar accelerated caramelization, allowing the fillets to develop a good crust before the flesh overcooked. A simple pineapple and jalapeño salsa was the perfect foil to brighten up the rich salmon. Try to purchase center-cut salmon fillets of similar size so that they cook at the same rate. We find it

A quick pineapple salsa with jalapeño and cilantro gives buttery broiled salmon a fresh tropical accent.

easiest to buy fresh pineapple that has already been peeled and cored. To make this salsa spicier, add the chile seeds. For the nutritional information for this recipe, see page 414.

SALSA
- ¾ cup ¼-inch pineapple pieces
- 1 scallion, sliced thin
- ½ jalapeño chile, stemmed, seeded, and minced
- 2 teaspoons lime juice
- 1 teaspoon minced fresh cilantro
  Salt and pepper

SALMON
- Vegetable oil spray
- 2 teaspoons honey
- ¼ teaspoon water
- ½ teaspoon brown sugar
- ½ teaspoon ground coriander
- ¼ teaspoon ground ginger
- ¼ teaspoon granulated garlic
- ¼ teaspoon pepper
- ⅛ teaspoon salt
- 2 (6- to 8-ounce) skinless salmon fillets, 1½ inches thick

1. FOR THE SALSA: Combine all ingredients in bowl and season with salt and pepper to taste; set aside.

2. FOR THE SALMON: Adjust oven rack 6 inches from broiler element and heat broiler. Line rimmed baking sheet with aluminum foil and spray with vegetable oil spray. Stir honey and water together in bowl. In second bowl, combine sugar, coriander, ginger, granulated garlic, pepper, and salt.

3. Pat salmon dry with paper towels and place skinned side down on prepared sheet. Brush each fillet with honey mixture. Sprinkle spice mixture evenly over fillets and press gently to adhere. Spray tops of fillets with vegetable oil spray.

4. Broil salmon until nicely browned and center is still translucent when checked with tip of paring knife and registers 125 degrees (for medium-rare), 6 to 9 minutes. Serve with salsa.

VARIATIONS

Broiled Salmon with Mango Salsa

For the nutritional information for this recipe, see page 414.

Substitute ½ mango, peeled and cut into ¼-inch pieces, for pineapple.

Broiled Salmon with Honeydew and Radish Salsa

You can substitute cantaloupe for the honeydew melon. For the nutritional information for this recipe, see page 414.

Substitute ¾ cup ¼-inch honeydew pieces for pineapple, 2 chopped radishes for jalapeño, and 2 teaspoons lemon juice for lime juice.

Skinning Salmon Fillets

If you can't find skinless salmon at the store, you can easily remove the skin yourself.

1. Using tip of boning knife (or sharp chef's knife), begin to cut skin away from fish at corner of fillet.

2. When enough skin is exposed, grasp it firmly with piece of paper towel, hold it taut, and carefully slice rest of skin off flesh.

For a new spin on fish cakes, we swap the usual white fish for rich, buttery salmon with a light bread-crumb and mayonnaise binder.

Crispy Salmon Cakes with Sweet and Tangy Tartar Sauce

SERVES 2

☑ **WHY THIS RECIPE WORKS:** We wanted to give classic New England cod cakes a new spin by swapping in rich, meaty salmon. We were after pure salmon flavor with just a few choice ingredients and minimal binder. Fresh salmon easily beat out canned, and we ditched the typical potato binder in favor of mayonnaise and bread crumbs. To chop the salmon, we quickly pulsed 1-inch pieces in the food processor. This gave us both larger chunks for a substantial texture and smaller pieces that helped the cakes hold together. Coating the cakes in ultracrisp panko bread crumbs ensured a good crust. Dijon mustard, shallot, lemon juice, and parsley boosted the flavor of the cakes, and a quick tartar sauce completed our dish. Be sure to use raw salmon here; do not substitute cooked salmon. Do not overprocess the salmon in step 2 or the cakes will have a pasty texture. If you purchase skin-on fillets, follow the instructions at left to remove the skin.

TARTAR SAUCE

- ⅓ cup mayonnaise
- 1 tablespoon sweet pickle relish
- 1½ teaspoons capers, rinsed and minced
- 1 teaspoon white wine vinegar
- ¼ teaspoon Worcestershire sauce

  Salt and pepper

SALMON CAKES

- 1 (10-ounce) skinless salmon fillet, cut into 1-inch pieces
- 2 tablespoons plus ½ cup panko bread crumbs
- 1 tablespoon minced fresh parsley
- 1 tablespoon mayonnaise
- 1 small shallot, minced
- 2 teaspoons lemon juice
- ½ teaspoon Dijon mustard

  Salt and pepper

  Pinch cayenne pepper

- ⅓ cup vegetable oil

1. FOR THE TARTAR SAUCE: Whisk all ingredients together in bowl and season with salt and pepper to taste; set aside.

2. FOR THE SALMON CAKES: Pulse salmon in food processor until there is an even mix of finely minced and coarsely chopped pieces of salmon, about 2 pulses, scraping down sides of bowl as needed.

3. Combine 2 tablespoons panko, parsley, mayonnaise, shallot, lemon juice, mustard, ½ teaspoon salt, ¼ teaspoon pepper, and cayenne in bowl. Gently fold in processed salmon until just combined.

4. Spread remaining ½ cup panko in shallow dish. Scrape salmon mixture onto small baking sheet. Divide mixture into 4 equal portions and gently flatten each portion into 1-inch-thick patty. Carefully coat each cake with panko, then return to sheet.

5. Line large plate with triple layer of paper towels. Heat oil in 10-inch skillet over medium-high heat until shimmering. Gently place salmon cakes in skillet and cook, without moving, until golden brown and crisp on both sides, 2 to 3 minutes per side. Drain cakes briefly on paper towel–lined plate. Serve with tartar sauce.

VARIATION

Crispy Salmon Cakes with Smoked Salmon, Capers, and Dill

Reduce amount of fresh salmon to 8 ounces and salt to ⅛ teaspoon. Substitute 1 tablespoon chopped fresh dill for parsley. Fold in 2 ounces finely chopped smoked salmon and 1½ teaspoons rinsed and minced capers with processed salmon in step 3.

A bold marinade of oil, garlic, lemon zest, and anise-flavored ouzo plus a spicy tomato sauce give this shrimp dish layers of flavor.

Greek-Style Shrimp with Tomatoes and Feta

SERVES 2

✓ WHY THIS RECIPE WORKS: Quick-cooking shrimp is one of the easiest things to make for two; for an exciting one-dish shrimp dish to add to our repertoire, we turned to shrimp *saganaki*, a Greek specialty of tender shrimp baked in a tomato sauce under crumbles of feta. First we marinated the shrimp with oil, garlic, lemon zest, and sweet, anise-flavored ouzo. For the tomato sauce, we sautéed bell pepper and shallot then added garlic, pepper flakes, ouzo, white wine, and canned diced tomatoes. Even nestled in the sauce, the shrimp baked unevenly in the oven, so we moved the dish to the stovetop. Simmered gently in the sauce over medium-low heat, the shrimp came out perfectly tender. This dish is fairly spicy; to make it milder, reduce the amount of red pepper flakes. To substitute jumbo-size shrimp (16 to 20 per pound), increase the cooking time to 7 to 11 minutes. You can substitute 1 tablespoon Pernod or 1 tablespoon vodka plus ⅛ teaspoon anise seeds for the ouzo. Serve with crusty bread or white rice.

12 ounces extra-large shrimp (21 to 25 per pound),
       peeled and deveined
2 tablespoons extra-virgin olive oil
1½ tablespoons ouzo
3 garlic cloves, minced
½ teaspoon grated lemon zest
       Salt and pepper
2 shallots, minced
½ red or green bell pepper, cut into ¼-inch pieces
¼ teaspoon red pepper flakes
1 (14.5-ounce) can diced tomatoes, drained with
       ¼ cup juice reserved
2 tablespoons dry white wine
3 ounces feta cheese, crumbled (¾ cup)
1 tablespoon minced fresh dill

1. Toss shrimp with 1½ teaspoons oil, 1½ teaspoons ouzo, one-third of garlic, and lemon zest in bowl. Season with salt and pepper and set aside.

2. Heat 1 tablespoon oil in 10-inch skillet over medium heat until shimmering. Add shallots, bell pepper, and ⅛ teaspoon salt, cover, and cook, stirring occasionally, until vegetables release their moisture, 3 to 5 minutes. Uncover and continue to cook, stirring occasionally, until moisture evaporates and vegetables have softened, 3 to 5 minutes. Stir in remaining garlic and pepper flakes and cook until fragrant, about 30 seconds. Stir in remaining 1 tablespoon ouzo, tomatoes and reserved juice, and wine. Bring to simmer and cook, stirring occasionally, until flavors meld and sauce is slightly thickened, about 5 minutes. Season with salt and pepper to taste.

3. Stir in shrimp with any accumulated juices. Reduce heat to medium-low, cover, and simmer, stirring occasionally, until shrimp are opaque throughout, 6 to 9 minutes. Off heat, sprinkle with feta and dill and drizzle with remaining 1½ teaspoons oil. Serve.

Pan-Seared Shrimp with Spicy Orange Glaze

SERVES 2 **FAST** **LIGHT**

✔ **WHY THIS RECIPE WORKS:** A good recipe for pan-seared shrimp is hard to find. Most recipes produce shrimp that are either dry and flavorless or pale, tough, and gummy. We wanted shrimp that were well caramelized but still moist and tender. We sometimes brine shrimp to boost flavor and texture, but brining the peeled shrimp inhibited browning. Instead we seasoned the shrimp with salt, pepper, and sugar, which brought out their natural sweetness and

Our super easy recipe uses just four ingredients to make a sweet and spicy orange glaze to flavor tender pan-seared shrimp.

encouraged browning. Since we only needed enough for two, we could easily cook the shrimp in a single batch without overcrowding. A piping-hot skillet browned the shrimp in just 90 seconds, then we coated the shrimp with a sweet and spicy orange glaze (made in minutes with just four ingredients) and simmered it until the glaze was nicely thickened. If using smaller or larger shrimp, be sure to adjust the cooking time accordingly. This dish is fairly spicy; to make it milder, use less chili-garlic sauce. Serve with rice. For the nutritional information for this recipe, see page 414.

GLAZE
1 tablespoon minced fresh cilantro
1 teaspoon sugar
½ teaspoon Asian chili-garlic sauce
½ teaspoon grated orange zest plus 2 tablespoons juice

SHRIMP
12 ounces extra-large shrimp (21 to 25 per pound),
       peeled and deveined
⅛ teaspoon sugar
       Salt and pepper
2 teaspoons vegetable oil

1. **FOR THE GLAZE:** Whisk all ingredients together in bowl.

2. **FOR THE SHRIMP:** Pat shrimp dry with paper towels and season with sugar, salt, and pepper. Heat oil in 10-inch nonstick skillet over medium-high heat until just smoking. Add shrimp in single layer and cook until curled and lightly browned, about 1½ minutes. Whisk glaze mixture to recombine, then add to skillet. Bring to simmer and cook, tossing shrimp to coat, until glaze is slightly thickened, about 30 seconds. Serve.

VARIATION

Pan-Seared Shrimp with Ginger-Hoisin Glaze

For the nutritional information for this recipe, see page 414.

Substitute the following ingredients for glaze; combine as directed: 1 thinly sliced scallion, 1 tablespoon hoisin sauce, 1 tablespoon water, 2 teaspoons grated fresh ginger, 1½ teaspoons rice vinegar, ¾ teaspoon soy sauce, and pinch red pepper flakes.

Stir-Fried Shrimp with Lemon-Ginger Sauce

SERVES 2   **FAST**   **LIGHT**

✔ **WHY THIS RECIPE WORKS:** For a bright-tasting shrimp stir-fry, we added a hefty dose of lemon juice and fresh ginger to our classic stir-fry sauce. Fresh asparagus and carrot gave our stir-fry heft and paired well with the lemony-ginger shrimp. Cooking the vegetables, shrimp, and aromatics in separate batches was important to ensure the pan stayed hot and the vegetables and shrimp cooked evenly and quickly. Steaming the vegetables before combining them with the shrimp and sauce yielded perfectly crisp-tender asparagus and carrots without adding extra oil. If using smaller or larger shrimp, be sure to adjust the cooking time accordingly. For the nutritional information for this recipe, see page 414.

¼   cup chicken broth

2   tablespoons lemon juice

2   tablespoons Chinese rice wine or dry sherry

1   tablespoon soy sauce

1   teaspoon sugar

1   teaspoon cornstarch

⅛   teaspoon pepper

12   ounces extra-large shrimp (21 to 25 per pound), peeled, deveined, and tails removed

2   teaspoons toasted sesame oil

2   scallions, minced

2   garlic cloves, minced

Plenty of lemon juice and fresh ginger give this easy shrimp stir-fry bright, bold flavor.

2   teaspoons grated fresh ginger

8   ounces asparagus, trimmed and cut on bias into 2-inch lengths

1   carrot, peeled and cut into 2-inch-long matchsticks

¼   cup water

1. Whisk broth, lemon juice, rice wine, soy sauce, sugar, cornstarch, and pepper together in small bowl. Toss shrimp with 1 teaspoon oil in medium bowl. In separate bowl, combine scallions, garlic, ginger, and remaining 1 teaspoon oil.

2. Cook asparagus, carrot, and water, covered, in 12-inch nonstick skillet over high heat until water is boiling and vegetables begin to soften, about 3 minutes. Uncover and continue to cook until water has evaporated and vegetables are crisp-tender, about 2 minutes; transfer to separate bowl.

3. Return now-empty skillet to high heat. Add shrimp and cook until nearly opaque, about 1 minute. Push shrimp to sides of skillet. Add garlic mixture and cook, mashing into skillet, until fragrant, about 30 seconds. Stir garlic mixture into shrimp.

4. Stir in cooked vegetables. Whisk sauce to recombine, then add to skillet. Cook, stirring constantly, until shrimp are opaque throughout and sauce is thickened, about 1 minute. Serve.

Kung Pao Shrimp

SERVES 2 **FAST** **LIGHT**

♥ **WHY THIS RECIPE WORKS:** Tired of dull, gloppy restaurant renditions of this Chinese classic, we set out to develop a *kung pao* shrimp recipe of our own. For a potent, syrupy sauce, we whisked together chicken broth, rice vinegar, oyster sauce, hoisin, and cornstarch. Sweet red bell pepper added just the right color and crunch to complement the shrimp. Steaming the red pepper ensured it had the perfect crisp-tender texture and helped keep the dish light. We briefly stir-fried the shrimp with flavorful toasted sesame oil, then added crumbled dried red chiles and peanuts. The chiles gave our dish some fire, and toasting the peanuts deepened their flavor. If using smaller or larger shrimp, be sure to adjust the cooking time accordingly. For a milder dish, use the lesser amount of chiles. You can substitute ½ teaspoon red pepper flakes for the chiles. For the nutritional information for this recipe, see page 414.

⅓	cup chicken broth
1½	teaspoons oyster sauce
1½	teaspoons hoisin sauce
1	teaspoon rice vinegar
1	teaspoon cornstarch
12	ounces extra-large shrimp (21 to 25 per pound), peeled, deveined, and tails removed
2	teaspoons toasted sesame oil
2	garlic cloves, minced
1	teaspoon grated fresh ginger
1	small red bell pepper, stemmed, seeded, and cut into 2-inch-long matchsticks
¼	cup water
¼	cup unsalted dry-roasted peanuts
1 to 3	small whole dried red chiles (each about 2 inches long), roughly crumbled
2	scallions, sliced thin

1. Whisk broth, oyster sauce, hoisin, vinegar, and cornstarch together in small bowl. Toss shrimp with 1 teaspoon oil in medium bowl. In separate bowl, combine garlic, ginger, and remaining 1 teaspoon oil.

2. Cook bell pepper and water, covered, in 12-inch nonstick skillet over high heat until water is boiling and pepper begins to soften, about 3 minutes. Uncover and continue to cook until water has evaporated and pepper is crisp-tender, about 2 minutes; transfer to separate bowl.

3. Return now-empty skillet to high heat. Add shrimp, peanuts, and chiles and cook until shrimp are nearly opaque and peanuts have darkened slightly, about 1 minute. Push shrimp

Shrimp 101

BUYING SHRIMP: Virtually all of the shrimp sold in supermarkets today have been previously frozen, either in large blocks of ice or by a method called "individually quick-frozen," or IQF for short. Supermarkets simply defrost the shrimp before displaying them on ice at the fish counter. We highly recommend purchasing bags of still-frozen shrimp and defrosting them as needed at home, since there is no telling how long "fresh" shrimp may have been kept on ice at the market. IQF shrimp have a better flavor and texture than shrimp frozen in blocks, and they are convenient for two because it's easy to defrost just the amount you need. Shrimp are sold both with and without their shells, but we find shell-on shrimp to be firmer and sweeter. Also, shrimp should be the only ingredient listed on the bag; some packagers add preservatives, but we find treated shrimp to have an unpleasant, rubbery texture.

SORTING OUT SHRIMP SIZES: Shrimp are sold both by size (small, medium, etc.) and by the number needed to make 1 pound, usually given in a range. Choosing shrimp by the numerical rating is more accurate, because the size label varies from store to store. Here's how the two sizing systems generally compare:

Small	51 to 60 per pound
Medium	41 to 50 per pound
Medium-Large	31 to 40 per pound
Large	26 to 30 per pound
Extra-Large	21 to 25 per pound
Jumbo	16 to 20 per pound

DEFROSTING SHRIMP: You can thaw frozen shrimp overnight in the refrigerator in a covered bowl. For a quicker thaw, place them in a colander under cold running water; they will be ready in a few minutes. Thoroughly dry the shrimp before cooking.

PEELING SHRIMP: Once shrimp is thawed, it is easy to peel. To peel shrimp, break the shell under the swimming legs; the legs will come off as the shell is removed. Leave the tail end intact if desired, or tug the tail end to remove the shell. If buying shrimp labeled "E-Z" peel (in which the shell has been split already), simply pull the shell around and off shrimp, leaving the tail end intact if desired. Note that you can freeze the shells for later use—they can be used to make shrimp broth or to flavor a liquid or sauce for seafood stews, pasta, or risotto recipes.

DEVEINING SHRIMP: Although the dark vein that runs along the back of the shrimp won't affect the flavor of the dish, it does affect appearance, so we prefer to remove it. Simply use a paring knife to make a shallow cut along the back of the shrimp to expose the vein, then use the tip of the knife to lift the vein out. Discard the vein by wiping the blade against a paper towel.

to sides of skillet. Add garlic mixture and cook, mashing mixture into skillet, until fragrant, about 30 seconds. Stir garlic mixture into shrimp.

4. Stir in cooked pepper. Whisk sauce to recombine, then add to skillet. Cook, stirring constantly, until shrimp are opaque throughout and sauce is thickened, about 1 minute. Sprinkle with scallions and serve.

Shrimp and Grits

SERVES 2

✓ **WHY THIS RECIPE WORKS:** A staple of the Southern table, grits are a great addition to any meal; we wanted to combine cheesy grits with plump shrimp for an easy one-pan dinner. We preferred quick grits over instant or old-fashioned for their creamy yet substantial texture. A mixture of water and heavy cream gave the grits a satisfying richness that we balanced with a little hot sauce. Once they were cooked, we stirred in shredded cheddar cheese, nestled in the shrimp, and moved the skillet to the oven to gently cook the shrimp through. A sprinkle of bright scallions was a fresh finishing touch. Do not substitute instant grits or old-fashioned grits in this recipe. If using smaller or larger shrimp, be sure to adjust the cooking time accordingly.

Tender, juicy shrimp poach right in our cheesy grits for a hearty but easy Southern-inspired supper.

8	ounces large shrimp (26 to 30 per pound), peeled, deveined, and tails removed
1	tablespoon olive oil
1	garlic clove, minced
	Pinch cayenne pepper
	Salt and pepper
1	tablespoon unsalted butter
½	cup finely chopped onion
1½	cups water
½	cup heavy cream
½	teaspoon hot sauce
½	cup quick grits
4	ounces extra-sharp cheddar cheese, shredded (1 cup)
1	scallion, sliced thin

1. Adjust oven rack to middle position and heat oven to 375 degrees. Toss shrimp with oil, garlic, and cayenne in bowl and season with salt and pepper. Cover and refrigerate while preparing grits.

2. Melt butter in 10-inch skillet over medium heat. Add onion and cook until softened, about 5 minutes. Stir in water, cream,

hot sauce, ½ teaspoon salt, and ¼ teaspoon pepper and bring to boil. Slowly whisk in grits, reduce heat to low, and cook, stirring often, until grits are thick and creamy, 5 to 7 minutes.

3. Off heat, whisk in cheddar until combined. Lay shrimp on their sides in pinwheel formation over grits, then press on them lightly to submerge them about halfway. Transfer skillet to oven and bake until shrimp are opaque throughout, 5 to 7 minutes. Sprinkle with scallion before serving.

VARIATIONS

Shrimp and Grits with Bacon

Cook 2 slices bacon, chopped fine, in 10-inch skillet over medium heat until crisp, 5 to 7 minutes. Using slotted spoon, transfer bacon to paper towel–lined plate. Pour off all but 1 tablespoon fat from skillet; substitute bacon fat for butter in step 2. Proceed with recipe, sprinkling dish with crisp bacon along with scallion before serving.

Shrimp and Grits with Chipotle Chile

For a spicier dish, use the larger amount of chipotle.

Substitute 1 to 2 teaspoons minced chipotle chile for hot sauce.

South Carolina Shrimp Boil

SERVES 2

✓ **WHY THIS RECIPE WORKS:** While New England has its clambakes and New Orleans its crawfish boils, the seafood boils of South Carolina boast shell-on shrimp, smoked sausage, corn on the cob, and potatoes simmered in broth seasoned with Old Bay. Downsizing this crowd-pleaser proved to be a challenge; it's designed to be a one-pot meal, but cooking everything at once resulted in blown-out potatoes and rubbery shrimp. The key to success was adding the ingredients in stages; first we browned the sausage, then we added the broth, potatoes, and corn. To keep the broth from watering down the flavors, we used just enough to cover the vegetables. This also allowed us to layer the shrimp on top of the vegetables so they could gently steam; once the potatoes were just tender, we added the shrimp and in just 3 minutes, everything was perfectly cooked through. This dish is made with shell-on shrimp; if you prefer peeled shrimp, use only ¼ teaspoon Old Bay in step 2. If you can't find andouille sausage, kielbasa can be substituted. Use small red potatoes measuring 1 to 2 inches in diameter.

 1 teaspoon vegetable oil
 6 ounces andouille sausage, cut into 2-inch lengths
 1 (8-ounce) bottle clam juice
 1 cup water
2½ teaspoons Old Bay seasoning
 2 garlic cloves, peeled and smashed
 1 teaspoon tomato paste
 1 bay leaf
 2 ears corn, husks and silk removed, cut into 2-inch lengths
 8 ounces small red potatoes, unpeeled, halved
 8 ounces shell-on extra-large shrimp (21 to 25 per pound)
 1 tablespoon minced fresh parsley or scallions (optional)

1. Heat oil in medium saucepan over medium-high heat until just smoking. Add sausage and cook until well browned, about 5 minutes. Stir in clam juice, water, 2 teaspoons Old Bay, garlic, tomato paste, and bay leaf, scraping up any browned bits. Stir in corn and potatoes and bring to simmer. Reduce heat to medium-low, cover, and simmer until potatoes are barely tender, 15 to 20 minutes.

2. Toss shrimp with remaining ½ teaspoon Old Bay in bowl. Scatter shrimp in single layer on top of vegetables. Cover and simmer until bottoms of shrimp turn pink, about 1 minute.

3. Flip shrimp, remove saucepan from heat, cover, and let sit until shrimp are opaque throughout, about 2 minutes. Strain stew, reserving broth if desired, and discard garlic cloves and bay leaf. Sprinkle with parsley, if using, and serve.

Deveining Shrimp

Although the vein running along the back of shrimp has no adverse effect on flavor or texture, removing it improves the appearance.

1. After removing shell, use paring knife to make shallow cut along back of shrimp so that vein is exposed.

2. Use tip of knife to lift vein out of shrimp. Discard vein by wiping blade against paper towel.

Pan-Seared Scallops

SERVES 2 **FAST**

✓ **WHY THIS RECIPE WORKS:** Producing crisp-crusted restaurant-style scallops at home means overcoming a major obstacle: weak stovetops. We wanted pan-seared scallops with perfectly brown crusts and moist, tender centers. Blotting the scallops dry, waiting until the oil was just smoking to add them to the skillet, and switching to a nonstick skillet were all steps in the right direction. But it wasn't until we tried a restaurant technique—butter basting—that our scallops really improved. We seared the scallops on one side then added butter to the skillet to encourage browning. (Butter contains milk proteins and sugars that brown rapidly when heated.) We then used a large spoon to ladle the foaming butter over the scallops. Adding the butter partway through cooking ensured that it had just enough time to work its browning magic on the scallops but not enough time to burn. We recommend buying "dry" scallops, which don't have chemical additives and taste better than "wet." Dry scallops will look ivory or pinkish; wet scallops are bright white.

12 ounces large sea scallops, tendons removed
 Salt and pepper
 1 tablespoon vegetable oil
 1 tablespoon unsalted butter
 Lemon wedges

1. Place scallops on large plate lined with clean dish towel. Place second clean dish towel on top of scallops and press gently on towel to blot liquid. Let scallops sit at room temperature for 10 minutes while towels absorb moisture.

2. Season scallops with salt and pepper. Heat oil in 12-inch nonstick skillet over high heat until just smoking. Add scallops flat side down in single layer and cook, without moving, until well browned, 1½ to 2 minutes.

3. Add butter to skillet. Using tongs, flip scallops and continue to cook, using large spoon to baste scallops with melted butter (tilt skillet so butter runs to 1 side) until sides of scallops are firm and centers are opaque, 30 to 90 seconds (remove smaller scallops as they finish cooking). Serve immediately with lemon wedges.

VARIATIONS

Pan-Seared Scallops with Lemon Browned Butter
Cook 2 tablespoons unsalted butter in small saucepan over medium heat, swirling saucepan constantly, until butter is golden brown and has nutty aroma, 3 to 4 minutes. Add 1 minced small shallot and cook until fragrant, about 30 seconds. Off heat, stir in 2 teaspoons minced fresh parsley, ¼ teaspoon minced fresh thyme, and 1 teaspoon lemon juice. Season with salt and pepper to taste. Cook scallops as directed and serve with sauce.

Pan-Seared Scallops with Tomato-Ginger Sauce
Cook 3 tablespoons unsalted butter in small saucepan over medium heat, swirling saucepan constantly, until butter turns golden brown and has nutty aroma, 3 to 4 minutes. Add 1 small plum tomato, cored, seeded, and chopped fine, 1½ teaspoons grated fresh ginger, 1½ teaspoons lemon juice, and pinch red pepper flakes. Cook, stirring constantly, until fragrant, about 1 minute. Season with salt to taste. Cook scallops as directed and serve with sauce.

NOTES FROM THE TEST KITCHEN

Dry vs. Wet Scallops

Wet scallops are dipped in preservatives to extend their shelf life. Unfortunately, these watery preservatives dull their flavor and ruin the texture. Unprocessed, or dry, scallops have much more flavor and a creamy, smooth texture, plus they brown very nicely. Dry scallops will look ivory or pinkish; wet scallops are bright white.

DISTINGUISHING DRY FROM WET: If your scallops are not labeled, you can find out if they are wet or dry with this quick microwave test: Place one scallop on a paper towel–lined microwave-safe plate and microwave for 15 seconds. A dry scallop will exude very little water, while a wet scallop will leave a sizable ring of moisture on the paper towel. (The microwaved scallop can be cooked as is.)

TREATING WET SCALLOPS: When you can find only wet scallops, you can hide the off-putting taste of the preservative by soaking the scallops in a solution of 1 quart cold water, ¼ cup lemon juice, and 2 tablespoons salt for 30 minutes. Be sure to pat the scallops very dry after soaking them. Even with this treatment, these scallops will be harder to brown than untreated dry scallops.

To get scallops with nicely browned crusts and juicy interiors, pat the scallops dry and use a large, smoking-hot skillet.

Seared Scallops with Butternut Squash
SERVES 2

✔ **WHY THIS RECIPE WORKS:** For an elegant scallop supper for two, we had to re-create the blazing heat of a professional stovetop. To keep the scallops' liquid from inhibiting browning, we patted them dry and cooked them in a roomy 12-inch skillet. Waiting until the oil was just smoking ensured that the pan was hot enough to give the scallops golden-brown crusts and juicy, medium-rare centers. To complement the scallops we made a quick and easy butternut squash puree in the same skillet, then we finished the dish with a rich browned butter sauce to drizzle over the plate. We recommend buying "dry" scallops, which don't have chemical additives and taste better than "wet." Dry scallops will look ivory or pinkish; wet scallops are bright white. Cream or whole milk can be substituted for the half-and-half.

    1 pound butternut squash, peeled, seeded, and cut into
        1-inch pieces (2½ cups)
    2 tablespoons unsalted butter, cut into 4 equal pieces
 1½ teaspoons half-and-half
      Salt and pepper
      Pinch cayenne pepper
   12 ounces large sea scallops, tendons removed
    1 tablespoon vegetable oil
    1 small shallot, minced
    1 teaspoon minced fresh sage
 1½ teaspoons lemon juice

1. Add squash and ½ cup water to 12-inch nonstick skillet. Cover and cook over medium heat until squash is tender, about 10 minutes. Drain squash and transfer to food processor. Add 1 piece butter, half-and-half, ¼ teaspoon salt, and cayenne and process until smooth, about 30 seconds, scraping down sides of bowl as needed. Season with salt and pepper to taste, transfer to serving bowl, and cover to keep warm.

2. Place scallops on large plate lined with clean dish towel. Place second clean dish towel on top of scallops and press gently on towel to blot liquid. Let scallops sit at room temperature for 10 minutes while towels absorb moisture.

3. Season scallops with salt and pepper. Heat oil in now-empty skillet over medium-high heat until just smoking. Add scallops flat side down in single layer and cook, without moving, until well browned, 1½ to 2 minutes. Using tongs, flip scallops and continue to cook until sides are firm and centers are opaque, 30 to 90 seconds longer. Transfer to platter and cover.

4. Add remaining pieces butter to now-empty skillet and cook over medium heat until melted and just starting to brown, about 30 seconds. Add shallot and sage and cook until fragrant, about 1 minute. Off heat, stir in lemon juice and season with salt and pepper to taste. Pour sauce over scallops and serve with pureed squash.

Preparing Scallops

The small, crescent-shaped muscle that is sometimes attached to the scallop will be incredibly tough when cooked. Use your fingers to peel this muscle away from the side of each scallop before cooking.

For an elegant but easy clam dish, we combine large-grained Israeli couscous and steamed clams with cherry tomatoes and kielbasa.

Clams with Israeli Couscous, Kielbasa, and Fennel

SERVES 2

✔ **WHY THIS RECIPE WORKS:** To infuse this simple clam dish with big flavor, we added spicy kielbasa and bright scallions to white wine for a potent broth to steam the clams. A pat of butter contributed ample richness to counter the bright, briny notes of the wine and clams. To make this dish a well-rounded meal, we added juicy cherry tomatoes, fennel, and couscous. Using larger-grained Israeli couscous instead of the more traditional, small-grain Moroccan couscous gave our dish great texture and visual appeal. To cook the couscous, we simply simmered it like pasta, drained it, then tossed it into the broth once the clams had steamed open so it could absorb the bright, briny flavors. Small quahogs or cherrystones are good alternatives to the littleneck clams. Be sure to use Israeli couscous in this dish; regular (or fine) couscous won't work here.

1 cup Israeli couscous
1 tablespoon unsalted butter
1 small onion, chopped coarse
1 small fennel bulb (8 ounces), stalks discarded,
   bulb halved, cored, and chopped coarse
4 ounces kielbasa sausage, halved lengthwise and
   sliced ½ inch thick
1 garlic clove, minced
¼ cup dry white wine or dry vermouth
1½ pounds littleneck clams, scrubbed
6 ounces cherry tomatoes, quartered
¼ cup coarsely chopped fresh parsley

1. Bring 2 quarts water to boil in medium saucepan. Add couscous and cook, stirring often, until al dente; drain well.

2. Meanwhile, melt butter in large saucepan over medium heat. Add onion, fennel, and kielbasa; cook until vegetables are softened, about 5 minutes. Stir in garlic and cook until fragrant, about 30 seconds. Stir in wine, scraping up any browned bits, and cook until slightly reduced, about 30 seconds. Stir in clams, cover, and cook, stirring occasionally, until clams open, 8 to 10 minutes.

3. Using slotted spoon, transfer opened clams to large bowl; discard any clams that have not opened. Stir drained couscous, tomatoes, and parsley into cooking liquid left in saucepan and season with salt and pepper to taste. Portion couscous into individual bowls, top with clams, and serve.

NOTES FROM THE TEST KITCHEN

Mussels and Clams 101

For the best flavor and texture, mussels and clams should be as fresh as possible. They should smell clean, not sour or sulfurous, and the shells should look moist. Look for tightly closed mussels and clams—avoid any that are cracked, broken, or sitting in a puddle of water. Some shells may gape slightly, but they should close when they are tapped. Discard any that won't close; they may be dead and should not be eaten. Most mussels and clams today are farmed and virtually free of grit. Soft-shell clams, however, almost always contain a lot of sand and should be submerged in a large bowl of cold water and drained several times before cooking. Both clams and mussels need to be scrubbed and rinsed before cooking; simply use a brush to scrub away any sand trapped in the outer shell. Some mussels may also need to be debearded; simply trap the small, weedy beard between the side of a small knife and your thumb and pull to remove it. The best way to store mussels and clams is in the refrigerator in a colander of ice set over a bowl; discard any water that accumulates so that the shellfish are never submerged.

Steamed Mussels in White Wine with Parsley
SERVES 2

✔ **WHY THIS RECIPE WORKS:** This French bistro classic, known as *moules à la marinière*, has just a few simple ingredients—mussels, shallot, parsley, white wine, and butter—but the effect is astonishing. The mussels are tender and briny, and the rich broth is perfect for sopping up with chunks of a rustic baguette. To make our own version, we sautéed a shallot plus a little garlic in butter, added wine and a bay leaf, and nestled in the mussels to gently steam in the broth. Once the mussels opened, we removed them and enriched the broth with butter and heavy cream. A sprinkling of fresh parsley finished this remarkably easy dish. Any type of mussel will work here; littlenecks or cherrystone clams can also be substituted (large clams will require 9 to 10 minutes of steaming time). Serve with crusty bread, garlic toasts, or rice.

2 tablespoons unsalted butter
1 shallot, minced
2 garlic cloves, minced
⅔ cup dry white wine
1 bay leaf
2 pounds mussels, scrubbed and debearded
2 tablespoons heavy cream
3 tablespoons minced fresh parsley
   Salt and pepper

1. Melt 1 tablespoon butter in Dutch oven over medium heat. Add shallot and cook until softened, about 2 minutes. Stir in garlic and cook until fragrant, about 30 seconds. Stir in wine and bay leaf, bring to simmer, and cook until flavors meld, about 2 minutes.

2. Increase heat to high and add mussels. Cover and cook, stirring occasionally, until mussels open, 3 to 7 minutes.

Debearding Mussels

Occasionally, mussels have a harmless weedy piece (known as a beard) protruding from the shells. Because it's fairly small, it can be difficult to tug out of place. To remove it easily, use this technique.

Trap beard between side of small knife and your thumb and pull to remove it.

3. Using slotted spoon, transfer opened mussels to large serving bowl, leaving cooking liquid in pot. Discard bay leaf and any mussels that have not opened.

4. Stir remaining 1 tablespoon butter and cream into cooking liquid, bring to simmer, and cook until butter is melted and liquid is slightly thickened, about 1 minute. Off heat, stir in parsley and season with salt and pepper to taste. Pour sauce over mussels and serve immediately.

VARIATIONS

Steamed Mussels in Coconut Milk with Cilantro

Add 1 sliced jalapeño chile to pot with shallot. Substitute ¾ cup canned coconut milk for wine and 3 tablespoons minced fresh cilantro for parsley. Stir in 1 teaspoon lime juice, 1 teaspoon packed brown sugar, and 1 teaspoon fish sauce with cilantro in step 4.

Steamed Mussels in White Wine with Tomato and Basil

Substitute 3 tablespoons chopped fresh basil for parsley. Add 1 finely chopped tomato with basil in step 4.

Maryland Crab Cakes

SERVES 2

✓ **WHY THIS RECIPE WORKS:** When it comes to crab cakes, Maryland is king. We wanted authentic Maryland-style crab cakes for two. We kept the ingredients simple: Just a little mustard, hot sauce, scallion, and Old Bay seasoning gave us plenty of flavor without overwhelming the crab. We liked the flavor of saltines for our binder, but our crab cakes fell apart in the pan. Adding a little mayonnaise and an egg yolk, patting the crabmeat dry with paper towels, and broiling rather than pan-frying the cakes were easy fixes. To give our cakes a little extra succulence, we added a tablespoon of melted butter to the crab mixture. Greasing the baking sheet with butter helped the bottoms of the cakes crisp to a perfect golden brown. Jumbo lump crabmeat is available at the fish counter of most grocery stores. If you can't find it, you can use pasteurized lump crabmeat.

- 7 **square or 8 round saltines**
- 8 **ounces lump crabmeat, picked over for shells**
- 2 **scallions, minced**
- 1 **tablespoon unsalted butter, melted, plus**
  1 tablespoon softened
- 1 **tablespoon mayonnaise**

Broiling, rather than pan-frying, our meaty Maryland-style crab cakes eliminates both the flipping and the fuss.

- 1 **egg yolk**
- 1½ **teaspoons Dijon mustard**
- 1 **teaspoon hot sauce**
- ½ **teaspoon Old Bay seasoning**
  Lemon wedges

1. Process saltines in food processor until finely ground, about 25 seconds; transfer to shallow dish. Dry crabmeat well with paper towels. Using rubber spatula, gently combine crabmeat, 2 tablespoons saltine crumbs, scallions, melted butter, mayonnaise, egg yolk, mustard, hot sauce, and Old Bay in large bowl.

2. Divide mixture into 2 equal portions and shape into tight, mounded cakes. Press 1 side of each cake in remaining crumbs. Place cakes crumb side down on large plate and refrigerate, covered, for at least 1 hour or up to 8 hours.

3. Adjust oven rack 8 inches from broiler element and heat broiler. Grease 8 by 4-inch area in center of rimmed baking sheet with softened butter. Transfer crab cakes to greased portion of prepared sheet, crumb side down. Broil until crab cakes are golden brown, 12 to 15 minutes. Serve with lemon wedges.

Vegetarian Mains

■ FAST (Start to finish in about 30 minutes)

■ LIGHT (See page 414 for nutritional information)

Opposite: Stuffed Tomatoes with Goat Cheese and Zucchini; Mushroom and Farro Ragout; Tempeh Tacos

Stuffed Acorn Squash with Barley

SERVES 2

✔ WHY THIS RECIPE WORKS: For a vegetable entrée that would satisfy even an ardent carnivore, we turned to stuffed winter squash. A single acorn squash, split in half and stuffed, was just right for two servings. Stuffing the raw squash and then roasting it gave us undercooked squash and dry filling, so we roasted the squash on its own first. Placing it cut side down on a baking sheet helped to caramelize the flesh, concentrating its sweet, nutty flavor. After trying various grains and rice in the filling, rustic, hearty barley was the clear favorite—we simply boiled it like pasta until tender. For a fresh crunch and rich flavor, we added sautéed fennel, shallot, garlic, coriander, thyme, Parmesan, and pine nuts. But our filling was a little dry and crumbly. To solve this problem, we scooped out the moist, tender roasted squash, mixed it with the filling, then mounded it all into the squash shells for a great texture and an attractive presentation. Make sure to use pearl barley, not hulled barley, in this recipe—hulled barley takes much longer to cook.

For stuffed squash with a moist and flavorful filling, we mix barley, fennel, pine nuts, and cheese with the creamy roasted squash.

1   **acorn squash (1½ pounds), halved pole to pole and seeded**

2   **tablespoons olive oil**

    Salt and pepper

¼   **cup pearl barley**

½   **fennel bulb, stalks discarded, bulb cored and chopped fine**

1   **shallot, minced**

3   **garlic cloves, minced**

½   **teaspoon ground coriander**

¼   **teaspoon minced fresh thyme or pinch dried**

1½   **ounces Parmesan cheese, grated (¾ cup)**

2   **tablespoons minced fresh parsley**

2   **tablespoons pine nuts, toasted**

1   **tablespoon unsalted butter**

    Balsamic vinegar

1. Adjust oven racks to upper-middle and lower-middle positions and heat oven to 400 degrees. Line rimmed baking sheet with aluminum foil and spray with vegetable oil spray.

2. Brush cut sides of squash with 1 tablespoon oil, season with salt and pepper, and lay cut side down on prepared sheet. Roast on lower rack until tender and tip of paring knife inserted into flesh meets no resistance, 45 to 55 minutes. Remove squash from oven and increase oven temperature to 450 degrees.

3. Meanwhile, bring 2 cups water to boil in small saucepan. Stir in barley and ¼ teaspoon salt and cook until barley is tender, 20 to 25 minutes; drain and set aside. Wipe saucepan dry.

4. Heat remaining 1 tablespoon oil in now-empty saucepan over medium heat until shimmering. Add fennel and shallot and cook until softened and lightly browned, 5 to 7 minutes. Stir in garlic, coriander, and thyme and cook until fragrant, about 30 seconds. Off heat, stir in cooked barley, ½ cup Parmesan, parsley, pine nuts, and butter. Season with salt and pepper to taste.

5. Flip roasted squash over and scoop out flesh, leaving ⅛-inch thickness of flesh in each shell. Gently fold cooked squash into barley mixture, then mound mixture evenly in squash shells. Sprinkle squash with remaining ¼ cup Parmesan and bake on upper rack until heated through and cheese is melted, 5 to 10 minutes. Drizzle with vinegar to taste and serve.

Stuffed Eggplant

SERVES 2

✔ **WHY THIS RECIPE WORKS:** Most recipes for stuffed eggplant combine soggy eggplant and bland fillings. We wanted a stuffed eggplant with creamy, earthy flesh and a hearty, flavorful filling. Getting perfectly cooked eggplant required a few tricks. Roasting gave us the best flavor and texture. When roasted whole, the skins split, so we halved the eggplants lengthwise first. Then we brushed the halves with oil and roasted them skin side down on a baking sheet. Finally, covering the sheet with foil trapped steam so that the eggplants cooked through without turning tough. For a fresh and satisfying filling, we mixed sautéed onion and fresh plum tomatoes with crunchy toasted pine nuts and salty Pecorino Romano cheese. Bright red wine vinegar plus oregano, cinnamon, and a little cayenne rounded out the flavors. This dish can be served hot or at room temperature.

- 2   **Italian eggplants (10 ounces each), halved lengthwise**
- 2   **tablespoons olive oil**
-     **Salt and pepper**
- 1   **small onion, chopped fine**
- 4   **garlic cloves, minced**
- 1   **teaspoon minced fresh oregano or ¼ teaspoon dried**
- ¼   **teaspoon ground cinnamon**
-     **Pinch cayenne pepper**
- 2   **plum tomatoes, cored, seeded, and chopped**
- 1   **ounce Pecorino Romano cheese, grated (½ cup)**
- 2   **tablespoons pine nuts, toasted**
- 1   **tablespoon red wine vinegar**
- 2   **tablespoons minced fresh parsley**

1. Adjust oven racks to upper-middle and lowest positions, place rimmed baking sheet on lower rack, and heat oven to 400 degrees.

2. Brush cut sides of eggplants with 1 tablespoon oil and season with salt and pepper. Lay eggplants cut side down on hot sheet in oven and carefully cover with aluminum foil. Roast eggplants until golden brown and tender, 45 to 55 minutes. Carefully transfer eggplants cut side down to paper towel–lined platter and let drain.

3. Meanwhile, heat remaining 1 tablespoon oil in 10-inch skillet over medium heat until shimmering. Add onion and ¼ teaspoon salt and cook until softened and lightly browned, 5 to 7 minutes. Stir in garlic, oregano, cinnamon, and cayenne and cook until fragrant, about 30 seconds. Stir in tomatoes, ¼ cup Pecorino, pine nuts, and vinegar and cook until heated through, about 1 minute. Season with salt and pepper to taste.

4. Return roasted eggplants to sheet, cut side up. Using 2 forks, gently push flesh to sides of each eggplant half to make room in center for filling. Mound filling evenly in eggplants. Sprinkle eggplants with remaining ¼ cup Pecorino and bake on upper rack until heated through and cheese is melted, 5 to 10 minutes. Sprinkle with parsley and serve.

Preparing Eggplant for Stuffing

Using 2 forks, gently push flesh to sides of each eggplant half to make room in center for filling.

NOTES FROM THE TEST KITCHEN

Getting to Know Eggplant

The eggplant is a member of the nightshade family, related to the potato and tomato. Though it's commonly thought of as a vegetable, eggplant is actually a fruit. Eggplants are available year-round. When shopping, look for eggplants that are firm, with smooth skin and no soft or brown spots. They should feel heavy for their size. Eggplants are very perishable and will get bitter if they overripen, so aim to use them within a day or two. They can be stored in a cool, dry place short-term, but for more than one or two days, refrigeration is best.

There are many varieties of eggplant. They can be anywhere from 2 to 12 inches long, round or oblong, ranging in color from dark purple to white. Here are a few of the most common varieties:

GLOBE
The most common variety in the United States, globe eggplant has a mild flavor and tender texture that works well in most applications. It is extremely watery, however, so often it's best to salt and drain it before cooking.

ITALIAN
Also called baby eggplant, Italian eggplant looks like a smaller version of a globe eggplant. It has moderately moist flesh and a distinct spicy flavor.

CHINESE
Chinese eggplant has firm, somewhat dry flesh with an intense, slightly sweet taste. It is best for sautéing, stewing, and stir-frying.

THAI
With crisp, applelike flesh and a bright, grassy flavor with a hint of spiciness, Thai eggplant can be eaten raw. It also works well when sautéed or stir-fried.

Stuffed Tomatoes with Goat Cheese and Zucchini

SERVES 2

✔ **WHY THIS RECIPE WORKS:** Warm summer nights call for a simple supper that makes the most of the season's fresh produce: bright, juicy tomatoes. Filled with zucchini, cheese, and nuts and served alongside a light green salad and a crusty baguette, stuffed tomatoes make a perfect light meal for two. We salted the tomatoes and let them drain to rid them of excess water that would otherwise turn the stuffing to mush. For the filling, we started with easy-to-make couscous. Toasting the couscous before cooking gave it a rich, nutty flavor and ensured fluffy, distinct grains in the finished dish. Chopped zucchini and fennel freshened up the filling, and sautéed shallot and garlic deepened the flavors. A combination of nutty Parmesan and tangy goat cheese contributed a rich creaminess and made the filling more cohesive, and toasted walnuts added crunch and nutty flavor. Finally, fresh basil added a bright, herbal note that nicely accented our summery supper.

- 4 **large tomatoes (8 ounces each)**
- **Salt and pepper**
- 3 **tablespoons extra-virgin olive oil**
- ½ **fennel bulb, stalks discarded, bulb cored and chopped fine**
- 1 **shallot, minced**
- 1 **small zucchini, cut into ¼-inch pieces**
- ¼ **cup couscous**
- 2 **garlic cloves, minced**
- ⅓ **cup vegetable broth**
- 1 **ounce Parmesan cheese, grated (½ cup)**
- 1 **ounce goat cheese, crumbled (¼ cup)**
- ¼ **cup walnuts, toasted and chopped coarse**
- 2 **tablespoons chopped fresh basil**

1. Adjust oven rack to upper-middle position and heat oven to 375 degrees. Slice off ⅛ inch of stem end of each tomato and remove core and seeds. Sprinkle inside of each tomato with ⅛ teaspoon salt, place cut side down on paper towel–lined plate, and let drain for 30 minutes.

2. Meanwhile, heat 1 tablespoon oil in medium saucepan over medium heat until shimmering. Add fennel and shallot and cook until softened, 5 to 7 minutes. Stir in zucchini and cook until tender, about 10 minutes. Stir in couscous and garlic and cook until fragrant, about 1 minute.

3. Stir in broth and bring to brief simmer. Off heat, cover and let sit until liquid is absorbed and grains are tender, about 5 minutes. Uncover and fluff grains with fork. Stir in ¼ cup Parmesan, goat cheese, walnuts, and basil. Season with salt and pepper to taste.

4. Line 8-inch square baking dish with aluminum foil and spray with vegetable oil spray. Pat insides of tomatoes dry with paper towels and brush cut edges with 2 teaspoons oil. Mound filling evenly in tomatoes, then arrange cut side up in prepared baking dish. Sprinkle tomatoes with remaining ¼ cup Parmesan and drizzle with remaining 4 teaspoons oil. Bake until cheese is lightly browned and tomatoes are tender, about 20 minutes. Serve.

Preparing Tomatoes for Stuffing

1. Using sharp knife, slice off top ⅛ inch of stem end of tomato.

2. Using your fingers or paring knife, remove and discard tomato core and seeds.

3. Sprinkle inside of cored tomatoes with salt, then place cut side down on paper towel–lined plate to drain for 30 minutes.

Vegetable and Bean Tostadas

SERVES 2

✔ **WHY THIS RECIPE WORKS:** Warm tostadas loaded with peppers and onions and creamy beans make a speedy and satisfying supper. For fresh, crisp tortilla shells in just 10 minutes—without the hassle of deep-frying—we baked store-bought tortillas until they were crisp and browned. For the beans, we found that we could get a surprisingly smooth, creamy texture from canned pinto beans by simply mashing the beans with their canning liquid. Picked jalapeños, along with some of their brine, added a nice amount of heat and tang. To let the fresh flavor of the peppers and onions shine through, we cooked them briefly in a hot skillet and seasoned them with just a squeeze of fresh lime juice. The beans, peppers, and onions made a great-tasting tostada, but we wanted to add some freshness. Topping the tostadas with crunchy coleslaw mix flavored with more of the spicy jalapeño brine did the trick. If you prefer, you can substitute ready-made tostadas. Queso fresco is a fresh, soft Mexican cheese available in many markets; if it's not available, feta works well, too. Do not drain the canned pinto beans, as the canning liquid is part of the recipe.

Pickled jalapeños—plus some of their brine—lend spicy, tangy flavor to peppers, onions, and coleslaw mix in these easy tostadas.

6	(6-inch) corn tortillas
	Vegetable oil spray
1	tablespoon vegetable oil
1½	green bell peppers, stemmed, seeded, and sliced thin
1	onion, halved and sliced thin
2	garlic cloves, minced
1½	tablespoons lime juice
	Salt and pepper
1	(15-ounce) can pinto beans, liquid reserved
1½	teaspoons minced jarred jalapeños, plus 2 tablespoons brine
2	cups (5½ ounces) shredded green coleslaw mix
2	ounces queso fresco or feta cheese, crumbled (½ cup)
¼	cup sour cream
1	tablespoon minced fresh cilantro

1. Adjust oven rack to middle position and heat oven to 450 degrees. Spray tortillas with oil spray and spread on rimmed baking sheet. Bake until lightly browned and crisp, 8 to 10 minutes.

2. Meanwhile, heat 1½ teaspoons oil in 10-inch skillet over medium heat until shimmering. Add bell peppers and onion and cook until softened and lightly browned, 5 to 7 minutes. Stir in garlic and cook until fragrant, about 30 seconds. Off heat, stir in 1½ teaspoons lime juice and season with salt and pepper to taste. Transfer vegetables to bowl and cover to keep warm.

3. Heat remaining 1½ teaspoons oil in now-empty skillet over medium heat until shimmering. Add beans and their liquid, jalapeños, and 1½ teaspoons jalapeño brine. Cook, mashing beans with potato masher, until mixture is thickened, about 5 minutes. Season with salt and pepper to taste.

4. Toss coleslaw mix with remaining 1½ tablespoons jalapeño brine in bowl and season with salt and pepper to taste.

5. Spread bean mixture evenly over crisp tortillas, then top with queso fresco, cooked vegetables, and slaw. Whisk sour cream and remaining 1 tablespoon lime juice together and drizzle over top. Sprinkle with cilantro and serve.

Making Tostadas

To turn store-bought tortillas into crispy tostadas, spray tortillas with vegetable oil spray and bake on rimmed baking sheet until lightly browned and crisp, 8 to 10 minutes.

Layering slices of tomatoes and zucchini on a creamy ricotta filling gives these tarts fresh flavor and a pretty presentation.

Zucchini, Tomato, and Ricotta Tarts

SERVES 2

✔ WHY THIS RECIPE WORKS: A great vegetable tart boasts a tender crust, a rich layer of cheese, and plenty of fresh vegetables. We started with our recipe for All-Butter Tart Shells, using the food processor to cut the butter into the flour quickly, then pressing the dough into two individual-size tart pans. Parbaking the crusts ensured they wouldn't slump, shrink, or get soggy. Next, a layer of chewy mozzarella and creamy ricotta made a rich base layer for our vegetables. For the vegetables, fresh zucchini and tomatoes nicely balanced the cheese and rich, buttery crust and were conveniently quick-cooking. Salting and draining the vegetables before layering them in the tart shells kept the tarts from getting waterlogged. For a final boost of flavor, we drizzled garlic-spiked olive oil over the tarts before baking. Yellow squash can be substituted for the zucchini.

9 cherry tomatoes
   Salt and pepper
½ small zucchini (3 ounces), halved lengthwise and
   sliced ⅛ inch thick
2 tablespoons extra-virgin olive oil
1 small garlic clove, minced
2 ounces (¼ cup) whole-milk or part-skim ricotta cheese
2 tablespoons shredded whole-milk mozzarella cheese
1 recipe All-Butter Tart Shells (page 378), fully baked
   and cooled
1 tablespoon chopped fresh basil

1. Slice 7 tomatoes into ⅛-inch-thick rounds (you should get about 5 slices from each tomato); quarter remaining 2 tomatoes. Toss tomatoes with ¼ teaspoon salt and spread out onto paper towel–lined plate. Toss zucchini with ¼ teaspoon salt and spread out onto paper towel–lined plate. Let vegetables drain for 30 minutes; gently blot vegetables dry before using.

2. Meanwhile, adjust oven rack to middle position and heat oven to 425 degrees. Combine 1 tablespoon oil and garlic in small bowl. In separate bowl, combine remaining 1 tablespoon oil, ricotta, and mozzarella and season with salt and pepper to taste.

3. Spread ricotta mixture evenly over bottom of cooled prebaked tart shells. Shingle alternating slices of tomato and zucchini around outside edge of tarts. Place quartered tomatoes in center of tarts. Drizzle garlic-oil mixture over vegetables.

4. Bake tarts on rimmed baking sheet until cheese is bubbling and vegetables are slightly wilted, 20 to 25 minutes. Let tarts cool on baking sheet for 20 minutes.

5. To serve, remove outer metal ring of each tart pan, slide thin metal spatula between tart and tart pan bottom, and carefully slide tart onto plate. Sprinkle with basil and serve warm or at room temperature.

Layering Tomato and Zucchini Tarts

Shingle alternating slices of tomato and zucchini around outside edge of tart. Place quartered tomatoes in center of each tart.

Fennel, Olive, and Goat Cheese Tarts

SERVES 2

✓ **WHY THIS RECIPE WORKS:** We wanted to make elegant savory tarts inspired by the flavors of the Mediterranean. To keep it easy enough for a weeknight dinner, we pulled store-bought puff pastry from the freezer to form the base. For the filling, fresh, anise-flavored fennel and briny cured olives made a light but flavorful combination. Tangy goat cheese brightened with fresh basil contrasted nicely with the rich, flaky pastry and helped bind the vegetables and pastry together. Parbaking the pastry without the weight of the filling allowed it to puff up nicely. To keep the filling firmly in place, we cut a border around the edges of the baked crusts and lightly pressed down the centers to make neat beds for the cheese and vegetables. Just 5 minutes more in the oven heated the filling through and browned the crusts beautifully. To thaw frozen puff pastry, let it sit either in the refrigerator for 24 hours or on the counter for 30 minutes to 1 hour.

½   (9½ by 9-inch) sheet puff pastry, thawed
4   ounces goat cheese, softened
¼   cup chopped fresh basil
1½ tablespoons extra-virgin olive oil
½   teaspoon grated lemon zest plus 2 teaspoons juice
    Salt and pepper
½   fennel bulb, stalks discarded, bulb cored and sliced thin
1   garlic clove, minced
¼   cup dry white wine
¼   cup pitted oil-cured black olives, chopped

Making Puff Pastry Tart Shells

Creating a bed for the filling within the tart shell ensures that none of the filling will leak during baking.

1. Lay pastry squares on parchment paper–lined baking sheet and poke them all over with fork. Bake pastry until puffed and golden, 12 to 15 minutes.

2. Using tip of paring knife, cut ½-inch border into top of each pastry shell and press center down with your fingertips to create bed for filling.

Store-bought puff pastry makes a simple and delicious crust for a flavorful tart filling of goat cheese, fennel, basil, and olives.

1. Adjust oven rack to middle position and heat oven to 425 degrees. Line baking sheet with parchment paper. Cut pastry sheet in half widthwise to make 2 squares and lay on prepared sheet. Poke pastry squares all over with fork and bake until puffed and golden brown, 12 to 15 minutes, rotating sheet halfway through baking. Using tip of paring knife, cut ½-inch-wide border into top of each pastry shell, then press centers down with your fingertips.

2. While pastry bakes, mix goat cheese, 2 tablespoons basil, 2 teaspoons oil, lemon zest, and ¼ teaspoon pepper together in small bowl. Heat remaining 2½ teaspoons oil in 8-inch skillet over medium heat until shimmering. Add fennel and cook until softened and lightly browned, about 5 minutes. Stir in garlic and cook until fragrant, 30 seconds. Stir in wine, scraping up any browned bits, cover, and cook for 5 minutes. Uncover and continue to cook until liquid has evaporated and fennel is very soft, 3 to 5 minutes. Off heat, stir in lemon juice and olives.

3. Spread goat cheese mixture evenly over centers of prebaked tart shells, leaving raised edges clean, then spoon fennel mixture evenly over cheese layer. Transfer filled tarts to oven and bake until cheese is heated through and crust is deep golden brown, about 5 minutes. Sprinkle with remaining 2 tablespoons basil and season with salt and pepper to taste. Serve.

Savory Spinach Strudel

SERVES 2

✔ **WHY THIS RECIPE WORKS:** *Spanakopita* is a savory spinach and feta pie with roots in Greek culture. We wanted a streamlined version for two with a zesty spinach filling and a crispy phyllo crust. Spinach, feta, and ricotta flavored with scallions, raisins, pine nuts, oregano, and garlic made a rich, satisfying filling. Using store-bought phyllo was an easy time-saver. And rather than assembling it into a fussy pie, we simply greased and stacked several phyllo sheets, mounded the filling on top, then rolled it up to make an easy spanakopita strudel. Cutting a few steam vents into the top of the strudel kept the top crust crisp. Make sure to thoroughly squeeze the spinach dry, or the filling will leak. Phyllo dough is also available in larger 18 by 14-inch sheets; if using, cut them in half to make 14 by 9-inch sheets. Don't thaw the phyllo in the microwave; let it sit in the refrigerator overnight or on the countertop for 4 to 5 hours.

    2 ounces feta cheese, crumbled (½ cup)
    2 ounces (¼ cup) whole-milk ricotta cheese
    3 scallions, sliced thin
    ¼ cup golden raisins
    1 tablespoon pine nuts, toasted
    1 tablespoon minced fresh oregano
    1 tablespoon lemon juice
    1 garlic clove, minced
    ¼ teaspoon ground nutmeg
    5 ounces frozen spinach, thawed, squeezed dry, and
       chopped coarse
       Salt and pepper
    5 (14 by 9-inch) phyllo sheets, thawed
       Olive oil

Squeezing Spinach Dry

To rid thawed spinach of excess moisture that would otherwise water down your dish, simply wrap it in cheesecloth or clean dish towel and squeeze it firmly over bowl.

1. Adjust oven rack to middle position and heat oven to 400 degrees. Line rimmed baking sheet with parchment paper. Mix feta, ricotta, scallions, raisins, pine nuts, oregano, lemon juice, garlic, and nutmeg together in medium bowl. Stir in spinach until well combined. Season with salt and pepper to taste.

2. Lay 1 phyllo sheet on clean counter with short side facing you and brush with oil, making sure to cover entire surface. Repeat and layer with remaining 4 phyllo sheets, brushing each with oil.

3. Mound spinach mixture into narrow log along bottom edge of phyllo, leaving 2-inch border at bottom and ½-inch border on sides. Fold bottom edge of dough over filling, then continue to roll dough around filling into tight log, leaving ends open.

4. Gently transfer strudel seam side down to prepared sheet and brush with oil. Cut four 1½-inch vents diagonally across top of strudel.

5. Bake strudel until golden brown, 20 to 25 minutes, rotating sheet halfway through baking. Let cool on sheet for 10 minutes before serving.

Making Spinach Strudel

1. On clean counter, layer phyllo sheets on top of one another, brushing each sheet with olive oil.

2. Mound spinach mixture into narrow log along bottom edge of phyllo, leaving 2-inch border at bottom and ½-inch border on sides.

3. Fold bottom edge of dough over filling, then continue to roll dough around filling into tight log, leaving sides open.

4. Transfer strudel seam side down to prepared baking sheet and brush with olive oil. Cut four 1½-inch vents diagonally across top of strudel.

Risotto Primavera

SERVES 2

✔ **WHY THIS RECIPE WORKS:** Most risotto recipes require constant stirring from start to finish, but with just two to feed, we weren't willing to spend all that time glued to the stove. To streamline the process, we tried cooking the risotto hands-off until it was partially tender, then stirring constantly while it finished cooking. We found that just 6 minutes of stirring at the end was enough to release the necessary starch to give us remarkably creamy risotto. To make the risotto a meal, we added vegetables inspired by pasta primavera: asparagus, mushrooms, onion, and peas. Sautéing the mushrooms and onion in the pan before adding the rice deepened their flavor. Lemon juice and fresh basil brightened the dish, and Parmesan and butter added richness. White, shiitake, or portobello (caps only) mushrooms can be substituted for the cremini in this recipe. High-quality Parmesan makes a big difference here.

Our easy shortcut method produces remarkably rich and creamy risotto with a fraction of the usual effort.

1¾ cups vegetable broth

½ cup water

4 teaspoons olive oil

3 ounces cremini mushrooms, trimmed and sliced thin

Salt and pepper

1 small onion, chopped fine

½ cup Arborio rice

3 ounces asparagus, trimmed and cut into ½-inch pieces

¼ cup frozen peas

¼ cup grated Parmesan cheese, plus extra for serving

2 tablespoons chopped fresh basil

1 tablespoon unsalted butter

2 teaspoons lemon juice

1. Bring broth and water to simmer in small saucepan over medium heat. Remove from heat, cover, and keep warm.

2. Heat 2 teaspoons oil in medium saucepan over medium heat until shimmering. Add mushrooms and ¼ teaspoon salt and cook, covered, until just starting to brown, about 4 minutes; transfer to bowl. Return now-empty saucepan to medium heat, add remaining 2 teaspoons oil, and heat until shimmering. Add onion and ¼ teaspoon salt and cook until just beginning to soften, about 2 minutes. Add rice and cook, stirring constantly, until grains are translucent around edges, about 1 minute.

3. Stir in 1½ cups warm broth, reduce heat to medium-low, cover, and simmer until almost all liquid is absorbed, about 12 minutes. Stir in asparagus, cover, and cook for 2 minutes. Add ½ cup broth and cook, stirring constantly, until broth is absorbed, about 3 minutes. Add remaining broth and peas and cook, stirring constantly, until rice is creamy and al dente, about 3 minutes.

4. Off heat, stir in cooked mushrooms, cover, and let sit until heated through, about 2 minutes. Stir in Parmesan, basil, butter, and lemon juice. Season with salt and pepper to taste. Serve, passing extra Parmesan separately.

Skillet Brown Rice and Beans with Corn and Tomatoes

SERVES 2 `LIGHT`

✔ **WHY THIS RECIPE WORKS:** The hearty, sustaining combination of rice and beans is found in many cuisines. We wanted to make a simple weeknight version with bold South American flavor. Although white rice is traditional, we preferred the texture, chew, and robust flavor of brown rice. After sautéing an onion, we added fresh corn and the uncooked rice to the skillet and toasted them until fragrant. Then we stirred in vegetable broth and simmered the rice until tender. Canned black beans kept the dish easy; to keep them from getting blown out and mushy, we stirred them in partway through cooking. Garlic, cumin, and cayenne gave the dish a potent aromatic backbone, and a flavorful salsa of grape tomatoes, scallions, cilantro, and lime juice added a fresh counterpoint to the rich, spicy rice and beans. We prefer the flavor of fresh corn; however, ¾ cup frozen corn, thawed and patted dry, can be substituted. For the nutritional information for this recipe, see page 414.

4 teaspoons extra-virgin olive oil

1 small onion, chopped fine

1 ear corn, kernels cut from cob

½ cup long-grain brown rice, rinsed

2 garlic cloves, minced

½ teaspoon ground cumin

Pinch cayenne pepper

2 cups vegetable broth

¾ cup canned black beans, rinsed

Salt and pepper

6 ounces grape tomatoes, quartered

2 scallions, sliced thin

2 tablespoons minced fresh cilantro

2 teaspoons lime juice

1. Heat 2 teaspoons oil in 10-inch nonstick skillet over medium heat until shimmering. Add onion and cook until softened and lightly browned, 5 to 7 minutes. Stir in corn and cook until lightly browned, about 4 minutes. Stir in rice, garlic, cumin, and cayenne and cook until fragrant, about 30 seconds.

2. Stir in broth, scraping up any browned bits, and bring to simmer. Reduce heat to medium-low, cover, and simmer gently, stirring occasionally, for 25 minutes.

3. Stir in beans, cover, and continue to simmer until liquid has been absorbed and rice is tender, 20 to 25 minutes. Season with salt and pepper to taste.

4. Meanwhile, combine remaining 2 teaspoons oil, tomatoes, scallions, cilantro, and lime juice in bowl and season with salt and pepper to taste. Sprinkle tomato mixture over rice and beans before serving.

VARIATION

Spanish-Style Skillet Brown Rice and Chickpeas

For the nutritional information for this recipe, see page 414.

Substitute 1 finely chopped red bell pepper for corn and pinch saffron threads, crumbled, for cumin. Substitute ¾ cup rinsed canned chickpeas for black beans. Substitute 2 tablespoons minced fresh parsley for cilantro and 2 teaspoons lemon juice for lime juice.

Farro makes a hearty, satisfying, whole-grain risotto—without the constant stirring or incremental additions of broth.

Farro Risotto with Arugula, Cherry Tomatoes, and Lemon
SERVES 2

✓ **WHY THIS RECIPE WORKS:** Farro, a whole-grain relative of wheat, is commonly used in Italy to make *farrotto*, a dish similar to risotto but with a distinct nutty flavor and satisfying chew. We wanted to come up with our own recipe for farrotto—one that would simplify the tedious risotto-cooking method. We quickly found that this hearty grain didn't require the nonstop stirring or incremental additions of liquid traditionally used to make risotto. We simply added all the liquid to the grain and simmered it uncovered, stirring every few minutes, until the farro was tender. Then we added classic risotto flavorings (Parmesan, butter, and lemon) plus bright cherry tomatoes and peppery arugula for a fresh and hearty meal. Farro is a grain that can be found alongside other grains or near the pasta in specialty or gourmet markets. For a creamy texture, be sure to stir the farro often in step 2. Serve with a simple green salad.

1 tablespoon olive oil
1 small onion, chopped fine
   Salt and pepper
1 garlic clove, minced
½ teaspoon minced fresh thyme or ⅛ teaspoon dried
¾ cup farro
1½ cups vegetable broth
1 cup water
6 ounces cherry tomatoes, quartered
2 ounces (2 cups) baby arugula
¼ cup grated Parmesan cheese
1 tablespoon unsalted butter
¼ teaspoon grated lemon zest plus 1 teaspoon juice

1. Heat oil in medium saucepan over medium heat until shimmering. Add onion and pinch salt and cook until softened, about 5 minutes. Stir in garlic and thyme and cook until fragrant, about 30 seconds.

2. Stir in farro and cook until lightly toasted, about 2 minutes. Stir in broth and water and bring to simmer. Reduce heat to medium-low and continue to simmer, stirring often, until farro is tender, 20 to 25 minutes.

3. Stir in tomatoes and arugula and cook until vegetables are softened, about 1 minute. Off heat, stir in Parmesan, butter, and lemon zest and juice. Season with salt and pepper to taste and serve.

VARIATION

Farro Risotto with Fennel, Radicchio, and Balsamic Vinegar

Substitute ½ fennel bulb, cored and chopped fine, for onion. Substitute ½ small head radicchio, cored and sliced thin, for tomatoes and arugula. Substitute 2 teaspoons balsamic vinegar for lemon zest and juice. Drizzle with additional balsamic vinegar to taste before serving.

Mushroom and Farro Ragout

SERVES 2 `LIGHT`

✔ **WHY THIS RECIPE WORKS:** A mushroom ragout is a rich, intensely flavorful stew made with a variety of exotic wild mushrooms. We wanted a version that tasted just as good but that relied on mushrooms easily available at the supermarket. We chose meaty, substantial portobellos, savory shiitakes, and white mushrooms, which were inexpensive and bulked up the stew nicely. For deep, complex flavor, we also

included ¼ ounce of dried porcini mushrooms. To make our ragout even heartier, we wanted to include a grain. Delicate quinoa disappeared next to the big bites of mushrooms, and wheat berries took too long to cook, but farro was a hit: Its nutty flavor and chewy texture complemented the mushrooms nicely. Tomatoes and a splash of dry sherry cut through the richness. Farro is a grain that can be found alongside other grains or near the pasta in specialty or gourmet markets. You can substitute Madeira wine for the dry sherry if necessary. For the nutritional information for this recipe, see page 414.

2 tablespoons unsalted butter
1 small onion, chopped fine
¼ ounce dried porcini mushrooms, rinsed and minced
   Salt and pepper
2 portobello mushroom caps, gills removed, caps halved and sliced ½ inch thick
5 ounces white mushrooms, trimmed and halved if small or quartered if large
2 ounces shiitake mushrooms, stemmed and sliced ¼ inch thick
2 garlic cloves, minced
1 teaspoon minced fresh thyme or ¼ teaspoon dried
2 tablespoons dry sherry
3 cups vegetable broth
½ cup canned whole peeled tomatoes, drained with juice reserved, chopped coarse
½ cup farro
1 tablespoon minced fresh parsley
¾ teaspoon balsamic vinegar

1. Melt 1 tablespoon butter in medium saucepan over medium heat. Add onion, porcini mushrooms, and ⅛ teaspoon salt and cook until softened and lightly browned, 8 to 10 minutes.

2. Stir in portobello mushrooms, white mushrooms, and shiitake mushrooms, cover, and cook, stirring occasionally, until mushrooms have released their moisture, 8 to 10 minutes. Uncover and continue to cook until dark fond forms on bottom of saucepan, 10 to 15 minutes.

3. Stir in garlic and thyme and cook until fragrant, about 30 seconds. Stir in sherry, scraping up any browned bits, and cook until almost completely evaporated, about 1 minute.

4. Stir in broth, tomatoes and reserved juice, and farro and bring to boil. Reduce heat to medium-low, partially cover, and simmer gently until ragout is thickened and farro is tender, 30 to 35 minutes. Off heat, stir in remaining 1 tablespoon butter, parsley, and vinegar. Season with salt and pepper to taste and serve.

Our Favorite Grains

Dozens of grains are sold at the supermarket, but the following are the ones we use most often. We've also included cornmeal and couscous here since they are prepared and served like grains. You can store many grains in the pantry—just make sure they are in an airtight container, and use them within six months. To prevent oxidation, whole grains like farro are best stored in the freezer.

BARLEY

This high-fiber grain has a nutty, subtly sweet flavor that makes it an ideal accompaniment to meat, chicken, and fish. Both hulled and pearl barley (the most widely available varieties) are stripped of their tough outer covering, but we prefer quicker-cooking pearl barley, which has been polished to remove the bran layer as well.

FARRO

A favorite in Tuscan cuisine, these hulled whole-wheat kernels boast a sweet, nutty flavor and chewy bite. Farro is available in three sizes, but the midsize type (*farro medio*) is most common in the United States. When cooked, the grains are tender with a slight chew, similar to al dente pasta. Farro takes best to the pasta cooking method because abundant water cooks the grains evenly.

QUINOA

Quinoa is often called a "super-grain" because it's a nutritionally complete protein. We love the small seeds (which can be white, red, black, or purple) for their faint crunch and mineral taste. When cooked, the grains will unfurl and expand to about three times their size. Quinoa should be rinsed carefully to remove its bitter coating (known as saponin). Toast quinoa in a dry pot before adding water; we've found that toasting it in fat gives the grain a slightly bitter flavor.

WHEAT BERRIES

These are whole husked wheat kernels that have a rich, earthy flavor and firm chew. Because they're unprocessed, they remain firm (though softened), smooth, and distinct when cooked, which makes them great for salads. We toast wheat berries in oil before adding them to the water, because it brings out their nutty flavor.

CORNMEAL/POLENTA

When shopping for polenta, avoid instant and quick-cooking polenta, which are parcooked and comparatively bland. Though we love the flavor of whole-grain cornmeal, we find it slightly gritty. We prefer degerminated cornmeal, in which the hard hull and germ are removed (check the back label or ingredient list; if it's not labeled as degerminated, you can assume it's whole-grain). As for grind, we found coarser grains are best for polenta, while finer grinds work well for baking muffins or cornbread.

COUSCOUS

Couscous is a starch made from high-protein wheat flour. Traditional Moroccan couscous is made by rubbing coarse-ground durum semolina and water between the hands to form small granules which are then steamed. The boxed couscous found in most supermarkets is a precooked version that needs only a few minutes of steeping in hot liquid. Israeli couscous, also known as pearl couscous, is larger than traditional couscous (about the size of a caper) and is not precooked. It has a unique, nutty flavor.

A surprisingly hearty combination of quinoa, chickpeas, kale, and carrots adds up to more than the sum of its parts.

Moroccan-Style Quinoa and Kale with Raisins and Pine Nuts

SERVES 2

✔ **WHY THIS RECIPE WORKS:** We combined two protein-packed vegetarian staples—quinoa and chickpeas—in one pot for this unique pilaf-style dish. Hearty kale helped tie the dish together, and golden raisins and carrot imparted sweet, earthy notes. To play up the Moroccan flavors, we spiced the dish with fragrant coriander and hot red pepper flakes and stirred in toasted pine nuts, tangy feta, and a squeeze of lemon juice. With as much protein as it has flavor, the hearty combination of quinoa, chickpeas, and kale makes a great vegetarian dish for two. Be sure to rinse the quinoa to remove its bitter coating (known as saponin). Don't dry the greens completely after washing; a little extra water clinging to the leaves will help them wilt when cooking.

2   **tablespoons olive oil**
1   **small onion, chopped fine**
1   **carrot, peeled and cut into ¼-inch pieces**

2 garlic cloves, minced
¼ teaspoon ground coriander
⅛ teaspoon red pepper flakes
½ cup quinoa, rinsed
1½ cups vegetable broth
¾ cup canned chickpeas, rinsed
2 tablespoons golden raisins
   Salt and pepper
6 ounces kale, stemmed and chopped into 1-inch pieces
2 tablespoons pine nuts, toasted
¼ teaspoon lemon zest plus 1 teaspoon juice
2 tablespoons crumbled feta cheese

1. Heat 1 tablespoon oil in medium saucepan over medium heat until shimmering. Add onion and carrot and cook until onion is softened, about 5 minutes. Stir in garlic, coriander, and pepper flakes and cook until fragrant, about 30 seconds. Stir in quinoa and cook, stirring often, until lightly toasted and aromatic, about 3 minutes.

2. Stir in broth, chickpeas, raisins, and ⅛ teaspoon salt. Place kale on top and bring to simmer. Reduce heat to low, cover, and simmer until quinoa is transparent and tender, 18 to 20 minutes. Off heat, gently stir in remaining 1 tablespoon oil, pine nuts, and lemon zest and juice. Sprinkle with feta and season with salt and pepper to taste. Serve.

Quinoa Cakes
SERVES 2

✅ **WHY THIS RECIPE WORKS:** Thanks to its high protein content, quinoa makes a satisfying entrée. We set out to develop a recipe for hearty quinoa patties with bright, fresh flavors. To keep our cakes from turning out dry and crumbly, we simmered the quinoa in extra liquid so that it cooked up moist. For the binder, a whole egg plus some cheese worked best—we chose Monterey Jack for its flavor and meltability. Chilling the patties for 30 minutes after forming them ensured that they stayed together in the pan. A combination of scallions, lemon zest and juice, and spinach added freshness. Sun-dried tomatoes and garlic gave the cakes a savory boost, and using the oil from the sun-dried tomatoes to sauté the scallions and garlic wasn't only convenient; it deepened the flavor as well. Be sure to rinse the quinoa to remove its bitter coating (known as saponin). To keep the patties from falling apart, be sure to wait until they are well browned on the first side before attempting to flip them. Serve over mixed greens with a creamy yogurt sauce such as tzatziki.

2 tablespoons coarsely chopped oil-packed sun-dried tomatoes, plus 1 tablespoon packing oil
2 scallions, chopped fine
2 garlic cloves, minced
1½ cups water
½ cup quinoa, rinsed
½ teaspoon salt
1 large egg, lightly beaten
1 ounce (1 cup) baby spinach, chopped
1 ounce Monterey Jack cheese, shredded (¼ cup)
¼ teaspoon grated lemon zest plus 1 teaspoon juice
1 tablespoon olive oil

1. Heat tomato oil in medium saucepan over medium heat until shimmering. Add scallions and cook until softened, about 3 minutes. Stir in garlic and cook until fragrant, about 30 seconds. Stir in water, quinoa, and salt and bring to simmer. Reduce heat to medium-low, cover, and simmer until quinoa is tender but still soupy, 16 to 18 minutes. Off heat, cover and let quinoa mixture sit until liquid is fully absorbed and grains are tender, about 10 minutes. Transfer to large bowl and let cool for 15 minutes.

2. Add tomatoes, egg, spinach, Monterey Jack, and lemon zest and juice to cooled quinoa and mix until uniform. Divide mixture into 2 firmly packed balls, flatten each ball into 1-inch-thick patty, and place on large plate. Refrigerate, uncovered, until patties are chilled and firm, about 30 minutes.

3. Heat olive oil in 10-inch nonstick skillet over medium heat until shimmering. Gently place patties in skillet and cook until well browned on first side, 8 to 10 minutes. Gently flip patties and continue to cook until golden on second side, 8 to 10 minutes. Serve.

Chickpea Cakes with Cucumber-Yogurt Sauce
SERVES 2 **FAST** **LIGHT**

✅ **WHY THIS RECIPE WORKS:** Buttery, nutty chickpeas make a great foundation for a light yet satisfying veggie burger. To break down the firm chickpeas, we gave them a quick spin in the food processor. Processing them just until we had both some finely chopped beans (to help the patties hold together) and some larger pieces (for a satisfying texture) was key. One egg bound the cakes together nicely and some Greek yogurt added moisture and a subtle tang. Garam masala gave the cakes complex flavor and a pinch of cayenne added just enough heat. A simple, creamy cucumber-yogurt sauce

Creamy, protein-packed chickpeas are the perfect base for a light but satisfying pan-fried bean cake.

perfectly balanced the rich chickpea cakes. Be careful not to overprocess the chickpeas in step 2, or the cakes will have a mushy texture. To keep the patties from falling apart, be sure to wait until they are well browned on the first side before attempting to flip them. Serve over mixed greens. For the nutritional information for this recipe, see page 414.

½ cucumber, peeled, halved lengthwise, seeded, and shredded
  Salt and pepper
½ cup plus 2 tablespoons 2 percent Greek yogurt
3 scallions, sliced thin
3 tablespoons minced fresh cilantro
¾ cup canned chickpeas, rinsed
1 large egg
4 teaspoons olive oil
¼ teaspoon garam masala
  Pinch cayenne pepper
⅓ cup panko bread crumbs
1 small shallot, minced
  Lime wedges

1. Toss cucumber and ¼ teaspoon salt together and let drain in colander for 15 minutes. Combine drained cucumber, ½ cup yogurt, 1 tablespoon scallions, and 1 tablespoon cilantro in bowl and season with salt and pepper to taste; set aside.

2. Pulse chickpeas in food processor to coarse puree with large pieces remaining, 5 to 8 pulses, scraping down sides of bowl as needed. In medium bowl, whisk egg, 2 teaspoons oil, garam masala, ⅛ teaspoon salt, and cayenne together. Gently stir in panko, processed chickpeas, remaining 2 tablespoons yogurt, remaining scallions, remaining 2 tablespoons cilantro, and shallot until just combined. Divide bean mixture into 2 lightly packed balls and gently flatten each ball into 1-inch-thick patty.

3. Heat remaining 2 teaspoons oil in 10-inch nonstick skillet over medium heat until shimmering. Gently place patties in skillet and cook until well browned on first side, 4 to 5 minutes. Gently flip patties and continue to cook until well browned on second side, 4 to 5 minutes. Serve with cucumber-yogurt sauce and lime wedges.

Black Bean Burgers

SERVES 2 FAST

✔ WHY THIS RECIPE WORKS: Our black bean burgers are a far cry from the heavy, dry, dense varieties of frozen veggie burgers you'll find in the supermarket. We found that mashing most of the beans while leaving a third of them whole made a burger that was neither too soft and crumbly nor too dense and pasty. To bind the burgers, we added an egg and some bread crumbs. Cayenne and cumin added warmth, and chopped red bell pepper and cilantro contributed fresh flavor. Best of all, these burgers are a snap to make: We just mixed the ingredients, shaped the patties, and browned them in a skillet. Avoid overmixing the bean mixture in step 1 or the texture of the burgers will be mealy. To keep the patties from falling apart, be sure to wait until they are well browned on the first side before attempting to flip them. Serve with your favorite burger toppings, or omit the buns and serve over mixed greens.

1 large egg
2 tablespoons olive oil
½ teaspoon ground cumin
¼ teaspoon salt
⅛ teaspoon cayenne pepper
1 (15-ounce) can black beans, rinsed

1 cup panko bread crumbs

½ red bell pepper, chopped fine

2 tablespoons minced fresh cilantro

1 small shallot, minced

2 hamburger buns, toasted (optional)

1. Whisk egg, 1 tablespoon oil, cumin, salt, and cayenne together in small bowl. In separate bowl, mash 1¼ cups beans with potato masher until mostly smooth. Gently stir in egg mixture, remaining beans, panko, bell pepper, cilantro, and shallot until just combined. Divide bean mixture into 2 lightly packed balls and gently flatten each ball into 1-inch-thick patty.

2. Heat remaining 1 tablespoon oil in 10-inch nonstick skillet over medium heat until shimmering. Gently place patties in skillet and cook until well browned on first side, 4 to 5 minutes. Gently flip patties and continue to cook until well browned on second side, 4 to 5 minutes. Serve on buns, if desired.

VARIATION

Black Bean Burgers with Corn and Chipotle

Substitute 1½ teaspoons minced canned chipotle chile in adobo sauce for cayenne. Stir in ⅓ cup frozen corn, thawed and patted dry, with bell pepper.

White Bean and Rosemary Gratin with Parmesan Croutons

SERVES 2

✓ **WHY THIS RECIPE WORKS:** We loved the idea of a hearty Tuscan-style white bean casserole, but casseroles can be time-consuming and typically feed a crowd. To speed up this dish, we started with canned beans, which needed only a few minutes of cooking to become tender and creamy. The trick with this dish, however, was infusing the beans with flavor before they overcooked and became mushy. We started building flavor by sautéing onion, celery, and carrot along with some aromatic garlic and fresh rosemary. Once we had a rich and aromatic flavor base, we added bright, fruity canned tomatoes and hearty, healthy chopped kale. For a sauce with great body and flavor, we pureed some of the beans with broth until smooth. Finally, to make our casserole a toasty, cheesy gratin, we topped it with chunks of baguette tossed with Parmesan and baked it until golden brown. Canned navy or great Northern beans can be substituted for the cannellini beans.

1 (15-ounce) can cannellini beans, rinsed

1 cup vegetable broth

2 tablespoons olive oil

1 small onion, chopped fine

1 celery rib, chopped

1 carrot, peeled and chopped

3 garlic cloves, minced

½ teaspoon minced fresh rosemary or ⅛ teaspoon dried

½ cup canned diced tomatoes, drained with ¼ cup juice reserved

¼ cup water

4 ounces kale or collard greens, stemmed and cut into 1-inch pieces

Salt and pepper

4 ounces French or Italian bread, cut into 1-inch cubes (2 cups)

1 ounce Parmesan cheese, grated (½ cup)

1. Adjust oven rack to middle position and heat oven to 450 degrees. Process ½ cup beans and broth in blender until smooth, about 30 seconds.

2. Heat 1 tablespoon oil in 10-inch ovensafe skillet over medium heat until shimmering. Add onion, celery, and carrot, and cook until vegetables are softened, about 5 minutes. Stir in garlic and rosemary and cook until fragrant, about 30 seconds.

3. Stir in tomatoes and cook until softened and dry, about 2 minutes. Stir in broth mixture, remaining beans, reserved tomato juice, and water, scraping up any browned bits. Bring to simmer and cook until beans are heated through, about 5 minutes.

4. Stir in kale, 1 handful at a time, and cook until liquid has thickened slightly and begins to fall below level of vegetables and mixture measures about 3 cups, about 5 minutes. Season with salt and pepper to taste.

5. Toss bread with remaining 1 tablespoon oil and Parmesan in bowl, sprinkle over top of bean mixture, and transfer skillet to oven. Bake until cheese has melted and croutons are golden brown, about 15 minutes. Let casserole cool for 10 minutes before serving.

Tempeh Tacos

SERVES 2

✓ **WHY THIS RECIPE WORKS:** Sold alongside tofu in most supermarkets, tempeh is made by fermenting cooked soybeans and then forming the mixture into a dense cake. With its firm texture and nutty flavor, tempeh added just the right meatiness to these easy tacos. We found it worked best to crumble the tempeh well with our hands before adding it to the pan. We browned it to deepen its flavor before simmering it in a quick tomato sauce seasoned with chili powder, garlic, oregano, and a touch of brown sugar. Cilantro and lime juice stirred in at the end rounded out the sweet-tart flavor of the sauce. Any type of tempeh will work well here. Serve with your favorite taco toppings.

  1   tablespoon vegetable oil
  1   small onion, chopped fine
1½   tablespoons chili powder
  2   garlic cloves, minced
  2   teaspoons minced fresh oregano or
       ½ teaspoon dried
  1   (8-ounce) package tempeh, crumbled into
       ¼-inch pieces
  ¾   cup vegetable broth
  ½   cup canned tomato sauce
  ½   teaspoon light brown sugar
  1   tablespoon minced fresh cilantro
1½   teaspoons lime juice
       Salt and pepper
  6   taco shells, warmed

1. Heat oil in 10-inch nonstick skillet over medium heat until shimmering. Add onion and cook until softened, about 5 minutes. Stir in chili powder, garlic, and oregano and cook until fragrant, about 30 seconds. Stir in tempeh and cook until lightly browned, about 5 minutes. Stir in broth, tomato sauce, and sugar, bring to simmer, and cook until thickened, about 2 minutes.

2. Off heat, stir in cilantro and lime juice and season with salt and pepper to taste. Serve with warm taco shells.

NOTES FROM THE TEST KITCHEN

What Is Tempeh?

While tofu has hit the mainstream, its soy-based cousin, tempeh, might not be as familiar. Tempeh is made by fermenting cooked soybeans then forming the mixture into a firm, dense cake. Some versions of tempeh also contain beans, grains, and flavorings. It serves as a good meat substitute and is a mainstay of many vegetarian diets—it's particularly popular in Southeast Asia. It has a strong nutty flavor, but it also will absorb flavors easily. And because it's better than tofu at holding its shape when cooked, it's a versatile choice for many dishes from chilis and stews to sandwiches and tacos. It is also a healthy choice, since it's high in protein, contains many essential vitamins and minerals, and is cholesterol-free and low in fat. Tempeh is sold in most supermarkets and can be found with different grain and flavoring combinations. We use five-grain tempeh in our recipes, but any variety will work.

Glazed Caribbean Tofu with Rice and Pigeon Peas

SERVES 2

✓ **WHY THIS RECIPE WORKS:** For a Caribbean-inspired vegetarian dinner, we paired tofu with a flavor-packed glaze. Pan-searing the tofu gave it a crisp, golden-brown crust. Firm tofu cut into large pieces held its shape best in the pan. To keep the glaze easy, we relied on pineapple preserves brightened with lime juice and seasoned with red pepper flakes. We also made an easy rice dish with onion, jalapeño, and pigeon peas to serve on the side. Cooking the rice in coconut milk made it rich and creamy—a perfect counterpart to the sweet and spicy tofu. Black-eyed peas or kidney beans can be substituted for the pigeon peas. Do not substitute full-fat coconut milk, or your rice will turn out greasy. You can substitute apricot preserves for the pineapple preserves in this recipe. To make this dish spicier, add the reserved chile seeds with the jalapeño in step 2.

  14   ounces firm tofu
         Salt and pepper
1½   teaspoons curry powder
  4   teaspoons vegetable oil
  1   small onion, chopped
  1   jalapeño chile, stemmed, seeds reserved, and minced
  ½   cup long-grain white rice
  ¾   cup canned pigeon peas, rinsed
  ¾   cup canned light coconut milk
  ⅓   cup plus 1½ tablespoons water
  ¼   cup pineapple preserves
  1   tablespoon lime juice
  ⅛   teaspoon red pepper flakes

1. Line baking sheet with triple layer of paper towels. Cut tofu in half lengthwise, then cut each half crosswise into 6 slices. Spread tofu over prepared sheet and let drain for 15 minutes. Gently pat tofu dry with paper towels and season with salt, pepper, and curry powder.

2. Meanwhile, heat 1 teaspoon oil in medium saucepan over medium-high heat until shimmering. Add onion and jalapeño and cook until softened, about 5 minutes. Stir in rice and cook until opaque, about 1 minute. Stir in peas, coconut milk, ⅓ cup water, and ¼ teaspoon salt and bring to boil. Reduce heat to low, cover, and simmer until rice is tender, 20 to 25 minutes. Season with salt and pepper to taste.

3. Place preserves in small bowl and microwave until bubbling, about 30 seconds. Whisk in remaining 1½ tablespoons water, lime juice, and pepper flakes.

4. Heat remaining 1 tablespoon oil in 12-inch nonstick skillet over medium-high heat until just smoking. Lay tofu

in skillet and cook until golden brown and crisp on all sides, about 5 minutes, turning tofu as needed. Add pineapple mixture and simmer, turning tofu to coat, until glaze thickens, about 1 minute. Serve with rice and pea mixture.

Crispy Tofu with Sweet Chili Sauce

SERVES 2

✅ **WHY THIS RECIPE WORKS:** Fresh soybean curd, or tofu, is perfect for pan-frying; its crust becomes crisp and makes a terrific contrast to its creamy interior. We wanted to start there and pair the mild tofu with a lively sweet-and-spicy chili sauce. To ensure the tofu would get a good crust in the pan, it was important to dry it. We sliced the tofu into fingers and drained it of its excess moisture on paper towels. For the coating, a mix of cornstarch and cornmeal gave us a crunchy, golden-brown crust. For a quick sauce with bold flavor, we whisked chili-garlic sauce with sugar, water, and vinegar and simmered it until thick and glossy. We prefer the softer, creamier texture of medium-firm or soft tofu here, but firm or extra-firm tofu will also work (they will taste drier). Be sure to handle the tofu gently or it may break apart. Serve with white rice.

14	ounces medium-firm or soft tofu
3	tablespoons sugar
¼	cup water
¼	cup rice vinegar
2	teaspoons plus ¾ cup cornstarch
1	tablespoon Asian chili-garlic sauce
¼	cup cornmeal
	Salt and pepper
¾	cup vegetable oil

1. Line baking sheet with triple layer of paper towels. Slice tofu crosswise into 1-inch slabs, then slice each slab in half lengthwise. Spread tofu over prepared sheet and let drain for 15 minutes.

2. Meanwhile, whisk sugar, water, vinegar, 2 teaspoons cornstarch, and chili-garlic sauce together in small saucepan. Bring to simmer over medium-high heat and cook, whisking constantly, until thickened, about 4 minutes. Remove from heat and cover to keep warm.

3. Set wire rack in rimmed baking sheet. Combine remaining ¾ cup cornstarch and cornmeal in shallow dish. Gently pat tofu dry with paper towels and season with salt and pepper. Working with a few pieces at a time, coat tofu thoroughly with cornstarch mixture, pressing gently to adhere, then transfer to prepared rack.

4. Line large plate with triple layer of paper towels. Heat oil in 12-inch nonstick skillet over medium-high heat until shimmering. Carefully lay tofu in skillet and cook until golden brown and crisp on all sides, about 4 minutes, turning tofu as needed. Drain tofu briefly on prepared plate. Season with salt to taste. Serve with sauce.

Cutting Tofu into Fingers

1. Slice block of tofu crosswise into 1-inch-thick slabs.

2. Slice each slab in half into 2 fingers.

3. Spread tofu out over rimmed baking sheet lined with several layers of paper towels and let sit for 15 minutes to drain. Gently pat tofu dry with paper towels.

Asian Braised Tofu with Butternut Squash and Eggplant

SERVES 2

✅ **WHY THIS RECIPE WORKS:** Braising is a great method for preparing tofu because the tofu will literally soak up the flavors of the braising liquid as it cooks. We decided to use rich, creamy coconut milk as the base of an Asian-inspired braise. Sautéed onion, garlic, ginger, and lemon grass gave the sauce a bold aromatic foundation. Cutting the tofu into cubes maximized its surface area, allowing it to absorb the most flavor. To round out the dish, we wanted hearty, earthy vegetables that would benefit from a quick braise: Sweet, creamy butternut squash and meaty eggplant won tasters over.

To deepen their flavors, we browned them in the pan before adding the tofu and braising liquid. If using prepeeled and seeded squash from the supermarket, you will need 8 ounces for this recipe. The tofu and vegetables are delicate and can break apart easily, so be gentle when stirring.

14 ounces extra-firm tofu, cut into ¾-inch pieces
1 tablespoon vegetable oil
1 pound butternut squash, peeled, seeded, and cut into ½-inch pieces (1½ cups)
½ eggplant (8 ounces), cut into ½-inch pieces
1 small onion, chopped fine
4 garlic cloves, minced
1 tablespoon grated fresh ginger
1 lemon grass stalk, trimmed to bottom 6 inches and bruised with back of knife
¾ cup vegetable broth
½ cup canned light coconut milk
2 teaspoons soy sauce
¼ cup minced fresh cilantro
2 teaspoons lime juice
Salt and pepper

1. Line baking sheet with triple layer of paper towels. Spread tofu over prepared sheet and let drain for 15 minutes.

All About Tofu

WHAT IS TOFU? Tofu is made from curds of soy milk, which are pressed into blocks and sold either fresh or vacuum-packed in water. A good choice for vegetarians, tofu is high in protein as well as iron, calcium, and an omega-3 fatty acid. It is also relatively low in fat and calories and is cholesterol-free. We love tofu in the test kitchen because it takes to a wide variety of preparations from stir-frying and sautéing to roasting, braising, grilling, and scrambling, and it soaks up the flavor of the dish as it cooks.

BUYING AND PREPARING TOFU: You can find tofu in a variety of textures: silken, soft, medium-firm, firm, and extra-firm. We like firm or extra-firm tofu in stir-fries because it holds its shape well in the pan. In recipes where we want a contrast between a crunchy crust and a creamy interior, we use soft or medium-firm tofu. Before cooking, we drain the tofu to prevent the excess liquid from waterlogging the dish: Simply place the cut tofu on several layers of paper towels and let it sit for 15 minutes, then gently pat it dry.

STORING TOFU: Tofu is perishable and should be kept well chilled to maximize its shelf life. We prefer to use it within a few days of opening. If you want to keep an open package of tofu for several days, cover the tofu with fresh water and store it in the refrigerator in an airtight container, changing the water daily. Any hint of sourness means the tofu is past its prime.

2. Meanwhile, heat 1 teaspoon oil in 10-inch nonstick skillet over medium-high heat until shimmering. Add squash and cook until spotty brown and tender, 7 to 10 minutes; transfer to bowl. Return now-empty skillet to medium-high heat, add 1 teaspoon oil, and heat until shimmering. Add eggplant and cook until golden brown, 5 to 7 minutes; transfer to bowl with squash.

3. Heat remaining 1 teaspoon oil in again-empty skillet over medium heat until shimmering. Add onion and cook until softened and lightly browned, 5 to 7 minutes. Stir in garlic, ginger, and lemon grass and cook until fragrant, about 30 seconds. Gently stir in tofu, broth, coconut milk, soy sauce, and cooked vegetables and bring to simmer. Reduce heat to medium-low, cover, and cook, stirring occasionally, until vegetables are softened, about 10 minutes. Uncover and continue to simmer until sauce is slightly thickened, about 2 minutes.

4. Off heat, discard lemon grass. Stir in cilantro and lime juice and season with salt and pepper to taste. Serve.

Bruising Lemon Grass

Smashing lemon grass helps release its flavorful oils. To smash lemon grass, set stalk on cutting board and smash it with meat pounder or back of knife. This keeps stalk intact so it can be easily removed from dish.

Spicy Asian Soy and Rice Lettuce Wraps

SERVES 2   **FAST**

✔ **WHY THIS RECIPE WORKS:** Asian lettuce wraps are traditionally filled with seasoned ground meat. Our fast, flavor-packed vegetarian version swaps the meat for soy crumbles, which are made from seasoned, textured soy and have a satisfying texture similar to that of ground meat. We added some crisp, sweet red bell pepper and cooked rice to bulk up the filling. For a flavorful sauce, we started with chili-garlic sauce and punched it up with soy sauce, fresh ginger, and a little brown sugar. Piled into a crisp lettuce leaf, our meaty vegetarian filling kept tasters coming back for more. To make a lettuce cup, put a spoonful of soy and rice mixture in the middle of a lettuce leaf, fold the leaf edges up around the filling, and eat with your hands. You can use leftover or store-bought precooked rice here.

Crisp lettuce cups are the perfect vessel for tender soy crumbles and fresh bell pepper seasoned with a sweet and spicy chili sauce.

¼ cup vegetable broth
1½ teaspoons Asian chili-garlic sauce
1½ teaspoons soy sauce
1½ teaspoons packed brown sugar
¼ teaspoon cornstarch
1 tablespoon vegetable oil
1 small red bell pepper, stemmed, seeded, and cut into ¼-inch pieces
6 ounces soy crumbles
1 cup cooked rice
1 teaspoon grated fresh ginger
2 scallions, sliced thin
1 tablespoon minced fresh cilantro
6 Bibb or Boston lettuce leaves (½ head)

1. Whisk broth, chili-garlic sauce, soy sauce, sugar, and cornstarch together in bowl. Heat oil in 10-inch nonstick skillet over medium-high heat until shimmering. Add bell pepper and cook until softened, about 5 minutes. Stir in soy crumbles, rice, and ginger and cook until fragrant, about 30 seconds.

2. Whisk sauce to recombine, then add to skillet. Cook, stirring constantly, until mixture is thickened, about 30 seconds. Off heat, stir in scallions and cilantro. Serve in lettuce leaves.

The Asian Pantry

Many supermarkets now carry a wide array of Asian ingredients, making it easy to give dishes authentic flavor. Here are some common Asian ingredients that you'll find in many of our recipes.

CHILE SAUCES

Used both in cooking and as condiments, chile sauces come in a variety of styles. Sriracha contains garlic and is made from chiles ground into a smooth paste. Chili-garlic sauce is similar to Sriracha, but uses coarsely ground chiles. Sambal oelek is made purely from ground chiles without garlic or other spices, adding heat but not additional flavor. Thai-style sweet chili sauce lies at the other end of the spicy spectrum. This sweet, thick sauce is made primarily from palm sugar, pickled chiles, vinegar, and garlic. It makes a good dipping sauce, and we also use it as a glaze. These sauces will keep for several months in the refrigerator.

SOY SAUCE

Soy sauce is a dark, salty, fermented liquid made from soybeans and roasted grain. It is used throughout Asia to enhance flavor and contribute complexity to food. It's rich in the amino acid glutamate, which contributes potent savory, meaty flavor to dishes. Pasteurized soy sauce can be stored at room temperature, but unpasteurized soy sauce should be refrigerated.

HOISIN SAUCE

Hoisin sauce is a thick, reddish-brown mixture of soybeans, sugar, vinegar, garlic, chiles, and spices, particularly five-spice powder. It is used in many classic Chinese dishes, including barbecued pork, Peking duck, and *kung pao* shrimp, and as a table condiment, much like ketchup. The ideal hoisin sauce balances sweet, salty, pungent, and spicy elements so that no one flavor dominates.

OYSTER SAUCE

This thick, salty, brown sauce is a concentrated mixture of oysters, soy sauce, brine, and seasonings. It is used to enhance the flavor of many dishes and is the base for many Asian dipping sauces.

MISO

Made from a fermented mixture of soybeans and rice, barley, or rye, miso is incredibly versatile, suitable for use in soups, braises, dressings, and sauces or for topping grilled foods. This salty, deep-flavored paste ranges in strength and color from a mild, pale yellow (referred to as white) to stronger-flavored red or brownish black, depending on the fermentation method and ingredients.

FISH SAUCE

Fish sauce is a salty amber-colored liquid made from fermented fish. It is used as an ingredient and condiment in Asian cuisines, most commonly in Southeast Asia. In very small amounts, it adds a well-rounded, salty flavor to sauces, soups, and marinades. Note that the lighter the color of the fish sauce, the lighter its flavor.

SESAME OIL

Raw sesame oil is very mild and light in color and is used mostly for cooking, while toasted sesame oil, which has a deep amber color and an intense nutty flavor, is primarily used for seasoning. Just a few drops will give stir-fries, noodle dishes, or salad dressings a deep, rich flavor. Purchase sesame oil in tinted glass and refrigerate it to extend its shelf life.

Pasta and Asian Noodle Dishes

■ FAST (Start to finish in about 30 minutes)

■ LIGHT (See page 414 for nutritional information)

Opposite: Beef Lo Mein with Broccoli and Bell Pepper; Skillet Pasta with Fresh Tomato Sauce; Classic Lasagna

Spaghetti with Garlic and Olive Oil

SERVES 2

✔ **WHY THIS RECIPE WORKS:** Made from kitchen staples—pasta, olive oil, garlic, and red pepper flakes—pasta with garlic and oil, or *aglio e olio*, is the perfect last-minute pantry supper for two. To make the most of its flavors, we started by sautéing the garlic slowly and gently over low heat until it developed a mellow, nutty, rich flavor. For a little kick we also stirred a small amount of raw garlic minced to a paste into the pasta. Three tablespoons of extra-virgin olive oil (using good olive oil was a must in this simple dish) was just enough to coat the pasta and evenly distribute the garlic without making the dish greasy. Minced parsley, fresh lemon juice, and a dash of red pepper flakes brightened the flavors. A rasp-style grater makes quick work of turning the garlic into a paste.

- 3 tablespoons extra-virgin olive oil
- 5 garlic cloves, minced, plus 1 garlic clove, minced to paste
- ⅛ teaspoon red pepper flakes
- Salt and pepper
- 6 ounces spaghetti
- 2 tablespoons minced fresh parsley
- 1 teaspoon lemon juice
- Grated Parmesan cheese

1. Cook 2 tablespoons oil, minced garlic, pepper flakes, and ¼ teaspoon salt in 10-inch nonstick skillet over low heat, stirring often, until garlic foams and is sticky and straw-colored, about 10 minutes. Transfer to bowl and stir in remaining 1 tablespoon oil and garlic paste.

NOTES FROM THE TEST KITCHEN

The Best Extra-Virgin Olive Oil

For most cooked dishes we're perfectly happy reaching for an inexpensive olive oil, but sometimes only a good-quality olive oil will do. Extra-virgin oils range wildly in price, color, and quality, so it's hard to know which to buy. While many things can affect the quality and flavor of olive oil, the type of olive, the time of harvest (earlier means greener, more bitter, and pungent; later, more mild and buttery), and processing are the most important factors. The best-quality oil comes from olives pressed as quickly as possible without heat (which coaxes more oil from the olives at the expense of flavor). Out of those we tasted, our favorite oils were produced from a blend of olives and, thus, were well rounded. Composed of a blend of intense Picual, mild Hojiblanca, Ocal, and Arbequina olives, **Columela Extra Virgin Olive Oil** took top honors for its buttery, fruity flavor and excellent balance.

2. Meanwhile, bring 4 quarts water to boil in large pot. Add pasta and 1 tablespoon salt and cook, stirring often, until al dente. Reserve ½ cup cooking water, then drain pasta and return it to pot. Add 1 tablespoon reserved cooking water to garlic mixture to loosen it. Add garlic mixture, parsley, and lemon juice to pasta and toss to combine. Season with salt and pepper to taste, and adjust consistency with remaining reserved cooking water as needed. Serve with Parmesan.

VARIATIONS

Spaghetti with Garlic, Olive Oil, and Fennel

After transferring cooked garlic mixture to bowl in step 1, cook 1 fennel bulb, cored and sliced thin, ½ cup water, and 2 teaspoons more extra-virgin olive oil, covered, in now-empty skillet over medium-high heat until fennel is crisp-tender, about 3 minutes. Uncover and continue to cook until water has evaporated and fennel is lightly browned and fully tender, about 5 minutes. Add cooked fennel to pasta with garlic mixture.

Spaghetti with Garlic, Olive Oil, and Artichokes

To thaw the artichokes quickly, microwave them in a covered bowl for about 3 minutes.

After transferring cooked garlic mixture to bowl in step 1, heat 2 teaspoons more extra-virgin olive oil in now-empty skillet over medium-high heat until shimmering. Add 9 ounces frozen artichoke hearts, thawed and patted dry, and ⅛ teaspoon salt and cook until artichokes are lightly browned and tender, 4 to 6 minutes. Add cooked artichokes to pasta with garlic mixture.

Spaghetti with Pecorino Romano and Black Pepper

SERVES 2　**FAST**

✔ **WHY THIS RECIPE WORKS:** The classic Roman dish *pasta cacio e pepe* (pasta with cheese and pepper) comes together quickly and offers great flavor from just a few ingredients, making it an ideal weeknight meal for two. The key to this dish was finding a way to prevent the cheese from clumping. A combination of starchy pasta cooking water and a little cream kept the sauce perfectly smooth. We cooked the pasta in just one-quarter of the usual water to concentrate the starch for an even creamier sauce. A generous amount of black pepper gave our pasta plenty of bite. Look for imported Pecorino Romano, not the bland domestic cheese labeled "Romano." Use the small holes of a box grater to grate the cheese and the large holes to shred it. Be sure to measure the amount of water; the thick, starchy pasta cooking water is necessary for the consistency of the sauce. Stir the pasta often during cooking to prevent clumping.

Six pantry-friendly ingredients are all you need to make our rich and creamy Spaghetti with Pecorino Romano and Black Pepper.

3 ounces Pecorino Romano cheese, 2 ounces grated (1 cup) and 1 ounce shredded (½ cup)

6 ounces spaghetti

½ teaspoon salt

1 tablespoon heavy cream

1 teaspoon extra-virgin olive oil

¾ teaspoon pepper

1. Place grated Pecorino in medium bowl. Set colander in large bowl.

2. Bring 1 quart water to boil in large pot. Add pasta and salt and cook, stirring often to prevent clumping, until al dente. Drain pasta in prepared colander, reserving cooking water, and return pasta to pot.

3. Slowly whisk ½ cup reserved cooking water into grated Pecorino until smooth, then whisk in cream, oil, and pepper. Gradually pour cheese mixture over pasta, tossing to coat. Let pasta rest for 1 to 2 minutes, tossing frequently and adjusting consistency with remaining cooking water as needed. Serve with shredded Pecorino.

Pasta with Tomato and Almond Pesto

SERVES 2 **FAST**

✔ **WHY THIS RECIPE WORKS:** For a fresh spin on classic basil pesto, we looked to a Sicilian variation featuring almonds and tomatoes. Cherry tomatoes worked best, offering fruity vibrancy and reliable quality year-round. We found that slivered almonds browned evenly and were preferable to whole almonds (their papery skins proved problematic). Basil played a supporting role here; just ¼ cup offered freshness without dominating the other ingredients. A dash of red wine vinegar contributed brightness, and some Parmesan cheese finished our dish with a nutty richness, for a satisfying meal that came together in no time. You can substitute grape tomatoes for the cherry tomatoes.

6 ounces cherry tomatoes

¼ cup fresh basil leaves

2 tablespoons slivered almonds, toasted

1 small garlic clove, minced

Salt

¼ teaspoon red wine vinegar

⅛ teaspoon red pepper flakes (optional)

3 tablespoons extra-virgin olive oil

6 ounces spaghetti or linguine

¼ cup grated Parmesan cheese, plus extra for serving

1. Process tomatoes, basil, almonds, garlic, ½ teaspoon salt, vinegar, and pepper flakes, if using, in food processor until smooth, about 1 minute, scraping down sides of bowl as needed. With processor running, slowly add oil until incorporated, about 30 seconds.

2. Meanwhile, bring 4 quarts water to boil in large pot. Add pasta and 1 tablespoon salt and cook, stirring often, until al dente. Reserve ½ cup cooking water, then drain pasta and return it to pot. Add pesto and Parmesan and toss to combine. Season with salt to taste, and adjust consistency with reserved cooking water as needed. Serve with extra Parmesan.

VARIATION

Pasta with Tomato, Pine Nut, and Arugula Pesto

Substitute ½ cup baby arugula for basil and 2 tablespoons toasted pine nuts for almonds. Add ¾ teaspoon grated lemon zest plus ½ teaspoon juice with tomatoes in step 1.

Linguine with Quick Tomato Sauce

SERVES 2 `LIGHT`

✓ **WHY THIS RECIPE WORKS:** While popping open a jar of tomato sauce is easy enough, the truth is, preparing a simple, from-scratch sauce doesn't take that much longer—and the flavor can't be beat. Canned tomatoes provided more consistent results than fresh, and whole tomatoes processed briefly in the food processor gave our sauce just the right consistency: mostly smooth, with just a few small bites of tomato. Draining the tomatoes before processing allowed our sauce to become nicely thickened in just a short amount of time, which was essential for retaining fresh tomato flavor. A little bit of sugar provided a sweetness that balanced the acidity of the tomatoes. Garlic and basil contributed classic background notes, and some fruity extra-virgin olive oil offered just enough richness. For a spicy sauce, add ½ teaspoon red pepper flakes to the oil with the garlic. For the nutritional information for this recipe, see page 414.

- 1 **(28-ounce) can whole peeled tomatoes, drained**
- 5 **teaspoons extra-virgin olive oil**
- 2 **garlic cloves, minced**
- 2 **tablespoons chopped fresh basil**
  Sugar
  Salt and pepper
- 6 **ounces linguine**

1. Pulse tomatoes in food processor until coarsely chopped and no large pieces remain, 6 to 8 pulses. Cook oil and garlic in medium saucepan over medium heat, stirring often, until fragrant but not browned, about 2 minutes. Stir in pulsed tomatoes, bring to simmer, and cook until slightly thickened, 10 to 15 minutes. Off heat, stir in basil and ¼ teaspoon sugar. Season with salt and additional sugar to taste.

2. Meanwhile, bring 4 quarts water to boil in large pot. Add pasta and 1 tablespoon salt and cook, stirring often, until al dente. Reserve ½ cup cooking water, then drain pasta and return it to pot. Add sauce and toss to combine. Season with salt and pepper to taste, and adjust consistency with reserved cooking water as needed. Serve.

VARIATION

Linguine with Quick Fire-Roasted Tomato Sauce

For the nutritional information for this recipe, see page 414.

Substitute 1 (28-ounce) can drained whole fire-roasted tomatoes for whole tomatoes. Add ¼ teaspoon smoked paprika to oil with garlic.

Spaghetti with Classic Marinara Sauce

SERVES 2

✓ **WHY THIS RECIPE WORKS:** Marinara sauce gets its rich, complex flavor from a long, slow simmer; we wanted to achieve that authentic, long-cooked flavor in under an hour. Canned whole tomatoes crushed by hand offered bright flavor and optimum texture, and sautéing them concentrated their flavor. Since we were just making enough sauce for two, we realized that we could switch from a saucepan to a skillet; the larger surface area allowed the sauce to concentrate more quickly, adding complexity in short order. Red wine, oregano, and basil provided acidity and floral notes, and a pinch of sugar kept the flavors in balance. Finally, reserving a portion of the tomatoes to add at the end of cooking added a nice freshness. Be sure to use whole tomatoes packed in juice (not puree). If you prefer a chunkier sauce, pulse it three or four times in the food processor in step 4. Feel free to substitute another pasta for the spaghetti.

- 1 **(28-ounce) can whole peeled tomatoes**
- 3 **tablespoons extra-virgin olive oil**
- 1 **small onion, chopped fine**
- 2 **garlic cloves, minced**
- 1 **teaspoon minced fresh oregano or ¼ teaspoon dried**
- 2 **tablespoons dry red wine**
- 1½ **tablespoons chopped fresh basil**
  Salt and pepper
  Sugar
- 6 **ounces spaghetti**
  Grated Parmesan cheese

1. Drain tomatoes in fine-mesh strainer set over medium bowl. Open tomatoes with your hands and remove and discard seeds and fibrous cores; let tomatoes drain, about 3 minutes. Measure out ⅓ cup tomatoes and set aside. Reserve 1¼ cups drained tomato juice; discard remaining tomato juice.

2. Heat 1 tablespoon oil in 10-inch skillet over medium heat until shimmering. Add onion and cook until softened and lightly browned, 5 to 7 minutes. Stir in garlic and oregano and cook until fragrant, about 30 seconds.

3. Stir in 1 tablespoon oil and drained tomatoes and increase heat to medium-high. Cook, stirring occasionally, until liquid has evaporated and tomatoes begin to brown and stick to bottom of skillet, 8 to 10 minutes. Stir in wine and cook until nearly evaporated, about 30 seconds. Stir in reserved tomato juice, scraping up any browned bits. Bring to simmer and cook, stirring occasionally, until sauce is thickened, 7 to 9 minutes.

4. Transfer sauce to food processor, add reserved ⅓ cup drained tomatoes, and pulse until sauce is mostly smooth, about 8 pulses. Return sauce to now-empty skillet, stir in basil and remaining 1 tablespoon oil. Season with salt, pepper, and sugar to taste.

5. Meanwhile, bring 4 quarts water to boil in large pot. Add pasta and 1 tablespoon salt and cook, stirring often, until al dente. Reserve ½ cup cooking water, then drain pasta and return it to pot. Add sauce and toss to combine. Season with salt and pepper to taste, and adjust consistency with reserved cooking water as needed. Serve with Parmesan.

NOTES FROM THE TEST KITCHEN

Cooking Pasta 101

Cooking pasta seems simple, but perfect pasta takes some finesse. Here's how we do it in the test kitchen.

USE PLENTY OF WATER: To prevent sticking, you'll need 4 quarts of water to cook up to 1 pound of dried pasta. Pasta leaches starch as it cooks; without plenty of water to dilute it, the starch will coat the noodles and they will stick. Use a pot with at least a 6-quart capacity so that the water won't boil over.

SALT THE WATER: Adding salt to the pasta cooking water is essential; it seasons and adds flavor to the pasta. Add 1 tablespoon of salt per 4 quarts of water. Be sure to add the salt with the pasta, not before, so it will dissolve and not stain the pot.

SKIP THE OIL: It's a myth that adding oil to pasta cooking water prevents the pasta from sticking together as it cooks. Adding oil to cooking water just creates a slick on the surface of the water, doing nothing for the pasta. And when you drain the pasta, the oil prevents the pasta sauce from adhering. To prevent pasta from sticking, simply stir the pasta for a minute or two when you add it to the boiling water, then stir occasionally while it's cooking.

CHECK OFTEN FOR DONENESS: The timing instructions given on the box are almost always too long and will result in mushy, over-cooked pasta. Tasting is the best way to check for doneness. We typically prefer pasta cooked al dente, when it still has a little bite left in the center.

RESERVE SOME WATER: Reserve about ½ cup cooking water before draining the pasta—the water is flavorful and can help loosen a thick sauce.

DON'T RINSE: Drain the pasta in a colander, but don't rinse the pasta; it washes away starch and makes the pasta taste watery. Do let a little cooking water cling to the cooked pasta to help the sauce adhere.

KEEP IT HOT: If you're using a large serving bowl for the pasta, place it under the colander while draining the pasta. The hot water heats up the bowl, which keeps the pasta warm longer.

Pasta with Creamy Tomato Sauce

SERVES 2

✔ **WHY THIS RECIPE WORKS:** The best creamy tomato sauces balance the acidity of fruity tomatoes with the richness of dairy, but many recipes produce sauces that are too sharp, too sweet, or lacking in tomato flavor. We wanted a smooth, full-flavored sauce in which the tomatoes and cream complemented each other. Diced tomatoes pureed in the food processor yielded a smooth sauce with bright tomato flavor. Sautéing a little tomato paste with the aromatics contributed depth to our sauce, and for a truly bold tomato presence we added some sun-dried tomatoes as well. Although tomato-cream sauce is traditionally pureed, we tried skipping the extra step and found that we preferred the slightly chunky texture. Reserving a splash of wine and some of the tomatoes to stir in at the end brightened our sauce considerably and cut through the richness of the cream. Other pasta shapes can be substituted for the fusilli; however, their cup measurements may vary (see page 228).

- 1 **(14.5-ounce) can diced tomatoes**
- 2 **tablespoons unsalted butter**
- 1 **small onion, chopped fine**
- ½ **ounce thinly sliced prosciutto, chopped fine**
- 1 **bay leaf**
  Pinch red pepper flakes
  Salt and pepper
- 2 **garlic cloves, minced**
- 1½ **tablespoons coarsely chopped oil-packed sun-dried tomatoes**
- 1 **tablespoon tomato paste**
- 3 **tablespoons dry white wine or dry vermouth**
- ¼ **cup heavy cream**
- 6 **ounces (2⅓ cups) fusilli**
- 2 **tablespoons shredded fresh basil**
  Grated Parmesan cheese

1. Process diced tomatoes and their juice in food processor until smooth, about 10 seconds. Measure out 1 tablespoon tomatoes and set aside.

2. Melt butter in medium saucepan over medium heat. Add onion, prosciutto, bay leaf, pepper flakes, and ⅛ teaspoon salt and cook, stirring occasionally, until onion is softened and lightly browned, 5 to 7 minutes. Stir in garlic and cook until fragrant, about 30 seconds. Stir in sun-dried tomatoes and tomato paste and cook until slightly darkened, about 1 minute. Stir in 2 tablespoons wine and cook until evaporated, about 1 minute.

3. Stir in processed tomatoes, scraping up any browned bits, and bring to simmer. Reduce heat to low, partially cover, and simmer, stirring occasionally, until sauce is thickened, 10 to 12 minutes. Discard bay leaf. Stir in cream, reserved 1 tablespoon processed tomatoes, and remaining 1 tablespoon wine. Season with salt and pepper to taste.

4. Meanwhile, bring 4 quarts water to boil in large pot. Add pasta and 1 tablespoon salt and cook, stirring often, until al dente. Reserve ½ cup cooking water, then drain pasta and return it to pot. Add sauce and toss to combine. Season with salt and pepper to taste, and adjust consistency with reserved cooking water as needed. Stir in basil. Serve with Parmesan.

Shredding Basil

To shred basil or other leafy herbs, simply stack several leaves on top of one another, roll them up, and slice. For basil, we find rolling leaves from tip to tail minimizes bruising and browning.

Salting and microwaving the eggplant before sautéing ensures it's nicely browned and tender—not soggy—in our pasta alla norma.

Pasta alla Norma

SERVES 2

✔ **WHY THIS RECIPE WORKS:** To make it work for two, we wanted to streamline the preparation required for pasta *alla norma*—a pasta dish featuring tender eggplant, rich tomato sauce, and salty, milky shreds of ricotta salata. Salting the eggplant drew out excess moisture, then we microwaved it to cause its air pockets to collapse and compress. This meant that the eggplant soaked up much less oil when sautéed, resulting in perfectly browned—not soggy or greasy—eggplant. Pureeing canned diced tomatoes gave us a quick tomato sauce to complement the tender eggplant. Just one minced anchovy plus a little garlic, basil, and red pepper flakes gave the sauce savory depth. Do not peel the eggplant, as the skin helps the eggplant hold together during cooking. Other pasta shapes can be substituted for the rigatoni; however, their cup measurements may vary (see page 228). Ricotta salata is traditional, but French feta, Pecorino Romano, and Cotija (a firm, crumbly Mexican cheese) are acceptable substitutes.

1 (14.5-ounce) can diced tomatoes
1 pound eggplant, cut into ¾-inch pieces
    Salt and pepper
3 tablespoons extra-virgin olive oil, plus extra for serving
2 garlic cloves, minced
1 anchovy fillet, rinsed, patted dry, and minced
⅛ teaspoon red pepper flakes
1 cup water
3 tablespoons chopped fresh basil
6 ounces (2⅓ cups) rigatoni
1½ ounces ricotta salata cheese, shredded (⅓ cup)

1. Process tomatoes and their juice in food processor until smooth, about 10 seconds.

2. Line large plate with double layer of coffee filters and lightly spray with vegetable oil spray. Toss eggplant with ¼ teaspoon salt, then spread out over coffee filters. Microwave eggplant until dry to touch and slightly shriveled, 8 to 10 minutes, tossing halfway through microwaving. Let cool slightly.

3. Transfer eggplant to large bowl, drizzle with 1 teaspoon oil, and toss gently to coat. Heat 1 tablespoon oil in 12-inch nonstick skillet over medium-high heat until shimmering. Add eggplant and cook, stirring occasionally, until well browned and fully tender, about 8 minutes; transfer to clean plate.

4. Let skillet cool slightly, about 1 minute. Add 2 teaspoons oil, garlic, anchovy, and pepper flakes to now-empty skillet and cook over medium heat until fragrant, about 30 seconds. Stir in processed tomatoes and water, bring to simmer, and cook until slightly thickened, about 8 minutes. Stir in eggplant and continue to simmer, stirring occasionally, until eggplant is heated through, 3 to 5 minutes. Stir in basil and remaining 1 tablespoon oil and season with salt and pepper to taste.

5. Meanwhile, bring 4 quarts water to boil in large pot. Add pasta and 1 tablespoon salt and cook, stirring often, until al dente. Reserve ½ cup cooking water, then drain pasta and return it to pot. Add sauce and toss to combine. Season with salt and pepper to taste and adjust consistency with reserved cooking water as needed. Serve with ricotta salata and extra oil.

VARIATION

Pasta with Eggplant, Olives, and Capers
Substitute 1 tablespoon minced fresh parsley for basil and add ¼ cup thinly sliced pitted kalamata olives and 1 tablespoon drained and rinsed capers to sauce with parsley and oil in step 4.

Pasta with Mushroom Ragu

SERVES 2

✔ **WHY THIS RECIPE WORKS:** Although less well known than traditional long-simmered meat ragu, mushroom ragu is an equally satisfying dish with a distinct earthy flavor. For ultimate mushroom flavor we combined the naturally hearty texture of fresh mushrooms with the intense concentrated flavor of dried. Just one portobello offered plenty of meatiness; we chopped it into bite-size pieces so that it had a noticeable presence in the sauce. A generous dose of dried porcini gave our sauce an earthy richness, and straining the rehydrating liquid and adding it to the sauce gave our ragu even more mushroom flavor. Rendering some pancetta in the pan before sautéing the mushrooms gave them great meaty flavor. Chopped whole tomatoes reinforced the hearty texture of the dish, and a little minced rosemary enhanced the woodsy flavor of the mushrooms. Be sure to scrape the dark brown gills from the portobello cap, or the ragu will look and taste muddy.

½ cup chicken broth

½ ounce dried porcini mushrooms, rinsed

2 tablespoons extra-virgin olive oil

2 ounces pancetta, cut into ½-inch pieces

1 large portobello mushroom cap, gills removed, cut into ½-inch pieces

2 garlic cloves, sliced thin

2 teaspoons tomato paste

1 teaspoon minced fresh rosemary or ¼ teaspoon dried

1 (14.5-ounce) can whole peeled tomatoes, drained and chopped coarse

Salt and pepper

6 ounces spaghetti

Grated Pecorino Romano cheese

1. Microwave broth and porcini mushrooms together in covered bowl until steaming, about 1 minute. Let sit until softened, about 5 minutes. Drain mushrooms through fine-mesh strainer lined with coffee filter, reserve broth, and finely chop mushrooms.

2. Heat 1 tablespoon oil in 10-inch skillet over medium heat until shimmering. Add pancetta and cook until rendered and crisp, 3 to 5 minutes. Add chopped porcini, remaining 1 tablespoon oil, portobello mushroom, garlic, tomato paste, and rosemary and cook, stirring occasionally, until all liquid has evaporated and tomato paste starts to brown, 5 to 7 minutes. Stir in reserved broth and tomatoes, scraping up any browned bits. Bring to simmer and cook, stirring occasionally, until thickened, 15 to 20 minutes. Season with salt and pepper to taste.

3. Meanwhile, bring 4 quarts water to boil in large pot. Add pasta and 1 tablespoon salt and cook, stirring often, until al dente. Reserve ½ cup cooking water, then drain pasta and return it to pot. Add sauce and toss to combine. Season with salt and pepper to taste, and adjust consistency with reserved cooking water as needed. Serve with Pecorino.

Removing Portobello Mushroom Gills

The black gills on the underside of a portobello mushroom cap can make a sauce, soup, or stew taste muddy and appear unappetizingly dark. To remove mushroom gills, simply scrape off using spoon before cooking.

Classic Pork Ragu

SERVES 2

☑ **WHY THIS RECIPE WORKS:** Featuring tender, shredded meat in a rich tomato sauce, classic pork ragu is a rustic alternative to more complicated meat sauces and delivers big, meaty flavor without a lot of work. Determining the right cut of pork was our biggest challenge, since many of the most flavorful cuts of pork are also the largest. Country-style ribs proved ideal; they are available in smaller portions and have plenty of fat and connective tissue to keep the meat moist during the long cooking time. Slowly simmered with a can of whole tomatoes and flavored with shallot, garlic, rosemary, and red wine, these meaty ribs delivered rich, savory flavor. Pork spareribs can be substituted for the country-style ribs. To prevent the sauce from becoming greasy, trim all external fat from the ribs before browning. Other pasta shapes can be substituted for the ziti; however, their cup measurements may vary (see page 228).

- 1 **(28-ounce) can whole peeled tomatoes, drained with ¼ cup juice reserved**
- 12 **ounces bone-in country-style pork ribs, trimmed**
  Salt and pepper
- 2 **teaspoons olive oil**
- 1 **large shallot, minced**
- 2 **garlic cloves, minced**
- 1½ **teaspoons minced fresh rosemary**
- ½ **cup dry red wine**
- 6 **ounces (2 cups) ziti**
  Grated Pecorino Romano cheese

1. Pulse tomatoes in food processor until coarsely chopped and no large pieces remain, 6 to 8 pulses.

2. Pat pork dry with paper towels and season with salt and pepper. Heat oil in 10-inch skillet over medium-high heat until just smoking. Brown pork well on all sides, 8 to 10 minutes; transfer to plate.

3. Add shallot and ¼ teaspoon salt to fat left in skillet and cook over medium heat until softened, 2 to 3 minutes. Stir in garlic and rosemary and cook until fragrant, about 30 seconds. Stir in wine, scraping up any browned bits. Bring to simmer and cook until reduced by half, about 2 minutes.

4. Stir in pulsed tomatoes and reserved juice. Nestle browned ribs into sauce, along with any accumulated juices, and bring to simmer. Reduce heat to low, cover, and simmer gently, turning ribs occasionally, until meat is very tender and falling off bones, about 1½ hours.

5. Transfer ribs to plate, let cool slightly, then shred into bite-size pieces using 2 forks, discarding fat and bones. Return shredded meat to sauce, bring to simmer, and cook until

For a supremely rich and meaty ragu, we use country-style pork ribs, which stay moist and tender throughout the slow simmer.

heated through and slightly thickened, 2 to 3 minutes. Season with salt and pepper to taste.

6. Meanwhile, bring 4 quarts water to boil in large pot. Add pasta and 1 tablespoon salt and cook, stirring often, until al dente. Reserve ½ cup cooking water, then drain pasta and return it to pot. Add sauce and toss to combine. Season with salt and pepper to taste, and adjust consistency with reserved cooking water as needed. Serve with Pecorino.

Pasta with Roasted Cauliflower, Garlic, and Walnuts

SERVES 2

☑ **WHY THIS RECIPE WORKS:** For a warming winter pasta dinner, we wanted to unite a roasted vegetable, pasta, and cheese with a simple sauce. Focusing first on the vegetable, we selected cauliflower, which becomes sweet and nutty when roasted. Cutting it into small pieces and sprinkling it with a little sugar maximized caramelization, and cooking it on a preheated baking sheet significantly reduced the roasting time. Roasted garlic turned out to be a key ingredient in our sauce—mashed with a little extra-virgin olive oil and lemon juice, it created a creamy puree with an earthy, nutty sweetness. Parsley, toasted walnuts, and Parmesan provided additional texture and layers of flavor. Other pasta shapes can be substituted for the campanelle; however, their cup measurements may vary (see page 228). For efficiency's sake, consider preparing the cauliflower after you put the garlic in the oven.

1 head garlic, outer papery skins removed and top quarter of head cut off and discarded

½ teaspoon plus 3 tablespoons extra-virgin olive oil

1 tablespoon lemon juice, plus extra for seasoning

⅛ teaspoon red pepper flakes

½ head cauliflower (1 pound), cored and cut into 1-inch florets

Salt and pepper

⅛ teaspoon sugar

6 ounces (2 cups) campanelle

¼ cup grated Parmesan cheese, plus extra for serving

2 teaspoons minced fresh parsley

2 tablespoons chopped toasted walnuts

1. Adjust oven racks to middle and lower-middle positions and heat oven to 500 degrees. Place garlic head cut side up in center of 12-inch square of aluminum foil. Drizzle ½ teaspoon oil over garlic and wrap securely. Place packet on lower rack and place rimmed baking sheet on upper rack. Roast garlic for 35 minutes. Transfer packet to cutting board, let cool for 10 minutes, then unwrap garlic. Gently squeeze to remove cloves from skin, transfer cloves to small bowl, and mash smooth with fork. Stir in lemon juice and pepper flakes, then slowly whisk in 2 tablespoons oil.

2. While garlic roasts, toss cauliflower, remaining 1 tablespoon oil, ½ teaspoon salt, ⅛ teaspoon pepper, and sugar together in large bowl. Working quickly, carefully arrange cauliflower in single layer on hot sheet. Roast cauliflower until well browned and tender, 10 to 15 minutes, stirring cauliflower halfway through cooking. Transfer cauliflower to cutting board, let cool slightly, then chop into ½-inch pieces.

3. Meanwhile, bring 4 quarts water to boil in large pot. Add pasta and 1 tablespoon salt and cook, stirring often, until al dente. Reserve ½ cup cooking water, then drain pasta and return it to pot. Add garlic sauce, chopped cauliflower, 2 tablespoons of reserved cooking water, Parmesan, and parsley and toss to combine. Season with salt, pepper, and extra lemon juice to taste, and adjust consistency with remaining reserved cooking water as needed. Sprinkle individual portions with walnuts. Serve with extra Parmesan.

Pasta with Roasted Broccoli, Garlic, and Almonds

Substitute 12 ounces broccoli florets for cauliflower and reduce roasting time to 8 to 10 minutes in step 2. Substitute ¼ cup grated Manchego cheese for Parmesan, 2 tablespoons chopped fresh basil for parsley, and 2 tablespoons toasted slivered almonds for walnuts. Serve with extra grated Manchego.

Pasta with Roasted Mushrooms, Garlic, and Pine Nuts

Substitute 1½ pounds portobello mushroom caps, gills removed, caps sliced ¾ inch thick, for cauliflower and reduce amount of salt to ⅛ teaspoon in step 2; roast as directed, flipping mushrooms halfway through cooking. Substitute ¼ cup grated Pecorino Romano cheese for Parmesan, 1 teaspoon minced fresh rosemary for parsley, and 2 tablespoons toasted pine nuts for walnuts. Serve with extra Pecorino.

Preparing Garlic for Roasting

1. Rinse garlic head and remove outer papery skin. Cut top quarter off of garlic head so that tops of cloves are exposed.

2. Place garlic head cut side up in center of 12-inch square of aluminum foil, drizzle with oil, and wrap securely.

3. After roasted garlic head has cooled, remove from foil. Using your hand or flat edge of chef's knife, squeeze garlic cloves from skins, starting from root end and working up.

All About Canned Tomatoes

Since canned tomatoes are processed at the height of freshness, they deliver more flavor than off-season fresh tomatoes. But with all the options lining supermarket shelves, it's not always clear what you should buy. We tested a variety of canned tomato products to determine the best uses for each and our favorite brands.

WHOLE TOMATOES

Whole tomatoes are peeled tomatoes packed in their own juice or puree. They are best when fresh tomato flavor is a must. Whole tomatoes are quite soft and break down quickly when cooked. We found that those packed in juice had a livelier, fresher flavor. Our top-rated brand is **Progresso Italian-Style Whole Peeled Tomatoes with Basil**. (Progresso sells whole tomatoes packed both in juice and in puree, so check the label.)

DICED TOMATOES

Diced tomatoes are peeled, machine-diced, and packed in their own juice or puree. Many brands contain calcium chloride, a firming agent that helps the chunks maintain their shape. Diced tomatoes are best for rustic tomato sauces with a chunky texture and in long-cooked stews and soups where you want the tomatoes to hold their shape. We favor diced tomatoes packed in juice because they have a fresher flavor than those packed in puree. Our preferred brand is **Hunt's Diced Tomatoes**, which has a fresh flavor and a good balance of sweet and tart notes.

CRUSHED TOMATOES

Crushed tomatoes are whole tomatoes ground very finely, then enriched with tomato puree. They work well in smoother sauces, and their thicker consistency makes them ideal when you want to make a sauce quickly. We prefer fresh-tasting **Tuttorosso Crushed Tomatoes in Thick Puree with Basil** (not to be confused with Tuttorosso's New World Style Crushed Tomatoes, which we don't recommend). **Muir Glen Organic Crushed Tomatoes with Basil** came in a close second. If you can't find either brand, crush your own canned diced tomatoes in a food processor.

TOMATO PUREE

Tomato puree is made from cooked tomatoes that have been strained to remove their seeds and skins. Tomato puree works well in long-simmered, smooth, thick sauces with a deep, hearty flavor. We like **Hunt's Tomato Puree**, with its thick consistency and tomatoey flavor, though most supermarket brands will work just fine.

TOMATO PASTE

Tomato paste is tomato puree that has been cooked to remove almost all moisture. Because it's naturally full of glutamates, tomato paste brings out subtle depths and savory notes. We use it in a variety of recipes, including both long-simmered sauces and quicker-cooking dishes, to lend a deeper, well-rounded tomato flavor and color. Our preferred brand is **Goya Tomato Paste**, for its fresh, full tomato flavor.

Pasta with Roasted Cherry Tomatoes, Garlic, and Basil

SERVES 2   `LIGHT`

 WHY THIS RECIPE WORKS: Typically we turn to canned tomatoes when we want a sauce we can make year-round, but we thought that a recipe for fresh tomato sauce we could make any time of year was a worthy goal. Cherry tomatoes offer the most reliable flavor and texture out of season, and roasting them is a surefire way to enhance their sweetness and intensify their flavor; just 30 minutes of roasting in a moderate oven yielded tomatoes with sweet, concentrated flavor and an appealing texture. Roasting some garlic and shallot along with the tomatoes streamlined our dish, and we liked the tartness and heat provided by a little balsamic vinegar and red pepper flakes. You can substitute grape tomatoes for the cherry tomatoes. Other pasta shapes can be substituted for the penne; however, their cup measurements may vary (see page 228). For the nutritional information for this recipe, see page 414.

1   **small shallot, sliced thin**
2   **tablespoons olive oil**
1   **pound cherry tomatoes, halved**
3   **garlic cloves, sliced thin**
1½   **teaspoons balsamic vinegar**
¾   **teaspoon sugar**
   Salt and pepper
⅛   **teaspoon red pepper flakes**
6   **ounces (2 cups) penne**
2   **tablespoons chopped fresh basil**

1. Adjust oven rack to middle position and heat oven to 350 degrees. Toss shallot with 1 teaspoon oil in small bowl. In medium bowl, gently toss remaining 5 teaspoons oil, tomatoes, garlic, vinegar, sugar, ¼ teaspoon salt, ⅛ teaspoon pepper, and pepper flakes together. Spread tomato mixture evenly into 13 by 9-inch baking dish and scatter shallot mixture over top. Roast vegetables, without stirring, until edges of shallot begin to brown and tomato skins are slightly shriveled but tomatoes still retain their shape, about 30 minutes. Remove vegetables from oven and let cool slightly, about 5 minutes.

2. Meanwhile, bring 4 quarts water to boil in large pot. Add pasta and 1 tablespoon salt and cook, stirring often, until al dente. Reserve ½ cup cooking water, then drain pasta and return it to pot. Transfer vegetable mixture to pot with pasta, add basil, and toss to combine. Season with salt and pepper to taste, and adjust consistency with reserved cooking water as needed. Serve.

Spaghetti and Turkey-Pesto Meatballs

SERVES 2

✓ **WHY THIS RECIPE WORKS:** Turkey meatballs make a great alternative to the traditional beef and pork meatballs—if you can find a way to infuse them with flavor and keep them moist. One convenient product helped us on both fronts. Store-bought basil pesto offered big garlic and herb flavors without any prep, and it contributed richness and kept our meatballs moist. Panko bread crumbs helped to bind the mixture, and grated Parmesan added a rich savory flavor. After browning the meatballs, we simmered them in a simple tomato sauce (seasoned with just a little garlic and sugar) to finish cooking through. Be sure to use ground turkey, not ground turkey breast (also labeled 99 percent fat free), in this recipe. You can make your own pesto or use your favorite store-bought brand from the refrigerated section of the supermarket—they have a fresher flavor than jarred pesto sold in the grocery aisles.

- 8 ounces ground turkey
- ⅓ cup panko bread crumbs
- ¼ cup prepared basil pesto
  Salt and pepper
- 1 tablespoon olive oil
- 1 garlic clove, minced
- 1 (28-ounce) can crushed tomatoes
- ¼ teaspoon sugar, plus extra for seasoning
- 6 ounces spaghetti
- 1 tablespoon shredded fresh basil
  Grated Parmesan cheese

1. Gently mix ground turkey, panko, pesto, ¼ teaspoon salt, and ⅛ teaspoon pepper together in bowl using your hands until uniform. Roll mixture into eight 1-inch meatballs. Heat oil in 10-inch skillet over medium-high heat until just smoking. Brown meatballs well on all sides, about 8 minutes; transfer to paper towel–lined plate.

2. Add garlic to fat left in skillet and cook over medium heat until fragrant, about 30 seconds. Stir in tomatoes and sugar, scraping up any browned bits. Bring to simmer and cook until sauce is slightly thickened, 5 to 8 minutes. Return meatballs to skillet and reduce heat to medium-low. Cover and simmer gently, turning meatballs occasionally, until meatballs are cooked through, about 5 minutes. Season with salt, pepper, and extra sugar to taste.

3. Meanwhile, bring 4 quarts water to boil in large pot. Add pasta and 1 tablespoon salt and cook, stirring often, until al dente. Reserve ½ cup cooking water, then drain pasta and return it to pot. Add several large spoonfuls of tomato sauce

(without meatballs) and toss to combine. Season with salt and pepper to taste, and adjust consistency with reserved cooking water as needed. Divide pasta between 2 bowls, top each bowl with remaining sauce and meatballs, and sprinkle with basil. Serve with Parmesan.

Pasta with Chicken, Broccoli, and Sun-Dried Tomatoes

SERVES 2

✓ **WHY THIS RECIPE WORKS:** Popular versions of this recipe often produce bland chicken and limp broccoli, drowning in a fatty cream sauce. We wanted a fresh sauce that would highlight the fresh, crisp broccoli and tender chicken. Lightly browning chicken breast strips in butter built great flavor. We kept the chicken tender and added flavor by letting it finish cooking in the sauce, and we kept the broccoli crisp by blanching it in the boiling pasta water. But our real breakthrough was to replace the typical cream sauce with a broth-based sauce, which we rounded out with a little butter, Asiago cheese, and some sun-dried tomatoes. Other pasta shapes can be substituted for the ziti; however, their cup measurements may vary (see page 228). Parmesan cheese can be substituted for the Asiago. To make the chicken easier to slice, freeze it for 15 minutes.

- 1 (8-ounce) boneless, skinless chicken breast, trimmed and sliced ¼ inch thick
  Salt and pepper
- 3 tablespoons unsalted butter
- 1 small onion, chopped fine
- 3 garlic cloves, minced
- 1 teaspoon minced fresh thyme or ¼ teaspoon dried
- 1 teaspoon all-purpose flour
- ⅛ teaspoon red pepper flakes
- 1 cup chicken broth
- ½ cup dry white wine
- 12 ounces broccoli, florets cut into 1-inch pieces, stalks peeled and sliced ¼ inch thick
- 6 ounces (2 cups) ziti
- 1 ounce Asiago cheese, grated (½ cup), plus extra for serving
- ½ cup oil-packed sun-dried tomatoes, patted dry and cut into ¼-inch strips
- 1 tablespoon chopped fresh parsley

1. Pat chicken dry with paper towels and season with salt and pepper. Melt 1 tablespoon butter in 10-inch nonstick skillet over high heat until beginning to brown. Add chicken, break up any clumps, and cook, without stirring, until beginning to brown, about 1 minute. Stir chicken and continue to cook until nearly cooked through, about 2 minutes; transfer to bowl.

2. Melt 1 tablespoon butter in now-empty skillet over medium heat. Add onion and ⅛ teaspoon salt and cook until softened and lightly browned, 5 to 7 minutes. Stir in garlic, thyme, flour, and pepper flakes and cook until fragrant, about 30 seconds. Whisk in broth and wine, bring to simmer, and cook until sauce is slightly thickened and measures about ⅔ cup, about 10 minutes. Remove from heat and cover to keep warm.

3. Meanwhile, bring 4 quarts water to boil in large pot. Add broccoli florets and stalks and 1 tablespoon salt and cook, stirring often, until florets are crisp-tender, about 2 minutes. Using slotted spoon, transfer broccoli to paper towel–lined plate.

4. Return pot of water to boil. Add pasta and cook, stirring often, until al dente. Reserve ½ cup cooking water, then drain pasta and return it to pot. Stir remaining 1 tablespoon butter, browned chicken and any accumulated juices, Asiago, and tomatoes into sauce, bring to simmer, and cook until chicken is cooked through, about 1 minute. Add chicken mixture, broccoli, and parsley to pasta and toss to combine. Season with salt and pepper to taste, and adjust consistency with reserved cooking water as needed. Serve with extra Asiago.

NOTES FROM THE TEST KITCHEN

Freezing Cheese

FREEZING FRESH CHEESES: Fresh cheeses like mozzarella, feta, and ricotta contain a lot of water, so their texture and flavor suffer more significantly than aged cheeses when frozen. In our tests, we've found that thawed ricotta is objectionably granular when tossed with pasta. However, in recipes like lasagna or cheesecake where the ricotta is cooked, the difference between frozen and fresh ricotta is negligible. So if you have trouble using up fresh cheeses before they spoil, go ahead and freeze them—just be sure to use them in a recipe where they will be cooked.

FREEZING AGED CHEESES: Hard and soft cheeses such as cheddar and Brie can be stored in the refrigerator, wrapped in parchment paper followed by a loose covering of aluminum foil, for as long as a month. But we wondered whether cheese could last even longer in the freezer or whether the ice and fat crystals that form would rupture their protein network, leading to breakage and weeping upon thawing. To find out, we wrapped a variety of cheeses (extra-sharp cheddar, Brie, fresh goat cheese, and Pecorino Romano) tightly in plastic wrap, sealed them in zipper-lock bags, and froze them for six weeks. Then we let them defrost overnight in the fridge (a 2½-hour rest on the counter also works). To our surprise, all samples were essentially identical to never-frozen controls. The frozen cheddar even melted properly. As long as you wrap the cheeses well (or vacuum-seal them) to prevent freezer burn, it's fine to freeze cheese for up to two months.

Orecchiette with Broccoli Rabe and Italian Sausage

SERVES 2

✔ **WHY THIS RECIPE WORKS:** The Italian region of Puglia is known for its simple, rustic cuisine. We wanted to create a version of one popular dish that features orecchiette paired with bitter broccoli rabe and sweet Italian sausage. Boiling the broccoli rabe allowed the stalks to become tender without overcooking the florets, and as a bonus we were able to use the richly flavored water to cook the pasta. Browning the sausage provided a good flavor base for the sauce. Chicken broth plus garlic and red pepper flakes contributed a rich backbone, and just one minced anchovy fillet deepened the overall flavor of the dish immensely. A little flour thickened our sauce to a luxurious consistency. Other pasta shapes can be substituted for the orecchiette; however, their cup measurements may vary (see page 228). Don't confuse broccoli rabe with broccoli or broccolini; broccoli rabe is a member of the turnip family and has a peppery bite. Chicory or turnip greens can be substituted for the broccoli rabe.

2 tablespoons extra-virgin olive oil
8 ounces sweet Italian sausage, casings removed
3 garlic cloves, minced
1 anchovy fillet, rinsed, patted dry, and minced
1 teaspoon all-purpose flour
¼ teaspoon red pepper flakes
¾ cup chicken broth
½ pound broccoli rabe, trimmed and cut into 1½-inch pieces
   Salt
6 ounces (1¾ cups) orecchiette
¼ cup grated Pecorino Romano cheese, plus extra for serving

1. Heat oil in 12-inch nonstick skillet over medium-high heat until shimmering. Add sausage and cook, breaking up meat with wooden spoon, until browned and crisp, 5 to 7 minutes. Stir in garlic, anchovy, flour, and pepper flakes and cook until fragrant, about 30 seconds. Stir in broth, scraping up any browned bits. Bring to simmer and cook, stirring occasionally, until sauce is slightly thickened, about 1 minute. Remove from heat and cover to keep warm.

2. Meanwhile, bring 4 quarts water to boil in large pot. Add broccoli rabe and 1 tablespoon salt and cook, stirring often, until broccoli rabe turns bright green, about 2 minutes. Using slotted spoon, transfer broccoli rabe to paper towel–lined plate.

3. Return pot of water to boil. Add pasta and cook, stirring often, until al dente. Reserve ½ cup cooking water, then drain pasta and return it to pot. Return sausage mixture to simmer. Add to pasta with broccoli rabe and Pecorino; toss to combine. Season with salt and pepper to taste, and adjust consistency with reserved cooking water as needed. Serve with extra Pecorino.

VARIATION

Orecchiette with Broccoli Rabe and White Beans

Omit sausage and anchovy. Increase amount of garlic to 4 cloves and substitute ¾ cup vegetable broth for chicken broth. Add ¾ cup rinsed canned cannellini beans to skillet with broth. Add 2 tablespoons toasted pine nuts and 1½ teaspoons red wine vinegar to pasta with sauce in step 3.

Removing Sausage from its Casing

Italian sausage is sold in links, bulk-style tubes, and patties. If using links, remove meat from its casing before cooking so that you can crumble it into bite-size pieces. Hold sausage firmly at 1 end and squeeze meat out of opposite end.

For the caramelized flavor of roasted garlic in a weeknight pasta dish, we separate the cloves and roast them for just 20 minutes.

Campanelle with Roasted Garlic, Shrimp, and Feta

SERVES 2

☑ **WHY THIS RECIPE WORKS:** Restaurant versions of shrimp scampi often run the gamut from boiled shrimp and tomato sauce on a bed of pasta to rubbery shrimp overloaded in butter or olive oil. We wanted lightly cooked, moist shrimp in a light garlic sauce. Rather than sautéing the garlic, we decided to roast it to bring a sweet, nutty dimension to our sauce. We found that we could speed up the roasting time if we separated and peeled the cloves before putting them in a covered baking dish with some olive oil. After 20 minutes we had soft, caramelized cloves of garlic, which we mashed with the oil to form a savory sauce. Adding the shrimp right to the garlic and oil mixture to cook through instilled it with big flavor quickly, and a little crumbled feta added a salty tang that complemented the sweetness of the roasted garlic and shrimp. If using smaller or larger shrimp, be sure to adjust the cooking time accordingly in step 1. Other pasta shapes can be substituted for the campanelle; however, their cup measurements may vary (see page 228).

2½ tablespoons olive oil
6 garlic cloves, peeled
Salt and pepper
8 ounces medium-large shrimp (31 to 40 per pound), peeled, deveined, and tails removed
6 ounces (2 cups) campanelle
1½ ounces feta cheese, crumbled (⅓ cup)
⅓ cup chopped fresh basil

1. Adjust oven rack to upper-middle position and heat oven to 425 degrees. Combine oil, garlic, ⅛ teaspoon salt, and ¼ teaspoon pepper in small baking dish and cover with aluminum foil. Bake, stirring occasionally, until garlic is caramelized and soft, about 20 minutes. Let cool slightly, then mash garlic and oil into paste with fork. Stir in shrimp and continue to bake, uncovered, until shrimp are opaque throughout, about 10 minutes.

2. Meanwhile, bring 4 quarts water to boil in large pot. Add pasta and 1 tablespoon salt and cook, stirring often, until al dente. Reserve ½ cup cooking water, then drain pasta and return it to pot. Add shrimp mixture, feta, and basil and toss to combine. Season with salt and pepper to taste, and adjust consistency with reserved cooking water as needed. Serve.

Pasta Shapes and Sizes

MEASURING PASTA: It's easy enough to measure out a pound of pasta, as most packages are sold in this quantity. But a pound of pasta is way too much when cooking for two; most of the recipes in this book call for 6 ounces. Obviously, you can weigh out partial pounds of pasta using a scale or judge by how full the box is, but we think it's easier to measure short pasta shapes using a dry measuring cup and strand pasta by determining the diameter.

PASTA TYPE	4 OUNCES	6 OUNCES
Elbow Macaroni and Small Shells	1 cup	1½ cups
Orecchiette	1 cup	1¾ cups
Penne, Ziti, and Campanelle	1¼ cups	2 cups
Rigatoni, Rotini, Fusilli, Medium Shells, Wagon Wheels, and Wide Egg Noodles	1½ cups	2⅓ cups
Farfalle	1⅔ cups	2½ cups

*These amounts do not apply to whole-wheat pasta.

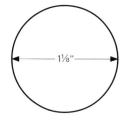

When 6 ounces of uncooked strand pasta are bunched together into a tight circle, the diameter measures about 1⅛ inches.

MATCHING PASTA SHAPES AND SAUCES: Pairing a pasta shape with the right sauce might be an art form in Italy, but we think there's only one basic rule to follow: Thick, chunky sauces go with short pastas, and thin, smooth, or light sauces with strand pasta. (Of course, there are a few exceptions—but that's where the art comes in.) Although we specify pasta shapes for every recipe in this book, you should feel free to substitute other pasta shapes. Short tubular or molded pasta shapes do an excellent job of trapping and holding on to chunky sauces. Sauces with very large chunks are best with rigatoni or other large tubes. Sauces with small chunks make more sense with fusilli or penne. Long strands are best with smooth sauces or sauces with very small chunks. In general, wider noodles, such as pappardelle and fettuccine, can support slightly chunkier sauces, like a classic ragu.

Spaghetti with Lemon, Basil, and Shrimp

SERVES 2

✔ **WHY THIS RECIPE WORKS:** For an easy shrimp and pasta dish we could get on the table in short order, we opted for a no-cook sauce: A combination of extra-virgin olive oil, lemon juice, and garlic provided the base for a simple vinaigrette we could toss with the warm pasta. Lemon zest added more citrus flavor without adding more acidity; some Parmesan cheese helped thicken the sauce slightly and contributed a nutty flavor; and a pat of butter added richness and rounded out the flavor of the sauce. We cooked the pasta in the same water we used to cook the shrimp, saving us from dirtying an extra pan. The flavor of this dish depends on high-quality extra-virgin olive oil, fresh-squeezed lemon juice, and fresh basil. A rasp-style grater makes quick work of turning the garlic into a paste.

   3 **tablespoons extra-virgin olive oil**
   1 **teaspoon grated lemon zest plus 2½ tablespoons juice**
   1 **garlic clove, minced to paste**
      Salt and pepper
   1 **ounce Parmesan cheese, grated (½ cup)**
   8 **ounces extra-large shrimp (21 to 25 per pound), peeled, deveined, and tails removed**
   6 **ounces spaghetti**
   2 **tablespoons shredded fresh basil**
   1 **tablespoon unsalted butter, softened**

1. Whisk oil, lemon zest and juice, garlic, and ¼ teaspoon salt together in bowl, then stir in Parmesan until thick and creamy.

2. Meanwhile, bring 4 quarts water to boil in large pot. Add shrimp and 1 tablespoon salt and cook until opaque throughout, about 1 minute. Using slotted spoon, transfer shrimp to bowl, season with salt and pepper to taste, and cover to keep warm.

3. Return pot of water to boil. Add pasta and cook, stirring often, until al dente. Reserve ½ cup cooking water, then drain pasta and return it to pot. Add oil-garlic mixture, cooked shrimp, basil, and butter and toss to combine. Season with salt and pepper to taste, and adjust consistency with reserved cooking water as needed. Serve.

To infuse our rich pasta sauce with briny flavor, we steam the clams right in the sauce before tossing it all with tender linguine.

Linguine with Fresh Clam Sauce

SERVES 2

✓ **WHY THIS RECIPE WORKS:** Clams cook quickly and can be purchased in any quantity, making them an ideal ingredient for two. We wanted a recipe for a fresh clam sauce that we could serve atop linguine for an easy, flavorful meal. Littleneck clams worked best in this dish; they cooked in minutes and offered sweet, briny flavor. To streamline our method, we used the same pan to steam our clams and build the sauce. White wine and a chopped tomato provided a pleasantly acidic background, shallot and garlic offered the right aromatic notes, and a dash of red pepper flakes and some fresh herbs rounded out the flavors. Finally, a little butter offered richness without weighing down the dish. When shopping for clams, choose the smallest ones you can find. Be sure to scrub the clams thoroughly to get rid of grit and sand before cooking. Note that the clams can be very briny, so be sure to taste the final dish before seasoning with additional salt.

1 tablespoon extra-virgin olive oil
1 shallot, minced
1 garlic clove, minced
⅛ teaspoon red pepper flakes
2 pounds littleneck or cherrystone clams, scrubbed
¼ cup dry white wine
1 bay leaf
1 tomato, cored and chopped fine
3 tablespoons unsalted butter, cut into ¼-inch pieces
2 tablespoons chopped fresh parsley
1 teaspoon minced fresh oregano or ¼ teaspoon dried
   Salt and pepper
6 ounces linguine

1. Heat oil in large saucepan over medium-high heat until shimmering. Add shallot and cook until softened, about 2 minutes. Stir in garlic and pepper flakes and cook until fragrant, about 30 seconds. Stir in clams, wine, and bay leaf. Cover and simmer, shaking pan occasionally, until clams begin to open, about 6 minutes.

2. Uncover and continue to simmer until all clams have opened and sauce is slightly reduced, about 2 minutes. Discard any clams that have not opened and remove bay leaf. (If clams release sand into sauce, remove clams and strain sauce; return sauce and clams to clean pot and continue.) Gently stir in tomato, butter, parsley, and oregano. Continue to cook until butter has melted and tomatoes are heated through, about 1 minute longer. Off heat, season with pepper to taste.

3. Meanwhile, bring 4 quarts water to boil in large pot. Add pasta and 1 tablespoon salt and cook, stirring often, until al dente. Reserve ½ cup cooking water, then drain pasta and return it to pot. Add clam mixture and toss to combine. Season with salt and pepper to taste, and adjust consistency with reserved cooking water as needed. Serve.

VARIATION

Spanish-Style Linguine with Clams and Chorizo

This pasta is inspired by the Spanish tradition of combining clams and pork sausage.

Add 2 ounces chorizo sausage, halved lengthwise and sliced ¼ inch thick, to oil in step 1; cook until lightly browned, about 5 minutes, then add shallot and proceed with recipe. Omit parsley and oregano. Before serving, stir 2 cups coarsely chopped arugula into pasta until wilted.

These easy, inventive pestos (like roasted red pepper and pistachio) are perfect for dressing up convenient store-bought ravioli.

Cheese Ravioli with Roasted Red Pepper and Pistachio Pesto

SERVES 2

✓ **WHY THIS RECIPE WORKS:** Store-bought ravioli make for a convenient weeknight dinner, but because they trap so much water during cooking, they tend to dilute whatever sauce accompanies them. To solve this problem, we ditched the traditional tomato sauce and paired our ravioli with pesto; its thick texture and concentrated flavor held up well once tossed with the hot ravioli. For an updated version of simple basil pesto, we combined roasted red peppers and sweet pistachios with the classic basil, garlic, and Parmesan cheese. Blanching the garlic mellowed its bite, and the Parmesan helped thicken our pesto to the proper consistency. This recipe calls for fresh ravioli, but you can substitute 12 ounces frozen ravioli.

 1   garlic clove, unpeeled
 ¾   cup jarred roasted red peppers, rinsed and patted dry
 ½   cup fresh basil leaves
 ⅓   cup grated Parmesan cheese
 ¼   cup shelled pistachios, toasted
 2   tablespoons extra-virgin olive oil
     Salt and pepper
 1   (9-ounce) package fresh cheese ravioli

1. Bring 4 quarts water to boil in large pot. Add garlic to water and cook for 1 minute. Using slotted spoon, transfer garlic to bowl and rinse under cold water to stop cooking. Peel and mince garlic.

2. Pulse garlic, red peppers, basil, Parmesan, and pistachios in food processor until smooth, 20 to 30 pulses, scraping down sides of bowl as needed. With processor running, slowly add oil until incorporated, about 30 seconds. Transfer to bowl and season with salt and pepper to taste.

3. Return pot of water to boil. Add pasta and 1 tablespoon salt and cook, stirring often, until tender. Reserve ½ cup cooking water, then drain pasta and return it to pot. Add ½ cup pesto and gently toss to combine. Season with salt and pepper to taste, and adjust consistency with reserved cooking water as needed. Serve, passing remaining pesto separately.

VARIATIONS

Cheese Ravioli with Sage, Walnut, and Browned Butter Pesto

Melt 3 tablespoons butter in 8-inch skillet over medium-high heat. Continue to cook, swirling skillet constantly, until butter is golden brown and has nutty aroma, 2 to 4 minutes. Off heat, add ¼ cup chopped fresh sage and let sit until cool, about 10 minutes. Omit oil and substitute butter-sage mixture for roasted red peppers, ½ cup fresh parsley leaves for basil, and ¼ cup toasted walnuts for pistachios in step 2.

Cheese Ravioli with Green Olive, Almond, and Orange Pesto

Substitute ¼ cup pitted green olives for roasted red peppers, ¾ cup fresh parsley leaves for basil, and ¼ cup toasted slivered almonds for pistachios. Add ¼ teaspoon grated orange zest plus 1 tablespoon juice to food processor in step 2 and increase amount of oil to ¼ cup.

Cheese Ravioli with Kale and Sunflower Seed Pesto

Substitute 1 cup chopped stemmed kale for roasted red peppers and ¼ cup toasted sunflower seeds for pistachios. Add ⅛ teaspoon red pepper flakes to food processor in step 2 and increase amount of oil to ¼ cup.

Classic Lasagna

SERVES 2

☑ **WHY THIS RECIPE WORKS:** Lasagna is a crowd-pleaser: What's not to love about a dish layered with tender noodles, meaty sauce, and gooey cheese baked until golden and bubbling? But it's also time-consuming to prepare. We didn't think this hearty and satisfying favorite should be off-limits when cooking for less than a crowd. Our goal was a streamlined version for two. For an easy meaty tomato sauce, we found that meatloaf mix lent more flavor and richness than ground beef. A little cream with diced tomatoes and canned tomato sauce gave us a velvety sauce reminiscent of a Bolognese. Swapping traditional noodles for no-boil noodles was an easy timesaver. A baking dish made far too much for two, but the noodles fit perfectly in a loaf pan. We simply layered noodles with the sauce and a combination of mozzarella, ricotta, and Parmesan for a perfectly proportioned two-person lasagna. Meatloaf mix is a combination of equal parts ground beef, pork, and veal and is available in most grocery stores. If you can't find meatloaf mix, substitute 4 ounces each of ground pork and 90 percent lean ground beef. Do not substitute fat-free ricotta here.

SAUCE

- 1 tablespoon olive oil
- 1 small onion, chopped fine
  Salt and pepper
- 2 garlic cloves, minced
- 8 ounces meatloaf mix
- 2 tablespoons heavy cream
- 1 (14.5-ounce) can diced tomatoes, drained with
  ¼ cup juice reserved
- 1 (8-ounce) can tomato sauce

FILLING, NOODLES, AND CHEESE

- 4 ounces (½ cup) whole-milk or part-skim ricotta cheese
- 1 ounce Parmesan cheese, grated (½ cup), plus
  2 tablespoons, grated
- 3 tablespoons chopped fresh basil
- 1 large egg, lightly beaten
- ⅛ teaspoon salt
- ⅛ teaspoon pepper
- 4 no-boil lasagna noodles
- 4 ounces whole-milk mozzarella cheese, shredded (1 cup)

1. FOR THE SAUCE: Adjust oven rack to middle position and heat oven to 400 degrees. Heat oil in large saucepan over medium heat until shimmering. Add onion and ⅛ teaspoon salt and cook until softened, about 5 minutes. Stir in garlic and cook until fragrant, about 30 seconds. Stir in meatloaf mix and cook, breaking up meat with wooden spoon, until no longer pink, about 2 minutes.

2. Stir in cream, bring to simmer, and cook until liquid evaporates, about 2 minutes. Stir in tomatoes and reserved juice and tomato sauce. Bring to simmer and cook until flavors are blended, about 2 minutes. Season with salt and pepper to taste.

3. FOR THE FILLING, NOODLES, AND CHEESE: Combine ricotta, ½ cup Parmesan, basil, egg, salt, and pepper in bowl.

4. Spread ½ cup sauce over bottom of loaf pan, avoiding large chunks of meat. Lay 1 noodle in pan, spread one-third of ricotta mixture over noodle, sprinkle with ¼ cup mozzarella, and top with ½ cup sauce; repeat layering 2 more times. Lay remaining noodle in pan and top with remaining sauce, remaining ¼ cup mozzarella, and remaining 2 tablespoons Parmesan.

5. Cover pan tightly with aluminum foil that has been sprayed with vegetable oil spray. Bake until sauce bubbles lightly around edges, 25 to 30 minutes. Remove foil and continue to bake until hot throughout and cheese is browned in spots, about 10 minutes. Let cool for 20 minutes before serving.

Baked Manicotti

SERVES 2

☑ **WHY THIS RECIPE WORKS:** Well-made versions of this Italian-American classic, with tender pasta tubes stuffed with rich ricotta filling and blanketed with tomato sauce, can be eminently satisfying. But when cooking for two, the hassle of putting it all together hardly seems worth it. Could we find a simpler, better method for making manicotti? Stuffing and baking raw pasta tubes proved problematic, but soaking no-boil noodles until just pliable and rolling them up around the filling worked perfectly—and saved us the trouble of boiling the pasta separately. To ensure our filling was thick and creamy, not thin and runny, we mixed ricotta with a generous amount of mozzarella. Finally, just six ingredients whirred in the food processor gave us a fresh, bright tomato sauce in minutes. As the manicotti baked, the tomato sauce reduced just enough that it didn't taste raw and kept the manicotti moist and tender. Do not substitute fat-free ricotta cheese here.

SAUCE

- 1 (14.5-ounce) can diced tomatoes
- 1 tablespoon extra-virgin olive oil
- 2 garlic cloves, minced
- ¼ teaspoon salt
- ⅛ teaspoon red pepper flakes (optional)
- 1 tablespoon chopped fresh basil

FILLING AND PASTA

- 8 ounces (1 cup) whole-milk or part-skim ricotta cheese
- 3 ounces whole-milk mozzarella cheese, shredded (¾ cup)
- 2 ounces Parmesan cheese, grated (1 cup)
- 1 large egg, lightly beaten
- 1 tablespoon chopped fresh basil
- ¼ teaspoon salt
- ⅛ teaspoon pepper
- 6 no-boil lasagna noodles

1. FOR THE SAUCE: Adjust oven rack to middle position and heat oven to 400 degrees. Process tomatoes and their juice, olive oil, garlic, salt, and pepper flakes, if using, in food processor until smooth, about 10 seconds. Transfer mixture to bowl and stir in basil.

2. FOR THE FILLING AND PASTA: Combine ricotta, mozzarella, ½ cup Parmesan, egg, basil, salt, and pepper in bowl.

3. Fill large bowl halfway with boiling water. Slip noodles into water, one at a time. Let noodles soak until pliable, about 5 minutes, separating noodles with tip of knife to prevent sticking. Remove noodles from water and place in single layer on clean dish towels.

Making Manicotti

1. Soak no-boil lasagna noodles in boiling water for 5 minutes until pliable, using tip of paring knife to separate noodles and prevent them from sticking together.

2. Using spoon, spread about ¼ cup of filling evenly over bottom three-quarters of each noodle, leaving top quarter of noodles exposed.

3. Starting at bottom, roll each noodle up around filling, and lay in prepared loaf pan, seam side down.

4. Spread ½ cup sauce over bottom of 9 by 5-inch loaf pan. Transfer noodles to counter with short sides facing you. Spread ¼ cup ricotta mixture evenly over bottom three-quarters of each noodle. Roll noodles up around filling and lay them seam side down in pan. Spoon remaining sauce over top to cover noodles completely. Sprinkle with remaining ½ cup Parmesan.

5. Cover pan tightly with aluminum foil and bake until bubbling, about 25 minutes. Remove foil and continue to bake until cheese is browned in spots, about 10 minutes. Let cool for 15 minutes before serving.

Skillet Pasta with Fresh Tomato Sauce

SERVES 2 `LIGHT`

✔ **WHY THIS RECIPE WORKS:** Most of the year, canned tomatoes offer better tomato flavor than their fresh counterparts do, but when fully ripe, juicy tomatoes are at their peak, we like to go with the real deal. For an effortless but flavorful pasta dinner featuring fresh tomatoes, we simmered the tomatoes briefly so they'd break down and release their juice, then added the pasta right to the pan to cook through. Not only did the released pasta starch help to thicken the sauce, making it nicely clingy, but the pasta picked up good flavor from cooking in the sauce. A little tomato paste added depth, and a small amount of white wine contributed a brightness that rounded out the flavor of our sauce. Other pasta shapes can be substituted for the campanelle; however, their cup measurements may vary (see page 228). Serve with Parmesan cheese. For the nutritional information for this recipe, see page 414.

- 1 tablespoon extra-virgin olive oil
- 1 small onion, chopped fine
- 2 garlic cloves, minced
- 1½ teaspoons tomato paste
- 1 pound tomatoes, cored and cut into ½-inch pieces
  Salt and pepper
- ¼ cup dry white wine
- 2 cups water, plus extra as needed
- 6 ounces (2 cups) campanelle
- 2 tablespoons chopped fresh basil

1. Heat oil in 12-inch nonstick skillet over medium heat until shimmering. Add onion and cook until softened, about 5 minutes. Stir in garlic and tomato paste and cook until fragrant, about 1 minute. Stir in tomatoes, ½ teaspoon salt, and

¼ teaspoon pepper and cook until tomato pieces lose their shape, 5 to 7 minutes. Stir in wine and simmer for 2 minutes.

2. Stir in water and pasta. Cover, increase heat to medium-high, and cook at vigorous simmer, stirring often, until pasta is nearly tender, 10 to 12 minutes.

3. Uncover and continue to simmer, tossing pasta gently, until pasta is tender and sauce is thickened, 3 to 5 minutes; if sauce becomes too thick, add extra water as needed. Off heat, stir in basil and season with salt and pepper to taste. Serve with Parmesan.

Skillet Pasta Quattro Formaggi

SERVES 2

✔ **WHY THIS RECIPE WORKS:** We love mac and cheese, but sometimes we crave a more refined cheesy pasta dish. *Pasta ai quattro formaggi*, or pasta with four cheeses, fills the bill but its preparation can be fussy. We decided to reinvent it as an easy skillet pasta without sacrificing flavor or the silkiness of the sauce. A blend of Italian fontina, Gorgonzola, Pecorino Romano, and Parmesan offered the best balance of creaminess and flavor, and adding the cheese at the end of cooking prevented it from curdling or separating. We simmered our pasta in a combination of water and cream. A little wine—used to deglaze the pan—cut through the richness of the sauce. If you don't have both Parmesan and Pecorino, you can omit one and use ¼ cup of the other. Other pasta shapes can be substituted for the penne; however, their cup measurements may vary (see page 228).

1	tablespoon unsalted butter
1	shallot, minced
	Salt and pepper
⅓	cup dry white wine
4	cups water, plus extra as needed
6	ounces (2 cups) penne
½	cup heavy cream
1	ounce Gorgonzola cheese, crumbled (¼ cup)
1	ounce Italian fontina cheese, shredded (¼ cup)
2	tablespoons grated Pecorino Romano cheese
2	tablespoons grated Parmesan cheese

1. Melt butter in 12-inch nonstick skillet over medium heat. Add shallot and ¼ teaspoon salt and cook until softened, about 2 minutes. Stir in wine, increase heat to medium-high, and simmer until nearly evaporated, about 1 minute.

2. Stir in water, pasta, and cream. Bring to vigorous simmer and cook, stirring often, until pasta is tender and sauce

is thickened, 15 to 18 minutes; if sauce becomes too thick, add extra water as needed. Off heat, stir in Gorgonzola, fontina, Pecorino, and Parmesan, one at a time, until melted and combined. Season with salt and pepper to taste and serve.

NOTES FROM THE TEST KITCHEN

All About Parmesan

Parmesan is classified as a grana-type cheese: a hard, grainy cheese made from cow's milk. It has a rich, sharp flavor and a melt-in-your mouth texture. We frequently reach for it to sprinkle on top of pasta dishes or to add a rich, salty flavor to sauces, soups, and stews.

BUYING PARMESAN: We recommend authentic Italian Parmigiano-Reggiano, which has a complex flavor and smooth, melting texture that none of the others can match. Most of the other Parmesan-type cheeses are too salty and one-dimensional. When shopping, make sure some portion of the words "Parmigiano-Reggiano" is stenciled on the golden rind. To ensure that you're buying a properly aged cheese, examine the condition of the rind. It should be a few shades darker than the straw-colored interior and penetrate about ½ inch deep (younger or improperly aged cheeses will have a paler, thinner rind). And closely scrutinize the center of the cheese. Those small white spots found on many samples are actually good things—they signify the presence of calcium phosphate crystals, which are formed only after the cheese has been aged for the proper amount of time.

STORING PARMESAN: After a number of tests to find the optimal storage method for Parmesan, we found that the best way to preserve its flavor and texture is to wrap it in parchment paper, then aluminum foil. However, if you have just a small piece of cheese, tossing it in a zipper-lock bag works almost as well; just be sure to squeeze out as much air as possible before sealing the bag. Note that these methods also work for Pecorino Romano.

PARMESAN VS. PECORINO ROMANO: While Parmesan is a cow's milk cheese, Pecorino Romano is made from sheep's milk, but the two do have a similar texture and flavor and often you'll see one as an alternative to the other in recipes. We have found that Parmesan and Pecorino Romano generally can be used interchangeably, especially when the amount called for is moderate. However, when Parmesan is called for in larger quantities, it is best to stick with the Parmesan, as Pecorino Romano can be fairly pungent.

CAN YOU PREGRATE YOUR OWN PARMESAN? We've never been tempted by tasteless, shelf-stable powdered Parmesan cheese, and even the higher-quality grated Parmesan in the refrigerator section of the supermarket is uneven in quality. But what about grating your own Parmesan to have at the ready? Do you sacrifice any flavor for convenience? In a side-by-side tasting, we found that tasters were hard-pressed to detect any difference between freshly grated Parmesan and cheese that had been grated and stored for up to three weeks. To grind Parmesan, cut a block into 1-inch chunks. Place the chunks in a food processor and process until ground into coarse particles, about 20 seconds. Refrigerate in an airtight container until ready to use.

Skillet Penne with Chicken, Mushrooms, and Gorgonzola

SERVES 2

✓ **WHY THIS RECIPE WORKS:** Looking for a hearty one-skillet pasta supper to add to our repertoire, we decided to pair tender chicken with earthy mushrooms and rich Gorgonzola cheese. Briefly sautéing a thinly sliced chicken breast was easy and created a flavorful fond on which we could build our sauce. Cooking the pasta right in the sauce was beneficial on two fronts: The starch from the pasta helped thicken the sauce, while the pasta itself absorbed maximum flavor as it simmered. Cooking the mushrooms over medium heat and not crowding them in the skillet ensured that they browned rather than steamed. Gorgonzola cheese added a rich creaminess and sharp flavor. Other pasta shapes can be substituted for the penne; however, their cup measurements may vary (see page 228).

1   **(8-ounce) boneless, skinless chicken breast, trimmed and sliced ¼ inch thick**
    Salt and pepper
2   **tablespoons olive oil**
4   **ounces white mushrooms, trimmed and quartered**
3   **garlic cloves, minced**
1   **teaspoon minced fresh oregano or ¼ teaspoon dried**
    Pinch red pepper flakes
½   **cup dry white wine**
6   **ounces (2 cups) penne**
1½ **cups chicken broth**
1   **cup water, plus extra as needed**
1   **ounce Gorgonzola cheese, crumbled (¼ cup), plus extra for serving**
1   **tablespoon unsalted butter**
1   **tablespoon minced fresh parsley**

1. Pat chicken dry with paper towels and season with salt and pepper. Heat 1 tablespoon oil in 10-inch nonstick skillet over medium-high heat until just smoking. Add chicken, break up any clumps, and cook, without stirring, until beginning to brown, about 1 minute. Stir chicken and continue to cook until nearly cooked through, about 2 minutes; transfer to bowl.

2. Add remaining 1 tablespoon oil and mushrooms to now-empty skillet and cook over medium heat, stirring occasionally, until mushrooms have released their moisture and are golden brown, 7 to 10 minutes. Stir in garlic, oregano, and pepper flakes and cook until fragrant, about 30 seconds. Stir in wine, bring to simmer, and cook until nearly evaporated, about 2 minutes.

3. Stir in pasta, broth, water, and ¼ teaspoon salt. Cover, increase heat to medium-high, and cook at vigorous simmer, stirring often, until pasta is tender and sauce is thickened, 12 to 15 minutes; if sauce becomes too thick, add extra water as needed.

4. Reduce heat to low and stir in cooked chicken and any accumulated juices, Gorgonzola, and butter. Cook, uncovered, tossing pasta gently, until well coated with sauce, 1 to 2 minutes. Season with salt and pepper to taste and sprinkle with parsley. Serve with extra Gorgonzola.

VARIATIONS

Skillet Penne with Chicken, Cherry Tomatoes, and Olives

Substitute 1 small finely chopped onion for mushrooms and cook until softened, about 5 minutes. Add 6 ounces quartered cherry tomatoes and ¼ cup coarsely chopped pitted kalamata olives to pasta along with cooked chicken in step 4. Substitute ½ cup grated Parmesan cheese for Gorgonzola.

Skillet Penne with Chicken, Arugula, Pine Nuts, and Lemon

Substitute 1 small finely chopped onion for mushrooms and cook until softened, about 5 minutes. Add 3 ounces baby arugula to pasta along with cooked chicken in step 4. Substitute ½ cup grated Parmesan cheese for Gorgonzola. Stir 2 tablespoons toasted pine nuts and ¼ teaspoon grated lemon zest plus 1½ teaspoons juice into pasta along with parsley.

Skillet Weeknight Bolognese with Linguine

SERVES 2

✓ **WHY THIS RECIPE WORKS:** Recipes for Bolognese typically feed a crowd and require hours of simmering, so we wanted to reinvent this dish as a weeknight meal for two. Skipping the step of browning the ground meat reduced the simmering time needed to make the meat tender; to replace the flavor lost from not browning the meat we added pancetta, dried porcini, and a little minced anchovy. Chopping our aromatic ingredients in the food processor cut down on prep time, and cooking the pasta right in the sauce eliminated extra dirty dishes. Meatloaf mix is a combination of equal parts ground beef, pork, and veal and is available in most grocery stores. If you can't find meatloaf mix, substitute 3 ounces each of ground pork and 90 percent lean ground beef. When adding the pasta in step 4, stir gently to avoid breaking the noodles; after a minute or two they will soften enough to be stirred more easily.

1 small onion, cut into 1-inch pieces
1 carrot, peeled and cut into 1-inch pieces
1½ ounces pancetta, cut into 1-inch pieces
¼ ounce dried porcini mushrooms, rinsed
½ anchovy fillet, rinsed and patted dry
1 (14.5-ounce) can diced tomatoes
1 tablespoon unsalted butter
1 garlic clove, minced
½ teaspoon sugar
6 ounces meatloaf mix
¾ cup whole milk
1 tablespoon tomato paste
¼ cup dry white wine
2 cups water, plus extra as needed
6 ounces linguine
   Salt and pepper
   Grated Parmesan cheese

1. Pulse onion, carrot, pancetta, porcini, and anchovy in food processor until finely chopped, 10 to 15 pulses; transfer to bowl. Pulse tomatoes and their juice until mostly smooth, about 8 pulses.

2. Melt butter in 12-inch nonstick skillet over medium heat. Add pulsed onion mixture and cook until softened and lightly browned, 5 to 7 minutes. Stir in garlic and sugar and cook until fragrant, about 30 seconds. Stir in meatloaf mix, breaking up meat with wooden spoon, and cook for 1 minute. Stir in milk, scraping up any browned bits. Bring to simmer and cook until milk is almost completely evaporated, 8 to 10 minutes.

3. Stir in tomato paste and cook for 1 minute. Stir in wine, bring to simmer, and cook until almost completely evaporated, 3 to 5 minutes.

4. Stir in pulsed tomatoes, water, and pasta. Cover, increase heat to medium-high, and cook at vigorous simmer, stirring often, until pasta is tender and sauce is thickened, 12 to 16 minutes; if sauce becomes too thick, add extra water as needed. Off heat, season with salt and pepper to taste. Serve with Parmesan.

Rinsing Dried Porcini

To remove dirt or grit from dried porcini, place porcini in fine-mesh strainer and run under water, using fingers as needed to rub grit out of crevices.

Skillet Mussels Marinara with Spaghetti
SERVES 2 LIGHT

✓ **WHY THIS RECIPE WORKS:** Mussels are inexpensive, are easy to purchase in small quantities, and require minimal prep, making them the ideal centerpiece of a weeknight meal for two. And creating a one-skillet mussels marinara—featuring mussels draped in a mildly spicy, brothy tomato sauce—turned out to be easier than we thought. Not only could we cook the pasta right in the sauce, but we could add the mussels to the simmering sauce as well, which saved us the step of steaming them in a separate pot. Any type of mussel will work here. When adding the pasta in step 3, stir gently to avoid breaking the noodles; after a minute or two they will soften enough to be stirred more easily. For the nutritional information for this recipe, see page 414.

1 (28-ounce) can whole peeled tomatoes
4 teaspoons extra-virgin olive oil, plus extra for serving
1 small onion, chopped fine
3 garlic cloves, minced
½ anchovy fillet, rinsed, patted dry, and minced
¼ teaspoon red pepper flakes
1½ cups water, plus hot water as needed
½ cup bottled clam juice
6 ounces spaghetti
1 pound mussels, scrubbed and debearded
2 tablespoons minced fresh parsley
   Salt and pepper

1. Pulse tomatoes and their juice in food processor until coarsely chopped and no large pieces remain, 6 to 8 pulses.

2. Heat 1 tablespoon oil in 12-inch nonstick skillet over medium heat until shimmering. Add onion and cook until softened, about 5 minutes. Stir in garlic, anchovy, and pepper flakes and cook until fragrant, about 30 seconds. Stir in pulsed tomatoes, bring to gentle simmer, and cook, stirring occasionally, until tomatoes no longer taste raw, about 10 minutes.

3. Stir in water, clam juice, and pasta. Cover, increase heat to medium-high, and cook at vigorous simmer, stirring often, for 12 minutes. Stir in mussels, cover, and continue to simmer vigorously until pasta is tender and mussels have opened, about 2 minutes.

4. Reduce heat to low and stir in remaining 1 teaspoon oil and parsley. Cook, uncovered, tossing pasta gently, until pasta is well coated with sauce, 1 to 2 minutes. If sauce is too thick, add hot water, 1 tablespoon at a time, as needed. Discard any mussels that have not opened and season with salt and pepper to taste. Drizzle individual portions with extra oil and serve.

Skillet Tortellini with Crispy Prosciutto and Spring Vegetables

SERVES 2

✔ **WHY THIS RECIPE WORKS:** The convenience of store-bought tortellini is undeniable, but when simply topped with store-bought pasta sauce, it can be bland and uninspired. We wanted properly cooked tortellini, fresh vegetables, and a luxurious, flavor-packed sauce—all cooked in one skillet. Simmering the tortellini in chicken broth rather than water infused it with savory flavor. A little cream added sweet richness to our sauce, and some lemon juice contributed a contrasting brightness. Fennel, spinach, and peas offered color and fresh spring flavor, and a sprinkling of salty, crisp prosciutto provided a welcome meatiness. Fresh tortellini won out over frozen or dried for its superior texture and flavor. Because the tortellini cooks right in the sauce, fresh tortellini should be used; do not substitute dried or frozen tortellini.

- 1 ounce thinly sliced prosciutto, cut into ¼-inch pieces
- 1 tablespoon unsalted butter
- 1 small fennel bulb, stalks discarded, bulb halved, cored, and cut into ½-inch pieces
- 2 garlic cloves, minced
- 2 cups chicken broth
- 1 (9-ounce) package fresh cheese tortellini
- 3 ounces (3 cups) baby spinach
- ½ cup frozen peas
- ¼ cup heavy cream
- ¼ cup grated Parmesan cheese, plus extra for serving
- 2 teaspoons lemon juice
  Salt and pepper

1. Cook prosciutto in 12-inch nonstick skillet over medium heat until browned and crisp, 5 to 7 minutes. Using slotted spoon, transfer prosciutto to paper towel–lined plate; set aside.

2. Add butter to fat left in skillet and heat over medium heat until melted. Add fennel and cook until softened and lightly browned, 6 to 9 minutes. Stir in garlic and cook until fragrant, about 30 seconds.

3. Stir in broth and pasta. Cover, increase heat to medium-high, and cook at vigorous simmer, stirring often, until pasta is tender and sauce is thickened, 6 to 9 minutes; if sauce becomes too thick, add water as needed.

4. Reduce heat to low, stir in spinach, peas, and cream, and cook, stirring gently but constantly, until spinach is wilted and pasta is well coated with sauce, 2 to 3 minutes. Off heat, stir in Parmesan and lemon juice and season with salt and pepper to taste. Sprinkle individual portions with reserved crisp prosciutto and serve with extra Parmesan.

Italian sausage gives our meaty tomato sauce lots of flavor, and we simmer ravioli right in the sauce for a satisfying one-dish meal.

Skillet Ravioli with Meat Sauce

SERVES 2

✔ **WHY THIS RECIPE WORKS:** A staple on every Italian restaurant menu, cheese-stuffed ravioli covered in meaty tomato sauce is the ultimate comfort food. For an effortless take on this dish, we cooked fresh store-bought ravioli right in the sauce. This not only eliminated extra pans, but it allowed the ravioli to soak up even more flavor. For the base of the sauce, we processed canned diced tomatoes to a smooth puree. We substituted crumbled fresh Italian sausage for the usual ground meat. Because it comes preseasoned, the sausage added welcome herbal and aromatic notes to our dish on top of its meaty flavor. A little minced porcini enhanced the sauce's savory depth in short order, and a small can of diced tomatoes plus a little water provided the base of the sauce as well as the liquid in which we simmered our pasta. Because the ravioli cooks right in the sauce, fresh ravioli should be used; do not substitute frozen ravioli.

1 (14.5-ounce) can diced tomatoes
1 tablespoon olive oil
1 small onion, chopped fine
2 garlic cloves, minced
⅛ ounce dried porcini mushrooms, rinsed and minced
8 ounces sweet Italian sausage, casings removed
   Salt and pepper
1½ cups water, plus extra as needed
1 (9-ounce) package fresh cheese ravioli
2 tablespoons chopped fresh basil
   Grated Parmesan cheese

1. Process tomatoes and their juice in food processor until smooth, about 10 seconds. Heat oil in 12-inch skillet over medium heat until shimmering. Add onion and cook until softened and lightly browned, 5 to 7 minutes. Stir in garlic and porcini and cook until fragrant, about 1 minute.

2. Add sausage and cook, breaking up meat with wooden spoon, for 1 minute. Stir in processed tomatoes and ⅛ teaspoon pepper, bring to simmer, and cook until sauce is slightly thickened, 8 to 10 minutes.

3. Stir in water and pasta, bring to vigorous simmer, and cook, stirring often, until pasta is tender and sauce is thickened, 6 to 9 minutes; if sauce becomes too thick, add extra water as needed. Off heat, stir in basil and season with salt and pepper to taste. Serve with Parmesan.

Meaty Skillet Lasagna

SERVES 2

❤ **WHY THIS RECIPE WORKS:** We wanted a recipe for meaty lasagna that we could make entirely on the stovetop, and we wanted to scale it down in size—without losing its comfort-food appeal. Half a pound of 85 percent lean ground beef offered good flavor and the right amount of richness. One large can of whole tomatoes, pulsed briefly in the food processor, gave our sauce a slightly chunky and substantial texture—and provided enough liquid to cook the noodles. Breaking the noodles into smaller pieces ensured they would fit in the pan and also made them easy to serve and eat. Stirring in the mozzarella and Parmesan provided a cohesive structure to the dish, but we decided to dollop the ricotta on top so that it remained its own distinct element. Do not substitute no-boil lasagna noodles for the traditional, curly-edged lasagna noodles here because the no-boil noodles will fall apart. You can substitute part-skim ricotta if desired, but do not use nonfat ricotta, which has a very dry texture and bland flavor.

1 (28-ounce) can whole peeled tomatoes
2 teaspoons olive oil
1 small onion, chopped fine
   Salt and pepper
1 garlic clove, minced
   Pinch red pepper flakes
8 ounces 85 percent lean ground beef
5 curly-edged lasagna noodles, broken into 2-inch lengths
¼ cup shredded mozzarella cheese
2 tablespoons grated Parmesan cheese
3 ounces (⅓ cup) whole-milk ricotta cheese
2 tablespoons chopped fresh basil

1. Pulse tomatoes and their juice in food processor until coarsely ground and no large pieces remain, 6 to 8 pulses.

2. Heat oil in 10-inch nonstick skillet over medium heat until shimmering. Add onion and ¼ teaspoon salt and cook until softened, about 5 minutes. Stir in garlic and pepper flakes and cook until fragrant, about 30 seconds. Add ground beef and cook, breaking up meat with wooden spoon, until no longer pink, 3 to 5 minutes.

3. Scatter noodles over meat, then pour pulsed tomatoes over pasta. Cover, increase heat to medium-high, and cook at vigorous simmer, stirring often, until pasta is tender, about 20 minutes.

4. Off heat, stir in 2 tablespoons mozzarella and 1 tablespoon Parmesan. Season with salt and pepper to taste. Dollop heaping tablespoons of ricotta over noodles, then sprinkle with remaining 2 tablespoons mozzarella and remaining 1 tablespoon Parmesan. Off heat, cover and let sit until cheese is melted, 2 to 4 minutes. Sprinkle with basil and serve.

VARIATION

Skillet Lasagna with Italian Sausage and Bell Pepper

Substitute 8 ounces hot or sweet Italian sausage, casings removed, for ground beef. Add ½ red bell pepper, chopped coarse, to skillet with onion.

Breaking Lasagna Noodles

To make sure lasagna noodles cook through evenly in skillet, we break them into 2-inch pieces using our hands. Be sure to use traditional curly-edged, not no-boil, lasagna noodles here.

Creamy, earthy eggplant pairs nicely with nutty, chewy soba noodles in this simple Asian-inspired dish.

2 tablespoons sugar
1 tablespoon oyster sauce
1 tablespoon toasted sesame oil
1½ teaspoons Asian chili-garlic sauce
2 teaspoons sake or dry vermouth
4 ounces soba noodles
¼ cup fresh cilantro leaves
1 teaspoon sesame seeds, toasted

1. Adjust oven rack to middle position and heat oven to 450 degrees. Line rimmed baking sheet with aluminum foil and brush with 1½ teaspoons vegetable oil. Toss eggplant with remaining 1½ tablespoons vegetable oil and 1½ teaspoons soy sauce, then spread on prepared sheet. Roast until well browned and tender, 25 to 30 minutes, stirring halfway through roasting.

2. In small saucepan, whisk remaining 1½ tablespoons soy sauce, sugar, oyster sauce, sesame oil, chili-garlic sauce, and sake together. Cook over medium heat until sugar has dissolved, about 1 minute; cover and set aside.

3. Meanwhile, bring 4 quarts water to boil in large pot. Add noodles and cook, stirring often, until tender. Reserve ½ cup cooking water, then drain noodles and return them to pot. Add roasted eggplant, sauce, and cilantro and toss to combine. Adjust consistency with reserved cooking water as needed. Sprinkle individual portions with sesame seeds. Serve.

Soba Noodles with Roasted Eggplant and Sesame
SERVES 2

◉ WHY THIS RECIPE WORKS: With their unique flavor and chewy texture, Japanese soba noodles require little adornment, so we thought they would make a quick and substantial meal for two. The creamy texture and mild flavor of cooked eggplant was the perfect foil to the rich, nutty noodles. Roasting proved an easy, hands-off way to cook the eggplant; we tossed it with soy sauce beforehand to help season the vegetable and draw out its moisture. For a richly flavored sauce, we started with soy sauce and added oyster sauce, Asian chili-garlic sauce, sake, and toasted sesame oil for a nice balance of sweet and spicy flavors. A garnish of toasted sesame seeds was the perfect finishing touch. Do not substitute other types of noodles for the soba noodles here.

2 tablespoons vegetable oil
1 pound eggplant, cut into 1-inch pieces
2 tablespoons soy sauce

Sesame Noodles with Shredded Chicken
SERVES 2

◉ WHY THIS RECIPE WORKS: For sesame noodles we could make at home whenever the craving struck, we started with the noodles themselves. We found that fresh Chinese noodles have a chewier texture and cleaner flavor than dried versions; rinsing them under cold water and tossing them with a little oil prevented clumping. The addition of one chicken breast turned our noodles into a meal, and broiling ensured that it cooked through quickly without drying out. Asian sesame paste is what gives this dish its distinct flavor, but it can be hard to find; happily, we found that peanut butter was a surprisingly good substitute. Garlic, ginger, soy sauce, rice vinegar, hot sauce, and brown sugar rounded out our sauce, and thinly sliced red bell pepper, cucumbers, and shredded carrot added color and fresh crunch to the dish. Conventional chunky peanut butter works best in this recipe because it tends to be sweeter than natural or old-fashioned versions; however, creamy peanut butter can be substituted.

SAUCE

2½ tablespoons soy sauce
2 tablespoons chunky peanut butter
1½ tablespoons sesame seeds, toasted
1 tablespoon rice vinegar
1 tablespoon packed light brown sugar
1½ teaspoons grated fresh ginger
1 garlic clove, minced
½ teaspoon hot sauce
3 tablespoons hot tap water

CHICKEN AND NOODLES

1 (8-ounce) boneless, skinless chicken breast, trimmed and pounded if necessary
8 ounces fresh Chinese noodles or 6 ounces dried spaghetti or linguine
1 tablespoon salt
1 tablespoon toasted sesame oil
½ red bell pepper, cut into ¼-inch-wide strips
½ cucumber, peeled, halved lengthwise, seeded, and sliced ¼ inch thick
1 carrot, peeled and shredded
2 scallions, sliced thin on bias
1 tablespoon chopped fresh cilantro (optional)
1 tablespoon sesame seeds, toasted

1. FOR THE SAUCE: Process soy sauce, peanut butter, sesame seeds, vinegar, sugar, ginger, garlic, and hot sauce together in blender until smooth, about 30 seconds. With blender running, slowly add hot water, 1 tablespoon at a time, until sauce has consistency of heavy cream (you may not need all of water).

2. FOR THE CHICKEN AND NOODLES: Adjust oven rack 6 inches from broiler element and heat broiler. Spray broiler pan top with vegetable oil spray. Pat chicken dry with paper towels and lay on prepared pan. Broil chicken until lightly golden on both sides and chicken registers 160 degrees, 10 to 12 minutes, flipping chicken halfway through cooking. Transfer chicken to cutting board, let cool slightly, then shred into bite-size pieces using 2 forks.

3. Meanwhile, bring 4 quarts water to boil in large pot. Add noodles and salt and cook, stirring often, until tender. Drain noodles, rinse with cold water, then drain again, leaving noodles slightly wet. Transfer noodles to large bowl and toss with oil. Add sauce, shredded chicken, bell pepper, cucumber, carrot, scallions, and cilantro, if using, and toss to combine. Sprinkle individual portions with sesame seeds and serve.

All About Asian Noodles

While Italian pasta is typically made from durum wheat flour, Asian noodles can be made from a variety of grains and even rice. Here are some of the most common types of Asian noodles.

FRESH CHINESE NOODLES

You can find fresh Chinese noodles in the refrigerated section of many supermarkets as well as Asian markets. Some noodles are cut thin, and others are cut slightly wider. Their texture is a bit more starchy and chewy than that of dried noodles, and their flavor is cleaner (less wheaty) than Italian pasta, making them an excellent match with well-seasoned sauces and soups. Fresh Chinese noodles cook quickly, usually in no more than three to four minutes in boiling water.

RICE NOODLES

Rice noodles are made from rice powder and water. They come in several widths (¼ inch wide, which is similar to linguine; ⅜ inch wide; and thin vermicelli). Since they can overcook quickly, we often soften them off the heat in hot water before adding them to whatever dish we're making toward the end of cooking. We've also had some success boiling the noodles as long as we carefully watch the time, and we usually rinse them after draining to ensure they cool quickly and don't overcook.

SOBA NOODLES

Soba noodles possess a rich, nutty flavor and delicate texture. They get their unusual flavor from buckwheat flour. Buckwheat flour contains no gluten, so a binder, usually wheat, is added to give the noodles structure and hold them together during cooking. Soba noodles must contain a minimum of 30 percent buckwheat flour, and the higher the percentage, the higher the price. Soba noodles are traditionally served cold, but we also like them warm.

UDON NOODLES

These Japanese noodles made from wheat are available in varying thicknesses and can be round or squared. They are typically used in soups and have an appealing chewy texture. You can find them alongside the tofu in the refrigerator section in most grocery stores as well as Asian markets. They can contain quite a bit of salt (up to 4,000 milligrams of sodium per 12 ounces); because of that, we don't add salt to the cooking water when boiling them.

RAMEN NOODLES

Typically fried in oil then dried and packaged, ramen noodles take only a few minutes to cook, making them a more convenient, quicker-cooking choice than other dried-noodle options. In the test kitchen we don't like ramen noodles when they are prepared with the salty, stale-tasting seasoning packet they often come with. However, we do sometimes use plain ramen noodles as the pasta component in Asian-inspired recipes; we just get rid of the seasoning packet and add our own mix of fresh herbs and spices.

Drunken Noodles with Chicken

SERVES 2

☑ **WHY THIS RECIPE WORKS:** For our version of drunken noodles with chicken—a spicy, potent Thai noodle dish—we selected the widest rice noodles we could find and soaked them in hot water until they were pliable but not fully limp. Then we tossed the noodles over medium heat with a combination of soy sauce, lime juice, dark brown sugar, and chili-garlic sauce (for heat and spicy flavor) to ensure that they would absorb the sauce's flavors and finish cooking. Baby bok choy provided textural contrast, and thin slices of chicken, quickly stir-fried, made our noodle dish hearty and filling. Do not substitute other types of noodles for the rice noodles here. This dish is spicy; to make it less spicy, use 1 tablespoon of chili-garlic sauce. To make the chicken easier to slice, freeze it for 15 minutes.

   6 ounces (⅜-inch-wide) rice noodles
   1 (6-ounce) boneless, skinless chicken breast, trimmed and sliced ¼ inch thick
  1½ teaspoons plus ¼ cup soy sauce
   ⅓ cup packed dark brown sugar
  2½ tablespoons lime juice (2 limes), plus lime wedges for serving
  1-2 tablespoons Asian chili-garlic sauce
   2 tablespoons vegetable oil
   2 heads baby bok choy (4 ounces each), stalks and greens separated and sliced ½ inch thick
   ½ cup coarsely chopped fresh Thai basil or cilantro
   1 scallion, sliced thin on bias

1. Cover noodles with very hot tap water in large bowl and stir to separate. Let noodles soak until softened, pliable, and limp but not fully tender, 25 to 30 minutes; drain.

2. Meanwhile, toss chicken with 1½ teaspoons soy sauce in bowl, cover, and marinate in refrigerator for at least 10 minutes or up to 1 hour. In separate bowl, whisk remaining ¼ cup soy sauce, sugar, lime juice, and chili-garlic sauce together.

3. Heat 1 teaspoon oil in 12-inch nonstick skillet over high heat until just smoking. Add chicken, break up any clumps, and cook, without stirring, until beginning to brown, about 1 minute. Stir chicken and continue to cook until nearly cooked through, about 2 minutes; transfer to bowl.

4. Add 1 teaspoon oil to now-empty skillet and heat over high heat until just smoking. Add bok choy stalks and cook, stirring often, until spotty brown, about 2 minutes. Stir in leaves and cook until wilted, about 1 minute; transfer to bowl with chicken.

Crisp baby bok choy, scallions, and tart lime juice balance the spicy sauce in this classic Thai noodle stir-fry.

5. Wipe again-empty skillet clean, add remaining 4 teaspoons oil, and heat over medium heat until shimmering. Add drained rice noodles, soy sauce mixture, and 1 cup water and cook, tossing gently, until noodles are tender and well coated, 5 to 10 minutes. Stir in chicken-vegetable mixture and basil and cook until chicken is heated through, about 1 minute. Sprinkle with scallion and serve with lime wedges.

Skillet Pork Lo Mein

SERVES 2

☑ **WHY THIS RECIPE WORKS:** At its best, pork lo mein features an addictive contrast of textures and flavors— springy noodles, tender, smoky pork, and a combination of crisp and tender vegetables. Meaty, flavorful country-style ribs were a good stand-in for the usual large cut of pork. Since we wanted to make our lo mein all in one skillet, we opted for dried linguine over fresh Chinese noodles, which require large amounts of water to cook properly. Napa cabbage, scallions, and shiitake mushrooms provided crunch, color, and heft. When adding the pasta in step 4, stir gently to avoid breaking the noodles; after a minute or two they will soften enough to be stirred more easily. This dish is moderately spicy; to make it less spicy, use ½ teaspoon Asian chili-garlic sauce. To make the pork easier to slice, freeze it for 15 minutes.

5 teaspoons soy sauce, plus extra for serving
1 tablespoon oyster sauce
1 tablespoon hoisin sauce
1 teaspoon toasted sesame oil
8 ounces boneless country-style pork ribs, trimmed and sliced thin crosswise
5 teaspoons vegetable oil
2 tablespoons Chinese rice wine or dry sherry
4 ounces shiitake mushrooms, stemmed, halved if large
4 scallions, white parts sliced thin, green parts cut into 1-inch pieces
1 garlic clove, minced
1 teaspoon grated fresh ginger
2½ cups water
6 ounces dried linguine
½ small head napa cabbage, cored and shredded (4 cups)
1 teaspoon Asian chili-garlic sauce

1. Whisk soy sauce, oyster sauce, hoisin sauce, and sesame oil together in medium bowl. Measure 1 tablespoon of mixture into separate bowl, then stir in pork. Cover and marinate pork in refrigerator for at least 15 minutes or up to 1 hour.

2. Heat 2 teaspoons vegetable oil in 12-inch nonstick skillet over high heat until just smoking. Add pork, break up any clumps, and cook, without stirring, until beginning to brown, about 1 minute. Stir pork and continue to cook until nearly cooked through, 1 to 2 minutes. Stir in wine and cook until almost completely evaporated, about 1 minute; transfer to clean bowl.

3. Add remaining 1 tablespoon vegetable oil to now-empty skillet and heat over high heat until just smoking. Add mushrooms and cook until light golden brown, about 5 minutes. Stir in scallion whites, garlic, and ginger and cook until fragrant, about 30 seconds.

4. Stir in water and pasta, bring to vigorous simmer, and cook, stirring often, until pasta is tender, 12 to 16 minutes. Stir in cabbage and continue to cook until cabbage is wilted and sauce is thickened, about 2 minutes.

5. Reduce heat to low and stir in remaining soy sauce mixture, browned pork, chili-garlic sauce, and scallion greens. Cook, tossing pasta gently, until well coated with sauce, about 2 minutes. Season with soy sauce to taste and serve.

Beef Lo Mein with Broccoli and Bell Pepper
SERVES 2

✔ **WHY THIS RECIPE WORKS:** For a full-flavored, not bland, beef lo mein—one featuring flavorful, chewy strands of noodles mingled with thin slices of perfectly cooked beef coated in a light, tangy sauce—we started by building bold, complex flavor from a few key ingredients: soy sauce, hoisin sauce, and toasted sesame oil. Marinating thinly sliced flank steak in this mixture before stir-frying ensured that it was well seasoned. Broccoli and red bell pepper gave the lo mein freshness and crunch. To guarantee crisp-tender broccoli, we steamed it first, then cooked it uncovered so it could brown. A generous amount of scallions added a sweet, grassy pungency. To make the beef easier to slice, freeze it for 15 minutes.

3 tablespoons hoisin sauce
2 tablespoons soy sauce
2 teaspoons toasted sesame oil
1 (8-ounce) flank steak, trimmed and sliced thin against grain
⅓ cup chicken broth
½ teaspoon cornstarch
1 garlic clove, minced
1 teaspoon grated fresh ginger
1 tablespoon vegetable oil
6 ounces broccoli florets, cut into 1-inch pieces
2½ tablespoons water
½ red bell pepper, cut into ½-inch-wide strips and halved crosswise
6 scallions, white parts sliced thin, greens parts cut into 1-inch pieces
6 ounces fresh Chinese noodles or 4 ounces dried linguine
1½ teaspoons Asian chili-garlic sauce

1. Whisk hoisin sauce, soy sauce, and sesame oil together in medium bowl. Measure 1½ tablespoons of mixture into separate bowl, then stir in beef. Cover and marinate beef in refrigerator for at least 15 minutes or up to 1 hour. Whisk broth and cornstarch into remaining mixture. In separate small bowl, combine garlic, ginger, and ½ teaspoon vegetable oil.

2. Heat 1 teaspoon vegetable oil in 10-inch nonstick skillet over high heat until just smoking. Add beef, break up any clumps, and cook, without stirring, for 1 minute. Stir beef and continue to cook until browned, about 1 minute; transfer to large clean bowl.

3. Wipe now-empty skillet clean, add ½ teaspoon vegetable oil, and heat over high heat until just smoking. Add broccoli and cook for 30 seconds. Add water, cover, and steam until broccoli is bright green and begins to soften, about 2 minutes. Uncover and continue to cook until water has evaporated and broccoli begins to brown, about 2 minutes; transfer to bowl with beef.

4. Add remaining 1 teaspoon vegetable oil and bell pepper to again-empty skillet and cook over high heat until crisp-tender and spotty brown, about 2 minutes. Stir in scallions and continue to cook until wilted, 2 to 3 minutes. Push vegetables to sides of skillet. Add garlic mixture to center and cook, mashing mixture into skillet until fragrant, about 30 seconds. Stir garlic mixture into vegetables, then stir in cooked beef and broccoli with any accumulated juices. Whisk broth mixture to recombine, then add to skillet and simmer until sauce has thickened, about 1 minute. Remove from heat and cover to keep warm.

5. Meanwhile, bring 4 quarts water to boil in large pot. Add noodles and cook, stirring often, until tender. Reserve ½ cup cooking water, then drain noodles and return them to pot. Add beef mixture and chili-garlic sauce and toss to combine. Adjust consistency with reserved cooking water as needed. Serve.

Singapore Noodles with Shrimp
SERVES 2 **LIGHT**

✔ **WHY THIS RECIPE WORKS:** Stir-fried rice vermicelli noodles with curry—Singapore noodles—is a dish with a devoted following. For a flavorful home-cooked version of this takeout dish, we made a sauce with soy sauce, mirin, and chicken broth for an ideal salty-sweet balance. Soaking the noodles in hot water softened them just enough so that they cooked up with a pleasantly tender chew. Sliced shallots and red bell pepper added crunch and freshness, and seared shrimp turned our noodles into a one-dish meal. Do not substitute other types of noodles for the rice vermicelli here. If using smaller or larger shrimp, be sure to adjust the cooking time accordingly. For the nutritional information for this recipe, see page 414.

For a fast and healthy noodle stir-fry, we combine rice vermicelli, bell pepper, shallots, and shrimp with a sweet and salty sauce.

  4 ounces rice vermicelli
  8 ounces extra-large shrimp (21 to 25 per pound), peeled, deveined, and tails removed
1½ teaspoons curry powder
 ⅛ teaspoon sugar
  4 teaspoons vegetable oil
  3 shallots, sliced thin
  1 red bell pepper, stemmed, seeded, and cut into ¼-inch-wide strips
  1 garlic clove, minced
 ½ cup chicken broth
  3 tablespoons soy sauce
  2 teaspoons mirin
 ½ teaspoon Sriracha sauce
  2 ounces (1 cup) bean sprouts
 ¼ cup minced fresh cilantro

1. Cover noodles with very hot tap water in large bowl and stir to separate. Let noodles soak until softened, pliable, and limp but not fully tender, about 20 minutes; drain.

2. Meanwhile, pat shrimp dry with paper towels and toss with ¼ teaspoon curry powder and sugar. Heat 2 teaspoons oil in 12-inch nonstick skillet over medium-high heat until just smoking. Add shrimp in single layer and cook, without stirring, until beginning to brown, about 1 minute. Stir shrimp and continue to cook until spotty brown and just pink around edges, about 30 seconds; transfer to bowl.

3. Add remaining 2 teaspoons oil to now-empty skillet and heat over medium heat until shimmering. Add shallots, bell pepper, and remaining 1¼ teaspoons curry powder and cook until vegetables are softened, about 5 minutes. Stir in garlic and cook until fragrant, about 30 seconds.

4. Stir in drained noodles, shrimp and any accumulated juices, broth, soy sauce, mirin, and Sriracha and cook, tossing gently, until noodles, shrimp, and vegetables are well coated with sauce, 2 to 3 minutes. Stir in bean sprouts and cilantro and serve.

Pad Thai with Shrimp

SERVES 2

✔ **WHY THIS RECIPE WORKS:** We wanted a recipe for pad thai that cut the mile-long ingredient list without sacrificing authentic flavor. Soaking the rice noodles in just-boiled water ensured they remained loose and separate. For the requisite sweet, salty, sour, and spicy notes, we added sugar, fish sauce, rice vinegar, and cayenne. To replicate the sweet-tart flavor of hard-to-find tamarind paste, we combined lime juice and dark brown sugar. Tender shrimp, lightly scrambled eggs, chopped peanuts, bean sprouts, and a sprinkling of scallion and fresh cilantro rounded out our streamlined pad thai. We prefer the rich molasses flavor of dark brown sugar in this recipe, but you can substitute light brown sugar. Do not substitute other types of noodles for the rice noodles here. Because this dish cooks very quickly, it is important to have everything prepared when you begin cooking. If using smaller or larger shrimp, be sure to adjust the cooking time accordingly.

SAUCE

- 3 tablespoons lime juice (2 limes)
- 3 tablespoons water
- 2½ tablespoons packed dark brown sugar
- 2 tablespoons fish sauce
- 1½ tablespoons vegetable oil
- 2 teaspoons rice vinegar
- ⅛ teaspoon cayenne pepper

NOODLES, SHRIMP, AND GARNISH

- 4 ounces (¼-inch-wide) rice noodles
- 6 ounces medium shrimp (41 to 50 per pound), peeled, deveined, and tails removed
- 2 tablespoons vegetable oil
- 1 small shallot, minced
- 1 garlic clove, minced
  Salt
- 1 large egg, lightly beaten
- 2 ounces (1 cup) bean sprouts
- 2 tablespoons chopped unsalted dry-roasted peanuts, plus extra for garnish
- 2 scallions, green parts only, sliced thin
- 2 tablespoons fresh cilantro leaves

1. FOR THE SAUCE: Whisk all ingredients together in bowl and set aside.

2. FOR THE NOODLES, SHRIMP, AND GARNISH: Cover noodles with very hot tap water in large bowl and stir to separate. Let noodles soak until softened, pliable, and limp but not fully tender, 20 to 25 minutes; drain.

We create the salty, sweet, sour, and spicy flavors of pad thai with easy-to-find ingredients: fish sauce, sugar, vinegar, and cayenne.

3. Pat shrimp dry with paper towels. Heat 1 tablespoon oil in 10-inch nonstick skillet over medium-high heat until just smoking. Add shrimp in single layer and cook, without stirring, until beginning to brown, about 1 minute. Stir shrimp and continue to cook until spotty brown and just pink around edges, about 30 seconds; transfer to bowl.

4. Add remaining 1 tablespoon oil, shallot, garlic, and pinch salt to now-empty skillet and cook over medium heat, stirring constantly, until shallot is light golden brown, about 1½ minutes. Stir in egg and cook, stirring vigorously, until scrambled and barely moist, about 20 seconds.

5. Add drained rice noodles and toss to combine. Add sauce, increase heat to medium-high, and cook, tossing gently, until noodles are well coated with sauce, about 1 minute. Add cooked shrimp with any accumulated juices, bean sprouts, peanuts, and half of scallions and continue to cook, tossing constantly, until noodles are tender, about 2 minutes. (If not yet tender, add 2 tablespoons water to skillet and continue to cook until tender.)

6. Transfer noodles to serving platter; sprinkle with remaining scallions, cilantro, and extra peanuts; and serve.

CHAPTER 10

Grilling

■ FAST (Start to finish in about 30 minutes)

▦ LIGHT (See page 415 for nutritional information)

Opposite: Grilled Herbed Chicken and Vegetable Kebabs; Grill-Smoked Salmon with Creamy Cucumber-Dill Salad; Grilled Tuscan Steak with Olive Oil and Lemon

Grilled Chicken Fajitas

SERVES 2

✓ **WHY THIS RECIPE WORKS:** Too often, chicken fajitas need to be slathered with guacamole, sour cream, and salsa to mask the bland flavor of the soggy underlying ingredients. We wanted a simple combination of smoky grilled vegetables and strips of juicy chicken wrapped up in warm flour tortillas. Marinating the chicken in a high-acid mixture gave it a bright, tangy flavor. We built a two-level fire by pouring two-thirds of the coals over one half of the grill and the remaining one-third of the coals over the other half. Creating a hotter side and a cooler side allowed us to grill the chicken and the peppers and onions simultaneously. When both the chicken and vegetables were spottily browned, we finished them with a burst of fresh flavor by tossing them with some reserved marinade and then we served them in tortillas briefly warmed on the grill. Do not marinate the chicken for longer than 15 minutes or the lime juice will make the meat mushy. To make this dish spicier, add the chile seeds to the marinade. You will need one 12-inch metal skewer for this recipe. See page 252 for information on how to set up a two-level fire. Serve with your favorite fajita toppings.

- 5 tablespoons vegetable oil
- ¼ cup lime juice (2 limes)
- 2 tablespoons chopped fresh cilantro
- 3 garlic cloves, minced
- 1 tablespoon Worcestershire sauce
- 1½ teaspoons packed brown sugar
- 1 jalapeño chile, stemmed, seeded, and minced
  Salt and pepper
- 2 (6- to 8-ounce) boneless, skinless chicken breasts, trimmed and pounded if necessary
- 1 small red onion, sliced into ½-inch rings (do not separate rings)
- 1 red, yellow, or orange bell pepper, stemmed, seeded, and quartered
- 6 (6-inch) flour tortillas

1. Whisk ¼ cup oil, lime juice, cilantro, garlic, Worcestershire, sugar, jalapeño, ½ teaspoon salt, and ½ teaspoon pepper together in bowl. Transfer ¼ cup marinade to separate bowl; set aside for serving.

2. Add ½ teaspoon salt to remaining marinade, combine with chicken in 1-gallon zipper-lock bag, seal bag tightly, and toss to coat. Let chicken marinate in refrigerator for 15 minutes. Thread onion rings, from side to side, onto 12-inch metal skewer. Brush onion and bell pepper with remaining 1 tablespoon oil and season with salt and pepper.

3A. FOR A CHARCOAL GRILL: Open bottom vent completely. Light large chimney starter filled with charcoal briquettes (6 quarts). When top coals are partially covered with ash, pour two-thirds evenly over half of grill, then pour remaining coals over other half of grill. Set cooking grate in place, cover, and open lid vent completely. Heat grill until hot, about 5 minutes.

3B. FOR A GAS GRILL: Turn all burners to high, cover, and heat grill until hot, about 15 minutes. Leave primary burner on high and turn other burner(s) to medium. (Adjust burners as needed to maintain hot fire and medium fire on separate sides of grill.)

4. Clean and oil cooking grate. Remove chicken from marinade and place on hotter side of grill. Place onion rings and bell pepper on cooler side of grill. Cook (covered if using gas), turning chicken and vegetables as needed, until chicken is browned and registers 160 degrees and vegetables are spottily charred, 8 to 12 minutes. Transfer chicken and vegetables to cutting board, tent loosely with aluminum foil, and let rest while grilling tortillas.

5. Place tortillas on hotter side of grill in single layer and cook until warmed and lightly browned on both sides, about 15 seconds per side. Stack grilled tortillas in foil packet to keep warm and soft until serving.

6. Separate onion rings and slice bell pepper into ¼-inch strips. Toss vegetables with half of reserved marinade in bowl. Slice chicken into ¼-inch strips and toss with remaining marinade in separate bowl. Arrange chicken and vegetables on serving platter and serve with warm tortillas.

VARIATION

Grilled Beef Fajitas

Substitute 12 ounces flank steak for chicken; marinate as directed. Grill steak over hotter side of grill, turning as needed, until well browned and registers 120 to 125 degrees (for medium-rare), about 8 minutes. Slice steak thin against grain before tossing with marinade.

Grilling Tortillas

Grill tortillas in single layer until soft and lightly charred, about 15 seconds per side. Stack grilled tortillas in foil packet to keep them warm and soft until serving time.

Grilled Herbed Chicken and Vegetable Kebabs

SERVES 2

✓ **WHY THIS RECIPE WORKS:** Chicken kebabs are an obvious choice when cooking for two—they cook quickly and are a snap to assemble. The problem is that the small chunks of chicken quickly turn dry and chalky. We wanted moist, well-seasoned chicken alongside a mix of lightly charred vegetables. We preferred boneless chicken thighs to breasts; thanks to their extra fat, they stayed juicy on the grill. To give the chicken a head start on flavor, we marinated it with fresh herbs and garlic. Reserving some marinade to drizzle over the chicken at the end added another layer of flavor. For the vegetables, we found that a zucchini, a red pepper, and a small onion gave us a great mix of flavors and textures without any leftovers. You will need four 12-inch metal skewers for this recipe. If the chicken pieces are smaller than 1½ inches, thread two small pieces together. See page 255 for information on how to set up a single-level fire.

¼ cup olive oil

2 tablespoons minced fresh parsley, chives, basil, tarragon, or oregano

3 garlic cloves, minced

¾ teaspoon salt

½ teaspoon pepper

2 teaspoons lemon juice

1 pound boneless, skinless chicken thighs, trimmed and cut into 1½-inch pieces

1 red bell pepper, stemmed, seeded, and cut into 1½-inch pieces

1 small red onion, quartered through root end, each quarter cut into 1-inch pieces

1 zucchini, sliced ½ inch thick

1. Whisk oil, parsley, garlic, salt, and pepper together in large bowl. Transfer 1½ tablespoons marinade to separate bowl and stir in lemon juice; set aside for serving. Transfer 2 tablespoons marinade to 1-gallon zipper-lock bag, add chicken, seal bag tightly, and toss to coat. Let chicken marinate in refrigerator for at least 30 minutes or up to 1 hour.

2. Add bell pepper, onion, and zucchini to remaining marinade and toss to coat. Thread chicken and vegetables evenly onto four 12-inch metal skewers, starting and ending with chicken.

3A. FOR A CHARCOAL GRILL: Open bottom vent completely. Light large chimney starter filled with charcoal briquettes (6 quarts). When top coals are partially covered with ash, pour evenly over grill. Set cooking grate in place, cover, and open lid vent completely. Heat grill until hot, about 5 minutes.

3B. FOR A GAS GRILL: Turn all burners to high, cover, and heat grill until hot, about 15 minutes.

4. Clean and oil cooking grate. Place kebabs on grill and cook (covered if using gas) until chicken is well browned on all sides and vegetables are tender, 8 to 12 minutes, turning as needed. Transfer kebabs to serving platter, tent loosely with aluminum foil, and let rest for 5 to 10 minutes. Drizzle with reserved marinade and serve.

VARIATIONS

Grilled Curried Chicken and Vegetable Kebabs

Substitute 2 tablespoons minced fresh cilantro (or mint) for parsley and 2 teaspoons lime juice for lemon juice. In step 1, whisk 1 teaspoon curry powder into oil mixture before reserving some for serving.

Grilled Southwestern Chicken and Vegetable Kebabs

Substitute 2 tablespoons minced fresh cilantro for parsley and 2 teaspoons lime juice for lemon juice. In step 1, whisk 1 tablespoon minced chipotle chile and 1 teaspoon chili powder into oil mixture before reserving some for serving.

Preparing Onion for Kebabs

1. Peel onion, trim off stem and root ends, then quarter onion.

2. Pull onion apart into sections that are 3 layers thick.

3. Cut each 3-layered section into 1-inch pieces.

4. Skewer onion through center of each piece.

Grilled Bone-In Chicken Breasts with Cherry Tomatoes

SERVES 2

✔ **WHY THIS RECIPE WORKS:** For the perfect easy summer meal, we wanted juicy, tender chicken breasts and bright cherry tomatoes together on the grill. Grilling bone-in chicken breasts over blazing hot coals caused flare-ups from the rendered fat and dried out the delicate meat. Instead, we spread the coals on one half of the grill to make a hotter side for crisping the skin and a cooler side where the chicken could cook gently. Tenting it with foil helped it to cook more evenly. Then, while the chicken rested, we tossed the tomatoes in oil and grilled them until they were nicely blistered but still fresh-tasting. If using kosher chicken, do not brine. If brining the chicken, do not season with salt in step 1. You will need two or three 12-inch metal skewers for this recipe depending on the size of your tomatoes. See page 250 for information on how to set up a half-grill fire.

Juicy, blistered cherry tomatoes and tender grilled chicken make the perfect fresh and easy summer supper.

12 ounces cherry tomatoes
¼ cup extra-virgin olive oil
2 tablespoons chopped fresh basil, cilantro, or tarragon
1 tablespoon red wine vinegar
1 garlic clove, minced
 Salt and pepper
2 (12-ounce) bone-in split chicken breasts, trimmed and brined if desired (see page 115)

1. Toss tomatoes with 1 tablespoon oil and thread, through stem ends, onto two or three 12-inch metal skewers. Mix remaining 3 tablespoons oil, basil, vinegar, garlic, ¼ teaspoon salt, and ⅛ teaspoon pepper together in small bowl; set aside for serving. Pat chicken breasts dry with paper towels and season with salt and pepper.

2A. FOR A CHARCOAL GRILL: Open bottom vent completely. Light large chimney starter three-quarters filled with charcoal briquettes (4½ quarts). When top coals are partially covered with ash, pour evenly over half of grill. Set cooking grate in place, cover, and open lid vent completely. Heat grill until hot, about 5 minutes.

2B. FOR A GAS GRILL: Turn all burners to high, cover, and heat grill until hot, about 15 minutes. Turn primary burner to medium-high and turn off other burner(s). (Adjust primary burner as needed to maintain grill temperature around 350 degrees.)

3. Clean and oil cooking grate. Place chicken, skin side down, on cooler side of grill with thicker ends of breasts facing hotter side of grill. Tent chicken loosely with aluminum foil, cover grill, and cook until chicken is browned and registers 150 degrees, 25 to 35 minutes.

4. Discard foil and slide chicken to hotter side of grill. Cook (covered if using gas), turning as needed, until chicken is well browned, skin is crisp, and chicken registers 160 degrees, 5 to 10 minutes. Transfer chicken to serving platter and let rest while grilling tomatoes.

5. Place tomato skewers on hotter side of grill and cook, turning skewers as needed, until skins begin to blister and wrinkle, 3 to 6 minutes. Remove skewers from grill and carefully slide tomatoes off skewers and onto platter with chicken. Drizzle vinaigrette over chicken and tomatoes. Serve.

Measuring Charcoal

To easily measure charcoal by volume, you can use 1 empty half-gallon milk or juice carton. Each full carton equals roughly 2 quarts.

Barbecued Dry-Rubbed Chicken

SERVES 2

✓ **WHY THIS RECIPE WORKS:** Simply brushing grilled chicken with barbecue sauce only flavors the surface of the meat, and worse, it turns the skin flabby. We wanted classic barbecued chicken that was flavored through and though. Our solution was to swap the barbecue sauce for a dry spice rub. Spread over and under the skin before cooking, it flavored the chicken down to the bone, and it didn't prevent the skin from crisping on the grill. To keep the chicken juicy, we let it rest while the salt in the rub penetrated the meat. We also added a generous amount of sugar to the rub; as it melted in the heat, it gave our chicken the glazed sweetness of a sauce. A second coating of the rub partway through cooking thickened the glaze even more. To keep the sugar from burning, we cooked the chicken over indirect heat. Apply the second coating of spices with a light hand or it won't melt into a glaze.

- 1 tablespoon packed dark brown sugar
- 1 teaspoon paprika
- ¾ teaspoon chili powder
- ¾ teaspoon pepper
- ½ teaspoon dry mustard
- ½ teaspoon onion powder
- ¼ teaspoon salt
- Pinch cayenne pepper
- 2 (12-ounce) bone-in split chicken breasts, trimmed

1. Combine sugar, paprika, chili powder, pepper, mustard, onion powder, salt, and cayenne in bowl. Transfer 1½ tablespoons spice mixture to shallow dish; set aside. Pat chicken dry with paper towels. Use your fingers to gently loosen center portion of skin covering each breast, then rub remaining spice mixture over and underneath skin. Transfer chicken to large plate, cover with plastic wrap, and refrigerate for at least 30 minutes or up to 1 hour.

2A. FOR A CHARCOAL GRILL: Open bottom vent completely. Light large chimney starter three-quarters filled with charcoal briquettes (4½ quarts). When top coals are partially covered with ash, pour evenly over half of grill. Set cooking grate in place, cover, and open lid vent completely. Heat grill until hot, about 5 minutes.

2B. FOR A GAS GRILL: Turn all burners to high, cover, and heat grill until hot, about 15 minutes. Turn primary burner to medium-high and turn off other burner(s). (Adjust primary burner as needed to maintain grill temperature around 350 degrees.)

3. Clean and oil cooking grate. Place chicken, skin side down, on cooler side of grill with thicker ends of breasts facing

Basic Grilling Methods

The words "grilling" and "barbecuing" are often used interchangeably, but they are actually different cooking techniques. Whereas grilling works best with quick-cooking foods that are smallish in size (such as shrimp and skewered meats) or foods that are individually portioned (such as steaks and chops), barbecuing and grill roasting work best with larger, slower-cooking foods.

GRILLING: Grilling is the speediest and simplest cooking method performed on the grill, and typically uses high or moderately high heat. Most of the cooking takes place directly over the fire, often without the lid, especially on a charcoal grill. Grilled foods derive their "grilled" flavor from the dripping juices and fat that hit the heat source, creating smoke that seasons the exterior of the food.

GRILL ROASTING: Grill roasting involves longer cooking times than grilling simply because the foods are larger, and this method calls for heat that is more moderate. The grill is set up for indirect cooking—that is, part of the grill is left free of coals, or some of the gas burners are turned off. The lid is employed to create an ovenlike cooking environment. As a result, foods can be cooked through without danger of scorching the exterior.

BARBECUING: Barbecuing takes even longer than grill roasting—often several hours—because the beef, pork, or poultry is cooked until proteins break down to a meltingly tender texture. This type of cooking requires low, gentle heat. As with grill roasting, food is not cooked directly over the coals or the lit burner. Barbecued foods derive their "barbecued" flavor from wood chips or chunks. The wood generates an intense smoke that permeates the food.

Creating Custom Grill Fires

Just as you don't cook everything on high heat on your stovetop, you don't cook only on high heat on the grill. Thin steaks need only high heat to give them a good sear and cook them through, but if you tried that method with thick-cut pork chops, the outside would be charred by the time they cooked through—different types of food need different types of fires. Here are the types of fires we use.

SINGLE-LEVEL FIRE: A single-level fire delivers a uniform level of heat and is good for small, quick-cooking foods like hamburgers and fish fillets. For a charcoal grill, distribute lit coals in an even layer across the bottom of the grill. For a gas grill, turn all burners to the directed heat setting. (See page 255.)

TWO-LEVEL FIRE: This fire has two cooking zones: a hotter area for searing and a slightly cooler area to cook food more gently. We use it for thick chops and bone-in chicken pieces. For a charcoal grill, evenly distribute two-thirds of the lit coals over half of the grill, then distribute the remaining coals in an even layer over the other half of the grill. For a gas grill, leave the primary burner on high and turn the other burner(s) to medium. (See page 252.)

HALF-GRILL FIRE: Like a two-level fire, this fire has two cooking zones, but the difference in temperature is more dramatic. This setup is best for foods that require longer cooking times. For a charcoal grill, distribute the lit coals in an even layer over half of the grill only. For a gas grill, turn the primary burner to the directed heat setting and turn off the other burner(s). (See page 250.)

hotter side of grill. Tent chicken loosely with aluminum foil, cover grill, and cook until chicken is browned and registers 140 degrees, 20 to 25 minutes.

4. Discard foil. Using tongs, lightly dredge skin side of breasts in reserved spice rub. Return chicken, skin side up, to cooler side of grill with thicker ends of breasts facing hotter side of grill. Cover grill and cook until rub has melted into glaze and chicken registers 160 degrees, about 15 minutes. Transfer chicken to serving platter and let rest for 5 to 10 minutes. Serve.

Building a Half-Grill Fire

This method creates a fire with a hot zone to allow searing over the coals and a cooler zone for cooking lean and easily overcooked meats. Foods placed over the empty part of the grill will still cook, but the heat is very gentle and little browning will occur here.

Pile all lit coals into half of grill to create hot place for searing, but leave remaining portion of grill empty.

NOTES FROM THE TEST KITCHEN

How to Light a Grill

LIGHTING A CHARCOAL FIRE WITH A CHIMNEY STARTER: Our favorite way to start a charcoal fire is with a chimney starter, also known as a flue starter. Simply fill the bottom section with crumpled newspaper, set the starter on the grill grate, and fill the top with charcoal. (A large starter holds about 6 quarts of charcoal.) When you light the newspaper, flames will shoot up through the charcoal, igniting it. Match-light charcoal has been soaked in lighter fluid and we find that it imparts an off-flavor to foods. Plain charcoal briquettes are a much better option.

LIGHTING A CHARCOAL FIRE WITHOUT A CHIMNEY STARTER: If you don't have a chimney starter, place eight crumpled sheets of newspaper below the rack on which the charcoal sits. With the bottom air vent open, pile the charcoal on the rack and light the paper. After about 20 minutes, the coals should be covered with fine gray ash and ready for cooking. Arrange lit coals as directed.

LIGHTING A GAS GRILL: Gas grills are simpler to use than charcoal grills, but there are a few important points to keep in mind before you get going. First and foremost, read all the instructions in your owner's manual thoroughly and follow the directions regarding the order in which the burners must be lit. On most grills, an electric igniter lights the burners, though we have found that electric igniters can fail occasionally, especially in windy conditions. For these situations, most models have a hole for lighting the burners with a match. Be sure to wait several minutes (or as directed) between attempts at lighting the grill. This waiting time allows excess gas to dissipate and is an important safety measure.

Grilled Indian-Spiced Chicken with Raita

SERVES 2

✓ **WHY THIS RECIPE WORKS:** Inspired by tandoori chicken, yogurt-marinated chicken cooked in an Indian tandoor oven, this dish packs in surprising flavor from a short ingredient list. As with authentic tandoori recipes, we marinated the chicken in yogurt. For the spice rub, curry powder alone tasted harsh and one-dimensional. Garam masala added complexity, but the raw taste remained. Adding the spices to the yogurt marinade solved the problem—the yogurt kept the chicken moist and tender, plus it helped to bloom, or deepen, the flavor of the spices once they hit the grill. To prevent the yogurt marinade from burning, we built a half-grill fire and started the chicken on the cooler side of the grill, then finished it on the hotter side so it would get an authentic char. More yogurt, flavored with garlic and cilantro, provided a cool, creamy counterpoint to the grilled meat. Low-fat yogurt can be substituted for the whole-milk yogurt; however, the sauce will taste a bit lean. Do not substitute nonfat yogurt.

⅔ cup plain whole-milk yogurt
1½ teaspoons curry powder
1½ teaspoons garam masala
   Salt and pepper
2 (12-ounce) bone-in split chicken breasts, trimmed
1 tablespoon minced fresh cilantro
1 small garlic clove, minced

1. Combine ⅓ cup yogurt, curry powder, garam masala, ½ teaspoon salt, and pinch pepper in 1-gallon zipper-lock bag. Add chicken to bag, seal bag tightly, and toss to coat. Let chicken marinate in refrigerator for at least 1 hour or up to 6 hours. Combine cilantro, garlic, and remaining ⅓ cup yogurt in bowl and season with salt and pepper to taste; cover and refrigerate.

2A. FOR A CHARCOAL GRILL: Open bottom vent completely. Light large chimney starter three-quarters filled with charcoal briquettes (4½ quarts). When top coals are partially covered with ash, pour evenly over half of grill. Set cooking grate in place, cover, and open lid vent completely. Heat grill until hot, about 5 minutes.

2B. FOR A GAS GRILL: Turn all burners to high, cover, and heat grill until hot, about 15 minutes. Turn primary burner to medium-high and turn off other burner(s). (Adjust primary burner as needed to maintain grill temperature around 350 degrees.)

3. Clean and oil cooking grate. Remove chicken from marinade and place, skin side down, on cooler side of grill with thicker ends of breasts facing hotter side of grill. Tent chicken loosely with aluminum foil, cover grill, and cook until chicken is browned and registers 150 degrees, 25 to 35 minutes.

4. Discard foil and slide chicken to hotter side of grill. Cook (covered if using gas), turning as needed, until chicken is lightly charred, skin is crisp, and chicken registers 160 degrees, 5 to 10 minutes. Transfer chicken to serving platter and let rest for 5 to 10 minutes. Serve with cilantro-yogurt sauce.

Grilled Jerk Chicken Breasts

SERVES 2

✔ **WHY THIS RECIPE WORKS:** Native to Jamaica, smoky, spicy "jerk" chicken is made by seasoning chicken with herbs and spices and cooking it over pimento wood for a distinctive smoky flavor. We wanted to bring the jerk flavors—hot chiles, warm spices, and charred meat—into our own backyard. Thyme and allspice mimicked the unique smoke of Jamaican pimento wood. We mixed the spices with fresh habanero, scallions, garlic, and molasses to make a potent paste, then rubbed the paste under and over the skin and let the chicken rest to fully absorb the flavors. A half-grill fire allowed us to cook the chicken through gently then char it over the hotter side. This dish is very spicy; to make it less spicy, remove the habanero seeds and ribs before processing. Be careful when handling the habanero as its oils can cause your skin to burn; be sure to use latex gloves when handling the pureed mixture in step 1. If you cannot find a habanero, substitute two jalapeño chiles. See page 250 for information on how to set up a half-grill fire.

    4   scallions, chopped
    2   tablespoons vegetable oil
    1   tablespoon light or mild molasses
    1   habanero chile, stemmed
    2   garlic cloves, peeled
    1½ teaspoons dried thyme
    1   teaspoon ground allspice
        Salt
    2   (12-ounce) bone-in split chicken breasts, trimmed
        Lime wedges

1. Process scallions, oil, molasses, habanero, garlic, thyme, allspice, and 1 teaspoon salt together in food processor (or blender) until almost smooth, about 15 seconds. Use your fingers to gently loosen center portion of skin covering each breast. Wearing latex gloves, rub 1 tablespoon marinade

NOTES FROM THE TEST KITCHEN

Essential Equipment for the Grill

Outdoor cooking requires some specialized equipment, starting with the grill. If you are using a charcoal grill, it's also helpful to keep a water-filled spray bottle handy to squelch any flare-ups from fat dripping on the coals (if using a gas grill, check the drip pan and empty excess fat regularly).

CHARCOAL GRILL

The test kitchen's charcoal grill standard is the 22-inch kettle grill. Some grills also have features that make them easier to use. A generous cooking surface is always best, a deep lid can cover large foods like a whole turkey, a built-in thermometer is a handy tool, and a side table is the ultimate convenience.

CHARCOAL

For consistently great results, we prefer regular charcoal briquettes to hardwood charcoal (aka lump charcoal), which burns too quickly. We avoid using instant-lighting briquettes because we find that they have a slightly off-odor as they burn and because we prefer to use a less-processed product.

CHIMNEY STARTER

For igniting charcoal briquettes, nothing is safer or more effective than a chimney starter (aka flue starter). We prefer large chimney starters—ones that can hold at least 6 quarts of briquettes. See page 250 for instructions on lighting a grill with a chimney starter.

GAS GRILL

A gas grill is convenient and easy to use. When choosing a grill, even heat distribution and good fat drainage are two important factors. We also like our gas grills to have a generous cooking surface area—at least 350 square inches—and three independently operating burners.

GRILL BRUSH

Nothing works better than a good grill brush for getting burnt-on gunk off a cooking grate. Most feature stiff metal bristles, but sticky goo can quickly get stuck in the bristles. We prefer grill brushes with replaceable scouring pads as the scrubbers. Make sure that the brush has a long, preferably wooden, handle to keep your hands a safe distance from the fire.

TONGS

Tongs are the most useful tool for turning anything from slender asparagus spears to racks of ribs. But tongs made especially for grilling are cumbersome to use, particularly for smaller items. We prefer a pair of 16-inch kitchen tongs, which keep your hands a safe distance from the fire and afford you ample dexterity.

BARBECUE MITT

A good grilling mitt is invaluable. It should meet two basic requirements: enough heat resistance to keep hands from burning and enough pliability to keep you from inadvertently dropping grates or smashing food.

BASTING BRUSH

Look for a basting brush with a long handle made from a heat-resistant material that is dishwasher-safe. An angled brush head facilitates basting. We prefer silicone brush bristles, which won't melt or singe, to nylon or boar bristles.

underneath skin of each breast. Combine chicken and remaining marinade in 1-gallon zipper-lock bag, seal bag tightly, and toss to coat. Let chicken marinate in refrigerator for at least 2 hours or up to 24 hours.

2A. FOR A CHARCOAL GRILL: Open bottom vent completely. Light large chimney starter three-quarters filled with charcoal briquettes (4½ quarts). When top coals are partially covered with ash, pour evenly over half of grill. Set cooking grate in place, cover, and open lid vent completely. Heat grill until hot, about 5 minutes.

2B. FOR A GAS GRILL: Turn all burners to high, cover, and heat grill until hot, about 15 minutes. Turn primary burner to medium-high and turn off other burner(s). (Adjust primary burner as needed to maintain grill temperature around 350 degrees.)

3. Clean and oil cooking grate. Remove chicken from marinade and place, skin-side down, on cooler side of grill with thicker ends of breasts facing hotter side of grill. Tent chicken loosely with aluminum foil, cover grill, and cook until chicken is browned and registers 150 degrees, 25 to 35 minutes.

4. Discard foil and slide chicken to hotter side of grill. Cook (covered if using gas), turning as needed, until chicken is lightly charred, skin is crisp, and chicken registers 160 degrees, 5 to 10 minutes. Transfer chicken to serving platter and let rest for 5 to 10 minutes. Serve with lime wedges.

Grilled Turkey Burgers

SERVES 2   `FAST`

✔ **WHY THIS RECIPE WORKS:** A lean, fully cooked turkey burger simply seasoned with salt and pepper is a dry, tasteless stand-in for an all-beef burger. Add the dry heat of the grill to the equation and things only get worse. We wanted a turkey burger that grilled up juicy and full of flavor—one that would rival a beef burger. We started with easy ground turkey and found that mixing in moist, rich ricotta cheese greatly improved the texture and flavor of the meat. A little Worcestershire sauce and Dijon mustard seasoned the burgers nicely. The burgers cooked up quickly on the hot grill and stayed tender and juicy thanks to the ricotta and seasonings. Be sure to use ground turkey, not ground turkey breast (also labeled 99 percent fat free), in this recipe. We prefer the richer flavor and softer texture of whole-milk ricotta here, but part-skim or fat-free will also work. Serve with your favorite burger toppings.

12 ounces ground turkey
2 ounces (¼ cup) whole-milk ricotta cheese
1 teaspoon Worcestershire sauce
1 teaspoon Dijon mustard
¼ teaspoon salt
¼ teaspoon pepper
2 hamburger buns

1. Break turkey into small pieces in bowl. Add ricotta, Worcestershire, mustard, salt, and pepper and gently knead until well incorporated. Divide meat mixture into 2 lightly packed balls, gently flatten each ball into 1-inch-thick patty, and press shallow divot in center of each patty. Transfer to plate, cover with plastic wrap, and refrigerate until grill is ready.

2A. FOR A CHARCOAL GRILL: Open bottom vent completely. Light large chimney starter filled with charcoal briquettes (6 quarts). When top coals are partially covered with ash, pour two-thirds evenly over half of grill, then pour remaining coals over other half of grill. Set cooking grate in place, cover, and open lid vent completely. Heat grill until hot, about 5 minutes.

2B. FOR A GAS GRILL: Turn all burners to high, cover, and heat grill until hot, about 15 minutes. Leave primary burner on high and turn other burner(s) to medium. (Adjust burners as needed to maintain hot fire and medium fire on separate sides of grill.)

3. Clean and oil cooking grate. Place burgers on hotter side of grill and cook (covered if using gas) until well browned on both sides, 5 to 7 minutes, flipping burgers halfway through cooking.

4. Slide burgers to cooler side of grill. Cover grill and cook, turning as needed, until burgers register 160 degrees, 5 to 7 minutes. Transfer burgers to serving platter, tent loosely with aluminum foil, and let rest for 5 minutes. Serve on buns.

VARIATION
Grilled Southwestern Turkey Burgers
In step 1, omit Worcestershire sauce and add 1 minced garlic clove, 1 teaspoon minced chipotle chile, and ½ teaspoon cumin.

Building a Two-Level Fire

This kind of fire permits searing over very hot coals and slower cooking over moderate coals to cook through thicker cuts.

Spread two-thirds of coals evenly over half of grill, then pour remaining third of coals over other half of grill.

Grilled Steak Burgers

SERVES 2

☑ **WHY THIS RECIPE WORKS:** Burgers often come off the grill tough, dry, and bulging in the middle. We wanted a moist and juicy burger with a texture that was tender and cohesive, not dense and heavy. Just as important, we wanted a flavorful, deeply caramelized crust and a nice flat surface capable of holding as many condiments as we could pile on. For robustly flavored meat, we opted for ultrabeefy ground sirloin. Because sirloin is about 90 percent lean (unlike ground chuck, which is 80 percent lean), we kneaded in some melted butter to ensure our patties stayed tender and juicy. We formed the meat into thick patties and indented the center of each patty to ensure they wouldn't puff up on the grill. For a rich, flavorful steak sauce to top our juicy burgers, we simmered more butter with tomato paste, beef broth, raisins, mustard, balsamic vinegar, and Worcestershire sauce. See page 255 for information on how to set up a single-level fire. We prefer these burgers cooked to medium-rare, but if you prefer them more or less done, see our guidelines on page 155. Serve with your favorite burger toppings.

Ultrabeefy ground sirloin enriched with melted butter gives us exceptionally tender, juicy, and meaty beef burgers.

4	tablespoons unsalted butter
1	garlic clove, minced
	Salt and pepper
1	tablespoon tomato paste
⅓	cup beef broth
3	tablespoons raisins
1	tablespoon Dijon mustard
1	tablespoon balsamic vinegar
1½	teaspoons Worcestershire sauce
12	ounces 90 percent lean ground sirloin
2	hamburger buns

1. Melt butter in 8-inch skillet over medium-low heat. Add garlic, ½ teaspoon salt, and ½ teaspoon pepper and cook until fragrant, about 1 minute. Pour all but 1 tablespoon butter mixture into bowl and let cool, about 5 minutes.

2. Meanwhile, add tomato paste to skillet with remaining butter mixture and cook over medium heat until paste begins to darken, 1 to 2 minutes. Stir in broth, raisins, mustard, vinegar, and Worcestershire and simmer until raisins plump, about 5 minutes. Transfer sauce to blender and process until smooth, about 30 seconds; transfer to bowl.

3. Combine 2 tablespoons cooled butter mixture with ground sirloin and gently knead until well incorporated. Divide meat mixture into 2 lightly packed balls, gently flatten each ball into ¾-inch-thick patty, and press shallow divot in center of each patty; transfer to plate. Measure out 1 tablespoon sauce and brush onto both sides of patties; cover burgers and refrigerate until grill is ready. Combine remaining 1 tablespoon butter mixture with 2 tablespoons sauce and brush onto cut sides of buns.

4A. FOR A CHARCOAL GRILL: Open bottom vent completely. Light large chimney starter filled with charcoal briquettes (6 quarts). When top coals are partially covered with ash, pour evenly over grill. Set cooking grate in place, cover, and open lid vent completely. Heat grill until hot, about 5 minutes.

4B. FOR A GAS GRILL: Turn all burners to high, cover, and heat grill until hot, about 15 minutes.

5. Clean and oil cooking grate. Place burgers on grill and cook (covered if using gas) until they register 120 to 125 degrees (for medium-rare), 6 to 8 minutes, flipping burgers halfway through cooking. Transfer burgers to plate, tent loosely with aluminum foil, and let rest for 5 to 10 minutes.

6. While burgers rest, cook buns until warm and lightly charred, about 30 seconds. Serve burgers on buns with remaining sauce.

Grilled Beef and Vegetable Kebabs with Lemon-Rosemary Marinade

SERVES 2

✔ **WHY THIS RECIPE WORKS:** Most beef kebabs are disappointing, with chewy meat and vegetables that are either raw or mushy. We wanted a foolproof approach to getting chunks of marinated beef with caramelized char on the outside and a juicy interior paired with nicely browned vegetables. We chose well-marbled steak tips for their beefy flavor and tender texture. For the marinade, we included salt for moisture, oil for flavor, and sugar for browning. For even more depth, we used tomato paste, lemon zest, rosemary, and beef broth. Grilling over a two-level fire with hotter and cooler areas allowed us to cook the vegetables gently while the beef seared over the hotter area. Steak tips, also known as flap meat, are sold as whole steak, cubes, and strips. To ensure evenly sized pieces, we prefer to purchase whole steak tips and cut them ourselves. However, if you have long, thin pieces of meat, roll or fold them into approximately 2-inch cubes before skewering. You will need three 12-inch metal skewers for this recipe.

MARINADE
- 1 small onion, chopped coarse
- 3 tablespoons beef broth
- 3 tablespoons vegetable oil
- 1½ tablespoons tomato paste
- 3 garlic cloves, chopped
- 2 teaspoons minced fresh rosemary
- 1½ teaspoons grated lemon zest
- 1 teaspoon salt
- ¾ teaspoon sugar
- ½ teaspoon pepper

BEEF AND VEGETABLES
- 12 ounces sirloin steak tips, trimmed and cut into 2-inch pieces
- 1 zucchini or summer squash, halved lengthwise and sliced 1 inch thick
- 1 red or green bell pepper, stemmed, seeded, and cut into 1½-inch pieces
- 1 small red onion, quartered through root end, each quarter cut into 1-inch pieces

1. FOR THE MARINADE: Process all ingredients together in blender until smooth, about 45 seconds. Transfer ½ cup marinade to medium bowl; set aside.

2. FOR THE BEEF AND VEGETABLES: Pat steak tips dry with paper towels and prick on all sides with fork. Combine remaining marinade and beef in 1-gallon zipper-lock bag, seal

A bold marinade of lemon, rosemary, garlic and onion gives these simple beef and vegetable kebabs lots of bright flavor.

bag tightly, and toss to coat. Let meat marinate in refrigerator for at least 1 hour or up to 2 hours. Meanwhile, toss zucchini, bell pepper, and onion with reserved marinade, cover, and let sit at room temperature for 30 minutes.

3. Remove beef from marinade and pat dry with paper towels. Thread beef tightly onto one 12-inch metal skewer. Thread vegetables onto two 12-inch metal skewers in alternating pattern of zucchini, pepper, and onion.

4A. FOR A CHARCOAL GRILL: Open bottom vent completely. Light large chimney starter mounded with charcoal briquettes (7 quarts). When top coals are partially covered with ash, pour evenly over center of grill, leaving 2-inch gap

Ensuring Evenly Cooked Meat for Kebabs

It can be hard to find thick, even pieces of beef for kebabs that will cook through evenly. To ensure that thinner pieces cook at same rate as larger chunks, slice tapered beef into 2-inch by 4-inch pieces and roll or fold to create thicker pieces for skewer.

between entire grill wall and charcoal. Set cooking grate in place, cover, and open lid vent completely. Heat grill until hot, about 5 minutes.

4B. FOR A GAS GRILL: Turn all burners to high, cover, and heat grill until hot, about 15 minutes. Leave primary burner on high and turn other burner(s) to medium-low.

5. Clean and oil cooking grate. Place meat skewer on hotter part of grill and vegetable skewers on cooler part of grill (near edge of coals if using charcoal). Cook (covered if using gas), turning skewers every 3 to 4 minutes, until beef is well browned and vegetables are tender and lightly charred, 17 to 21 minutes. Transfer skewers to serving platter, tent loosely with aluminum foil, and let rest for 5 to 10 minutes. Serve.

VARIATIONS
Grilled Beef and Vegetable Kebabs with North African Marinade

Omit lemon zest and rosemary from marinade and add 10 cilantro sprigs, 1 teaspoon paprika, ¾ teaspoon ground cumin, and ¼ teaspoon cayenne pepper.

Grilled Beef and Vegetable Kebabs with Red Curry Marinade

Omit lemon zest and rosemary from marinade and add ¼ cup fresh basil leaves, 1½ tablespoons red curry paste, 1½ teaspoons grated lime zest, and 1 teaspoon grated ginger.

Grilled Steakhouse Steak Tips

SERVES 2

✓ **WHY THIS RECIPE WORKS:** Grilled steak tips are a steakhouse favorite for a reason: The tender cut of beef takes well to potent marinades and easily picks up flavorful char. Plus, steak tips are a perfect cut for serving two. We wanted steak tips with deep flavor and tender texture. For the meat, we chose sirloin steak tips, also known as flap meat, an affordable cut that stayed tender and moist during a brief stint on the grill. To further tenderize and season the meat, we used a soy sauce–based marinade flavored with garlic, paprika, cayenne, and tomato paste. Letting the steak tips rest for five to 10 minutes after grilling helped to ensure juicy meat. Steak tips, also known as flap meat, are sold as whole steak, cubes, and strips. To ensure evenly sized pieces, we prefer to purchase whole steak tips and cut them ourselves. We also prefer these steak tips cooked to medium, but if you prefer them more or less done, see our guidelines on page 155.

3   **tablespoons soy sauce**
3   **tablespoons vegetable oil**
1½ **tablespoons packed dark brown sugar**
3   **garlic cloves, minced**
1½ **teaspoons tomato paste**
1½ **teaspoons paprika**
¼   **teaspoon pepper**
⅛   **teaspoon cayenne pepper**
12 **ounces sirloin steak tips, trimmed and cut into 2½-inch pieces**

1. Whisk soy sauce, oil, sugar, garlic, tomato paste, paprika, pepper, and cayenne together in bowl until sugar dissolves. Pat steak tips dry with paper towels and prick on all sides with fork. Combine marinade and steak in 1-gallon zipper-lock bag, seal bag tightly, and toss to coat. Let meat marinate in refrigerator for at least 2 hours or up to 24 hours.

2A. FOR A CHARCOAL GRILL: Open bottom vent completely. Light large chimney starter filled with charcoal briquettes (6 quarts). When top coals are partially covered with ash, pour evenly over grill. Set cooking grate in place, cover, and open lid vent completely. Heat grill until hot, about 5 minutes.

2B. FOR A GAS GRILL: Turn all burners to high, cover, and heat grill until hot, about 15 minutes.

3. Clean and oil cooking grate. Remove meat from marinade and place on grill. Cook (covered if using gas), turning as needed, until beef is charred on both sides and registers 130 to 135 degrees (for medium), 8 to 10 minutes. Transfer to serving platter, tent loosely with aluminum foil, and let rest for 5 to 10 minutes. Serve.

Building a Single-Level Fire

This kind of fire delivers even heat and is best for quick searing at a moderate temperature.

Arrange lit charcoal in even layer in bottom of grill.

Grilled Cowboy Steaks

SERVES 2 **FAST**

✔ **WHY THIS RECIPE WORKS:** The big, beefy flavor of strip steaks holds up well to spice rubs. To that end, we set out to develop a recipe for grilled strip steak imbued with a smoky, spicy Southwestern-flavored rub. We rubbed the steaks evenly with an assertive mixture of chili powder, paprika, brown sugar, and garlic and threw them on a blazing hot grill to sear. Placing a packet of soaked wood chips directly on the coals gave the steaks a subtle smokiness. Resting the steaks before serving was key—if sliced into right off the grill, the meat would lose its flavorful juices and be dry. Although we prefer hickory wood chips, any variety of chip except mesquite will work. See page 255 for information on how to set up a single-level fire. We prefer these steaks cooked to medium-rare, but if you prefer them more or less done, see our guidelines on page 155.

    ¼   cup wood chips, soaked in water for 15 minutes and
         drained
    1   tablespoon paprika
    1½   teaspoons packed light brown sugar
    1½   teaspoons chili powder
    ½   teaspoon granulated garlic
    ¼   teaspoon salt
    ¼   teaspoon pepper
    ⅛   teaspoon cayenne pepper
    2   (8-ounce) boneless strip steaks, ¾ inch thick,
         trimmed
    1   tablespoon vegetable oil

1. Using piece of heavy-duty aluminum foil, wrap soaked chips in foil packet and cut several vent holes in top. Combine paprika, sugar, chili powder, garlic, salt, pepper, and cayenne in bowl. Pat steaks dry with paper towels, brush both sides with oil, and rub spice mixture evenly over both sides.

2A. FOR A CHARCOAL GRILL: Open bottom vent halfway. Light large chimney starter filled with charcoal briquettes (6 quarts). When top coals are partially covered with ash, pour

Making a Foil Packet for Wood Chips

After soaking wood chips in water for 15 minutes, spread drained chips in center of 15 by 12-inch piece of heavy-duty aluminum foil. Fold to seal edges, then cut several slits to allow smoke to escape.

evenly over grill. Place wood chip packet on coals. Set cooking grate in place, cover, and open lid vent halfway. Heat grill until hot and wood chips are smoking, about 5 minutes.

2B. FOR A GAS GRILL: Remove cooking grate and place wood chip packet directly on primary burner. Set grate in place, turn all burners to high, cover, and heat grill until hot and wood chips are smoking, about 15 minutes.

3. Clean and oil cooking grate. Place steaks on grill and cook (covered if using gas), turning as needed, until well browned and meat registers 120 to 125 degrees (for medium-rare), 6 to 8 minutes. Transfer steaks to cutting board, tent loosely with foil, and let rest for 5 to 10 minutes. Serve.

Grilled Flank Steak with Chimichurri Sauce

SERVES 2

✔ **WHY THIS RECIPE WORKS:** Traditionally Argentine steaks are thick-cut and slow-smoked to give them a nice char and smoky flavor, but we wanted to speed things up. We chose quick-cooking flank steak for its beefy flavor and moist meat. Then, to give our steaks that authentic wood-smoked flavor, we rubbed them with smoked paprika, sugar, salt, and pepper. Carefully patting them dry ensured they took on lots of char over the hot fire. But when we added the spice rub directly to the dry steaks, it was dusty and raw-tasting. An easy fix was to brush the steaks with oil before adding the spice rub, allowing the flavors of the rub to bloom and deepen as the steaks cooked. Finally we whipped up the traditional chimichurri sauce, made with parsley, cilantro, oregano, garlic, red wine vinegar, salt, and pepper and emulsified with extra-virgin olive oil. See page 255 for information on how to set up a single-level fire. We prefer this steak cooked to medium-rare, but if you prefer it more or less done, see our guidelines on page 155.

    1   teaspoon hot water
    ¼   teaspoon dried oregano
    3   tablespoons extra-virgin olive oil
    3   tablespoons minced fresh parsley
    2   tablespoons minced fresh cilantro
    1   tablespoon red wine vinegar
    1   small garlic clove, minced
         Salt and pepper
         Sugar
    1   (1-pound) flank steak, trimmed
    1   tablespoon smoked paprika

A spice rub of sugar and paprika gives our flank steak the char and smoky flavor of authentic Argentinean-style grilled steak.

Grilled Marinated Skirt Steak
SERVES 2

✔ **WHY THIS RECIPE WORKS:** Intensely beefy skirt steak is a popular cut because its shaggy grain makes it ideal for soaking up a flavorful marinade. But while a marinade might add flavor, it usually causes the meat to steam on the grill. To achieve a charred crust, we seasoned our steak with salt, pepper, and sugar before grilling and didn't marinate it until after it came off the grate. And since the marinade never touched raw meat, we also could serve it as a sauce on the side. Keep the marinade at room temperature or it will cool down the steak. See page 250 for information on how to set up a half-grill fire. We prefer this steak cooked to medium-rare, but if you prefer it more or less done, see our guidelines on page 155.

¼ cup soy sauce
2 tablespoons Worcestershire sauce
4 teaspoons sugar
1 scallion, sliced thin
2 garlic cloves, minced
1½ teaspoons Dijon mustard
1 teaspoon balsamic vinegar
Salt and pepper
2 tablespoons olive oil
1 (12-ounce) skirt steak, cut crosswise into 4-inch pieces and trimmed

1. Combine hot water and oregano in small bowl and let sit for 5 minutes. Whisk in 2 tablespoons oil, parsley, cilantro, vinegar, garlic, ¼ teaspoon salt, pinch pepper, and pinch sugar; set aside for serving. Pat steak dry with paper towels, then brush with remaining 1 tablespoon oil. Combine paprika, ¼ teaspoon salt, ⅛ teaspoon pepper, and ⅛ teaspoon sugar in bowl, then rub evenly over steak.

2A. FOR A CHARCOAL GRILL: Open bottom vent completely. Light large chimney starter filled with charcoal briquettes (6 quarts). When top coals are partially covered with ash, pour evenly over grill. Set cooking grate in place, cover, and open lid vent completely. Heat grill until hot, about 5 minutes.

2B. FOR A GAS GRILL: Turn all burners to high, cover, and heat grill until hot, about 15 minutes. Leave all burners on high.

3. Clean and oil cooking grate. Place steak on grill. Cook (covered if using gas), turning as needed, until steak is lightly charred on both sides and registers 120 to 125 degrees (for medium-rare), 6 to 8 minutes. Transfer to cutting board, tent loosely with aluminum foil, and let rest for 5 to 10 minutes. Slice steak thin against grain. Serve with sauce.

1. Combine soy sauce, Worcestershire, 1 tablespoon sugar, scallion, garlic, mustard, vinegar, and ¾ teaspoon pepper in bowl. Slowly whisk in oil until incorporated and sugar has dissolved. Pat steak dry with paper towels and season with ¼ teaspoon salt, ¼ teaspoon pepper, and remaining 1 teaspoon sugar.

2A. FOR A CHARCOAL GRILL: Open bottom vent completely. Light large chimney starter mounded with charcoal briquettes (7 quarts). When top coals are partially covered with ash, pour evenly over half of grill. Set cooking grate in place, cover, and open lid vent completely. Heat grill until hot, about 5 minutes.

2B. FOR A GAS GRILL: Turn all burners to high, cover, and heat grill until hot, about 15 minutes.

3. Clean and oil cooking grate. Place steak on grill (directly over coals if using charcoal). Cook (covered if using gas) until well browned and meat registers 120 to 125 degrees (for medium-rare), 2 to 4 minutes per side.

4. Transfer steak to 8-inch square baking pan and poke all over with fork. Pour marinade over steak, tent with aluminum foil, and let rest for 5 to 10 minutes. Transfer steak to cutting board and slice thin against grain. Pour marinade into serving vessel and serve with steak.

Grilled Tuscan Steak with Olive Oil and Lemon

SERVES 2

✔ **WHY THIS RECIPE WORKS:** Grilled Tuscan-style steaks can be raw on the inside even when the outer crust is perfectly seared, and often the flavor of the olive oil and lemon juice just doesn't come through. We wanted perfectly grilled steak accented by olive oil to complement the flavor of the meat and lemon juice to sharpen the flavors of the dish and balance its richness. For our version, we built a half-grill fire and seared the steaks on the hotter side, then moved them to the cooler side of the grill to finish cooking. To bring out the full, fresh flavor of the olive oil and lemon juice, we drizzled them over the steak after cooking rather than before, as many recipes recommend. Be sure to buy steaks that are at least 1 inch thick. See page 250 for information on how to set up a half-grill fire. We prefer this steak cooked to medium-rare, but if you prefer it more or less done, see our guidelines on page 155.

- 1 (1¾-pound) porterhouse or T-bone steak, 1 to 1½ inches thick, trimmed
  Salt and pepper
- 1 garlic clove, cut in half
- 2 tablespoons extra-virgin olive oil
  Lemon wedges

1. Pat steak dry with paper towels, season with salt and pepper, and rub cut sides of garlic clove over bone and meat.

2A. FOR A CHARCOAL GRILL: Open bottom vent completely. Light large chimney starter three-quarters filled with charcoal briquettes (4½ quarts). When top coals are partially covered with ash, pour evenly over half of grill. Set cooking grate in place, cover, and open lid vent completely. Heat grill until hot, about 5 minutes.

2B. FOR A GAS GRILL: Turn all burners to high, cover, and heat grill until hot, about 15 minutes. Leave primary burner on high and turn other burner(s) to low.

3. Clean and oil cooking grate. Place steak on hotter part of grill with tenderloin sides (smaller side of T-bone) facing cooler part of grill. Cook (covered if using gas) until dark crust forms, 6 to 8 minutes. Flip steak and turn so that tenderloin side is facing cooler side of grill. Continue to cook (covered if using gas) until dark brown crust forms on second side, 6 to 8 minutes.

4. Slide steak to cooler side of grill with bone side facing hotter side of grill. Cover grill and continue to cook until meat registers 120 to 125 degrees (for medium-rare), 2 to 4 minutes longer, flipping halfway through cooking.

5. Transfer steak to cutting board, tent loosely with aluminum foil, and let rest for 5 to 10 minutes. Cut strip and tenderloin pieces off bone, then cut each piece crosswise into ¼-inch-thick slices. Transfer to serving platter and drizzle with oil. Serve with lemon wedges.

Carving Porterhouse and T-Bone Steaks

1. After meat has rested, cut along bone to remove large top loin, or strip, section.

2. Cut smaller tenderloin section off bone. Cut each large piece crosswise into ¼-inch-thick slices for serving.

Grilled Glazed Pork Chops

SERVES 2

✔ **WHY THIS RECIPE WORKS:** Quick-cooking pork chops are great for two, but because they're relatively lean, they can easily overcook and turn dry. For chops with deeply browned crusts and tender, juicy meat all the way to the bone, we started with well-marbled bone-in, thick-cut rib chops. As with chicken breasts, we found that a two-level fire allowed us to sear the chops then finish cooking them gently over the cooler side of the grill. To flavor the chops, we made a sweet and tangy maple and mustard glaze. We brushed the seared chops with the glaze and tented them with foil on the cooler side of the grill. Just 10 minutes later, they had a crisp crust and tender, juicy meat. If the pork is enhanced (injected with a salt solution), do not brine. If brining the pork, do not season with salt in step 2. See page 252 for information on how to set up a two-level fire.

- 2 tablespoons maple syrup
- 2 tablespoons Dijon mustard
- 2 tablespoons whole-grain mustard
- 2 tablespoons extra-virgin olive oil
  Pinch cayenne pepper
  Salt and pepper
- 2 (12- to 14-ounce) bone-in pork rib or center-cut chops, about 1½ inches thick, trimmed and brined if desired (see page 150)

1. Whisk maple syrup, Dijon mustard, whole-grain mustard, oil, cayenne, pinch salt, and pinch pepper together in bowl. Transfer ¼ cup glaze to separate bowl; set aside for serving.

2. Cut 2 slits about 2 inches apart through outer layer of fat and silverskin on each chop. Pat chops dry with paper towels and season with salt and pepper.

3A. FOR A CHARCOAL GRILL: Open bottom vent completely. Light large chimney starter filled with charcoal briquettes (6 quarts). When top coals are partially covered with ash, pour two-thirds evenly over half of grill, then pour remaining coals over other half of grill. Set cooking grate in place, cover, and open lid vent completely. Heat grill until hot, about 5 minutes.

3B. FOR A GAS GRILL: Turn all burners to high, cover, and heat grill until hot, about 15 minutes. Leave primary burner on high and turn other burner(s) to medium. (Adjust burners as needed to maintain hot fire and medium fire on separate sides of grill.)

4. Clean and oil cooking grate. Place chops on hotter side of grill. Cook (covered if using gas), turning as needed, until well browned on both sides, 6 to 10 minutes. Slide chops to cooler side of grill and brush with glaze. Tent loosely with aluminum foil, cover grill, and cook until chops register 145 degrees, 7 to 9 minutes, flipping and brushing them with glaze halfway through cooking.

5. Transfer chops to serving platter, tent loosely with foil, and let rest for 5 to 10 minutes. Serve with reserved glaze.

Grill-Smoked Pork Chops

SERVES 2 LIGHT

✔ **WHY THIS RECIPE WORKS:** For great grill-smoked pork chops with rosy, ultramoist meat and smoke flavor throughout, we built a half-grill fire and started the chops on the cooler side of the grill. Then we brushed on a few coats of sauce and seared the glazed chops over the hotter side to give them a beautiful crust. Bone-in chops worked best; the bones lent flavor and suppleness to the meat, and we used this cut to our advantage by cooking each chop upright on its bone instead of laying it flat. To keep the chops from toppling over, we speared them together with skewers, leaving space between them to allow smoke to circulate. If the pork is enhanced (injected with a salt solution), do not brine. If brining the pork, do not season with salt in step 2. Use the large holes of a box grater to grate the onion for the sauce. You will need two 12-inch metal skewers for this recipe. If desired, a disposable aluminum roasting pan can be placed under the grate on a charcoal grill to catch the pork drippings. See page 250 for information on how to set up a half-grill fire. For the nutritional information for this recipe, see page 415.

For great grill-smoked pork chops, we use low heat to gently infuse the chops with smoky flavor then brown them over high heat.

¼	cup ketchup
2	tablespoons light or mild molasses
1	tablespoon grated onion
1	tablespoon Worcestershire sauce
1	tablespoon Dijon mustard
1	tablespoon cider vinegar
1½	teaspoons packed brown sugar
	Salt and pepper
1	cup wood chips, soaked in water for 15 minutes and drained
2	(12- to 14-ounce) bone-in pork rib or center-cut chops, about 1½ inches thick, trimmed and brined if desired (see page 150)

1. Simmer ketchup, molasses, onion, Worcestershire, mustard, vinegar, and sugar in small saucepan over medium heat, stirring often, until sauce is thickened and measures ½ cup, 3 to 5 minutes. Season with salt and pepper to taste. Transfer ¼ cup glaze to bowl; set aside for serving. Using piece of heavy-duty aluminum foil, wrap soaked chips in foil packet and cut several vent holes in top.

2. Cut 2 slits, about 2 inches apart, through outer layer of fat and silverskin on each chop. Pat chops dry with paper towels and season with salt and pepper. Stand chops on their rib bones, side by side and facing in same direction. Pass two 12-inch metal skewers through loin muscle of each chop, close to bone, about 1 inch from each end. Once chops have been threaded onto skewers, pull them apart to create 2-inch space between them.

3A. FOR A CHARCOAL GRILL: Open bottom vent halfway. Light large chimney starter filled with charcoal briquettes (6 quarts). When top coals are partially covered with ash, pour evenly over half of grill. Place wood chip packet on coals. Set cooking grate in place, cover, and open lid vent halfway. Heat grill until hot and wood chips are smoking, about 5 minutes.

3B. FOR A GAS GRILL: Remove cooking grate and place wood chip packet directly on primary burner. Set grate in place, turn all burners to high, cover, and heat grill until hot and wood chips are smoking, about 15 minutes. Leave primary burner on high and turn off other burner(s). (Adjust burner as needed to maintain grill temperature around 350 degrees.)

4. Clean and oil cooking grate. Stand chops, bone side down, on cooler side of grill. Cover (positioning lid vent over chops if using charcoal) and cook until chops register 120 degrees, 20 to 25 minutes.

5. Carefully remove chops from skewers and brush one side with half of glaze. Grill, glazed side down, over hotter side of grill (covered if using gas) until browned, 3 to 6 minutes. Brush second side of chops with remaining sauce, flip, and cook until second side is browned and chops register 145 degrees, 3 to 6 minutes. Transfer chops to serving platter, tent loosely with foil, and let rest for 5 to 10 minutes. Serve with reserved glaze.

Grill-Smoking Pork Chops

1. To stand pork chops on grill, pass two skewers through loin muscle of each chop. Then pull chops apart to create space to allow smoke to circulate.

2. Stand skewered chops, bone side down, on cooking grate on cooler side of grill.

We rub juicy pork tenderloin with bright coriander and brown sugar then drizzle it with a parsley-rosemary oil before serving.

Grilled Coriander-Rubbed Pork Tenderloin with Herbs

SERVES 2

✔ **WHY THIS RECIPE WORKS:** Thanks to its compact size and shape, pork tenderloin is a good candidate for both the grill and dinner for two. But its leanness can make it a challenge to cook: Less fat translates to little flavor and meat that easily dries out. We needed a technique that would yield pork with a well-browned crust and a perfectly cooked interior. A half-grill fire was an easy solution. We browned the pork over the hotter side of the grill, then moved it to the cooler side to cook through gently. Tenting the pork with foil helped it to cook through more quickly. To flavor the lean pork, we rubbed it with bright, citrusy coriander, brown sugar, and salt before grilling, then drizzled it with a fresh herb oil before serving. If the pork is enhanced (injected with a salt solution), do not brine. If brining the pork, omit salt in rub in step 1. See page 250 for information on how to set up a half-grill fire.

3 tablespoons extra-virgin olive oil

1 tablespoon minced fresh parsley

½ teaspoon minced fresh rosemary

1 small garlic clove, minced

Salt and pepper

¾ teaspoon brown sugar

½ teaspoon ground coriander

1 (12-ounce) pork tenderloin, trimmed and brined if desired (see page 150)

1. Whisk 2 tablespoons oil, parsley, rosemary, garlic, ⅛ teaspoon salt, and ⅛ teaspoon pepper together in bowl; set aside for serving. In separate bowl, combine sugar, coriander, ½ teaspoon salt, and ¼ teaspoon pepper. Pat tenderloin dry with paper towels, rub with remaining 1 tablespoon oil, and coat with sugar mixture, pressing to help it adhere.

2A. FOR A CHARCOAL GRILL: Open bottom vent completely. Light large chimney starter filled with charcoal briquettes (6 quarts). When top coals are partially covered with ash, pour evenly over half of grill. Set cooking grate in place, cover, and open lid vent completely. Heat grill until hot, about 5 minutes.

2B. FOR A GAS GRILL: Turn all burners to high, cover, and heat grill until hot, about 15 minutes. Leave primary burner on high and turn off other burner(s).

3. Clean and oil cooking grate. Place pork on hotter side of grill. Cook (covered if using gas), turning as needed, until well browned on all sides, 10 to 12 minutes. Slide pork to cooler side of grill, tent loosely with aluminum foil, and cook until pork registers 145 degrees, 5 to 8 minutes.

4. Transfer pork to cutting board, tent loosely with foil, and let rest for 5 to 10 minutes. Slice pork into ¼-inch-thick slices and drizzle with herb-oil mixture. Serve.

Checking the Fuel Level in a Gas Tank

There's nothing worse than running out of fuel halfway through grilling. If your grill doesn't have a gas gauge, use this technique to estimate how much gas is left in the tank.

1. Bring about 1 cup of water to boil. Pour water over side of tank.

2. Where water has warmed metal, the tank is empty; where metal remains cool to touch, there is propane inside.

Juicy, well-browned lamb chops paired with a fresh zucchini and Parmesan salad make an elegant summer meal.

Grilled Lamb Chops with Shaved Zucchini Salad

SERVES 2 FAST

✓ **WHY THIS RECIPE WORKS:** Lamb doesn't need to be reserved for weekends or special occasions. Our quick-cooking lamb loin chops can be on the table in less than 30 minutes for an easy and delicious weeknight meal. Lamb loin chops are especially tender and tend to dry out if cooked past medium-rare, so we used a medium-hot fire and only cooked the chops for a few minutes per side. A quick, fresh zucchini salad, with the bright flavor and acidity of lemon juice tamed by cool mint, was the perfect complement to the mild gaminess of the lamb. And slicing the zucchini into ribbons meant that it didn't need to be cooked; the thin slices were tender, with a pleasing bite. We finished the salad with a drizzle of extra-virgin olive oil and thin shavings of salty Parmesan that mimicked the zucchini ribbons in shape and texture. Look for small zucchini, which are younger and have thinner skins than large zucchini. See page 255 for information on how to set up a single-level fire.

2½ tablespoons extra-virgin olive oil

2 teaspoons minced fresh rosemary

1 garlic clove, minced

Salt and pepper

4 (4-ounce) lamb loin or rib chops, ¾ to 1 inch thick, trimmed

1 zucchini

1½ teaspoons lemon juice

1 ounce Parmesan cheese, shaved

1 tablespoon minced fresh mint or basil

1. Combine 1 tablespoon oil, rosemary, garlic, ⅛ teaspoon salt, and pinch pepper in bowl; set aside. Pat chops dry with paper towels, rub chops with ½ tablespoon oil, and sprinkle with salt and pepper.

2A. FOR A CHARCOAL GRILL: Open bottom vent completely. Light large chimney starter filled with charcoal briquettes (6 quarts). When top coals are partially covered with ash, pour evenly over grill. Set cooking grate in place, cover, and open lid vent completely. Heat grill until hot, about 5 minutes.

2B. FOR A GAS GRILL: Turn all burners to high, cover, and heat grill until hot, about 15 minutes.

3. Clean and oil cooking grate. Place chops on grill and cook, brushing with rosemary-garlic oil and flipping as needed, until both sides are well browned and chops register 120 to 125 degrees (for medium-rare), 4 to 8 minutes. Transfer chops to serving platter; tent loosely with aluminum foil and let rest while making salad.

4. Use vegetable peeler or mandoline to slice zucchini lengthwise into very thin ribbons. Gently toss zucchini with salt and pepper and arrange on serving platter. Drizzle with remaining 1 tablespoon oil and lemon juice, then sprinkle with Parmesan and mint. Serve with lamb chops, passing rosemary-garlic oil separately.

Making Zucchini Ribbons

Using vegetable peeler or mandoline, slice zucchini lengthwise into very thin ribbons.

Grilled Fish Tacos

SERVES 2

WHY THIS RECIPE WORKS: Southwestern fish tacos combine grilled pieces of fish and crisp shredded cabbage with a tangy white sauce, all wrapped up in warm, soft corn tortillas. Tasters liked the meaty flavor and firm texture of mahi-mahi. To flavor the fish, we rubbed it with a mix of chili powder, salt, and pepper. Over the blazing heat of the grill, the fish developed a nicely crisped crust before its quick-cooking interior was overdone. We liked the crisp crunch of raw cabbage, but its flavor was a bit bland. Tossing it with cilantro, lime juice, and salt and pepper gave it just enough bright flavor. Halibut, swordfish, or red snapper can be substituted for the mahi-mahi. See page 255 for information on how to set up a single-level fire. Be sure to oil the cooking grate well in step 4; fish is delicate and tends to stick on the grill. To make this dish more or less spicy, adjust the amount of chipotle chiles.

¼ small head green cabbage, cored and shredded (2 cups)

3 tablespoons chopped fresh cilantro

2 tablespoons vegetable oil

1½ tablespoons lime juice

Salt and pepper

⅓ cup mayonnaise

1–2 teaspoons minced canned chipotle chiles in adobo sauce

1 small garlic clove, minced

2 (6- to 8-ounce) skinless mahi-mahi fillets, 1 inch thick

1 teaspoon chili powder

6 (6-inch) corn tortillas

Lime wedges

1. Toss cabbage, 2 tablespoons cilantro, 1 tablespoon oil, 1 tablespoon lime juice, ⅛ teaspoon salt, and pinch pepper together in bowl; set aside for serving. In separate bowl, combine mayonnaise, chipotle, garlic, remaining 1 tablespoon cilantro, and remaining 1½ teaspoons lime juice and season with salt and pepper to taste; set aside for serving.

2. Pat mahi-mahi dry with paper towels and brush with remaining 1 tablespoon oil. Combine chili powder, ¼ teaspoon salt, and ⅛ teaspoon pepper, then rub evenly over fillets.

3A. FOR A CHARCOAL GRILL: Open bottom vent completely. Light large chimney starter filled with charcoal briquettes (6 quarts). When top coals are partially covered with ash, pour evenly over grill. Set cooking grate in place, cover, and open lid vent completely. Heat grill until hot, about 5 minutes.

3B. FOR A GAS GRILL: Turn all burners to high, cover, and heat grill until hot, about 15 minutes. Leave all burners on high.

4. Clean cooking grate, then repeatedly brush grate with well-oiled paper towels until grate is black and glossy, 5 to

For the ultimate fish tacos, we grill fillets of meaty mahi-mahi and wrap them up with crisp coleslaw in lightly grilled corn tortillas.

10 times. Place fillets on grill and cook (covered if using gas) until fish flakes apart when gently prodded with paring knife and registers 140 degrees, 10 to 14 minutes, gently flipping fillets with 2 spatulas halfway through cooking. Transfer fillets to cutting board and tent loosely with aluminum foil.

5. Place tortillas on grill in single layer and cook until warmed and lightly browned on both sides, about 15 seconds per side. Stack grilled tortillas in foil packet to keep warm and soft. To serve, cut each fillet into 3 equal pieces. Smear warm tortillas with mayonnaise mixture, top with cabbage and fish, and serve with lime wedges.

Preventing Fish from Sticking

To prevent fish and shellfish from sticking, always clean and oil hot grill grates thoroughly. Scrape grate clean with brush, then wipe it 5 to 10 times with paper towels dipped in vegetable oil until grate is black and glossy, dipping paper towels in oil between applications.

Grilled Mediterranean Swordfish Skewers

SERVES 2   FAST

✔ **WHY THIS RECIPE WORKS:** Swordfish has a robust taste all its own and needs co-starring ingredients with just as much flavor. For these skewers, we paired swordfish with artichoke hearts and chunks of lemon. Once grilled, the artichoke hearts softened slightly yet retained some texture, and the lemon flavor went from tart and acidic to intensely sweet and rich. A simple basil oil, brushed over our skewers once they came off the grill, complemented the bright lemon flavor. Tossing the swordfish with a bit of ground coriander added complexity and provided a base of flavor that popped with the lemon and basil. We like the flavor of swordfish here but you can substitute other sturdy, firm-fleshed fish such as mahi-mahi or halibut. You will need two 12-inch metal skewers for this recipe. See page 255 for information on how to set up a single-level fire.

¼ **cup pitted kalamata olives, chopped**
3 **tablespoons extra-virgin olive oil**
1 **tablespoon chopped fresh basil**
½ **garlic clove, minced**
   Salt and pepper
1 **(12-ounce) skinless swordfish steak, cut into ¾-inch pieces**
2 **teaspoons ground coriander**
4 **ounces frozen artichoke hearts, thawed and patted dry**
½ **lemon, quartered**

1. Combine olives, 2 tablespoons oil, basil, garlic, ¼ teaspoon salt, and pinch pepper in bowl; set aside for serving. Pat swordfish dry with paper towels and season with coriander, salt, and pepper. Thread fish, artichokes, and lemon evenly onto two 12-inch metal skewers in alternating pattern. Brush skewers with remaining 1 tablespoon oil.

2A. FOR A CHARCOAL GRILL: Open bottom vent completely. Light large chimney starter three-quarters filled with charcoal briquettes (4½ quarts). When top coals are partially covered with ash, pour evenly over grill. Set cooking grate in place, cover, and open lid vent completely. Heat grill until hot, about 5 minutes.

2B. FOR A GAS GRILL: Turn all burners to high, cover, and heat grill until hot, about 15 minutes. Turn all burners to medium-high.

3. Clean cooking grate, then repeatedly brush grate with well-oiled paper towels until grate is black and glossy, 5 to 10 times. Place skewers on grill and cook (covered if using gas), turning as needed, until fish is lightly charred and registers 140 degrees, 10 to 12 minutes. Transfer skewers to serving platter and brush with olive mixture. Serve.

Grilled Blackened Red Snapper

SERVES 2 LIGHT

✔ **WHY THIS RECIPE WORKS:** Blackened fish is usually prepared in a cast-iron skillet, but it can lead to a relentlessly smoky kitchen. We thought we'd solve this issue by moving our fish to the grill, but this introduced a host of new challenges—curled fillets that stuck to the grill and spices that tasted raw and harsh. To prevent curling fillets, we simply scored the skin. We solved the sticking problem by thoroughly oiling the grate. Finally, to give the fish a flavorful blackened —but not burnt—coating, we bloomed our spice mixture in melted butter, allowed it to cool, then brushed it on the fish. Once on the grill, the spice crust acquired depth and richness while the fish cooked through. Striped bass, halibut, or grouper can be substituted for the snapper. See page 250 for information on how to set up a half-grill fire. Be sure to oil the grate well in step 4; fish is delicate and tends to stick to the grill. For the nutritional information for this recipe, see page 415.

- 1 tablespoon paprika
- 1 teaspoon onion powder
- 1 teaspoon granulated garlic
- ½ teaspoon ground coriander
- ⅛ teaspoon cayenne pepper
- Salt and pepper
- 2 tablespoons unsalted butter
- 2 (6- to 8-ounce) skin-on red snapper fillets, ¾ inch thick
- Lime wedges

1. Combine paprika, onion powder, garlic, coriander, cayenne, ½ teaspoon salt, and ¼ teaspoon pepper in bowl. Melt butter in 8-inch skillet over medium heat. Stir in spice mixture and cook, stirring constantly, until fragrant and spices turn dark rust color, about 2 minutes. Transfer mixture to shallow dish and let cool to room temperature, then use fork to break up any large clumps.

2. Using sharp knife, make 3 or 4 shallow slashes about 1 inch apart along skin side of each fillet, being careful not to cut into flesh. Pat fillets dry with paper towels. Rub spice mixture evenly over both sides of fillets. Lay fish on wire rack set over baking sheet and refrigerate until grill is ready.

3A. FOR A CHARCOAL GRILL: Open bottom vent completely. Light large chimney starter three-quarters filled with charcoal briquettes (4½ quarts). When top coals are partially covered with ash, pour evenly over half of grill. Set cooking grate in place, cover, and open lid vent completely. Heat grill until hot, about 5 minutes.

3B. FOR A GAS GRILL: Turn all burners to high, cover, and heat grill until hot, about 15 minutes.

4. Clean cooking grate, then repeatedly brush grate with well-oiled paper towels until grate is black and glossy, 5 to 10 times. Place snapper on hotter side of grill, skin side down and perpendicular to bars of cooking grate. Cook until exterior is dark brown and fish is opaque and flakes apart when gently prodded with paring knife, 10 to 14 minutes, gently flipping fillets with 2 spatulas halfway through cooking. Serve with lime wedges.

Grilled Salmon Steaks

SERVES 2

✔ **WHY THIS RECIPE WORKS:** Salmon steaks are perfect for the grill: They're a sturdier cut than a fillet, but they still cook relatively quickly, making them a great choice for weeknight dining. We started our testing by developing a method for evenly cooked steaks. Because salmon steaks have thinner belly flaps that can easily overcook, we wrapped and tied our steaks into neat medallions that would cook evenly. A half-grill fire allowed us to sear the steaks over the hot side of the grill then finish cooking them gently on the cooler side. To flavor our rich salmon, we made a lemon and shallot butter sauce in a disposable aluminum pie plate set alongside the steaks. Once the steaks were nicely seared, we transferred them to the pie plate to finish cooking through right in the sauce, flavoring the fish all the way through. See page 250 for information on how to set up a half-grill fire. Before serving, lift out the small circular bone from the center of each steak.

- 2 (10-ounce) salmon steaks, 1 to 1½ inches thick
- 1 tablespoon olive oil
- Salt and pepper
- 1 small shallot, minced
- 2 tablespoons unsalted butter, cut into 2 pieces
- 1½ teaspoons capers, rinsed
- ½ teaspoon grated lemon zest plus 3 tablespoons juice
- 1 (9-inch) disposable aluminum pie plate
- 1 tablespoon minced fresh parsley

1. Pat salmon dry with paper towels. Working with 1 steak at a time, carefully trim 1½ inches of skin from 1 tail. Tightly wrap other tail around skinned portion and tie steaks with kitchen twine. Brush steaks with oil and season with salt and pepper. Combine shallot, butter, capers, lemon zest and juice, and ⅛ teaspoon salt in disposable pie plate.

2A. FOR A CHARCOAL GRILL: Open bottom vent completely. Light large chimney starter filled with charcoal briquettes (6 quarts). When top coals are partially covered with ash, pour evenly over half of grill. Set cooking grate in place, cover, and open lid vent completely. Heat grill until hot, about 5 minutes.

2B. FOR A GAS GRILL: Turn all burners to high, cover, and heat grill until hot, about 15 minutes. Leave primary burner on high and turn off other burner(s).

3. Clean cooking grate, then repeatedly brush grate with well-oiled paper towels until grate is black and glossy, 5 to 10 times. Place steaks on hotter side of grill and cook (covered if using gas) until browned, 2 to 3 minutes per side. Meanwhile, place pie plate on cooler side of grill and heat until butter has melted, about 2 minutes.

4. Transfer steaks to pie plate and gently turn to coat with melted butter. Cover grill and cook until center of fish is still translucent when checked with tip of paring knife and registers 125 degrees (for medium-rare), 6 to 14 minutes, flipping steaks and rotating pie plate halfway through grilling.

5. Transfer salmon to serving platter, leaving sauce in pan, and remove twine. Whisk parsley into sauce and drizzle over steaks. Serve.

Preparing Salmon Steaks

1. To make salmon steaks sturdy enough to grill, first remove 1½ inches of skin from 1 tail of each steak.

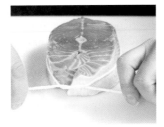

2. Next, tuck skinned portion into center of steak, wrap other tail around it, and tie with kitchen twine.

NOTES FROM THE TEST KITCHEN

How Hot Is Your Fire?

If you don't have a grill thermometer on hand, you can use this simple method to check the intensity of a fire. Once the grill is preheated, take the temperature of the fire by holding your hand 5 inches above the cooking grate and counting how long you can comfortably leave it in place.

INTENSITY OF FIRE	TIME YOU CAN HOLD YOUR HAND 5 INCHES ABOVE GRATE
Hot fire	2 seconds
Medium-hot fire	3 to 4 seconds
Medium fire	5 to 6 seconds
Medium-low fire	7 seconds

Grill-Smoked Salmon with Creamy Cucumber-Dill Salad

SERVES 2

✓ **WHY THIS RECIPE WORKS:** We wanted to capture the intense, smoky flavor of hot-smoked fish and the firm but silky texture of the cold-smoked type—without turning the recipe into a day-long project. First, to prepare the salmon for smoking, we quick-cured our fillets with a mixture of salt and sugar to draw moisture from the flesh and firm it up and to season it inside and out. We then cooked the fish indirectly over a gentle fire with ample smoke to produce salmon that was sweet, smoky, and tender. A creamy cucumber-yogurt sauce made the perfect complement to our silky, smoky fillets. Try to purchase center-cut salmon fillets of similar size so that they cook at the same rate. Although we prefer hickory wood chips, any variety of chips except mesquite will work. Low-fat Greek yogurt can be substituted for the whole-milk Greek yogurt; however, the sauce will taste a bit lean. Do not substitute nonfat yogurt.

- 2 (6- to 8-ounce) skin-on salmon fillets, 1½ inches thick
- 2 teaspoons sugar
  Kosher salt and pepper
- 2 cups wood chips, half of chips soaked in water for 15 minutes and drained
- 1 cucumber, peeled, halved lengthwise, seeded, and sliced ¼ inch thick
- ⅓ cup plain whole-milk Greek yogurt
- 1 tablespoon lemon juice
- 1 tablespoon minced fresh dill
- 1 scallion, minced

1. Set wire rack in rimmed baking sheet and lay salmon on rack. Combine sugar and 1 teaspoon salt, then sprinkle evenly over top and sides of salmon. Refrigerate, uncovered, for 1 hour. Using paper towels, brush excess salt and sugar from salmon and blot dry. Return fillets to wire rack and refrigerate, uncovered, until ready to grill. Using piece of heavy-duty aluminum foil, wrap soaked and unsoaked chips together in foil packet and cut several vent holes in top.

2A. FOR A CHARCOAL GRILL: Open bottom vent halfway. Light large chimney starter one-third filled with charcoal briquettes (2 quarts). When top coals are partially covered with ash, pour into steeply banked pile against side of grill. Place wood chip packet on coals. Set cooking grate in place, cover, and open lid vent halfway. Heat grill until hot and wood chips are smoking, about 5 minutes.

2B. FOR A GAS GRILL: Remove cooking grate and place wood chip packet directly on primary burner. Set grate in place, turn primary burner to high (leave other burners off), cover, and heat grill until hot and wood chips are smoking, 15 to 25 minutes. Turn primary burner to medium. (Adjust primary burner as needed to maintain grill temperature around 275 degrees.)

3. Clean and oil cooking grate. Fold piece of heavy-duty foil into 6 by 6-inch square. Place foil square over cooler side of grill and place fillets on foil, spaced at least ½ inch apart. Cover grill (positioning lid vent over fillets if using charcoal) and cook until center of fish is still translucent when checked with tip of paring knife and registers 125 degrees (for medium-rare), 30 to 40 minutes. Transfer fillets to serving platter and tent loosely with foil.

4. Meanwhile, toss cucumber and ¼ teaspoon salt together and let drain in colander for 15 minutes. Just before serving, combine yogurt, lemon juice, dill, and scallion in bowl, stir in drained cucumber, and season with salt and pepper to taste. Serve with fillets.

Grilled Shrimp Skewers

SERVES 2

✔ **WHY THIS RECIPE WORKS:** Shrimp can turn from moist and juicy to rubbery and dry in the blink of an eye—especially when grilled. For tender, juicy, boldly seasoned grilled shrimp we seasoned peeled shrimp with salt, pepper, and sugar (to help browning) and set them over a very hot fire. Jumbo shrimp are less likely to overcook but cost as much as $25 per pound, so we created faux jumbo shrimp by cramming a skewer with several extra-large shrimp pressed tightly together. Our final step was to take the shrimp off the fire before they were completely cooked but after they had picked up attractive grill marks. We finished cooking them in a heated sauce waiting on the cool side of the grill; this final simmer infused them with bold flavor. The shrimp and sauce will finish cooking together on the grill, so be sure to have the sauce prepared before you begin to cook. You will need two 12-inch metal skewers for this recipe. See page 250 for information on how to set up a half-grill fire.

- 12 **ounces extra-large shrimp (21 to 25 per pound), peeled and deveined**
- 1 **tablespoon olive oil**
  Salt and pepper
- ⅛ **teaspoon sugar**
- 1 **recipe sauce (recipes follow)**
  Lemon wedges

For caramelized grilled shrimp that are tender and juicy, we crowd the shrimp on the skewers to insulate them from the heat.

1. Pat shrimp dry with paper towels and thread tightly onto two 12-inch metal skewers, alternating direction of heads and tails. Brush both sides of shrimp with oil and season with salt and pepper. Sprinkle 1 side of each skewer evenly with sugar.

2A. FOR A CHARCOAL GRILL: Open bottom vent completely. Light large chimney starter filled with charcoal briquettes (6 quarts). When top coals are partially covered with ash, pour evenly over half of grill. Set cooking grate in place, cover, and open lid vent completely. Heat grill until hot, about 5 minutes.

2B. FOR A GAS GRILL: Turn all burners to high, cover, and heat grill until hot, about 15 minutes. Leave primary burner on high and turn other burner(s) to medium-low.

3. Clean cooking grate, then repeatedly brush grate with well-oiled paper towels until grate is black and glossy, 5 to 10 times. Place disposable pan with sauce ingredients on hotter side of grill and cook, stirring sauce occasionally, until butter melts, about 1½ minutes. Slide pan to cooler side of grill.

4. Place shrimp skewers, sugared side down, on hotter side of grill and use tongs to push shrimp together on skewers if they have separated. Cook shrimp until lightly charred, 4 to 5 minutes. Using tongs, flip and continue to cook until second side is pink and slightly translucent, 1 to 2 minutes longer.

5. Using potholder, carefully lift each skewer from grill and use tongs to slide shrimp off skewers into pan with sauce. Toss shrimp and sauce to combine. Place pan on hotter side of grill and cook, stirring, until shrimp are opaque throughout, about 30 seconds. Remove from grill, add remaining sauce ingredients as directed and toss to combine. Transfer to serving platter. Serve with lemon wedges.

Spicy Lemon-Garlic Sauce
MAKES ABOUT 3 TABLESPOONS

- 2 tablespoons unsalted butter, cut into 2 pieces
- 2 tablespoons lemon juice
- 1 large garlic clove, minced
- ¼ teaspoon red pepper flakes
  Pinch salt
- 1 (9-inch) disposable aluminum pie plate
- 2 tablespoons minced fresh parsley

Combine butter, lemon juice, garlic, pepper flakes, and salt in disposable pie plate. Add parsley just before serving.

Chermoula Sauce
MAKES ABOUT 3 TABLESPOONS

- 3 tablespoons extra-virgin olive oil
- 1 small garlic clove, minced
- ½ teaspoon ground cumin
- ½ teaspoon paprika
- ⅛ teaspoon cayenne pepper
- ⅛ teaspoon salt
- 1 (9-inch) disposable aluminum pie plate
- ¼ cup minced fresh cilantro
- 1 tablespoon lemon juice

Combine oil, garlic, cumin, paprika, cayenne, and salt in disposable pie plate. Add cilantro and lemon juice just before serving.

Grilled Shrimp Masala
SERVES 2 **FAST**

✓ WHY THIS RECIPE WORKS: For an exotic dinner for two that's ready in no time, we rubbed easy grilled shrimp with a potent paste made from garam masala, chili powder, sweet paprika, ginger, and garlic. To ensure that the shrimp cooked through evenly, we packed them tightly onto two skewers. To get a nicely browned crust without overcooking the delicate shrimp, we grilled them briefly over a hot single-level fire. An easy-to-make yogurt dipping sauce flavored with fresh mint served as a cooling counterpoint to the boldly spiced shrimp. Low-fat Greek yogurt can be substituted for the whole-milk Greek yogurt; however, the sauce will taste a bit lean. Do not substitute nonfat yogurt. You will need two 12-inch metal skewers for this recipe. See page 255 for information on how to set up a single-level fire.

- 2 teaspoons garam masala
- 1½ teaspoons grated fresh ginger
- 1 garlic clove, minced
- 1 teaspoon paprika
- ½ teaspoon grated lemon zest plus 2½ tablespoons juice
- ½ teaspoon chili powder
- ½ teaspoon sugar
  Salt and pepper
- ¼ cup plain whole-milk Greek yogurt
- 2 tablespoons minced fresh mint or basil
- 2 tablespoons vegetable oil
- 12 ounces extra-large shrimp (21 to 25 per pound), peeled and deveined

1. In large bowl, combine garam masala, ginger, garlic, paprika, lemon zest and juice, chili powder, sugar, and ¼ teaspoon salt to make paste. In separate bowl, combine

Crowding Shrimp onto a Skewer

Packing shrimp tightly onto skewers insulates them from overcooking and helps them to cook evenly. Pass skewer through center of each shrimp, alternating direction of heads and tails, about 8 shrimp per skewer. Shrimp should be crowded and touching.

¼ teaspoon spice paste, yogurt, and mint and season with salt and pepper to taste; set aside for serving.

2. Stir oil into remaining spice paste, breaking up any clumps, then add shrimp and toss to coat. Thread shrimp tightly onto two 12-inch metal skewers, alternating direction of heads and tails.

3A. FOR A CHARCOAL GRILL: Open bottom vent completely. Light large chimney starter mounded with charcoal briquettes (7 quarts). When top coals are partially covered with ash, pour evenly over grill. Set cooking grate in place, cover, and open lid vent completely. Heat grill until hot, about 5 minutes.

3B. FOR A GAS GRILL: Turn all burners to high, cover, and heat grill until hot, about 15 minutes. Leave all burners on high.

4. Clean cooking grate, then repeatedly brush grate with well-oiled paper towels until grate is black and glossy, 5 to 10 times. Place shrimp on grill and cook until lightly charred and opaque throughout, 2 to 3 minutes per side. Transfer shrimp to serving platter and serve with yogurt sauce.

Grilled Scallops with Fennel and Orange Salad

SERVES 2 **FAST** **LIGHT**

✔ **WHY THIS RECIPE WORKS:** Grilled scallops need little embellishment—their sweet, briny richness becomes even more intense on a hot grill, and their exterior develops a flavorful, nicely charred crust. With just oil, salt, and pepper plus a sprinkling of ground pink peppercorns for color and fruity flavor, our scallops were ready for the grill. To turn our tender scallops into a satisfying supper, we created a simple salad to go with them. A trio of grilled fennel, orange pieces, and chopped mint kept the dish bright and fresh-tasting. A quick stint in the microwave helped soften the fennel so it didn't need too long on the grill. You will need four 12-inch metal skewers for this recipe. We recommend buying "dry" scallops, which don't have chemical additives and taste better than "wet." Dry scallops will look ivory or pinkish; wet scallops are bright white. See page 255 for information on how to set up a single-level fire. For the nutritional information for this recipe, see page 415.

 1 **orange**
 1 **fennel bulb, stalks discarded, bulb halved, cored, and sliced thin**
 1 **tablespoon minced fresh basil**
 2 **tablespoons extra-virgin olive oil**
    Salt and pepper
 8 **large sea scallops, tendons removed**
 2 **teaspoons pink peppercorns, crushed**

To complement these juicy grilled scallops, we serve them with a bright salad of fresh fennel, sweet orange pieces, and mint.

1. Cut away peel and pith from orange. Quarter orange, then slice crosswise into ¼-inch-thick pieces. Toss orange, fennel, basil, and 1 tablespoon oil in bowl and season with salt and pepper to taste; set aside for serving.

2. Pat scallops dry with paper towels and thread onto doubled 12-inch metal skewers, 4 scallops per doubled skewer. Brush scallops with remaining 1 tablespoon oil and season with peppercorns, salt, and pepper.

3A. FOR A CHARCOAL GRILL: Open bottom vent completely. Light large chimney starter mounded with charcoal briquettes (7 quarts). When top coals are partially covered with ash, pour

Skewering Scallops for the Grill

To double-skewer scallops, which makes flipping them much easier, thread 4 scallops onto one 12-inch metal skewer, then place second skewer through scallops parallel to and about ¼ inch from first skewer.

evenly over grill. Set cooking grate in place, cover, and open lid vent completely. Heat grill until hot, about 5 minutes.

3B. FOR A GAS GRILL: Turn all burners to high, cover, and heat grill until hot, about 15 minutes.

4. Clean cooking grate, then repeatedly brush grate with well-oiled paper towels until grate is black and glossy, 5 to 10 times. Place scallop skewers on grill and cook (covered if using gas), turning as needed, until lightly charred and centers of scallops are opaque, about 6 minutes. Serve with salad.

Grilled Vegetable and Bread Salad

SERVES 2

✔ **WHY THIS RECIPE WORKS:** Grilled vegetables are the perfect basis for a summer supper, when all kinds of produce are at the height of ripeness. We wanted to pair nicely charred vegetables with chunks of rustic bread, fresh herbs, and a bright vinaigrette for a summery take on Italian-style vegetable and bread salad. To keep with our Mediterranean theme, we chose zucchini, red bell pepper, and sweet red onion for the vegetables. After 10 minutes on the grill, the vegetables were perfectly browned and tender and full of smoky flavor. We brushed slices of rustic Italian bread with oil and quickly toasted them over the grill. Then we simply tossed everything with a vinaigrette of basil, lemon, garlic, and mustard. A rustic round loaf, or a baguette sliced on the extreme bias, works best for this recipe. Be sure to use high-quality bread. You will need one 12-inch metal skewer for this recipe. See page 255 for information on how to set up a single-level fire.

¼ cup extra-virgin olive oil
1 tablespoon chopped fresh basil
½ teaspoon grated lemon zest plus 2 teaspoons juice
1 small garlic clove, minced
½ teaspoon Dijon mustard
  Salt and pepper
1 small red onion, sliced into ¾-inch-thick rounds
1 red bell pepper, stemmed, seeded, and quartered
1 zucchini, halved lengthwise
3 ounces French or Italian bread, cut into 1-inch-thick slices
2 ounces goat cheese, crumbled (½ cup)

1. Whisk 2 tablespoons oil, basil, lemon zest and juice, garlic, mustard, ⅛ teaspoon salt, and ⅛ teaspoon pepper together in large bowl; set vinaigrette aside.

2. Thread onion rounds from side to side onto 12-inch metal skewer. Brush onion, bell pepper, zucchini, and bread with remaining 2 tablespoons oil and season with salt and pepper.

3A. FOR A CHARCOAL GRILL: Open bottom vent completely. Light large chimney starter half filled with charcoal briquettes (3 quarts). When top coals are partially covered with ash, pour evenly over grill. Set cooking grate in place, cover, and open lid vent completely. Heat grill until hot, about 5 minutes.

3B. FOR A GAS GRILL: Turn all burners to high, cover, and heat grill until hot, about 15 minutes. Turn all burners to medium.

4. Clean and oil cooking grate. Place vegetables on 1 side of grill and cook (covered if using gas) until spottily charred on both sides, 10 to 15 minutes, flipping them halfway through cooking. Transfer vegetables to cutting board and carefully remove onion from skewer.

5. While vegetables cook, place bread slices on grill, opposite vegetables, and cook (covered if using gas) until golden brown on both sides, about 4 minutes, flipping them halfway through cooking. Transfer bread to cutting board with vegetables.

6. Cut vegetables and bread into 1-inch pieces. Add vegetables and bread to bowl with vinaigrette and toss to coat. Divide salad evenly between 2 plates and sprinkle evenly with goat cheese. Serve.

Skewering Onion for Grilling

After slicing onion crosswise into ¾-inch-thick rounds, slide skewer completely through each onion slice from side to side.

Grilled Portobello Burgers with Garlicky Eggplant

SERVES 2

✔ **WHY THIS RECIPE WORKS:** For a hearty, flavorful vegetarian entrée off the grill, we turned to portobello mushroom burgers. But in our initial tests, the mushrooms oozed moisture, turning the buns soggy; and even worse, they tasted bland. Luckily, the solutions to these problems were simple. To rid the mushroom caps of their excess moisture, we scored them before grilling. For bold flavor, we brushed them with a garlic and thyme oil halfway through cooking. Then we topped the burgers with grilled onion, creamy goat cheese,

We top our meaty portobello burgers with grilled red onion, creamy goat cheese, peppery arugula, and juicy tomato.

baby arugula, and juicy tomato. For an easy side dish, we drizzled thick rounds of eggplant with more of the garlicky oil and grilled them alongside the burgers. If your mushrooms are larger or smaller, you may need to adjust the cooking time accordingly. You will need one 12-inch metal skewer for this recipe. See page 255 for information on how to set up a single-level fire.

- 6 tablespoons olive oil
- 3 garlic cloves, minced
- 1 teaspoon minced fresh thyme or ¼ teaspoon dried
  Salt and pepper
- 12 ounces eggplant, sliced into ¾-inch-thick rounds
- 1 small red onion, sliced into ¾-inch-thick rounds
- 2 large portobello mushroom caps (4 to 5 inches in diameter)
- 2 ounces goat cheese, crumbled (½ cup)
- 2 hamburger buns
- ½ cup baby arugula
- 1 tomato, cored and sliced thin

1. Cook oil, garlic, thyme, ¼ teaspoon salt, and ¼ teaspoon pepper in 8-inch skillet over medium heat until fragrant, about 1 minute; transfer to bowl. Brush both sides of eggplant rounds with 2 tablespoons garlic oil and season with salt and pepper. Thread onion rounds from side to side onto 12-inch metal skewer, brush with 1 tablespoon garlic oil, and season with salt and pepper. Using paring knife, lightly score top of each mushroom cap in diagonal crosshatch pattern.

2A. FOR A CHARCOAL GRILL: Open bottom grill vent completely. Light large chimney starter three-quarters filled with charcoal briquettes (4½ quarts). When top coals are partially covered with ash, pour evenly over grill. Set cooking grate in place, cover, and open lid vent completely. Heat grill until hot, about 5 minutes.

2B. FOR A GAS GRILL: Turn all burners to high, cover, and heat grill until hot, about 15 minutes. Turn all burners to medium-high.

3. Clean and oil cooking grate. Place mushrooms, gill side down; onion skewer; and eggplant rounds on grill. Cook mushrooms (covered if using gas) until lightly charred and beginning to soften, 4 to 6 minutes. Flip mushrooms, brush with 1 tablespoon garlic oil, and cook until tender and browned on second side, 4 to 6 minutes. Sprinkle goat cheese over mushrooms and cook until cheese softens, about 2 minutes.

4. Meanwhile, cook onion and eggplant, turning as needed, until spottily charred on both sides, 8 to 12 minutes. Transfer mushrooms, onion, and eggplant to large plate and tent loosely with aluminum foil. Grill buns until warm and lightly charred, about 30 seconds; transfer to separate plate.

5. Toss arugula with 1 teaspoon garlic oil in bowl and season with salt and pepper to taste. Carefully remove onion from skewer and separate rings. Assemble mushroom caps, onion rings, arugula, and tomato on buns. Drizzle remaining garlic oil over eggplant rounds. Serve with burgers.

Scoring Portobellos for Grilling

To help mushrooms release excess moisture on grill, use tip of sharp knife to lightly score top of each mushroom cap on diagonal in crosshatch pattern.

Grilled Pizza with Charred Romaine and Red Onion Salad

SERVES 2

✓ **WHY THIS RECIPE WORKS:** Pizza is a natural fit for the grill: The super-hot fire mimics a professional pizza oven, giving the crust great char and crispness. Since grilled pizza is all about the crust, that's where we started. We made a batch of our basic pizza dough, shaped it into two individual crusts, and grilled them over a medium-hot fire. Leaving one-quarter of the grill bottom free of coals gave us a cooler zone to move the crusts to if they started to burn. After cooking the dough on one side, we flipped the crusts and topped them with mozzarella, Parmesan, and tomato sauce. For an easy sauce, we salted, drained, and seasoned chopped plum tomatoes. A quick charred romaine salad rounded out our meal. You can substitute store-bought pizza dough for the dough in this recipe. Let the dough sit out at room temperature while preparing the remaining ingredients; otherwise, it will be difficult to stretch. You will need one 12-inch metal skewer for this recipe. Do not remove the core from the lettuce; it will help keep the leaves together on the grill.

PIZZA

- 12 ounces plum tomatoes, cored, seeded, and cut into ½-inch pieces
  - Salt and pepper
- 2 tablespoons chopped fresh basil
- 2 tablespoons extra-virgin olive oil
- 1 small garlic clove, minced
- ⅛ teaspoon red pepper flakes
- 3 ounces mozzarella cheese, shredded (¾ cup)
- ¼ cup grated Parmesan cheese
- 1 recipe Basic Pizza Dough (page 93), room temperature

SALAD

- 3 tablespoons extra-virgin olive oil
- 2 teaspoons balsamic vinegar
- 1 teaspoon honey
- ½ teaspoon Dijon mustard
- 1 small garlic clove, minced
  - Salt and pepper
- 1 red onion, sliced into ¾-inch-thick rounds
- 1 large romaine lettuce heart, halved lengthwise through core
- 1 ounce Parmesan cheese, shaved

The high heat of the grill gives us a parlor-quality pizza crust: crisp and lightly charred with a satisfyingly chewy interior.

1. FOR THE PIZZA: Toss tomatoes with ¼ teaspoon salt, spread on paper towel–lined plate, and let drain for 15 minutes. Combine drained tomatoes, basil, 1 tablespoon oil, garlic, and pepper flakes in bowl and season with salt and pepper to taste. In separate bowl, combine mozzarella and Parmesan.

2. Place dough on lightly floured counter and divide into 2 equal pieces. Working with 1 piece at a time, press and roll dough into 9-inch rounds. (If dough shrinks when rolled out, cover with plastic wrap and let rest for 5 minutes.) Lay dough rounds on separate pieces of parchment paper dusted with flour; they can be stacked on top of one another. Cover with plastic wrap.

3. FOR THE SALAD: Whisk 2 tablespoons oil, vinegar, honey, mustard, and garlic together in small bowl. Season with salt and pepper to taste; set dressing aside. Thread onion rounds from side to side onto 12-inch metal skewer. Brush skewered onion and romaine with remaining 1 tablespoon oil and season with salt and pepper.

4A. FOR A CHARCOAL GRILL: Open bottom vent completely. Light large chimney starter filled with charcoal briquettes (6 quarts). When top coals are partially covered with ash, pour in even layer over three-quarters of grill, leaving one quadrant free of coals. Set cooking grate in place, cover, and open lid vent completely. Heat grill until hot, about 5 minutes.

4B. FOR A GAS GRILL: Turn all burners to high, cover, and heat grill until hot, about 15 minutes. Leave primary burner on high and turn off other burner(s). (Adjust primary burner as needed to maintain hot fire on one side.)

5. Clean and oil cooking grate. Place skewered onion on hotter part of grill and cook (covered if using gas) until spottily charred on both sides, 8 to 10 minutes, flipping onion halfway through cooking. Meanwhile, cook romaine on hotter part of grill next to onion until spottily charred on all sides, about 2 minutes, turning as needed. Transfer onion and romaine to serving platter. Carefully remove onion from skewer, separate rings, and tent vegetables loosely with aluminum foil to keep warm.

6. Lightly flour rimless (or inverted) baking sheet. Invert 1 dough round onto prepared sheet, peel off parchment, and reshape as needed. Working quickly, carefully slide round onto hotter part of grill. Repeat with second dough round. Cook (covered if using gas) until top of dough is covered with bubbles and bottom is spotty brown, about 1 minute, poking large bubbles with tongs as needed. (Check bottom of crust continually and slide to cooler part of grill if browning too quickly.)

7. Using tongs, return crusts to inverted sheet, browned sides up. Brush with remaining 1 tablespoon oil, sprinkle with cheese mixture, then top with tomato mixture. Return pizzas to hotter part of grill, cover, and cook until bottoms are well browned and cheese is melted, 2 to 4 minutes, checking bottoms frequently to prevent burning. Transfer pizzas to cutting board.

8. Drizzle onion and romaine with reserved dressing and sprinkle with Parmesan. Slice pizzas and serve with salad.

Making Grilled Pizza

1. To easily and safely transfer dough to grill, use tongs to slide dough from baking sheet onto grill. Repeat with second dough round.

2. When dough is covered with bubbles and bottom is spotty brown, return pizza crusts to baking sheet, browned sides up. Then, add toppings and slide rounds back onto grill.

Grilled Glazed Tofu with Warm Cabbage Slaw

SERVES 2

✅ **WHY THIS RECIPE WORKS:** We wanted custardy tofu with a crisp, browned crust paired with crunchy cabbage slaw. Tasters liked firm tofu the best; it held together on the grill and had a moist, creamy texture. Cutting the tofu into two thin planks maximized its surface area, giving us lots of browning without lots of flipping. To flavor the mild tofu, we made a thick glaze of soy sauce, sugar, mirin, garlic, and ginger. For the slaw, we quartered napa cabbage and grilled it until just the outer leaves were charred before tossing it with a quick Asian-inspired dressing. Mirin is a sweet Japanese rice wine available in the international aisle of most supermarkets; sherry or white wine can be substituted. Do not remove the core from the cabbage; it will help keep the leaves together on the grill. See page 252 for information on how to set up a two-level fire.

- 14 ounces firm tofu
- ⅓ cup soy sauce
- 2 tablespoons mirin
- 1½ teaspoons grated fresh ginger
- 1 garlic clove, minced
- ¼ cup chopped fresh cilantro
- 2 teaspoons toasted sesame oil
- 1 teaspoon rice vinegar
- ⅓ cup water
- 3 tablespoons sugar
- ½ teaspoon cornstarch
- 2 tablespoons vegetable oil
- 1 small head napa cabbage (1½ pounds), quartered lengthwise through core
  Pepper

1. Cut tofu horizontally into 2 slabs. Spread tofu over paper towel–lined baking sheet and let drain for 15 minutes.

2. While tofu drains, combine soy sauce, mirin, ginger, and garlic in small saucepan. Transfer 2 tablespoons soy sauce mixture to medium bowl, then stir in cilantro, sesame oil, and vinegar; set dressing aside. Whisk water, sugar, and cornstarch into remaining soy sauce mixture in saucepan. Bring to simmer and cook until thickened and measures ⅓ cup, about 5 minutes.

3. Gently pat tofu dry with paper towels, brush with 1 tablespoon vegetable oil, and season with pepper. Brush cabbage with remaining 1 tablespoon vegetable oil and season with pepper.

4A. FOR A CHARCOAL GRILL: Open bottom vent completely. Light large chimney starter filled with charcoal briquettes (6 quarts). When top coals are partially covered with ash, pour

A flavorful Asian-inspired glaze helps our grilled tofu develop a crisp browned crust that contrasts nicely with its creamy interior.

two-thirds evenly over half of grill, then pour remaining coals over other half of grill. Set cooking grate in place, cover, and open lid vent completely. Heat grill until hot, about 5 minutes.

4B. FOR A GAS GRILL: Turn all burners to high, cover, and heat grill until hot, about 15 minutes. (Adjust burners as needed to maintain a hot fire.)

5. Clean and oil cooking grate. Place tofu and cabbage, cut side down, on grill (on hotter part of grill if using charcoal). Cook tofu (covered if using gas), until lightly browned on both sides, 6 to 10 minutes, gently flipping it with 2 spatulas halfway through cooking. Meanwhile, cook cabbage, turning as needed, until slightly wilted and browned on all sides, 6 to 10 minutes. Transfer cabbage to plate and tent loosely with aluminum foil.

6. Slide tofu to cooler part of grill if using charcoal, or turn all burners to medium if using gas (adjust burners as needed to maintain medium fire). Brush tofu with glaze and cook until well browned on both sides, 2 to 4 minutes, flipping and brushing tofu with more glaze halfway through cooking. Transfer tofu to separate plate and brush with remaining glaze.

7. Cut cabbage crosswise into thin strips, discarding core. Transfer cabbage to bowl with reserved dressing and toss to combine. Divide cabbage evenly between 2 plates. Halve tofu planks on the diagonal and place on top of cabbage. Serve.

Cutting Tofu for the Grill

Carefully cut tofu in half horizontally to make 2 slabs before draining it on paper towels.

NOTES FROM THE TEST KITCHEN

Grilling Vegetables at a Glance

To easily grill a vegetable to serve alongside dinner, use this chart as a guide. Brush or toss the vegetables with oil before grilling. Grill vegetables over a medium-hot fire (see page 265).

VEGETABLE	PREPARATION	GRILLING DIRECTIONS
Asparagus	Snap off tough ends.	Grill, turning once, until tender and streaked with light grill marks, 5 to 7 minutes.
Bell Pepper	Core, seed, and cut into large wedges.	Grill, turning every 2 minutes, until streaked with dark grill marks, 8 to 10 minutes.
Corn	Remove all but last layer of husk.	Grill, turning every 2 minutes, until husk chars and peels away at tip, 8 to 10 minutes.
Endive	Cut in half lengthwise through stem end.	Grill, flat side down, until streaked with dark grill marks, 5 to 7 minutes.
Eggplant	Remove ends. Cut into ¾-inch-thick rounds or strips.	Grill, turning once, until flesh is darkly colored, 8 to 10 minutes.
Fennel	Slice bulb through base into ¼-inch-thick pieces.	Grill, turning once, until streaked with dark grill marks and quite soft, 7 to 9 minutes.
White or Cremini Mushrooms	Trim thin slice from stems then thread onto skewers.	Grill, turning several times, until golden brown, 6 to 7 minutes.
Onions	Peel and cut into ½-inch-thick slices.	Grill, turning occasionally, until lightly charred, 10 to 12 minutes.
Cherry Tomatoes	Remove stems then thread onto skewers.	Grill, turning several times, until streaked with dark grill marks, 3 to 6 minutes.
Plum Tomatoes	Cut in half lengthwise and seed.	Grill, turning once, until streaked with dark grill marks, about 6 minutes.
Zucchini or Summer Squash	Remove ends. Slice lengthwise into ½-inch-thick strips.	Grill, turning once, until streaked with dark grill marks, 8 to 10 minutes.

CHAPTER 11

Slow-Cooker Favorites

▥ LIGHT (See page 415 for nutritional information)

Opposite: Slow-Cooker Tomatillo Chili with Pork and Hominy; Slow-Cooker Asian-Style Braised Short Ribs; Slow-Cooker Curried Chicken Breasts

Slow-Cooker Black Bean Soup

SERVES 2

COOKING TIME 6 TO 7 HOURS ON LOW OR
4 TO 5 HOURS ON HIGH

✓ **WHY THIS RECIPE WORKS:** Black bean soup should be thick, hearty, and full of flavor. Unfortunately, most black bean soups from a slow cooker come out watery and bland. We vowed to up the flavor while ensuring that it was a snap to pull together. To give our stew the thick, rich texture we were after, we cooked the beans until tender, then mashed a portion of them with a potato masher to thicken the broth. A few slices of bacon infused our soup with smoky, savory depth, and a good amount of chili powder provided some heat. Coating the inside of the slow cooker with vegetable oil spray before adding the ingredients prevented our scaled-down dish from sticking and burning. Serve with minced red onion, sour cream, and hot sauce.

1	onion, chopped fine
1	tablespoon vegetable oil
3	garlic cloves, minced
2	teaspoons chili powder
1½	cups chicken broth, plus extra as needed
1	cup water
¾	cup dried black beans, picked over and rinsed
3	slices bacon
1	celery rib, cut into ½-inch pieces
1	carrot, peeled and cut into ½-inch pieces
	Salt and pepper
1	tablespoon minced fresh cilantro

1. Lightly spray inside of slow cooker with vegetable oil spray. Microwave onion, oil, garlic, and chili powder in bowl, stirring occasionally, until onion is softened, about 5 minutes; transfer to prepared slow cooker. Stir in broth, water, beans, bacon, celery, carrot, ½ teaspoon salt, and ½ teaspoon pepper. Cover and cook until beans are tender, 6 to 7 hours on low or 4 to 5 hours on high.

2. Discard bacon. Transfer ½ cup of bean mixture to bowl and mash with potato masher until mostly smooth. Stir mashed bean mixture into soup and let sit until heated through, about 5 minutes. Adjust soup consistency with extra broth as needed. Stir in cilantro and season with salt and pepper to taste. Serve.

Slow-Cooker Red Lentil Stew

SERVES 2

COOKING TIME 3 TO 4 HOURS ON LOW OR
2 TO 3 HOURS ON HIGH

✓ **WHY THIS RECIPE WORKS:** Indian dals are deeply flavored, exotically spiced, thick lentil stews. For our scaled-down version, we started with red lentils, which cooked down nicely in the slow cooker. Fork-friendly bites of carrot, chopped tomatoes, and peas added color and substance. To capture the complex flavors of Indian cuisine without reaching for several spice jars, we opted for garam masala, a spice blend that contains dried chiles, cinnamon, cardamom, coriander, and other spices. Coconut milk ensured that our stew was rich and creamy; to keep its flavor from becoming muted, we added it with the peas and some bright tomatoes in the last few minutes of cooking. You cannot substitute other varieties of lentils for the red lentils here; they will not cook down to the proper consistency. Do not use light coconut milk here. Serve over white rice.

1	tablespoon vegetable oil
2	garlic cloves, minced
1½	teaspoons garam masala
	Pinch red pepper flakes
1¼	cups water, plus extra as needed
2	carrots, peeled and cut into ¼-inch pieces
½	cup red lentils, picked over and rinsed
	Salt and pepper
2	tomatoes, cored and cut into ½-inch pieces
¾	cup canned coconut milk
⅓	cup frozen peas
1	tablespoon minced fresh cilantro

1. Lightly spray inside of slow cooker with vegetable oil spray. Microwave oil, garlic, garam masala, and pepper flakes in bowl, stirring occasionally, until fragrant, about 1 minute; transfer to prepared slow cooker. Stir in water, carrots, lentils, ½ teaspoon salt, and ½ teaspoon pepper. Cover and cook until lentils are very tender and broken down, 3 to 4 hours on low or 2 to 3 hours on high.

2. Stir in tomatoes, coconut milk, and peas, cover, and cook on high until heated through, about 5 minutes. Adjust stew consistency with extra hot water as needed. Stir in cilantro and season with salt and pepper to taste. Serve.

Slow-Cooker Moroccan Chicken Stew

SERVES 2

COOKING TIME 3 TO 4 HOURS ON LOW

✔ **WHY THIS RECIPE WORKS:** For a slow-cooked Moroccan chicken stew for two that delivered authentic flavor, we started with chicken thighs and added chickpeas and dried apricots, which softened during the long cooking time and permeated the stew with their flavor. To keep our prep work to a minimum, we chose boneless, skinless chicken thighs, which could be simply seasoned and added to the stew; once they were tender, we shredded them into bite-size pieces. Chicken broth and white wine infused the chicken with flavor. For savory depth, we included a good amount of tomato paste. A bit of tapioca ensured that the sauce thickened nicely. Narrowing down the spice list to just the essentials—paprika and garam masala—gave us a dish that tasted like a true tagine without requiring obscure ingredients. Serve over couscous or white rice.

  2   tablespoons tomato paste
  1   tablespoon vegetable oil
  1   tablespoon paprika
  1   teaspoon garam masala
  1½   cups chicken broth, plus extra as needed
  1   (14-ounce) can chickpeas, rinsed
  ¼   cup dry white wine
  1   tablespoon instant tapioca
  1   pound boneless, skinless chicken thighs, trimmed
       Salt and pepper
  3   tablespoons chopped dried apricots

1. Lightly spray inside of slow cooker with vegetable oil spray. Microwave tomato paste, oil, paprika, and garam masala in bowl, stirring occasionally, until fragrant, about 1 minute; transfer to prepared slow cooker. Stir in broth, chickpeas, wine, and tapioca. Season chicken with salt and pepper and nestle into slow cooker. Cover and cook until chicken is tender, 3 to 4 hours on low.

2. Using large spoon, skim excess fat from surface of stew. Break chicken into 1-inch pieces with tongs. Stir in apricots and let sit until heated through, about 5 minutes. Adjust stew consistency with extra broth as needed. Season with salt and pepper to taste and serve.

Trimming Chicken Thighs

Trimming and removing excess fat from chicken thighs before adding them to the slow cooker reduces the amount of fat that will be rendered and helps to prevent the dish from becoming greasy.

Holding your hand on top of chicken thigh, trim off any excess fat with sharp knife.

NOTES FROM THE TEST KITCHEN

Choosing a Slow Cooker

Slow cookers come in a variety of sizes, from the ridiculously small (1 quart) to very large (7 quarts or more). For smaller households, a smaller slow cooker (around 4 quarts) can be convenient, particularly if your kitchen is short on space. However, we tested our recipes in slow cookers of nearly every size, and all of the recipes in this chapter can be made in a slow cooker that holds anywhere from 3½ to 7 quarts. If you don't know the size of your slow cooker, the underside of the insert is usually stamped with the size, or you can simply measure how much water it takes to fill the insert to just above the lip.

To find out which models performed best and which features really mattered, we tested seven large (6-quart capacity or more) and eight small (4-quart capacity) slow cookers. To determine each model's cooking performance, we made a variety of recipes in each cooker. We also paid attention to design; the features we liked most included programmable timers, warming modes, and clear glass lids (which allow the cook to assess the food as it cooks). Inserts that can be washed in the dishwasher and that have handles (which make it easy to remove the insert from the slow cooker) earned extra points. We also tested the maximum temperatures of the models on high and low settings and found that some models didn't get hot enough. The best models quickly brought food into the safe zone (above 140 degrees) then climbed slowly to the boiling point or just below it over a period of hours; those that reached the boiling point right away tended to overcook food.

The **Cuisinart 4-Quart Cook Central 3-in-1 Multicooker** was our favorite small slow cooker. A slow cooker that can also brown, sauté, and steam, it produced perfect chicken, steaks, and ribs. Its programmable timer can be set to cook for up to 24 hours then automatically switches to "keep warm." We liked its lightweight, easy-clean, sturdy metal insert with extra-large handles and its oval shape, clear lid, and intuitive controls. The browning function is a nice plus for searing food or reducing sauces. If you want the option of slow cooking for company, our favorite large slow cooker is the **Crock-Pot Touchscreen 6½-Quart Slow Cooker.** We found its control panel extremely easy to use, and the timer counted up to 20 hours, even on high. Sunday gravy thickened to the correct consistency, pot roast was tender and sliceable, and onions caramelized perfectly every time.

Swapping chuck roast for convenient steak tips gave us a stew boasting big beefy flavor with a lot less work.

1 tablespoon vegetable oil
1 tablespoon tomato paste
2 garlic cloves, minced
1 teaspoon minced fresh thyme or ¼ teaspoon dried
2 cups beef broth, plus extra as needed
8 ounces small red potatoes, unpeeled
2 carrots, peeled and sliced ½ inch thick
1 tablespoon instant tapioca
1 tablespoon soy sauce
  Salt and pepper
1 pound sirloin steak tips, trimmed and cut into 1½-inch pieces
⅔ cup frozen peas

1. Lightly spray inside of slow cooker with vegetable oil spray. Microwave oil, tomato paste, garlic, and thyme in bowl, stirring occasionally, until fragrant, about 1 minute; transfer to prepared slow cooker. Stir in broth, potatoes, carrots, tapioca, soy sauce, ½ teaspoon salt, and ½ teaspoon pepper. Season beef with pepper and stir into slow cooker. Cover and cook until beef is tender, 6 to 7 hours on low or 4 to 5 hours on high.

2. Using large spoon, skim excess fat from surface of stew. Stir in peas and let sit until heated through, about 5 minutes. Adjust stew consistency with extra broth as needed. Season with salt and pepper to taste and serve.

Slow-Cooker Hearty Beef Stew

SERVES 2

COOKING TIME 6 TO 7 HOURS ON LOW OR
4 TO 5 HOURS ON HIGH

✔ **WHY THIS RECIPE WORKS:** For such a humble dish, beef stew requires a lot of work. We wanted a small-batch stew with maximum flavor for minimum effort. To start, we swapped the traditional chuck roast for convenient steak tips, which were easy to cut into pieces and came out tender and flavorful. We skipped browning the meat and instead bolstered the beefy, savory notes of our broth with tomato paste and soy sauce. For the vegetables, we stuck with the traditional lineup of potatoes, carrots, and peas. Small red potatoes needed no prep and could be added to the slow cooker whole; frozen peas needed just a few minutes to heat through before serving. Steak tips, also known as flap meat, are sold as whole steak, cubes, and strips; look for either whole steak tips or strips that are easy to cut into large pieces for this recipe. Use small red potatoes measuring 1 to 2 inches in diameter; if your potatoes are larger, cut them into 1-inch pieces to ensure they cook through.

Slow-Cooker Weeknight Beef Chili

SERVES 2

COOKING TIME 5 TO 6 HOURS ON LOW OR
3 TO 4 HOURS ON HIGH

✔ **WHY THIS RECIPE WORKS:** Most slow-cooker recipes for beef chili make enough to serve a crowd. We wanted to scale down our chili, but it still had to offer all the rich, long-simmered flavor and thick, substantial texture we were craving. The trio of tomato sauce, diced tomatoes, and tomato paste ensured that our chili tasted bright yet complex and was the right consistency after a few hours of simmering. For big flavor, we incorporated generous amounts of chili powder, garlic, and cumin; minced chipotles added smoky undertones and heat. We also reached for a test kitchen favorite, soy sauce, to boost the meaty, savory notes. For the meat, we wanted ground beef, but it turned gritty after hours of slow cooking. The solution was to microwave it briefly so it became firm enough to break into coarse crumbles that didn't turn grainy in the slow cooker. Serve with your favorite chili garnishes.

To give our beef chili complex, satisfying flavor, we added plenty of chili powder, garlic, and cumin plus smoky, spicy chipotle chile.

1 pound 85 percent lean ground beef
2 tablespoons chili powder
2 tablespoons tomato paste
3 garlic cloves, minced
1½ teaspoons ground cumin
1 (15-ounce) can kidney beans, rinsed
1 (15-ounce) can tomato sauce
1 (14.5-ounce) can diced tomatoes
1½ tablespoons soy sauce
1½ teaspoons packed brown sugar
1 teaspoon minced canned chipotle chile in adobo sauce
Salt and pepper

1. Lightly spray inside of slow cooker with vegetable oil spray. Microwave ground beef, chili powder, tomato paste, garlic, and cumin in bowl, stirring occasionally, until beef is no longer pink, about 5 minutes. Transfer mixture to prepared slow cooker, breaking up any large pieces of meat with wooden spoon. Stir in beans, tomato sauce, tomatoes and their juice, soy sauce, sugar, chipotle, ½ teaspoon salt, and ½ teaspoon pepper. Cover and cook until beef is tender, 5 to 6 hours on low or 3 to 4 hours on high.

Slow-Cooker Basics

While all ovens set to 350 degrees will perform the same (assuming all the ovens are properly calibrated), heating varies tremendously among slow cookers. We tested more than a dozen models and prepared every recipe in this chapter in at least three different models. Here's what you need to know.

GET TO KNOW YOUR SLOW COOKER: Some models run hot and fast, while others heat more slowly and gently. Most models perform best on low, but it's hard to make blanket statements that will apply to all slow cookers. In our testing, we have found that some slow cookers run hot or cool on just one of the settings (either low or high). This is where the cook's experience comes into play. If you have been using a slow cooker for some time, ask yourself if recipes are generally done at the low or high end of the cooking times provided in recipes. The answer should tell you whether you have a "fast" slow cooker or a "slow" model. If you are just getting started with your slow cooker, check all recipes at the beginning of the time range but allow some extra time to cook food longer if necessary.

HOW TO USE TIME RANGES: Through extensive testing using multiple brands of slow cookers, we found that we could narrow the window of doneness, which is usually 2 hours or more in slow-cooker recipes, to just an hour, giving you a better expectation of when your food will be done or when you should be home to start checking. We found that this 1-hour time frame worked for all the models we tested. It is especially helpful to have a narrower range when cooking fish or lean meats, which are less forgiving than stews and braises.

KEEPING FOOD SAFE: For safety reasons, the internal temperature of meat and poultry should reach 140 degrees (the temperature at which bacteria cannot grow) by the 2-hour mark in the cooking time. When you first start using your slow cooker, we suggest that you check the temperature of meat or chicken at this stage to be sure this is happening. If your food doesn't reach this safety zone when cooking on low, you might be able to solve the problem by using the high setting. Note that putting frozen meat or other frozen food into any slow cooker is dangerous as it will dramatically increase the amount of time it takes your food to reach this safe zone.

2. Using large spoon, skim excess fat from surface of chili. Break up any remaining large pieces of beef with spoon. Season with salt and pepper to taste and serve.

VARIATION
Slow-Cooker Weeknight Turkey Chili

Be sure to use ground turkey, not ground turkey breast (also labeled 99 percent fat free), in this recipe. Do not cook this chili on high as it will cause the turkey to dry out.

Substitute 1 pound ground turkey for ground beef and 1 (15-ounce) can pinto beans for kidney beans. Cook chili until turkey is tender, 3 to 4 hours on low.

Slow-Cooker Tomatillo Chili with Pork and Hominy

SERVES 2

COOKING TIME 5 TO 6 HOURS ON LOW OR
3 TO 4 HOURS ON HIGH

✓ WHY THIS RECIPE WORKS: We wanted an easier, more streamlined take on classic Mexican green chili, *posole*, which stars tender pork, tangy tomatillos, and earthy hominy. To scale it down, we traded the traditional pork shoulder for boneless country-style pork ribs. To achieve the bold flavor of authentic recipes, we broiled the tomatillos, along with our aromatics and spices; once charred, the vegetables and spices took on an earthy, smoky flavor. Canned hominy added sweet, "corny" flavor, and a bit of tapioca helped give our chili just the right consistency. If you can't find fresh tomatillos, you can substitute one 11-ounce can of tomatillos, drained, rinsed, and patted dry; broil as directed in step 1. Try to buy country-style pork ribs with lots of fat and dark meat; stay away from ribs that look overly lean with pale meat, as they will taste very dry after the extended cooking time. Serve with your favorite chili garnishes.

- 6 ounces tomatillos, husks and stems removed, rinsed well, dried, and halved
- ½ onion, cut into 1-inch pieces
- 1 garlic clove, minced
- 1 teaspoon minced fresh oregano or ¼ teaspoon dried
- ¼ teaspoon ground cumin
- 1 tablespoon vegetable oil
- ¾ cup canned white or yellow hominy, rinsed
- ¾ cup chicken broth, plus extra as needed
- 2 poblano chiles, stemmed, seeded, and minced
- 1 tablespoon instant tapioca
- ½ teaspoon sugar
- 1 bay leaf
- 12 ounces boneless country-style pork ribs, trimmed
  Salt and pepper
- 1 tablespoon minced fresh cilantro

1. Lightly spray inside of slow cooker with vegetable oil spray. Adjust oven rack 6 inches from broiler element and heat broiler. Line rimmed baking sheet with aluminum foil. Toss tomatillos, onion, garlic, oregano, and cumin with oil and spread on prepared sheet. Broil until vegetables are blackened and begin to soften, 5 to 10 minutes, rotating sheet halfway through broiling. Let cool slightly.

2. Pulse cooled vegetables with accumulated juices in food processor until almost smooth, about 10 pulses; transfer to prepared slow cooker. Stir in hominy, broth, poblanos, tapioca, sugar, and bay leaf. Season pork with salt and pepper and nestle into slow cooker. Cover and cook until pork is tender, 5 to 6 hours on low or 3 to 4 hours on high.

3. Using large spoon, skim excess fat from surface of chili. Discard bay leaf. Break pork into about 1-inch pieces with tongs. Adjust chili consistency with extra broth as needed. Stir in cilantro and season with salt and pepper to taste. Serve.

NOTES FROM THE TEST KITCHEN

Tips for Ensuring Slow-Cooker Success

After hours of slow cooking, flavors can become muted or one-dimensional, and meat and vegetables can dry out. Here are some tips for turning out satisfying, full-flavored dishes.

SPRAY YOUR SLOW COOKER: When cooking a smaller amount of food in the slow cooker, as with our scaled-down recipes for two, more evaporation can occur, leading some dishes to stick to the sides of the slow-cooker insert and burn. To avoid this, be sure to spray the sides of the slow-cooker insert with vegetable oil spray before adding any food. This not only prevents your dishes from burning but also makes serving and cleanup easier.

DON'T SKIMP ON THE AROMATICS: You'll see hefty amounts of onions, garlic, herbs, and other flavorful ingredients in our recipes. This is because the moist heat environment and long cooking times that come with the slow cooker tend to dull flavors. Also, many recipes need a flavor boost at the end of the cooking time, which is why we often finish with fresh herbs, lemon juice, or other flavorful ingredients.

ADD TOMATO PASTE AND SOY SAUCE FOR MEATY FLAVOR:
To replicate the meaty flavor usually achieved by browning meat and vegetables, we turn to *umami*-rich ingredients, which offer savory depth and rich flavor. Tomato paste ramps up the meaty richness of everything from soups and stews to braised chicken. Soy sauce adds flavor to a number of non-Asian dishes, like our beef stew and smothered pork chops, without calling attention to itself.

ADD DELICATE VEGETABLES AT THE RIGHT TIME: Certain ingredients need just a short stint in the slow cooker to warm through and meld into the dish, so we save them until the end of cooking. Delicate vegetables, like frozen peas, baby spinach, and chopped tomatoes, turn mushy when added at the beginning, so we stir them in at the end; in just a few minutes, they're perfectly tender.

SKIM AWAY EXCESS FAT: During the long cooking time, meat will release fat into a stew or braise, but it is easy to remove it at the end of the cooking time. Simply turn off the slow cooker and let the food sit for a few minutes so the fat can rise to the top. Use a large spoon to skim the excess fat off the surface.

This distinctive New Mexican specialty features meltingly tender chunks of slow-cooked pork in a rich sauce with warm flavors.

3 tablespoons tomato paste

2 tablespoons chili powder

1 tablespoon vegetable oil

3 garlic cloves, minced

¾ cup chicken broth, plus extra as needed

¼ cup brewed coffee

1 tablespoon instant tapioca

2 teaspoons packed brown sugar

1 pound boneless country-style pork ribs, trimmed
    Salt and pepper

2 tablespoons minced fresh cilantro

½ teaspoon grated lime zest plus 1½ teaspoons juice

1. Lightly spray inside of slow cooker with vegetable oil spray. Microwave tomato paste, chili powder, oil, and garlic in bowl, stirring occasionally, until fragrant, about 1 minute; transfer to prepared slow cooker. Stir in broth, coffee, tapioca, and sugar. Season pork with salt and pepper and nestle into slow cooker. Cover and cook until pork is tender, 5 to 6 hours on low or 3 to 4 hours on high.

2. Using large spoon, skim excess fat from surface of chili. Break pork into about 1-inch pieces with tongs. Adjust chili consistency with extra broth as needed. Stir in cilantro and lime zest and juice and season with salt and pepper to taste. Serve.

Slow-Cooker New Mexican Red Pork Chili

SERVES 2

COOKING TIME 5 TO 6 HOURS ON LOW OR
3 TO 4 HOURS ON HIGH

✔ WHY THIS RECIPE WORKS: In this dish, pork butt is braised in a richly flavored red chile sauce for a chili that's spicy yet sweet and smoky yet bright. For our for-two version, we opted for country-style pork ribs, which were available in smaller quantities and became meltingly tender. Chicken broth, chili powder, tomato paste, and garlic provided a flavorful backbone. To balance the spicy chili powder, we added coffee, which offered robust, bittersweet notes. Lime juice and zest brightened our hearty dish. Try to buy country-style pork ribs with lots of fat and dark meat; stay away from ribs that look overly lean with pale meat, as they will taste very dry after the extended cooking time. You can substitute ¾ teaspoon of instant espresso powder dissolved in ¼ cup of boiling water for the brewed coffee if desired. Serve with your favorite chili garnishes.

Slow-Cooker Lemony Chicken Breasts and Potatoes

SERVES 2

COOKING TIME 2 TO 3 HOURS ON LOW

✔ WHY THIS RECIPE WORKS: Moving the classic duo of chicken and potatoes to the slow cooker gave us an easy yet satisfying dinner for two. We started with a pair of bone-in chicken breasts, which stayed moist during the long cooking time thanks to the insulation provided by the bones. Chicken broth provided a flavorful braising liquid, and a bit of tapioca ensured that it thickened nicely. To give our spuds a head start on cooking, we microwaved them briefly. A pat of butter and some minced garlic added richness and depth. Once the chicken was done, we set it aside and briefly steeped a rosemary sprig in the slow cooker to infuse our potatoes with earthy, woodsy notes. A squeeze of lemon juice and some lemon zest brightened this simple supper. If using kosher chicken, do not brine. If brining the chicken, do not season with salt in step 1. Be sure to use a small sprig of rosemary or its flavor will be overpowering.

12 ounces red potatoes, unpeeled, cut into 1-inch pieces
2   tablespoons unsalted butter
2   garlic cloves, minced
¼   cup chicken broth
1   teaspoon instant tapioca
    Salt and pepper
2   (12-ounce) bone-in split chicken breasts, trimmed and
    brined if desired (see page 115)
1   small sprig fresh rosemary
½   teaspoon grated lemon zest plus 1 teaspoon juice

1. Lightly spray inside of slow cooker with vegetable oil spray. Microwave potatoes, 1 tablespoon butter, and garlic in bowl, stirring occasionally, until potatoes are softened, about 5 minutes; transfer to prepared slow cooker. Stir in broth, tapioca, ¼ teaspoon salt, and ½ teaspoon pepper. Season chicken with salt and pepper and nestle into slow cooker. Cover and cook until chicken is tender, 2 to 3 hours on low.

2. Transfer chicken to serving platter, remove skin, and tent loosely with aluminum foil. Stir rosemary sprig into potatoes and cook on high until fragrant, about 10 minutes. Discard rosemary sprig. Stir in lemon zest and juice and remaining 1 tablespoon butter and season with salt and pepper to taste. Serve chicken with potatoes and sauce.

NOTES FROM THE TEST KITCHEN

Tapioca: Slow-Cooking Secret Ingredient

When we're making stovetop stews, braises, or pan sauces, we usually reach for either flour or cornstarch when we want to thicken things up. But we've found that both lose their thickening power after hours in the slow cooker. We tried adding extra to compensate for their diminished abilities, but the texture of the dish suffered. In search of a thickener that would work for the slow cooker, we hit upon tapioca. Tapioca is made from starch extracted from the root of the cassava plant (also called manioc or yuca). We found that just a teaspoon of tapioca gave our slow-cooker stews and braises a silky texture.

Tapioca is available in several forms, but flour, pearl, and instant are the most common. After the cassava starch grains are removed from the root's cells, they are heated and ruptured, which converts the starches into small, irregular masses. These masses are then baked into flakes that are finely ground to make tapioca flour, or they're forced through sieves and baked again to form pearl tapioca. Tapioca pearls are gelatinous spheres; they come in various sizes ranging from 1 to 8 millimeters in diameter and must be rehydrated before using. Minute or instant tapioca is made from tapioca flour and is precooked then coarsely ground. It dissolves quickly and doesn't require presoaking, making it our favorite choice for thickening. It is also the most widely available. Tapioca flour and pearl tapioca can be substituted for instant tapioca, but pearl tapioca will not fully dissolve and will lend a slightly grainy texture to the dish. Stored in a cool, dark place, all types of tapioca will keep indefinitely.

Slow-Cooker Curried Chicken Breasts

SERVES 2 `LIGHT`

COOKING TIME 2 TO 3 HOURS ON LOW

✔ WHY THIS RECIPE WORKS: Curries are well suited to the slow cooker because their deep and complex flavors hold up well even after hours of cooking. For this curried chicken dish, those flavors allowed us to forgo browning the chicken breasts or aromatics. Instead, we built the base of this dish by briefly microwaving curry powder with onion, garlic, ginger, and tomato paste before adding it to the slow cooker along with the chicken and some broth. To complement the bold curry flavor, we added plain yogurt to the finished sauce; the yogurt provided a creamy, tangy richness that brought the flavors of the dish together. Finally, a little fresh cilantro brightened everything up. If using kosher chicken, do not brine. If brining the chicken, do not season with salt in step 1. We prefer the richness of whole-milk yogurt for this recipe. Serve with couscous or white rice. For the nutritional information for this recipe, see page 415.

1   small onion, chopped fine
1   tablespoon vegetable oil
2   garlic cloves, minced
2   teaspoons grated fresh ginger
1   teaspoon curry powder
1   teaspoon tomato paste
¼   cup chicken broth
1   teaspoon instant tapioca
2   (12-ounce) bone-in split chicken breasts, trimmed and
    brined if desired (see page 115)
    Salt and pepper
2   tablespoons plain whole-milk yogurt
1   tablespoon minced fresh cilantro

1. Lightly spray inside of slow cooker with vegetable oil spray. Microwave onion, oil, garlic, ginger, curry powder, and tomato paste in bowl, stirring occasionally until onion is softened, about 5 minutes; transfer to prepared slow cooker. Stir in broth and tapioca. Season chicken with salt and pepper and nestle into slow cooker. Cover and cook until chicken is tender, 2 to 3 hours on low.

2. Transfer chicken to serving platter, remove skin, and tent loosely with aluminum foil. In small bowl, combine ¼ cup hot braising liquid with yogurt (to temper), then whisk mixture back into slow cooker until smooth. Stir in cilantro and season with salt and pepper to taste. Spoon ½ cup sauce over chicken and serve, passing remaining sauce separately.

Slow-Cooker Gingery Chicken Breasts

SERVES 2 `LIGHT`

COOKING TIME 2 TO 3 HOURS ON LOW

✔ **WHY THIS RECIPE WORKS:** We built this Asian-inspired dish of slightly sweet and boldly gingery chicken breasts around a foundation of shallot, garlic, soy sauce, sugar, and, of course, ginger. Microwaving the aromatics to intensify their flavors gave the finished sauce depth and richness. We found that after simmering for hours in the slow cooker, the flavor of the ginger had mellowed, so to achieve the bold punch we were after, we added more fresh ginger at the end. Just 1 teaspoon whisked into the sauce before serving gave us the right amount of spicy flavor. If using kosher chicken, do not brine. If brining the chicken, do not season with salt in step 1. Serve with white rice. For the nutritional information for this recipe, see page 415.

- 1 shallot, minced
- 1 tablespoon vegetable oil
- 1 tablespoon grated fresh ginger
- 2 garlic cloves, minced
- ¼ cup chicken broth
- 1 tablespoon soy sauce
- 1 teaspoon instant tapioca
- 1 teaspoon sugar
- 2 (12-ounce) bone-in split chicken breasts, trimmed and brined if desired (see page 115)
  Salt and pepper
- 1 scallion, sliced thin

1. Lightly spray inside of slow cooker with vegetable oil spray. Microwave shallot, oil, 2 teaspoons ginger, and garlic in bowl, stirring occasionally, until fragrant, about 1 minute; transfer to prepared slow cooker. Stir in broth, soy sauce, tapioca, and sugar. Season chicken with salt and pepper and nestle into slow cooker. Cover and cook until chicken is tender, 2 to 3 hours on low.

Grating Ginger

To grate ginger, first peel small section of large piece of ginger, then grate peeled portion with rasp-style grater, using unpeeled section of ginger as handle.

2. Transfer chicken to serving platter and remove skin. Whisk remaining 1 teaspoon ginger into sauce until smooth and season with salt and pepper to taste. Spoon ½ cup sauce over chicken, sprinkle with scallion, and serve, passing remaining sauce separately.

Slow-Cooker Chicken Provençal

SERVES 2

COOKING TIME 3 TO 4 HOURS ON LOW

✔ **WHY THIS RECIPE WORKS:** A French classic, chicken Provençal uses low, slow heat to produce chicken that's fall-off-the-bone tender with a thick, rich-tasting garlicky tomato sauce. For an easier version for two, we moved it to the slow cooker and traded the whole bird for chicken thighs. Removing the skin prior to cooking kept the sauce from becoming greasy, and a spoonful of tomato paste amped up the rich, savory notes of the dish in lieu of browning the meat. Canned whole tomatoes, processed until smooth, plus a potent blend of garlic, oregano, white wine, and niçoise olives gave us a bright-tasting sauce that rounded out our homage to simple yet satisfying French fare. We like serving this dish with polenta, but rice and crusty bread also make good accompaniments.

- 1 onion, chopped fine
- 4 garlic cloves, minced
- 1 tablespoon olive oil
- 1 tablespoon tomato paste
- ½ teaspoon minced fresh oregano or ⅛ teaspoon dried
- 1 (14.5-ounce) can whole peeled tomatoes
- 3 tablespoons dry white wine
- 4 (5- to 7-ounce) bone-in chicken thighs, skin removed, trimmed
  Salt and pepper
- 2 tablespoons coarsely chopped pitted niçoise olives
- 2 tablespoons minced fresh parsley

1. Lightly spray inside of slow cooker with vegetable oil spray. Microwave onion, garlic, oil, tomato paste, and oregano in bowl, stirring occasionally, until onion is softened, about 5 minutes; transfer to prepared slow cooker.

2. Pulse tomatoes and their juice in food processor until almost smooth, about 10 pulses. Stir tomatoes and wine into slow cooker. Season chicken with salt and pepper and nestle into slow cooker. Cover and cook until chicken is tender, 3 to 4 hours on low.

3. Transfer chicken to serving platter. Stir olives and parsley into sauce and season with salt and pepper to taste. Pour sauce over chicken and serve.

Slow-Cooker Balsamic-Braised Chicken with Swiss Chard

SERVES 2 · LIGHT

COOKING TIME 3 TO 4 HOURS ON LOW

✓ **WHY THIS RECIPE WORKS:** This Italian-inspired braise offers surprising intensity and flavor, even though it takes mere minutes to get it into the slow cooker and hit "start." Bone-in chicken thighs stayed moist and tender during the long cooking time, and removing the skin before cooking ensured that the dish wasn't greasy. Chicken broth provided a flavorful braising liquid, and tomato paste, which we microwaved with our aromatics, amped up the meaty depth of the dish. A little instant tapioca thickened the sauce to the proper consistency. Finally, for more substance and to reinforce the Italian character of our braise, we added some Swiss chard and cherry tomatoes; a brief stint in the slow cooker was all they needed to soften slightly but still retain their fresh flavors. Serve with polenta. For the nutritional information for this recipe, see page 415.

    1 tablespoon vegetable oil
    1 tablespoon tomato paste
    1 garlic clove, minced
    2 teaspoons minced fresh thyme or ½ teaspoon dried
       Pinch red pepper flakes
    ½ cup chicken broth
    2 tablespoons balsamic vinegar
    1 tablespoon instant tapioca
       Salt and pepper
    4 (5- to 7-ounce) bone-in chicken thighs, skin removed, trimmed
    1 pound Swiss chard, stemmed and cut into 1-inch pieces
    4 ounces cherry tomatoes, halved

1. Lightly spray inside of slow cooker with vegetable oil spray. Microwave oil, tomato paste, garlic, thyme, and pepper flakes in bowl, stirring occasionally, until fragrant, about 1 minute; transfer to prepared slow cooker. Stir in broth, vinegar, tapioca, and ½ teaspoon pepper. Season chicken with salt and pepper and nestle into slow cooker. Cover and cook until chicken is tender, 3 to 4 hours on low.

2. Transfer chicken to serving platter and tent loosely with aluminum foil. Stir Swiss chard and tomatoes into braising liquid, cover, and cook on high until chard is wilted, 15 to 20 minutes.

3. Return chicken and any accumulated juices to slow cooker and season with salt and pepper to taste. Let chicken sit until heated through, about 5 minutes. Serve.

Slow-Cooker Southern-Style Chicken and Dirty Rice

SERVES 2

COOKING TIME 4 TO 5 HOURS ON LOW

✓ **WHY THIS RECIPE WORKS:** In the South, chicken is often paired with dirty rice—a tasty side dish of rice, cured meats, vegetables, and seasonings. We wanted to transform this flavorful duo into a scaled-down slow-cooker casserole. Boneless, skinless thighs stayed moist even after a few hours of cooking and were easy to shred and stir back into the slow cooker once tender. Onion, bell pepper, and garlic plus some chili powder and thyme provided a flavorful backbone. For meaty, savory depth, we included bites of kielbasa. Uncooked rice never got fully tender, and leftover white rice resulted in mushy, blown-out grains, but store-bought precooked rice worked great and kept our recipe super-easy. Sliced scallions added a touch of color and freshness. Store-bought precooked rice is important to the success of this dish; it remains intact and retains the proper doneness. Don't shred the chicken too fine in step 2; it will break up more as it is stirred back into the slow cooker.

    4 ounces kielbasa sausage, cut into ½-inch pieces
    1 onion, chopped fine
    1 red bell pepper, stemmed, seeded, and cut into ½-inch pieces
    2 garlic cloves, minced
    2 teaspoons chili powder
    2 teaspoons minced fresh thyme or ½ teaspoon dried
    2 cups cooked rice
       Salt and pepper
    1 pound boneless, skinless chicken thighs, trimmed
    2 scallions, sliced thin

1. Lightly spray inside of slow cooker with vegetable oil spray. Microwave kielbasa, onion, bell pepper, garlic, chili powder, and thyme in bowl, stirring occasionally, until vegetables are softened, about 5 minutes; transfer to prepared slow cooker. Stir in rice, ¼ teaspoon salt, and ½ teaspoon pepper. Season chicken with salt and pepper and nestle into slow cooker. Cover and cook until chicken is tender, 4 to 5 hours on low.

2. Transfer chicken to cutting board, let cool slightly, then shred into bite-size pieces using 2 forks. Gently stir shredded chicken and scallions into slow cooker and season with salt and pepper to taste. Serve.

The moist, gentle heat of the slow cooker is the perfect environment for poaching buttery salmon fillets to perfection.

Slow-Cooker Poached Salmon

SERVES 2

COOKING TIME 1 TO 2 HOURS ON LOW

✔ **WHY THIS RECIPE WORKS:** Poaching is a gentle cooking method that promises to deliver moist, delicately flavored salmon. But rather than poach our salmon on the stovetop, we decided to move this dish to the slow cooker to take advantage of its walk-away convenience. We started with two salmon fillets. To prevent the bottom of our salmon from overcooking, we rested our fillets on flavorful lemon slices and dill stems, then added a small amount of water to the slow cooker to create a moist cooking environment. A foil sling made it easy to remove the delicate salmon from the slow cooker. For a simple serving sauce, we combined sour cream and Dijon mustard with more lemon and dill. Try to purchase center-cut salmon fillets of similar size so that they cook at the same rate. Because delicate fish can easily overcook in the slow cooker, be sure to check the temperature of the salmon after the first hour of cooking, then continue to check every 10 minutes until the salmon is done.

1 lemon, sliced ¼ inch thick, plus 1 tablespoon juice
1½ teaspoons minced fresh dill, stems reserved
2 (6- to 8-ounce) skin-on salmon fillets, 1½ inches thick
Salt and pepper
¼ cup sour cream
1 teaspoon Dijon mustard

1. Fold sheet of aluminum foil into 12 by 9-inch sling and press widthwise into slow cooker. Arrange lemon slices in tight single layer in bottom of prepared slow cooker. Scatter dill stems over lemon slices. Pour water into slow cooker until it is even with lemon slices (about ½ cup water). Season salmon with salt and pepper and place skin side down on top of lemon slices. Cover and cook until salmon is opaque throughout when checked with tip of paring knife and registers 135 degrees, 1 to 2 hours on low.

2. Combine sour cream, mustard, lemon juice, and minced dill in bowl and season with salt and pepper to taste. Using sling, transfer fillets to baking sheet. Gently lift and tilt fillets with spatula to remove dill stems and lemon slices and transfer fillets to individual plates. Serve with sauce.

Removing Salmon from a Slow Cooker

To make it easy to remove delicate salmon from the slow cooker, we use an aluminum foil sling. Fold sheet of foil into 12 by 9-inch rectangle and press widthwise into slow cooker. Before serving, use edges of sling as handles to lift fish out of slow cooker easily.

Slow-Cooker Braised Steaks with Mushrooms and Onion

SERVES 2

COOKING TIME 6 TO 7 HOURS ON LOW OR
4 TO 5 HOURS ON HIGH

✔ **WHY THIS RECIPE WORKS:** This dish features meltingly tender blade steaks smothered in a sauce of sweet onions and earthy mushrooms, a combination that works perfectly in the slow cooker. We found that blade steaks were ideal in this application because they have a relatively high and even distribution of fat; after hours of simmering in the slow cooker, they were supremely moist and tender. Since we weren't browning our steaks, we added a spoonful of soy sauce to enhance the meaty, savory notes of the dish. Microwaving the onions and mushrooms jump-started their cooking and deepened their flavor. A couple of teaspoons of tapioca turned the braising liquid into a full-fledged sauce that clung nicely to our fork-tender steaks. Serve over egg noodles or mashed potatoes.

 1 onion, halved and sliced ½ inch thick
 6 ounces white or cremini mushrooms, trimmed and sliced thin
 1 tablespoon vegetable oil
1½ teaspoons packed brown sugar
 1 garlic clove, minced
 1 teaspoon minced fresh thyme or ¼ teaspoon dried
 ½ cup beef broth
 1 tablespoon soy sauce
 2 teaspoons instant tapioca
 2 (6- to 8-ounce) beef blade steaks, ¾ to 1 inch thick
    Salt and pepper

1. Lightly spray inside of slow cooker with vegetable oil spray. Microwave onion, mushrooms, oil, sugar, garlic, and thyme in bowl, stirring occasionally, until vegetables are softened, about 5 minutes; transfer to prepared slow cooker. Stir in broth, soy sauce, and tapioca. Season steaks with salt and pepper and nestle into slow cooker. Cover and cook until beef is tender, 6 to 7 hours on low or 4 to 5 hours on high.

2. Transfer steaks to serving platter, tent loosely with aluminum foil, and let rest for 5 minutes. Using large spoon, skim excess fat from surface of sauce. Season with salt and pepper to taste. Pour sauce over steaks and serve.

Slow-Cooker Barbecued Steak Tips

SERVES 2

COOKING TIME 6 TO 7 HOURS ON LOW OR 4 TO 5 HOURS ON HIGH

✔ **WHY THIS RECIPE WORKS:** We wanted to use the gentle heat of the slow cooker to make exceptionally tender barbecued steak tips that tasted like they'd come off the grill. We quickly seared the steak tips to give them a rich, browned crust. Then we used the fond left in the pan to flavor a quick barbecue sauce that we added to the slow cooker. To keep our seared steak from steaming in the sauce, we elevated it on an inverted steamer basket. To prevent crowding, we skewered the steak tips. Six hours later, we had a sweet and tangy barbecue sauce and meaty, tender steak tips as good as grilled. Steak tips, also known as flap meat, are sold as whole steak, cubes, and strips; look for either whole steak tips or strips that are easy to cut into large

For barbecued flavor from the slow cooker, we elevate our steak tips above the simmering sauce to preserve their browned crust.

pieces for this recipe. If you have long, thin pieces of meat, roll or fold them into approximately 2-inch cubes before skewering.

 1 tablespoon soy sauce
 1 tablespoon tomato paste
 1 tablespoon packed dark brown sugar
    Salt and pepper
 1 pound sirloin steak tips, trimmed and cut into 2-inch pieces
 2 (8-inch) wooden skewers
 1 tablespoon vegetable oil
 1 shallot, minced
 1 small garlic clove, minced
 ½ cup water
 ½ cup tomato sauce
 ⅓ cup ketchup
 ¾ teaspoon cider vinegar
 ¼ teaspoon hot sauce

1. Lightly spray inside of slow cooker with vegetable oil spray. Combine soy sauce, tomato paste, sugar, and ⅛ teaspoon pepper in bowl. Pat beef dry with paper towels and thread onto skewers.

2. Heat oil in 10-inch skillet over medium-high heat until just smoking. Brown beef on all sides, about 5 minutes. Transfer skewers to plate and brush soy sauce mixture evenly on all sides of meat.

3. Add shallot and ⅛ teaspoon salt to fat left in skillet and cook over medium heat until softened and lightly browned, 2 to 3 minutes. Stir in garlic and cook until fragrant, about 30 seconds. Stir in water, tomato sauce, and half of ketchup, scraping up any browned bits, and bring to boil; transfer to prepared slow cooker.

4. Set inverted metal steamer basket in slow cooker. Place skewers on steamer basket, scraping excess soy sauce mixture over meat. Cover and cook until beef is tender and fork slips easily in and out of meat, 6 to 7 hours on low or 4 to 5 hours on high.

5. Transfer skewers to serving dish, slide beef off skewers, and tent loosely with aluminum foil. Remove steamer basket. Using large spoon, skim excess fat from surface of cooking liquid. Transfer liquid to small saucepan and stir in remaining ketchup. Bring to simmer and cook until sauce is reduced to ¾ cup, about 5 minutes. Stir in vinegar and hot sauce and season with salt and pepper to taste. Pour ¼ cup sauce over steak tips. Serve with remaining sauce.

Arranging Steak Skewers in a Slow Cooker

Set inverted steamer basket in slow cooker, then place skewers on top to keep them out of cooking liquid and preserve seared crust.

Slow-Cooker Asian-Style Braised Short Ribs

SERVES 2

COOKING TIME 8 TO 9 HOURS ON LOW OR 5 TO 6 HOURS ON HIGH

✓ **WHY THIS RECIPE WORKS:** For a boldly flavored, seriously satisfying dinner for two, we slow-cooked short ribs until meltingly tender in a sweet, spicy, and savory Asian-style sauce. The well-marbled ribs cooked down significantly, so to compensate we started with over a pound of ribs. Hoisin sauce and chili-garlic sauce provided an intensely flavored sauce with a nice sweetness and subtle heat, and chicken broth

added meatiness. To ensure a nicely thickened sauce by the end of the cooking time, we stirred in 2 teaspoons of tapioca. Thinly sliced scallion whites gave the sauce an aromatic presence. Once the ribs were tender, we defatted the sauce, then stirred the ribs back in and sprinkled the finished dish with scallion greens for freshness and a burst of color. Look for boneless short ribs that are well marbled and measure about 2 inches wide and 1 inch thick. Serve over egg noodles or rice.

½ **cup chicken broth**
⅓ **cup hoisin sauce**
3 **scallions, white parts minced, green parts sliced thin**
1 **tablespoon Asian chili-garlic sauce**
2 **teaspoons instant tapioca**
2 **(10-ounce) boneless beef short ribs, trimmed**
   Salt and pepper

1. Lightly spray inside of slow cooker with vegetable oil spray. Combine broth, hoisin, scallion whites, chili-garlic sauce, and tapioca in prepared slow cooker. Season beef with salt and pepper and nestle into slow cooker. Cover and cook until beef is tender, 8 to 9 hours on low or 5 to 6 hours on high.

2. Transfer short ribs to serving platter, tent loosely with aluminum foil, and let rest for 5 minutes. Using large spoon, skim excess fat from surface of sauce. Pour sauce over short ribs and sprinkle with scallion greens. Serve.

Slow-Cooker Smothered Pork Chops

SERVES 2

COOKING TIME 2 TO 3 HOURS ON LOW

✓ **WHY THIS RECIPE WORKS:** Pork chops are a convenient cut of pork when cooking for two, and smothering them in a hearty gravy adds richness to an otherwise lean dish. We started with blade-cut chops, which are cut from the shoulder end of the loin and contain fat and connective tissue that help them stay juicy in the slow cooker. Chicken broth provided a savory base for our onion gravy. Soy sauce added meaty notes, and tapioca helped to thicken it. A splash of cider vinegar and parsley offered brightness, and chopped bacon, microwaved briefly, gave us a crispy garnish. Look for bone-in chops with a good streak of dark meat running through the center of the chop or for chops with as much dark meat as possible. If the pork is enhanced (injected with a salt solution), do not brine. If brining the pork, do not season with salt in step 1. Serve over egg noodles or mashed potatoes.

1 onion, halved and sliced ½ inch thick

1 tablespoon vegetable oil

2 garlic cloves, minced

1 teaspoon minced fresh thyme or ¼ teaspoon dried

½ cup chicken broth

1 tablespoon soy sauce

2 teaspoons instant tapioca

Salt and pepper

2 (8- to 10-ounce) bone-in blade-cut pork chops, ¾ to 1 inch thick, trimmed and brined if desired (see page 150)

4 slices bacon, chopped

2 tablespoons minced fresh parsley

1½ teaspoons cider vinegar

1. Lightly spray inside of slow cooker with vegetable oil spray. Microwave onion, oil, garlic, and thyme in bowl, stirring occasionally, until onion is softened, about 5 minutes; transfer to prepared slow cooker. Stir in broth, soy sauce, tapioca, and ½ teaspoon pepper. Cut 2 slits, about 2 inches apart, through outer layer of fat and silverskin on each chop. Season chops with salt and pepper and nestle into slow cooker. Cover and cook until pork is tender, 2 to 3 hours on low.

2. Transfer chops to serving platter and tent loosely with aluminum foil. Line plate with double layer of coffee filters. Spread bacon in even layer over filters and microwave until crisp, about 5 minutes. Using large spoon, skim excess fat from surface of sauce. Stir in parsley and vinegar and season with salt and pepper to taste. Pour sauce over chops and sprinkle with crisp bacon. Serve.

Slow-Cooker Sweet-and-Sour Sticky Ribs

SERVES 2

COOKING TIME 3 TO 6 HOURS ON LOW

✔ **WHY THIS RECIPE WORKS:** Chinese-style sweet-and-sour ribs are a party favorite, but we wanted to scale this irresistible dish down for two. Leaving the membrane attached to the underside of our baby back ribs helped the rack hold together as it cooked and, as a bonus, shortened our prep time. Rubbing the ribs with a mixture of granulated garlic and ground ginger infused them with flavor. Once the ribs were tender, we brushed them with a tangy sauce and broiled them to develop a caramelized, lightly charred exterior. Avoid racks of baby back ribs that are larger than 2 pounds; they will be difficult to maneuver into the slow cooker. For more information on slow-cooker sizes, see page 277.

A few coats of sweet-and-sour glaze plus a few minutes under the broiler give our tender, meaty slow-cooked ribs a caramelized crust.

1½ teaspoons granulated garlic

1 teaspoon ground ginger

Salt and pepper

1 (1½- to 2-pound) rack baby back ribs, trimmed

⅓ cup apricot preserves

2 tablespoons ketchup

2 tablespoons soy sauce

2 tablespoons rice vinegar

1 tablespoon minced fresh cilantro

1. Mix garlic, ginger, 1 teaspoon salt, and 1 teaspoon pepper together in bowl and rub evenly over ribs.

2A. FOR A 3½- TO 4½-QUART SLOW COOKER: Lightly spray inside of slow cooker with vegetable oil spray. Arrange ribs along bottom and sides of prepared slow cooker, meaty side facing down. Cover and cook until ribs are tender, 5 to 6 hours on low.

2B. FOR A 5- TO 7-QUART SLOW COOKER: Lightly spray inside of slow cooker with vegetable oil spray. Arrange ribs along bottom and sides of prepared slow cooker, meaty side facing down. Cover and cook until ribs are tender, 3 to 4 hours on low.

3. Adjust oven rack 10 inches from broiler element and heat broiler. Set wire rack in aluminum foil–lined rimmed baking sheet and spray with oil spray. Whisk preserves, ketchup, soy sauce, and vinegar together. Transfer ribs meaty side up to prepared rack. Brush ribs with sauce, then broil until browned and sticky, 10 to 15 minutes, flipping and brushing with additional sauce every few minutes. Sprinkle with cilantro. Serve with remaining sauce.

Arranging Ribs in a Slow Cooker

Arrange rack with meaty side down across bottom of slow cooker. Ends of rack will come up against sides of slow cooker.

We use the gentle, steady heat of the slow cooker to get perfectly tender pulled pork without spending hours tending the grill.

Slow-Cooker Easy Pulled Pork

SERVES 2

COOKING TIME 5 TO 6 HOURS ON LOW OR 3 TO 4 HOURS ON HIGH

✔ **WHY THIS RECIPE WORKS:** To revamp this cookout classic for two, we ditched the usual pork shoulder in favor of boneless country-style ribs, which have plenty of marbling and are easy to purchase in smaller quantities. To guarantee that our pork offered the big flavor of authentic recipes, we applied a dry spice rub to our ribs. Simmering bacon slices with the ribs infused the pork with smoky flavor. Bottled barbecue sauce ensured that our recipe was effortless, and mixing it with the leftover braising liquid enhanced its flavor. Try to buy country-style pork ribs with lots of fat and dark meat, and stay away from ribs that look overly lean with pale meat, as they will taste very dry after the extended cooking time. If the pork is enhanced (injected with a salt solution), do not brine. If brining the pork, omit salt in step 1. Don't shred the pork too fine in step 2; it will break up more as it is combined with the sauce. Serve on hamburger buns with pickle chips.

½ cup chicken broth

2 slices bacon

1 tablespoon packed brown sugar

1 tablespoon paprika

1½ teaspoons chili powder

Salt and pepper

1 pound boneless country-style pork ribs, trimmed and brined if desired (see page 150)

¾ cup barbecue sauce

1. Lightly spray inside of slow cooker with vegetable oil spray. Combine broth and bacon in prepared slow cooker. Mix sugar, paprika, chili powder, ½ teaspoon salt, and ½ teaspoon pepper together in bowl and rub evenly over ribs. Nestle ribs into slow cooker, cover, and cook until pork is tender, 5 to 6 hours on low or 3 to 4 hours on high.

2. Transfer ribs to bowl and let cool slightly. Shred into bite-size pieces using 2 forks, discarding excess fat.

3. Discard bacon. Strain cooking liquid into fat separator and let sit for 5 minutes; reserve ½ cup defatted liquid. Combine reserved liquid and barbecue sauce in separate bowl. Stir ½ cup sauce into shredded pork, adding more sauce as needed to keep meat moist. Season with salt and pepper to taste and serve with remaining sauce.

CHAPTER 12

Vegetable Side Dishes

VEGETABLE SIDE DISHES A-Z

■ FAST (Start to finish in about 30 minutes)
▪ LIGHT (See page 415 for nutritional information)
Opposite: Roasted Carrots; Roasted Sweet Potatoes; Easy Creamed Spinach

To complement the delicate flavor of our roasted artichoke hearts, we toss them with a simple dressing of lemon, basil, oil, and garlic.

Roasted Artichoke Hearts with Lemon and Basil

SERVES 2

✔ **WHY THIS RECIPE WORKS:** For this quick side dish, we wanted to bring out the delicate, vegetal flavor of tender artichoke hearts without extensive hands-on time. Frozen artichoke hearts eliminated the tedious prep work that fresh artichokes required, but the frozen hearts contained a considerable amount of water, which prevented browning and diluted the flavor of our dish. To encourage deep caramelization, we preheated the baking sheet in a 450-degree oven. The excess water quickly evaporated on the sizzling-hot pan, giving us golden-brown, deeply flavored artichokes. Lining the baking sheet with foil made cleanup a snap. While the hearts roasted, we tossed together a simple dressing with just lemon juice, olive oil, basil, and roasted garlic to highlight the artichokes' flavor without overpowering them.

9 ounces frozen artichoke hearts, thawed and patted dry
1 garlic clove, peeled
5 teaspoons olive oil
    Salt and pepper
2 teaspoons lemon juice
2 teaspoons chopped fresh basil

1. Adjust oven rack to middle position, place aluminum foil–lined rimmed baking sheet on rack, and heat oven to 450 degrees. Toss artichokes with garlic, 1 tablespoon oil, ¼ teaspoon salt, and pinch pepper and carefully arrange in single layer on hot sheet. Roast artichokes until browned around edges, 15 to 20 minutes.

2. Mince roasted garlic. Whisk remaining 2 teaspoons oil, lemon juice, basil, and minced garlic together in large bowl. Add roasted artichokes and toss to coat. Season with salt and pepper to taste and serve.

VARIATIONS
Roasted Artichoke Hearts with Fennel, Mustard, and Tarragon

Roast 1 small fennel bulb, cored and thinly sliced, along with artichokes and garlic. Substitute 2 teaspoons minced fresh tarragon for basil and add 1 teaspoon whole-grain mustard to dressing in step 2.

Roasted Artichoke Hearts with Olives, Bell Pepper, and Lemon

Roast ¼ cup coarsely chopped pitted kalamata olives and 1 small red bell pepper, seeded and coarsely chopped, along with artichokes and garlic. Substitute 2 teaspoons minced fresh parsley for basil.

Pan-Roasted Asparagus

SERVES 2 FAST

✔ **WHY THIS RECIPE WORKS:** Asparagus can be a perfect no-fuss, quick-cooking side dish for two, but getting it right can be a challenge. To avoid overcooking, we started with thicker spears. To help the asparagus release moisture, encouraging caramelization and better flavor, we parcooked the spears, covered, with butter and oil. The water evaporating from the butter helped to steam the asparagus, cooking it through evenly. Then we removed the lid and turned up the heat to brown the spears. We found that we preferred the flavor of asparagus that had been browned on only one side, keeping the other side green and crisp-tender. This also allowed us to skip the tedious step of rotating individual spears. This recipe works best with asparagus that is at least ½ inch thick near the base. Do not use pencil-thin asparagus; it will overcook.

1 tablespoon unsalted butter
2 teaspoons olive oil
1 pound thick asparagus, trimmed
   Salt and pepper
1 teaspoon lemon juice

1. Heat butter and oil in 12-inch skillet over medium heat until butter is melted. Add half of asparagus to skillet with tips pointed in 1 direction and add remaining asparagus with tips pointed in opposite direction. Using tongs, distribute spears in even layer, cover, and cook until asparagus is bright green and still crisp, about 7 minutes.

2. Uncover, increase heat to medium-high, and cook until asparagus is tender and well browned on one side, 3 to 4 minutes, using tongs to transfer spears from center of skillet to edge of skillet to ensure even browning. Season with salt and pepper to taste, drizzle with lemon juice, and serve.

VARIATION

Pan-Roasted Asparagus with Toasted Garlic and Parmesan

Cook 2 thinly sliced garlic cloves and oil in 12-inch skillet over medium heat until garlic is crisp and golden, about 4 minutes. Transfer garlic to paper towel–lined plate and set aside, leaving oil in skillet. Add butter to garlic oil left in skillet and proceed with recipe. Sprinkle toasted garlic and 2 tablespoons grated Parmesan cheese over asparagus before serving.

Trimming Asparagus

1. Remove 1 spear of asparagus from bunch and bend it at thicker end until it snaps.

2. With broken asparagus spear as guide, trim tough ends from remaining asparagus bunch using chef's knife.

A crisp, browned Parmesan and bread-crumb coating transforms simple roasted asparagus into a sophisticated side dish.

Parmesan-Crusted Asparagus

SERVES 2

✔ **WHY THIS RECIPE WORKS:** A crunchy, flavorful coating of bread crumbs and grated Parmesan promised to jazz up our roasted asparagus, but only if we could figure out how to get rid of the vegetable's excess moisture. Poking holes in the asparagus and salting it worked wonders, driving off the extra moisture that would have made our asparagus rubbery and prevented the topping from sticking. From there, we dipped the spears in a combination of honey and egg white whipped to soft peaks and then coated them with a mixture of panko bread crumbs, Parmesan, melted butter, and a pinch of cayenne. Finally, to reinforce the Parmesan flavor, we topped the spears with an extra dose of cheese halfway through roasting. Avoid pencil-thin asparagus for this recipe. Since the recipe involves just one egg white, we recommend using a hand-held electric mixer to whip it rather than a stand mixer. Work quickly when tossing the asparagus with the egg white, as the salt will rapidly begin to deflate the white.

1 pound (½ inch thick) asparagus, trimmed
  Salt and pepper
1½ ounces Parmesan cheese, grated (¾ cup)
⅓ cup panko bread crumbs
½ tablespoon unsalted butter, melted and cooled
  Pinch cayenne
1 large egg white
½ teaspoon honey

1. Adjust oven rack to middle position and heat oven to 450 degrees. Line rimmed baking sheet with aluminum foil and spray with vegetable oil spray. Using fork, poke holes up and down asparagus spears. Toss asparagus with ¼ teaspoon salt and let stand for 30 minutes in single layer on large paper towel–lined platter.

2. Meanwhile, combine ½ cup Parmesan, panko, butter, ⅛ teaspoon salt, pinch pepper, and cayenne in bowl. Transfer half of panko mixture to shallow dish and reserve remaining mixture. Using electric mixer, whip egg white and honey together on medium-low speed until foamy, about 1 minute. Increase speed to medium-high and whip until soft peaks form, 2 to 3 minutes. Scrape egg white mixture into medium baking dish, then gently toss asparagus in mixture. Working with 1 spear at a time, dredge half of asparagus spears in panko and transfer to prepared baking sheet. Refill shallow dish with reserved panko mixture and repeat with remaining asparagus.

3. Bake asparagus until just beginning to brown, 6 to 8 minutes. Sprinkle with remaining ¼ cup Parmesan and continue to bake until cheese is melted and bread crumbs are golden brown, 6 to 8 minutes longer. Transfer to platter. Serve.

Making the Coating Stick

1. Use fork to poke holes in asparagus spears. Toss with salt and let drain on paper towel–lined baking sheet to draw out excess moisture that could saturate bread-crumb coating.

2. Gently toss asparagus spears in whipped egg white–honey mixture to help crumbs adhere, then, working with 1 spear at a time, dredge spears in panko bread-crumb mixture.

Garlicky Green Beans
SERVES 2 **FAST**

✔ **WHY THIS RECIPE WORKS:** Garlicky green beans are a classic side dish, but they run the risk of quickly becoming overcomplicated—or overcooked. We wanted to streamline the process to make this dish fresh, flavorful, and fast for two. We love the rich, mellow flavor of roasted garlic, but in the oven it takes the better part of an hour. We discovered that microwaving the garlic with oil and sugar gave us creamy, caramelized garlic (plus a flavorful cooking oil) in only 1 minute. To ensure crisp-tender beans, we added some water directly to a covered skillet so they could steam gently for a few minutes, then we uncovered the pan so they could brown in our flavorful garlic oil. Microwave temperatures can vary, so be sure to check the garlic after 30 seconds to see if it has softened.

6 garlic cloves, peeled and halved lengthwise
1 tablespoon extra-virgin olive oil
  Pinch sugar
8 ounces green beans, trimmed
2 tablespoons water
1½ teaspoons red or white wine vinegar
  Salt and pepper

1. Microwave garlic, oil, and sugar in small bowl until garlic is softened and fragrant, 30 to 60 seconds.

2. Heat 2 teaspoons garlic oil in 12-inch nonstick skillet over medium heat until shimmering. Add green beans and water, cover, and cook until green beans are bright green, about 3 minutes. Add remaining garlic oil without stirring and cook, covered, until green beans are almost tender, about 2 minutes.

3. Uncover and continue to cook, stirring occasionally, until green beans are spotty brown and garlic is golden, 3 to 4 minutes. Off heat, stir in vinegar, season with salt and pepper to taste, and serve.

Trimming Green Beans Quickly

Line up several green beans in row on cutting board. Trim about ½ inch from each end, then cut beans as directed in recipe.

VARIATION

Lemony Green Beans with Toasted Almonds

Omit garlic, sugar, and step 1. Heat 1 tablespoon oil in skillet in step 2 and proceed with recipe, substituting ⅛ teaspoon grated lemon zest plus 1½ teaspoons juice for vinegar. Sprinkle green beans with 2 tablespoons toasted sliced almonds before serving.

Skillet Broccoli with Olive Oil and Garlic

SERVES 2 **FAST**

WHY THIS RECIPE WORKS: Broccoli florets are quick-cooking, easy to prep, and sold in smaller quantities—perfect when cooking for two. The trick is getting the cores to cook through before the delicate outer buds overcook and begin to fall apart. Our solution was to use a two-step stir-fry method. An initial sear in hot oil browned the florets, adding color and flavor. Then we added water to the skillet to quickly steam the tough cores. To flavor the crisp-tender broccoli, we added garlic and thyme at the end of cooking, quickly blooming them in the hot skillet to deepen their flavor before stirring everything together.

> 2 tablespoons olive oil
> 1 garlic clove, minced
> ¼ teaspoon minced fresh thyme
> 8 ounces broccoli florets, cut into 1-inch pieces
>   Salt and pepper
> 2 tablespoons water

1. Combine 1 tablespoon oil, garlic, and thyme in bowl. Heat remaining 1 tablespoon oil in 10-inch skillet over medium-high heat until just smoking. Add broccoli and ¼ teaspoon salt and cook, without stirring, until beginning to brown, about 2 minutes.

2. Add water, cover, and cook until broccoli is bright green but still crisp, about 2 minutes. Uncover and continue to cook until water has evaporated and broccoli is crisp-tender, about 2 minutes.

3. Push broccoli to sides of skillet. Add garlic mixture and cook, mashing mixture into skillet, until fragrant, about 30 seconds. Stir garlic mixture into broccoli. Season with salt and pepper to taste and serve.

VARIATION

Skillet Broccoli with Sesame Oil and Ginger

Omit thyme. Substitute 2 teaspoons toasted sesame oil for 2 teaspoons of olive oil in garlic mixture in step 1; add 2 teaspoons grated fresh ginger to garlic mixture.

NOTES FROM THE TEST KITCHEN

All About Garlic

When shopping for garlic, choose unpackaged, loose garlic heads so you can examine them closely. Pick heads without spots, mold, or sprouting. Squeeze them to make sure they are not rubbery, have no soft spots, and aren't missing cloves. The garlic shouldn't have much of a scent; if it does, you're risking spoilage. Here are the types of garlic you will find at the market plus everything you need to know about preparing and cooking garlic.

SOFTNECK GARLIC
Of the various garlic varieties, your best bet is softneck garlic, since it stores well and is heat-tolerant. This variety features a circle of large cloves surrounding a small cluster at the center.

HARDNECK GARLIC
Distinguished by a stiff center staff surrounded by large, uniform cloves, hardneck garlic has a more intense, complex flavor. But since it's easily damaged and doesn't store as well as softneck garlic, wait to buy it at the farmers' market.

ELEPHANT GARLIC
The huge individual cloves of so-called elephant garlic—which is actually a member of the leek family—are often sold alongside regular garlic. We find its flavor too mild and don't recommend it.

STORING GARLIC: With proper storage, whole heads of garlic should last at least a few weeks. Store heads in a cool, dark place with plenty of air circulation to prevent spoiling and sprouting. (A small basket in the pantry is ideal.)

PREPARING GARLIC: When preparing garlic, keep in mind that a fine mince equals strong flavor. Garlic's pungency emerges only after its cell walls are ruptured, triggering the creation of a compound called allicin. The more a clove is broken down, the more allicin—and more flavor—is produced. Thus you can control the amount of bite garlic contributes to a recipe by how fine or coarse you cut it. It's also best not to cut garlic in advance; the longer cut garlic sits, the harsher its flavor.

COOKING GARLIC: Garlic's flavor is sharpest when raw. Once heated above 150 degrees, its enzymes are destroyed and no new flavor is produced. This is why roasted garlic, which is cooked slowly and takes longer to reach 150 degrees, has a mellow, slightly sweet flavor. Alternatively, garlic browned at very high temperatures (300 to 350 degrees) results in a more bitter flavor. To avoid the creation of bitter compounds, wait to add garlic to the pan until other aromatics or ingredients have softened. And don't cook garlic over high heat for much longer than 30 seconds; you want to cook it, stirring constantly, only until it turns fragrant.

GARLIC SUBSTITUTES: When garlic is a predominant flavor in a recipe, nothing comes close to fresh. However, garlic substitutes have a long shelf life and require no prep, so in recipes that only call for a clove or two, the convenience may be worth a little loss in flavor. Granulated garlic and garlic powder are both made from garlic cloves that are dehydrated and ground; dehydrated minced garlic is minced while fresh then dehydrated and packaged, but it must be reconstituted before use. We prefer granulated garlic; substitute ¾ teaspoon for every 1 teaspoon fresh minced garlic.

Roasted Broccoli

SERVES 2 `FAST`

✓ **WHY THIS RECIPE WORKS:** Roasting is a great way to deepen the flavor of vegetables, but broccoli can be tricky to roast given its awkward shape, dense, woody stalks, and shrubby florets. We wanted a roasted broccoli recipe that would give us evenly cooked broccoli with concentrated flavor and dappled browning. The way we prepared the broccoli was key. Because contact with the baking sheet was essential for browning, we cut the broccoli crown into uniform wedges to maximize its flat surface area. Then we cut the stalks into slightly smaller pieces so everything would cook through at the same rate. We further amped up browning by sprinkling the broccoli with a bit of sugar, which had the added benefit of bringing out the broccoli's natural sweetness. Preheating the baking sheet cut down on cooking time and therefore reduced the risk of charred buds. A simple squeeze of lemon brightened the finished dish.

 1 **pound broccoli**
 2 **tablespoons extra-virgin olive oil**
 ¼ **teaspoon sugar**
 ¼ **teaspoon salt**
 ¼ **teaspoon pepper**
   Lemon wedges

1. Adjust oven rack to lowest position, line rimmed baking sheet with aluminum foil, place sheet on rack, and heat oven to 500 degrees. Cut broccoli at juncture of florets and stalks and remove outer peel from stalk. Cut stalk into ½-inch-thick pieces. Cut crowns into 4 wedges if 3 to 4 inches in diameter, or into 6 wedges if 4 to 5 inches in diameter. Toss broccoli pieces with oil, sugar, salt, and pepper.

Cutting Broccoli Crown into Wedges

1. After cutting off stalk and setting aside (do not discard), place crown upside down, then cut in half through central stalk.

2. Lay each half on its cut side. For each half, if it is 3 to 4 inches in diameter, cut it into 4 wedges, or into 6 wedges if 4 to 5 inches in diameter.

2. Carefully arrange broccoli flat side down in single layer on hot sheet and roast until stem pieces are well browned and tender and florets are lightly browned, 9 to 11 minutes. Serve with lemon wedges.

VARIATIONS
Roasted Broccoli with Olives, Garlic, Oregano, and Lemon

While broccoli roasts, cook 1 tablespoon extra-virgin olive oil, 3 thinly sliced garlic cloves, and ¼ teaspoon red pepper flakes in 8-inch skillet over medium-low heat until garlic begins to brown, 5 to 7 minutes. Off heat, stir in 1 tablespoon chopped pitted kalamata olives, 1 teaspoon lemon juice, and ½ teaspoon minced fresh oregano. Toss roasted broccoli with olive mixture before serving.

Roasted Broccoli with Shallot, Fennel Seeds, and Parmesan

Use a vegetable peeler to shave the Parmesan.

While broccoli roasts, heat 2 teaspoons extra-virgin olive oil in 8-inch skillet over medium heat until shimmering. Add 1 thinly sliced large shallot and cook until softened and lightly browned, 5 to 7 minutes. Stir in ½ teaspoon coarsely chopped fennel seeds and continue to cook until shallot is golden brown, 1 to 2 minutes. Toss roasted broccoli with shallot mixture and ¼ cup shaved Parmesan cheese before serving.

Roasted Brussels Sprouts

SERVES 2

✓ **WHY THIS RECIPE WORKS:** For a streamlined recipe for roasted Brussels sprouts, we halved the sprouts to speed cooking and to create a flat surface for browning. Since we were making just enough sprouts for two, we found that a regular baking sheet was too big; the oil burned where the sheet was empty. So we roasted the sprouts in a 12-inch ovensafe skillet with a tight-fitting cover, eliminating the need for foil. We tossed the sprouts with a little water to create a steamy environment to cook the sprouts through plus a tablespoon of oil to ensure they didn't stick. Uncovering the pan partway through allowed the exteriors to caramelize, giving us tender sprouts with nicely browned exteriors. Look for Brussels sprouts that are about 1½ inches long; quarter sprouts longer than 2½ inches. Be careful not to cut off too much of the stem end when trimming the sprouts, or the leaves will fall away from the core.

Steaming then roasting Brussels sprouts ensures the insides are fully tender and the outsides are nicely browned and caramelized.

8   ounces Brussels sprouts, trimmed and halved
4   teaspoons water
1   tablespoon olive oil
    Salt and pepper

1. Adjust oven rack to upper-middle position and heat oven to 500 degrees. Toss Brussels sprouts with water, oil, ⅛ teaspoon salt, and pinch pepper and arrange cut side down in 12-inch ovensafe skillet.

2. Cover and roast sprouts for 10 minutes. Uncover and continue to roast until sprouts are well browned and tender, 10 to 12 minutes. Season with salt and pepper to taste and serve.

VARIATIONS
Roasted Brussels Sprouts with Garlic, Red Pepper Flakes, and Parmesan
While Brussels sprouts roast, heat 2 teaspoons olive oil in 8-inch skillet over medium-low heat until shimmering. Add 1 small minced garlic clove and pinch red pepper flakes and cook until garlic is golden and fragrant, about 1 minute. Remove from heat. Toss roasted sprouts with garlic oil, then season with salt and pepper to taste. Sprinkle with 1 tablespoon grated Parmesan cheese before serving.

Roasted Brussels Sprouts with Bacon and Pecans
While Brussels sprouts roast, halve 1 slice bacon crosswise and cook in 8-inch skillet over medium heat until crisp, 5 to 7 minutes. Using slotted spoon, transfer bacon to paper towel–lined plate and reserve bacon fat. Finely chop bacon. After transferring sprouts to platter, toss with 1½ teaspoons olive oil, reserved bacon fat, chopped bacon, and 2 tablespoons finely chopped toasted pecans. Season with salt and pepper to taste and serve.

Braised Brussels Sprouts
SERVES 2 FAST LIGHT

✔ **WHY THIS RECIPE WORKS:** Braising is a quick and fuss-free cooking method for producing tender, flavorful Brussels sprouts. We simply simmered the sprouts in a covered skillet until they were bright green and almost tender, then we removed the lid to cook the sprouts through and reduce the braising liquid into a sauce to coat the sprouts. Braising the sprouts in water worked well, but chicken broth gave them a much richer flavor. A shallot sautéed in butter further enhanced the dish's flavor, and the butter also thickened the sauce nicely. Don't use a larger skillet; it will cause the liquid to disappear too quickly. Look for Brussels sprouts that are about 1½ inches long; quarter sprouts longer than 2½ inches. Be careful not to cut off too much of the stem end when trimming the sprouts, or the leaves will fall away from the core. For the nutritional information for this recipe, see page 415.

1   tablespoon unsalted butter
1   small shallot, minced
    Salt and pepper
8   ounces Brussels sprouts, trimmed and halved
¾   cup chicken broth

1. Melt butter in 10-inch nonstick skillet over medium heat. Add shallot and ⅛ teaspoon salt and cook until softened, about 2 minutes. Add Brussels sprouts, broth, and pinch pepper and bring to simmer. Cover and cook until sprouts are bright green and almost tender, 7 to 10 minutes.

2. Uncover and continue to cook until sprouts are tender and braising liquid is slightly thickened, 3 to 5 minutes. Season with salt and pepper to taste and serve.

VARIATION
Braised Brussels Sprouts with Curry and Currants
For the nutritional information for this recipe, see page 415.
    Add ¾ teaspoon curry powder to skillet with shallot and add 1 tablespoon currants with Brussels sprouts.

Glazed Carrots

SERVES 2 `FAST`

✓ **WHY THIS RECIPE WORKS:** For well-seasoned carrots with a glossy, clingy, modestly sweet glaze, we started by slicing the carrots on the bias, which lent visual appeal without much work. Most glazed carrot recipes start by steaming, parboiling, or blanching the carrots prior to glazing. To make our glazed carrots a convenient one-dish operation, we steamed them directly in the skillet. Steaming them in chicken broth seasoned with a little sugar provided a savory backbone and complemented the sweetness of the carrots. When the carrots were just shy of done, we removed the lid and turned up the heat to reduce the liquid to a perfectly clingy glaze, adding some butter for a silky finish. Fresh lemon and ground black pepper offered brightness and bite and gave the sweet carrots extra depth.

- 3 carrots, peeled and sliced ¼ inch thick on bias
- ½ cup chicken broth
- 1 tablespoon sugar
- 1 tablespoon unsalted butter, cut into 4 pieces
- 1 teaspoon lemon juice
  Salt and pepper

1. Bring carrots, broth, and 2 teaspoons sugar to boil in 10-inch nonstick skillet over medium-high heat. Reduce heat to medium, cover, and simmer, stirring occasionally, until carrots are almost tender when poked with tip of paring knife, about 5 minutes.

2. Uncover, increase heat to medium-high, and simmer, stirring occasionally, until cooking liquid is reduced to about 1 tablespoon, 1 to 2 minutes. Stir in butter and remaining 1 teaspoon sugar and cook, stirring frequently, until carrots are completely tender and glaze is lightly golden, 1 to 2 minutes.

3. Off heat, stir in lemon juice and season with salt and pepper to taste. Serve.

Slicing Carrots on the Bias

Cut carrot on bias into pieces that are ¼ inch thick and 2 inches long.

VARIATIONS
Glazed Carrots with Ginger and Rosemary

Cut ½-inch piece fresh ginger in half. Add ginger to skillet with carrots in step 1 and add ¼ teaspoon minced fresh rosemary with butter in step 2. Discard ginger pieces before serving.

Glazed Carrots with Currants and Almonds

Lightly toasting the curry powder in a warm, dry skillet brings forth its full flavor. If currants are unavailable, substitute an equal amount of coarsely chopped raisins.

Toast ½ teaspoon curry powder in 10-inch nonstick skillet over medium heat until fragrant, about 30 seconds. Add carrots, broth, and sugar to skillet with curry powder, bring to boil, and proceed with recipe. Add 2 tablespoons currants to skillet with butter in step 2. Sprinkle carrots with 2 tablespoons toasted sliced almonds before serving.

Roasted Carrots

SERVES 2

✓ **WHY THIS RECIPE WORKS:** Roasting carrots draws out their natural sugars and intensifies their flavor—if you can prevent them from coming out dry and shriveled. Cutting the carrots into large batons about ½ inch wide gave us evenly cooked results with the best browning, and precooking the carrots before roasting kept their moisture in and minimized withering. We avoided dirtying a second pan by precooking the buttered, seasoned carrots right on the baking sheet, covered with foil to keep them from drying out. The butter, which has a high water content, helped create a steamy cooking environment. Then, when the carrots were almost tender, we removed the foil to brown and caramelize them. Be sure to cut the carrots into uniform batons before roasting; otherwise, they will not cook evenly or brown properly.

- 4 carrots, peeled, halved crosswise, and cut lengthwise into ½-inch-wide batons
- 1 tablespoon unsalted butter, melted
  Salt and pepper

1. Adjust oven rack to middle position and heat oven to 425 degrees. Line rimmed baking sheet with aluminum foil. Toss carrots with melted butter, ¼ teaspoon salt, and ⅛ teaspoon pepper and arrange in single layer on prepared sheet. Cover sheet tightly with foil and roast carrots until almost tender, about 15 minutes.

2. Carefully remove top piece of foil and continue to roast carrots, uncovered, until well browned and tender, 20 to 25 minutes, stirring twice during roasting. Season with salt and pepper to taste and serve.

VARIATIONS

Roasted Carrots and Fennel with Toasted Almonds and Parsley

Reduce number of carrots to 3. Toss ½ fennel bulb, cored and sliced ½ inch thick, with carrots, butter, and seasonings. Toss roasted vegetables with 2 tablespoons toasted sliced almonds, 1 teaspoon minced fresh parsley, and ½ teaspoon lemon juice before serving.

Roasted Carrots and Shallots with Lemon and Thyme

Reduce number of carrots to 3. Toss 3 shallots, peeled and halved lengthwise, and ½ teaspoon minced fresh thyme with carrots, butter, and seasonings. Toss roasted vegetables with ¾ teaspoon lemon juice before serving.

Preparing Carrots for Roasting

Cutting carrots to a uniform size is key to evenly cooked results when roasting.

A. For large carrots (over 1 inch in diameter), cut carrot in half crosswise, then quarter each section lengthwise to create total of 8 pieces.

B. For medium carrots (½ to 1 inch in diameter), cut carrot in half crosswise, then halve wider section lengthwise to create total of 3 pieces.

C. For small carrots (less than ½ inch in diameter), cut carrot in half crosswise, then leave both sections whole.

For beautifully browned roasted cauliflower, we cut the cauliflower into wedges to maximize contact with the hot baking sheet.

Roasted Cauliflower

SERVES 2

✔ **WHY THIS RECIPE WORKS:** We wanted to add flavor to cauliflower without drowning it in a blanket of cheese sauce, so we developed a recipe for roasted cauliflower with golden, nutty, well-browned edges and a sweet, tender interior. Since browning took place only where the cauliflower was in contact with the hot baking sheet, we sliced half a head of cauliflower into four wedges, creating more flat surface area than you'd get with florets. To keep the cauliflower from drying out, we started it covered in a hot oven, which allowed it to steam until barely soft. Then we removed the foil to caramelize and brown the wedges. Flipping each slice halfway through roasting ensured even cooking and color. Thanks to its natural sweetness and flavor, our roasted cauliflower needed little enhancement—just a drizzle of olive oil and a sprinkle of salt and pepper.

½ head cauliflower (1 pound)
2 tablespoons extra-virgin olive oil
  Salt and pepper

1. Adjust oven rack to lowest position and heat oven to 475 degrees. Line rimmed baking sheet with aluminum foil.

2. Trim outer leaves off cauliflower and cut stem flush with bottom. Cut cauliflower into 4 equal wedges. Arrange wedges cut side down on prepared sheet, drizzle with 1 tablespoon oil, and sprinkle with salt and pepper. Gently rub seasonings and oil into cauliflower, then flip cauliflower and season other cut side with remaining 1 tablespoon oil, salt, and pepper.

3. Cover sheet tightly with foil and roast cauliflower for 10 minutes. Carefully remove top piece of foil and continue to roast, uncovered, until bottoms of cauliflower pieces are golden, about 4 minutes. Remove sheet from oven, and, using spatula, carefully flip cauliflower. Return sheet to oven and continue to roast cauliflower until golden all over, about 4 minutes. Season with salt and pepper to taste. Serve.

VARIATIONS

Roasted Cauliflower with Lemon and Capers

Add 1 teaspoon minced fresh thyme to oil before rubbing on cauliflower. In medium bowl, whisk 1 tablespoon rinsed and chopped capers, additional 1 teaspoon olive oil, 1 teaspoon lemon juice, and ¼ teaspoon grated lemon zest together. Gently toss roasted cauliflower in oil mixture before serving.

Roasted Cauliflower with Chorizo and Smoked Paprika

Add 1 teaspoon smoked paprika to oil before rubbing on cauliflower. Spread 1 small red onion, halved and sliced ½ inch thick, and 3 ounces chorizo, halved lengthwise and sliced ½ inch thick, on baking sheet with cauliflower before roasting. In medium bowl, whisk 1 tablespoon minced fresh parsley, additional 1 teaspoon olive oil, and 1 teaspoon sherry vinegar together. Gently toss roasted cauliflower in oil mixture before serving.

Cutting Cauliflower into Wedges

1. Trim off outer leaves of cauliflower and cut stem flush with bottom of head. Place head upside down and cut in half through central stalk. Set aside one half for another use.

2. Lay remaining cauliflower half on its cut side and cut it into 4 wedges, keeping florets attached to pieces of central stalk.

Braised Cauliflower

SERVES 2 **FAST**

✓ **WHY THIS RECIPE WORKS:** Cauliflower is a perfect candidate for braising thanks to its porous surface, which allows it to absorb liquid—and therefore flavor—easily. Briefly sautéing the florets in olive oil added flavor to the finished dish and also conveniently reduced the total cooking time. We deglazed the pan with chicken broth, added a clove of garlic and some red pepper flakes, and covered the pan to let the cauliflower cook through. The simple flavors of the braising liquid highlighted the nutty, earthy flavor of the cauliflower without overwhelming it. We finished the dish with a sprinkle of minced fresh parsley. For the best texture and flavor, make sure to brown the cauliflower well in step 1.

2 tablespoons olive oil
1 garlic clove, minced
 Pinch red pepper flakes
½ head cauliflower (1 pound), cored and cut into 1-inch florets
 Salt and pepper
½ cup chicken broth
1 tablespoon minced fresh parsley

1. Combine 1 teaspoon oil, garlic, and pepper flakes in bowl. Heat remaining 5 teaspoons oil in 10-inch skillet over medium-high heat until shimmering. Add cauliflower and ⅛ teaspoon salt and cook, stirring occasionally, until florets are golden brown, 6 to 8 minutes.

2. Push cauliflower to sides of skillet. Add garlic mixture and cook, mashing mixture into skillet, until fragrant, about 30 seconds. Stir garlic mixture into cauliflower.

3. Stir in broth and bring to simmer. Cover and cook until cauliflower is crisp-tender, 4 to 5 minutes. Off heat, stir in parsley and season with salt and pepper to taste. Serve.

VARIATION

Braised Curried Cauliflower

Add 1 teaspoon curry powder to garlic mixture in step 1. Substitute ¼ cup plain yogurt for ¼ cup of chicken broth and 1 tablespoon minced fresh cilantro for parsley. Stir 1½ teaspoons lime juice into braised cauliflower with cilantro.

Convenient garlic-and-herb Boursin cheese makes a rich, flavorful, and easy cheese sauce for our Cauliflower Gratin.

Cauliflower Gratin

SERVES 2

✔ **WHY THIS RECIPE WORKS:** We wanted an effortless version of this casserole that would serve two, not 10. Cooking the cauliflower in the microwave gave us a big head start (no need to drag out a pot to steam it on the stovetop) and meant that our gratin needed just a short stint in the oven. For a speedy cheese sauce, we microwaved garlic-and-herb Boursin cheese with a small amount of heavy cream; after just a minute, it had thickened to the right consistency. Toasted panko bread crumbs ensured that our easy cauliflower gratin offered the same golden, crisp topping as traditional versions. You will need an 8½ by 5½-inch baking dish for this recipe.

½ cup panko bread crumbs

1½ teaspoons olive oil

10 ounces cauliflower florets, cut into 1-inch pieces

1 tablespoon water

½ (5.2-ounce) package Boursin Garlic and Fine Herbs cheese

¼ cup heavy cream

¼ teaspoon salt

⅛ teaspoon pepper

1. Adjust oven rack to middle position and heat oven to 450 degrees. Combine panko and oil in 8-inch nonstick skillet. Toast panko over medium-high heat, stirring often, until golden, about 3 minutes.

2. Meanwhile, microwave cauliflower and water together in covered bowl until tender, about 3 minutes; drain cauliflower.

3. Wipe bowl dry with paper towels. Microwave Boursin, cream, salt, and pepper in cleaned bowl until cheese is melted, about 1 minute. Whisk Boursin mixture until smooth, then add drained cauliflower and toss to coat.

4. Transfer cauliflower mixture to 8½ by 5½-inch baking dish and sprinkle with toasted panko. Bake until hot and lightly bubbling around edges, about 7 minutes. Transfer gratin to wire rack and let cool for 5 to 10 minutes before serving.

Braised Hearty Greens

SERVES 2

✔ **WHY THIS RECIPE WORKS:** The traditional Southern method for making braised greens—simmering the greens with a ham hock for hours—results in a rich and tasty dish, but the greens lose their deep color, firm texture, and earthy flavor. We wanted an easy one-pot recipe for fresh and flavorful braised greens. Since we just needed enough for two, we were able to cook all the greens at once instead of in batches. We wilted kale in a small amount of broth and then, when it was tender, we removed the lid to allow the liquid to evaporate. The result: perfectly tender but not waterlogged winter greens. Shallot, brown sugar, cider vinegar, and cayenne pepper rounded out the flavors. Don't dry the greens completely after washing; a little extra water clinging to the leaves will help them wilt when cooking. You can substitute mustard, turnip, or collard greens for the kale; if using collard greens, allow 2 to 3 extra minutes of cooking time in step 1.

2 tablespoons unsalted butter

1 shallot, sliced thin

1 pound kale, stemmed and cut into 1-inch pieces

½ cup chicken broth

1½ teaspoons packed brown sugar

Salt and pepper

⅛ teaspoon cayenne pepper

1½ teaspoons cider vinegar

1. Melt 1 tablespoon butter in medium saucepan over medium heat. Add shallot and cook until softened, about 2 minutes. Add kale, broth, sugar, ¼ teaspoon salt, and cayenne. Cover, reduce heat to medium-low, and cook, stirring occasionally, until kale is completely tender, about 10 minutes.

2. Uncover, increase heat to medium-high, and cook, stirring occasionally, until liquid is nearly evaporated, 10 to 12 minutes. Off heat, stir in remaining 1 tablespoon butter and vinegar. Season with salt and pepper to taste and serve.

VARIATIONS

Braised Hearty Greens with Pancetta and Pine Nuts

Cook 2 ounces chopped thinly sliced pancetta in medium saucepan over medium heat until browned and crisp, 6 to 8 minutes. Using slotted spoon, transfer pancetta to paper towel–lined plate; substitute fat left in saucepan for butter in step 1. Proceed with recipe, substituting 1½ teaspoons red wine vinegar for cider vinegar and topping braised greens with 1 tablespoon toasted pine nuts and crisp pancetta before serving.

Braised Hearty Greens with White Beans

Substitute 1 small onion, halved and thinly sliced, for shallot in step 1; cook until softened and lightly browned, 5 to 7 minutes. Add 1 minced garlic clove and cook until fragrant, about 30 seconds. Proceed with recipe, adding 1 cup rinsed canned small white beans to kale after removing lid in step 2.

Sautéed Mushrooms

SERVES 2

✔ **WHY THIS RECIPE WORKS:** Deeply browned and ultra-savory, sautéed mushrooms make a great side dish, but the mushrooms can quickly turn from silky and rich to rubbery and greasy. To make this dish foolproof, the first step was choosing the right mushrooms. We liked the robust flavor of cremini paired with a smaller amount of rich, earthy shiitakes. To keep the high water content of the cremini from inhibiting browning, we cooked them in a covered skillet until they released their liquid, then we uncovered the skillet to let the liquid evaporate and the mushrooms brown. A generous amount of butter kept the mushrooms from burning, and deglazing the pan with white wine picked up flavorful fond and provided a welcome acidic punch to our earthy mushrooms. Look for shiitakes that have caps between 2 and 2½ inches in diameter. You will need a 10-inch skillet with a tight-fitting lid for this recipe.

A combination of flavorful cremini and meaty shiitake mushrooms sautéed in butter and white wine makes a decadent side dish.

2	tablespoons unsalted butter
1	small shallot, sliced thin
8	ounces cremini or white mushrooms, trimmed and halved if small or quartered if large
4	ounces shiitake mushrooms, stemmed and sliced ½ inch thick
	Salt and pepper
¾	teaspoon minced fresh thyme or ⅛ teaspoon dried
1	small garlic clove, minced
2½	tablespoons dry white wine

1. Melt 1 tablespoon butter in 10-inch skillet over medium heat. Add shallot and cook until softened, about 2 minutes. Add cremini mushrooms, shiitake mushrooms, and ¼ teaspoon salt, cover, and cook, stirring occasionally, until mushrooms have released their moisture, 8 to 10 minutes.

2. Remove lid, add remaining 1 tablespoon butter, and cook, stirring occasionally, until mushrooms are deep golden brown and tender, 10 to 12 minutes. Stir in thyme and garlic and cook until fragrant, about 30 seconds. Stir in wine and cook, scraping up any browned bits, until liquid is nearly evaporated, about 30 seconds. Season with salt and pepper to taste and serve.

All About Mushrooms

Mushrooms are a common ingredient in the test kitchen because we love their complex meatiness in soups, sauces, meats, and stuffings, or simply stuffed, marinated, or sautéed on their own. There are many varieties of fresh mushrooms available at the supermarket nowadays: the humble white button mushroom, as well as cremini, shiitake, oyster, and portobello mushrooms, for starters. We find cremini mushrooms to be firmer and more flavorful than white mushrooms, but the two are interchangeable in any recipe. We also frequently reach for dried porcini mushrooms, which add potent flavor to recipes in small amounts and have a conveniently long shelf life.

BUYING FRESH MUSHROOMS: Buy mushrooms loose if possible so that you can inspect their quality and buy exactly what you need. When buying white or cremini mushrooms, look for mushrooms with whole, intact caps; avoid those with discoloration or dry, shriveled patches. Pick mushrooms with large caps and minimal stems.

PREPARING FRESH MUSHROOMS: When it comes to cleaning, you can ignore the advice against washing mushrooms, which exaggerates their ability to absorb water, as long as you wash them before they are cut. We found that 6 ounces of mushrooms only gained about a quarter ounce of water after washing, not nearly enough to make them taste soggy. If you plan to serve the mushrooms raw, however, you're better off brushing them with a dry toothbrush, as rinsing can cause discoloration.

STORING FRESH MUSHROOMS: Due to their high moisture content, mushrooms are very perishable; most mushrooms can be kept fresh only a few days. We recommend storing loose mushrooms in the crisper drawer in a partially open zipper-lock bag, which maximizes air circulation without letting the mushrooms dry out. Store packaged mushrooms in their original containers, as these are designed to "breathe," maximizing the life of the mushrooms. After opening the package, simply rewrap the box with plastic wrap.

BUYING AND STORING DRIED MUSHROOMS: When purchasing dried mushrooms, avoid packages filled with small, dusty pieces, full of small holes (which can indicate worms), or those labeled "wild mushroom mix"—they are often older and of lesser quality. Dried mushrooms should have an earthy (not musty or stale) aroma. Store dried mushrooms in an airtight container in a cool, dry place for up to one year.

PREPARING DRIED MUSHROOMS: Dried mushrooms are typically gritty and tough, so they should be rinsed thoroughly to remove any dirt and grit and then softened. An easy way to do this? Microwave dried mushrooms, covered, with at least twice the volume of water or broth (alternatively, they can be soaked in hot liquid for about 5 minutes) until they become pliable enough to chop. Don't throw the soaking liquid away—once strained, it adds a meaty, earthy flavor to soups, stews, and rice dishes. We use a fine-mesh strainer lined with a single paper towel or paper coffee filter for the job.

Sautéed Snow Peas with Lemon and Parsley

SERVES 2 FAST LIGHT

✔ **WHY THIS RECIPE WORKS:** We wanted to create a dish in which sweet, grassy snow peas would be the star component. To highlight and amplify the delicate flavor of the peas, we knew we needed to brown them to caramelize their flavor. We tried a traditional stir-fry technique, but the constant stirring gave us greasy, overcooked pods without any browning. Adding a sprinkle of sugar and cooking the peas without stirring for a short time helped to achieve a flavorful sear, then we continued to cook them, stirring constantly, until they were just crisp-tender. To boost flavor, we sautéed minced shallot flavored with lemon zest and then stirred everything together. A squeeze of lemon juice and parsley added just before serving kept this dish fresh and bright. For the nutritional information for this recipe, see page 415.

2 teaspoons vegetable oil
1 small shallot, minced
¾ teaspoon grated lemon zest plus ½ teaspoon juice
 Salt and pepper
⅛ teaspoon sugar
6 ounces snow peas, strings removed
1 tablespoon minced fresh parsley, chives, or tarragon

1. Combine 1 teaspoon oil, shallot, and lemon zest in small bowl. Combine ¼ teaspoon salt, ⅛ teaspoon pepper, and sugar in separate small bowl.

2. Heat remaining 1 teaspoon oil in 10-inch nonstick skillet over high heat until just smoking. Add snow peas, sprinkle with salt mixture, and cook, without stirring, for 30 seconds. Stir, then continue to cook, without stirring, until snow peas are beginning to brown, about 30 seconds. Continue to cook, stirring constantly, until peas are crisp-tender, 1 to 2 minutes.

3. Push peas to sides of skillet. Add shallot mixture and cook, mashing mixture into skillet, until fragrant, about 30 seconds. Stir shallot mixture into peas, transfer to bowl, and stir in lemon juice and parsley. Season with salt and pepper to taste and serve.

VARIATIONS

Sautéed Snow Peas with Ginger and Scallion

For the nutritional information for this recipe, see page 415.

Substitute 2 minced scallion whites, 1½ teaspoons grated fresh ginger, and 1 minced small garlic clove for shallot and lemon zest. Substitute pinch red pepper flakes for pepper in step 1. Substitute ½ teaspoon rice vinegar for lemon juice and 2 thinly sliced scallion greens for parsley.

Sautéed Snow Peas with Cumin and Cilantro

For the nutritional information for this recipe, see page 415.

Substitute 1 minced small garlic clove and ¼ teaspoon toasted cumin seeds for shallot. Substitute ½ teaspoon lime zest for lemon zest, ½ teaspoon lime juice for lemon juice, and 1 tablespoon minced fresh cilantro for parsley.

NOTES FROM THE TEST KITCHEN

All About Onions

Many supermarkets stock a half-dozen types of onions. They don't all look the same or taste the same. Here are the onions and their close relatives that you will find in most markets.

YELLOW ONIONS
These strong-flavored onions maintain their potency when cooked, making them our first choice for cooking.

WHITE ONIONS
These pungent onions are similar to yellow onions but lack some of their complexity.

RED ONIONS
These crisp onions have a sweet, peppery flavor when raw and are often used in salads and for pickling.

SWEET ONIONS
Vidalia, Maui, and Walla Wallas are three common sweet varieties. Their texture can become stringy when cooked, so these sugary onions are best used raw.

PEARL ONIONS
These crunchy, small onions are generally used in soups, stews, and side dishes. Peeling them is a chore, so we recommend buying frozen pearl onions that are already peeled.

SHALLOTS
Shallots have a complex, subtly sweet flavor. When cooked, they become very soft and almost melt away, making them the perfect choice for sauces.

SCALLIONS
Scallions have an earthy flavor and delicate crunch that work well in dishes that involve little or no cooking, like stir-fries.

BUYING ONIONS: Choose onions with dry, papery skins. They should be rock-hard, with no soft spots or powdery mold on the skin. Avoid onions with green sprouts.

STORING ONIONS: All varieties of onions and shallots should be stored in the same way: at cool room temperature, away from light. Don't store onions in the refrigerator, where their odors can permeate other foods. Delicate scallions are the exception; they do belong in the refrigerator. Stand them up in 1 inch of water in a tall container and cover them loosely with a plastic bag.

To make supremely rich scalloped potatoes, we simmer the potatoes in broth and cream then stir in plenty of cheddar cheese.

Cheesy Scalloped Potatoes

SERVES 2

✔ **WHY THIS RECIPE WORKS:** Casserole-style scalloped potatoes can take up to an hour to cook through and usually serve a crowd, but that doesn't mean smaller households should be denied their cheesy, creamy appeal. We wanted an easy version sized for two. To speed things up, we simmered the potatoes in chicken broth and cream in a skillet until they were nearly tender, then moved the skillet to the oven, where they needed just 15 minutes to brown and cook through. To ensure our potatoes had tons of cheesy flavor, we stirred ½ cup of cheddar right into the sauce and sprinkled Parmesan on top to give the dish a nicely browned topping. A bit of cornstarch pulled double duty, thickening the sauce and preventing the cheeses from making the dish greasy. Do not use preshredded cheese, which contains added starch that will interfere with the sauce. Do not substitute extra-sharp or sharp cheddar for the mild cheddar. Prepare and assemble all of the ingredients before slicing the potatoes or the potatoes will begin to turn brown.

2 ounces mild cheddar cheese, shredded (½ cup)

1½ teaspoons cornstarch

1 ounce Parmesan cheese, grated (½ cup)

1 teaspoon vegetable oil

½ cup finely chopped onion

1 garlic clove, minced

1 teaspoon minced fresh thyme or ¼ teaspoon dried

⅓ cup chicken broth

⅓ cup heavy cream

12 ounces russet potatoes, peeled and sliced ¼ inch thick

½ teaspoon salt

¼ teaspoon pepper

1. Adjust oven rack to upper-middle position and heat oven to 425 degrees. Toss cheddar and 1 teaspoon cornstarch together in bowl until well combined. Toss Parmesan and remaining ½ teaspoon cornstarch together in second bowl until well combined.

2. Heat oil in 8-inch nonstick ovensafe skillet over medium heat until shimmering. Add onion and cook until softened and lightly browned, 5 to 7 minutes. Stir in garlic and thyme and cook until fragrant, about 30 seconds. Stir in broth, cream, potatoes, salt, and pepper and bring to boil. Reduce heat to medium-low, cover, and simmer until potatoes are nearly tender, 10 to 12 minutes.

3. Off heat, stir in cheddar mixture and press potatoes into even layer, removing any air pockets. Sprinkle Parmesan mixture evenly over top and bake until golden brown, 12 to 14 minutes. Transfer potatoes to wire rack and let cool for 5 to 10 minutes before serving.

Potato Gratin

SERVES 2

✔ **WHY THIS RECIPE WORKS:** For our potato gratin, we wanted an elegant dish of tender sliced potatoes napped with a rich, velvety cream sauce. Heavy cream thickened with flour gave us a rich-tasting sauce that was stable enough to withstand the baking time without breaking. We enriched the sauce with garlic, shallot, thyme, and a pinch each of nutmeg and cayenne. We skipped tediously layering the potato slices; we got the same attractive presentation by simply pouring them into the dish and gently pressing them down into an even layer. A sprinkle of grated Gruyère imparted a nutty flavor to this refined side dish. Parmesan can be used in place of the Gruyère. Use a mandoline, a V-slicer, or a food processor fitted with a ⅛-inch-thick slicing blade to slice the potatoes. You will need a shallow 8½ by 5½-inch baking dish with sides that are no more than 2 inches high for this recipe.

1 large russet potato (12 ounces), peeled and sliced ⅛ inch thick

1 tablespoon unsalted butter

1 small shallot, minced

½ teaspoon salt

1 garlic clove, minced

1 teaspoon minced fresh thyme or ¼ teaspoon dried

¼ teaspoon pepper

Pinch ground nutmeg

Pinch cayenne pepper

2 teaspoons all-purpose flour

¾ cup heavy cream

¼ cup finely grated Gruyère cheese

1. Adjust oven rack to upper-middle position and heat oven to 400 degrees. Grease 8½ by 5½-inch baking dish. Place potato slices in medium bowl.

2. Melt butter in small saucepan over medium heat. Add shallot and salt and cook until softened, about 2 minutes. Stir in garlic, thyme, pepper, nutmeg, and cayenne and cook until fragrant, about 30 seconds. Stir in flour and cook until incorporated, about 10 seconds. Whisk in cream, bring to simmer, and cook until beginning to thicken, about 30 seconds.

3. Pour sauce over potato slices and toss to coat thoroughly. Transfer potato mixture to prepared dish and gently press potato slices into even layer, removing any air pockets. Cover dish tightly with aluminum foil and bake until potatoes are almost tender, 35 to 40 minutes.

4. Carefully remove foil and sprinkle with Gruyère. Continue to bake, uncovered, until cheese is lightly browned and potatoes are tender, about 10 minutes. Transfer gratin to wire rack and let cool for 5 to 10 minutes before serving.

Perfect Baked Potatoes

SERVES 2 `LIGHT`

✔ **WHY THIS RECIPE WORKS:** For the ultimate classic baked potato, it took a lot of experimentation to discover that the traditional low-and-slow method is best. The crisp yet tender skin of a potato baked at 350 degrees for an hour and 15 minutes simply has no peer. Rubbing the potatoes with a bit of vegetable oil and cooking them directly on the oven rack allowed heat to circulate evenly and crisped the skin on all sides. To ensure that our potatoes had light and fluffy flesh, we found the most important step was opening them wide when they were hot to let the steam escape, rather than getting trapped in the potatoes and making them soggy. For the nutritional information for this recipe, see page 415.

2 russet potatoes (8 ounces each)

2 teaspoons vegetable oil

Adjust oven rack to middle position and heat oven to 350 degrees. Rub each potato with 1 teaspoon oil, place directly on oven rack, and bake until skewer glides easily through flesh, about 1¼ hours. Remove potatoes from oven and pierce with fork to create dotted X. Press in at ends of potatoes to push flesh up and out. Serve.

Preparing Baked Potatoes for Serving

1. Use tines of fork to make dotted X on top of each potato.

2. Press in at ends of potato to push flesh up and out.

VARIATION

30-Minute Baked Potatoes

If you don't have time for our Perfect Baked Potatoes, this variation is the next best thing. For the nutritional information for this recipe, see page 415.

Heat oven to 450 degrees. Do not rub potatoes with oil. Poke potatoes several times with fork. Microwave potatoes until slightly soft to touch, 6 to 12 minutes, turning them over halfway through cooking. Place microwaved potatoes directly on oven rack and bake until skewer glides easily through flesh, about 20 minutes. Remove potatoes from oven and pierce with fork to create dotted X. Press in at ends of potatoes to push flesh up and out. Serve.

Easier French Fries

SERVES 2 **FAST**

✔ **WHY THIS RECIPE WORKS:** Even with their short ingredient list, making fries at home can seem daunting. And filling a pot with oil to make fries for only two feels wasteful. We wanted a recipe that would require fewer steps and less oil. We discovered that starting our fries in cold oil, then heating it, was an easy solution to both problems: The gradual increase in temperature gave the fries a chance to cook through and soften before the exteriors crisped, and this method required only

3 cups of oil versus the 2 to 3 quarts called for in most recipes. Compared to traditional russets, the higher water content of Yukon Gold potatoes made for crisp fries with creamy interiors, and thanks to their thin skins, we didn't even have to peel them. You will need a saucepan with a 4-quart capacity for this recipe; if your pan is larger you may need more oil to cover the potatoes. If desired, serve with Belgian-Style Dipping Sauce or Garlic Mayonnaise (recipes follow).

1½ pounds Yukon gold potatoes, unpeeled, sides squared, and cut lengthwise into ¼-inch-thick batons

3 cups peanut oil or vegetable oil

Kosher salt

1. Set wire rack in rimmed baking sheet lined with triple layer of paper towels. Combine potatoes and oil in large saucepan. Cook over high heat until oil has reached rolling boil, about 5 minutes. Continue to cook, without stirring, until potatoes are limp but exteriors are beginning to firm, 12 to 14 minutes.

2. Using tongs, stir potatoes, gently scraping up any that stick, and continue to cook, stirring occasionally, until fries are golden and crisp, 5 to 10 minutes. Using slotted spoon, transfer fries to prepared rack. Season with salt to taste and serve immediately.

Cutting Potatoes for French Fries

1. Square off potato by cutting ¼-inch-thick slice from each of its 4 long sides.

2. Cut potato lengthwise into ¼-inch-thick planks.

3. Stack 3 or 4 planks and cut into ¼-inch-thick batons. Repeat with remaining planks.

Belgian-Style Dipping Sauce

MAKES ABOUT ¼ CUP

For a spicier sauce, use the larger quantity of hot sauce.

3	tablespoons mayonnaise
1	tablespoon ketchup
¼–½	teaspoon hot sauce
¼	teaspoon minced garlic
⅛	teaspoon salt

Whisk all ingredients together in bowl. Refrigerate until flavors have melded, about 15 minutes.

Garlic Mayonnaise

MAKES ABOUT ¼ CUP

¼	cup mayonnaise
1	teaspoon lemon juice
½	teaspoon Dijon mustard
½	small garlic clove, minced
	Salt and pepper

Whisk all ingredients together in bowl and season with salt and pepper to taste. Refrigerate until flavors have melded, about 15 minutes.

Mashed Potatoes

SERVES 2

✔ **WHY THIS RECIPE WORKS:** We wanted creamy yet fluffy mashed potatoes with plenty of buttery richness, and we didn't want to spend a lot of time or effort pulling this simple side together. We sped things up by swapping the usual russet potatoes for Yukon Golds. Because Yukon Golds have less starch and are less absorbent than russets, they don't become soggy when simmered without their skins. This meant we were able to peel and slice the potatoes before cooking, cutting our simmering time in half. Returning the drained potatoes to the hot pan to mash them helped the remaining water evaporate before the potatoes became gluey. Mashing the potatoes by hand prevented overbeating, keeping them from turning pasty. And melting the butter before folding it in along with the half-and-half allowed it to coat the starch molecules quickly and easily so the potatoes turned out creamy and light. You can substitute whole milk for the half-and-half here, but the potatoes will taste a bit leaner. Make sure to cook the potatoes thoroughly; they are done if they break apart when a knife is inserted and gently wiggled.

Mashing Yukon Golds with melted butter and half-and-half gives these potatoes a rich and creamy yet fluffy texture.

1	pound Yukon Gold potatoes, peeled and sliced ½ inch thick
	Salt and pepper
⅓	cup half-and-half, room temperature
3	tablespoons unsalted butter, melted and cooled

1. Place potatoes and 1 tablespoon salt in medium saucepan and add water to cover by 1 inch. Bring to boil over medium-high heat, then reduce to simmer and cook, stirring once or twice, until potatoes are tender, 12 to 15 minutes.

2. Drain potatoes and return to saucepan set on still-hot burner. Using potato masher, mash potatoes until a few small lumps remain. Gently mix half-and-half and melted butter together in small bowl until combined. Add half-and-half mixture to potatoes and, using rubber spatula, fold gently to incorporate. Season with salt and pepper to taste and serve immediately.

VARIATION

Buttermilk Mashed Potatoes

Substitute ⅓ cup buttermilk for half-and-half.

We give these rustic mashed potatoes richness and bright flavor with butter, tangy cream cheese, and minced fresh chives.

NOTES FROM THE TEST KITCHEN

All About Potatoes

Since potatoes have varying textures (determined by starch level), you can't just reach for any potato and expect great results. Potatoes fall into three main categories—baking, boiling, or all-purpose—depending on texture.

BAKING POTATOES

These dry, floury potatoes contain more total starch (20 to 22 percent) than other categories, giving these varieties a dry, mealy texture. These potatoes are the best choice when baking and frying. In our opinion, they are also the best potatoes for mashing because they can drink up butter and cream. They work well when you want to thicken a stew or soup, but not when you want distinct chunks of potatoes. Common varieties: Russet, Russet Burbank, and Idaho.

ALL-PURPOSE POTATOES

These potatoes contain less total starch (18 to 20 percent) than dry, floury potatoes but more than firm, waxy potatoes. Although they are considered "in-between" potatoes, their texture is more mealy than that of waxy potatoes, putting them closer to dry, floury potatoes. All-purpose potatoes can be mashed or baked but won't be as fluffy as dry, floury potatoes. They can be used in salads and soups but won't be quite as firm as waxy potatoes. Common varieties: Yukon Gold, Yellow Finn, Purple Peruvian, Kennebec, and Katahdin.

BOILING POTATOES

These potatoes contain a relatively low amount of total starch (16 to 18 percent), which means they have a firm, smooth, and waxy texture. Often they are called "new" potatoes because they are less mature potatoes harvested in the late spring and summer. They are less starchy than "old" potatoes because they haven't had time to convert their sugar to starch. They also have thinner skins. Firm, waxy potatoes are perfect when you want the potatoes to hold their shape, as with potato salad. They are also a good choice when roasting or boiling. Common varieties: Red Bliss, French Fingerling, Red Creamer, and White Rose.

BUYING POTATOES: Look for potatoes that are firm and free of green spots, sprouts, and cracks. Potatoes with a greenish tinge beneath the skin have had too much exposure to light and should also be avoided. Try to buy loose potatoes rather than those sold in plastic bags, which can act like greenhouses and cause potatoes to sprout, soften, and rot.

STORING POTATOES: If stored under unsuitable heat and light circumstances, potatoes will germinate and grow. To avoid this, keep them in a cool, dark place. Store potatoes in a paper (not plastic) bag and keep them away from onions, which give off gases that will hasten sprouting. Most varieties should keep for several months. The exception is new potatoes—because of their thinner skins, they will keep for no more than one month.

Rustic Smashed Red Potatoes

SERVES 2

✔ **WHY THIS RECIPE WORKS:** For our version of rustic smashed potatoes, we wanted chunks of potato textured with skins and bound by a rich, creamy puree. Moist, low-starch red potatoes had pleasantly tender, thin skins that gave us the perfect chunky texture. Cooking the potatoes whole helped them retain their naturally creamy character and kept the dish from getting waterlogged. A spatula or wooden spoon worked best to smash the potatoes without making them overly smooth. A combination of tangy cream cheese and melted butter complemented the rich, earthy potatoes without dulling their flavor, and adding some of the starchy cooking water thinned the mash just enough to keep it from turning gluey as it cooled. Use small red potatoes measuring 1 to 2 inches in diameter. Try to purchase potatoes of equal size; if that's not possible, test the larger potatoes for doneness. White potatoes can be used instead of red, but their skins will lack the rosy color.

12 ounces small red potatoes, unpeeled
    Salt and pepper
1   bay leaf
3   tablespoons cream cheese, softened
1   tablespoon unsalted butter, melted
1   tablespoon minced fresh chives (optional)

1. Place potatoes, 1 teaspoon salt, and bay leaf in medium saucepan and add water to cover by 1 inch. Bring to boil over medium-high heat, then reduce to simmer and cook, stirring once or twice, until potatoes are tender, 10 to 15 minutes. Reserve ½ cup cooking water, then drain potatoes. Return potatoes to saucepan, discard bay leaf, and let steam escape for 2 minutes.

2. Meanwhile, whisk softened cream cheese and melted butter together in small bowl until smooth and fully incorporated. Stir in 2 tablespoons reserved cooking water, ¼ teaspoon salt, ¼ teaspoon pepper, and chives, if using.

3. Using rubber spatula or back of wooden spoon, smash potatoes just enough to break skins. Fold in cream cheese mixture until most of liquid has been absorbed and chunks of potatoes remain. Add remaining reserved cooking water as needed, 1 tablespoon at a time, until potatoes are slightly looser than desired (potatoes will thicken slightly with sitting). Season with salt and pepper to taste and serve immediately.

Roasted Red Potatoes

SERVES 2

✔ WHY THIS RECIPE WORKS: To arrive at our ideal roasted potatoes—ones with deep golden, crisp crusts and creamy, soft interiors—we took advantage of the naturally high moisture content of red potatoes. Covering them for part of the cooking time allowed the trapped moisture to steam the potatoes, giving them creamy flesh and allowing us to skip the extra step of parboiling, a welcome timesaver. Finishing the potatoes uncovered crisped the outsides to a perfect golden brown. We knew from past recipes that contact with the baking sheet was important to browning, so we flipped the potatoes partway through the browning process to achieve multi-sided crispness. We made these simple potatoes even easier by lining the baking sheet with foil, making for quick cleanup.

1   pound red potatoes, unpeeled, cut into ¾-inch wedges
1½   tablespoons olive oil
     Salt and pepper

1. Adjust oven rack to middle position and heat oven to 425 degrees. Line rimmed baking sheet with aluminum foil. Toss potatoes with oil, ¼ teaspoon salt, and ⅛ teaspoon pepper and arrange cut side down in single layer on prepared sheet. Cover sheet tightly with foil and roast potatoes for 20 minutes.

2. Carefully remove top piece of foil and continue to roast, uncovered, until bottoms of potatoes are golden and crusty, 8 to 10 minutes. Remove sheet from oven, and, using spatula, flip potatoes. Return sheet to oven and continue to roast potatoes until crusty and golden on second side, about 5 minutes. Season with salt and pepper to taste. Serve.

VARIATION

Roasted Red Potatoes with Garlic and Rosemary
Sprinkle potatoes with 1 tablespoon minced fresh rosemary during final 5 minutes of roasting in step 2. Toss roasted potatoes with 1 minced garlic clove before serving.

Spinach with Garlic Chips and Red Pepper Flakes

SERVES 2 **FAST** **LIGHT**

✔ WHY THIS RECIPE WORKS: To create a quick and healthy spinach side dish, we wilted the spinach in a saucepan and added garlic and red pepper flakes to complement the earthy, mineral flavor of the greens. First we sliced the garlic thin and fried it in hot oil until golden and crisp. The garlic chips added a nice flavorful crunch, and wilting the spinach in the rich garlic oil added another layer of flavor. In just a few minutes, we had a healthy, flavorful spinach dish. One pound of flat-leaf spinach (about 1½ bunches) can be substituted for the curly-leaf spinach, but do not use baby spinach; it is too delicate. Do not heat the oil before adding the garlic in step 1; heating them together over gentle heat prevents the garlic from burning. Don't dry the spinach completely after washing; a little extra water clinging to the leaves will help them wilt when cooking. For the nutritional information for this recipe, see page 415.

1   tablespoon olive oil
2   garlic cloves, sliced thin
     Pinch red pepper flakes
10   ounces curly-leaf spinach, stemmed and chopped coarse
     Salt and pepper

1. Cook oil and garlic in large saucepan over medium heat, stirring occasionally, until garlic is golden and very crisp, about 5 minutes. Using slotted spoon, transfer garlic chips to paper towel–lined plate.

2. Add pepper flakes to garlic oil and cook over medium heat until fragrant, about 30 seconds. Add spinach in handfuls, stirring and tossing each handful to wilt slightly before adding next. Cover saucepan, increase heat to medium-high, and cook, stirring occasionally, until spinach is tender and wilted but still bright green, 1 to 3 minutes. Off heat, season with salt and pepper to taste and toss with garlic chips. Serve.

Easy Creamed Spinach
SERVES 2 **FAST**

✔ **WHY THIS RECIPE WORKS:** We wanted super-easy, one-pot creamed spinach that still offered the rich flavor and creamy texture of an authentic steakhouse version. After wilting our spinach in a covered pot, we set it in a colander to drain the excess liquid while we used the same pot to make the sauce. We bypassed the usual work-intensive béchamel and started with creamy Boursin cheese flavored with garlic and herbs. Just 2 tablespoons of cream ensured that our sauce was the right thickness to coat our spinach nicely. One pound of flat-leaf spinach (about 1½ bunches) can be substituted for the curly-leaf spinach, but do not use baby spinach because it is too delicate. Don't dry the spinach completely after washing; a little extra water clinging to the leaves will help them wilt when cooking.

1½   teaspoons olive oil
10   ounces curly-leaf spinach, stemmed and chopped coarse
½   (5.2-ounce) package Boursin Garlic and Fine Herbs cheese
2   tablespoons heavy cream
     Salt and pepper

1. Heat oil in large saucepan over high heat until shimmering. Add spinach in handfuls, stirring and tossing each handful to wilt slightly before adding next. Continue to cook spinach, stirring constantly, until uniformly wilted, about 1 minute. Transfer spinach to colander and squeeze between tongs to release excess liquid.

2. Wipe saucepan dry with paper towels. Whisk Boursin and cream together in now-empty saucepan, bring to simmer over medium-high heat, and cook until thickened, about 2 minutes. Off heat, stir in spinach until evenly coated. Season with salt and pepper to taste and serve.

We brush acorn squash with a sweet maple syrup glaze spiked with cayenne and roast it until tender and caramelized.

Maple-Glazed Acorn Squash
SERVES 2

✔ **WHY THIS RECIPE WORKS:** Maple syrup is a natural counterpart for earthy and sweet acorn squash, but many recipes leave the glaze in pools in the squash halves—or stuck on the baking sheet. To taste the syrup in every bite, we needed the syrup to stick but not burn. Cutting our acorn squash into wedges increased its surface area to give the glaze more to stick to (and smaller pieces of squash also resulted in a shorter roasting time). Tossing the wedges with vegetable oil and a small amount of sugar before baking ensured that they browned quickly. At first, our simple glaze of maple syrup and melted butter—with salt and a little cayenne for kick—ran right off the squash, but slightly reducing the glaze in the microwave helped it coat the squash nicely. Avoid using pancake syrup here; pure maple syrup is important to the flavor of this dish.

1 acorn squash (1½ pounds), halved pole to pole, seeded, and cut into 8 wedges
1 tablespoon vegetable oil
1 teaspoon sugar
Salt and pepper
2 tablespoons maple syrup
2 tablespoons unsalted butter
Pinch cayenne pepper

1. Adjust oven rack to middle position and heat oven to 475 degrees. Line rimmed baking sheet with aluminum foil. Toss squash with oil, sugar, ¼ teaspoon salt, and ¼ teaspoon pepper and arrange cut side down in single layer on prepared sheet. Roast until bottoms of squash wedges are deep golden brown, about 15 minutes.

2. Meanwhile, microwave maple syrup, butter, cayenne, and pinch salt in bowl, stirring occasionally, until butter is melted and mixture is slightly thickened, about 90 seconds; cover to keep warm.

3. Remove sheet from oven, and, using spatula, carefully flip squash. Brush with half of glaze and continue to roast until squash is tender and deep golden, 5 to 8 minutes. Carefully flip squash, brush with remaining glaze, and serve.

Preparing Acorn Squash for Roasting

1. Set squash on damp kitchen towel to hold in place. Position chef's knife on top of squash and strike with mallet to drive it into squash. Continue to hit knife with mallet until it cuts completely through squash.

2. After scooping out seeds with spoon, place squash halves cut side down on cutting board and cut in half, pole to pole, using mallet if necessary.

3. Using your hand to steady squash quarters, carefully cut each into 2 wedges.

Butternut Squash Puree
SERVES 2

✓ **WHY THIS RECIPE WORKS:** With a silky-smooth texture and lightly sweet flavor, pureed butternut squash is a surefire winner. And although it requires a relatively long cooking time, it's almost entirely hands-off. Our first instinct was to braise the squash, but we found that the squash's subtle flavor was washing away and its texture was watery. It turned out that the squash exuded so much liquid as it cooked that we didn't need to include braising liquid at all. Simply cooking the squash pieces over low heat created a perfect steamy environment, coaxing the flavor out of the squash while breaking down its tough starches. A little cream and butter were all we needed to enrich the squash without overpowering its delicate flavor. Pureeing the squash in the food processor yielded a sumptuous, creamy texture. You can substitute delicata squash for the butternut squash.

1 pound butternut squash, peeled, seeded, and cut into 1-inch pieces
2 tablespoons unsalted butter, cut into 2 pieces
2 tablespoons heavy cream
½ teaspoon sugar
Salt and pepper
Pinch cayenne pepper

1. Combine squash, butter, 1 tablespoon cream, sugar, ¼ teaspoon salt, ⅛ teaspoon pepper, and cayenne in medium saucepan. Cover and cook squash over low heat until fall-apart tender, 40 to 50 minutes.

2. Transfer squash mixture to food processor, add remaining 1 tablespoon cream, and process until smooth, about 20 seconds, scraping down sides of bowl as needed. Transfer squash puree to bowl, season with salt and pepper to taste, and serve.

VARIATIONS

Butternut Squash Puree with Orange
Add 1½ teaspoons packed brown sugar and 1½ teaspoons orange marmalade to blender with cream in step 2.

Butternut Squash Puree with Honey and Chipotle Chile
Add 1½ teaspoons honey and ½ teaspoon minced chipotle chile in adobo sauce to blender with cream in step 2.

Mashed Sweet Potatoes

SERVES 2

✔ **WHY THIS RECIPE WORKS:** Deeply flavored, earthy, and subtly sweet, mashed sweet potatoes hardly need a layer of marshmallows to make them into a tempting side. For a silky and full-flavored mash, we found the secret was to thinly slice the potatoes and cook them covered on the stovetop over low heat with just a little butter and cream. This method allowed the potatoes to cook evenly in their own moisture, retaining all of their flavor. A teaspoon of sugar was all the enhancement the potatoes needed. Once the potatoes were fall-apart tender, they could be mashed to a silky smooth texture right in the pot—no draining, no straining, no fuss. Adding another spoonful of cream when we mashed the potatoes enriched them even more.

1 **pound sweet potatoes, peeled, quartered lengthwise and sliced ¼ inch thick**
2 **tablespoons unsalted butter, cut into 2 pieces**
2 **tablespoons heavy cream**
1 **teaspoon sugar**
  Salt and pepper

1. Combine potatoes, butter, 1 tablespoon cream, sugar, ¼ teaspoon salt, and ⅛ teaspoon pepper in medium saucepan. Cover and cook potatoes over low heat until fall-apart tender, 40 to 50 minutes.

2. Add remaining 1 tablespoon cream and mash sweet potatoes with potato masher until a few small lumps remain. Season with salt and pepper to taste and serve.

Roasted Sweet Potatoes

SERVES 2 LIGHT

✔ **WHY THIS RECIPE WORKS:** Too often, roasted sweet potatoes turn out starchy and bland. We wanted a method that gave us potatoes with a nicely caramelized exterior, a smooth, creamy interior, and an earthy sweetness. Slicing the potatoes into ¾-inch-thick rounds and laying them flat on a baking sheet ensured even cooking. A few experiments proved that a lower roasting temperature resulted in a sweeter potato, so we started the potatoes in a cold (versus preheated) oven, allowing plenty of time for their starches to convert to sugars as the oven came up to temperature. To prevent scorching, we covered the potatoes with aluminum foil to start, then removed the foil after 20 minutes and continued to roast the potatoes until crisp and browned. Choose potatoes that are as

even in width as possible. If you prefer not to peel the potatoes, simply scrub them well before cutting. For the nutritional information for this recipe, see page 415.

1 **pound sweet potatoes, peeled, ends trimmed, and cut into ¾-inch-thick rounds**
1 **tablespoon vegetable oil**
  Salt and pepper

1. Line rimmed baking sheet with aluminum foil and spray with vegetable oil spray. Toss potatoes with oil until evenly coated, then season with salt and pepper. Arrange potatoes in single layer on prepared sheet and cover tightly with foil. Adjust oven rack to middle position and place potatoes in cold oven. Turn oven to 425 degrees and roast potatoes for 20 minutes.

2. Carefully remove top piece of foil and continue to roast, uncovered, until bottom edges of potatoes are golden brown, 8 to 10 minutes. Remove sheet from oven, and, using spatula, carefully flip potatoes. Return sheet to oven and continue to roast until bottom edges of potatoes are golden brown, 8 to 10 minutes. Season with salt and pepper to taste and serve.

Sautéed Swiss Chard

SERVES 2 FAST

✔ **WHY THIS RECIPE WORKS:** We wanted a recipe for Swiss chard that would bring out its earthy flavor but wouldn't compromise its tender, delicate texture. We found sautéing to be the best way to cook the chard; this method took advantage of the greens' high moisture content to help them wilt and soften without turning mushy. The tougher stems took slightly longer to cook than the leaves, so we added the stems to the skillet first to give them a head start. Minced onions lent sweetness that balanced the slightly bitter greens, lemon juice brightened the dish, and a little thyme, added at the last stage of cooking, rounded out the earthy flavor. You can use green or red chard here; keep in mind that red chard has a stronger flavor. Don't dry the greens completely after washing; a little extra water clinging to the leaves will help them wilt when cooking in step 1.

2 **tablespoons plus 1 teaspoon extra-virgin olive oil**
12 **ounces Swiss chard, stems chopped, leaves cut into ½-inch pieces**
¼ **cup finely chopped onion**
  Salt and pepper
1 **garlic clove, minced**

1 teaspoon minced fresh thyme or ¼ teaspoon dried

1 teaspoon lemon juice

1. Heat 2 tablespoons oil in 12-inch skillet over medium heat until shimmering. Add chard stems, onion, and ¼ teaspoon salt and cook until vegetables are softened and lightly browned, 5 to 7 minutes. Stir in garlic and thyme and cook until fragrant, about 30 seconds. Stir in chard leaves, cover, and cook, stirring occasionally, until chard is wilted and tender, about 5 minutes.

2. Off heat, stir in lemon juice and season with salt and pepper to taste. Drizzle with remaining 1 teaspoon oil and serve.

Preparing Swiss Chard and Hearty Greens

1. To prepare Swiss chard and hearty greens, first cut away leafy green portion from either side of stalk using chef's knife.

2. Next, stack several leaves on top of one another and cut as directed. Wash and dry after leaves are cut, using salad spinner.

Tomato Gratin

SERVES 2

✔ **WHY THIS RECIPE WORKS:** It's hard to go wrong with a creamy, cheesy, vegetable side, yet most tomato gratins end up waterlogged and flavorless. We solved the problem of a watery gratin by salting the tomatoes for 30 minutes before whirling them in a salad spinner to remove excess moisture. Sautéed onion, flavored with garlic and fresh thyme, amped up the savory notes of the dish, and panko plus grated Parmesan cheese delivered a crispy, cheesy topping. Since the panko browned before the tomatoes were cooked, we gave the tomatoes a head start in the oven before sprinkling on the topping. You will need an 8½ by 5½-inch baking dish for this recipe.

12 ounces plum tomatoes, cored and sliced ¼ inch thick
  Salt and pepper

⅛ teaspoon sugar

¼ cup panko bread crumbs

¼ cup grated Parmesan cheese

For a tomato gratin that's juicy and flavorful—not waterlogged—we salt the tomatoes then whirl them dry in a salad spinner.

4 teaspoons extra-virgin olive oil

1 small onion, halved and sliced thin

1 small garlic clove, minced

½ teaspoon minced fresh thyme or ⅛ teaspoon dried

1. Adjust oven racks to lower-middle and upper-middle positions and heat oven to 450 degrees. Toss tomatoes, ½ teaspoon salt, and sugar together in bowl and let sit for 30 minutes. Combine panko, Parmesan, 2 teaspoons oil, ⅛ teaspoon salt, and pinch pepper in second bowl.

2. Heat remaining 2 teaspoons oil in 8-inch skillet over medium-high heat until shimmering. Add onion and cook until softened, about 5 minutes. Stir in garlic and thyme and cook until fragrant, about 30 seconds. Season with salt and pepper to taste. Spread onion mixture in bottom of 8½ by 5½-inch baking dish.

3. Transfer tomatoes to salad spinner and spin to remove excess moisture. Arrange tomatoes in even layer over onion mixture and sprinkle with pinch pepper. Transfer baking dish to lower rack and bake until tomatoes are tender and starting to bubble, about 15 minutes. Sprinkle evenly with panko mixture, transfer to upper rack, and bake until topping is golden brown, about 10 minutes. Transfer gratin to wire rack and let cool for 5 to 10 minutes before serving.

CHAPTER 13

Rice, Grains, and Beans

■ FAST (Start to finish in about 30 minutes)

■ LIGHT (See page 415 for nutritional information)

Opposite: Creamy Parmesan Polenta; Tabbouleh; Lentil Salad with Olives, Mint, and Feta

Getting to Know Rice

All rice (except wild rice) starts out as brown rice. A grain of rice is made up of endosperm, germ, bran, and a hull or husk. Brown rice is simply husked and cleaned. White rice has the germ and bran removed. This makes the rice cook up faster and softer, and it's more shelf-stable, but this process also removes much of the fiber, protein, and other nutrients, as well as flavor.

LONG-GRAIN WHITE RICE

This broad category includes generic long-grain rice as well as aromatic varieties such as basmati (see below), Texmati, and jasmine. The grains are slender and elongated and measure four to five times longer than they are wide. The rice cooks up light and fluffy with firm, distinct grains, making it good for pilafs and salads. Avoid converted rice, which is parboiled during processing. In our opinion, this tan-colored rice cooks up too separate, and the flavor is a bit off.

MEDIUM-GRAIN WHITE RICE

This category includes a wide variety of specialty rices used to make risotto (Arborio) and paella (Valencia), as well as many Japanese and Chinese brands. The grains are fat, measuring two to three times longer than they are wide. This rice cooks up a bit sticky (the starch is what makes risotto so creamy), and when simmered, the grains clump together, making this rice a common choice in Chinese restaurants.

SHORT-GRAIN WHITE RICE

The grains of short-grain rice are almost round, and the texture is quite sticky and soft when cooked. Most of us are familiar with short-grain rice through its use in sushi.

BROWN RICE

As with white rice, brown rice comes in a variety of grain sizes: short, medium, and long. Long-grain brown rice, the best choice for pilafs, cooks up fluffy, with separate grains. Medium-grain brown rice is a bit more sticky, perfect for risotto, paella, and similar dishes. Short-grain brown rice is the most sticky, ideal for sushi and other Asian dishes where getting the grains to clump together is desired.

BASMATI RICE

Prized for its nutty flavor and sweet aroma, basmati rice is eaten in pilafs and biryanis and with curries. Indian basmati is aged for a minimum of one year, though often much longer, before being packaged. Aging dehydrates the rice, which translates into grains that, once cooked, expand greatly. We don't recommend American-grown basmati.

WILD RICE

Wild rice is technically not in the same family as other rices; it's actually an aquatic grass. Wild rice is North America's only native grain. It grows naturally in lakes and also is cultivated in man-made paddies in Minnesota, California, and Canada. We prefer brands that parboil the grains during processing.

Simple White Rice

SERVES 2 LIGHT

✔ **WHY THIS RECIPE WORKS:** White rice seems like an easy enough dish to make, but it can be deceptively temperamental, quickly dissolving into unpleasant, gummy grains. For really great long-grain rice with distinct, separate grains that didn't clump together, we rinsed the rice of excess starch first. Then, to add a rich dimension, we sautéed the grains in oil before covering them with boiling water. After simmering the rice until all of the liquid was absorbed, we placed a dish towel between the lid and pot to absorb excess moisture and ensure dry, fluffy grains. You will need a small saucepan with a tight-fitting lid for this recipe. A nonstick saucepan will help prevent the rice from sticking. For the nutritional information for this recipe, see page 415.

1   teaspoon vegetable oil
¾   cup long-grain white, basmati, or jasmine rice, rinsed
1¼ cups water
¼   teaspoon salt

1. Heat oil in small saucepan over medium heat until shimmering. Stir in rice and cook until edges of grains begin to turn translucent, about 2 minutes. Stir in water and salt and bring to boil. Reduce heat to low, cover, and simmer until all liquid is absorbed, 18 to 22 minutes.

2. Remove saucepan from heat. Remove lid, place folded clean dish towel over saucepan, then replace lid. Let rice sit for 10 minutes, then gently fluff with fork. Serve.

Classic Rice Pilaf

SERVES 2

✔ **WHY THIS RECIPE WORKS:** Rice pilaf should be fragrant, fluffy, and tender. For the best pilaf, we started with traditional basmati rice. We tried a standard 1:2 ratio of rice to water, but we got the best results with a little less water. Bringing the water to a boil before measuring it so we didn't lose any to evaporation was also key. Rinsing the rice before cooking gave us beautifully separated grains, and sautéing the raw rice in butter before steaming gave our pilaf great flavor. Minced shallot added a subtle aromatic flavor. Long-grain white rice can be substituted here. You will need a small saucepan with a tight-fitting lid for this recipe. A nonstick saucepan will help

For fragrant, fluffy rice pilaf, we sauté basmati rice in butter before cooking to deepen its flavor and ensure nicely separate grains.

prevent the rice from sticking. For an accurate measurement of boiling water, bring a full kettle of water to a boil, then measure out the desired amount.

1   tablespoon unsalted butter or olive oil
1   small shallot, minced
¾   cup basmati rice, rinsed
1¼ cups boiling water
¼   teaspoon salt
⅛   teaspoon pepper

1. Melt butter in small saucepan over medium heat. Add shallot and cook until softened, about 2 minutes. Stir in rice and cook until edges of grains begin to turn translucent, about 2 minutes. Stir in boiling water, salt, and pepper, and bring rice to boil. Reduce heat to low, cover, and simmer until all liquid is absorbed, 12 to 15 minutes.

2. Remove saucepan from heat. Remove lid, place folded clean dish towel over saucepan, then replace lid. Let rice sit for 10 minutes, then gently fluff with fork. Serve.

VARIATIONS

Classic Rice Pilaf with Pine Nuts, Basil, and Lemon
Add ¼ cup shredded fresh basil, 2 tablespoons toasted pine nuts, and ¼ teaspoon grated lemon zest to saucepan when fluffing rice in step 2.

Classic Rice Pilaf with Saffron and Toasted Almonds
Add pinch saffron to saucepan with shallot. Add 2 tablespoons toasted sliced almonds to saucepan when fluffing rice in step 2.

Hands-Off Baked Brown Rice

SERVES 2

✓ **WHY THIS RECIPE WORKS:** Brown rice is considered a whole grain because each grain has the bran, the nutrient-rich coating, still attached. The bran gives brown rice its distinctly nutty flavor and great chew, but it also makes it more of a challenge to cook than white rice. The tough coating makes it difficult for liquid to permeate the grain, which can lead to uneven cooking and extended cooking times. To avoid the pitfalls of burnt rice and undercooked grains, we found the oven to be the perfect solution. Baking gave us more precise temperature control than the stovetop, and the steady, even heat eliminated the risk of scorching. Bringing the water to a boil before adding it to the pan sped up the cooking time. This foolproof method produced light and fluffy rice every time. The test kitchen's preferred loaf pan measures 8½ by 4½ inches; if you use a 9 by 5-inch loaf pan, start checking for doneness 5 minutes early. For an accurate measurement of boiling water, bring a full kettle of water to a boil, then measure out the desired amount.

1¼ cups boiling water
¾   cup long-grain, medium-grain, or short-grain
    brown rice, rinsed
2   teaspoons olive oil
    Salt and pepper

1. Adjust oven rack to middle position and heat oven to 375 degrees. Combine boiling water, rice, oil, and ¼ teaspoon salt in 8½ by 4½-inch loaf pan. Cover pan tightly with double layer of aluminum foil. Bake until rice is tender and no water remains, 45 to 55 minutes.

2. Remove pan from oven and fluff rice with fork, scraping up any rice that has stuck to bottom. Cover pan with clean dish towel, then re-cover loosely with foil. Let rice sit for 10 minutes. Season with salt and pepper to taste and serve.

VARIATIONS

Hands-Off Baked Brown Rice with Parmesan, Lemon, and Herbs

Add ¼ cup grated Parmesan cheese, 2 tablespoons minced fresh parsley, 2 tablespoons chopped fresh basil, and ½ teaspoon grated lemon zest plus ¼ teaspoon juice to pan when fluffing rice in step 2.

Hands-Off Baked Brown Rice with Peas, Feta, and Mint

Add ½ cup thawed frozen peas, 2 tablespoons chopped fresh mint, and ¼ teaspoon grated lemon zest to pan when fluffing rice in step 2. Sprinkle with ¼ cup crumbled feta cheese before serving.

Rinsing Rice

To remove excess starch, rinse rice in fine-mesh strainer under cold water until water runs clear. Then, set strainer over a bowl and let rice drain until needed.

Parmesan Risotto

SERVES 2

✔ **WHY THIS RECIPE WORKS:** Classic Parmesan risotto is incredibly satisfying, rich in both flavor and texture. But try to adapt this finicky recipe for two and you'll most likely be disappointed by sticky, gummy, and bland rice. For foolproof risotto for two, we had to find just the right proportion of liquid to rice. We settled on ¾ cup of Arborio rice as the right amount for two, and after lots of tests and tinkering, we found that 2½ cups water, 2 cups broth, and ½ cup white wine (for acidity and complexity) gave us tender, creamy risotto with a little bite. Although the liquid is traditionally added incrementally with constant stirring, we found we could simplify things by adding

To infuse our tender, creamy risotto with flavor, we simmer the rice in a combination of water, chicken broth, and dry white wine.

half of the liquid and cooking the rice hands-off until the liquid was absorbed. Then we added the rest of the broth in stages, stirring constantly, until the rice was perfectly cooked. The texture of the risotto will stiffen substantially as it sits; loosen with additional hot broth or water as needed before serving. Garnish with parsley and shaved Parmesan, if desired.

2½	cups water
2	cups chicken broth
2	tablespoons unsalted butter
1	small onion, chopped fine
	Salt and pepper
1	garlic clove, minced
¾	cup Arborio rice
½	cup dry white wine
1	ounce Parmesan cheese, grated (½ cup)

1. Bring water and broth to simmer in small saucepan over medium heat. Remove from heat, cover, and keep warm.

2. Melt 1 tablespoon butter in medium saucepan over medium-high heat. Add onion and ¼ teaspoon salt and cook until softened, about 5 minutes. Stir in garlic and cook until fragrant, about 30 seconds. Add rice and cook, stirring constantly, until grains are translucent around edges, about 1 minute. Add wine and cook, stirring frequently, until fully absorbed, 3 to 5 minutes.

3. Stir in 2 cups reserved warm broth. Reduce heat to medium-low, cover, and simmer until almost all liquid is absorbed, about 12 minutes.

4. Stir in ½ cup reserved warm broth and cook, stirring constantly, until absorbed, about 3 minutes. Repeat with additional broth 2 or 3 more times until rice is al dente (you may have broth left over). Off heat, stir in remaining 1 tablespoon butter and Parmesan. Season with salt and pepper to taste and serve.

VARIATION
Pesto Risotto

You can make your own pesto or use your favorite store-bought brand from the refrigerated section of the supermarket—they have a fresher flavor than jarred pesto sold in the grocery aisles.

Substitute ¼ cup prepared basil pesto for remaining 1 tablespoon butter and Parmesan in step 4.

Creamy Parmesan Polenta

SERVES 2

✔ **WHY THIS RECIPE WORKS:** If you don't stir polenta almost constantly, it forms intractable lumps. We wondered if there was a way to get creamy, smooth polenta with rich corn flavor but without the fussy process. We started with traditional dried polenta, which had a soft but hearty texture and a nutty flavor when cooked. To help break down the cornmeal's tough endosperm, we added a pinch of baking soda to the pot. This simple trick cut our cooking time in half and eliminated the need for stirring. We simply brought the pot to a boil, reduced the heat, and in just 15 minutes we had perfectly al dente polenta. Be sure to use traditional dried polenta here, not instant polenta or precooked; dried polenta looks like coarse-ground cornmeal and can be found alongside cornmeal or pasta in the supermarket. It is important to cook the polenta over very low heat, so use a flame tamer if your stovetop runs hot.

1⅔ **cups water**
Salt and pepper
Pinch baking soda
⅓ **cup polenta**
1 **tablespoon unsalted butter**
1 **ounce Parmesan cheese, grated (½ cup), plus extra for serving**

Sorting Out Polenta

In the supermarket, cornmeal can be labeled anything from yellow grits to corn semolina. Forget the names. When shopping for the right product to make polenta, there are three things to consider: "instant" or "quick-cooking" versus the traditional style, degerminated or full-grain meal, and grind size.

Instant and quick-cooking cornmeals are parcooked and comparatively bland—leave them on the shelf. Though we loved the full corn flavor of whole-grain cornmeal, it remains slightly gritty no matter how long you cook it. We prefer degerminated cornmeal, in which the hard hull and germ are removed from each kernel (check the back label or ingredient list to see if your cornmeal is degerminated; if it's not explicitly labeled as such, you can assume it's whole grain).

As for grind, we found coarser grains brought the most desirable and pillowy texture to our Creamy Parmesan Polenta. However, grind coarseness can vary dramatically from brand to brand since there are no standards to ensure consistency—one manufacturer's "coarse" may be another's "fine." To identify coarse polenta as really coarse, the grains should be about the size of couscous.

1. Bring water to boil in small saucepan over medium-high heat. Stir in ¼ teaspoon salt and baking soda. Slowly add polenta in steady stream, stirring constantly with wooden spoon or rubber spatula. Bring mixture to boil, stirring constantly, about 30 seconds. Reduce heat to lowest possible setting and cover.

2. After 5 minutes, whisk polenta to smooth out any lumps that may have formed, making sure to scrape down sides and bottom of saucepan. Cover and continue to cook, without stirring, until grains of cornmeal are tender but slightly al dente, 8 to 10 minutes longer. (Polenta should be loose and barely hold its shape; it will continue to thicken as it cools.)

3. Off heat, stir in butter and Parmesan and season with salt and pepper to taste. Cover and let sit for 5 minutes. Serve, passing extra Parmesan separately.

How to Make a Flame Tamer

A flame tamer (or heat diffuser) is a metal disk that can be fitted over an electric or gas burner to reduce the heat to a bare simmer. If you don't have a flame tamer (it costs less than $10 at most kitchen supply stores), you can easily make one.

Shape long sheet of heavy-duty aluminum foil into 1-inch-thick ring that will fit on your burner. Make sure ring is of even thickness so that saucepan will rest flat on it.

Cheesy Baked Grits

SERVES 2

✓ **WHY THIS RECIPE WORKS:** A staple of the Southern table, grits are a simple but satisfying side dish. We wanted a rich and cheesy version, baked until it was brown on the top and creamy in the middle. We began building flavor by sautéing some chopped onion in butter. Then we brought water—enriched with cream and spiked with a dash of hot sauce—to a boil and whisked in the grits. We found that convenient quick grits had a creamy yet substantial texture that tasters preferred over old-fashioned grits. Once they were thickened, we stirred in plenty of tangy extra-sharp cheddar cheese along with a beaten egg, which gave the finished dish an airy texture, and moved the grits to the oven to develop a nicely browned crust. A sprinkle of scallions was the finishing touch. Do not substitute instant grits or old-fashioned grits for the quick-cooking grits in this recipe, as they require different amounts of liquid for cooking.

1	tablespoon unsalted butter
¼	cup finely chopped onion
¾	cup water
¼	cup heavy cream
½	teaspoon salt
¼	teaspoon hot sauce
¼	cup quick grits
1	large egg, lightly beaten
⅛	teaspoon pepper
3	ounces extra-sharp cheddar cheese, shredded (¾ cup)
1	scallion, sliced thin

1. Adjust oven rack to middle position and heat oven to 375 degrees. Melt butter in 8-inch ovensafe nonstick skillet over medium heat. Add onion and cook until softened and lightly browned, 5 to 7 minutes. Stir in water, cream, salt, and hot sauce and bring to boil. Slowly whisk in grits. Reduce heat to low and cook, stirring often, until grits are thick and creamy, 5 to 7 minutes.

2. Off heat, stir in egg, pepper, and ½ cup cheddar until combined. Smooth grits into even layer and sprinkle with remaining ¼ cup cheddar. Transfer skillet to oven and bake until cheese is melted and golden, 15 to 20 minutes.

3. Using potholders (skillet handle will be hot), remove skillet from oven and transfer to wire rack. Let cool for 10 minutes, sprinkle with scallion, and serve.

Toasted Orzo with Chives and Lemon

SERVES 2 `LIGHT`

✓ **WHY THIS RECIPE WORKS:** Most versions of orzo pilaf are bland at best, little more than a stodgy starch used to bulk up a meal. We wanted a flavorful orzo pilaf that would hold its own when paired with any main dish. Toasting the orzo until golden brown before cooking it was the key to an outstanding pilaf. After sautéing an onion in butter, we added a combination of white wine and chicken broth and simmered the orzo over moderate heat. A handful of minced chives added fresh flavor and a shot of color. Lemon zest and juice brightened the dish, nicely balancing the hearty, nutty orzo. In step 1, watch the orzo closely toward the end of the toasting time—it can quickly go from browned to burnt. For the nutritional information for this recipe, see page 415.

⅔	cup orzo
1	tablespoon unsalted butter
1	small onion, chopped fine
1	garlic clove, minced
2	cups chicken broth
½	cup water
2	tablespoons dry white wine
1	tablespoon minced fresh chives
½	teaspoon grated lemon zest plus 1 teaspoon juice
	Salt and pepper

1. Toast orzo in 10-inch skillet over medium heat, stirring frequently, until golden brown, 6 to 8 minutes; transfer to bowl.

2. Melt butter in now-empty skillet over medium-high heat. Add onion and cook until softened, about 5 minutes. Stir in garlic and cook until fragrant, about 30 seconds. Stir in toasted orzo, broth, water, and wine and bring to simmer. Reduce heat to medium-low and cook, stirring every 5 minutes, until liquid has been absorbed and orzo is tender, about 15 minutes.

3. Stir in chives and lemon zest and juice and cook until heated through, about 1 minute. Season with salt and pepper to taste and serve.

VARIATION

Toasted Orzo with Tomatoes and Basil
For the nutritional information for this recipe, see page 415.

Omit lemon juice. Substitute 2 tablespoons chopped fresh basil for chives. Add ½ cup chopped tomatoes and ¼ cup grated Parmesan cheese with basil and lemon zest in step 3.

For a quick couscous dish with lots of fresh flavor, we add juicy plum tomatoes, scallions, lemon juice, and a pinch of cayenne.

Couscous with Tomato, Scallion, and Lemon

SERVES 2

✔ **WHY THIS RECIPE WORKS:** Couscous may look like a grain, but it is actually tiny pasta made from semolina flour. At its best, it's light and fluffy, and with its ability to absorb flavors, it can make a great addition to any meal. But it often falls flat, with a bland flavor and heavy, clumpy texture. Toasting the couscous grains deepened their flavor and helped them to cook up fluffy without clumping. And to bump up the flavor even further, we replaced half of the cooking water with chicken broth. Sautéed shallot and garlic added rich aromatic notes, and lemon zest and cayenne lent brightness and heat. Bites of juicy plum tomatoes and thinly sliced scallion rounded out the dish. Do not use Israeli couscous in this recipe; its larger size requires a different cooking method. Whole-wheat couscous can be substituted for regular couscous.

⅓ cup couscous
1 tablespoon extra-virgin olive oil
1 shallot, minced
1 garlic clove, minced
¼ teaspoon grated lemon zest plus 1 teaspoon juice
   Pinch cayenne pepper
¼ cup water
¼ cup chicken broth
1 plum tomato, cored, seeded, and chopped fine
½ scallion, sliced thin
   Salt and pepper

1. Toast couscous in small saucepan over medium-high heat, stirring often, until some grains begin to brown, about 3 minutes. Transfer couscous to medium bowl.

2. Heat 1½ teaspoons oil in now-empty saucepan over medium heat until shimmering. Add shallot and cook until softened, about 2 minutes. Stir in garlic, lemon zest, and cayenne and cook until fragrant, about 30 seconds. Stir in water and broth and bring to boil.

3. Pour boiling liquid over couscous in bowl, cover bowl tightly with plastic wrap, and let sit until couscous is tender, about 12 minutes. Uncover and fluff couscous with fork. Stir in remaining 1½ teaspoons oil, lemon juice, tomato, and scallion. Season with salt and pepper to taste and serve.

VARIATION
Couscous with Saffron, Raisins, and Toasted Almonds

Omit garlic and lemon zest, and add pinch crumbled saffron threads and pinch ground cinnamon to saucepan with cayenne. Omit tomato and scallions, and add ¼ cup raisins and 2 tablespoons toasted sliced almonds to couscous with oil and lemon juice in step 3.

Quinoa Pilaf

SERVES 2

✔ **WHY THIS RECIPE WORKS:** With its hearty flavor, chewy texture, and complete protein properties, quinoa has increasingly become a popular side dish. We set out to put this "super-grain" to work in a quick and easy quinoa pilaf. After rinsing the quinoa (to remove its bitter saponin coating), we toasted it in olive oil to deepen its flavor. This step also ensured that the pilaf had distinct individual grains, rather than cooking up in dense clumps. To give the pilaf rich, savory flavor, we simmered the toasted quinoa in chicken broth along with a little thyme. Once the grains were tender, we removed the pot from the heat and let it sit for 10 minutes before fluffing the grains with a fork. Placing a kitchen towel under the lid absorbed the steam, keeping the grains from getting soggy. Be sure to rinse the quinoa to remove its bitter coating (known as saponin).

1 tablespoon olive oil
1 small onion, chopped fine
  Salt and pepper
¾ cup quinoa, rinsed
1¼ cups chicken broth
1 teaspoon minced fresh thyme or ¼ teaspoon dried

1. Heat oil in medium saucepan over medium-high heat until shimmering. Add onion and ¼ teaspoon salt and cook until onion is softened, about 5 minutes.

2. Add quinoa and cook, stirring often, until quinoa is lightly toasted and aromatic, about 5 minutes. Stir in broth and thyme and bring to simmer. Reduce heat to low, cover, and simmer until quinoa is translucent and tender, 16 to 18 minutes.

3. Remove saucepan from heat. Remove lid, place folded clean kitchen towel over saucepan, then replace lid. Let quinoa sit for 10 minutes, then gently fluff with fork. Season with salt and pepper to taste and serve.

VARIATION

Quinoa Pilaf with Goat Cheese and Chives

Substitute 2 minced garlic cloves for onion; cook until fragrant, about 30 seconds, before adding quinoa. Add 1 tablespoon minced chives to saucepan when fluffing quinoa in step 3. Sprinkle with ¼ cup crumbled goat cheese before serving.

NOTES FROM THE TEST KITCHEN

Getting to Know Quinoa

Quinoa originated in the Andes Mountains of South America, and while it is generally treated as a grain, it is actually the seed of the goosefoot plant. Sometimes referred to as a "supergrain," quinoa is high in protein, and its protein is complete, meaning that it possesses all of the essential amino acids in the balanced amounts that our bodies require. The Food and Agricultural Organization of the United Nations has indicated that the amino acid profile of quinoa is superior to that of most other grains, and is similar to that of casein, the complete protein in cow's milk. Beyond its nutritional prowess, we love quinoa for its addictive crunch, nutty taste, and ease of preparation. Quinoa is also gluten-free and easy to digest. Cooked as a pilaf or for a salad, quinoa is ready in about 15 minutes. Unless labeled as "prewashed," quinoa should always be rinsed before cooking to remove its protective layer (called saponin), which is unpleasantly bitter.

A bright dressing of mustard, cumin and lime ties together nutty, hearty quinoa, crisp bell pepper, spicy jalapeño, and fresh cilantro.

Quinoa Salad with Red Bell Pepper and Cilantro

SERVES 2

✓ **WHY THIS RECIPE WORKS:** To take advantage of the versatility of quinoa, we wanted to make a protein-packed quinoa salad. We started by using our pilaf method to cook the grains until just tender. Then we spread the cooked quinoa over a baking sheet to cool it to room temperature quickly. Crisp, sweet bell pepper, jalapeño, shallot, and fresh cilantro provided a sweet and spicy contrast to the hearty, chewy quinoa. We tossed the vegetables and grains with a bright dressing flavored with lime juice, mustard, garlic, and cumin. Be sure to rinse the quinoa to remove its bitter coating (known as saponin). A nonstick saucepan will help prevent the rice from sticking. After 12 minutes of cooking, there will still be a little bit of water in the pan, but this will evaporate as the quinoa cools. To make this dish spicier, add the jalapeño seeds.

⅔ cup quinoa, rinsed

1 cup water

  Salt and pepper

2 tablespoons finely chopped red bell pepper

¼ jalapeño chile, stemmed, seeded, and minced

1 shallot, finely chopped

1 tablespoon minced fresh cilantro

2 tablespoons extra-virgin olive oil

2 teaspoons lime juice

1 teaspoon Dijon mustard

1 small garlic clove, minced

¼ teaspoon ground cumin

1. Toast quinoa in small saucepan over medium heat, stirring often, until lightly toasted and aromatic, about 5 minutes. Stir in water and ⅛ teaspoon salt and bring to simmer. Reduce heat to low, cover, and simmer until quinoa has absorbed most of water and is just tender, 12 to 14 minutes. Spread quinoa on rimmed baking sheet lined with clean dish towel and let cool for about 20 minutes.

2. When quinoa is cool, transfer to serving bowl. Stir in bell pepper, jalapeño, shallot, and cilantro. In separate bowl, whisk oil, lime juice, mustard, garlic, and cumin together until well combined. Pour over quinoa and toss to coat. Season with salt and pepper to taste and serve.

Tabbouleh

SERVES 2

✔ **WHY THIS RECIPE WORKS:** Tabbouleh is a traditional Middle Eastern salad made of bulgur, parsley, tomato, and onion steeped in a penetrating mint and lemon dressing. For tabbouleh for two, we started by salting the tomatoes to rid them of excess moisture that otherwise made our salad soggy. Soaking the bulgur in lemon juice and some of the drained tomato liquid, rather than water, allowed it to soak up lots of flavor. A whole chopped onion overwhelmed the salad, but a single scallion added just the right amount of oniony flavor. Bright parsley, mint, and a bit of cayenne pepper rounded out the dish. We added the herbs and vegetables while the bulgur was still soaking so the components had time to mingle, resulting in a cohesive, balanced dish. Serve the salad with the crisp inner leaves of romaine lettuce and wedges of pita bread. This salad tastes best the day it's made.

1 tomato, cored and cut into ½-inch pieces

  Salt and pepper

¼ cup medium-grain bulgur, rinsed and dried well

2 tablespoons lemon juice

¾ cup chopped fresh parsley

¼ cup chopped fresh mint

1 scallion, sliced thin

3 tablespoons extra-virgin olive oil

  Pinch cayenne pepper

1. Toss tomato with ⅛ teaspoon salt and let drain in fine-mesh strainer set over bowl, tossing occasionally, about 30 minutes.

2. In separate bowl, combine bulgur, 1 tablespoon lemon juice, and 1 tablespoon juice from drained tomatoes. Let stand until grains begin to soften, 30 to 40 minutes.

3. Layer drained tomato, parsley, mint, and scallion on top of bulgur. Whisk remaining 1 tablespoon lemon juice, oil, cayenne, and ⅛ teaspoon salt together, then drizzle over top and toss gently to combine. Cover and let sit at room temperature until flavors have blended and bulgur is tender, about 1 hour. Before serving, toss to recombine and season with salt and pepper to taste.

NOTES FROM THE TEST KITCHEN

Getting to Know Bulgur

Adding recipes using bulgur to your repertoire is a great way to add fiber, protein, iron, and magnesium to your diet. But cooking with bulgur requires an understanding of what it is and how to buy it. A product of the wheat berry, bulgur has been steamed, dried, ground, and then sorted by size (fine-grain, medium-grain, and coarse-grain). The result of this process is a fast-cooking, highly nutritious grain that can be used in a variety of applications. In the test kitchen, we like medium-grain bulgur for tabbouleh and salads because it requires little more than a soak to become tender and flavorful. Soaking it in flavorful liquids, such as lemon or lime juice, also imbues the whole grain with bright flavor. Coarse-grain bulgur, which requires simmering, is best for cooked applications like pilaf. Note that medium-grain bulgur can work in cooked applications if you make adjustments to cooking times. Cracked wheat, which is often sold alongside bulgur in the market, is not precooked and cannot be substituted for bulgur. Be sure to rinse bulgur, regardless of grain size, to remove excess starches that can turn the grain gluey.

Coarse-Grain Bulgur

Fine-Grain Bulgur

Braising convenient canned chickpeas in a skillet brings out their buttery, nutty flavor in just 10 minutes.

Braised Chickpeas with Garlic and Parsley

SERVES 2   **FAST**

✔ **WHY THIS RECIPE WORKS:** For many people, chickpeas are synonymous with hummus, but with their buttery, nutty flavor, these beans also make a great side dish. Convenient canned chickpeas needed only a few minutes of cooking to warm through, keeping our dish quick and simple. To develop a rich foundation of flavor, we first toasted garlic and red pepper flakes in oil, then added a minced shallot and cooked it until all was lightly browned and aromatic. We added the chickpeas and some chicken broth to this mixture and simmered it covered until the flavors blended, then turned up the heat and reduced the liquid to a light, flavorful glaze. A little parsley and lemon juice brightened and balanced the flavors. Make sure you rinse the chickpeas thoroughly before cooking to get rid of excess salt.

2   tablespoons extra-virgin olive oil
2   garlic cloves, sliced thin
    Pinch red pepper flakes
1   large shallot, minced
1   (15-ounce) can chickpeas, rinsed
½   cup chicken broth
1   tablespoon minced fresh parsley
1   teaspoon lemon juice
    Salt and pepper

1. Cook oil, garlic, and pepper flakes in 10-inch skillet over medium heat, gently shaking pan to prevent garlic from sticking, until garlic turns pale gold, about 1 minute. Stir in shallot and cook until softened and lightly browned, about 3 minutes. Stir in chickpeas and broth, cover, and cook until chickpeas have warmed through and flavors have blended, about 2 minutes.

2. Uncover, increase heat to high, and simmer until liquid has reduced slightly, about 3 minutes. Off heat, stir in parsley and lemon juice. Season with salt and pepper to taste and serve.

VARIATIONS

Braised Chickpeas with Red Bell Pepper and Basil

Add ½ red bell pepper, cut into ½-inch pieces, to skillet with shallot; cook until softened, about 5 minutes, before adding chickpeas. Substitute 1 tablespoon chopped fresh basil for parsley.

Braised Chickpeas with Smoked Paprika and Cilantro

Omit red pepper flakes and add ¼ teaspoon smoked paprika to skillet once shallot has softened. Substitute 1 tablespoon minced fresh cilantro for parsley and ½ teaspoon sherry vinegar for lemon juice.

Slicing Garlic Thin

Place flattest side of peeled garlic clove down on cutting board. Holding garlic securely, slice garlic thin using paring knife. Use tip of knife to pull out green stem, if present.

Braised White Beans with Rosemary and Parmesan

SERVES 2 `FAST`

✔ **WHY THIS RECIPE WORKS:** This Tuscan-inspired white bean braise should boast a rustic, rich texture and be lightly seasoned with garlic and rosemary. In traditional versions of this dish, dried beans are gently cooked for hours over low heat, allowing the beans to break down and bind together. To make it more practical as a side dish for two, we wanted to re-create this dish with convenient, time-saving canned beans. It took several failed attempts before we found the solution: Mashing some of the beans before adding them to the pot gave the finished dish the creamy, saucy texture of long-simmered beans in just 10 minutes. Simmering the beans in chicken broth allowed them to absorb rich savory flavor. We limited the supporting ingredients to the classics: onion, garlic, rosemary, and Parmesan. Make sure you rinse the beans thoroughly before cooking to get rid of excess salt.

- 1 **(15-ounce) can white or cannellini beans, rinsed**
- 1 **tablespoon extra-virgin olive oil**
- 1 **small onion, chopped fine**
- 1 **garlic clove, minced**
- 1 **teaspoon minced fresh rosemary or ¼ teaspoon dried**
- ¾ **cup chicken broth**
- 1 **ounce Parmesan cheese, grated (½ cup)**
  Salt and pepper

1. Mash ⅔ cup beans in bowl with potato masher until smooth. Heat oil in small saucepan over medium-high heat until shimmering. Add onion and cook until softened and lightly browned, 5 to 7 minutes. Stir in garlic and rosemary and cook until fragrant, about 30 seconds.

2. Stir in broth, mashed beans, and remaining whole beans. Bring to simmer and cook until slightly thickened, about 10 minutes. Off heat, sprinkle with Parmesan and season with salt and pepper to taste. Serve.

Rinsing Canned Beans

Before using canned beans, rinse beans thoroughly in fine-mesh strainer.

To make a great white bean salad, we infuse convenient canned cannellini beans with flavor by steeping them in a garlicky broth.

White Bean Salad

SERVES 2

✔ **WHY THIS RECIPE WORKS:** To liven up canned white beans for a boldly flavored bean salad for two, we started by steeping the beans in a garlicky broth. Sautéing the garlic first gave the salad a toasty, caramelized flavor. Marinating minced shallot in vinegar worked to tame its raw, harsh notes. Some red bell pepper added color and crunch, and chopped parsley and chives ramped up the freshness of the salad. Make sure you rinse the beans thoroughly before cooking to get rid of excess salt. The salad can be served chilled or at room temperature.

- 2 **tablespoons extra-virgin olive oil**
- 2 **garlic cloves, peeled and smashed**
  Salt and pepper
- 1 **(15-ounce) can cannellini beans, rinsed**
- 1 **tablespoon sherry vinegar**
- 1 **small shallot, minced**

½   red bell pepper, cut into ¼-inch pieces

2   tablespoons chopped fresh parsley

2   tablespoons chopped fresh chives

1. Cook 1½ teaspoons oil and garlic in small saucepan over medium-high heat until garlic just begins to brown, about 2 minutes. Let skillet cool slightly off heat, then carefully add ⅔ cup water and ¼ teaspoon salt. Bring to simmer over high heat. Off heat, add beans, cover, and let sit for 20 minutes. Meanwhile, combine vinegar and shallot in large bowl and let sit for 20 minutes.

2. Drain beans and discard garlic. Add drained beans, remaining 1½ tablespoons oil, bell pepper, parsley, and chives to shallot mixture and toss to combine. Season with salt and pepper to taste. Cover and let sit for 20 minutes. Serve.

Southwestern Black Bean Salad

SERVES 2   **FAST**

✔ **WHY THIS RECIPE WORKS:** For a great black bean salad, restraint, rather than a kitchen-sink approach, is important. We didn't want to lose the beans among an endless array of Tex-Mex ingredients. We found that a judicious mixture of black beans, corn, avocado, tomato, and cilantro gave us just the right combination of flavors and textures. Toasting the corn before we added it gave the salad deep, well-rounded flavor. And to give our simple dressing plenty of kick, we used a generous amount of bright lime juice, some spicy minced chipotle chile, and a little honey for balancing sweetness. Make sure you rinse the beans thoroughly before cooking to get rid of excess salt. Fresh corn is important for the flavor of this salad—don't substitute frozen or canned corn.

2   tablespoons olive oil

1   tablespoon lime juice

½   teaspoon minced canned chipotle chile in adobo sauce

¼   teaspoon honey

   Salt and pepper

1   ear corn, kernels cut from cob

¾   cup canned black beans, rinsed

1   small tomato, cored, seeded, and chopped fine

2   tablespoons minced fresh cilantro

½   avocado, cut into ½-inch pieces

Whisk 1 tablespoon oil, lime juice, chipotle, honey, ¼ teaspoon salt, and ¼ teaspoon pepper together in medium bowl. Heat remaining 1 tablespoon oil in 10-inch skillet over medium-high heat until shimmering. Add corn and cook, stirring occasionally,

We freshen up black bean salad with chopped tomatoes, creamy diced avocado, sweet corn, and cilantro.

until golden brown, 6 to 8 minutes. Transfer corn to bowl with dressing. Stir in beans, tomato, and cilantro. Gently fold in avocado. Season with salt and pepper to taste. Serve.

Lentil Salad with Olives, Mint, and Feta

SERVES 2

✔ **WHY THIS RECIPE WORKS:** We wanted a bright-tasting lentil salad with lentils that retained their shape and boasted a firm-tender bite. Brining the lentils in warm salted water helped to soften the lentils' skins, which led to fewer blowouts. Then we baked the lentils to heat them gently and uniformly. Once we had perfectly cooked lentils, all we had to do was pair the earthy legumes with a tart vinaigrette and a few boldly flavored additions. We chose kalamata olives, fresh mint, and creamy feta cheese for a Mediterranean flair. French green lentils, or *lentilles du Puy*, are our preferred choice for this recipe, but any type of lentil except red or yellow will work. Brining helps keep the lentils intact, but this step can be skipped if you're in a hurry. The salad can be served warm or at room temperature.

½ cup lentils, picked over and rinsed

Salt and pepper

1 cup chicken broth

2 garlic cloves, lightly crushed and peeled

1 bay leaf

2½ tablespoons extra-virgin olive oil

1½ tablespoons white wine vinegar

¼ cup coarsely chopped pitted kalamata olives

¼ cup chopped fresh mint

1 shallot, minced

2 tablespoons crumbled feta cheese

1. Place lentils and ½ teaspoon salt in bowl. Cover with 2 cups warm water and soak for 1 hour. Drain well. (Drained lentils can be refrigerated for up to 2 days before cooking.)

2. Adjust oven rack to middle position and heat oven to 325 degrees. Place drained lentils, 1 cup warm water, broth, garlic, bay leaf, and ¼ teaspoon salt in medium saucepan. Cover and bake until lentils are tender but remain intact, 40 minutes to 1 hour. Meanwhile, whisk oil and vinegar together in large bowl.

3. Drain lentils well, discarding garlic and bay leaf. Add drained lentils, olives, mint, and shallot to dressing and toss to combine. Season with salt and pepper to taste. Sprinkle with feta and serve.

VARIATION

Lentil Salad with Goat Cheese

Substitute red wine vinegar for white wine vinegar and add 1 teaspoon Dijon mustard to dressing in step 2. Omit olives and substitute 2 tablespoons chopped fresh parsley for mint. Substitute 1 ounce crumbled goat cheese for feta.

Dal (Spiced Red Lentils)

SERVES 2

WHY THIS RECIPE WORKS: Indian dal is a dish of red lentils simmered to a porridgelike consistency and seasoned with spices, tomatoes, and onions. Traditional recipes call for a laundry list of spices, but we got a similarly complex flavor with just garam masala and fresh ginger. It took some trial and error to get the consistency of the dal just right—too much water and it wound up thin and soupy; too little and it was thick and pasty. Two cups of chicken broth to ½ cup lentils turned out to be just right. After only about 20 minutes of simmering, the lentils were tender. We added chopped fresh tomatoes, minced cilantro, and a pat of butter for richness. Do not substitute brown lentils for the red lentils here; they will not break down to the proper consistency. Serve with white rice and lemon wedges.

1 tablespoon vegetable oil

1 small onion, chopped fine

2 garlic cloves, minced

1¼ teaspoons garam masala

1 teaspoon grated fresh ginger

Pinch cayenne pepper

2 cups chicken broth

½ cup red lentils, picked over and rinsed

1 tomato, cored, seeded, and chopped

2 tablespoons minced fresh cilantro

1 tablespoon unsalted butter

Salt and pepper

1. Heat oil in medium saucepan over medium-high heat until shimmering. Add onion and cook until softened, about 5 minutes. Stir in garlic, garam masala, ginger, and cayenne and cook until fragrant, about 30 seconds. Stir in broth and lentils and bring to simmer. Reduce heat to low and continue to simmer until lentils are tender and resemble thick, coarse puree, 20 to 25 minutes.

2. Off heat, stir in tomato, cilantro, and butter. Season with salt and pepper to taste and serve.

NOTES FROM THE TEST KITCHEN

Getting to Know Lentils

Lentils come from many parts of the world, in dozens of sizes and colors, with considerable differences in flavor and texture. Because they are thin-skinned, they require no soaking, which makes them a highly versatile legume. Here are the most commonly available types of lentils.

BROWN AND GREEN LENTILS
These larger lentils are what you'll find in every supermarket. They are a uniform drab brown or green. They have a mild, light, earthy flavor and a creamy texture. Because they hold their shape well when cooked, they are good all-purpose lentils, great in soups and salads or simmered then tossed with olive oil and herbs.

LENTILLES DU PUY
These dark green French lentils from the city of Le Puy are smaller than the more common brown and green varieties. They are a dark olive green, almost black. They have a rich, earthy, complex flavor and a firm but tender texture. This is the kind to use if you are looking for lentils that will keep their shape and look beautiful on the plate when cooked, so they're perfect for salads and dishes where the lentils take center stage.

RED AND YELLOW LENTILS
These Indian lentils are small and orange-red or golden yellow. They come split and skinless, so they completely disintegrate into a uniform consistency when cooked. If you are looking for lentils that will quickly break down into a thick puree, as in our recipe for Dal, this is the kind to use.

CHAPTER 14

Eggs and Breakfast

■ FAST (Start to finish in about 30 minutes)
▦ LIGHT (See page 415 for nutritional information)
Opposite: Soft-Cooked Eggs; Ten-Minute Steel-Cut Oatmeal; Buttermilk Waffles

Buying Eggs

There are numerous—and often confusing—options when buying eggs at the supermarket. And when eggs are the focal point of a dish, the quality of the eggs makes a big difference. Here's what we've learned about buying eggs in the test kitchen.

COLOR: The shell's hue depends on the breed of the chicken. The run-of-the-mill leghorn chicken produces the typical white egg. Brown-feathered birds, such as Rhode Island Reds, produce ecru- to coffee-colored eggs. Despite marketing hype extolling the virtues of nonwhite eggs, our tests proved that shell color has no effect on flavor.

FARM-FRESH AND ORGANIC: In our taste tests, farm-fresh eggs were standouts. The large yolks were bright orange and sat very high above the comparatively small whites, and the flavor of these eggs was exceptionally rich and complex. The organic eggs followed in second place, with eggs from hens raised on a vegetarian diet in third, and the standard supermarket eggs last. Differences were easily detected in egg-based dishes like an omelet or a frittata but not in cakes or cookies.

EGGS AND OMEGA-3s: Several companies are marketing eggs with a high level of omega-3 fatty acids, the healthful unsaturated fats also found in some fish. In our taste test, we found that more omega-3s translated into a richer egg flavor and a deeper yolk color. Why? Commercially raised chickens usually peck on corn and soy, while chickens on an omega-3-enriched diet have supplements of greens, flaxseeds, and algae, which also add flavor, complexity, and color. Read labels carefully and look for brands that guarantee at least 200 milligrams omega-3s per egg.

HOW OLD ARE MY EGGS? Egg cartons are marked with both a sell-by date and a pack date. The pack date is the day the eggs were graded and packed, which is generally within a week of when they were laid but may be as much as 30 days later. The sell-by date is within 30 days of the pack date, which is the legal limit set by the U.S. Department of Agriculture (USDA). In short, a carton of eggs may be up to two months old by the end of the sell-by date. Even so, according to the USDA, eggs are still fit for consumption for an additional three to five weeks past the sell-by date.

EGG SIZES: Eggs vary in size, which will make a difference in recipes, especially those that call for several eggs. We use large eggs in all of our recipes, but you can substitute one size for another. For instance, four jumbo eggs are equivalent to five large eggs—both weigh 10 ounces. (See page 8 for more information on substituting egg sizes.)

EGG SIZES	APPROXIMATE WEIGHTS
Medium	1.75 ounces
Large	2.00 ounces
Extra-Large	2.25 ounces
Jumbo	2.50 ounces

Frying our eggs in a combination of butter and vegetable oil gives us the perfect tender yet crisp-edged diner-style fried eggs.

Perfect Fried Eggs

SERVES 2   FAST

✔ **WHY THIS RECIPE WORKS:** There are few things better than a perfect diner-style fried egg, but crispy edges, tender whites, and runny yolks can be elusive. In our search for the perfect fried egg, we uncovered a few tricks. We knew that cracking the eggs one by one into the pan would cause them to cook unevenly, so we cracked them into bowls and tipped them into the pan all at once. Heating the oil for a full 5 minutes ensured that the whites set quickly, and a bit of butter added to the oil aided browning. Covering the eggs and cooking them for 1 minute then letting them sit off the heat for an additional 15 to 45 seconds gave us the opaque, tender whites and warm, runny yolks we were craving. When checking the eggs for doneness, lift the lid just a crack to prevent loss of steam. To cook two eggs, use an 8- or 9-inch nonstick skillet and halve the amounts of oil and butter. When cooked, the thin layer of white surrounding the yolk will turn opaque, but the yolk should remain runny.

2 teaspoons vegetable oil
4 large eggs
   Salt and pepper
2 teaspoons unsalted butter, cut into 4 pieces and chilled

1. Heat oil in 12- or 14-inch nonstick skillet over low heat for 5 minutes. Meanwhile, crack eggs into 2 small bowls (2 eggs in each), and season with salt and pepper.

2. Increase heat to medium-high and heat until oil is shimmering. Add butter and quickly swirl to coat skillet. Working quickly, pour 1 bowl of eggs in 1 side of skillet and second bowl of eggs in other side. Cover and cook for 1 minute. Remove skillet from burner and let stand, covered, for 15 to 45 seconds for runny yolks (white around edge of yolk will be barely opaque), 45 to 60 seconds for soft but set yolks, and about 2 minutes for medium-set yolks. Slide eggs onto warm plates and serve immediately.

Hard-Cooked Eggs

SERVES 2 **FAST** **LIGHT**

✓ WHY THIS RECIPE WORKS: Hard-cooking an egg can be a crapshoot. There's no way to watch it cook inside its shell, and you certainly can't poke it with an instant-read thermometer. We finally got our foolproof recipe by tinkering with a technique recommended by the American Egg Board. We started the eggs in cold water, brought the water to a boil, then removed the pan from the heat and let the eggs steep for 10 minutes. This method consistently turned out perfect hard-cooked eggs with moist and creamy yolks, firm yet tender whites, and no trace of a green ring. You can halve or double this recipe as long as you use a pot large enough to hold the eggs in a single layer, covered by an inch of water. For the nutritional information for this recipe, see page 415.

4 large eggs

Place eggs in medium saucepan, cover with 1 inch water, and bring to boil over high heat. Remove pot from heat, cover, and let sit for 10 minutes. Meanwhile, fill medium bowl with 4 cups cold water and 4 cups ice cubes. Transfer eggs to ice bath with slotted spoon; let sit for 5 minutes. Peel eggs.

Soft-Cooked Eggs

SERVES 2 **FAST**

✓ WHY THIS RECIPE WORKS: Most methods for making soft-cooked eggs are hit or miss. We wanted a recipe that would produce any number of perfect eggs with set whites and fluid yolks. To eliminate temperature variables, we used fridge-cold eggs and boiling water. This also created the steepest temperature gradient, ensuring that the yolk at the center stayed fluid while the white cooked through. To keep the temperature of the water from dropping when we added the cold eggs, we decided to steam the eggs rather than boil them. This minimized the contact between the hot water and the cold surface of the eggs, maintaining the temperature of the water whether we cooked one egg or six. You can cook one to six large, extra-large, or jumbo eggs without altering the cooking time. Be sure to use eggs that have no cracks and are cold from the refrigerator. Because precise timing is vital to the success of this recipe, we strongly recommend using a digital timer. We recommend serving these eggs in egg cups with buttered toast for dipping.

4 large eggs
   Salt and pepper

1. Bring ½ inch water to boil in medium saucepan over medium-high heat. Using tongs, gently place eggs in boiling water (eggs will not be submerged). Cover saucepan and cook eggs for 6½ minutes.

2. Remove cover, transfer saucepan to sink, and place under cold running water for 30 seconds. Remove eggs from saucepan and serve immediately, seasoning with salt and pepper to taste.

VARIATIONS

Soft-Cooked Eggs with Sautéed Mushrooms
Heat 2 tablespoons olive oil in 12-inch skillet over medium-high heat until shimmering. Add 12 ounces sliced white mushrooms and pinch salt and cook, stirring occasionally, until liquid has evaporated and mushrooms are lightly browned, 5 to 6 minutes. Stir in 2 teaspoons chopped fresh herbs (chives, tarragon, parsley, or combination). Season with salt and pepper to taste and divide between 2 plates. Top each serving with 2 peeled soft-cooked eggs, split crosswise to release yolks, and season eggs with salt and pepper to taste.

Soft-Cooked Eggs with Steamed Asparagus
Look for asparagus that is at least ½ inch thick near the base.
Steam 12 ounces asparagus, trimmed, over medium heat until crisp-tender, 4 to 5 minutes. Divide asparagus between

2 plates, then top each serving with 1 tablespoon extra-virgin olive oil and 1 tablespoon grated Parmesan cheese. Top each serving with 2 peeled soft-cooked eggs, split crosswise to release yolks, and season eggs with salt and pepper to taste.

Soft-Cooked Eggs with Salad

Combine 3 tablespoons olive oil, 1 tablespoon balsamic vinegar, 1 teaspoon Dijon mustard, and 1 teaspoon minced shallot in jar, seal lid, and shake vigorously until emulsified, 20 to 30 seconds. Toss 5 ounces assertively flavored salad greens (arugula, radicchio, watercress, or frisée) with dressing. Season with salt and pepper to taste and divide between 2 plates. Top each serving with 2 peeled soft-cooked eggs, split crosswise to release yolks, and season eggs with salt and pepper to taste.

Ultimate Scrambled Eggs

SERVES 2   **FAST**

✔ **WHY THIS RECIPE WORKS:** For scrambled eggs that were fluffy and moist, not dried-out and tough, we put some science to work. The first step was to add salt to the uncooked eggs; salt dissolves some of the egg proteins, creating more tender curds. To avoid overbeating the eggs, we beat them until just combined using the gentle action of a fork rather than a whisk. For the dairy, we found that half-and-half produced clean-tasting curds that were both fluffy and stable. To replicate the richer flavor of farm-fresh eggs, we added extra yolks. Finally, we started the eggs on medium-high heat to create puffy curds, then finished them over low heat to ensure that they wouldn't overcook. It's important to follow visual cues, as pan thickness will affect cooking times. If using an electric stove, heat one burner on low heat and a second burner on medium-high heat; move the skillet between the burners for temperature adjustment. If you don't have half-and-half, you can substitute 4 teaspoons of whole milk and 2 teaspoons of heavy cream.

- 4 large eggs plus 1 large yolk
- 2 tablespoons half-and-half
- ⅛ teaspoon salt
- ⅛ teaspoon pepper
- ½ tablespoon unsalted butter, chilled

1. Beat eggs and yolk, half-and-half, salt, and pepper with fork until eggs are thoroughly combined and color is pure yellow; do not overbeat.

For foolproof, fluffy scrambled eggs, we add extra egg yolks, beat the eggs gently, and fold them rather than stir them as they cook.

2. Heat butter in 10-inch nonstick skillet over medium-high heat until foaming just subsides (butter should not brown), swirling to coat skillet. Add egg mixture and, using heat-resistant rubber spatula, constantly and firmly scrape along bottom and sides of skillet until eggs begin to clump and spatula just leaves trail on bottom of skillet, 45 to 75 seconds.

3. Reduce heat to low and continue to cook, gently but constantly folding eggs, until clumped and just slightly wet, 30 to 60 seconds. Transfer eggs to warm plates and season with salt to taste. Serve immediately.

Making Scrambled Eggs

Once spatula just leaves trail through eggs, that's your cue to turn heat to low and continue to cook until large, shiny, wet curds form.

Tofu Scramble with Shallot and Herbs

SERVES 2 **FAST**

✓ **WHY THIS RECIPE WORKS:** Tofu scrambles are increasingly common on restaurant breakfast menus as an alternative to scrambled eggs, but they often turn out dry and dull. We wanted to come up with a version of this dish that would appeal to carnivores and vegans alike. Soft tofu was essential for a creamy texture; we crumbled it into smaller and larger pieces to resemble different size egg curds. A small amount of curry powder added depth of flavor and a touch of color to the tofu without overwhelming the other flavors. A minced shallot added just the right amount of aromatic flavor, and fresh herbs gave a pop of brightness. Do not substitute firm tofu for the soft tofu in this recipe. Be sure to press the tofu dry thoroughly before cooking.

- 14 ounces soft tofu
- 2 teaspoons vegetable oil
- 1 shallot, minced
- ¼ teaspoon curry powder
- ¾ teaspoon salt
- ⅛ teaspoon pepper
- 2 tablespoons minced fresh basil, parsley, tarragon, or marjoram

Gently pat tofu dry with paper towels, then crumble into ¼- to ½-inch pieces. Heat oil in 10-inch nonstick skillet over medium heat until shimmering. Add shallot and cook until softened, about 2 minutes. Stir in tofu, curry powder, salt, and pepper and cook until tofu is hot, about 2 minutes. Off heat, stir in basil and serve.

VARIATIONS

Tofu Scramble with Spinach and Feta

Before adding tofu to skillet, cook 4 ounces baby spinach until wilted, about 1 minute. Add ½ cup crumbled feta cheese with tofu.

Tofu Scramble with Tomato, Scallions, and Parmesan

Add 1 tomato, seeded and chopped fine, and 1 minced garlic clove with shallot and cook until tomato is no longer wet, 3 to 5 minutes. Add ¼ cup grated Parmesan cheese and 2 tablespoons minced scallions with tofu.

Tofu Scramble with Shiitakes, Bell Pepper, and Goat Cheese

Add 4 ounces shiitake mushrooms, stemmed and sliced thin, 1 finely chopped small red bell pepper, and pinch red pepper flakes with shallot; cover and cook until mushrooms have released their liquid, about 5 minutes. Uncover and continue to cook until mushrooms are dry, about 2 minutes. Stir in tofu and seasonings along with ¼ cup crumbled goat cheese and continue to cook as directed.

Classic Filled Omelet

SERVES 2 **FAST**

✓ **WHY THIS RECIPE WORKS:** Omelets seem simple, but cooking the eggs properly in a hot pan can be a delicate matter. Add in cheese, which must melt before the omelet turns brown and rubbery, and you've got a truly temperamental dish on your hands. We wanted a foolproof cooking method for a creamy, supple omelet with perfectly melted cheese that didn't leak all over the pan. We found that a good-quality nonstick skillet and an easy-melting cheese were essential. A heatproof rubber spatula kept the eggs from tearing as we shaped the omelet with the sides of the pan. To ensure the cheese melted before the eggs overcooked, we shredded it fine for quick melting and removed the pan from the heat after adding the cheese. The residual heat was enough to melt the cheese without overcooking the eggs. This technique gave us the omelet we had been looking for; moist and creamy with plenty of perfectly melted cheese. You can substitute cheddar, Monterey Jack, or any semisoft, gratable cheese for the Gruyère.

- 6 large eggs
  Salt and pepper
- 1 tablespoon unsalted butter, plus 1 tablespoon melted butter for brushing omelets
- 6 tablespoons finely shredded Gruyère cheese
- 1 recipe filling (recipes follow)

1. Add 3 eggs to small bowl, season with salt and pepper, and beat with fork until thoroughly combined. Repeat with remaining 3 eggs in separate bowl.

2. Melt 1½ teaspoons butter in 10-inch nonstick skillet over medium-high heat. Add 1 bowl of egg mixture and cook until edges begin to set, 2 to 3 seconds. Using heat-resistant rubber spatula, stir eggs in circular motion until slightly thickened, about 10 seconds. Use spatula to pull cooked edges of eggs in toward center, then tilt skillet to 1 side so that uncooked eggs run to edge of skillet. Repeat until omelet is just set but still moist on surface, 20 to 25 seconds. Sprinkle 3 tablespoons Gruyère and half of filling across center of omelet.

3. Off heat, use spatula to fold lower third (portion nearest you) of omelet over filling; press gently with spatula to secure seams, maintaining fold.

4. Run spatula between outer edge of omelet and skillet to loosen. Pull skillet sharply toward you few times to slide unfolded edge of omelet up far side of skillet. Jerk skillet again so that unfolded edge folds over itself, or use spatula to fold edge over. Invert omelet onto warm plate. Tidy edges with spatula, brush with melted butter, and serve immediately.

5. Wipe out skillet and repeat with remaining 1½ teaspoons butter, remaining egg mixture, remaining 3 tablespoons Gruyère, remaining filling, and remaining melted butter.

Mushroom and Thyme Filling

    1   tablespoon unsalted butter
    1   small shallot, minced
    2   ounces white mushrooms, trimmed and
        sliced ¼ inch thick
    1   teaspoon minced fresh thyme
        Salt and pepper

Melt butter in 10-inch skillet over medium heat. Add shallot and cook until softened, about 2 minutes. Add mushrooms and cook until lightly browned, about 3 minutes. Off heat, stir in thyme and season with salt and pepper to taste. Transfer to small bowl, cover, and set aside until needed.

Bacon, Onion, and Scallion Filling
Smoked Gouda cheese is a good match for this filling.

    2   slices bacon, cut into ½-inch pieces
    ½   small onion, chopped fine
    1   scallion, sliced thin

Cook bacon in 10-inch skillet over medium heat until crisp, 5 to 7 minutes. Using slotted spoon, transfer bacon to paper towel–lined plate. Pour off all but 1 tablespoon fat from skillet, add onion, and cook over medium heat until softened and golden brown, about 3 minutes. Off heat, stir in scallion. Combine crisp bacon and onion mixture in small bowl, cover, and set aside until needed.

Bell Pepper, Mushroom, and Onion Filling
Monterey Jack or pepper Jack cheese will taste good with this filling.

    1   tablespoon unsalted butter
    ½   small onion, chopped fine
    1   ounce white mushrooms, trimmed and
        sliced ¼ inch thick
    ¼   red bell pepper, cut into ½-inch pieces
    1   teaspoon minced fresh parsley
        Salt and pepper

Melt butter in 10-inch skillet over medium heat. Add onion and cook until softened, about 2 minutes. Add mushrooms and cook until softened and beginning to brown, about 2 minutes. Add bell pepper and cook until softened, about 2 minutes. Off heat, stir in parsley and season with salt and pepper to taste. Transfer mixture to small bowl, cover, and set aside until needed.

Making a Filled Omelet

1. Pull cooked eggs from edges of skillet toward center, tilting skillet so any uncooked eggs run to skillet's edges.

2. Sprinkle cheese and filling across center of omelet. Off heat, fold lower third of omelet over filling, then press seam to secure.

3. Pull skillet sharply toward you so that unfolded edge of omelet slides up far side of skillet.

4. Fold far edge of omelet toward center and press to secure seam. Invert omelet onto plate.

Poached Egg Sandwiches with Goat Cheese, Tomato, and Spinach

SERVES 2

✔ **WHY THIS RECIPE WORKS:** Poached eggs are often written off for being too finicky, but we were determined to make them foolproof. We poached the eggs in a shallow skillet, which was easier to maneuver than a deep saucepan. Cracking the eggs into teacups made it easy to pour the eggs into the skillet all at once. As soon as we added the eggs, we took the skillet off the heat to allow the eggs to cook gently in the residual heat without the simmering water making the whites ragged. A splash of vinegar lowered the pH of the water, helping the eggs to cook more gently at a lower temperature. Once we had our perfectly poached eggs, we served them on crisp toasted English muffins spread with lemony goat cheese and topped with fresh tomato and lightly sautéed spinach. Do not omit the vinegar in the egg poaching water—in addition to adding flavor, it helps to ensure that the egg whites stay intact during cooking.

We dress up easy egg sandwiches with sautéed spinach, creamy goat cheese, and fresh tomato on a toasted English muffin.

- 2   ounces goat cheese, crumbled and softened (½ cup)
- 4   teaspoons olive oil
- 1   teaspoon lemon juice
      Salt and pepper
- 2   English muffins, split, toasted, and still warm
- 1   small tomato, cored and sliced thin
- 1   shallot, minced
- 1   small garlic clove, minced
- 4   ounces (4 cups) baby spinach
- 2   tablespoons distilled white vinegar
- 4   large eggs

1. Adjust oven rack to middle position and heat oven to 300 degrees. Combine goat cheese, 1 teaspoon oil, and lemon juice in bowl until smooth and season with salt and pepper to taste. Spread mixture evenly over warm English muffin halves, top with tomato slices, and arrange on rimmed baking sheet. Keep warm in oven.

2. Heat remaining 1 tablespoon oil in 12-inch nonstick skillet over medium heat until shimmering. Add shallot and ¼ teaspoon salt and cook until softened, about 2 minutes. Stir in garlic and cook until fragrant, about 30 seconds. Stir in spinach, 1 handful at a time, until wilted. Continue to cook, stirring frequently, until spinach is uniformly wilted and glossy, about 30 seconds. Using tongs, squeeze out any excess moisture from spinach, then divide evenly among English muffins and return to oven to keep warm.

3. Wipe skillet clean, then fill it nearly to rim with water. Add vinegar and 1 teaspoon salt and bring to boil. Meanwhile, crack eggs into 2 teacups (2 eggs in each).

4. Reduce water to gentle simmer. Lower rims of teacups into water and gently tip eggs into skillet simultaneously. Remove skillet from heat, cover, and poach eggs for 4 minutes (add 30 seconds for firm yolks).

5. Using slotted spoon, gently lift eggs from water and let drain before laying them on top of each English muffin. Season with salt and pepper to taste and serve immediately.

Pouring Eggs into Skillet

To add eggs to water at same time for poaching, crack 2 eggs each into 2 teacups. Simultaneously lower lips of cups into simmering water and tip eggs into water.

Storing Eggs

In the test kitchen, we've tasted two- and three-month-old eggs and found them perfectly palatable. However, at four months, the white was very loose and the yolk had off-flavors, though it was still edible. Our advice is to use your discretion; if eggs smell odd or are discolored, pitch them. Older eggs also lack the structure-lending properties of fresh eggs, so beware when baking.

IN THE REFRIGERATOR: Eggs often suffer more from improper storage than from age. If your refrigerator has an egg tray in the door, don't use it—eggs should be stored on a shelf, where the temperature is below 40 degrees (the average refrigerator door temperature in our kitchen is closer to 45 degrees). Eggs are best stored in their cardboard carton, which protects them from absorbing flavors from other foods. The carton also helps maintain humidity, which slows down the evaporation of the eggs' moisture.

IN THE FREEZER: Extra whites can be frozen for later use, but we have found their rising properties compromised. Frozen whites are best in recipes that call for small amounts (like an egg wash) or don't depend on whipping (an omelet). Yolks can't be frozen as is, but adding sugar syrup (microwave 2 parts sugar to 1 part water, stirring occasionally, until sugar is dissolved) to the yolks allows them to be frozen. Stir a scant ¼ teaspoon sugar syrup per yolk into the yolks before freezing. Defrosted yolks treated this way will behave just like fresh yolks in custards and other recipes.

This unusual but appealing dish combines a spicy, chunky tomato sauce, crispy bacon, and perfectly poached eggs all in one skillet.

Cajun-Style Eggs in Purgatory with Cheesy Grits

SERVES 2

✓ WHY THIS RECIPE WORKS: For a hearty but simple egg dish, we loved the idea of the dish called eggs in purgatory, where eggs are poached directly in a tomato sauce. We started with a simple sauce of canned tomatoes, green pepper, sautéed onion, garlic, and a little tomato paste. Replacing the plain canned tomatoes with chile-laced, spiced Ro-tel tomatoes gave the sauce punch and dimension without extra effort. A little bacon lent smoky meatiness. We cracked the eggs into divots we made in the sauce, then covered the skillet so the tops of the eggs would gently steam. A side of simple quick grits with plenty of cheddar rounded out our Cajun-inspired meal. Do not substitute instant grits or old-fashioned grits in this recipe.

2 cups water
½ cup quick grits
  Salt and pepper
2 ounces sharp cheddar cheese, shredded (½ cup)
2 slices bacon, cut into ½-inch pieces
1 small onion, chopped fine
½ green bell pepper, cut into ¼-inch pieces
1 tablespoon tomato paste
1 garlic clove, minced
1 (10-ounce) can Ro-tel Diced Tomatoes & Green Chilies
4 large eggs

1. Combine 1¾ cups water, grits, and ⅛ teaspoon salt in medium bowl, cover, and microwave until grits are tender and water is absorbed, 6 to 8 minutes. Stir in cheddar and season with salt and pepper to taste. Cover to keep warm.

2. Meanwhile, cook bacon in 10-inch nonstick skillet over medium heat until crisp, 5 to 7 minutes. Using slotted spoon, transfer bacon to paper towel–lined plate. Add onion and bell pepper to fat left in skillet and cook over medium-high heat until softened, about 5 minutes. Stir in tomato paste and garlic and cook until fragrant, about 30 seconds. Stir in tomatoes and their juice, and remaining ¼ cup water. Bring to simmer and cook until sauce is thickened, 8 to 10 minutes.

3. Make 4 shallow indentations (about 2 inches wide) in surface of sauce. Crack 1 egg into each indentation and season with salt and pepper. Cover, reduce heat to medium-low, and cook until eggs are just set, about 5 minutes. Off heat, sprinkle with bacon and serve immediately with grits.

Bacon, Potato, and Cheddar Frittata

SERVES 2

✓ **WHY THIS RECIPE WORKS:** Thick frittatas loaded with meat and vegetables often end up dry, overstuffed, and over-cooked. We wanted a frittata with a nice balance of egg to filling, firm yet moist eggs, and a supportive browned crust. A 10-inch skillet gave us a frittata that was neither too thick nor too thin. A nonstick skillet was also important to this recipe; the extra oil required for a traditional skillet made the eggs greasy. For a balanced ratio of ingredients, we used six eggs, one potato, and four slices of bacon. A little half-and-half added a touch of creaminess, and cubing the cheese, rather than shredding it, added a complementary texture. Cooking the frittata either in the oven or on the stovetop produced sub-par results, so we used a dual cooking method, starting the frittata on the stove and then finishing it under the broiler to give it a spotty-brown crust. Because broilers can vary in intensity, watch the frittata carefully as it cooks.

- 6 large eggs
- 2 tablespoons half-and-half
  Salt and pepper
- 4 slices bacon, cut into ¼-inch pieces
- 1 Yukon Gold potato (8 ounces), peeled and cut into ½-inch pieces
- 1 shallot, minced
- 1½ ounces cheddar cheese, cut into ¼-inch cubes (⅓ cup)

1. Adjust oven rack 6 inches from broiler element and heat broiler. Whisk eggs, half-and-half, ¼ teaspoon salt, and ⅛ teaspoon pepper together in bowl for 30 seconds; set aside.

2. Cook bacon in 10-inch ovensafe nonstick skillet over medium-low heat until crisp, about 10 minutes. Using slotted spoon, transfer bacon to paper towel–lined plate.

3. Pour off all but 1 tablespoon fat from skillet, then add potato, ¼ teaspoon salt, and ⅛ teaspoon pepper. Cook over medium heat, stirring occasionally, until potato begins to brown and is almost tender, about 10 minutes. Stir in shallot and cook until potato is tender and shallot is softened, 4 to 6 minutes.

4. Stir crisp bacon and cheddar into egg mixture. Add egg mixture to skillet and cook, using heat-resistant rubber spatula to stir and scrape bottom of skillet, until large curds form and spatula begins to leave wake but eggs are still very wet, about 1 minute. Shake skillet to distribute eggs evenly and continue to cook without stirring to let bottom set, about 30 seconds.

5. Slide skillet under broiler and cook until surface is puffed and spotty brown, yet center remains slightly wet and runny when cut into with paring knife, 1 to 2 minutes.

6. Using potholders (skillet handle will be hot), remove skillet from oven. Let sit until eggs in middle are just set, about 3 minutes. Using rubber spatula, loosen frittata from skillet, then slide onto cutting board and slice into wedges. Serve immediately.

VARIATION

Sun-Dried Tomato, Potato, and Mozzarella Frittata

Omit bacon and substitute 1 tablespoon vegetable oil for bacon fat in step 3. Substitute mozzarella cheese for cheddar cheese. Add ¼ cup oil-packed sun-dried tomatoes, minced, and 2 tablespoons chopped fresh basil to egg mixture before cooking in step 4.

Skillet Strata with Cheddar and Thyme

SERVES 2

✓ **WHY THIS RECIPE WORKS:** Strata at its most basic consists of day-old bread, eggs, milk, and cheese layered into a casserole dish and baked. To downsize this dish for two, we switched from a casserole dish to an 8-inch skillet. Whole milk provided richness without overwhelming the dish. Toasting bite-size squares of bread in the skillet ensured that they maintained some structure when doused in custard. We liked cheddar cheese for its sharp flavor, and sautéed onion and thyme lent aromatic notes. Baking the strata in the same skillet in which we sautéed the onions and toasted the bread made for easier cleanup. Be sure to use an 8-inch skillet; it is crucial to obtaining proper thickness and texture in this dish. Do not trim the crusts from the bread or the strata will be too dense and eggy. Make sure to remove the strata from the oven when it is still slightly loose; it will continue to set as it cools.

- 3 large eggs
- ¾ cup whole milk
- 1 teaspoon minced fresh thyme or ¼ teaspoon dried
  Salt and pepper
- 2 ounces cheddar cheese, shredded (½ cup)
- 2 tablespoons unsalted butter
- 1 small onion, chopped fine
- 2 slices hearty white sandwich bread, cut into 1-inch pieces

1. Adjust oven rack to middle position and heat oven to 425 degrees. Whisk eggs, milk, thyme, ¼ teaspoon salt, and ¼ teaspoon pepper together in bowl. Stir in cheese and set aside.

2. Melt butter in 8-inch ovensafe nonstick skillet over medium heat. Add onion and cook until softened and lightly browned, 5 to 7 minutes. Add bread and cook, using heat-resistant rubber spatula to fold bread and onion together, until bread is lightly toasted, about 3 minutes.

3. Off heat, fold in egg mixture until slightly thickened and well combined with bread. Gently press down on bread to help it soak up egg mixture. Bake until edges and center of strata are puffed and edges have pulled away slightly from sides of skillet, 12 to 15 minutes.

4. Using potholders (skillet handle will be hot), remove skillet from oven. Let sit for 5 minutes before serving.

VARIATION
Skillet Strata with Sausage and Gruyère
Substitute ½ cup shredded Gruyère cheese for cheddar cheese. Reduce amount of butter to 1 tablespoon and add 4 ounces crumbled raw breakfast sausage to skillet with onion in step 2.

Classic Cheese Quiche
SERVES 2

✔ **WHY THIS RECIPE WORKS:** To tailor a classic quiche to serve two, we first needed to ditch our full-size pie plate. A 6-inch pie plate produced a perfect-size quiche for two people. For a crisp, flaky crust, we parbaked the dough to keep the filling from turning the crust soggy. For the filling, two eggs and ⅔ cup of half-and-half gave us a creamy texture and lightly eggy flavor. Cheddar cheese and minced herbs rounded out the flavor. Taking the quiche out of the oven when the center looked slightly underdone allowed carryover cooking to produce a perfectly cooked quiche. You will need a 6-inch pie plate for this recipe. We prefer the buttery flavor and flaky texture of homemade pie dough; however, you can substitute 1 (9-inch) store-bought pie dough round if desired. It is important to add the custard to the crust while it is still warm; if the crust has cooled, rewarm it in the oven for 5 minutes before adding the custard.

1 recipe Classic Single-Crust Pie Dough (page 369)
⅔ cup half-and-half
2 large eggs, lightly beaten
2 teaspoons minced fresh chives or parsley
⅛ teaspoon salt
⅛ teaspoon pepper
2 ounces cheddar cheese, shredded (½ cup)

1. Roll dough into 10-inch circle, about ⅜ inch thick, on lightly floured counter. Loosely roll dough around rolling pin and gently unroll it onto 6-inch pie plate, letting excess dough hang over edge. Ease dough into plate by gently lifting edge of dough with your hand while pressing into plate bottom with your other hand, letting excess dough overhang plate

2. Trim overhang to ½ inch beyond lip of pie plate. Tuck overhang under itself; folded edge should be flush with edge of pie plate. Crimp dough evenly around edge of pie using your fingers. Wrap dough-lined pie plate loosely in plastic wrap and place in freezer until dough is fully chilled and firm, about 20 minutes.

3. Adjust oven rack to lower-middle position and heat oven to 375 degrees. Line chilled pie shell with parchment paper or double layer of aluminum foil, covering edges to prevent burning, and fill with pie weights. Bake until pie dough looks dry and is light in color, 25 to 30 minutes. Transfer pie plate to wire rack and remove weights and parchment. (Crust must still be warm when custard filling is added.)

4. Reduce oven temperature to 350 degrees. Line rimmed baking sheet with aluminum foil. Whisk half-and-half, eggs, chives, salt, and pepper together in 4-cup liquid measuring cup. Stir in cheddar until well combined.

5. Place warm baked pie crust on prepared sheet and return shell to oven. Carefully pour egg mixture into crust until it reaches about ½ inch from top edge of crust (you may have extra egg mixture). Bake quiche until top is lightly browned, very center still jiggles and looks slightly underdone, and knife inserted about 1 inch from edge comes out clean, 30 to 40 minutes. Let quiche cool on wire rack for 30 minutes to 1 hour. Serve slightly warm or at room temperature.

VARIATIONS
Quiche Lorraine
While crust bakes in step 3, cook 2 slices bacon, cut into ¼-inch pieces, in 8-inch skillet over medium-low heat until crisp, about 10 minutes. Using slotted spoon, transfer bacon to paper towel–lined plate. Pour off all but 1 tablespoon fat from skillet, add ¼ cup finely chopped onion, and cook over medium heat until softened and lightly browned, 5 to 7 minutes; set aside. Substitute 2 ounces Gruyère cheese for cheddar cheese and whisk bacon and onion into egg mixture in step 4.

Ham and Swiss Quiche
Substitute 2 ounces Swiss cheese for cheddar cheese. Whisk 2 ounces thinly sliced deli ham, cut into ¼-inch pieces, into egg mixture in step 4.

Our classic buttermilk pancakes boast a crisp, golden crust, a light, tender center, and a lightly sweet, tangy flavor.

Buttermilk Pancakes

SERVES 2

✓ WHY THIS RECIPE WORKS: We wanted truly tangy buttermilk pancakes with a slightly crisp, golden crust surrounding a fluffy, tender center with enough structure to withstand a good pour of maple syrup. We loved the tangy flavor that the buttermilk imparted, but too much made our batter runny; we found that supplementing the buttermilk with sour cream gave us the tang we were after without diluting the batter. For pancakes that were lightly sweet, we decided that 1 tablespoon of sugar was the perfect amount. A combination of baking powder and baking soda provided the best rise. Gently folding the wet and dry ingredients together was essential for a tender texture; overmixed batter made for tough pancakes. Letting the batter sit while the skillet heated allowed the batter to thicken slightly, resulting in perfect light, fluffy pancakes. The pancakes can be cooked on an electric griddle; set the griddle temperature to 350 degrees and cook as directed.

1 cup (5 ounces) all-purpose flour
1 tablespoon sugar
½ teaspoon baking powder
¼ teaspoon baking soda
¼ teaspoon salt
1 cup buttermilk
2 tablespoons sour cream
2 tablespoons unsalted butter, melted and cooled
1 large egg
1 teaspoon vegetable oil, plus extra as needed

1. Adjust oven rack to middle position and heat oven to 200 degrees. Set wire rack in rimmed baking sheet, spray with vegetable oil spray, and place in oven.

2. Whisk flour, sugar, baking powder, baking soda, and salt together in medium bowl. Whisk buttermilk, sour cream, melted butter, and egg together in separate bowl until smooth. Gently fold buttermilk mixture into flour mixture with rubber spatula until just combined. (Batter will be lumpy with a few spots of dry flour; do not overmix.) Let batter rest for 10 minutes before cooking.

3. Heat oil in 12-inch nonstick skillet over medium heat until shimmering. Using wad of paper towels, carefully wipe out oil, leaving thin film of oil on bottom and sides of skillet. Using ¼-cup dry measure, portion batter into skillet in 3 places. Cook until edges are set, first side is golden brown, and bubbles on surface are just beginning to break, 2 to 3 minutes.

4. Using thin, wide spatula, flip pancakes and continue to cook until second side is golden brown, 1 to 2 minutes. Transfer pancakes to prepared wire rack (don't overlap them) in warm oven. Repeat with remaining batter, using more oil as needed. Serve.

Getting Perfectly Cooked Pancakes

1. To ensure pancakes are same size, use ¼-cup dry measure to portion batter.

2. Cook pancakes until large bubbles begin to appear, about 2 minutes. Flip pancakes and cook until golden brown on second side, about 1½ minutes.

Key Tips to Better Pancakes

Here are our tips for getting perfectly fluffy, golden-brown pancakes every time.

MAKE A WELL WHEN MIXING: Make a well in the center of the dry ingredients, pour the liquid ingredients into the well, and gently whisk together until just incorporated. We like this method when making liquidy batters, because it helps incorporate the wet ingredients into the dry without overmixing.

LEAVE SOME LUMPS: When whisking the batter, be careful not to overmix it—the batter should actually have a few lumps. Overmixed batter makes for dense pancakes.

GET THE SKILLET HOT BUT NOT SCORCHING: Heat the oil in a 12-inch nonstick skillet over medium heat for 3 to 5 minutes. If the skillet is not hot enough before cooking the pancakes, the pancakes will be pale and dense. Knowing when the skillet is hot enough can take some practice; if you're not sure if the skillet is ready, try cooking just one small pancake to check.

WIPE OUT EXCESS OIL: Before adding the batter, use a wad of paper towels to carefully wipe out the excess oil, leaving a thin film of oil in the pan. If you use too much oil, the delicate cakes will taste greasy and dense.

USE A ¼-CUP MEASURE: Add the batter to the skillet in ¼-cup increments (two or three pancakes will fit at a time). Using a measuring cup ensures that the pancakes are the same size and that they cook at the same rate. Don't crowd the pan or the pancakes will run together and be difficult to flip.

FLIP WHEN YOU SEE BUBBLES: Cook the pancakes on the first side until large bubbles begin to appear, about 2 minutes. The bubbles indicate that the pancakes are ready to be flipped. If the pancakes are not browned when flipped, the skillet needs to be hotter; if the pancakes are overly browned, turn down the heat.

All About Maple Syrup

Maple syrup is the reduced sap of the sugar maple tree and is separated by quality into three grades: A, B, and C. Grade A is the purest (and most mild) syrup from the earliest sap of the season. Grade B is slightly darker and possesses a more assertive flavor. Grade C maple syrup is characterized by a harsh, almost molasses-like flavor and is generally only available for commercial use. Although Grade A is the most widely available, we prefer the richer flavor of Grade B syrup, which won praise from our tasters for its subtle vanilla and rum overtones and its potent maple flavor. That said, you should rely on your personal preference in deciding whether to use Grade A or Grade B syrup; they are interchangeable in recipes. Note that pure maple syrup and pancake syrup are not the same. Real maple syrup is nothing but sap from the sugar maple tree that has been boiled down (from about 40 gallons to 1). In the process, the sap caramelizes and develops its characteristic flavor. Pancake syrup, on the other hand, is flavored corn syrup and contains no real maple syrup. Unopened, maple syrup will last several years stored in a cool, dark place. Once opened, it will keep six months to a year in the refrigerator.

Multigrain Pancakes

SERVES 2

✔ **WHY THIS RECIPE WORKS:** Bland, dense, and gummy, most multigrain pancakes are more about appeasing your diet than pleasing your palate. We wanted flavorful, fluffy, and healthful flapjacks. We found that muesli had all the ingredients we wanted in one convenient package—raw whole oats, wheat germ, rye, barley, toasted nuts, and dried fruit. But pancakes made with whole muesli were too chewy and gummy. We ground the muesli in the food processor and then found the perfect combination of muesli "flour," all-purpose flour, whole-wheat flour, and leaveners to achieve the lightness we wanted. We added a little butter, vanilla, and brown sugar and cut the acidity by replacing the buttermilk with a blend of milk and lemon juice. If you can't find muesli without sugar, use muesli with sugar and reduce the brown sugar in the recipe to 1½ teaspoons. The pancakes can be cooked on an electric griddle; set the griddle temperature to 350 degrees and cook as directed.

1 cup whole milk
2 teaspoons lemon juice
¾ cup (3½ ounces) plus 1½ tablespoons no-sugar-added muesli
6 tablespoons (1¾ ounces) all-purpose flour
¼ cup (1⅓ ounces) whole-wheat flour
1 tablespoon packed brown sugar
1 teaspoon baking powder
¼ teaspoon baking soda
¼ teaspoon salt
1 large egg
2 tablespoons unsalted butter, melted and cooled
½ teaspoon vanilla extract
1 teaspoon vegetable oil, plus extra as needed

1. Adjust oven rack to middle position and heat oven to 200 degrees. Set wire rack in rimmed baking sheet, spray with vegetable oil spray, and place in oven. Whisk milk and lemon juice together in 2-cup liquid measuring cup and set aside to thicken.

2. Process ¾ cup muesli in food processor until finely ground, about 2 minutes. Transfer processed muesli to large bowl and whisk in remaining 1½ tablespoons muesli, all-purpose flour, whole-wheat flour, sugar, baking powder, baking soda, and salt.

3. Add egg, melted butter, and vanilla to milk mixture and whisk until combined. Make well in center of dry ingredients, add milk mixture to well, and whisk very gently until just combined. (Batter will be lumpy with a few spots of dry flour; do not overmix.) Let batter rest for 15 minutes before cooking.

4. Heat oil in 12-inch nonstick skillet over medium heat until shimmering. Using wad of paper towels, carefully wipe out oil, leaving thin film of oil on bottom and sides of skillet. Using ¼-cup dry measure, portion batter into skillet in 3 places. Cook until edges are set, first side is golden brown, and bubbles on surface are just beginning to break, 2 to 3 minutes.

5. Using thin, wide spatula, flip pancakes and continue to cook until second side is golden brown, 1 to 2 minutes. Transfer pancakes to prepared wire rack (don't overlap them) in warm oven. Repeat with remaining batter, using extra oil as needed. Serve.

Buttermilk Waffles

SERVES 2

✔ **WHY THIS RECIPE WORKS:** Most "waffle" recipes are merely repurposed pancake recipes that rely on butter and maple syrup to mask the mediocre results. Our waffles had to have a crisp, golden-brown crust with a moist, fluffy interior. We started by adapting buttermilk pancake batter, but this produced a gummy, wet interior and not much crust. We needed a drier batter with much more leavening oomph. We found the key to lightening our waffles in recipes for tempura batter, which often call for seltzer because the tiny bubbles inflate the batter the same way as a chemical leavener. We tried replacing the buttermilk in our recipe with a mixture of seltzer and powdered buttermilk, plus baking soda for browning. The resulting waffles were light and perfectly browned and crisp. The waffles will be more crisp if rested in a warm oven for 10 minutes. Buttermilk powder is available in most supermarkets near the dried-milk products or in the baking aisle. Do not substitute sparkling water such as Perrier for the seltzer water.

    1 cup (5 ounces) all-purpose flour
    ¼ cup (1¼ ounces) buttermilk powder
    1½ teaspoons sugar
    ¼ teaspoon salt
    ¼ teaspoon baking soda
    ¼ cup sour cream
    1 large egg
    2 tablespoons vegetable oil
    ⅛ teaspoon vanilla extract
    ⅔ cup seltzer water

1. Adjust oven rack to middle position and heat oven to 200 degrees. Set wire rack in rimmed baking sheet, spray with vegetable oil spray, and place in oven.

2. Whisk flour, buttermilk powder, sugar, salt, and baking soda together in large bowl. Whisk sour cream, egg, oil, and vanilla together in medium bowl, then gently stir in seltzer. Make well in center of dry ingredients, add seltzer mixture to well, and stir

gently with rubber spatula until just combined. (Batter will be lumpy with a few spots of dry flour; do not overmix.)

3. Heat waffle iron and bake waffles according to manufacturer's instructions (use about ⅓ cup batter for 7-inch round iron). Transfer waffles to prepared wire rack in warm oven; repeat with remaining batter. Serve.

Ten-Minute Steel-Cut Oatmeal

SERVES 2   LIGHT

✔ **WHY THIS RECIPE WORKS:** Most oatmeal fanatics agree that steel-cut oats offer the best flavor and texture, but many balk at the 40-minute cooking time. We were determined to find a way to make really good oatmeal that would take just 10 minutes before serving. Our solution was to jump-start the oats' cooking by stirring them into boiling water the night before so they gently hydrated and softened overnight. In the morning, we simply added more water and simmered the oats for just 4 to 6 minutes. Then we briefly rested the oatmeal off the heat so that it could thicken to the perfect consistency: creamy with a subtle chew and nutty flavor. The oatmeal will thicken as it cools. If you prefer a looser consistency, thin the oatmeal with boiling water. Serve with toppings such as brown sugar, toasted nuts, maple syrup, or dried fruit. For the nutritional information for this recipe, see page 415.

    2 cups water
    ½ cup steel-cut oats
       Pinch salt

1. Bring 1½ cups water to boil in small saucepan over high heat. Off heat, stir in oats and salt, cover, and let sit overnight.

2. Stir remaining ½ cup water into oats and bring to boil over medium-high heat. Reduce heat to medium and cook, stirring occasionally, until oats are softened but still retain some chew and mixture thickens and resembles warm pudding, 4 to 6 minutes. Remove saucepan from heat and let sit for 5 minutes. Stir and serve, passing desired toppings separately.

VARIATIONS

Apple-Cinnamon Steel-Cut Oatmeal

For the nutritional information for this recipe, see page 415.

Increase salt to ¼ teaspoon. Substitute ¼ cup apple cider and ¼ cup whole milk for water in step 2. Stir ¼ cup peeled and grated Golden Delicious, Fuji, or Gala apple, 1 tablespoon packed dark brown sugar, and ¼ teaspoon ground cinnamon into oatmeal with cider and milk. Sprinkle each serving with 1 tablespoon coarsely chopped toasted walnuts.

Carrot-Spice Steel-Cut Oatmeal

For the nutritional information for this recipe, see page 415.

Increase salt to ¼ teaspoon. Substitute ¼ cup carrot juice and ¼ cup whole milk for water in step 2. Stir ¼ cup peeled and finely shredded carrot, 2 tablespoons packed dark brown sugar, 3 tablespoons dried currants, and ¼ teaspoon ground cinnamon into oatmeal with carrot juice and milk. Sprinkle each serving with 1 tablespoon coarsely chopped toasted pecans.

Cranberry-Orange Steel-Cut Oatmeal

For the nutritional information for this recipe, see page 415.

Increase salt to ¼ teaspoon. Substitute ¼ cup orange juice and ¼ cup whole milk for water in step 2. Stir ¼ cup dried cranberries, 1½ tablespoons packed dark brown sugar, and pinch ground cardamom into oatmeal with orange juice and milk. Sprinkle each serving with 1 tablespoon toasted sliced≈almonds.

NOTES FROM THE TEST KITCHEN

Understanding Oat Types

Even with so many types of oats from which to choose, we found only one that was just right for our ideal bowl of oatmeal. Sometimes called Scottish or Irish oats, steel-cut oats are simply whole oats that have been cut into smaller pieces. They take longer to cook than regular rolled oats, but the outcome is very much worth the wait—and with our easy recipe, most of the time is hands-off. The hot cereal made with steel-cut oats had a faint nutty flavor, and while its consistency was surprisingly creamy, it also had a pleasing chewy quality. Rolled oats, on the other hand, resulted in bland, gummy oatmeal.

	UNCOOKED	COOKED
Oat Groats	Whole oats hulled and cleaned	These have a flavor reminiscent of brown rice and a very coarse texture.
Steel-Cut Oats	Groats cut crosswise into a few pieces	These make a creamy yet chewy hot cereal with a nutty flavor.
Rolled Oats	Groats steamed and pressed into flat flakes; also known as old-fashioned or regular	These American-style oats make a drab, gummy bowl of oatmeal.
Quick Oats	Groats rolled extra-thin	Cooked, these are flavorless and quick to cool into a flabby, pastelike consistency.
Instant Oats	Precooked rolled oats	These make a gummy, gelatinous cereal.

To get satisfyingly crisp granola, we firmly pack the raw granola into a pan, bake it, then break it up into big crunchy clusters.

Almond Granola with Dried Fruit

MAKES ABOUT 5 CUPS

✔ **WHY THIS RECIPE WORKS:** Store-bought granola suffers from many shortcomings. It's often loose and gravelly and infuriatingly expensive. We wanted to make our own granola at home with big, satisfying clusters and a crisp texture. The secret was to firmly pack the granola mixture into a 13 by 9-inch pan before baking. Once it was baked, we had granola "bark" that we could break into crunchy clumps of any size. A combination of just a few tablespoons each of maple syrup and brown sugar gave us granola with a subtle, not cloying, sweetness. Chopping the almonds by hand is best for superior texture and crunch. If you prefer not to hand-chop, substitute an equal quantity of slivered or sliced almonds. (A food processor does a poor job of chopping whole nuts evenly.) Do not use quick oats. You can substitute 1 cup of your favorite dried fruit(s) for the raisins.

2½ tablespoons maple syrup
2½ tablespoons packed light brown sugar
2 teaspoons vanilla extract
¼ teaspoon salt
¼ cup vegetable oil
2½ cups (7½ ounces) old-fashioned rolled oats
1 cup whole almonds, chopped coarse
1 cup raisins, chopped

1. Adjust oven rack to upper-middle position and heat oven to 325 degrees. Make parchment paper sling for 13 by 9-inch baking pan by folding 2 long sheets of parchment; first sheet should be 13 inches wide and second sheet should be 9 inches wide. Lay sheets of parchment in pan perpendicular to each other, with extra parchment hanging over edges of pan. Push parchment into corners and up sides of pan, smoothing parchment flush to pan.

2. Whisk maple syrup, sugar, vanilla, and salt together in large bowl, then whisk in oil. Fold in oats and almonds until thoroughly coated.

3. Transfer oat mixture to prepared pan and spread across bottom into thin, even layer. Using stiff metal spatula, compress oat mixture until very compact. Bake until lightly browned, 30 to 35 minutes, rotating pan halfway through baking.

4. Remove granola from oven and let cool on wire rack to room temperature, about 1 hour. Using parchment overhang, lift granola out of pan. Break cooled granola into pieces of desired size and transfer to large clean bowl. Add raisins and gently toss to combine. (Granola can be stored in airtight container for up to 2 weeks.)

VARIATIONS

Pecan-Orange Granola with Dried Cranberries

Add 1 tablespoon grated orange zest and 1¼ teaspoons ground cinnamon to maple syrup mixture in step 2. Substitute 1 cup pecans for almonds and 1 cup dried cranberries for raisins.

Tropical Granola with Dried Mango

Reduce amount of vanilla extract to 1 teaspoon and add ¾ teaspoon ground ginger and ¼ teaspoon ground nutmeg to maple syrup mixture in step 2. Substitute 1 cup macadamia nuts for almonds and ¾ cup unsweetened shredded coconut for ½ cup of oats. Substitute 1 cup chopped dried mango or pineapple for raisins.

Hazelnut Granola with Dried Pear

Substitute 1 cup toasted and skinned hazelnuts for almonds and 1 cup chopped dried pears for raisins.

Breakfast Smoothies with Strawberries and Banana
SERVES 2 FAST LIGHT

WHY THIS RECIPE WORKS: Smoothies are perfect for a quick breakfast on mornings when you can't sit down to eggs or pancakes. They're healthy, easy to make, and conveniently portable. Since we were only making smoothies for two, we wanted to keep the ingredient list simple, using pantry staples and items that could be easily saved for another recipe. Frozen fruit fit the bill perfectly. Not only did we not have to buy a lot of highly perishable fresh fruit, but because frozen fruit is picked at the peak of ripeness, it is sweeter than out-of-season fresh fruit. Additionally, it saves on prep time and eliminates the need for ice cubes. We simply combined frozen strawberries with a banana, a little sugar, and plain yogurt in the blender until smooth. You can substitute 1½ cups fresh, hulled strawberries and 10 ice cubes for frozen strawberries. For the nutritional information for this recipe, see page 415.

1½ cups plain low-fat yogurt
7 ounces (1½ cups) frozen strawberries
1 banana, peeled, halved lengthwise, and sliced 1 inch thick
1 tablespoon sugar, plus extra for seasoning
Pinch salt

Place yogurt in blender, then layer other ingredients on top. Process mixture on low speed until combined but still coarse in texture, about 10 seconds. Increase speed to high and continue to process until mixture is completely smooth, 20 to 40 seconds. Season with extra sugar to taste and serve.

VARIATIONS

Breakfast Smoothies with Pineapple and Mango

You can substitute ¾ cup 1-inch fresh pineapple pieces, ¾ cup fresh chopped mango, and 10 ice cubes for the frozen pineapple and mango. For the nutritional information for this recipe, see page 415.

Substitute ¾ cup frozen pineapple chunks and ¾ cup frozen chopped mango for strawberries and banana.

Breakfast Smoothies with Blueberries and Pomegranate

You can substitute 1½ cups fresh blueberries and 10 ice cubes for the frozen blueberries. For the nutritional information for this recipe, see page 415.

Substitute 1½ cups frozen blueberries and ½ cup pomegranate juice for strawberries and banana.

CHAPTER 15

Quick Breads

Opposite: Simple Currant Cream Scones; Banana Bread; Cinnamon Streusel Coffee Cake

Simple Drop Biscuits

MAKES 4 BISCUITS

✓ **WHY THIS RECIPE WORKS:** We wanted a drop biscuit recipe we could make anytime—and this would be no ordinary drop biscuit. It should possess the same rich flavor and tender crumb of a rolled and cut biscuit, but with less work. Replacing the usual milk with buttermilk gave the biscuits a rich, buttery tang. The buttermilk also encouraged a crisp crust and a fluffy interior. Stirring melted butter into the buttermilk created clumps that seemed problematic at first, but when we tried making a batch with the lumpy buttermilk, the result was a surprisingly better biscuit. The water in the lumps of butter turned to steam in the oven, creating additional height. A combination of baking powder and baking soda gave us even more rise for the lightest, fluffiest biscuits. If you have one, a spring-loaded ice cream scoop makes portioning these biscuits particularly easy. You will need about 1 teaspoon of melted butter for brushing the tops of the biscuits.

Melted butter and buttermilk plus a double dose of leaveners produce the richest, fluffiest, easiest-ever drop biscuits.

- ⅔ **cup (3⅓ ounces) all-purpose flour**
- ¾ **teaspoon baking powder**
- ¼ **teaspoon baking soda**
- ⅛ **teaspoon sugar**
- ⅛ **teaspoon salt**
- ⅓ **cup buttermilk, chilled**
- 2 **tablespoons unsalted butter, melted and hot, plus extra for brushing**

1. Adjust oven rack to middle position and heat oven to 450 degrees. Line baking sheet with parchment paper.

2. Whisk flour, baking powder, baking soda, sugar, and salt together in medium bowl. In separate bowl, stir chilled buttermilk and melted butter together until butter forms small clumps. Stir buttermilk mixture into flour mixture with rubber spatula until just incorporated and dough pulls away from sides of bowl.

3. Using greased ¼-cup dry measure or #16 ice cream scoop, scoop out and drop 4 mounds of dough onto prepared sheet, spacing them about 1½ inches apart. Bake until biscuit tops are golden brown and crisp, 12 to 15 minutes, rotating sheet halfway through baking.

4. Brush baked biscuits with extra melted butter, transfer to wire rack, and let cool for 5 minutes. Serve warm.

VARIATIONS

Fresh Herb Simple Drop Biscuits

Whisk 2 teaspoons minced fresh mild herbs (such as tarragon, cilantro, chives, parsley, or dill) or 1 teaspoon minced fresh hearty herbs (such as thyme, sage, or rosemary) into the flour mixture.

Black Pepper and Bacon Simple Drop Biscuits

Whisk 2 slices fried, crumbled bacon and ¼ teaspoon coarsely ground black pepper into flour mixture.

Rosemary and Parmesan Simple Drop Biscuits

Whisk ¼ cup grated Parmesan and pinch minced fresh rosemary into flour mixture.

Making Drop Biscuits

When melted butter is stirred into cold buttermilk, the butter clumps. Although it looks like a mistake, it's not; the clumps of butter turn to steam in the oven, ensuring the biscuits have a light and fluffy interior.

Judging Doneness in Quick Breads

There are two ways to judge doneness in quick breads. Fully baked items should feel springy and resilient when the center is gently pressed. If your finger leaves an impression—or if the center jiggles—the item is not done. This works best with biscuits, scones, and loaf-style quick breads. The other option is to insert a skewer or toothpick into the center of the item; it should emerge fairly clean, with perhaps just a few crumbs attached. If you see moist batter, the item needs to bake longer. This test works well with muffins and loaf breads.

Storing Quick Breads and Muffins

Most leftover biscuits, scones, and muffins can be stored in a zipper-lock bag at room temperature for up to three days. If the leftover quick breads include perishable flavorings like bacon, it is best to refrigerate them, but in general the refrigerator causes baked goods to dry out and so is not our first choice for storage. When ready to serve, refresh quick breads by placing them on a baking sheet and warming them in a 300-degree oven for about 10 minutes.

Simple Currant Cream Scones

MAKES 4 SCONES

✔ **WHY THIS RECIPE WORKS:** Traditional British scones are essentially fluffy biscuits. They should be sweet, but not too sweet, so that they can be enjoyed with jam and perhaps clotted cream. For a light, tender texture, we tried cake flour, but it made gummy scones. All-purpose flour, on the other hand, gave us light, feathery scones. A modest amount of sugar kept the sweetness level in check. Heavy cream gave our scones a rich, not-too-dry character. A food processor made quick work of incorporating the butter into the flour; we stirred in the cream by hand and then lightly kneaded the dough before cutting it into wedges. We also found that it was important to get the scones into the oven immediately after cutting them out for the best rise. Resist the urge to eat the scones hot out of the oven; letting them cool for at least 10 minutes allows them to firm up and improves their texture.

1	cup (5 ounces) all-purpose flour
2	tablespoons sugar
1½	teaspoons baking powder
¼	teaspoon salt
3	tablespoons unsalted butter, cut into ¼-inch pieces and chilled
¼	cup dried currants
½	cup heavy cream

1. Adjust oven rack to middle position and heat oven to 375 degrees. Line baking sheet with parchment paper.

2. Process flour, sugar, baking powder, and salt in food processor until combined, about 5 seconds. Scatter butter over top and pulse until mixture resembles coarse cornmeal with some slightly larger butter lumps, about 6 pulses. Transfer mixture to large bowl and stir in currants. Stir in cream with rubber spatula until dough begins to form, about 30 seconds.

3. Turn dough and any floury bits onto lightly floured counter and knead until rough, slightly sticky ball forms, 5 to 10 seconds. Shape dough into 5-inch round, about ¾ inch thick. Cut dough into 4 wedges.

4. Place wedges on prepared sheet. Bake until scone tops are light golden brown, 18 to 22 minutes, rotating sheet halfway through baking. Transfer scones to wire rack and let cool for at least 10 minutes before serving.

VARIATIONS
Simple Maple-Pecan Cream Scones

Omit sugar and substitute ¼ cup pecans, toasted and chopped, for currants. Whisk 1½ tablespoons maple syrup into heavy cream before adding to flour mixture. While scones bake, whisk 3 tablespoons confectioners' sugar and 1 tablespoon maple syrup together in bowl to make glaze. Let baked scones cool to room temperature, about 20 minutes, then drizzle with glaze. Let glaze set for 5 to 10 minutes before serving.

Simple Ginger Cream Scones

Substitute ¼ cup chopped crystallized ginger for currants.

Simple Cranberry-Orange Cream Scones

Add ½ teaspoon finely grated orange zest to flour mixture with butter and substitute ¼ cup dried cranberries for currants.

Making Simple Cream Scones

1. Pat dough into 5-inch round, about ¾ inch thick.

2. Using metal bench scraper or knife, cut dough into 4 evenly sized wedges.

Corn Muffins

MAKES 4 MUFFINS

✔ **WHY THIS RECIPE WORKS:** A corn muffin should taste like corn, but not overpoweringly so, and should be moist with a tender crumb and a crunchy top. We wanted a recipe that struck just the right balance in both texture and flavor. The cornmeal itself proved to be an important factor; degerminated cornmeal just didn't have enough corn flavor. A fine-ground, whole-grain meal provided better flavor and texture. Butter, milk, and sour cream provided moisture and richness plus acidity for its tenderizing effect. We tried mixing the ingredients with both the quick-bread and creaming methods; creaming resulted in overly airy, cakey muffins, so we stuck with the easier quick-bread method. We got our crunchy browned top from a 400-degree oven. Any muffin tin with standard-size cups will work here, and the batter can be placed in any of the cups. We prefer stone-ground cornmeal because it has a full flavor.

- ⅔ cup (3⅓ ounces) all-purpose flour
- ⅓ cup (1⅔ ounces) stone-ground cornmeal
- ½ teaspoon baking powder
- ½ teaspoon baking soda
- ¼ teaspoon salt
- ⅓ cup sour cream
- ¼ cup (1¾ ounces) sugar
- 1 large egg, room temperature
- 3 tablespoons unsalted butter, melted and cooled
- 2 tablespoons whole milk

1. Adjust oven rack to middle position and heat oven to 400 degrees. Spray 4 cups of muffin tin with baking spray with flour.

2. Whisk flour, cornmeal, baking powder, baking soda, and salt together in large bowl. In separate bowl, whisk sour cream, sugar, egg, melted butter, and milk together until smooth. Gently fold sour cream mixture into flour mixture with rubber spatula until just combined. (Batter will be lumpy with a few spots of dry flour; do not overmix.)

3. Using dry measuring cup or ice cream scoop, divide batter evenly among prepared muffin cups. Bake until muffins are golden brown and toothpick inserted in center of muffin comes out clean, 12 to 17 minutes, rotating muffin tin halfway through baking.

4. Let muffins cool in muffin tin on wire rack for 10 minutes. Remove muffins from muffin tin and let cool for at least 10 minutes before serving.

VARIATIONS

Apricot-Orange Corn Muffins
Add ¼ teaspoon finely grated orange zest and ⅓ cup dried apricots, chopped fine, to sour cream mixture in step 2.

Cheddar Cheese and Scallion Corn Muffins
Reduce sugar to 2 tablespoons. Add 2 thinly sliced scallions and ½ cup shredded cheddar cheese to sour cream mixture in step 2. Sprinkle muffins with 2 tablespoons shredded cheddar cheese before baking.

Blueberry Muffins

MAKES 4 MUFFINS

✔ **WHY THIS RECIPE WORKS:** Blueberry muffins, for all of their simple, warm appeal, have a host of problems, as they often emerge from the oven too sweet, too dense, or just plain bland, with little blueberry flavor. We wanted delicate muffins with a balanced fresh blueberry flavor. To achieve a delicate texture, we decided to forgo creaming the butter and sugar and instead folded melted butter into the batter. Plain yogurt added moisture and a nice tang, and a little lemon zest complemented the sweet blueberries nicely. Sprinkling the muffins with lemon-sugar topping was the perfect finishing touch. Any muffin tin with standard-size cups will work here, and the batter can be placed in any of the cups. Frozen blueberries can be substituted for the fresh blueberries; rinse and dry the frozen blueberries (do not thaw) before folding into the batter.

TOPPING
- 1 tablespoon sugar
- ¼ teaspoon finely grated lemon zest

MUFFINS
- ¾ cup (3¾ ounces) all-purpose flour
- ¼ cup (1¾ ounces) sugar
- 1 teaspoon baking powder
- ⅛ teaspoon baking soda
- ⅛ teaspoon salt
- ¼ cup whole-milk or low-fat plain yogurt
- 1 large egg, room temperature
- ¼ teaspoon finely grated lemon zest
- 3 tablespoons unsalted butter, melted and cooled
- 2½ ounces (½ cup) fresh blueberries

We sprinkle our moist and tender blueberry muffins with lemon sugar for a bright sweet-tart crunch.

1. FOR THE TOPPING: Adjust oven rack to middle position and heat oven to 325 degrees. Spray 4 cups of muffin tin with baking spray with flour. Combine sugar and lemon zest in bowl; set aside.

2. FOR THE MUFFINS: Whisk flour, sugar, baking powder, baking soda, and salt together in large bowl. In separate bowl, whisk yogurt, egg, and lemon zest together until smooth. Gently fold yogurt mixture into flour mixture with rubber spatula until just combined, then fold in melted butter and blueberries.

3. Using dry measure or ice cream scoop, divide batter evenly among prepared muffin cups. Sprinkle sugar topping over muffins. Bake until muffins are golden brown and toothpick inserted in center of muffin comes out clean, 20 to 24 minutes, rotating muffin tin halfway through baking.

4. Let muffins cool in muffin tin on wire rack for 10 minutes. Remove muffins from muffin tin and let cool for at least 10 minutes before serving.

Troubleshooting Muffins

Sure, muffins are quick and easy to make, but who hasn't run into a few problems such as squat muffins, unevenly sized muffins, or muffins that simply wouldn't come out of the pan? Here are a few tricks that will help you become a muffin master.

PROBLEM: Stuck muffins
SOLUTION: Give the tin a good greasing
To make sure your muffins slide effortlessly out of the tins, start by using a good nonstick muffin tin—this will make a huge difference in your success rate with muffins. Next, it's important to grease the tin thoroughly; we like to use baking spray with flour. We get this pan prep out of the way first, before we start making the batter. To prevent the spray from getting all over the counter or floor, we suggest spraying the muffin tin over the sink, a garbage can, or even an open dishwasher door.

PROBLEM: Tough, squat muffins
SOLUTION: Don't overmix the batter
Overmixing encourages gluten development, which inhibits rise and makes tougher muffins. To avoid this, blend the wet and dry ingredients separately and mix the two gently until just combined.

PROBLEM: Overflowing muffin tins
SOLUTION: Portion the batter carefully
For neat, evenly portioned muffins it's important to have a strategy for filling the tins—especially because every recipe has a slightly different yield. If you don't you'll end up with muffins of different sizes and/or batter that overflows the cups, making it nearly impossible to get the muffins out without breaking them. Our foolproof way for filling muffin tins is to portion ⅓ cup of the batter into each cup, and then circle back and evenly add the remaining batter using a spoon. A spring-loaded #12 ice cream scoop (which holds ⅓ cup batter) makes it easy to portion batter into the cups without making a mess around the edges of the pan. Whether you are using an ice cream scoop or a measuring cup, spray it first with vegetable oil spray so that all the batter slides off easily.

PROBLEM: Overdone or underdone muffins
SOLUTION: Poke them with a toothpick
The best way to test a muffin for doneness is to poke it with a toothpick. A toothpick inserted into the center of the muffin should come out with only a few crumbs attached.

PROBLEM: Broken muffins
SOLUTION: Cool them in the tins
Be sure to let the muffins cool in the tins for at least 10 minutes to help them set up so that they are easier to remove without breaking. Trying to remove muffins from a hot tin never works—they are too delicate to be handled at this point and will break apart.

For truly nutty cranberry-nut muffins, we stir ground pecans into the batter then top the muffins with a crunchy pecan streusel.

Cranberry-Pecan Muffins

MAKES 4 MUFFINS

✓ **WHY THIS RECIPE WORKS:** We wanted cranberry-nut muffins punctuated by zingy but not harsh cranberries and rich-tasting, crunchy nuts. Our first job was to tame the bite of the cranberries, so we chopped them in a food processor with a little confectioners' sugar and salt. For big, nutty flavor, we supplemented the all-purpose flour with our own nut flour (made by grinding pecans in a food processor). Letting the batter rest for 30 minutes ensured that the small amount of flour became more hydrated, resulting in a properly thickened batter that baked up perfectly domed with a tender crumb. A pecan-streusel topping added even more nuttiness and a nice crunch. Any muffin tin with standard-size cups will work here, and the batter can be placed in any of the cups. If fresh cranberries aren't available, you can substitute frozen; simply microwave them in a bowl until they're partially but not fully thawed, 30 to 45 seconds.

STREUSEL TOPPING

- 2½ tablespoons all-purpose flour
- 1½ tablespoons unsalted butter, cut into ½-inch pieces and softened
- 1 tablespoon packed brown sugar
- 1 tablespoon granulated sugar
  Pinch salt
- 3 tablespoons chopped pecans

MUFFINS

- 6 tablespoons (1¾ ounces) all-purpose flour
- ¼ teaspoon baking powder
  Salt
- ½ cup pecans, toasted and cooled
- ¼ cup (1¾ ounces) granulated sugar
- 1 large egg, room temperature
- 3 tablespoons whole milk
- 1½ tablespoons unsalted butter, melted and cooled
- 2 ounces (½ cup) fresh cranberries
- 1 teaspoon confectioners' sugar

1. FOR THE STREUSEL TOPPING: Adjust oven rack to upper-middle position and heat oven to 375 degrees. Spray 4 cups of muffin tin with baking spray with flour. Mix flour, butter, brown sugar, granulated sugar, and salt together with your fingers in small bowl until mixture resembles wet sand. Stir in pecans; set aside.

2. FOR THE MUFFINS: Whisk flour, baking powder, and ¼ teaspoon salt together in bowl; set aside.

3. Process pecans and granulated sugar in food processor until mixture resembles coarse sand, 10 to 15 seconds. Transfer mixture to large bowl and whisk in egg, milk, and melted butter until combined. Whisk flour mixture into egg mixture until just moistened and no streaks of flour remain. Set aside for 30 minutes to thicken.

4. Pulse cranberries, confectioners' sugar, and pinch salt in food processor until very coarsely chopped, 3 to 5 pulses. Gently fold cranberry mixture into batter with rubber spatula. Using dry measuring cup or ice cream scoop, divide batter evenly among prepared muffin cups. Sprinkle streusel topping over muffins, gently pressing into batter to adhere.

5. Bake until muffins are golden brown and toothpick inserted in center of muffin comes out clean, 18 to 20 minutes, rotating muffin tin halfway through baking.

6. Let muffins cool in muffin tin on wire rack for 10 minutes. Remove muffins from muffin tin and let cool for at least 10 minutes before serving.

Reducing the exuded fruit juice from the pineapple and apple ensures flavorful and moist, not soggy, Morning Glory Muffins.

Morning Glory Muffins

MAKES 4 MUFFINS

✔ **WHY THIS RECIPE WORKS:** Morning glory muffins are chock-full of nuts, fruit, carrots, and spices. But all these tasty add-ins can make for heavy, sodden muffins, so we aimed to lighten them up. Our first move was to strain the fruit and press out the extra juice to prevent our muffins from being soggy. To keep the bright, fruity flavor intact, we saved the fruit juice, reduced it on the stovetop, and added the concentrated syrup back to the batter. To keep the nuts and coconut from becoming mealy or soggy in the finished muffins, we toasted and processed them. At last, our muffins were truly glorious. Any muffin tin with standard-size cups will work here, and the batter can be placed in any of the cups. We prefer golden raisins in these muffins but ordinary raisins will work, too.

⅓ cup canned crushed pineapple
1 small Granny Smith apple, peeled and shredded
¼ cup (¾ ounce) sweetened shredded coconut, toasted
¼ cup walnuts, toasted

¾ cup (3¾ ounces) all-purpose flour
¼ cup (1¾ ounces) sugar
½ teaspoon baking soda
¼ teaspoon baking powder
¼ teaspoon ground cinnamon
¼ teaspoon salt
3 tablespoons unsalted butter, melted and cooled
1 large egg, room temperature
¼ teaspoon vanilla extract
⅓ cup shredded carrot (1 carrot)
⅓ cup golden raisins

1. Adjust oven rack to middle position and heat oven to 350 degrees. Spray 4 cups of muffin tin with baking spray with flour. Place pineapple and shredded apple in fine-mesh strainer set over liquid measuring cup. Press fruit dry, reserving juice; juice should measure about ⅓ cup. Bring juice to boil in 8-inch skillet over medium-high heat and cook until reduced to 2 tablespoons, 3 to 5 minutes; let cool slightly.

2. Process coconut and walnuts in food processor until finely ground, about 15 seconds. Add flour, sugar, baking soda, baking powder, cinnamon, and salt and process until combined, about 5 seconds; transfer to medium bowl.

3. In separate bowl, whisk cooled juice, melted butter, egg, and vanilla together until smooth. Gently fold juice mixture into flour mixture with rubber spatula until just combined, then fold in drained pineapple-apple mixture, carrot, and raisins.

4. Using dry measuring cup or ice cream scoop, divide batter evenly among prepared muffin cups. Bake until muffins are golden brown and toothpick inserted in center of muffin comes out clean, 24 to 28 minutes, rotating muffin tin halfway through baking.

5. Let muffins cool in muffin tin on wire rack for 10 minutes. Remove muffins from muffin tin and let cool for at least 10 minutes before serving.

NOTES FROM THE TEST KITCHEN

Muffin Tin Myth Buster

Did your mother ever tell you that if you're baking a small batch of muffins using a 12-cup tin, you should fill the empty cups with water? The theory is that the water acts as a "heat sink" to ensure that muffins next to empty cups heat evenly (avoiding stunted growth or spotty browning). But when we tested this theory by baking a small batch of muffins and leaving the extra cups empty, all the muffins had the same height, texture, and color, and none of the tins warped. The reason? In a full 12-cup muffin tin, all but the two center muffins are directly exposed to the oven's heat on at least one side to no ill effect. So when making a small batch of muffins, you can place the batter in any of the cups and your muffins will bake just fine.

Baking Soda vs. Baking Powder

BAKING SODA

Baking soda is a leavener that provides lift to muffins, biscuits, cakes, and other baked goods. When baking soda, which is alkaline, encounters an acidic ingredient (such as sour cream, buttermilk, or brown sugar), carbon and oxygen combine to form carbon dioxide. The tiny bubbles of carbon dioxide then lift up the dough. Baking soda also promotes browning.

BAKING POWDER

Baking powder also creates carbon dioxide to provide lift to a wide range of baked goods. The active ingredients in baking powder are baking soda and an acidic element, such as cream of tartar. It also contains cornstarch to absorb moisture and keep the powder dry. Cooks use baking powder rather than baking soda when there is no natural acidity in the batter.

There are two kinds of baking powder. A single-acting baking powder has only one acid combined with the baking soda: a quick-acting acid that begins to work when liquid is added to the batter. A double-acting baking powder (like most supermarket brands) has two acids added to the baking soda: The second acid (often sodium aluminum sulfate) begins to work only when the dish is put in the oven, after the temperature has climbed above 120 degrees.

We recommend using double-acting baking powder in all recipes—baked goods rise higher since most of the rise with baking powder occurs at oven temperatures. Double-acting baking powder also provides sufficient lift in the oven to allow you to bake frozen dough. Also, we have found that single-acting baking powder doesn't provide sufficient leavening for doughs with little liquid, such as scones or muffins.

STORING CHEMICAL LEAVENERS: Keep baking powder and baking soda in a cool, dark dry place in the pantry. Despite most manufacturer claims of one year, our tests have proven baking powder loses its potency after six months.

Coffee Cake Muffins

MAKES 4 MUFFINS

✓ **WHY THIS RECIPE WORKS:** The perfect coffee cake muffin should have a texture somewhere between the delicate, buttery crumb of coffee cake and the slightly coarser, chewier crumb of a muffin. To make our ideal version, we started by testing different fats. Sour cream gave the muffins a light texture and a nice tanginess, but sour cream alone also made the batter too wet. Swapping in some butter fixed the problem and enriched the muffins' flavor. A combination of granulated and dark brown sugar gave the muffins the right sweetness. For the streusel topping, we liked a combination of flour, sugar, brown

To ensure our decadent coffee cake muffins have plenty of sweet, rich streusel, we layer it inside the muffin to ensure it stays put.

sugar, and cinnamon. But when sprinkled on top of the muffins, the streusel refused to stay put. Our solution was to layer it inside the muffin instead; we filled the muffin cups partway with batter, added the streusel, and dolloped the rest of the batter on top. This gave us muffins with an attractive swirl of streusel in the center. Any muffin tin with standard-size cups will work here, and the batter can be placed in any of the cups.

⅓ cup (2⅓ ounces) granulated sugar
⅓ cup (1⅔ ounces) plus 8 teaspoons all-purpose flour
8 teaspoons packed dark brown sugar
1 teaspoon ground cinnamon
⅛ teaspoon baking powder
⅛ teaspoon baking soda
⅛ teaspoon salt
4 tablespoons unsalted butter, cut into 4 pieces and chilled
1 large egg, room temperature
2 tablespoons plus 2 teaspoons sour cream
Confectioners' sugar

1. Adjust oven rack to middle position and heat oven to 350 degrees. Spray 4 cups of muffin tin with baking spray with flour.

2. Pulse granulated sugar, 8 teaspoons flour, and 4 teaspoons brown sugar in food processor until combined, about 3 pulses. Transfer 2 tablespoons processed sugar mixture to small bowl (leaving rest in food processor) and whisk in remaining 4 teaspoons brown sugar and cinnamon to make streusel; set aside.

3. Add remaining ⅓ cup flour, baking powder, baking soda, and salt to sugar mixture left in food processor and pulse to combine, about 5 pulses. Scatter butter over top and pulse until mixture breaks down into small pebbly pieces, about 8 pulses. Add egg and sour cream and pulse until batter is well combined and thick, about 8 pulses, scraping down sides of bowl as needed.

4. Portion generous tablespoon batter into each muffin cup, then sprinkle each with scant 1 tablespoon streusel mixture. Spoon remaining batter over streusel in each cup. Bake until muffins are golden brown and toothpick inserted in center of muffin comes out clean, 20 to 24 minutes, rotating muffin tin halfway through baking.

5. Let muffins cool in muffin tin on wire rack for 10 minutes. Remove muffins from muffin tin and let cool for at least 10 minutes. Dust muffins with confectioners' sugar before serving.

Cinnamon Streusel Coffee Cake
SERVES 2

✔ WHY THIS RECIPE WORKS: For a well-balanced coffee cake sized for two that delivered both tender cake and a crunchy, cinnamon-y streusel topping, we started by building a simple cake with just the right amount of moisture and structure. We cut back on the butter so our cake wouldn't be greasy, but we needed to find another ingredient to bump up the moistness and richness. Buttermilk worked perfectly and it imparted a nice subtle tang. All-purpose flour ensured that our cake was sturdy enough to support a generous amount of pecan-and-cinnamon streusel topping. You will need a 6-inch round cake pan for this recipe. You can substitute 3 tablespoons of plain whole-milk or low-fat yogurt mixed with 1 tablespoon of milk for the buttermilk if necessary.

STREUSEL TOPPING

1½   tablespoons all-purpose flour
1½   tablespoons granulated sugar
1½   tablespoons packed light brown sugar
  1   tablespoon unsalted butter, softened
  ¾   teaspoon ground cinnamon
  ⅓   cup pecans or walnuts, chopped

CAKE

  ¾   cup (3¾ ounces) all-purpose flour
  ¼   teaspoon baking powder
  ¼   teaspoon baking soda
  ¼   teaspoon ground cinnamon
        Pinch salt
  ¼   cup buttermilk
  ¼   cup (1¾ ounces) granulated sugar
  ¼   cup packed (1¾ ounces) light brown sugar
  1   large egg, room temperature
  2   tablespoons unsalted butter, melted and cooled

1. FOR THE STREUSEL TOPPING: Adjust oven rack to middle position and heat oven to 350 degrees. Grease 6-inch round cake pan, line with parchment paper, grease parchment, and flour pan. Mix flour, granulated sugar, brown sugar, butter, and cinnamon together with your fingers in medium bowl until mixture resembles wet sand. Stir in pecans; set aside.

2. FOR THE CAKE: Whisk flour, baking powder, baking soda, cinnamon, and salt together in separate medium bowl. Whisk buttermilk, granulated sugar, brown sugar, egg, and melted butter together in small bowl until smooth. Gently fold egg mixture into flour mixture with rubber spatula until combined.

3. Scrape batter into prepared pan and smooth top. Sprinkle streusel evenly over top of cake. Bake until cake is golden brown and toothpick inserted in center comes out with a few moist crumbs attached, about 30 minutes, rotating pan halfway through baking.

4. Let cake cool in pan on wire rack for 10 minutes. Remove cake from pan, discarding parchment, and let cool for at least 10 minutes before serving.

NOTES FROM THE TEST KITCHEN

Buttermilk Options

For small households, buying liquid buttermilk by the quart is often a waste since recipes usually call for less than a cup. Luckily, when it comes to baking with buttermilk, you have options: liquid (or fresh) buttermilk, powdered buttermilk, and soured milk (just add 1½ teaspoons lemon juice or white vinegar to ½ cup milk). To see how these options stack up, we pitted them against one another in a biscuit recipe and a chocolate cake recipe.

We noted only small differences in flavor and texture among these recipes. Overall, the powdered buttermilk (rehydrated using the package instructions) produced baked goods with a more delicate, even texture and a milder flavor. Both the liquid buttermilk and the soured milk produced slightly coarser textures. Tasters preferred the strong, tangy flavor of the liquid buttermilk, while the soured milk was downgraded for tasting flat. In short, we prefer to use either fresh or powdered buttermilk; however, soured milk is a fine substitute in a pinch. (For information on freezing buttermilk, see page 7.)

Banana Bread

SERVES 2

✔ **WHY THIS RECIPE WORKS:** Our ideal banana bread is simple enough—a moist, tender loaf that really tastes like bananas. We set out to scale down banana bread to fit in a mini loaf pan but keep all the flavor intact. A single ultraripe banana infused the bread with flavor. A combination of butter and a little yogurt kept our loaf rich and moist without making it greasy. We liked the addition of toasted walnuts for crunch and a little vanilla to enhance the overall flavor. Creaming the butter and sugar resulted in overmixed batter and a dense loaf, so we gently folded everything together using the quick-bread method to ensure that our loaf stayed tender with a delicate texture. You will need a 5½ by 3-inch loaf pan or a pan of similar size for this recipe. The key to this recipe is using a very ripe, soft, darkly speckled banana.

- ½ cup (2½ ounces) all-purpose flour
- ¼ cup walnuts, toasted and chopped coarse
- ¼ cup sugar
- ½ teaspoon baking soda
- ⅛ teaspoon salt
- 1 small ripe banana, peeled and mashed well (¼ cup)
- 1 large egg, room temperature
- 1 tablespoon unsalted butter, melted and cooled
- 1 tablespoon plain yogurt
- ½ teaspoon vanilla extract

1. Adjust oven rack to middle position and heat oven to 350 degrees. Grease 5½ by 3-inch loaf pan.

2. Whisk flour, walnuts, sugar, baking soda, and salt together in medium bowl. In separate bowl, whisk mashed banana, egg, melted butter, yogurt, and vanilla together until smooth. Gently fold banana mixture into flour mixture with rubber spatula until just combined. (Batter will be lumpy with a few spots of dry flour; do not overmix.)

3. Scrape batter into prepared pan and smooth top. Bake until loaf is golden brown and toothpick inserted in center comes out clean, 30 to 40 minutes, rotating pan halfway through baking.

4. Let loaf cool in pan on wire rack for 5 minutes. Remove loaf from pan and let cool for at least 1 hour before serving.

VARIATION

Banana-Chocolate Bread

Add ¾ ounce grated bittersweet chocolate to flour mixture in step 2.

Storing Bananas

MAKING BANANAS LAST: Most people store bananas on the countertop, but we wondered if chilling the fruit could slow ripening. To find out, we left 12 pounds of bananas at room temperature for three days until they were perfectly ripe (with a firm but yielding texture). We then moved half of the bananas into the refrigerator, leaving the remainder at room temperature.

After four days, the room-temperature fruit became markedly soft and mushy, while the refrigerated fruit remained firm, despite blackened skins. We continued to taste the refrigerated bananas after the room-temperature samples had been discarded and were delighted to discover that they lasted an additional five days (almost two weeks after purchase). The explanation is simple: As a banana ripens, it emits a gas called ethylene and develops acids that aid in ripening. Cool temperatures slow down this process, thereby decelerating ripening. Note that refrigeration also causes the cell walls of the peel to break down, releasing enzymes that cause the formation of black-brown pigments.

RIPENING BANANAS: The abundance of natural sugars in overripe bananas is the secret to big flavor and serious moisture in baked goods. Yellow bananas don't have as much sweet flavor and will remain starchy even after baking. Strategies for speeding ripening in bananas abound, but we've found most of them ineffective. One theory, for example, holds that freezing or roasting underripe bananas in their skins will quickly render them sweet and soft enough for baking. While these methods do turn the bananas black—giving them the appearance of their super-sweet, over-ripe brethren—they actually do little to encourage the necessary conversion of starch to sugar. The best way to ripen bananas is to enclose them in a paper bag for a few days. The bag will trap the ethylene gas produced by fruit that hastens ripening, while still allowing some moisture to escape. Since fully ripe fruit emits the most ethylene, placing a ripe banana or other ripe fruit in the bag will speed the process along by a day or two.

Zucchini Bread

SERVES 2

✔ **WHY THIS RECIPE WORKS:** It can be difficult to muster enthusiasm for your typical bland, soggy loaf of zucchini bread. We wanted a zucchini bread worth eating, subtly spiced, with great summery zucchini flavor, and with a moist—but not wet—crumb. To start, we had to confront the downfall of most zucchini breads—the excess moisture from the zucchini. Shredding the zucchini and then squeezing it dry in a dish towel not only rid the zucchini of excess moisture, but also intensified the zucchini flavor for a better-tasting bread. Many zucchini bread recipes use oil, but we preferred the rich

With a moist and tender crumb, subtle warm spices, and lots of summery zucchini flavor, this is not your typical zucchini bread.

flavor of butter. Cinnamon and allspice along with lemon juice perked the flavor up further, as did the tang of yogurt. Finally, for nutty flavor in every bite, we stirred toasted chopped nuts into the batter. You will need a 5½ by 3-inch loaf pan or a pan of similar size for this recipe. Be sure to squeeze the zucchini thoroughly of moisture before adding it to the batter, or the bread will turn out soggy.

½   zucchini (4 ounces)
½   cup (2½ ounces) all-purpose flour
½   teaspoon baking powder
½   teaspoon baking soda
¼   teaspoon ground cinnamon
¼   teaspoon ground allspice
⅛   teaspoon salt
½   cup (3½ ounces) sugar
1   large egg, room temperature
1   tablespoon unsalted butter, melted and cooled
1   tablespoon plain yogurt
1   teaspoon lemon juice
¼   cup pecans or walnuts, toasted and chopped coarse

1. Adjust oven rack to middle position and heat oven to 350 degrees. Grease 5½ by 3-inch loaf pan.

2. Shred zucchini on holes of coarse grater. Squeeze shredded zucchini in clean dish towel or several layers of paper towels until very dry.

3. Whisk flour, baking powder, baking soda, cinnamon, allspice, and salt together in medium bowl. In separate bowl, whisk sugar, egg, melted butter, yogurt, and lemon juice together until smooth. Gently fold shredded zucchini, yogurt mixture, and pecans into flour mixture with rubber spatula until just combined. (Do not overmix.)

4. Scrape batter into prepared pan and smooth top. Bake until loaf is golden brown and toothpick inserted into center comes out clean, 35 to 45 minutes, rotating pan halfway through baking.

5. Let loaf cool in pan on wire rack for 5 minutes. Remove loaf from pan and let cool for at least 1 hour before serving.

Removing Moisture from Zucchini

1. To prevent soggy zucchini bread, it's important to remove excess moisture. Shred zucchini on holes of coarse grater.

2. Squeeze shredded zucchini in clean dish towel or several layers of paper towels until dry.

Cheddar Cheese Bread

SERVES 2

✔ **WHY THIS RECIPE WORKS:** We were after the ultimate cheese bread, one that was cheesy inside and out. To find the best recipe, we tested lots of cheese and techniques. First, for the batter, we found that extra-sharp cheddar cheese worked best, and cutting it into small chunks rather than shredding it gave the bread luscious, chewy pockets of cheese. For a cheesy crust on top and bottom, we sprinkled Parmesan in the bottom of our loaf pan before filling it with batter and then topped the batter with more Parmesan. You will need a 5½ by 3-inch loaf pan or a pan of similar size for this recipe. Use the large holes of a box grater to shred the Parmesan; do not substitute

For the cheesiest cheese bread, we use lots of extra-sharp cheddar and add Parmesan and a pinch of cayenne to round out its flavor.

2. Whisk flour, baking powder, salt, cayenne, and pepper together in medium bowl. Fold in cheddar, breaking up any clumps, until cheese is coated with flour mixture. In separate bowl, whisk milk, sour cream, egg, and melted butter together until smooth. Gently fold milk mixture into flour mixture with rubber spatula until just combined. (Batter will be heavy and thick; do not overmix.)

3. Scrape batter into prepared pan, smooth top, and sprinkle with remaining Parmesan. Bake until loaf is golden brown and toothpick inserted into center comes out with a few crumbs attached, 30 to 40 minutes, rotating pan halfway through baking.

4. Let loaf cool in pan on wire rack for 5 minutes. Remove loaf from pan and let cool for at least 1 hour before serving.

Skillet Olive Bread

SERVES 2

✔ **WHY THIS RECIPE WORKS:** Most savory breads serve a crowd and require long rest periods and kneading. Not ours. We stirred together an effortless quick bread and baked it in a small cast-iron skillet, which gave us just enough for two. We started with all-purpose flour and added whole milk and sour cream for a moist texture. A whole egg lent richness and structure. Shredded Parmesan, minced garlic, chopped kalamata olives, and fresh basil ensured that our bread was robustly flavored, and our cast-iron pan guaranteed a crisp, golden-brown crust. Using the large holes of a box grater to shred the Parmesan adds a nice texture to the bread and helps prevent the cheese from burning. Do not substitute finely grated or pregrated Parmesan. We prefer to use an 8-inch cast-iron skillet here because it makes the best crust, but you can also use an 8-inch ovensafe skillet; increase the baking time by 10 to 15 minutes.

finely grated or pregrated Parmesan. A mild, soft Asiago cheese, crumbled into ¼-inch pieces, is a nice substitute for the cheddar. The texture of the bread improves as it cools.

- 1 ounce Parmesan cheese, shredded (⅓ cup)
- ¾ cup plus 2 tablespoons (4⅜ ounces) all-purpose flour
- 1 teaspoon baking powder
- ¼ teaspoon salt
  Pinch cayenne pepper
  Pinch pepper
- 2 ounces extra-sharp cheddar cheese, cut into ¼-inch cubes (½ cup)
- ¼ cup whole milk
- 3 tablespoons sour cream
- 1 large egg, room temperature
- 1 tablespoon unsalted butter, melted and cooled

1. Adjust oven rack to middle position and heat oven to 350 degrees. Grease 5½ by 3-inch loaf pan, then sprinkle 2 tablespoons Parmesan evenly over bottom of pan.

- 1 cup (5 ounces) all-purpose flour
- 1 tablespoon chopped fresh basil
- 1 teaspoon baking powder
- ¼ teaspoon salt
- 1½ ounces Parmesan cheese, shredded (½ cup)
- ½ cup whole milk
- 3 tablespoons sour cream
- 1 large egg, room temperature
- 2 tablespoons olive oil
- 1 garlic clove, minced
- ¼ cup pitted kalamata olives, chopped

This ultra-easy savory bread with olives, Parmesan, and garlic cooks right in a skillet for an exceptionally crisp, browned crust.

1. Adjust oven rack to lower-middle position and heat oven to 450 degrees.

2. Whisk flour, basil, baking powder, and salt together in medium bowl. Stir in ⅓ cup Parmesan, breaking up any clumps, until cheese is coated with flour. In separate bowl, whisk milk, sour cream, and egg together until smooth.

3. Heat oil in 8-inch cast-iron skillet over medium-high heat until shimmering. Add garlic and cook until fragrant, about 30 seconds. Pour all but 2 teaspoons garlic oil into milk mixture and whisk to incorporate. Gently fold milk mixture into flour mixture with rubber spatula until just combined, then fold in olives. (Batter will be heavy and thick; do not overmix.)

4. Working quickly, scrape batter into hot skillet, smooth top, and sprinkle with remaining Parmesan. Bake until loaf is golden brown and toothpick inserted into center comes out clean, 15 to 20 minutes, rotating skillet halfway through baking.

5. Let bread cool slightly in skillet on wire rack for 5 minutes. Remove loaf from skillet and serve warm or at room temperature.

Caring for Cast Iron

If you buy a preseasoned cast-iron pan (and you should), you can use the pan with little fuss. The number one rule: Don't wash the pan with soap or leave it in the sink to soak. Instead, rinse it out under hot running water, scrubbing with a brush to remove traces of food. (This is easiest while the pan is still warm.) Dry the pan thoroughly and put it back on the burner on low heat until all moisture disappears (this keeps rusting at bay). To protect the seasoning, put a few drops of vegetable oil in the warm, dry pan and wipe the interior with paper towels until it is lightly covered with oil. Using fresh paper towels, rub more firmly to burnish the surface and remove all excess oil. The pan shouldn't look or feel oily to the touch. Allow the pan to cool before putting it away.

HEAVY-DUTY CLEANING: If your pan has stuck-on food or is rusty or gummy, pour in ¼ inch of vegetable oil, then place the pan over medium-low heat for 5 minutes. Remove pan from heat and add ¼ cup kosher salt. Using potholder to grip hot handle, use thick cushion of paper towels to scrub pan. Warm oil will loosen food or rust, and kosher salt will have abrading effect. Rinse pan under hot running water, dry well, and repeat if necessary.

SEASONING CAST IRON: For years we've seasoned cast-iron cookware in the test kitchen by heating it and wiping out the pan with vegetable oil until its surface turns dark and shiny. When a pan starts to look patchy, we simply repeat the process. Then we heard about a method that creates a slick surface so indestructible that touch-ups are almost never necessary. Developed by blogger Sheryl Canter, the approach calls for treating the pan with multiple coats of flaxseed oil between hour-long stints in the oven.

We tried Canter's approach on new, unseasoned skillets—and the results amazed us. The flaxseed oil so effectively bonded to the skillets, forming a sheer, stick-resistant veneer, that even a run through our commercial dishwasher left them totally unscathed. This method works so well because flaxseed oil boasts six times the amount of omega-3 fatty acids compared to vegetable oil. Over prolonged exposure to high heat, these fatty acids combine to form a strong, solid matrix that polymerizes to the pan's surface. Although lengthy, seasoning with flaxseed oil is a mainly hands-off undertaking. We highly recommend the treatment:

1. Warm an unseasoned pan (new or stripped of seasoning*) for 15 minutes in a 200-degree oven to open its pores.

2. Remove the pan from the oven. Place 1 tablespoon flaxseed oil in the pan and, using tongs, rub the oil into the surface with paper towels. With fresh paper towels, thoroughly wipe out the pan to remove excess oil.

3. Place the oiled pan upside down in a cold oven, then set the oven to its maximum baking temperature. Once the oven reaches its maximum temperature, heat the pan for 1 hour. Turn off the oven; let the pan cool in the oven for at least 2 hours.

4. Repeat the process five more times, or until the pan develops a dark, semimatte surface.

* To strip seasoning, spray pan with oven cleaner, wait 30 minutes, wash with soapy water, and thoroughly wipe with paper towels.

CHAPTER 16

Fruit Desserts, Pies, and Tarts

FRUIT DESSERTS

■ FAST (Start to finish in about 30 minutes)
■ LIGHT (See page 415 for nutritional information)
Opposite: Key Lime Pie; Free-Form Summer Fruit Tartlets; Pecan Tarts

Skillet-Roasted Pear Halves with Caramel Sauce

SERVES 2 **FAST**

✓ **WHY THIS RECIPE WORKS:** Looking for an alternative to the classic autumn dessert of baked apples, we decided to develop a recipe with pears—and to really intensify their flavor and develop a sweet richness, we turned to roasting. For such a simple dessert, we knew the variety of pear would be important. We found that just-ripe Bosc and Bartlett fared well. Adding a caramel sauce provided a nutty contrast to the sweet fruit, and cooking them both in a skillet streamlined our recipe; we simply started the caramel before adding the pear halves, then poured in the cream to finish our sauce just as the pears finished browning. For this dessert, the pear should be ripe but firm, which means the flesh at the base of the stem should give slightly when gently pressed with a finger. Use caution around the caramel—it is extremely hot.

> 3 tablespoons water
> 3 tablespoons sugar
> 1 large ripe but firm Bartlett or Bosc pear, halved and cored
> ⅓ cup heavy cream
>   Salt

1. Pour water into 10-inch nonstick skillet, then pour sugar into center of skillet (don't let it hit skillet sides). Gently stir sugar with clean spatula to wet it thoroughly. Bring to boil over medium-high heat and cook, without stirring, until sugar has dissolved completely and liquid is bubbling, about 1 minute.

2. Add pear halves to skillet, cut side down. Reduce heat to medium, cover, and cook until pear halves are almost tender and fork inserted into center meets slight resistance, 13 to 15 minutes, reducing heat as needed to prevent caramel from getting too dark.

3. Uncover, reduce heat to medium-low, and continue to cook until sauce is golden brown and cut sides of pear are beginning to brown, 2 to 3 minutes. Pour cream around pear halves and let bubbling subside. Cook, shaking skillet until sauce is smooth and has deep caramel color, 2 to 3 minutes.

4. Off heat, transfer pear halves to individual plates. Season sauce with salt to taste, then drizzle over pears. Serve.

Gently heating the skillet over low heat for a full 10 minutes then shaking it while adding the batter guarantees thin, lacy crêpes.

Crêpes with Sugar and Lemon

SERVES 2

✓ **WHY THIS RECIPE WORKS:** Crêpes have a reputation for being fussy and finicky; we sought to demystify this French classic and develop a recipe just for two. For thin, lacy, rich-tasting crêpes, we discovered that the proper cooking technique was more important than the batter itself. Heating an oiled skillet over low heat for a full 10 minutes ensured that our pan was just the right temperature. Tilting and gently shaking the pan while adding the batter guaranteed even distribution. Finally, flipping the crêpes at just the right moment—when the top surface was dry and the edges were starting to brown—ensured each one was cooked to delicate golden-brown perfection. Crêpes will give off steam as they cook, but if at any point the skillet begins to smoke, remove it from the heat immediately and turn down the heat. Stacking the crêpes on a wire rack allows excess steam to escape so they won't stick together. To allow for practice, the recipe yields five crêpes; only four are needed for the dessert.

½ teaspoon vegetable oil
½ cup (2½ ounces) all-purpose flour
1½ tablespoons sugar
⅛ teaspoon salt
¾ cup whole milk
1 large egg
1 tablespoon unsalted butter, melted and cooled
   Lemon wedges

1. Heat oil in 12-inch nonstick skillet over low heat for at least 10 minutes.

2. While skillet is heating, whisk flour, ½ teaspoon sugar, and salt together in medium bowl. In separate bowl, whisk milk and egg together. Add half of milk mixture to flour mixture and whisk until smooth. Add melted butter and whisk until incorporated. Whisk in remaining milk mixture until smooth.

3. Wipe out skillet with paper towel, leaving thin film of oil on bottom and sides of skillet. Increase heat to medium and let skillet heat for 1 minute. After 1 minute, test heat of skillet by placing 1 teaspoon batter in center and cook for 20 seconds. If mini crêpe is golden brown on bottom, skillet is properly heated; if it is too light or too dark, adjust heat accordingly and retest.

4. Pour ¼ cup batter into far side of skillet and tilt and shake gently until batter evenly covers bottom of skillet. Cook crêpe without moving it until top surface is dry and edges are starting to brown, loosening crêpe from side of skillet with heat-resistant rubber spatula, about 25 seconds.

5. Gently slide spatula underneath edge of crêpe, grasp edge with your fingertips, and flip crêpe. Cook until second side is lightly spotted, about 20 seconds. Transfer cooked crêpe to wire rack, inverting so spotted side is facing up. Return skillet to heat and heat for 10 seconds before repeating with remaining batter. As crêpes are done, stack on wire rack.

6. Transfer stack of crêpes to large plate and invert second plate over crêpes. Microwave until crêpes are warm, 30 to 45 seconds (45 to 60 seconds if crêpes have cooled completely). Remove top plate and wipe dry with paper towel. Sprinkle half of top crêpe with 1 teaspoon sugar. Fold unsugared half over sugared half, then fold into quarters. Transfer sugared crêpe to second plate. Continue with remaining crêpes. Serve immediately with lemon wedges.

VARIATIONS

Crêpes with Banana and Nutella
Omit 4 teaspoons sprinkling sugar and lemon wedges. Spread 2 teaspoons Nutella over half of each crêpe followed by four to five ¼-inch-thick banana slices. Fold crêpes into quarters.

Crêpes with Honey and Toasted Almonds
Omit 4 teaspoons sprinkling sugar and lemon wedges. Drizzle 1 teaspoon honey over half of each crêpe and sprinkle with 2 teaspoons finely chopped toasted sliced almonds and small pinch salt. Fold crêpes into quarters.

Crêpes with Chocolate and Orange
Omit 4 teaspoons sprinkling sugar and lemon wedges. Using your fingertips, rub ½ teaspoon finely grated orange zest into 2 tablespoons sugar, then stir in 1 ounce finely grated bittersweet chocolate. Sprinkle 1½ tablespoons chocolate-orange mixture over half of each crêpe. Fold crêpes into quarters.

Making a Crêpe

1. Pour ¼ cup batter into far side of skillet.

2. Tilt and shake skillet gently until batter evenly covers bottom of skillet.

3. Gently slide spatula underneath edge of crêpe, grasp edge with your fingertips, and flip crêpe.

Berry Gratins

SERVES 2   LIGHT

✓ **WHY THIS RECIPE WORKS:** When the occasion demands something a bit more dressed up than berries with a dollop of whipped cream, our thoughts turn to berry gratin. While toppings for this baked dessert vary, our favorite is the light and creamy Italian custard, zabaglione. To ensure our zabaglione had the perfect, creamy consistency every time, we cooked the egg yolk, sugar, and wine in a glass bowl set over a pan of barely simmering water until it was nicely thickened, then folded in a little whipped cream. Broiling—rather than baking—the gratin ensured that the crust browned before the berries overcooked. Do not substitute frozen berries in this recipe. Make sure to cook the egg mixture in a glass bowl over water that is barely simmering; glass conducts heat more evenly and gently than metal. To prevent scorching, pay close attention to the gratins when broiling. You will need two shallow 6-ounce gratin dishes for this recipe, but a 3-cup broiler-safe baking dish (measuring approximately 7¼ by 5¼ inches) will also work. For the nutritional information for this recipe, see page 415.

BERRY MIXTURE

7½ ounces (1½ cups) blackberries, blueberries, raspberries, and/or strawberries (strawberries hulled and halved lengthwise if small, quartered if large)
1 teaspoon granulated sugar
Pinch salt

ZABAGLIONE

1 large egg yolk
1 tablespoon granulated sugar
1 tablespoon dry white wine
2 teaspoons packed light brown sugar
2 tablespoons heavy cream, chilled

1. FOR THE BERRY MIXTURE: Line rimmed baking sheet with aluminum foil. Gently toss berries, sugar, and salt together in bowl. Divide berry mixture evenly between 2 shallow 6-ounce gratin dishes and set on prepared sheet; set aside.

2. FOR THE ZABAGLIONE: Whisk egg yolk, 2 teaspoons granulated sugar, and wine together in medium glass bowl until sugar is dissolved, about 1 minute. Set bowl over small saucepan of barely simmering water (water should not touch bottom of bowl) and cook, whisking constantly, until mixture is frothy.

Making Zabaglione

When making zabaglione, it's important to pay attention to the visual cues to know when it's ready and prevent overcooking.

Once zabaglione is slightly thickened, creamy, and glossy, that's your cue to remove it from heat and begin whisking constantly to cool slightly.

3. Continue to cook, whisking constantly, until mixture is slightly thickened, creamy, and glossy, 5 to 10 minutes (mixture will form loose mounds when dripped from whisk). Remove bowl from saucepan and whisk constantly for 30 seconds to cool slightly. Transfer bowl to refrigerator and chill until egg mixture is completely cool, about 10 minutes.

4. Meanwhile, adjust oven rack 6 inches from broiler element and heat broiler. Combine brown sugar and remaining 1 teaspoon granulated sugar in bowl.

5. In separate bowl, whisk cream until soft peaks form. Using rubber spatula, gently fold whipped cream into cooled egg mixture until incorporated and no streaks remain. Spoon zabaglione over berries and sprinkle sugar mixture evenly on top; let sit at room temperature until sugar dissolves, about 10 minutes.

6. Broil gratins until sugar is bubbly and caramelized, 1 to 4 minutes. Serve immediately.

NOTES FROM THE TEST KITCHEN

Washing and Storing Berries

Washing berries before you use them is always a safe practice, and we think that the best way to wash them is to place the berries in a colander and rinse them gently under running water for at least 30 seconds. As for drying berries, we've tested a variety of methods and have found that a salad spinner lined with a buffering layer of paper towels is the best approach.

It's particularly important to store berries carefully, because they are prone to growing mold and rotting quickly. If the berries aren't to be used immediately, we recommend cleaning them with a mild vinegar solution (3 cups water mixed with 1 cup white vinegar), which will destroy the bacteria, before drying them and storing them in a paper towel–lined airtight container.

Easy Strawberry Shortcakes

SERVES 2

✓ **WHY THIS RECIPE WORKS:** Our ideal strawberry short-cakes are tender, flaky biscuits topped with juicy strawberries and a dollop of whipped cream. And because they're assembled individually, they're an ideal dessert for two. Slicing most of the strawberries made for an attractive presentation, while crushing a portion of them helped unify the sliced fruit and prevented it from sliding off the biscuits. Because the fruit isn't cooked, fresh, ripe berries were essential. Biscuits made with all-purpose flour were tender and cakey; an egg and some half-and-half contributed richness. With such a small amount of dough, we found it best to shape the biscuits by hand (rather than stamp them out) to ensure that none went to waste. Fresh blueberries, raspberries, or halved blackberries can be substituted for some or all of the strawberries. Fresh fruit is key to the success of these shortcakes; do not substitute frozen strawberries.

FRUIT

- 10 ounces strawberries, hulled (2 cups)
- 5 teaspoons sugar

BISCUITS

- ⅔ cup (3⅓ ounces) all-purpose flour
- 2 tablespoons sugar
- 1 teaspoon baking powder
- ⅛ teaspoon salt
- 4 tablespoons unsalted butter, cut into ½-inch pieces and chilled
- 2 tablespoons half-and-half
- 1 large egg, lightly beaten, plus 1 large white, lightly beaten

- 1 recipe Whipped Cream (recipe follows)

1. FOR THE FRUIT: Crush ¾ cup strawberries in medium bowl with potato masher. Slice remaining 1¼ cups strawberries. Stir sliced strawberries and sugar into crushed strawberries. Set aside until sugar has dissolved and strawberries are juicy, at least 30 minutes or up to 2 hours.

2. FOR THE BISCUITS: Meanwhile, adjust oven rack to middle position and heat oven to 425 degrees. Line rimmed baking sheet with parchment paper. Process flour, 5 teaspoons sugar, baking powder, and salt in food processor until combined, about 5 seconds. Scatter butter over top and pulse until mixture resembles coarse cornmeal, about 15 pulses. Transfer mixture to medium bowl.

3. In separate bowl, whisk half-and-half and whole egg together, then stir into flour mixture with rubber spatula until large clumps form. Turn dough and any floury bits onto lightly floured counter and knead lightly until dough comes together (do not overwork dough). Divide dough into 2 even pieces, then, with well-floured hands, shape each into 2½-inch round, about 1 inch thick.

4. Arrange biscuits on prepared sheet. Brush tops with egg white and sprinkle evenly with remaining 1 teaspoon sugar. Bake biscuits until golden brown, 10 to 12 minutes, rotating sheet halfway through baking. Transfer biscuits to wire rack and let cool for 15 minutes.

5. To assemble, split each biscuit in half and place bottoms on individual serving plates. Spoon strawberries over each bottom, dollop with whipped cream, and cap with biscuit tops. Serve immediately.

Whipped Cream

MAKES ABOUT ¾ CUP

The whipped cream can be refrigerated in a fine-mesh strainer set over a small bowl, wrapped tightly with plastic wrap, for up to 8 hours.

- ⅓ cup heavy cream, chilled
- 1 teaspoon sugar
- ¼ teaspoon vanilla extract

Using hand-held mixer set at medium-low speed, beat cream, sugar, and vanilla in medium bowl until foamy, about 1 minute. Increase speed to high and beat until soft peaks form, 1 to 3 minutes.

NOTES FROM THE TEST KITCHEN

Secrets to Foolproof Whipped Cream

When is the best time to add sugar when making whipped cream? The old wives' tale says that you need to wait until the cream has whipped before adding the sugar. We made two batches of whipped cream to find out. We added the sugar at two different points: at the beginning of whipping and at the end. Although both batches whipped to the same volume, there was a difference in texture. When the sugar was added later in the process, the whipped cream had a slightly grainy texture. When added to the cream at the beginning of whipping, however, the granules had dissolved by the time the cream was fully whipped.

While sugar timing doesn't affect the cream's ability to whip up properly, the temperature of the cream does. Whipping the cream introduces air bubbles, whose walls are stabilized by tiny globules of fat. These fat globules hold the air bubbles in place as the whipping continues, forming what eventually becomes light, airy whipped cream. Because heat softens the butterfat in the cream, the liquid fat globules will collapse completely rather than hold together the air bubbles, preventing the cream from whipping up properly. To keep this from happening, it is crucial to use cream straight from the refrigerator. Chilling the bowl and beaters helps, too.

Working with Phyllo Dough

Phyllo dough, tissue-thin layers of pastry dough, can be used in a variety of recipes, both sweet and savory. Phyllo is available in two sheet sizes: full-size sheets that measure 18 by 14 inches (about 20 large sheets per box) and half-size sheets that are 14 by 9 inches (about 40 small sheets per box). The smaller sheets are more convenient for scaled-down desserts, but if you happen to buy the large sheets, simply cut them half. Here are some tips that make working with this delicate dough easier.

THAW THE PHYLLO DOUGH COMPLETELY BEFORE USING: Frozen phyllo dough must be thawed before using, and we've found that thawing it quickly in the microwave doesn't work—it makes the delicate sheets of dough stick together. We've had the best luck thawing the dough in the refrigerator overnight. (Our second choice is to thaw phyllo on the counter for 4 to 5 hours.) When the dough is completely thawed, it will be very flexible and will unfold easily without tearing.

THROW OUT BADLY TORN SHEETS OF DOUGH: Usually there are one or two badly torn sheets of phyllo per box that just can't be salvaged—throw them out. There are always a few extra sheets of phyllo in the package so you won't come up short. But don't worry about small rips; just make sure to adjust the orientation of the sheets as you stack them so that cracks in different sheets don't line up. And if phyllo sheets emerge from the box fused at their edges, don't try to separate the sheets. Instead, trim and discard the fused portion.

KEEP THE PHYLLO COVERED WHILE WORKING: Because each sheet is paper-thin, it dries out very quickly when exposed to air. As soon as the phyllo is removed from its plastic sleeve, unfold the dough and carefully smooth it with your hands to flatten. Cover with plastic wrap, then a damp kitchen towel.

DON'T REFREEZE LEFTOVER DOUGH: Leftover sheets can be rerolled, wrapped in plastic wrap, and stored in the refrigerator for up to five days. Don't try refreezing phyllo dough because it will become brittle and impossible to work with.

Quick Apple Strudel

SERVES 2

✔ **WHY THIS RECIPE WORKS:** Classic strudel requires hours of hands-on preparation; we wanted to simplify this dessert so it could round off a weeknight dinner for two. With homemade strudel pastry out of the question, we turned to store-bought phyllo dough. Sprinkling the dough with sugar and brushing it with melted butter helped the layers form a cohesive crust. One sliced apple made just the right amount of filling. Golden raisins simmered in apple brandy provided a pleasing textural contrast and another layer of apple flavor. Toasted bread crumbs helped absorb the juice from the apples and added richness to the moist filling. Phyllo dough is also available in larger 18 by 14-inch sheets; if using, cut them in half to make 14 by 9-inch sheets. Don't thaw the phyllo in the microwave; let it sit in the refrigerator overnight or on the counter for 4 to 5 hours.

¼   cup golden raisins
1   tablespoon Calvados or apple cider
2   tablespoons plain dried bread crumbs or panko
4   tablespoons unsalted butter, melted and cooled
1   McIntosh apple, peeled, cored, quartered, and sliced crosswise ¼ inch thick
3   tablespoons granulated sugar
½   teaspoon lemon juice
⅛   teaspoon ground cinnamon
    Pinch salt
5   (14 by 9-inch) phyllo sheets, thawed
    Confectioners' sugar

1. Adjust oven rack to lower-middle position and heat oven to 450 degrees. Line baking sheet with parchment paper.

Making Quick Apple Strudel

1. On large piece of parchment paper, layer phyllo sheets on top of one another, brushing each sheet with melted butter and sprinkling it with ½ teaspoon sugar.

2. Mound filling along bottom edge of phyllo, leaving 2½-inch border at bottom and 2-inch border on sides.

3. Fold dough on sides over apples. Fold dough on bottom over apples and continue to roll dough around filling to form strudel.

4. Brush strudel with remaining butter and sprinkle with remaining sugar, then cut four 1-inch vents across top of strudel with small knife.

Combine raisins and Calvados in small bowl, cover, and microwave until simmering, 30 seconds to 1 minute. Let sit, covered, until needed.

2. Toast bread crumbs with 1 tablespoon melted butter in 8-inch skillet over medium heat, stirring frequently, until golden brown, about 2 minutes; transfer to large bowl.

3. Drain raisins, discarding liquid. Add raisins, apple, 2 tablespoons granulated sugar, lemon juice, cinnamon, and salt to bowl with bread crumbs and toss to combine.

4. Place large sheet of parchment on counter. Lay 1 phyllo sheet on parchment with short side facing you, then brush with melted butter and sprinkle with ½ teaspoon granulated sugar. Repeat layering with remaining 4 phyllo sheets, brushing each layer with melted butter and sprinkling with ½ teaspoon granulated sugar.

5. Mound filling along bottom edge of phyllo, leaving 2½-inch border at bottom and 2-inch border on sides. Fold dough on sides over apples. Fold dough on bottom over apples and continue to roll dough around filling into strudel.

6. Gently transfer strudel seam side down to prepared sheet. Brush with remaining melted butter and sprinkle with remaining ½ teaspoon granulated sugar. Cut four 1-inch vents on diagonal across top of strudel and bake until golden brown, 12 to 15 minutes, rotating sheet halfway through baking.

7. Transfer strudel with sheet to wire rack and let cool until warm, about 20 minutes. Dust with confectioners' sugar before serving; slice with serrated knife and serve warm or at room temperature.

Skillet Cherry Cobbler

SERVES 2

✔ **WHY THIS RECIPE WORKS:** We wanted a streamlined, scaled-down recipe for cherry cobbler we could make any time of year. Jarred sour cherries are plump, tart, and available year-round. They're also already pitted and packed in a flavorful juice we could incorporate into our recipe. Switching from a baking dish to a skillet allowed us to simmer the sauce on the stovetop before adding the other elements and moving the skillet to the oven. Buttermilk contributed a light, tender texture to the biscuits, and dropping small spoonfuls of dough—rather than the standard large mounds—over the cherries allowed the biscuits to cook through in just 20 minutes. The amount of sugar you use in the filling will depend on the sweetness of your cherries. We prefer the crunchy texture of turbinado sugar sprinkled over the biscuits before baking, but granulated sugar can be substituted. Serve with vanilla ice cream or Whipped Cream (page 363).

Our easy Skillet Cherry Cobbler relies on jarred sour cherries so we can make this summery treat any time of year.

TOPPING
- ½ cup (2½ ounces) all-purpose flour
- 3 tablespoons granulated sugar
- ½ teaspoon baking powder
- ⅛ teaspoon baking soda
- ⅛ teaspoon salt
- ¼ cup buttermilk, chilled
- 2 tablespoons unsalted butter, melted and cooled

FILLING
- ¼–⅓ cup (1¾ to 2⅓ ounces) granulated sugar
- 1 tablespoon cornstarch
  Pinch salt
- 1⅓ cups jarred sour cherries in light syrup, drained with ¼ cup syrup reserved
- ¼ cup dry red wine
- ¼ teaspoon vanilla extract
- 1 small cinnamon stick
- 1 teaspoon turbinado sugar

1. FOR THE TOPPING: Adjust oven rack to middle position and heat oven to 400 degrees. Whisk flour, sugar, baking powder, baking soda, and salt together in medium bowl.

In separate bowl, stir chilled buttermilk and melted butter together until butter forms small clumps. Stir buttermilk mixture into flour mixture with rubber spatula until just incorporated. Cover and set aside.

2. FOR THE FILLING: Whisk granulated sugar, cornstarch, and salt together in 8-inch ovensafe skillet. Whisk in reserved ¼ cup cherry syrup, wine, and vanilla, then add cinnamon stick. Bring mixture to simmer over medium-high heat and cook, whisking frequently, until slightly thickened, 1 to 3 minutes. Off heat, remove cinnamon stick and stir in cherries.

3. Using large spoon, scoop and drop 1-inch pieces of dough, spaced about ½ inch apart, over cherry filling, then sprinkle with turbinado sugar. Bake until biscuits are golden brown and filling is thick and glossy, 20 to 25 minutes. Let cobbler cool in skillet on wire rack for at least 15 minutes before serving.

Skillet Apple Crisp

SERVES 2

✔ **WHY THIS RECIPE WORKS:** Most recipes for apple crisp result in unevenly cooked apples and a topping that's anything but crisp. To drive off excess moisture and allow the fruit to caramelize, we sautéed the apples in a little butter. Apple cider provided intense fruity flavor. Chewy rolled oats and crunchy pecans made a substantial crisp topping that was the perfect contrast to the tender apples underneath. We like Golden Delicious apples for this recipe, but any sweet, crisp apple such as Honeycrisp or Braeburn can be substituted; do not use Granny Smith apples. If your skillet is not ovensafe, prepare the recipe through step 3 and then transfer the filling to an 8½ by 4½-inch loaf pan; add the topping and bake as directed. Serve with vanilla ice cream or Whipped Cream (page 363).

TOPPING

¼ cup (1¼ ounces) all-purpose flour
¼ cup pecans, chopped fine
¼ cup (¾ ounce) old-fashioned rolled oats
3 tablespoons packed light brown sugar
1 tablespoon granulated sugar
¼ teaspoon ground cinnamon
¼ teaspoon salt
3 tablespoons unsalted butter, melted

FILLING

1½ pounds Golden Delicious apples, peeled, cored, halved, and cut into ½-inch-thick wedges
2 tablespoons granulated sugar
¼ teaspoon ground cinnamon (optional)

For an apple crisp with perfectly cooked apples and rich flavor, we sauté the apples in butter before topping and baking them.

½ cup apple cider
1 teaspoon lemon juice
1 tablespoon unsalted butter

1. FOR THE TOPPING: Adjust oven rack to middle position and heat oven to 450 degrees. Combine flour, pecans, oats, brown sugar, granulated sugar, cinnamon, and salt in medium bowl. Stir in melted butter until mixture is thoroughly moistened and crumbly; set aside.

2. FOR THE FILLING: In separate bowl, toss apples, sugar, and cinnamon, if using, together; set aside. Bring cider to simmer in 8-inch ovensafe skillet over medium heat and cook until reduced to ⅓ cup, 2 to 3 minutes. Transfer reduced cider to small bowl and stir in lemon juice.

3. Melt butter in now-empty skillet over medium heat. Add apple mixture and cook, stirring frequently, until apples begin to soften and become translucent, 12 to 14 minutes. (Do not fully cook apples.) Off heat, gently stir in cider mixture until apples are coated.

4. Sprinkle topping evenly over fruit, breaking up any large chunks. Place skillet on baking sheet and bake until fruit is tender and topping is deep golden brown, 15 to 20 minutes. Let crisp cool on wire rack for 15 minutes before serving.

VARIATION
Skillet Apple Crisp with Raspberries and Almonds

Substitute ¼ cup slivered almonds for pecans. Add ⅛ teaspoon almond extract to reduced cider with lemon juice in step 2. Stir ¼ cup raspberries into apple mixture along with reduced cider in step 3.

Coring Apples

A. CORING WITH A CORER:
Cut small slice from top and bottom of apple. Hold apple steady and push corer through. Cut apple according to recipe.

B. CORING WITHOUT A CORER:
Cut sides of apple squarely away from core. Cut each piece of apple according to recipe.

Individual Pear Crisps

SERVES 2

✔ **WHY THIS RECIPE WORKS:** Simply substituting pears for apples in this classic American dessert is a recipe for disaster; pears exude so much moisture that a traditional crisp topping will sink into the filling. To solve this problem, we found that selecting ripe yet firm pears of the right variety (Bartlett or Bosc worked best) was key. To compensate for all the liquid they released, we added a slurry of cornstarch and lemon juice. We also developed an extra-sturdy topping; melting the butter helped bind the flour to the other ingredients, and a generous amount of nuts guaranteed a thick, crunchy crust. For this crisp, the pears should be ripe but firm, which means the flesh at the base of the stem should give slightly when gently pressed with a finger. You will need two 12-ounce ramekins for this recipe, but an 8½ by 5½-inch baking dish will also work. Serve with vanilla ice cream or Whipped Cream (page 363).

2 tablespoons granulated sugar
1 teaspoon lemon juice
¼ teaspoon cornstarch
 Salt
2 ripe but firm Bartlett or Bosc pears, peeled, halved, cored, and cut into 1½-inch pieces

⅓ cup whole almonds or pecans, chopped fine
¼ cup (1¼ ounces) all-purpose flour
2 tablespoons packed light brown sugar
⅛ teaspoon ground cinnamon
 Pinch ground nutmeg
3 tablespoons unsalted butter, melted and cooled

1. Adjust oven rack to lower-middle position and heat oven to 425 degrees. Line rimmed baking sheet with aluminum foil. Combine 1 tablespoon granulated sugar, lemon juice, cornstarch, and pinch salt in medium bowl. Gently toss pears with sugar mixture and divide evenly between two 12-ounce ramekins.

2. Mix almonds, flour, brown sugar, cinnamon, nutmeg, pinch salt, and remaining 1 tablespoon granulated sugar together in medium bowl. Drizzle melted butter over top and stir until mixture resembles crumbly wet sand. Pinch mixture between your fingers into small pea-size pieces (with some smaller loose bits). Sprinkle topping evenly over pears, breaking up any large chunks.

3. Place crisps on prepared sheet and bake until filling is bubbling around edges and topping is deep golden brown, 20 to 25 minutes, rotating sheet halfway through baking. Let crisps cool on wire rack for 15 minutes before serving.

VARIATION
Individual Peach Crisps

Microwave 1 pound frozen peaches in bowl at 50 percent power, stirring occasionally, until thawed and slightly warm, 5 to 7 minutes; drain peaches well. Substitute thawed and drained peaches for pears.

Individual Blueberry Crumbles

SERVES 2

✔ **WHY THIS RECIPE WORKS:** We wanted an easy blueberry crumble with fresh flavor and a substantial crumble topping. To avoid a soupy filling, we preferred to add a thickener rather than cook the berries; a little cornstarch thickened the blueberry filling nicely while preserving the berries' summery flavor. A combination of butter, flour, brown sugar, oats, and a sprinkle of cinnamon provided the best flavor and texture for the streusel topping. Leaving the streusel in dime-size pieces kept it from sinking into the filling. Avoid instant or quick oats here. In step 2, do not press the topping into the berry mixture or it may sink and become soggy. Do not substitute frozen berries in this recipe. You will need two 12-ounce ramekins for this recipe, but an 8½ by 5½-inch baking dish will also work. Serve with vanilla ice cream or Whipped Cream (page 363).

Fresh blueberries tossed with a little sugar then topped with buttery oats make the ultimate effortless fruit dessert.

¼–⅓ cup (1¾ to 2⅓ ounces) granulated sugar

1½ teaspoons cornstarch

Salt

10 ounces (2 cups) blueberries

½ cup (2½ ounces) all-purpose flour

⅓ cup (1 ounce) old-fashioned rolled oats

¼ cup packed (1¾ ounces) light brown sugar

¼ teaspoon ground cinnamon

4 tablespoons unsalted butter, cut into 4 pieces and chilled

1. Adjust oven rack to lower-middle position and heat oven to 375 degrees. Line rimmed baking sheet with aluminum foil. Combine ¼ cup granulated sugar, cornstarch, and pinch salt in medium bowl. Gently toss blueberries with sugar mixture. (If blueberries taste tart, add up to 4 teaspoons more sugar.) Divide blueberries evenly between two 12-ounce ramekins.

2. Mix flour, oats, brown sugar, cinnamon, and pinch salt together in medium bowl. Add butter and, using your fingers, blend butter into dry ingredients until dime-size clumps form. Pinch together any powdery parts, then sprinkle topping evenly over blueberries.

3. Place crumbles on prepared sheet and bake until filling is bubbling around edges and topping is deep golden brown, about 30 minutes, rotating sheet halfway through baking. Let crumbles cool on wire rack for 15 minutes before serving.

Classic Double-Crust Pie Dough

MAKES ENOUGH FOR ONE 6-INCH PIE

✓ **WHY THIS RECIPE WORKS:** Vegetable shortening makes pie dough easy to handle and yields a crust that is remarkably flaky. But nothing beats the rich flavor of a crust made with butter. We set out to create a basic pie dough that combined the right fats and the right proportion of fat to flour to give us a supremely tender and flaky crust that was also rich and buttery. We experimented with a variety of combinations and ultimately settled on 5 tablespoons of butter to 3 tablespoons of shortening for the best flavor and texture. We found that 1¼ cups of flour was just the right amount, producing a dough that was easy to work and a baked crust that was extremely tender and flavorful. While this pie dough can be made by hand, the food processor is faster and easier and does the best job of cutting the fat into the flour. If you don't have a food processor, see "Hand-Mixing Pie Dough" on page 369.

1¼ cups (6¼ ounces) all-purpose flour

1 tablespoon sugar

½ teaspoon salt

3 tablespoons vegetable shortening, cut into ½-inch pieces and chilled

5 tablespoons unsalted butter, cut into ¼-inch pieces and chilled

4–6 tablespoons ice water

1. Process flour, sugar, and salt in food processor until combined, about 5 seconds. Scatter shortening over top and process until mixture resembles coarse cornmeal, about 10 seconds. Scatter butter over top and pulse until mixture resembles coarse crumbs, about 10 pulses.

2. Transfer mixture to bowl. Sprinkle 4 tablespoons ice water over mixture. Using rubber spatula, stir and press dough until it sticks together. If dough does not come together, stir in remaining water, 1 tablespoon at a time, until it does.

3. Divide dough in half and form each half into 3-inch disk. Wrap disks tightly in plastic wrap and refrigerate for 1 hour. Let chilled dough sit on counter to soften slightly, about 10 minutes, before rolling. (Wrapped dough can be refrigerated for up to 2 days or frozen for up to 2 months. If frozen, let dough thaw completely on counter before rolling.)

VARIATION
Classic Single-Crust Pie Dough

MAKES ENOUGH FOR ONE 6-INCH PIE

If you don't have a food processor, see "Hand-Mixing Pie Dough."

- 1 cup (5 ounces) all-purpose flour
- 1 teaspoon sugar
- ½ teaspoon salt
- 2 tablespoons vegetable shortening, cut into ½-inch pieces and chilled
- 4 tablespoons unsalted butter, cut into ¼-inch pieces and chilled
- 3-5 tablespoons ice water

1. Process flour, sugar, and salt in food processor until combined, about 5 seconds. Scatter shortening over top and process until mixture resembles coarse cornmeal, about 10 seconds. Scatter butter over top and pulse until mixture resembles coarse crumbs, about 10 pulses.

2. Transfer mixture to bowl. Sprinkle 3 tablespoons ice water over mixture. Using rubber spatula, stir and press dough until it sticks together. If dough does not come together, stir in remaining water, 1 tablespoon at a time, until it does.

3. Form dough into 3-inch disk, wrap tightly in plastic wrap, and refrigerate for 1 hour. Let chilled dough sit on counter to soften slightly, about 10 minutes, before rolling. (Wrapped dough can be refrigerated for up to 2 days or frozen for up to 2 months. If frozen, let dough thaw completely on counter before rolling.)

Hand-Mixing Pie Dough

While a food processor makes quick work of mixing pie dough, you can also cut the fats into the flour by hand. Here's how.

1. Freeze butter in its stick form until very firm. Whisk flour, sugar, and salt together in large bowl. Sprinkle chilled vegetable shortening over flour mixture and press it into flour using fork.

2. Grate frozen butter on coarse grater into flour mixture. Using two butter or dinner knives, cut mixture together until it resembles coarse crumbs. Add water as directed, stirring with rubber spatula.

NOTES FROM THE TEST KITCHEN

Tips for Better Pie Crusts

Pie dough seems easy enough to prepare. Mix flour, salt, and sugar together, cut in some fat, add water just until the dough sticks together, roll it out, and bake. Yet it can all go wrong so easily, resulting in a crust that's dense and tough instead of tender and flaky. To ensure a perfect pie crust every time, we use these tricks.

KEEP EVERYTHING COLD: Keeping the fat cold when mixing it into the flour is the key to a tender, flaky dough. Always chill the butter and shortening before making the dough and make sure that your water is ice cold. On particularly warm days, we even recommend chilling the flour and mixing bowl. And once the dough comes together, wrap it in plastic wrap and refrigerate it for at least one hour before attempting to roll it out. Cool dough is easier to manage and less apt to break or tear. Before rolling it out, let the dough soften slightly on counter for about 10 minutes. If it softens too much when rolling or shaping, slide it onto a baking sheet and place it in the refrigerator or freezer to firm up.

ROLL IT OUT RIGHT: Keeping the dough as evenly round as possible when rolling makes fitting it into a pie plate easy. The dough should be in the shape of a flat disk before you start to roll it, and the counter should be lightly floured. Every few times you roll the dough, rotate it a quarter turn and lightly flour the counter to prevent it from sticking. Keep checking the dough as you roll it: If it starts becoming lopsided, use your hands or a bench scraper to reshape the dough.

CHILL THE CRUST: The biggest risk when baking a pie crust is that the dough can shrink in the oven. If this happens, the pie won't look as nice. More important, the shell won't be able to hold all the filling and your pie may overflow. A cold pie shell will hold its shape better in the oven, in part because the chilling gives the gluten in the dough time to relax.

BAKE ON A FOIL-LINED BAKING SHEET: Juicy, fruit-filled pies can be prone to bubbling over, and the sugary juice will burn and smoke if it hits the bottom of the oven. To avoid this, place the pie on a rimmed baking sheet that has been lined with foil and bake on the lowest oven rack. The sheet catches any splatters and the foil makes cleanup easy and reduces the risk of spills smoking and burning. The sheet also conducts heat well and thus promotes better browning, preventing a soggy bottom crust. Placing the sheet on the lowest rack ensures that it gets nice and hot.

PROTECT THE CRUST: Sometimes the crimped crust around the edge of the pie can get quite brown before the pie has finished baking. If this happens, simply wrap a piece of foil loosely around the rim of the pie. The foil will help to deflect the heat and prevent the rim of the crust from getting too dark or burning.

BAKE UNTIL WELL BROWNED: Bake your pie in a glass pie plate; glass holds heat well and promotes better browning. Before taking a pie out of the oven, lift up the pie plate and check to make sure the bottom is nicely browned. For a double-crust pie in particular, since the bottom crust is more likely to be undercooked (and therefore soggy) than the top crust, be patient and don't pull the pie out of the oven too early.

Raspberry-Nectarine Pie

SERVES 2

✓ **WHY THIS RECIPE WORKS:** For a fresh take on summer fruit pie, we turned to a vibrant combination of nectarines and raspberries. Granulated sugar sweetened our pie without competing with the fruit's flavor, and a little lemon juice added brightness. To account for the varying ripeness and juiciness of the nectarines, we found that macerating the fruit and sugar for 20 minutes then draining off most of the liquid prevented a soupy filling. A little cornstarch helped thicken the filling nicely. Starting with a hot oven and lowering the temperature partway through baking ensured that both the top and bottom crust were baked to golden-brown perfection. We prefer the buttery flavor and flaky texture of homemade pie dough here; however, you can substitute two 9-inch store-bought pie dough rounds, if desired. You will need a 6-inch pie plate for this recipe.

We take a classic fruit pie and give it a fresh new flavor with a combination of sweet raspberries and juicy nectarines.

1 recipe Classic Double-Crust Pie Dough (page 368)

2 nectarines, halved, pitted, and sliced ⅓ inch thick

5 ounces (1 cup) raspberries

¼–⅓ cup (1¾ to 2⅓ ounces) plus 1 teaspoon sugar

2 teaspoons cornstarch

¼ teaspoon grated lemon zest plus ¾ teaspoon juice

Pinch salt

1 large egg white, lightly beaten

1. Adjust oven rack to lowest position and heat oven to 425 degrees. Roll 1 disk of dough into 9-inch circle on lightly floured counter. Loosely roll dough around rolling pin and gently unroll it onto 6-inch pie plate, letting excess dough hang over edge. Ease dough into plate by gently lifting edge of dough with your hand while pressing into plate bottom with your other hand. Leave any dough that overhangs plate in place. Wrap dough-lined pie plate loosely in plastic wrap and refrigerate until dough is firm, about 30 minutes. Roll other disk of dough into 9-inch circle on lightly floured counter, then transfer to parchment paper–lined baking sheet; cover with plastic and refrigerate for 30 minutes.

Making a Double-Crust Pie

1. Unroll untrimmed top piece of dough over filled pie, taking care not to stretch it and create thin spots.

2. Trim overhanging edges of both crusts to about ½ inch beyond lip of pie plate.

3. Pinch edges of top and bottom crusts firmly together to prevent leaking, then tuck overhang under itself to make it flush with edge of pie plate.

4. Use index finger of one hand and thumb and index finger of other hand to create fluted ridges perpendicular to edge of pie plate. Use small knife to make 1-inch vents in center of top crust, depending on recipe.

2. Meanwhile, gently toss nectarines, raspberries, and ¼ cup sugar together in bowl and let sit, tossing occasionally, until fruit releases its juice, about 20 minutes.

3. Drain fruit in colander set in large bowl. Measure out and reserve 1 tablespoon juice; discard remaining juice. Add drained fruit, reserved juice, cornstarch, lemon zest and juice, and salt to now-empty bowl and gently toss to combine. (If fruit tastes tart, add up to 4 teaspoons more sugar.)

4. Transfer fruit mixture to dough-lined pie plate, mounding it slightly in middle. Loosely roll remaining dough round around rolling pin and gently unroll it onto filling. Trim overhang to ½ inch beyond lip of pie plate. Pinch edges of top and bottom crusts firmly together. Tuck overhang under itself; folded edge should be flush with edge of pie plate. Crimp dough evenly around edge of pie plate using your fingers. Cut three 1-inch vents in center of top crust. Brush surface with beaten egg white and sprinkle with remaining 1 teaspoon sugar.

5. Place pie on foil-lined rimmed baking sheet and bake until crust is light golden brown, 20 to 25 minutes. Reduce oven temperature to 375 degrees, rotate sheet, and continue to bake until juices are bubbling and crust is deep golden brown, 20 to 25 minutes. Let pie cool on wire rack until filling has set, about 1½ hours; serve slightly warm or at room temperature.

Sweet Cherry Pie

SERVES 2

✅ **WHY THIS RECIPE WORKS:** While sweet cherries are typically best eaten out of hand, sour cherries are more suited to baking, where their bright fruit flavor shines. But fresh sour cherries can be hard to find, so we set out to develop a cherry pie that would taste great using easily available sweet cherries. Adding a plum in with the cherries provided a subtle tartness that tamed the cherries' sweetness. We processed the plum with a small portion of the cherries to create a puree that we mixed in with the unprocessed cherries for a moist, juicy filling. We prefer the buttery flavor and flaky texture of homemade pie dough here; however, you can substitute two 9-inch store-bought pie dough rounds, if desired. You can substitute 12 ounces frozen sweet cherries for the fresh cherries; to preserve their juice, thaw them only partway before using. You will need a 6-inch pie plate for this recipe. Grind the tapioca to a fine powder in a spice grinder for 30 seconds or in a mortar and pestle.

1	recipe Classic Double-Crust Pie Dough (page 368)
14	ounces fresh sweet cherries, pitted and halved
1	red plum, quartered and pitted
¼	cup (1¾ ounces) sugar
2	teaspoons instant tapioca, ground
1½	teaspoons lemon juice
	Pinch salt
	Pinch ground cinnamon (optional)
1	tablespoon unsalted butter, cut into ¼-inch pieces
1	large egg white, lightly beaten

1. Adjust oven rack to lowest position and heat oven to 425 degrees. Roll 1 disk of dough into 9-inch circle on lightly floured counter. Loosely roll dough around rolling pin and gently unroll it onto 6-inch pie plate, letting excess dough hang over edge. Ease dough into plate by gently lifting edge of dough with your hand while pressing into plate bottom with your other hand. Leave any dough that overhangs plate in place. Wrap dough-lined pie plate loosely in plastic wrap and refrigerate until dough is firm, about 30 minutes. Roll other disk of dough into 9-inch circle on lightly floured counter, then transfer to parchment paper–lined baking sheet; cover with plastic and refrigerate for 30 minutes.

2. Meanwhile, process ½ cup cherries and plum together in food processor until smooth, about 1 minute, scraping down sides of bowl as necessary. Strain puree through fine-mesh strainer into large bowl, pressing on solids to extract liquid; discard solids. Stir remaining halved cherries, sugar, ground tapioca, lemon juice, salt, and cinnamon, if using, into puree and let sit for 15 minutes.

3. Transfer cherry mixture with its juices to dough-lined pie plate, mounding it slightly in middle (pie plate will be very full). Scatter butter pieces over top. Loosely roll remaining dough round around rolling pin and gently unroll it onto filling. Trim overhang to ½ inch beyond lip of pie plate. Pinch edges of top and bottom crusts firmly together. Tuck overhang under itself; folded edge should be flush with edge of pie plate. Crimp dough evenly around edge of pie plate using your fingers. Cut five 1-inch vents in center of top crust. Brush surface with beaten egg white and freeze for 20 minutes.

4. Place pie on foil-lined rimmed baking sheet and bake until crust is light golden brown, 20 to 25 minutes. Reduce oven temperature to 350 degrees, rotate sheet, and continue to bake until juices are bubbling and crust is deep golden brown, 25 to 35 minutes. Let pie cool on wire rack until filling has set, about 1½ hours; serve slightly warm or at room temperature.

Icebox Strawberry Pie

SERVES 2

✔ **WHY THIS RECIPE WORKS:** For a no-bake strawberry pie bursting with berry flavor and boasting a firm, sliceable texture, we discovered a few key steps. Simmering a portion of the berries concentrated their juice, which reinforced the strawberry flavor of our filling and made it less watery. Leaving some berries uncooked added a freshness that was missing when we cooked all the berries. But since the fresh berries released some water as the pie chilled, we added a small amount of unflavored gelatin to help our filling firm up to just the right consistency. We prefer the buttery flavor and flaky texture of homemade pie dough here; however, you can substitute one 9-inch store-bought pie dough round, if desired. You will need a 6-inch pie plate for this recipe. In step 4, be sure to cook the strawberry mixture until it measures ½ cup in a liquid measuring cup.

1 recipe Classic Single-Crust Pie Dough (page 369)

FILLING

8 ounces (1¾ cups) frozen strawberries
1½ teaspoons lemon juice
1 teaspoon water
¾ teaspoon unflavored gelatin
⅓ cup (2⅓ ounces) sugar
   Pinch salt
5 ounces fresh strawberries, hulled and sliced thin (¾ cup)

TOPPING

½ cup heavy cream, chilled
1 ounce cream cheese, softened
1 tablespoon sugar
¼ teaspoon vanilla extract

Picking Ripe Strawberries

Few fruits have as uncanny an ability to look perfect yet taste disappointingly bland as strawberries. Unlike climacteric fruits such as bananas and peaches that continue to ripen after picking, strawberries (nonclimacteric fruit) don't get any sweeter once off the vine, so it's vital to select the sweetest ones you can find. Strawberries continue to develop a deep red pigment (called anthocyanin), but a berry that looks redder is not necessarily a berry that tastes sweeter.

What, then, is the best way to pick out a ripe pint of strawberries? Being upstanding citizens, we would never officially recommend one method: tearing open a berry or two to see if the red pigment extends all the way to the core, which can be a reliable sign. (Or, better yet, stealing a quick taste.) The third-best method? Taking a whiff. A sweet, fruity aroma is a much better indicator of what lies beneath the rosy exterior than the rosy exterior itself.

1. Roll dough into 10-inch circle, about ⅜ inch thick, on lightly floured counter. Loosely roll dough around rolling pin and gently unroll it onto 6-inch pie plate, letting excess dough hang over edge. Ease dough into plate by gently lifting edge of dough with your hand while pressing into plate bottom with your other hand. Leave any dough that overhangs plate in place.

2. Trim overhang to ½ inch beyond lip of pie plate. Tuck overhang under itself; folded edge should be flush with edge of pie plate. Crimp dough evenly around edge of pie plate using your fingers. Wrap dough-lined pie plate loosely in plastic wrap and place in freezer until dough is fully chilled and firm, about 20 minutes, before using.

3. Adjust oven rack to lower-middle position and heat oven to 375 degrees. Line chilled pie shell with parchment paper or double layer of aluminum foil, covering edges to prevent burning, and fill with pie weights. Bake until pie dough looks

Fitting the Dough and Finishing a Single-Crust Pie

1. Loosely roll dough around rolling pin, then gently unroll it onto pie plate, letting excess hang over plate.

2. Lift dough around edges and gently press it into corners of pie plate.

3. To finish, trim overhanging edge of crust to about ½ inch beyond lip of pie plate, then tuck overhang under itself to make it flush with edge of pie plate.

4. Use index finger of one hand and thumb and index finger of other hand to create fluted ridges perpendicular to edge of pie plate.

dry and is light in color, 25 to 30 minutes. Remove weights and parchment and continue to bake crust until deep golden brown, 10 to 12 minutes. Transfer pie plate to wire rack and let crust cool completely, about 1 hour.

4. FOR THE FILLING: Meanwhile, cook frozen strawberries in small saucepan over low heat until berries begin to release their juice, about 3 minutes. Increase heat to medium-low and continue to cook, stirring frequently, until mixture measures ½ cup and is thick and jamlike, 10 to 15 minutes.

5. Combine lemon juice and water in small bowl, sprinkle gelatin over liquid, and let sit until gelatin softens, about 5 minutes. Stir gelatin mixture, sugar, and salt into cooked berry mixture, return to simmer, and cook for about 1 minute. Transfer to medium bowl and let cool to room temperature, about 30 minutes.

6. Fold fresh strawberries into cooled berry mixture. Spread filling evenly over bottom of baked and cooled pie crust and refrigerate until set, at least 4 hours or up to 24 hours.

7. FOR THE TOPPING: Using hand-held mixer set at medium-low speed, beat cream, cream cheese, sugar, and vanilla in medium bowl until combined, about 1 minute. Increase speed to high and beat until stiff peaks form, 1 to 3 minutes. Spread topping evenly over pie and serve.

Banana Cream Pie

SERVES 2

✔ **WHY THIS RECIPE WORKS:** Banana cream pie is utterly addictive—unless the pastry cream ends up soupy, stiff, and bland. Using cornstarch instead of flour gave us a nicely thickened pastry cream that held up to slicing. Rather than relying on artificial banana extract or liqueur (an impractical purchase when we needed only a splash), we got roasted banana flavor by infusing the pastry cream with sautéed bananas. Be sure to buy all-yellow to lightly spotted bananas for this recipe. We prefer the buttery flavor and flaky texture of homemade pie dough here; however, you can substitute one 9-inch store-bought pie dough round, if desired. You will need a 6-inch pie plate for this recipe. Peel and slice the bananas just before using. When straining the half-and-half mixture in step 5, do not press on the bananas or the custard will turn gray as it sits.

1 recipe Classic Single-Crust Pie Dough (page 369)
2 ripe bananas
2 tablespoons unsalted butter
1¼ cups half-and-half
5 tablespoons (2¼ ounces) granulated sugar
3 large egg yolks

To give our cream pie real banana flavor, we skip the extracts and liqueurs and infuse the pastry cream with sautéed ripe bananas.

⅛ teaspoon salt
1 tablespoon cornstarch
¾ teaspoon vanilla extract
1 tablespoon orange juice
¼ cup heavy cream, chilled
2 teaspoons confectioners' sugar

1. Roll dough into 10-inch circle, about ⅜ inch thick, on lightly floured counter. Loosely roll dough around rolling pin and gently unroll it onto 6-inch pie plate, letting excess dough hang over edge. Ease dough into plate by gently lifting edge of dough with your hand while pressing into plate bottom with your other hand. Leave any dough that overhangs plate in place.

2. Trim overhang to ½ inch beyond lip of pie plate. Tuck overhang under itself; folded edge should be flush with edge of pie plate. Crimp dough evenly around edge of pie plate using your fingers. Wrap dough-lined pie plate loosely in plastic wrap and place in freezer until dough is fully chilled and firm, about 20 minutes, before using.

3. Adjust oven rack to lower-middle position and heat oven to 375 degrees. Line chilled pie shell with parchment paper or double layer of aluminum foil, covering edges to prevent burning, and fill with pie weights. Bake until pie dough looks dry and is light in color, 25 to 30 minutes. Remove weights and parchment and continue to bake crust until deep golden brown, 10 to 12 minutes. Transfer pie plate to wire rack and let crust cool completely, about 1 hour.

4. Meanwhile, peel and slice 1 banana ½ inch thick. Melt 1 tablespoon butter in small saucepan over medium-high heat. Add banana slices and cook until they begin to soften, about 2 minutes. Add half-and-half, bring to boil, and cook for 30 seconds. Remove pot from heat, cover, and let sit for 40 minutes.

5. Whisk granulated sugar, egg yolks, and salt together in medium bowl until smooth. Whisk in cornstarch. Strain cooled half-and-half mixture through fine-mesh strainer into yolk mixture—do not press on banana—and whisk until incorporated; discard cooked banana.

6. Transfer mixture to clean saucepan. Cook over medium heat, whisking constantly, until thickened to consistency of warm pudding (180 degrees), 4 to 6 minutes. Off heat, whisk in remaining 1 tablespoon butter and ½ teaspoon vanilla. Transfer pastry cream to bowl, press greased parchment directly against surface, and let cool for about 1 hour.

7. Peel and slice remaining banana ¼ inch thick and toss with orange juice. Whisk pastry cream briefly, then spread half over bottom of baked and cooled pie crust. Arrange sliced bananas on pastry cream. Top with remaining pastry cream.

8. Using hand-held mixer set at medium-low speed, beat cream, confectioners' sugar, and remaining ¼ teaspoon vanilla in medium bowl until foamy, about 1 minute. Increase speed to high and beat until soft peaks form, 1 to 3 minutes. Spread whipped cream attractively over center of pie. Refrigerate until set, at least 5 hours or up to 24 hours. Serve.

Key Lime Pie

SERVES 2

✔ **WHY THIS RECIPE WORKS:** For a Key lime pie with bold lime flavor, we used a combination of lime juice and zest in the filling. Sweetened condensed milk provided a creamy richness, and two egg yolks thickened our filling to just the right consistency. A buttery graham cracker crust contributed caramel notes that complemented the sweet-tart filling, and adding the filling while the crust was still warm ensured it would adhere to the crust even when sliced. We developed our recipe using regular supermarket Persian limes. Feel free to use Key limes if desired; note that you'll need about 10 Key limes to yield ¼ cup juice. You will need a 6-inch pie plate for this recipe. It is important to add the filling to the crust while it is still warm; if the crust has cooled, rewarm it in the oven for 5 minutes before adding the filling.

FILLING
- 2 **large egg yolks**
- 2 **teaspoons grated lime zest plus ¼ cup juice (2 limes)**
- ⅔ **cup sweetened condensed milk**

CRUST
- 4 **whole graham crackers, broken into 1-inch pieces**
- 2 **tablespoons unsalted butter, melted and cooled**
- 4 **teaspoons granulated sugar**

TOPPING
- ¼ **cup heavy cream, chilled**
- 2 **teaspoons confectioners' sugar**
- ⅛ **teaspoon vanilla extract**

1. FOR THE FILLING: Whisk egg yolks and lime zest together in medium bowl until mixture has light green tint, about 1 minute. Whisk in condensed milk until smooth, then whisk in lime juice. Cover mixture and set aside at room temperature until thickened, about 30 minutes.

2. FOR THE CRUST: Meanwhile, adjust oven rack to middle position and heat oven to 325 degrees. Process graham cracker pieces in food processor to fine, even crumbs, about 30 seconds. Sprinkle melted butter and sugar over crumbs and pulse to incorporate, about 5 pulses.

3. Sprinkle mixture into 6-inch pie plate. Using bottom of measuring cup, press crumbs into even layer on bottom and sides of pie plate. Bake until crust is fragrant and beginning to brown, 13 to 18 minutes. Transfer pie plate to wire rack; do not turn oven off. (Crust must still be warm when filling is added.)

4. Pour thickened filling into warm pie crust. Bake pie until center is firm but jiggles slightly, 15 to 20 minutes. Let pie cool slightly on wire rack, about 1 hour; cover loosely with plastic wrap and refrigerate until filling is chilled and set, about 3 hours.

5. FOR THE TOPPING: Using hand-held mixer set at medium-low speed, beat cream, sugar, and vanilla in medium bowl until foamy, about 1 minute. Increase speed to high and beat until soft peaks form, 1 to 3 minutes. Spread whipped cream attractively over top of chilled pie and serve.

Making a Graham Cracker Crust

To make graham cracker crust, press crumb mixture firmly and evenly across bottom and up sides of pie plate, using bottom of measuring cup.

Store-bought puff pastry makes this elegant, special-occasion apple galette deceptively easy and delicious.

Easy Apple Galette

SERVES 2

✔ **WHY THIS RECIPE WORKS:** For an ultraeasy apple galette for two, we bypassed the labor-intensive, time-consuming homemade pastry and reached for store-bought frozen puff pastry instead. Forming an attractive crust was as easy as folding over the edges of the pastry. We found that Granny Smith apples worked best; the slices stayed moist in the oven and maintained their shape throughout cooking. Sprinkling a little sugar on the apples prevented them from drying out and also helped them brown nicely. A simple glaze made from apple jelly and a small amount of water was the perfect finishing touch, contributing an attractive sheen and fruity tartness to our scaled-down apple galette. Be sure to let the puff pastry thaw completely before using; otherwise, it can crack and break apart. To thaw frozen puff pastry, let it sit either in the refrigerator for 24 hours or on the counter for 30 minutes to 1 hour.

Using Store-Bought Puff Pastry

Store-bought frozen puff pastry is convenient and works really well, but it can present the uninitiated with some minor obstacles. For the perfect puff, the pastry should never come to room temperature. Thawing the dough in the refrigerator overnight is the most foolproof method. Defrosting on the counter works fine if you take care not to let it sit out too long. Depending on the temperature of your kitchen, it may take between 30 and 60 minutes to thaw. Once thawed, the dough should unfold easily but still feel firm. If the seams crack, rejoin them by rolling them smooth with a rolling pin. If the dough warms and softens, freeze it until firm.

½ (9½ by 9-inch) sheet puff pastry, thawed
1 large Granny Smith apple (8 ounces), peeled, cored, halved, and sliced ⅛ inch thick
½ tablespoon unsalted butter, cut into ¼-inch pieces
2 teaspoons sugar
1 tablespoon apple jelly
1 teaspoon water

1. Adjust oven rack to middle position and heat oven to 400 degrees. Line rimmed baking sheet with parchment paper. Transfer puff pastry to prepared sheet and fold edges over by ¼ inch; crimp to create ¼-inch-thick border.

2. Starting in 1 corner of tart, shingle apple slices into crust in tidy diagonal rows, overlapping them by about half, until surface is completely covered. Dot apple with butter and sprinkle evenly with sugar. Bake until bottom of tart is deep golden brown and apple has caramelized, 40 to 45 minutes, rotating sheet halfway through baking.

3. Combine apple jelly and water in bowl and microwave until mixture begins to bubble, about 30 seconds. Brush glaze over apple and let tart cool slightly on sheet for 15 minutes. Serve warm or at room temperature.

Making Easy Apple Galette

1. Fold edges of dough over by ¼ inch and crimp to create ¼-inch-thick border.

2. Starting in 1 corner, shingle sliced apples to form even rows across dough, overlapping each slice by about half.

Free-Form Summer Fruit Tartlets

SERVES 2

✔ **WHY THIS RECIPE WORKS:** For an easy yet elegant take on summer fruit pie, we wanted a recipe for individual free-form fruit tarts. We started with an all-butter crust for the best flavor and tender texture. We turned to the French *fraisage* method to make the pastry, which calls for smearing the dough with the heel of your hand to spread the butter into long, thin streaks, creating lots of flaky layers when the dough is baked. Then we simply rolled out the chilled dough and pleated it loosely around the fruit filling. Taste the fruit before adding sugar to it; use the lesser amount if the fruit is very sweet, more if it is tart. However much sugar you use, do not add it to the fruit until you are ready to fill and form the tart. Serve with vanilla ice cream or Whipped Cream (page 363).

DOUGH

¾ **cup (3¾ ounces) all-purpose flour**

¼ **teaspoon salt**

5 **tablespoons unsalted butter, cut into ½-inch pieces and chilled**

2–3 **tablespoons ice water**

FILLING

8 **ounces peaches, nectarines, apricots, or plums, halved, pitted, and cut into ½-inch wedges**

2½ **ounces (½ cup) blackberries, blueberries, or raspberries**

3–5 **tablespoons sugar**

1. FOR THE DOUGH: Process flour and salt in food processor until combined, about 5 seconds. Scatter butter over top and pulse until mixture resembles coarse crumbs and butter pieces

Making Flaky Tart Dough

Starting at farthest end of dough pile, use heel of hand to smear small amount of dough against counter. Continue to smear dough until all crumbs have been worked. Gather smeared crumbs together and repeat process.

are about size of small peas, 6 to 8 pulses. Continue to pulse, adding 1 tablespoon ice water at a time, until dough begins to form small curds and holds together when pinched with fingers (dough will be crumbly), about 10 pulses.

2. Turn dough crumbs onto lightly floured counter and gather into rectangular-shaped pile about 8 inches long and 3 inches wide, with short side facing you. Starting at farthest end, use heel of your hand to smear small amount of dough against counter. Continue to smear dough until all crumbs have been worked. Gather smeared crumbs together into another rectangular-shaped pile and repeat process. Divide dough in half and form each half into 3-inch disk. Wrap disks tightly in plastic wrap and refrigerate for 1 hour. Let chilled dough sit on counter to soften slightly, about 10 minutes, before rolling. (Wrapped dough can be refrigerated for up to 2 days or frozen for up to 2 months. If frozen, let dough thaw completely on counter before rolling.)

3. Roll each disk of dough into 7-inch circle between 2 small sheets of floured parchment. (If dough sticks to parchment, gently loosen and lift sticky area with bench scraper and dust parchment with additional flour.) Slide dough circles, still between parchment sheets, onto rimmed baking sheet and refrigerate

Making Free-Form Summer Fruit Tartlets

1. Roll each chilled disk of dough into 7-inch circle between 2 small sheets of lightly floured parchment paper. Slide dough circles with parchment onto rimmed baking sheet and refrigerate until firm.

2. Mound half of fruit in center of each circle, leaving 1½-inch border around edge of fruit.

3. Being careful to leave ½-inch border of dough around edge of fruit, fold outermost 1 inch of dough over fruit, pleating it every 1 to 2 inches as needed.

4. Quickly brush top and sides of dough with water and sprinkle with sugar.

until firm, 15 to 30 minutes. (If refrigerated longer and dough is hard and brittle, let sit at room temperature until pliant.)

4. FOR THE FILLING: Adjust oven rack to lower-middle position and heat oven to 400 degrees. Gently toss peaches and blackberries and 2 tablespoons sugar together in bowl. (If fruit tastes tart, add up to 2 tablespoons more sugar.) Remove top sheet of parchment from each dough circle. Mound half of fruit in center of 1 circle, leaving 1½-inch border around edge of fruit. Being careful to leave ½-inch border of dough around edge of fruit, fold outermost 1 inch of dough over fruit, pleating it every 1 to 2 inches as needed; gently pinch pleated dough to secure, but do not press dough into fruit. Repeat with remaining fruit and dough circle.

5. Working quickly, brush top and sides of dough with water and sprinkle tartlets evenly with remaining 1 tablespoon sugar. Bake until crust is deep golden brown and fruit is bubbling, 40 to 45 minutes, rotating sheet halfway through baking.

6. Transfer tartlets with sheet to wire rack and let cool for 10 minutes, then use parchment to gently transfer tartlets to wire rack. Use metal spatula to loosen tartlets from parchment and remove parchment. Let tartlets cool on rack until juices have thickened, about 20 minutes; serve slightly warm or at room temperature.

Pear Tarte Tatin

SERVES 2

✔ **WHY THIS RECIPE WORKS:** This classic French dessert is the original skillet dessert—fruit is caramelized, topped with a crust, then served upside down. To transform this labor-intensive classic into a streamlined yet still impressive dessert for two, we started by nixing the homemade pastry in favor of convenient store-bought puff pastry. To give it a modern spin, we used pears in place of the traditional apples. Quartering them before cooking them in the caramel gave the fruit time to absorb the buttery flavor without turning to mush. Then we simply topped the pears with the puff pastry and baked it until golden brown. The pears should be ripe but firm—the flesh at the base of the stem should give slightly when gently pressed with a finger. Be sure to let the puff pastry thaw completely before using; otherwise, it can crack and break apart. To thaw frozen puff pastry, let it sit either in the refrigerator for 24 hours or on the counter for 30 minutes to 1 hour. Use caution around the caramel—it is extremely hot. Serve with vanilla ice cream or Whipped Cream (page 363).

1 (9½ by 9-inch) sheet puff pastry, thawed
2 tablespoons unsalted butter
½ cup (3½ ounces) sugar
3 small ripe but firm Bosc or Bartlett pears (6 ounces each), peeled, halved, cored, and each half halved lengthwise

1. Adjust oven rack to upper-middle position and heat oven to 425 degrees. Roll puff pastry into 10-inch square on lightly floured counter. Using sharp knife, cut pastry into 10-inch circle, then cut four 1-inch vents in center of dough. Slide pastry onto lightly floured large plate, cover, and refrigerate until needed.

2. Melt butter in 8-inch ovensafe nonstick skillet over medium-high heat. Stir in sugar and cook until sugar has dissolved completely and mixture is light golden, about 2 minutes.

3. Off heat, place 1 pear quarter cut side down around edge of skillet, with peeled side touching skillet wall. Continue to shingle 9 more pear quarters around edge of skillet, with

Making Pear Tarte Tatin

1. Arrange pear quarters cut side down around edge of skillet, with narrow ends slightly raised. Then place remaining pear quarters cut side down in middle of skillet.

2. After cooking pears in skillet until light golden brown and caramel is darkly colored, slide chilled dough circle over pears.

3. Carefully fold back edge of dough so that it fits snugly into skillet.

4. Once baked tart has cooled, run thin knife around edge of skillet. Place serving platter over skillet, hold tightly, and invert skillet and platter. Set platter on counter and lift skillet off, leaving tart behind.

narrow ends slightly raised. Place remaining pear quarters cut side down in skillet middle. Cook pears over medium heat until they are light golden brown and caramel is darkly colored, 9 to 11 minutes, turning pears over so peeled sides are facing down, halfway through cooking.

4. Off heat, slide chilled dough circle over pears in skillet. Being careful not to burn your fingers, fold back edge of dough so that it fits snugly into skillet. Bake tart until crust is golden brown and crisp, 20 to 25 minutes, rotating skillet halfway through baking.

5. Using potholder (skillet handle will be hot), remove skillet from oven. Let tart cool in skillet for 30 minutes. Run thin knife around edge, place inverted serving platter (or cutting board) over top and gently flip tart onto platter, using mitts or kitchen towels if skillet is still hot. Scrape out any pears that stick to skillet and put them back into place on tart. Serve.

All-Butter Tart Shells

MAKES TWO 4-INCH TART SHELLS

✔ **WHY THIS RECIPE WORKS:** While pie crust is tender and flaky, classic tart crust should be rich, crisp, and crumbly—almost like shortbread. We love the flavor of an all-butter crust, but the dough can be difficult to work with. To make it easier, we skipped rolling out the dough and instead turned to a pat-in-the-pan style crust. We started by cutting the butter into the flour (the food processor was an easy way to speed up this task). Once the dough came together, we simply tore it into pieces and pressed it into the pan until we had a cohesive crust. The dough baked as evenly as traditional rolled tart dough, and since the butter was evenly distributed throughout the dough, the crust was exceptionally rich and crisp. You will need two 4-inch fluted tart pans with removable bottoms for this recipe.

½ **cup plus 2 tablespoons (3⅛ ounces) all-purpose flour**
1½ **teaspoons sugar**
¼ **teaspoon salt**
4 **tablespoons unsalted butter, cut into ½-inch pieces and chilled**
2–3 **tablespoons ice water**

1. Grease two 4-inch tart pans with removable bottoms. Process flour, sugar, and salt in food processor until combined, about 5 seconds. Scatter butter over top and pulse until mixture resembles coarse cornmeal, about 15 pulses. Add 2 tablespoons ice water and continue to pulse until large clumps of dough form and no powdery bits remain, about 5 pulses. If dough doesn't clump, add remaining water, 1 teaspoon at a time, and pulse until it does.

2. Divide dough into 2 equal pieces. Tear each piece of dough into walnut-size clumps and spread evenly in bottom of prepared pans. Working outward from center of each pan, press dough into even layer, then press it up sides and into fluted edges of pan. Use your thumb to level off top edges and remove excess dough; use excess dough to patch any holes. Lay plastic wrap over dough in each pan and smooth out any bumps or shallow areas using your fingertips. Place dough-lined tart pans on large plate and freeze until fully chilled and firm, at least 30 minutes or up to 1 day.

3. Adjust oven rack to middle position and heat oven to 375 degrees. Set dough-lined tart pans on rimmed baking sheet. Press parchment paper or double layer of aluminum foil into frozen tart shells, covering edges to prevent burning, and fill with pie weights.

4. Bake tart shells until top edges of dough just start to color and surface of dough under parchment no longer looks wet, about 30 minutes. Carefully remove weights and parchment and continue to bake tart shells until golden brown, 5 to 10 minutes. Transfer tart shells with sheet to wire rack. Use shells while still warm or let cool completely (see individual recipe instructions.)

Making a Tart Shell

1. Tear 1 piece of dough into clumps and distribute evenly in bottom of prepared tart pan.

2. Working from center, press dough into even layer and up sides into fluted edges of pan.

3. Use your thumb to level off top edge. Use excess dough to patch any holes.

4. Lay plastic wrap over dough and smooth out any bumps using your fingertips.

We use ¼ cup of fresh lemon juice and a whole tablespoon of zest to give these rich tarts unmistakable, bright lemon flavor.

Lemon Tarts

SERVES 2

✓ **WHY THIS RECIPE WORKS:** We wanted a proper lemon tart, filled with a creamy lemon curd that possessed a perfectly balanced sweet-tart flavor. For serious lemon flavor, we used ¼ cup of juice and a whopping tablespoon of zest. Then we added just enough sugar—⅓ cup—to balance the bracing acidity of the lemons. To ensure our lemon curd was creamy and dense with a vibrant yellow color, we used one whole egg along with three egg yolks. A little butter added richness. For a smooth, light texture, we strained the curd, then stirred in heavy cream just before baking. Once the lemon curd ingredients are combined, cook the curd immediately; otherwise, it will have a grainy consistency. It is important to add the filling to the tart shell while it is still warm; if the shell has cooled, rewarm it in the oven for 5 minutes before adding the filling. Dust with confectioners' sugar or serve with Whipped Cream (page 363).

NOTES FROM THE TEST KITCHEN

Juicing Lemons

We've tried countless methods and gizmos for juicing lemons and dismissed most of them. Our favorite method for easily juicing lemons is simply rolling them vigorously on a hard surface before slicing them open. Rolling the lemon bruises, breaks up, and softens the rind's tissues while it tears the membranes of the juice vesicles (tear-shaped juice sacs), filling the inside of the lemon with juice even before it is squeezed. After rolling, we recommend either a wooden reamer, which effectively digs into and tears the lemon to extract as much juice as possible, or a good citrus juicer. However you squeeze them, we strongly recommend that you squeeze lemons at the last minute; their flavor mellows quickly and the juice will taste bland in a short time.

1   **large egg plus 3 large yolks**
⅓   **cup (2⅓ ounces) sugar**
1   **tablespoon grated lemon zest plus ¼ cup juice (2 lemons)**
    Pinch salt
2   **tablespoons unsalted butter, cut into 2 pieces**
1   **tablespoon heavy cream, chilled**
1   **recipe All-Butter Tart Shells (page 378), still warm**

1. Adjust oven rack to middle position and heat oven to 375 degrees. Whisk egg and yolks together in small saucepan. Whisk in sugar until combined, then whisk in lemon zest and juice and salt. Add butter and cook over medium-low heat, stirring constantly, until mixture thickens slightly and registers 170 degrees, 5 to 7 minutes. Immediately pour mixture through fine-mesh strainer into bowl and stir in cream.

2. Divide warm lemon filling evenly between warm prebaked tart shells and smooth tops. Place tarts on rimmed baking sheet and bake until filling is opaque and centers jiggle slightly when gently shaken, about 10 minutes, rotating sheet halfway through baking.

3. Transfer tarts with sheet to wire rack and let cool to room temperature, about 1½ hours. To serve, remove outer metal ring of tart pans, slide thin metal spatula between tarts and tart pan bottoms, and carefully slide tarts onto individual plates.

Nutella Tarts

SERVES 2

✓ **WHY THIS RECIPE WORKS:** For amazingly simple yet showstopping individual tarts, we started with our flaky and flavorful All-Butter Tart Shells. For the base of the filling, we relied on Nutella, a creamy and incredibly addictive hazelnut-chocolate spread. To the Nutella we added heavy cream,

Creamy hazelnut-and-chocolate flavored Nutella plus bittersweet chocolate, cream, and butter make an easy but decadent tart filling.

3. Refrigerate tarts until filling is just set, about 15 minutes. Arrange reserved whole hazelnuts evenly around edge of tarts and continue to refrigerate until filling is firm, about 1½ hours. To serve, remove outer metal ring of tart pans, slide thin metal spatula between tarts and tart pan bottoms, and carefully slide tarts onto individual plates.

Pecan Tarts

SERVES 2

✔ **WHY THIS RECIPE WORKS:** We wanted a recipe for individual pecan tarts with a rich, smooth, cohesive filling that was subtly sweet. We used our easy pat-in-the-pan All-Butter Tart Shells as the base for the filling. Dark brown sugar added rich caramel notes that nicely complemented the pecans, and swapping some of the sugar for a little corn syrup ensured the filling was smooth, not gritty. A pinch of salt balanced the sweetness, preventing the tarts from being cloying. A little vanilla extract rounded out all the flavors, and just one egg yolk was all we needed to ensure the filling set up properly. Because the pecans were the star the show, we chopped them coarse before adding them to the filling to ensure we had nuts in every bite. Serve with vanilla ice cream or Whipped Cream (page 363).

butter, and a little bittersweet chocolate for silky richness. A sprinkling of chopped hazelnuts in the bottom of each tart shell added a welcome crunch and textural contrast to the smooth, creamy filling. And because this easy filling required no baking, all we had to do was pour it into the tart shells and let it set. Garnished with whole toasted hazelnuts, these tarts are sure to impress. Serve with Whipped Cream (page 363).

⅓ cup hazelnuts, toasted and skinned
1 recipe All-Butter Tart Shells (page 378), cooled
½ cup Nutella
3 tablespoons heavy cream
1 ounce bittersweet chocolate, chopped
1 tablespoon unsalted butter

¼ cup packed (1¾ ounces) dark brown sugar
3 tablespoons light corn syrup
2 tablespoons unsalted butter
   Pinch salt
1 large egg yolk
½ teaspoon vanilla extract
½ cup pecans, toasted and chopped coarse
1 recipe All-Butter Tart Shells (page 378), cooled

1. Reserve 16 whole hazelnuts for garnish, then chop remaining hazelnuts coarse. Sprinkle half of chopped hazelnuts in bottom of each cooled prebaked tart shell.

2. Microwave Nutella, cream, chocolate, and butter together in covered bowl at 30 percent power, stirring often, until mixture is smooth and glossy, about 1 minute (do not overheat). Divide warm Nutella filling evenly between tart shells and smooth tops.

1. Adjust oven rack to middle position and heat oven to 325 degrees. Heat sugar and corn syrup together in small saucepan over medium heat, stirring occasionally, until sugar dissolves, about 2 minutes. Off heat, whisk in butter and salt until butter is melted. Whisk in egg yolk and vanilla until combined. Stir in pecans.

2. Divide warm pecan mixture evenly between cooled prebaked tart shells and smooth tops. Place tarts on rimmed baking sheet and bake until centers jiggle slightly when gently shaken, 10 to 15 minutes, rotating sheet halfway through baking.

3. Transfer tarts with sheet to wire rack and let cool to room temperature, about 1½ hours. To serve, remove outer metal ring of tart pans, slide thin metal spatula between tarts and tart pan bottoms, and carefully slide tarts onto individual plates.

Rustic Walnut Tarts

SERVES 2

✓ **WHY THIS RECIPE WORKS:** For an elegant addition to our for-two repertoire, we wanted to create individual walnut tarts with rich caramel flavor, crunchy nuts, and a buttery crust. We started by making a simple all-butter dough quickly in the food processor. To give the crust a subtle flavor that would complement the filling, we added brown sugar and a handful of ground toasted walnuts. For the filling, we swapped the granulated sugar for a combination of corn syrup, which ensured a smooth, cohesive filling, and light brown sugar, which lent a subtle caramelized flavor. A dash of vanilla and a pinch of salt balanced the sweetness of the filling and rounded out the flavors. Finally, a little bourbon brought the nutty, caramel notes of our tart to the forefront. Pecans can be substituted for the walnuts if desired. You will need two 4-inch fluted tart pans with removable bottoms for this recipe. Serve with vanilla ice cream or Whipped Cream (page 363).

TART SHELLS

½ cup (2½ ounces) all-purpose flour
2 tablespoons packed light brown sugar
2 tablespoons coarsely chopped walnuts, toasted
⅛ teaspoon baking powder
⅛ teaspoon salt
4 tablespoons unsalted butter, cut into ½-inch pieces and chilled

FILLING

⅓ cup packed (2⅓ ounces) light brown sugar
3 tablespoons light corn syrup
2 tablespoons unsalted butter, melted and cooled
2 teaspoons bourbon or dark rum
½ teaspoon vanilla extract
Pinch salt
1 large egg
⅓ cup walnuts, chopped coarse

1. FOR THE TART SHELLS: Grease two 4-inch tart pans with removable bottoms. Process flour, sugar, walnuts, baking powder, and salt in food processor until combined, about 5 seconds. Scatter butter over top and pulse until mixture is pale yellow and resembles coarse cornmeal, about 8 pulses.

2. Sprinkle mixture evenly into prepared pans. Using bottom of measuring cup, press crumbs firmly into even layer on bottom and sides of pans. Use your thumb to level off top edges and remove excess crumbs. Use excess crumbs to patch

For a walnut tart with nutty flavor throughout, we add ground walnuts to the crust as well as to the caramel-flavored filling.

any holes. Place crumb-lined tart pans on large plate, cover with plastic wrap, and freeze until fully chilled and firm, at least 30 minutes or up to 1 day.

3. Adjust oven rack to middle position and heat oven to 350 degrees. Set crumb-lined tart pans on rimmed baking sheet. Press parchment paper or double layer of aluminum foil into frozen tart shells, covering edges to prevent burning, and fill with pie weights.

4. Bake tart shells until golden brown and set, 20 to 25 minutes, rotating sheet halfway through baking. Carefully remove weights and parchment; transfer tarts with sheet to wire rack and let cool slightly while making filling.

5. FOR THE FILLING: Whisk sugar, corn syrup, melted butter, bourbon, vanilla, and salt together in medium bowl until sugar dissolves. Whisk in egg until combined. Pour filling evenly into tart shells and sprinkle with walnuts. Bake tarts until filling is set and walnuts begin to brown, 25 to 30 minutes, rotating sheet halfway through baking.

6. Transfer tarts with sheet to wire rack and let cool to room temperature, about 1½ hours. To serve, remove outer metal ring of tart pans, slide thin metal spatula between tarts and tart pan bottoms, and carefully slide tarts onto individual plates.

CHAPTER 17

Cookies, Cakes, and Custards

◼ FAST (Start to finish in about 30 minutes)

◻ LIGHT (See page 415 for nutritional information)

Opposite: Coffee-Toffee Cookies; Bold and Spicy Gingerbread Cakes; Crème Brûlée

Melted butter gives our classic chocolate chip cookies a super-chewy texture and makes them extra easy to throw together.

1 cup (5 ounces) all-purpose flour
½ teaspoon baking soda
¼ teaspoon salt
½ cup packed (3½ ounces) light brown sugar
¼ cup (1¾ ounces) granulated sugar
5 tablespoons unsalted butter, melted and cooled
1 large egg
1½ teaspoons vanilla extract
1 cup (6 ounces) semisweet chocolate chips

1. Adjust oven rack to middle position and heat oven to 350 degrees. Line baking sheet with parchment paper. Whisk flour, baking soda, and salt together in bowl.

2. Whisk brown sugar and granulated sugar together in medium bowl. Whisk in melted butter until combined. Whisk in egg and vanilla until smooth. Gently stir in flour mixture with rubber spatula until soft dough forms. Fold in chocolate chips.

3. Working with 2 tablespoons dough at a time, roll into balls and space them 2 inches apart on prepared sheet.

4. Bake cookies until edges are set but centers are still soft and puffy, about 14 minutes, rotating sheet halfway through baking. Let cookies cool slightly on sheet. Serve warm or at room temperature. (Cookies can be stored at room temperature for up to 3 days.)

Chewy Chocolate Chip Cookies

MAKES 12 COOKIES   `FAST`

✔ **WHY THIS RECIPE WORKS:** Most cookie recipes leave the baker with a yield that's far larger than what can be eaten by two before they go stale. We wanted to develop a recipe for the perfect chewy chocolate chip cookie that would yield a mini batch of 12 cookies. To keep our recipe quick and convenient, we also wanted to eliminate the need to lug out an electric mixer. Rather than creaming the butter and sugar, we melted the butter so that we could simply stir everything together in one bowl. Gently folding the dry ingredients into the wet ingredients ensured that our cookies were tender and chewy, not tough. A combination of granulated and brown sugars plus a dash of vanilla extract gave the cookies a subtle caramelized flavor. To avoid overbaking, pull the cookies out of the oven when they are still slightly underbaked in the center; they will finish cooking on the baking sheet.

Oatmeal-Raisin Cookies

MAKES 12 COOKIES

✔ **WHY THIS RECIPE WORKS:** It took 30 batches of oatmeal cookies before we figured out how to make our ideal oatmeal cookie, with lots of oat flavor, crisp around the edges, and chewy in the middle. To pack the cookies with oat flavor, we used a high ratio of oats to flour. Old-fashioned rolled oats provided the best flavor; instant and quick oats lacked oat flavor and made the cookies dry and mealy. Swapping some of the granulated sugar for brown sugar complemented the nutty oats and gave us moister, chewier cookies. Since the oats weighed down the batter, we needed to add extra liquid to get the cookies to spread correctly and to ensure they weren't dry or crumbly. Milk added more body and flavor than plain water; just a couple of tablespoons did the trick. Do not substitute quick or instant oats in this recipe.

1¼ cups (3¾ ounces) old-fashioned rolled oats
½ cup plus 2 tablespoons (3⅛ ounces) all-purpose flour
¼ teaspoon baking powder
¼ teaspoon salt

Our oatmeal-raisin cookies boast plenty of oats with great nutty flavor, crisp edges, and tender, chewy centers.

⅛ teaspoon ground cinnamon
½ cup packed (3½ ounces) brown sugar
¼ cup (1¾ ounces) granulated sugar
6 tablespoons unsalted butter, melted and cooled
1 large egg yolk
2 tablespoons whole milk
¾ teaspoon vanilla extract
⅓ cup raisins

1. Adjust oven rack to middle position and heat oven to 350 degrees. Line baking sheet with parchment paper. Whisk oats, flour, baking powder, salt, and cinnamon together in bowl.

2. Whisk brown sugar and granulated sugar together in medium bowl. Whisk in melted butter until combined. Whisk in egg yolk, milk, and vanilla until smooth. Gently stir in oat mixture with rubber spatula until soft dough forms. Fold in raisins.

3. Working with heaping 1½ tablespoons dough at a time, roll into balls and space them 2 inches apart on prepared sheet. Using bottom of greased drinking glass, flatten dough balls until 2½ inches in diameter.

4. Bake cookies until edges are set and beginning to brown, about 15 minutes, rotating sheet halfway through baking. Let cookies cool slightly on sheet. Serve warm or at room temperature. (Cookies can be stored at room temperature for up to 3 days.)

Coffee-Toffee Cookies

MAKES 12 COOKIES **FAST**

✔ **WHY THIS RECIPE WORKS:** Cookies aren't just for kids. We wanted a cookie with sophisticated allure, so we combined the rich flavor of coffee with buttery, nutty toffee. To build intense coffee flavor, we started with the strong stuff: espresso. Instant espresso powder, with its concentrated flavor and fine texture, was a quick and easy way to add bold coffee flavor. We dissolved a few teaspoons in warm water (we tried to add it directly in the melted butter, but since instant espresso is water soluble, it needed the water to dissolve). We then added the butter and sugar directly to the "brewed" espresso. A little vanilla extract balanced and softened the espresso's bite. Finally, we folded in plenty of toffee pieces to add texture and rich caramel flavor. You can substitute espresso granules for the espresso powder; however, they might not dissolve as readily in water.

1 cup (5 ounces) all-purpose flour
¼ teaspoon baking soda
¼ teaspoon salt
4 teaspoons instant espresso powder
1½ teaspoons warm tap water
½ cup plus 2 tablespoons (4⅓ ounces) sugar
5 tablespoons unsalted butter, melted and cooled
1 large egg
½ teaspoon vanilla extract
¼ cup Heath toffee bits

NOTES FROM THE TEST KITCHEN

Freezing Cookie Dough

Keeping frozen cookie dough on hand means that you can bake as many, or as few, cookies as you like. To freeze the dough, form it into balls, arrange the balls on a baking sheet, and place the sheet in the freezer. Once the individual balls of dough are frozen, place them in a zipper-lock freezer bag and store them in the freezer. To bake, line a baking sheet with parchment paper and place on top of a second baking sheet. Arrange the frozen cookies (do not thaw) on the prepared sheet and bake as directed, increasing the baking time by 5 to 10 minutes.

1. Adjust oven rack to middle position and heat oven to 350 degrees. Line baking sheet with parchment paper. Whisk flour, baking soda, and salt together in bowl.

2. Whisk espresso powder and water together in medium bowl until espresso powder dissolves, then whisk in sugar and melted butter until combined. Whisk in egg and vanilla until smooth. Gently stir in flour mixture with rubber spatula until soft dough forms. Fold in toffee bits.

3. Working with 2 tablespoons dough at a time, roll into balls and space them 2 inches apart on prepared sheet.

4. Bake cookies until edges are set but centers are still soft and puffy, about 13 minutes, rotating sheet halfway through baking. Let cookies cool slightly on sheet. Serve warm or at room temperature. (Cookies can be stored at room temperature for up to 3 days.)

Molasses Spice Cookies

MAKES 12 COOKIES

✔ **WHY THIS RECIPE WORKS:** Our ultimate molasses spice cookie is soft, chewy, and gently spiced with deep, dark molasses flavor. To achieve this ideal, we started with all-purpose flour and butter for full, rich flavor. Using just the right amount of molasses and brown sugar and flavoring the cookies with a combination of vanilla, ginger, cinnamon, cloves, and black pepper gave these spiced cookies the warm flavor and subtle bite that we were after. Baking soda was essential to create the traditional cracks and crinkles so characteristic of these charming cookies, and rolling the dough in granulated sugar before baking gave the soft cookies sparkling sweet crunch. We pulled the cookies from the oven when the edges were just set; residual heat finished the baking and kept the cookies chewy and moist. For the best results, use fresh spices. Light or mild molasses gives the cookies a milder flavor; for a stronger flavor, use robust or full molasses.

 1 cup plus 2 tablespoons (5⅔ ounces) all-purpose flour
 ¾ teaspoon ground cinnamon
 ¾ teaspoon ground ginger
 ½ teaspoon baking soda
 ¼ teaspoon ground cloves
 ⅛ teaspoon finely ground pepper
 ⅛ teaspoon salt

 ¼ cup (1¾ ounces) plus 2 tablespoons granulated sugar
 3 tablespoons packed dark brown sugar
 6 tablespoons unsalted butter, melted and cooled
 ¼ cup molasses
 1 large egg yolk
 ½ teaspoon vanilla extract

1. Adjust oven rack to middle position and heat oven to 350 degrees. Line baking sheet with parchment paper. Whisk flour, cinnamon, ginger, baking soda, cloves, pepper, and salt together in bowl. Place 2 tablespoons granulated sugar in shallow dish.

2. Whisk brown sugar and remaining ¼ cup granulated sugar together in medium bowl. Whisk in melted butter until combined. Whisk in molasses, egg yolk, and vanilla until smooth. Gently stir in flour mixture with rubber spatula until soft dough forms.

3. Working with heaping 1½ tablespoons dough at a time, roll into balls. Roll dough balls in granulated sugar to coat, then space balls 2 inches apart on prepared sheet. Using bottom of greased drinking glass, flatten dough balls until 2 inches in diameter. Sprinkle tops of cookies evenly with 2 teaspoons of granulated sugar remaining in shallow dish from rolling. Discard remaining sugar.

4. Bake cookies until edges are set and beginning to brown, 10 to 12 minutes, rotating sheet halfway through baking. Let cookies cool slightly on sheet. Serve warm or at room temperature. (Cookies can be stored at room temperature for up to 3 days.)

Shaping Molasses Spice Cookies

1. Take 1½ tablespoons dough and roll it between your palms into ball. Roll ball of dough in sugar, then place it on prepared sheet.

2. Use greased drinking glass with flat bottom or measuring cup to flatten balls of dough until 2 inches in diameter. Sprinkle tops with sugar.

Cornmeal Olive Oil Cookies

MAKES 12 COOKIES **FAST**

✔ WHY THIS RECIPE WORKS: For these lightly sweetened Italian-style cookies, we combined subtly sweet cornmeal and aromatic rosemary with peppery extra-virgin olive oil. To hold the savory flavors of these cookies in check, we used two different types of sugar. One-quarter cup of granulated sugar in the dough contributed a mild sweetness and cakey texture, while rolling the warm cookies in confectioners' sugar lent a second layer of sweetness. Fresh rosemary provided deep floral and herbal notes. These sophisticated cookies pair equally well with a hot cup of tea or coffee, or a glass of wine. Regular olive oil can be substituted for the extra-virgin olive oil; however, the cookies will have a less pronounced olive oil flavor.

¾ cup (3¾ ounces) all-purpose flour

¼ cup (1¼ ounces) cornmeal

½ teaspoon baking powder

⅛ teaspoon salt

⅓ cup extra-virgin olive oil

¼ cup (1¾ ounces) granulated sugar

1 large egg

½ teaspoon minced fresh rosemary

⅓ cup (1⅓ ounces) confectioners' sugar, plus extra as needed

1. Adjust oven rack to middle position and heat oven to 375 degrees. Line baking sheet with parchment paper. Whisk flour, cornmeal, baking powder, and salt together in bowl.

2. Whisk oil and granulated sugar together in medium bowl until combined. Whisk in egg and rosemary until smooth. Gently stir in flour mixture with rubber spatula until soft dough forms.

3. Working with 1 tablespoon dough at a time, roll into balls and space them 2 inches apart on prepared sheet.

4. Bake cookies until edges are lightly golden and centers puff and split open, about 13 minutes, rotating sheet halfway through baking. Let cookies cool slightly on sheet. Place confectioners' sugar in bowl, then gently roll warm cookies in sugar to coat. Dust with extra confectioners' sugar as desired before serving. Serve warm or at room temperature. (Cookies can be stored at room temperature for up to 3 days.)

All About Sugar

Sugar not only adds sweetness to baked goods, it affects texture too. The amount or type of sugar can make a cookie crisp or chewy. Here are the most common types of sugar we use in baking.

WHITE GRANULATED SUGAR
Made either from sugar cane or sugar beets, this is the type of sugar used most often in our recipes. It has a clean flavor, and its evenly ground, loose texture ensures that it incorporates well with butter when creaming and dissolves easily into batters.

CONFECTIONERS' SUGAR
Also called powdered sugar, this is the most finely ground sugar. It is most commonly used for dusting cakes and cookies and for making quick glazes and icings. To prevent clumping, confectioners' sugar contains a small amount of cornstarch. You can also approximate confectioners' sugar with this method: For 1 cup of confectioners' sugar, process 1 cup of granulated sugar with 1 tablespoon of cornstarch in a blender (not a food processor) until fine, 30 to 40 seconds.

TURBINADO AND DEMERARA SUGAR
These "raw" sugars have large crystals that do not readily dissolve—a reason to avoid them in dough. Instead, we like to sprinkle them on muffin tops to create crunch or use them to form the caramel crust on Crème Brûlée (page 409).

BROWN SUGAR
Brown sugar is simply granulated white sugar that has been combined with molasses. (When necessary, our ingredient list will indicate "light" or "dark" brown sugar. If either can be used, we simply list "brown sugar.") Store brown sugar in an airtight container to prevent it from drying out. To approximate 1 cup of light brown sugar, pulse 1 cup of granulated sugar with 1 tablespoon of mild molasses in a food processor until blended. Use 2 tablespoons of molasses for dark brown sugar.

MEASURING SUGAR: Weighing sugar is always the most accurate, but if you're measuring sugar by volume, it's important to use the best method. White sugar should be measured with the dip-and-sweep method: Dip the measuring cup into the sugar and sweep away the excess with a straight-edged object like the back of a butter knife. Brown sugar, on the other hand, is so moist and clumpy that it must be packed into the measuring cup to get an accurate measurement. Fill the dry measure with brown sugar and use the next smallest cup to pack it down. For instance, if you need ⅓ cup of packed brown sugar, use the bottom of the ¼-cup measure to pack it down. When properly packed, 1 cup of brown sugar should weigh the same as 1 cup of granulated sugar: 7 ounces.

REVIVING HARDENED BROWN SUGAR: If your brown sugar dries out, place the sugar in a zipper-lock bag, add a slice of bread, and set it aside overnight until the sugar is soft again. Or, quicker yet, put the brown sugar in a microwave-safe bowl with the bread and tightly cover with plastic wrap. Microwave until the sugar is moist, 15 to 30 seconds.

For a batch of classic chewy, fudgy brownies scaled for two, we swap the standard large baking pan for a perfectly sized loaf pan.

Fudgy Brownies

MAKES 8 BROWNIES

✔ **WHY THIS RECIPE WORKS:** Everyone loves brownies, but a full pan of brownies for two is way too much for even the most ardent brownie lovers. To scale back our batch of fudgy brownies, we ditched the large baking dish in favor of a loaf pan, which made just eight brownies—perfect for two people to enjoy over a few days. Two types of chocolate—semisweet chocolate and cocoa powder—gave us plenty of fudgy flavor. To make our batter easy to mix by hand, we melted the semisweet chocolate quickly in the microwave. A whole egg plus an extra yolk made our brownies rich, moist, and chewy. The deep sides of the loaf pan made it hard to cut the brownies neatly, so we lined the pan with a foil sling that allowed us to lift the brownies out in one piece before cutting. Be careful not to overbake these brownies or they will have a very dry, cakey texture. The test kitchen's preferred loaf pan measures 8½ by 4½ inches; if you use a 9 by 5-inch loaf pan, start checking for doneness 5 minutes earlier than advised in the recipe.

3½ ounces semisweet chocolate, chopped
4 tablespoons unsalted butter, cut into 4 pieces
1 tablespoon unsweetened cocoa powder
½ cup plus 2 tablespoons (4⅓ ounces) sugar
1 large egg plus 1 large yolk
1 teaspoon vanilla extract
¼ teaspoon salt
½ cup (2½ ounces) all-purpose flour

1. Adjust oven rack to middle position and heat oven to 350 degrees. Make foil sling for 8½ by 4½-inch loaf pan by folding 2 long sheets of aluminum foil; first sheet should be 8½ inches wide and second sheet should be 4½ inches wide. Lay sheets of foil in pan perpendicular to each other, with extra foil hanging over edges of pan. Push foil into corners and up sides of pan, smoothing foil flush to pan. Grease foil.

2. Microwave chocolate, butter, and cocoa in bowl at 50 percent power, stirring occasionally, until melted and smooth, 1 to 3 minutes; let cool slightly. Whisk sugar, egg and yolk, vanilla, and salt together in medium bowl until combined. Whisk in melted chocolate mixture until combined. Stir in flour with rubber spatula until just combined.

3. Transfer batter to prepared pan; spread batter into corners of pan and smooth surface. Bake until toothpick inserted in center comes out with a few moist crumbs attached, 24 to 28 minutes, rotating pan halfway through baking. Let brownies cool completely in pan on wire rack. Remove brownies from pan using foil, loosening sides with paring knife, if needed. Cut brownies into 2-inch squares and serve. (Brownies can be stored at room temperature for up to 3 days.)

Making a Foil Sling

1. Place 2 sheets of aluminum foil perpendicular to each other in loaf pan, pushing foil into corners. Smooth foil flush to pan.

2. Use foil handles to lift baked brownies or bars from pan.

Blondies

MAKES 8 BARS

✔ **WHY THIS RECIPE WORKS:** Although blondies are baked in a pan like brownies, the flavorings are similar to those in chocolate chip cookies—vanilla, butter, and brown sugar, often laced with nuts and chocolate chips. But blondies can be bland, floury, and dry. We set out to fix the blondie so it would be chewy but not dense, sweet but not cloying, and loaded with nuts and chocolate. For deep caramelized flavor, we eliminated the granulated sugar and used only brown sugar to make our bars. A combination of semisweet and white chocolate chips highlighted the vanilla and caramel flavors, and chopped pecans added crunch and nutty richness. Walnuts can be substituted for the pecans. The test kitchen's preferred loaf pan measures 8½ by 4½ inches; if you use a 9 by 5-inch loaf pan, start checking for doneness 5 minutes earlier than advised in the recipe.

½ cup (2½ ounces) all-purpose flour
½ teaspoon baking powder
¼ teaspoon salt
½ cup packed (3½ ounces) light brown sugar
3 tablespoons unsalted butter, melted and cooled
1 large egg
1½ teaspoons vanilla extract
⅓ cup pecans, toasted and chopped
2 tablespoons semisweet chocolate chips
2 tablespoons white chocolate chips

1. Adjust oven rack to middle position and heat oven to 350 degrees. Make foil sling for 8½ by 4½-inch loaf pan by folding 2 long sheets of aluminum foil; first sheet should be 8½ inches wide and second sheet should be 4½ inches wide. Lay sheets of foil in pan perpendicular to each other, with extra foil hanging over edges of pan. Push foil into corners and up sides of pan, smoothing foil flush to pan. Grease foil.

2. Whisk flour, baking powder, and salt together in bowl. In large bowl, whisk sugar and melted butter until combined. Whisk in egg and vanilla until smooth. Stir in flour mixture with rubber spatula until just combined. Fold in pecans and semisweet and white chocolate chips.

3. Transfer batter to prepared pan; spread batter into corners of pan and smooth surface. Bake until toothpick inserted in center comes out clean, 20 to 25 minutes, rotating pan halfway through baking. Let bars cool completely in pan on wire rack. Remove bars from pan using foil, loosening sides with paring knife, if needed. Cut into 2-inch squares and serve. (Bars can be stored at room temperature for up to 3 days.)

Chocolate and Peanut Butter Oatmeal Bars

MAKES 8 BARS

✔ **WHY THIS RECIPE WORKS:** Chocolate and peanut butter are an irresistible combination. Add nutty, buttery oats to make easy no-cook treats and you've got a surefire winner. But old-fashioned, instant, and quick-cooking oats each tasted dry and dusty in the bars. Granola, which is already fully cooked, proved to be the solution; it tasted great right out of the package. For the chocolate, we mixed crumbled chocolate wafers in with the oats and peanut butter, then topped the bars with a layer of melted semisweet chocolate. Look for a simply flavored oat-and-nut-based granola; avoid granola with dried fruit. If the granola has large clumps, place it in a zipper-lock bag and gently break it into small pieces with a mallet or rolling pin. Do not substitute crunchy peanut butter here. You can substitute ⅓ cup semisweet chocolate chips for the semisweet chocolate.

3 ounces chocolate wafer cookies, crumbled
½ cup (2 ounces) granola, crushed into small pieces
¼ cup (1 ounce) confectioners' sugar
2 tablespoons unsalted butter
½ cup smooth peanut butter
2 ounces semisweet chocolate, chopped

1. Make foil sling for 8½ by 4½-inch loaf pan by folding 2 long sheets of aluminum foil; first sheet should be 8½ inches wide and second sheet should be 4½ inches wide. Lay sheets of foil in pan perpendicular to each other, with extra foil hanging over edges of pan. Push foil into corners and up sides of pan, smoothing foil flush to pan. Grease foil.

2. Process crumbled chocolate wafers in food processor to fine, even crumbs, about 30 seconds. Combine wafer crumbs, granola, and sugar in medium bowl. Microwave butter in second medium bowl until melted, about 30 seconds, then whisk in 6 tablespoons peanut butter until combined. Stir peanut butter mixture into wafer-granola mixture until combined. Scrape mixture into prepared pan and press firmly into even layer with greased spatula. Freeze, uncovered, until firm, about 20 minutes.

3. Microwave chocolate in bowl at 50 percent power, stirring occasionally, until melted and smooth, about 2 minutes. Spread melted chocolate evenly over top of frozen mixture. Microwave remaining 2 tablespoons peanut butter in clean bowl until warm, about 1 minute, then drizzle attractively over top. Freeze, uncovered, until chocolate has hardened, about 10 minutes.

4. Remove bars from pan using foil, loosening sides with paring knife, if needed. Cut into 2-inch squares and serve. (Bars can be stored at room temperature for up to 2 days.)

Flour and Baking

Flour is essential for providing structure to most baked goods. The amount and type of flour that you use can be the difference between a tough, leaden cake and a light, tender one.

ALL-PURPOSE FLOUR VERSUS CAKE FLOUR: The main difference between types of flour is their protein content. All-purpose is by far the most versatile flour available. With a protein content between 10 percent and 11.7 percent, it provides enough structure to make good sandwich bread, yet it's light enough to use for cakes of a medium-to-coarse crumb. Cake flour has a lower protein content—about 6 to 8 percent—and thus yields cakes and pastries with less gluten, which translates to a finer, more delicate crumb. We use cake flour for light or fine-grained cakes, such as pound cake and angel food cake. It is possible to approximate 1 cup of cake flour by using 2 tablespoons of cornstarch plus ⅞ cup of all-purpose flour. Cake flour is usually bleached, but when buying all-purpose flour, we prefer unbleached. Bleached flours in our tests did not perform as well as the unbleached flours and were sometimes criticized for tasting flat or carrying off-flavors.

MEASURING FLOUR: The way you measure flour can make a big difference in your recipe. Too little flour can turn out baked goods that are flat, wet, or lacking in structure. Too much flour can result in tough, dry baked goods. For the ultimate in accuracy, nothing beats weighing flour, but our research has shown that the dip-and-sweep method is also reliable. You might be surprised to learn that if you are spooning your flour into a measuring cup and then leveling it off, you could end up with 20 percent less flour than with the dip-and-sweep method. For the dip-and-sweep method, simply dip the measuring cup into the container of flour and sweep away the excess with a straight-edged object like the back of a butter knife.

SIFTING FLOUR: Sifting flour is a chore, but sometimes it is important. When making a delicate cake like an angel food cake that requires flour to be folded into beaten eggs and sugar, sifted flour can be added quickly and distributed evenly (because sifting aerates the flour), thereby reducing the risk of deflating the batter. To sift flour, simply place the flour in a fine-mesh strainer and shake or tap the strainer over the bowl or a sheet of parchment paper.

STORING FLOUR: Refined flours, including all-purpose, bread, and cake flour, can be stored in airtight containers in your pantry for up to one year. A wide-mouthed plastic container allows you to scoop out what you need without making a floury mess of your countertop. Make sure the container can hold the entire contents of a 5-pound bag. A tight-fitting lid is also essential.

Whole-wheat flour and others made from whole grains contain more fat than refined flours and can turn rancid quickly at room temperature. For this reason, we recommend storing these flours in the freezer. In various tests, we found that using flour straight from the freezer inhibited rise and yielded denser baked goods. Therefore, it's best to bring chilled flour to room temperature before baking.

Summer Berry Snack Cakes

SERVES 2

✓ **WHY THIS RECIPE WORKS:** Unlike fancy layer cakes, snack cakes come together in just minutes with little effort, making them a perfect no-fuss dessert for two. We wanted to make two simple single-serving vanilla-scented cakes dotted with juicy bites of fresh berries. Miniature 1-cup Bundt pans were the perfect size, and gave the cakes an appealing shape. Getting the right ratio of tart berries to sweet cake was key; too many berries made the cakes wet and dense, but ½ cup of berries gave us just the right balance. To give the cakes a light, airy texture, we creamed the softened butter and sugar together before adding egg, vanilla, flour, and milk. Finally, simply dusting the cooled cakes with powdered sugar gave them a pretty, delicate finish. You will need two 1-cup Bundt pans for this recipe—the center tube is necessary to facilitate even baking.

½   cup (2½ ounces) all-purpose flour
½   teaspoon baking powder
⅛   teaspoon salt
3   tablespoons unsalted butter, softened
¼   cup (1¾ ounces) granulated sugar
1   large egg, room temperature
¼   teaspoon vanilla extract
2   tablespoons whole milk, room temperature
2½ ounces (½ cup) blueberries and/or raspberries
    Confectioners' sugar

1. Adjust oven rack to middle position and heat oven to 350 degrees. Spray two 1-cup Bundt pans with baking spray with flour. Whisk flour, baking powder, and salt together in bowl.

2. Using hand-held mixer set at low speed, beat butter and granulated sugar in medium bowl until sugar is moistened, about 1 minute. Increase speed to medium-high and beat mixture until pale and fluffy, about 3 minutes, scraping down sides of bowl as needed. Add egg and vanilla and beat until combined, about 30 seconds. Reduce speed to low and add flour mixture in 3 additions, alternating with milk in 2 additions (batter will be quite thick). Gently fold in blueberries with rubber spatula.

3. Divide batter evenly between prepared pans, smooth tops, and gently tap each pan on counter to release air bubbles. Wipe any drops of batter off sides of pans. Place pans on rimmed baking sheet and bake cakes until toothpick inserted in center comes out clean, 20 to 30 minutes, rotating sheet halfway through baking.

4. Let cakes cool in pans on wire rack for 10 minutes. Remove cakes from pans and let cool completely on rack, about 1 hour. Dust with confectioners' sugar and serve.

Angel Food Cakes

SERVES 2 `LIGHT`

✔ WHY THIS RECIPE WORKS: At its heavenly best, an angel food cake should have a snowy-white, tender interior and a thin, delicate, golden crust. Because it requires a delicate balance of ingredients, it's particularly tricky to scale for two. Two small, 2-cup tube pans made elegant single-serving cakes. For voluminous whipped egg whites, cream of tartar offered extra insurance against deflation. Cake flour was essential for a delicate crumb. Inverting the pans while the cakes rested ensured the cakes didn't sink as they cooled. You will need two 2-cup tube pans and either two 5- or 6-inch kitchen funnels or two chopsticks and two empty beer bottles for this recipe. If your tube pans do not have removable bottoms, line the bottoms with parchment paper. Serve with fresh berries and Whipped Cream (page 363). For the nutritional information for this recipe, see page 415.

- **6 tablespoons (1½ ounces) cake flour**
- **½ cup (3½ ounces) sugar**
- **Pinch salt**
- **3 large egg whites, room temperature**
- **½ teaspoon cream of tartar**
- **¼ teaspoon vanilla extract**

1. Adjust oven rack to lower-middle position and heat oven to 325 degrees. Whisk flour, ¼ cup sugar, and salt together in bowl.

2. Using hand-held mixer set at medium-low speed, beat egg whites and cream of tartar in large bowl until foamy, about 1 minute. Increase speed to medium-high and beat whites to soft, billowy mounds, about 1 minute. Gradually add remaining ¼ cup sugar and beat until glossy, soft peaks form, 1 to 3 minutes. Whisk in vanilla by hand.

3. Sift flour mixture over egg whites in 2 additions, folding gently with rubber spatula after each addition until combined.

Two Ways to Cool Angel Food Cakes

A. Set two 5- or 6-inch kitchen funnels upside down on counter. Invert 1 cake over each funnel.

B. Place chopstick in empty bottle; repeat setup. Invert each cake over 1 chopstick, balancing it on mouth of bottle.

Getting just the right proportions of ingredients ensures light and tender angel food cakes with a delicate, airy crumb.

4. Divide batter evenly between two 2-cup tube pans and smooth tops. Wipe any drops of batter off sides of pans. Place pans on rimmed baking sheet and bake cakes until toothpick inserted in center comes out clean and any cracks in cakes appear dry, 30 to 35 minutes.

5. Invert each cake pan over upside-down kitchen funnel or over empty beer bottle with chopstick set inside. Let cakes cool completely in pans, about 1 hour. Run thin knife around edges of cakes to loosen, then gently tap pans upside down on counter to release cakes. Turn cakes right side up onto plates and serve.

VARIATIONS
Chocolate-Almond Angel Food Cakes
For the nutritional information for this recipe, see page 415.

Substitute ¼ teaspoon almond extract for vanilla extract and add ½ ounce finely grated bittersweet chocolate to egg whites with flour mixture in step 3.

Café au Lait Angel Food Cakes
For the nutritional information for this recipe, see page 415.

Add ½ teaspoon instant espresso powder to flour mixture in step 1. Substitute ½ teaspoon coffee liqueur, such as Kahlúa, for vanilla extract in step 2.

Lemon–Poppy Seed Pound Cake

SERVES 2

✔ **WHY THIS RECIPE WORKS:** Lemon–poppy seed pound cake is a classic, but most versions lack true lemon flavor. We wanted an easy recipe for a truly lemony pound cake that would serve just two. Adjusting the size was an easy fix: We ditched our regular loaf pan in favor of a small, 5½ by 3-inch loaf pan. Next, we set out to make the cake foolproof. Cake flour and baking powder produced a tender crumb. Mixing the poppy seeds with a small amount of flour helped to distribute them evenly in the cake. For bold lemon flavor throughout, we used both lemon zest and fresh lemon juice. To finish it off, we brushed the cake with a simple lemon glaze, poking small holes in the cake to help the glaze sink in. Substituting all-purpose flour for cake flour will result in a denser cake. You will need a 5½ by 3-inch loaf pan or a 2½-cup pan of a similar shape for this recipe.

CAKE

- ½ cup (2 ounces) cake flour
- ¼ teaspoon baking powder
- ⅛ teaspoon salt
- 4 teaspoons poppy seeds
- ⅓ cup (2⅓ ounces) sugar
- 4 tablespoons unsalted butter, melted and cooled
- 1 large egg, room temperature
- 1½ teaspoons grated lemon zest plus ½ teaspoon juice
- ¼ teaspoon vanilla extract

LEMON GLAZE

- 2 tablespoons sugar
- 1 tablespoon lemon juice

1. FOR THE CAKE: Adjust oven rack to middle position and heat oven to 325 degrees. Grease and flour 5½ by 3-inch loaf pan.

2. Whisk flour, baking powder, and salt together in bowl. In small bowl, combine 1 tablespoon flour mixture and poppy seeds.

3. In medium bowl, whisk sugar, melted butter, egg, lemon zest and juice, and vanilla together until smooth. Whisk in remaining flour mixture in 2 additions until a few streaks of flour remain. Gently whisk in poppy seed mixture until most of lumps are gone (do not overmix). Give batter final stir with rubber spatula.

4. Scrape batter into prepared pan and smooth top. Wipe any drops of batter off sides of pan and gently tap pan on counter to release air bubbles. Bake cake until toothpick inserted in center comes out with a few moist crumbs attached, 30 to 40 minutes, rotating pan halfway through baking. Let cake

For our buttery lemon–poppy seed pound cake, we found that lots of lemon zest plus a little juice gave us the brightest lemon flavor.

cool in pan on wire rack for 10 minutes, then turn onto rack. Poke cake's top and sides with toothpick.

5. FOR THE LEMON GLAZE: Combine sugar and lemon juice in bowl and microwave until sugar dissolves and mixture thickens slightly, about 1 minute, stirring halfway through microwaving. Brush top and sides of cake with warm glaze and let cool completely on rack, about 1 hour, before serving.

Glazed Lemon Bundt Cakes

SERVES 2

✔ **WHY THIS RECIPE WORKS:** For a simple Bundt cake with potent lemon flavor, we had to keep the acidity of the lemon juice from ruining its texture. To maximize the lemon flavor, we turned to lemon zest; 2 teaspoons gave the cake a perfumed lemon flavor. Increasing the butter and replacing the milk with buttermilk gave us a rich, tender cake with a light crumb. Creaming the butter and sugar was essential to creating a light and even crumb. For the glaze, a simple mixture of lemon zest and juice and confectioners' sugar gave our cakes an extra burst of citrus flavor. Two mini Bundt pans produced perfect single-serving cakes. You will need two 1-cup Bundt pans for this recipe—the center tube is necessary to facilitate even baking.

CAKES

- ½ cup (2½ ounces) all-purpose flour
- ¼ teaspoon salt
- ¼ teaspoon baking powder
- ⅛ teaspoon baking soda
- 2 tablespoons buttermilk, room temperature
- 2 teaspoons grated lemon zest plus 1 teaspoon juice
- ½ teaspoon vanilla extract
- 3 tablespoons unsalted butter, softened
- ⅓ cup (2⅓ ounces) granulated sugar
- 1 large egg, room temperature

LEMON GLAZE

- ⅓ cup (1⅓ ounces) confectioners' sugar, plus extra as needed
- ¼ teaspoon grated lemon zest plus 2¾ teaspoons juice
  Pinch salt

1. FOR THE CAKES: Adjust oven rack to lower-middle position and heat oven to 350 degrees. Spray two 1-cup Bundt pans with baking spray with flour.

2. Whisk flour, salt, baking powder, and baking soda together in bowl. In small bowl, whisk buttermilk, lemon zest and juice, and vanilla together.

3. Using hand-held mixer set at low speed, beat butter and sugar in medium bowl until sugar is moistened, about 1 minute. Increase speed to medium-high and beat mixture until pale and fluffy, about 3 minutes, scraping down sides of bowl as needed. Add egg and beat until combined, about 30 seconds. Reduce speed to low and add flour mixture in 3 additions, alternating with buttermilk mixture in 2 additions. Increase speed to medium-high and beat until mixture is completely smooth, about 30 seconds. Give batter final stir by hand.

4. Divide batter evenly between prepared pans, smooth tops, and gently tap each pan on counter to release air bubbles. Wipe any drops of batter off sides of pans. Place pans on rimmed baking sheet and bake cakes until light golden brown and toothpick inserted in center comes out clean, 20 to 22 minutes, rotating sheet halfway through baking.

5. Let cakes cool in pans on wire rack set over baking sheet for 10 minutes. Remove cakes from pans and let cool completely on rack, about 1 hour.

6. FOR THE LEMON GLAZE: Whisk sugar, lemon zest and juice, and salt together in bowl until smooth, adding extra sugar as needed to achieve thick but still pourable consistency. Pour glaze over tops of cooled cakes, letting glaze drip down sides. Let glaze set before serving, about 25 minutes.

The Importance of Temperature in Baking

EGGS AND MILK

Temperature plays an important role in the behavior of ingredients in baking. Cakes and cookies often use room-temperature eggs and milk. Room-temperature eggs and milk are more easily incorporated than cold, and the additional mixing necessary to incorporate cold ingredients may adversely affect the batter and, ultimately, the texture of the baked good. Because recipes for two call for only small amounts of liquid ingredients like milk and buttermilk, you can simply set them on the counter while you prep the rest of the recipe. Eggs, however, take about an hour to come to room temperature on their own. To warm them quickly, put whole eggs in a small bowl of warm water (about 110 degrees) for about 5 minutes. This trick also works well for softening cream cheese—simply place the foil-wrapped block in warm water for about 10 minutes.

BUTTER

The temperature of butter in particular makes a difference in many recipes and can dramatically affect the texture of finished baked goods. For example, pie dough made with warm or room-temperature butter rather than chilled butter will be nearly impossible to roll out, and the resulting crust will be hard and tough rather than tender and flaky. On the other hand, many cakes and cookies require softened butter for creaming; softened butter blends easily with the sugar, and this action incorporates air into the dough or batter, creating tender baked goods.

Generally, recipes will call for butter chilled, softened, or melted and cooled. Chilled butter (about 35 degrees) should be cold and unyielding when pressed with a finger. To chill butter quickly, cut it into small pieces and freeze until very firm, 10 to 15 minutes. Softened butter (65 to 67 degrees) will bend easily without breaking and will give slightly when pressed. To soften butter quickly, you can place cold butter in a plastic bag and use a rolling pin to pound it to the desired consistency, or you can cut the butter into small pieces and let it sit until softened. (For our microwave method, see below.) For melted and cooled butter (85 to 90 degrees), melt the butter on the stovetop or in the microwave then let it cool for about 5 minutes.

SOFTENING BUTTER IN THE MICROWAVE: If you're going to soften butter in the microwave, here's how to keep it from melting. Microwave 4 tablespoons butter in one piece for 1 minute at 10 percent power. Press on the butter with your finger to see if it is sufficiently softened; if not, heat for an additional 20 seconds at 10 percent power. For each additional 2 tablespoons of butter, increase the second microwave intervals by 10 seconds.

RESCUING OVERSOFTENED BUTTER: The fat in butter is partially crystalline and highly sensitive to temperature changes. When butter is properly softened to 65 or 70 degrees, the tiny crystals surround and stabilize the air bubbles that are generated during creaming. When heated to the melting point, however, these crystals are destroyed. They can be reestablished but only if the butter is rapidly chilled. To quickly cool partially melted butter, mix the butter with a few ice cubes. Once the butter has cooled to a softened stage—right below 70 degrees—remove the ice.

For a supremely chocolaty Bundt cake, we bloom the chocolate with hot water and add vanilla and espresso to bring out its flavor.

Rich Chocolate Bundt Cakes

SERVES 2

✔ WHY THIS RECIPE WORKS: Too often, chocolate Bundt cakes look better than they taste: all those pretty fluted edges usually boast only muted chocolate flavor. To infuse our Bundt cake with serious chocolate flavor, we used both bittersweet chocolate and cocoa powder. Borrowing a technique from devil's food cake, we poured boiling water over the chocolate to bloom its flavor and help the cocoa particles distribute more evenly through the batter. Vanilla and espresso powder complemented the floral nuances of the chocolate, adding more depth of flavor. For deeper caramelized flavor and extra moisture, we swapped out white sugar for brown. As a final touch, we greased the pans using cocoa powder instead of flour to avoid an unattractive white film. You will need two 1-cup Bundt pans for this recipe—the center tube is necessary to facilitate even baking. For an accurate measurement of boiling water, bring a full kettle of water to a boil and then measure out the desired amount.

3 tablespoons unsweetened cocoa powder
2 tablespoons unsalted butter, softened, plus 1 tablespoon melted, for pans
1½ ounces bittersweet chocolate, chopped fine
¼ teaspoon instant espresso powder or instant coffee powder
2 tablespoons boiling water
3 tablespoons sour cream, room temperature
½ teaspoon vanilla extract
⅓ cup (1⅔ ounces) all-purpose flour
¼ teaspoon baking soda
¼ teaspoon salt
⅓ cup packed (2⅓ ounces) light brown sugar
1 large egg, room temperature
Confectioners' sugar

1. Adjust oven rack to middle position and heat oven to 350 degrees. Mix 1 tablespoon cocoa and melted butter into paste. Using pastry brush, thoroughly coat interior of two 1-cup Bundt pans with paste.

2. Combine chocolate, espresso powder, and remaining 2 tablespoons cocoa in small bowl. Pour boiling water over mixture, cover, and let sit until chocolate is melted, 3 to 5 minutes. Whisk mixture gently until smooth. Let cool to room temperature, then whisk in sour cream and vanilla. In separate bowl, whisk flour, baking soda, and salt together.

3. Using hand-held mixer set at low speed, beat brown sugar and softened butter in medium bowl until sugar is moistened, about 1 minute. Increase speed to medium-high and beat mixture until pale and fluffy, about 3 minutes, scraping down sides of bowl as needed. Add egg and beat until combined, about 30 seconds (batter may look slightly curdled). Reduce speed to low and add flour mixture in 2 additions, alternating with chocolate mixture. Give batter final stir by hand.

Preparing a Bundt Pan

Our preferred method for preparing a Bundt pan is to coat it thoroughly with baking spray with flour, which contains both oil and flour. However, if you don't have baking spray, this method works just as well.

Make paste with 1 tablespoon flour or cocoa powder (for chocolate cakes) and 1 tablespoon melted butter. Apply paste to inside of Bundt pans with pastry brush, taking care to reach all nooks and crannies.

4. Divide batter evenly between prepared pans, smooth tops, and gently tap each pan on counter to release air bubbles. Wipe any drops of batter off sides of pans. Place pans on rimmed baking sheet and bake cakes until toothpick inserted in center comes out with a few moist crumbs attached, 20 to 22 minutes, rotating sheet halfway through baking.

5. Let cakes cool in pans on wire rack for 10 minutes. Remove cakes from pans and let cool completely on rack, about 1 hour. Dust with confectioners' sugar and serve.

Bold and Spicy Gingerbread Cakes

SERVES 2

✔ **WHY THIS RECIPE WORKS:** Most gingerbread cakes miss the mark, with a cloying sweetness and ginger that is either too harsh or too muted. We wanted a moist cake with bold, spicy ginger flavor and balanced sweetness. Creaming the butter and sugar made the cakes too fluffy, but simply melting the butter and mixing everything together gave us the rich, dense texture we were after. We liked robust molasses for a fuller flavor. A combination of ground dried ginger and grated fresh ginger was key to creating the bite we were after. Cinnamon, allspice, and a pinch of pepper complemented the ginger nicely, and blooming the spices in the melted butter rounded out their flavors. If desired, you can substitute 1 teaspoon water for the bourbon in the glaze. You will need two 1-cup Bundt pans for this recipe—the center tube is necessary to facilitate even baking.

CAKES

⅓ cup (1⅔ ounces) all-purpose flour
¼ teaspoon baking powder
⅛ teaspoon baking soda
⅛ teaspoon salt
2 tablespoons unsalted butter
¼ teaspoon ground ginger
¼ teaspoon ground cinnamon
⅛ teaspoon ground allspice
Pinch finely ground pepper
1 large egg, room temperature
3 tablespoons granulated sugar
½ teaspoon grated fresh ginger
2 tablespoons robust or full molasses
1 tablespoon water

BOURBON GLAZE

½ cup (2 ounces) confectioners' sugar, plus extra as needed
1½ teaspoons water
1 teaspoon bourbon

1. FOR THE CAKES: Adjust oven rack to middle position and heat oven to 375 degrees. Spray two 1-cup Bundt pans with baking spray with flour.

2. Whisk flour, baking powder, baking soda, and salt together in bowl. Melt butter in small saucepan over medium heat. Add ground ginger, cinnamon, allspice, and pepper and cook until fragrant, about 30 seconds. Off heat, let cool slightly.

3. Whisk egg, sugar, and fresh ginger together in medium bowl until light and frothy. Whisk in cooled butter mixture, molasses, and water until smooth and thoroughly combined. Gently whisk in flour mixture until just combined. Give batter final stir with rubber spatula.

4. Divide batter evenly between prepared pans, smooth tops, and gently tap each pan on counter to release air bubbles. Wipe any drops of batter off sides of pans. Place pans on rimmed baking sheet and bake cakes until toothpick inserted in center comes out with a few moist crumbs attached, 20 to 25 minutes, rotating sheet halfway through baking.

5. Let cakes cool in pans on wire rack set over baking sheet for 10 minutes. Remove cakes from pans and let cool completely on rack, about 1 hour.

6. FOR THE BOURBON GLAZE: Whisk sugar, water, and bourbon together in bowl until smooth, adding extra sugar as needed to achieve thick but still pourable consistency. Pour glaze over tops of cooled cakes, letting glaze drip down sides. Let glaze set before serving, about 25 minutes.

Checking a Cake for Doneness

To check cake for doneness, insert toothpick into center; it should come out with just a few moist crumbs attached. If you see raw batter, continue to bake cake, checking every few minutes.

Almond Cakes

SERVES 2

✔ **WHY THIS RECIPE WORKS:** Almond cake is a versatile dessert, as good eaten plain as it is adorned with a simple sauce, whipped cream, or fresh berries. It should be lightly sweet, with a texture like coarse pound cake. We found that a cup of ground almonds and ¼ cup of cake flour created the rustic texture we were after without making the cake too heavy and dense. To prevent the almonds from turning into nut butter when ground, we processed them with 2 tablespoons of sugar. Another 5 tablespoons of sugar in the cake provided just enough sweetness—any more and the cake formed a sickly sweet, candylike crust. Adding 2 tablespoons of milk gave our batter just the right consistency without dulling any of the almond flavor. You will need two 4½-inch springform pans for this recipe. Be careful not to overtoast the almonds or the cakes will have a dry, crumbly texture. Serve with Whipped Cream (page 363) and fresh berries.

1 cup slivered almonds, toasted
7 tablespoons (3 ounces) granulated sugar
Pinch salt
¼ cup (1 ounce) cake flour
¼ teaspoon baking powder
2 tablespoons unsalted butter, softened
1 large egg, room temperature
2 tablespoons whole milk, room temperature
Confectioners' sugar

1. Adjust oven rack to middle position and heat oven to 325 degrees. Grease two 4½-inch springform pans.

2. Process almonds, 2 tablespoons granulated sugar, and salt in food processor until very finely ground, about 15 seconds. Add flour and baking powder and pulse to incorporate, about 5 pulses.

3. Using hand-held mixer set at low speed, beat butter and remaining 5 tablespoons granulated sugar in medium bowl until sugar is moistened, about 1 minute. Increase speed to medium-high and beat mixture until pale and fluffy, about 3 minutes, scraping down sides of bowl as needed. Add egg and beat until combined, about 30 seconds. Reduce speed to low and slowly add ground almond mixture until combined, 15 to 30 seconds. Add milk and beat until combined, 15 to 30 seconds. Give batter final stir by hand.

4. Divide batter evenly between prepared pans, smooth tops, and gently tap each pan on counter to release air bubbles. Wipe any drops of batter off sides of pans. Place pans on rimmed baking sheet and bake cakes until tops are golden brown and toothpick inserted in center comes out with a few moist crumbs attached, 25 to 30 minutes, rotating sheet halfway through baking.

5. Let cakes cool in pans on wire rack for 10 minutes. Run thin knife around edges of cakes, remove sides of pans, and let cool slightly, about 30 minutes. Slide thin metal spatula between cakes and pan bottoms to loosen, then slide cakes onto individual serving plates. Dust with confectioners' sugar and serve warm.

Rustic Peach Cakes

SERVES 2

✔ **WHY THIS RECIPE WORKS:** We wanted a recipe for a rustic yellow cake studded with chunks of juicy fresh peaches. To develop a cake sturdy enough to support the peaches, we altered our recipe for yellow cake. Substituting all-purpose flour for the cake flour gave the cake a sturdier crumb, as did replacing the milk with sour cream. Swapping some of the white sugar for light brown sugar added a subtle caramel flavor. To get rid of some of the peaches' excess moisture, we tossed them with cinnamon and sugar and let them sit while we prepared the batter. Scattering dried peaches over the batter added an extra layer of peach flavor without adding more moisture. Look for barely ripe peaches that give slightly to the touch; overly ripe peaches will make this cake soggy. You will need two 4½-inch springform pans for this recipe. Serve with vanilla ice cream or Whipped Cream (page 363).

¼ cup (1¾ ounces) granulated sugar
⅛ teaspoon ground cinnamon
1 peach, peeled, halved, pitted, and cut into 8 wedges
½ cup (2½ ounces) all-purpose flour
½ teaspoon baking powder
⅛ teaspoon salt
4 tablespoons unsalted butter, softened
2 tablespoons packed light brown sugar
1 large egg, room temperature
1 tablespoon sour cream, room temperature
½ teaspoon vanilla extract
3 tablespoons finely chopped dried peaches or apricots

1. Adjust oven rack to middle position and heat oven to 350 degrees. Grease two 4½-inch springform pans.

2. Combine 2 tablespoons granulated sugar and cinnamon in medium bowl. Measure out and reserve 1 tablespoon cinnamon sugar. Add peach wedges to bowl with remaining cinnamon sugar and toss to coat.

3. In separate bowl, whisk flour, baking powder, and salt together. Using hand-held mixer set at low speed, beat butter, brown sugar, and remaining 2 tablespoons granulated sugar in second medium bowl until sugar is moistened, about 1 minute. Increase speed to medium-high and beat mixture until pale and fluffy, about 3 minutes, scraping down sides of bowl as needed. Add egg, sour cream, and vanilla and beat until combined, about 30 seconds. Reduce speed to low and slowly add flour mixture. Give batter final stir by hand.

4. Divide batter evenly between prepared pans, smooth tops, and gently tap each pan on counter to release air bubbles. Wipe any drops of batter off sides of pans. Scatter dried peaches evenly over batter, then arrange 4 sugared peach wedges in pinwheel pattern over top in each pan. Sprinkle reserved cinnamon sugar mixture evenly over peaches.

5. Place pans on rimmed baking sheet and bake cakes until tops are golden brown and toothpick inserted in center comes out with a few moist crumbs attached, 30 to 35 minutes, rotating sheet halfway through baking.

6. Let cakes cool completely in pans on wire rack, about 1½ hours. Run thin knife around edges of cakes and remove sides of pans. Slide thin metal spatula between cakes and pan bottoms to loosen, then slide cakes onto individual serving plates. Serve.

Pineapple Upside-Down Cake

SERVES 2

✔ **WHY THIS RECIPE WORKS:** Pineapple upside-down cake is a classic American dessert, but it can be difficult to achieve perfectly caramelized pineapple and a cake that is tender yet sturdy enough to support the fruit. We wanted all the elements to be perfect—and we wanted it to serve just two people. A 6-inch cake pan made a nice size cake for two, and a moist butter cake was a nice foil for the bright, fruity pineapple. To streamline our recipe, we skipped cooking the pineapple separately on the stovetop. Instead, we melted butter right in the cake pan in the oven, stirred in brown sugar until it dissolved, and placed the pineapple directly on top. To maximize the amount of pineapple we could fit in the smaller pan, we traded in the usual rings for smaller chunks, which we could nestle tightly together. Do not substitute canned pineapple. You will need a 6-inch round cake pan for this recipe. To ensure a clean release, let the cake cool in the pan for no more than 10 minutes before inverting it.

  6 **tablespoons unsalted butter, cut into 6 pieces and softened**
 ⅓ **cup packed (2⅓ ounces) light brown sugar**
1½ **cups ½-inch pineapple pieces**
 ¾ **cup (3¾ ounces) all-purpose flour**
 ¾ **teaspoon baking powder**
 ¼ **teaspoon salt**
 ⅓ **cup (2⅓ ounces) granulated sugar**
 1 **large egg, room temperature**
 ½ **teaspoon vanilla extract**
 3 **tablespoons whole milk, room temperature**

1. Adjust oven rack to lower-middle position and heat oven to 350 degrees. Place 2 tablespoons butter in 6-inch round cake pan and place in oven until butter melts, 2 to 4 minutes.

Using rubber spatula, stir brown sugar into pan with melted butter, then pat mixture into even layer. Place pineapple pieces on top of sugar mixture and press into single layer.

2. Whisk flour, baking powder, and salt together in bowl. Using hand-held mixer set at low speed, beat remaining 4 tablespoons butter and granulated sugar in medium bowl until sugar is moistened, about 1 minute. Increase speed to medium-high and beat mixture until pale and fluffy, about 3 minutes, scraping down sides of bowl as needed. Add egg and vanilla and beat until combined, about 30 seconds. Reduce speed to low and add flour mixture in 2 additions, alternating with milk (batter will be quite thick). Give batter final stir by hand.

3. Scrape batter into pan over pineapple, smooth top, and gently tap pan on counter to release air bubbles. Wipe any drops of batter off side of pan. Bake cake until toothpick inserted in center comes out with a few moist crumbs attached, 45 to 50 minutes, rotating pan halfway through baking.

4. Let cake cool in pan on wire rack for 10 minutes. Place inverted serving platter over pan, flip pan and plate together, and let sit until cake releases itself from pan (do not shake or tap pan), about 1 minute. Gently remove pan, replacing any pineapple pieces that fall off. Let cake cool completely, about 1 hour, before serving.

Cutting Up a Pineapple

1. Trim off bottom and top of pineapple so it sits flat on counter.

2. Rest pineapple on trimmed bottom and cut off skin in thin strips from top to bottom, using sharp paring, chef's, or serrated knife.

3. Quarter pineapple lengthwise, then cut tough core from each quarter. Slice pineapple according to recipe.

With decadent, creamy chocolate frosting, our fluffiest-ever yellow cake is the perfect dessert for any special occasion for two.

Fluffy Yellow Layer Cake

SERVES 2

✔ **WHY THIS RECIPE WORKS:** We wanted a yellow layer cake with the same ethereal texture and supreme fluffiness as the cakes that come from a box—without the mysterious chemical additives. We found that the secret was to use a chiffon cake method (whipping egg whites separately and folding them into the batter at the end) to lighten the cake and a combination of fats (butter plus vegetable oil) to keep the butter flavor intact while improving the moistness of the cake. For extra tenderness, we increased the sugar and substituted buttermilk for milk. Two 6-inch cake pans gave us a perfectly sized layer cake for two. Be sure to bring all of the ingredients to room temperature before beginning this recipe. You will need two 6-inch round cake pans for this recipe. We recommend using a small offset spatula to easily and neatly frost the cake. You can use Chocolate Frosting (recipe follows) or Vanilla Frosting (page 400) in this recipe.

2 large egg yolks plus 1 large white, room temperature
½ cup (3½ ounces) sugar
¾ cup (3 ounces) cake flour
½ teaspoon baking powder
⅛ teaspoon baking soda
¼ teaspoon salt
⅓ cup buttermilk, room temperature
3 tablespoons unsalted butter, melted and cooled
1 tablespoon vegetable oil
¾ teaspoon vanilla extract
2 cups frosting

1. Adjust oven rack to middle position and heat oven to 350 degrees. Grease two 6-inch round cake pans, line with parchment paper, grease parchment, and flour pans.

2. Using hand-held mixer set at medium-low speed, beat egg white in medium bowl until foamy, about 1 minute. Increase speed to medium-high and beat white to soft, billowy mounds, about 1 minute. Gradually add 2 tablespoons sugar and beat until glossy, stiff peaks form, 1 to 2 minutes, scraping down sides of bowl as needed; set aside.

3. Whisk flour, baking powder, baking soda, salt, and remaining 6 tablespoons sugar together in second medium bowl. In small bowl, whisk buttermilk, melted butter, oil, vanilla, and egg yolks together. Using hand-held mixer set at low speed, gradually pour butter mixture into flour mixture and mix until almost combined (a few streaks of dry flour will remain), 15 to 30 seconds. Scrape down bowl, then beat on medium-low speed until smooth and fully combined, 10 to 15 seconds.

4. Using rubber spatula, stir one-third of whites into batter, then add remaining whites and gently fold into batter until no white streaks remain. Divide batter evenly between prepared pans, smooth tops, and gently tap each pan on counter to release air bubbles. Wipe any drops of batter off sides of pans. Bake cakes until toothpick inserted in center comes out with a few moist crumbs attached, 16 to 18 minutes, rotating pans halfway through baking.

5. Let cakes cool in pans on wire rack for 10 minutes. Run knife around edge of cakes to loosen. Remove cakes from pans, discarding parchment, and let cool completely on rack, about 1 hour. (Cooled cakes can be wrapped tightly in plastic wrap and stored at room temperature for up to 1 day. Wrapped tightly in plastic, then aluminum foil, cakes can be frozen for up to 1 month. Defrost cakes at room temperature before unwrapping and frosting.)

6. Line edges of cake platter with 4 strips of parchment paper to keep platter clean. Place 1 cake layer on platter. Spread ½ cup frosting evenly over top, right to edge of cake. Top with second cake layer, press lightly to adhere, then spread ½ cup frosting evenly over top. Spread remaining 1 cup frosting evenly over sides of cake. To smooth frosting, run edge of offset spatula around cake sides and over top, or create billows by pressing back of spoon into frosting and twirling spoon as you lift away. Carefully remove parchment strips before serving. (Assembled cake can be refrigerated for up to 1 day. Bring to room temperature before serving.)

Chocolate Frosting

MAKES ABOUT 2 CUPS

To make this frosting for cupcakes, cut all ingredients in half.

- 6 ounces milk, bittersweet, or semisweet chocolate, chopped
- 14 tablespoons unsalted butter, softened
- ⅔ cup (2⅔ ounces) confectioners' sugar
- ½ cup (1½ ounces) unsweetened cocoa powder
  Pinch salt
- ½ cup light corn syrup
- 1 teaspoon vanilla extract

Microwave chocolate in bowl at 50 percent power, stirring occasionally, until melted and smooth, 2 to 4 minutes. Let cool slightly. Process butter, sugar, cocoa, and salt in food processor until smooth, about 10 seconds, scraping down sides of bowl as needed. Add corn syrup and vanilla and process until just combined, 5 to 10 seconds. Add melted chocolate and pulse until smooth and creamy, about 5 pulses. (Frosting can be kept at room temperature for up to 3 hours before using or refrigerated for up to 3 days. If refrigerated, let sit at room temperature for 1 hour before using.)

Two Ways to Chop Chocolate

A. WITH A KNIFE: Hold knife at 45-degree angle to corner of block of chocolate and bear down evenly. After cutting about 1 inch from corner, repeat with other corners.

B. WITH A LARGE FORK: Alternatively, use sharp 2-tined meat fork to break chocolate into smaller pieces.

Chocolate Layer Cake

SERVES 2

✅ **WHY THIS RECIPE WORKS:** A beautifully frosted chocolate layer cake is the perfect dessert for any special occasion, but in a small household, most of it will go stale and dry out before it can be enjoyed. To make a petite layer cake suited for two, we needed to scale back our recipe to fill two 6-inch cake pans. For rich chocolate flavor, we used both cocoa powder and unsweetened chocolate. A small amount of instant espresso powder further enhanced the chocolate flavor. We added boiling water to the chocolate mixture to dissolve the espresso powder and intensify the chocolate flavor. Sour cream ensured that the cake stayed moist, and brown sugar provided subtle caramelized notes. You will need two 6-inch round cake pans for this recipe. For an accurate measurement of boiling water, bring a full kettle of water to a boil and then measure out the desired amount. We recommend using a small offset spatula to easily and neatly frost the cake. You can use Vanilla Frosting (recipe follows) or Chocolate Frosting (at left) in this recipe.

- 1½ ounces unsweetened chocolate, chopped
- 3 tablespoons unsweetened cocoa powder
- ¼ teaspoon instant espresso powder or instant coffee powder
- ½ cup boiling water
- ¼ cup sour cream, room temperature
- ¼ teaspoon vanilla extract
- ½ cup (2½ ounces) all-purpose flour
- ½ teaspoon baking soda
- ⅛ teaspoon baking powder
- ¼ teaspoon salt
- 4 tablespoons unsalted butter, softened
- ½ cup packed (3½ ounces) light brown sugar
- 1 large egg, room temperature
- 2 cups frosting

1. Adjust oven rack to middle position and heat oven to 350 degrees. Grease two 6-inch round cake pans, line with parchment paper, grease parchment, and flour pans.

2. Combine chocolate, cocoa, and espresso powder in small bowl. Pour boiling water over mixture, cover, and let sit until chocolate is melted, 3 to 5 minutes. Whisk mixture gently until smooth. Let cool to room temperature, then whisk in sour cream and vanilla. In separate bowl, whisk flour, baking soda, baking powder, and salt together.

3. Using hand-held mixer set at low speed, beat butter and sugar in medium bowl until sugar is moistened, about 1 minute. Increase speed to medium-high and beat mixture until pale and fluffy, about 3 minutes, scraping down sides of bowl as needed. Add egg and beat until combined, about 30 seconds. Reduce speed to low and add flour mixture in 2 additions, alternating with chocolate mixture. Give batter final stir by hand.

4. Divide batter evenly between prepared pans, smooth tops, and gently tap each pan on counter to release air bubbles. Wipe any drops of batter off sides of pans. Bake cakes until toothpick inserted in center comes out with a few moist crumbs attached, 20 to 25 minutes, rotating pans halfway through baking.

5. Let cakes cool in pans on wire rack for 10 minutes. Run knife around edge of cakes to loosen. Remove cakes from pans, discarding parchment, and let cool completely on rack, about 1 hour. (Cooled cakes can be wrapped tightly in plastic wrap and stored at room temperature for up to 1 day. Wrapped tightly in plastic, then aluminum foil, cakes can be frozen for up to 1 month. Defrost cakes at room temperature before unwrapping and frosting.)

6. Line edges of cake platter with 4 strips of parchment paper to keep platter clean. Place 1 cake layer on platter. Spread ½ cup frosting evenly over top, right to edge of cake. Top with second cake layer, press lightly to adhere, then spread ½ cup frosting evenly over top. Spread remaining 1 cup frosting evenly over sides of cake. To smooth frosting, run edge of offset spatula around cake sides and over top, or create billows by pressing back of spoon into frosting and twirling spoon as you lift away. Carefully remove parchment strips before serving. (Assembled cake can be refrigerated for up to 1 day. Bring to room temperature before serving.)

Vanilla Frosting
MAKES ABOUT 2 CUPS

To make this frosting for cupcakes, cut all ingredients in half. Be sure to use unsalted butter here. For fun, consider adding some color to the frosting by stirring in a few drops of food coloring.

2	tablespoons heavy cream
1½	teaspoons vanilla extract
⅛	teaspoon salt
16	tablespoons unsalted butter, softened
2	cups (8 ounces) confectioners' sugar

Stir cream, vanilla, and salt together in bowl until salt dissolves. Using hand-held mixer set at medium-high speed, beat butter in medium bowl until smooth, 30 to 60 seconds, scraping down sides of bowl as needed. Reduce speed to medium-low, gradually add sugar, and beat until smooth, about 2 minutes. Add cream mixture and beat until combined, about 30 seconds. Increase speed to medium-high and beat until frosting is pale and fluffy, about 5 minutes.

VARIATIONS
Coffee Frosting
To make this frosting for cupcakes, cut all ingredients in half.

Add 4 teaspoons instant espresso powder or instant coffee powder to cream mixture.

Coconut Frosting
To make this frosting for cupcakes, cut all ingredients in half.

Add 2 teaspoons coconut extract to cream mixture.

NOTES FROM THE TEST KITCHEN

How to Bake a Perfect Layer Cake

Layer cakes aren't difficult to make, but sometimes problems can occur. Here are a few tips to help you avoid some common pitfalls.

PREP THE PANS: To ensure a dependable cake release every time, first grease the inside of the pan evenly with a thin coat of butter or vegetable shortening. Next, fit the pans with a piece of parchment paper. The paper prevents the formation of a tough outer crust and helps the cake hold together when it is removed from the pan. The trick to getting a piece of parchment that fits the bottom of a cake pan is to trace the outline of the bottom of the pan onto the parchment. When cutting out the outline, cut on the inside of the line so that the round fits snugly inside the pan. Fit the trimmed piece of parchment into the pan, then grease the paper. Finally, sprinkle flour (or cocoa powder for chocolate cakes) in the cake pan, then shake and rotate to coat evenly with the flour; shake out any remaining flour.

PORTION THE BATTER CAREFULLY: Portioning the batter evenly is essential to making level cake layers that stack easily when layered. Weighing the filled pans is the most accurate way to gauge even portions. If you don't have a scale, use a ruler to measure the space between the top of the batter and the top of the pan, then re-portion the batter if needed.

SLICE OFF DOMED TOPS: Cake layers with a domed top are difficult to stack and frost. To prevent domed layers, make sure your oven is running at the right temperature by using an oven thermometer. If it's too hot, the heat can cause your cakes to crack and dome. That said, if your cakes do crack and dome, you can simply slice the domed section off to make a level layer.

BEFORE FROSTING, BRUSH THE CAKE WITH A PASTRY BRUSH: To get a crumb-free finish, brush the cake layers gently with a pastry brush to remove any unwanted crumbs before frosting the cake. This will prevent the crumbs from getting embedded in the frosting. Also be sure to cool the cake completely before frosting it; warm cake is more delicate and likely to tear.

FOR PERFECT SLICES, RUN THE KNIFE UNDER HOT WATER: For neat slices of cake, it is helpful to clean the knife with hot water before slicing each piece—you can do this at the sink or in a pitcher of hot water if you're cutting the cake at the table—and wipe the knife dry before slicing. This prevents the cake and frosting (or cheesecake filling) from sticking to the knife, which can make a mess as you try to slice your third or fourth piece of cake.

Carrot Cake with Cream Cheese Frosting

SERVES 2

✔ **WHY THIS RECIPE WORKS:** We wanted a carrot cake that was moist and rich—not soggy or greasy—with a tender crumb and balanced spice flavor. Getting the ingredient proportions just right was tricky. Too much oil made the cake heavy and greasy; too little made it lean and lacking in richness. Too much spice overpowered the sweet carrot flavor, but too little left the cake bland. And the shredded carrots could quickly turn the whole thing soggy. We tried precooking the carrots to rid them of some of their moisture, but precooked carrots turned to mush in the cake. Instead, we scaled back the carrots until we had just the right amount of moisture; one small carrot was enough to give the cake its distinct flavor. For a rich, decadent cream cheese frosting, we added vanilla extract and a pinch of salt to give the frosting a rich flavor that wasn't cloying.

CAKE

- ⅔ cup (3⅓ ounces) all-purpose flour
- ½ teaspoon ground cinnamon
- ¼ teaspoon baking powder
- ⅛ teaspoon baking soda
- ⅛ teaspoon salt
- ⅛ teaspoon ground nutmeg
- Pinch ground cloves
- ⅓ cup (2⅓ ounces) granulated sugar
- ¼ cup vegetable oil
- 1 large egg, room temperature
- 2 tablespoons packed light brown sugar
- 1 small carrot, peeled and shredded

FROSTING

- 4 ounces cream cheese, softened
- 2 tablespoons unsalted butter, softened
- ½ teaspoon vanilla extract
- Pinch salt
- ½ cup (2 ounces) confectioners' sugar

1. FOR THE CAKE: Adjust oven rack to middle position and heat oven to 350 degrees. Grease 7¼ by 5¼-inch baking dish, line with parchment paper, grease parchment, and flour dish.

2. Whisk flour, cinnamon, baking powder, baking soda, salt, nutmeg, and cloves together in bowl. In medium bowl, whisk granulated sugar, oil, egg, and brown sugar together until smooth and thoroughly combined. Gently whisk in flour mixture until just combined. Stir in carrot.

3. Scrape batter into prepared dish, smooth top, and gently tap dish on counter to release air bubbles. Wipe any drops of batter off side of dish. Bake cake until toothpick inserted in center comes out with a few moist crumbs attached, 30 to 40 minutes, rotating dish halfway through baking.

4. Let cake cool in dish on wire rack for 10 minutes. Run knife around edge of cake to loosen. Remove cake from dish, discarding parchment, and let cool completely on rack, about 1 hour.

5. FOR THE FROSTING: Using hand-held mixer set at medium-high speed, beat cream cheese, butter, vanilla, and salt in medium bowl until smooth, 1 to 2 minutes, scraping down sides of bowl as needed. Reduce speed to medium-low, gradually add sugar, and beat until smooth, 2 to 3 minutes. Increase speed to medium-high and beat until frosting is pale and fluffy, 2 to 3 minutes. Spread frosting evenly over cake and serve. (Cake can be refrigerated for up to 1 day. Bring to room temperature before serving.)

Vanilla Cupcakes

MAKES 4 CUPCAKES

✔ **WHY THIS RECIPE WORKS:** Cupcakes are a natural choice when you want a small-scale dessert, but most recipes produce at least a dozen. We wanted a recipe for just four fluffy, tender, snowy-white cupcakes. Using cake flour and doubling up on leaveners ensured that our cupcakes had golden, rounded tops and a tender crumb. Buttermilk gave the cupcakes a tangy richness. To avoid having to pull out our electric mixer, we melted the butter and simply stirred everything together by hand. Make sure not to overmix the batter or the cupcakes will turn out tough. Any muffin tin with standard-size cups will work here, and the batter can be placed in any of the cups. We recommend using a small offset spatula to easily and neatly frost the cupcakes. You can use Vanilla Frosting (page 400) or Chocolate Frosting (page 399) in this recipe.

- ¾ cup (3 ounces) cake flour
- ¼ teaspoon baking powder
- ⅛ teaspoon baking soda
- ⅛ teaspoon salt
- ¼ cup (1¾ ounces) sugar
- 1 large egg, room temperature
- 3 tablespoons unsalted butter, melted and cooled
- ¼ cup buttermilk, room temperature
- ½ teaspoon vanilla extract
- 1 cup frosting

1. Adjust oven rack to middle position and heat oven to 325 degrees. Line 4 cups of muffin tin with paper or foil liners.

2. Whisk flour, baking powder, baking soda, and salt together in bowl. In medium bowl, whisk sugar, egg, and melted butter together until smooth. Whisk in buttermilk and vanilla until thoroughly combined. Sift flour mixture over egg mixture in 2 additions, whisking gently after each addition until a few streaks of flour remain. Continue to whisk batter until most of lumps are gone (do not overmix).

3. Using dry measuring cup or ice cream scoop, divide batter evenly among prepared muffin cups. Bake cupcakes until golden brown and toothpick inserted in center comes out clean, 18 to 22 minutes, rotating muffin tin halfway through baking.

4. Let cupcakes cool in muffin tin on wire rack for 10 minutes. Remove cupcakes from muffin tin and let cool completely on rack, about 1 hour. Spread 3 to 4 tablespoons frosting over each cooled cupcake and serve.

Chocolate Cupcakes

MAKES 4 CUPCAKES

✔ **WHY THIS RECIPE WORKS:** Developing a recipe for decadent chocolate cupcakes wasn't as easy as adding chocolate to our white cupcakes. We found that cake flour didn't provide enough structure to support the added chocolate, giving us crumbly cupcakes that fell apart in our hands. All-purpose flour proved to be a better option. The flavor of the buttermilk was out of place here, but a few tablespoons of whole milk gave us a tender crumb without affecting the flavor. A combination of bittersweet chocolate and cocoa powder gave us decadent chocolate flavor. A little salt and vanilla extract rounded out the flavors. Any muffin tin with standard-size cups will work here, and the batter can be placed in any of the cups. We recommend using a small offset spatula to easily and neatly frost the cupcakes. You can use Vanilla Frosting (page 400) or Chocolate Frosting (page 399) in this recipe.

¼ cup (1¼ ounces) all-purpose flour

¼ teaspoon baking powder

⅛ teaspoon baking soda

⅛ teaspoon salt

4 tablespoons unsalted butter, cut into 3 pieces

1½ ounces bittersweet chocolate, chopped

3 tablespoons unsweetened cocoa powder

¼ cup (1¾ ounces) sugar

1 large egg, room temperature

3 tablespoons whole milk, room temperature

½ teaspoon vanilla extract

1 cup frosting

A combination of bittersweet chocolate and cocoa powder gives these easy cupcakes intense chocolate flavor.

1. Adjust oven rack to middle position and heat oven to 325 degrees. Line 4 cups of muffin tin with paper or foil liners. Whisk flour, baking powder, baking soda, and salt together in bowl.

2. In separate bowl, microwave butter, chocolate, and cocoa at 50 percent power, stirring occasionally, until melted and smooth, about 1 minute; let cool slightly. Whisk sugar and egg together in medium bowl until smooth. Whisk in milk and vanilla until combined. Whisk in cooled chocolate mixture until well combined. Sift flour mixture over chocolate mixture in 2 additions, whisking gently after each addition until a few streaks of flour remain (batter will be thick). Continue to whisk batter until most of lumps are gone (do not overmix).

3. Using dry measuring cup or ice cream scoop, divide batter evenly among prepared muffin cups. Bake cupcakes until toothpick inserted into center comes out clean, 18 to 22 minutes, rotating muffin tin halfway through baking.

4. Let cupcakes cool in pan on wire rack for 10 minutes. Remove cupcakes from muffin tin and let cool completely on rack, about 1 hour. Spread 3 to 4 tablespoons frosting over each cooled cupcake and serve.

Lemon Pudding Cake

SERVES 2

✔ **WHY THIS RECIPE WORKS:** Somewhere between a cake and a custard, lemon pudding cake should separate into two layers as it bakes, with light, airy cake topping a creamy, lemony pudding. The cakey top layer depends on whipped egg whites to rise to the top while baking, so stabilizing the egg whites with some sugar was important. A high proportion of liquid—½ cup of milk—was necessary to get the pudding layer to sink. To make sure that our pudding was thick and rich, not soupy, we added a bit of cornstarch. To get the burst of bright lemon flavor we wanted, we added both lemon zest and juice. You will need a 3-cup baking dish (measuring approximately 7¼ by 5¼ inches) or dish of a similar size for this recipe. It's important to use a metal pan for the water bath—a glass baking dish may crack when you add the boiling water.

    2   large eggs, separated, room temperature
    ½   cup (3½ ounces) sugar
    4   teaspoons all-purpose flour
    ½   teaspoon cornstarch
    2   tablespoons unsalted butter, softened
    2   teaspoons grated lemon zest plus ¼ cup juice (2 lemons)
    ½   cup whole milk, room temperature

1. Adjust oven rack to lowest position and heat oven to 325 degrees. Place dish towel in bottom of 13 by 9-inch baking pan. Grease 7¼ by 5¼-inch baking dish and set on towel. Bring kettle of water to boil.

2. Using hand-held mixer set at medium-low speed, beat egg whites in large bowl until foamy, about 1 minute. Increase speed to medium-high and beat whites to soft, billowy mounds, about 1 minute. Gradually add 6 tablespoons sugar and beat until glossy, stiff peaks form, 2 to 6 minutes; set aside.

3. Whisk flour and cornstarch together in small bowl. Using hand-held mixer set at medium-high speed, beat butter, lemon zest, and remaining 2 tablespoons sugar in medium bowl until pale and fluffy, about 3 minutes, scraping down sides of bowl as needed. Add egg yolks and beat until combined, about 30 seconds. Reduce speed to low and slowly add flour mixture until combined, about 30 seconds. Add milk and lemon juice and beat until just combined.

4. Using rubber spatula, stir one-third of whites into batter, then add remaining whites and gently fold into batter until no white streaks remain. Scrape batter into prepared dish and smooth top. Set pan on oven rack. Taking care not to splash water into dish, pour enough boiling water into pan to reach halfway up sides of dish. Bake cake until surface is golden brown and edges are set (center should jiggle slightly when gently shaken), about 1 hour.

5. Carefully transfer baking dish to wire rack and let cake cool until warm, about 30 minutes. Serve warm or at room temperature.

Making a Water Bath

1. To prevent baking dish (or ramekins) from sliding, line bottom of metal baking pan with dish towel. Then place baking dish on top.

2. Add batter to baking dish set inside baking pan; transfer pan to oven. Then carefully pour boiling water into pan, halfway up sides of baking dish.

Warm Chocolate Fudge Cakes

SERVES 2

✔ **WHY THIS RECIPE WORKS:** To bring this restaurant favorite home for two, we started by building a rich, brownie-like cake batter with an intense chocolate flavor. Moderate amounts of vegetable oil and chocolate ensured that our cakes were plenty moist and boasted a good jolt of chocolaty flavor. Half an egg also contributed to our cakes' moistness and richness, and a small amount of flour gave our cakes more structure and lift. Finally, for a gooey center, we pressed a square of chocolate into each ramekin before baking, giving us individual cakes with a big burst of chocolate and a rich, fudgy center. You will need two 6-ounce ramekins for this recipe. Serve these cakes warm in their ramekins and top them with vanilla ice cream, if desired.

    6   tablespoons (1¾ ounces) all-purpose flour
    ¼   teaspoon baking powder
    ⅛   teaspoon baking soda
    ⅛   teaspoon salt
    3   ounces bittersweet chocolate (2 ounces chopped, 1 ounce broken into two ½-ounce pieces)
    ¼   cup whole milk, room temperature

For chocolate fudge cakes with rich, gooey centers, we press a piece of chocolate into the center of each cake before baking.

3 tablespoons packed light brown sugar

2 tablespoons vegetable oil

2 tablespoons lightly beaten egg, room temperature

¼ teaspoon vanilla extract

1. Adjust oven rack to middle position and heat oven to 350 degrees. Grease and flour two 6-ounce ramekins. Whisk flour, baking powder, baking soda, and salt together in bowl.

2. Microwave 2 ounces chopped chocolate and milk in medium bowl at 50 percent power, stirring occasionally, until chocolate is melted and mixture is smooth, 1 to 3 minutes. Stir in sugar until dissolved; let cool slightly. Whisk in oil, egg, and vanilla until combined. Gently whisk in flour mixture until just combined. Give batter final stir with rubber spatula.

3. Divide batter evenly between prepared ramekins and gently tap each ramekin on counter to release air bubbles. Wipe any drops of batter off sides of ramekins. Gently press 1 square chocolate into center of each ramekin to submerge. Place ramekins on rimmed baking sheet and bake cakes until tops are just firm to touch and center is gooey when pierced with toothpick, about 15 minutes, rotating sheet halfway through baking. Let cool for 2 to 3 minutes before serving.

Tiramisù

SERVES 2

✔ **WHY THIS RECIPE WORKS:** *Tiramisù* (Italian for "pick me up") features delicate ladyfingers soaked in a spiked coffee mixture and layered with a sweet, creamy filling. To scale down this luxurious dessert, we found that a cup of mascarpone lightened with some cream made two generous servings, and just a tablespoon of dark rum added to the filling was enough for a subtly boozy backbone. Brewed espresso is impractical for most home cooks; luckily, instant espresso was an easy substitute. Soaking the ladyfingers in the flavorful liquid for just a few seconds was key for achieving the ideal saturated texture. A sprinkling of cocoa and grated chocolate made for an elegant finish. Be sure to use hard, not soft, ladyfingers. Brandy or whiskey can be substituted for the rum. You will need a 3-cup baking dish (measuring approximately 7¼ by 5¼ inches) or dish of a similar size for this recipe. Do not allow the mascarpone to warm to room temperature before using it or it may curdle. To make tiramisù without raw eggs, see page 405.

⅔ cup water, room temperature

2 tablespoons instant espresso powder

2 tablespoons dark rum

2 large egg yolks

¼ cup (1¾ ounces) sugar

Pinch salt

8 ounces (1 cup) mascarpone

¼ cup heavy cream, chilled

10–15 dried ladyfingers (savoiardi)

1 tablespoon unsweetened cocoa powder

1 tablespoon grated bittersweet or semisweet chocolate (optional)

1. Stir water, espresso powder, and 1 tablespoon rum together in shallow dish until espresso dissolves; set aside.

2. Using hand-held mixer set at low speed, beat egg yolks in large bowl until just combined, about 30 seconds. Increase speed to medium-high, add sugar and salt, and beat until pale yellow, 1 to 2 minutes, scraping down sides of bowl as needed. Add remaining 1 tablespoon rum and beat until combined, 15 to 30 seconds. Reduce speed to low, add mascarpone, and beat until no lumps remain, 15 to 30 seconds.

3. Using hand-held mixer set at medium-low speed, beat cream in small bowl until frothy, about 1 minute. Increase speed to high and beat until stiff peaks form, 1 to 3 minutes. Using rubber spatula, stir one-third of whipped cream into

Our tiramisù boasts elegant layers of espresso-and-rum-soaked ladyfingers, creamy mascarpone cheese, and whipped cream.

mascarpone mixture, then add remaining whipped cream and gently fold into mascarpone mixture until no white streaks remain.

4. Working with one at a time, drop half of ladyfingers into espresso mixture, roll to coat, remove, and transfer to 7¼ by 5¼-inch baking dish. (Do not submerge ladyfingers in espresso mixture; entire process should take no longer than 2 to 3 seconds for each cookie.) Arrange soaked cookies in single layer in dish, breaking or trimming ladyfingers as necessary to fit.

5. Spread half of mascarpone mixture over ladyfingers with spatula, spreading mixture to sides and into corners of dish, then smooth surface. Place 1½ teaspoons cocoa in fine-mesh strainer and dust cocoa over mascarpone mixture.

6. Repeat dipping and arrangement with remaining ladyfingers; spread remaining mascarpone mixture over ladyfingers and dust with remaining 1½ teaspoons cocoa. Wipe edges of dish clean with paper towel. Cover with plastic wrap and refrigerate for at least 6 hours or up to 24 hours. Sprinkle with grated chocolate, if using, and serve chilled. (Tiramisù can be refrigerated for up to 1 day.)

Tiramisù with Cooked Eggs

This recipe involves cooking the yolks in a double boiler, which requires a little more effort and makes for a slightly thicker mascarpone filling, but the results are just as good as with our traditional method. You will need an additional 2 tablespoons heavy cream.

In step 2, add 2 tablespoons cream to egg yolks after sugar and salt; do not whisk in rum. Set bowl with egg yolks over medium saucepan of barely simmering water (water should not touch bottom of bowl); cook, constantly scraping along bottom and sides of bowl with heat-resistant rubber spatula, until mixture coats back of spoon and registers 160 degrees, 3 to 5 minutes. Remove bowl from saucepan and stir vigorously to cool slightly, then set aside and let cool to room temperature, about 15 minutes. Whisk in remaining 1 tablespoon rum until combined. Using hand-held mixer set at low speed, beat egg yolk mixture and mascarpone together in large bowl until no lumps remain, 15 to 30 seconds. Proceed with recipe from step 3, using full amount of heavy cream specified (¼ cup).

New York Cheesecakes
SERVES 2

WHY THIS RECIPE WORKS: True New York–style cheesecake is a beautiful thing: the dense, velvety, tangy-sweet filling is supported by a crunchy graham-cracker crust. But with a dessert this rich, a full-size cake in a two-person household will mostly go to waste. We wanted to make foolproof individual cheesecakes for two. We started with a simple graham-cracker crust, prebaked to ensure it wouldn't turn soggy once we added the filling. We thinned the cream cheese with just a little tangy sour cream. One whole egg plus an extra yolk gave the cakes a lush texture that was dense but not heavy. A pinch of salt, a small dose of vanilla, and a squeeze of lemon juice perfected the flavors. Finally, we baked the cheesecakes using the classic New York method—first at 500 degrees to get a nicely browned top, then at 200 degrees to cook through gently. You will need two 4½-inch springform pans for this recipe. Serve as is or with fresh berries.

CRUST

- **3 whole graham crackers, broken into 1-inch pieces**
- **3 tablespoons unsalted butter, melted and cooled**
- **1 tablespoon sugar**

Our miniature New York–style cheesecakes feature a velvety, tangy-sweet filling and a crisp, buttery graham-cracker crust.

FILLING

10	ounces cream cheese, softened
⅓	cup (2⅓ ounces) sugar
	Pinch salt
4	teaspoons sour cream
½	teaspoon lemon juice
½	teaspoon vanilla extract
1	large egg plus 1 large yolk

1. FOR THE CRUST: Adjust oven rack to middle position and heat oven to 325 degrees. Process graham cracker pieces in food processor to fine, even crumbs, about 30 seconds.

Softening Cream Cheese Quickly

To speed up the softening of cold cream cheese, simply submerge the foil-wrapped package in a bowl of warm water for about 10 minutes.

Sprinkle 2 tablespoons melted butter and sugar over crumbs and pulse to incorporate, about 5 pulses. Divide mixture evenly between two 4½-inch springform pans. Using bottom of spoon, press crumbs firmly into even layer on bottom of pans, keeping sides as clean as possible. Bake crusts until fragrant and beginning to brown, about 10 minutes. Let crusts cool in pans on wire rack while making filling.

2. FOR THE FILLING: Increase oven temperature to 500 degrees. Using hand-held mixer set at medium-low speed, beat cream cheese in large bowl until smooth, 1 to 2 minutes. Scrape down sides of bowl. Add ¼ cup sugar and salt and beat until combined, 30 to 60 seconds. Scrape down bowl, add remaining sugar, and beat until combined, 30 to 60 seconds. Scrape down bowl, add sour cream, lemon juice, and vanilla and beat until combined, 15 to 30 seconds. Scrape down bowl, add egg and egg yolk and beat until combined, 30 to 60 seconds.

3. Being careful not to disturb baked crusts, brush inside of pans with remaining 1 tablespoon melted butter and place pans on rimmed baking sheet. Pour filling evenly into cooled crusts, smooth tops, and bake cheesecakes for 5 minutes. Without opening oven door, reduce temperature to 200 degrees and continue to bake until cakes register 150 degrees, 10 to 15 minutes, rotating sheet halfway through baking.

4. Let cheesecakes cool in pans on wire rack for 5 minutes, then run thin knife around edge of each cake. Let cakes continue to cool to room temperature, about 1 hour. Wrap pans tightly in plastic wrap and refrigerate until cold, at least 2 hours or up to 4 days.

5. To unmold cheesecakes, wrap hot dish towel around pans and let sit for 1 minute. Remove sides of pans. Slide thin metal spatula between crusts and pan bottoms to loosen, then slide cakes onto individual serving plates. Let cakes sit at room temperature for 30 minutes before serving. (Cheesecakes can be made up to 3 days in advance; however, crust will begin to lose its crispness after only 1 day.)

Making a Graham-Cracker Crust

To get an even, firmly packed graham-cracker crust for our New York–style cheesecake, use a spoon to press the crumb mixture firmly and evenly across the bottom of the pan.

Chocolate Pots de Crème

SERVES 2

✓ **WHY THIS RECIPE WORKS:** Classic *pots de crème* recipes can be finicky and laborious but deliver a dessert with a satiny texture and intense chocolate flavor. We wanted a user-friendly recipe for two. Since we were making only two custards, we decided that making them on the stovetop would be simpler than using the oven. First we cooked a simple custard in a small saucepan, then we poured the warm custard over the chocolate. Once the chocolate was melted, we divided the decadent mixture between two ramekins, and refrigerated the custards until chilled. Tasters liked bittersweet chocolate for its moderate sweetness, and a little instant espresso powder deepened the chocolate flavor. We prefer pots de crème made with 60 percent cacao bittersweet chocolate (our favorite brands are Ghirardelli and Callebaut). A teaspoon of strong brewed coffee may be substituted for the instant espresso and water. You will need two 5-ounce ramekins for this recipe.

POTS DE CRÈME

- 2½ ounces bittersweet chocolate, chopped fine
- 2 large egg yolks
- 4 teaspoons granulated sugar
- Pinch salt
- ¾ cup heavy cream
- 1 teaspoon water
- ⅛ teaspoon instant espresso powder
- 1 teaspoon vanilla extract

WHIPPED CREAM AND GARNISH

- ¼ cup heavy cream, chilled
- 2 teaspoons confectioners' sugar
- ⅛ teaspoon vanilla extract
- Cocoa powder (optional)
- Chocolate shavings (optional)

1. FOR THE POTS DE CRÈME: Place chocolate in medium bowl; set fine-mesh strainer over bowl and set aside.

2. Whisk egg yolks, sugar, and salt together in second medium bowl until combined, then whisk in cream. Transfer mixture to small saucepan and cook over medium-low heat, stirring constantly and scraping bottom of pot with rubber spatula, until it is thickened and silky and registers 175 to 180 degrees, 3 to 6 minutes. (Do not let custard overcook or simmer.)

3. Immediately pour custard through fine-mesh strainer over chocolate. Let mixture stand to melt chocolate, about 5 minutes; whisk gently until smooth. Combine water and espresso powder and stir to dissolve, then whisk dissolved espresso and vanilla into chocolate mixture. Pour mixture evenly into two 5-ounce ramekins. Gently tap ramekins on counter to release air bubbles.

4. Let pots de crème cool to room temperature, about 1 hour. Cover ramekins tightly with plastic wrap and refrigerate until chilled, at least 4 hours or up to 3 days. Before serving, let pots de crème stand at room temperature for 20 to 30 minutes.

5. FOR THE WHIPPED CREAM AND GARNISH: Using handheld mixer set at medium-low speed, beat cream, sugar, and vanilla in small bowl until foamy, about 1 minute. Increase speed to high and beat until soft peaks form, 1 to 3 minutes. Dollop pots de crème with whipped cream and garnish with cocoa powder and/or chocolate shavings, if desired. Serve.

Making Chocolate Shavings

To make chocolate shavings for decoration, use vegetable peeler and peel shavings off block of chocolate at least 1 inch thick. Slightly softened chocolate will be easier to shave; to soften chocolate, microwave on lowest power setting for 1 minute.

Flan

SERVES 2

✓ **WHY THIS RECIPE WORKS:** Flan is a deceptively simple, classic Spanish custard. It boasts a light, ultracreamy texture and a thin layer of caramel that pools over the custard when it is unmolded. To adapt this recipe for two, we swapped the large cake pan for two individual ramekins. First we made a quick caramel and poured it into the bottoms of the ramekins. For the custard, one whole egg plus one yolk gave us the perfect rich flavor and tender texture. Sweetened condensed milk made our flan rich and creamy but not overly heavy, and a touch of lemon zest added a balancing brightness. Any type of milk can be used in this recipe, resulting in varying degrees of richness. You will need two 6-ounce ramekins for this recipe. It's important to use a metal pan for the water bath—a glass baking pan may crack when you add the boiling water. Note that the custard will look barely set once it is ready to be removed from the oven.

3 tablespoons water

3 tablespoons sugar

1 large egg plus 1 large yolk, room temperature

½ cup 1 percent low-fat milk

½ cup sweetened condensed milk

⅛ teaspoon grated lemon zest

1. Adjust oven rack to middle position and heat oven to 350 degrees. Place dish towel in bottom of 8-inch square baking pan. Grease two 6-ounce ramekins and place them on towel (they should not touch). Bring kettle of water to boil.

2. Pour water into small saucepan, then pour sugar into center of saucepan (don't let it hit saucepan sides). Gently stir sugar with clean spatula to wet it thoroughly. Bring to boil over medium-high heat and cook, without stirring, until sugar has dissolved completely and liquid has faint golden color (about 300 degrees), 3 to 4 minutes.

3. Reduce heat to medium-low and continue to cook, stirring occasionally, until caramel has a dark amber color (about 350 degrees), 1 to 2 minutes. Carefully pour caramel evenly into ramekins and let cool until hardened, about 5 minutes.

4. Whisk egg and egg yolk together in medium bowl. Whisk in milk, sweetened condensed milk, and lemon zest until thoroughly combined. Pour custard evenly into ramekins. Set pan on oven rack. Taking care not to splash water into ramekins, pour enough boiling water into pan to reach halfway up sides of ramekins. Bake until centers of custards are just barely set and register 170 to 175 degrees, 25 to 30 minutes, checking temperature 5 minutes before recommended minimum time.

5. Carefully transfer ramekins to wire rack and let custards cool to room temperature, about 2 hours. Cover ramekins tightly with plastic wrap and refrigerate until cold, at least 2 hours or up to 1 day.

This surprisingly simple custard is made with just eggs, fresh milk, and sweetened condensed milk and topped with a quick caramel.

6. Run thin knife around 1 ramekin to loosen custard. Place inverted serving plate over top and quickly flip custard and plate together. Gently remove ramekin, drizzling any extra caramel sauce over top (some caramel will remain stuck in ramekin). Repeat with remaining custard and serve.

Unmolding Flan

1. Run thin knife around custard to loosen it, gently pressing custard away from side of dish.

2. Place inverted serving plate over top and quickly flip custard and plate together.

3. Shake ramekin gently to release custard and caramel. (Some caramel will remain stuck in ramekin.)

Crème Brûlée

SERVES 2

⚡ WHY THIS RECIPE WORKS: Crème brûlée is all about the contrast between the crisp, caramelized sugar crust and the silky custard underneath. We found that the secret to getting a custard with a soft, supple texture was to use only egg yolks rather than whole eggs. To make tempering the egg yolks easier, we heated just half of the cream until the sugar was fully dissolved, then added the remaining cold cream to bring the temperature down so we could add the egg yolks. Crunchy turbinado sugar made for an incredibly crackly crust. To substitute vanilla extract for the vanilla bean, skip the steeping time in step 2 and stir ½ teaspoon vanilla extract into the yolk mixture in step 3. Granulated sugar can be substituted for the turbinado sugar. You will need two 6-ounce ramekins for this recipe (two 4- to 5-ounce shallow fluted ramekins can also be used; you will have some custard left over). It's important to use a metal pan for the water bath—a glass baking pan may crack when you add the boiling water. Note that the custard will look barely set once it is ready to be removed from the oven; it will firm up as it cools.

    1   (3-inch) piece vanilla bean
    1   cup heavy cream, chilled
    3   tablespoons granulated sugar
        Pinch salt
    3   large egg yolks, room temperature
  2–3   teaspoons turbinado sugar

1. Adjust oven rack to middle position and heat oven to 300 degrees. Place dish towel in bottom of 8-inch square baking pan and place two 6-ounce ramekins on towel (they should not touch). Bring kettle of water to boil.

2. Cut vanilla bean in half lengthwise. Using tip of paring knife, scrape out seeds. Combine vanilla bean pod and seeds,

½ cup cream, granulated sugar, and salt in small saucepan. Bring mixture to simmer over medium heat, stirring occasionally to dissolve sugar. Off heat, let steep for 15 minutes.

3. After cream has steeped, stir in remaining ½ cup cream. Place egg yolks in medium bowl and slowly whisk in ½ cup of cream mixture until smooth. Whisk in remaining cream mixture until thoroughly combined. Strain custard through fine-mesh strainer into 2-cup liquid measuring cup; discard solids in strainer. Pour custard evenly into ramekins.

4. Set pan on oven rack. Taking care not to splash water into ramekins, pour enough boiling water into pan to reach halfway up sides of ramekins. Bake until centers of custards are just barely set and register 170 to 175 degrees, 30 to 35 minutes (25 to 30 minutes for shallow fluted dishes), checking temperature 5 minutes before recommended minimum time.

5. Carefully transfer ramekins to wire rack and let custards cool to room temperature, about 2 hours. Cover ramekins tightly with plastic wrap and refrigerate until cold, at least 2 hours or up to 3 days.

6. Uncover ramekins; if condensation has collected on custards, blot moisture with paper towel. Sprinkle each with about 1 teaspoon turbinado sugar (1½ teaspoons for shallow fluted dishes); tilt and tap each ramekin to distribute sugar evenly, dumping out excess sugar. Ignite torch and caramelize sugar. Refrigerate ramekins, uncovered, to rechill, 30 to 40 minutes. Serve.

VARIATION

Espresso Crème Brûlée

Add ½ teaspoon instant espresso powder or instant coffee powder to egg yolks in step 3.

Caramelizing Crème Brûlée

1. Sprinkle sugar over surface of custard, then tilt and tap ramekin to distribute sugar into thin, even layer. Pour out any excess sugar and wipe inside rim clean.

2. To caramelize sugar, sweep flame of torch from perimeter of custard toward middle, keeping flame about 2 inches above ramekin, until sugar is bubbling and deep golden brown.

Removing Seeds from a Vanilla Bean

1. Use small knife to cut piece of vanilla bean in half lengthwise.

2. Scrape vanilla seeds out of bean using tip of knife.

Easy Lemon Soufflé

SERVES 2 `LIGHT`

✓ **WHY THIS RECIPE WORKS:** Lemon soufflé, with its ethereal, airy texture and bright, tart lemon flavor, requires a precise balance of ingredients. To size this recipe for two and make it foolproof, we ditched the soufflé dish in favor of a small skillet. Using an equal number of egg whites and yolks made our soufflé lofty but still rich and creamy. Sugar and cream of tartar helped stabilize the whipped egg whites, ensuring that our soufflé stayed tall. We started cooking our batter on the stovetop, then allowed it to rise in the oven until beautifully puffed and golden. An 8-inch traditional (not non-stick) skillet is essential to getting the right texture and height here. Don't open the oven door during the first 5 minutes of baking, but do check the soufflé for doneness regularly during the final few minutes in the oven. The center of the soufflé should be creamy and slightly liquid when properly cooked. For the nutritional information for this recipe, see page 415.

    3 large eggs, separated
    ⅛ teaspoon cream of tartar
    6 tablespoons (2⅔ ounces) granulated sugar
    ⅛ teaspoon salt
    1 tablespoon all-purpose flour
    ¾ teaspoon grated lemon zest plus 3 tablespoons juice
    2 teaspoons unsalted butter
       Confectioners' sugar

1. Adjust oven rack to middle position and heat oven to 375 degrees. Using hand-held mixer set at medium-low speed, beat egg whites and cream of tartar in large bowl until foamy, about 1 minute. Increase speed to medium-high and beat whites to soft, billowy mounds, about 1 minute. Gradually add 2 tablespoons granulated sugar and salt and beat until glossy, stiff peaks form, 1 to 3 minutes.

2. Using hand-held mixer set at medium-high speed, beat egg yolks and remaining ¼ cup granulated sugar in second large bowl until pale and thick, about 2 minutes, scraping down sides of bowl as needed. Add flour and lemon zest and juice and beat until combined, about 30 seconds.

3. Fold one-quarter of whipped egg whites into yolk mixture until almost no white streaks remain. Gently fold in remaining egg whites until just combined.

4. Melt butter in 8-inch ovensafe skillet over medium-low heat. Swirl skillet to coat it evenly with melted butter, then gently scrape soufflé batter into skillet and cook until edges begin to set, about 1 minute.

5. Transfer skillet to oven and bake soufflé until puffed, center jiggles slightly when shaken, and surface is golden,

6 to 8 minutes. Using potholder (skillet handle will be hot), remove skillet from oven. Dust soufflé with confectioners' sugar and serve immediately.

Separating Eggs

To separate eggs, use either the broken shell halves or your hand.

A. To use broken shell halves, gently transfer egg yolk from one shell half to other, so white will drip into bowl and leave intact yolk behind.

B. To use your hand (make sure it's very clean), cup your hand over small bowl, transfer egg into your palm, and slowly allow white to slide through fingers, leaving yolk intact.

NOTES FROM THE TEST KITCHEN

Whipping Egg Whites

Perfectly whipped egg whites begin with a scrupulously clean bowl, as fat inhibits the whites from whipping properly. Plastic bowls retain an oily film even when washed and should not be used for whipping egg whites. Glass and ceramic should be avoided as well; their slippery surfaces make it hard for whites to billow up. The best choices are stainless steel and copper. Wash the bowl in soapy, hot-as-you-can-stand-it water, rinse with hot water, and dry with paper towels. (A dish towel may have traces of oil in its fibers.)

Start with eggs straight from the fridge—they will separate more easily than eggs at room temperature. Fresh eggs are also helpful; older eggs will not rise as well. Be careful not to puncture the yolk as you separate the eggs. Once separated, it's best to let the whites come to room temperature; they will whip more quickly, and if you are whipping sugar into the whites, it will dissolve better if the egg whites are not cold. With your whites in the bowl (some recipes also include cream of tartar for stabilization), start the mixer on low speed and whip the whites until foamy, about 1 minute. Then increase the mixer speed (adding sugar if required) and continue to whip the whites to their desired consistency. For soft peaks (left), beat until the whites droop slightly from the tip of the whisk or beater. For stiff peaks (right), beat until the whites stand up tall on their own on the tip of the whisk or beater.

Soft Peaks

Stiff Peaks

New Orleans Bourbon Bread Pudding

SERVES 2

✓ **WHY THIS RECIPE WORKS:** The best bourbon bread pudding is a rich, scoopable custard that envelops the bread with a perfect balance of sweetness, spice, and bourbon flavor. We wanted to do justice to each element, while scaling the recipe to serve two. To avoid unnecessary leftovers, we replaced the usual whole baguette with two small French rolls. Brown sugar gave the custard a rounded, caramelized flavor, and a few tablespoons of bourbon was enough for punch without making the pudding too boozy. Covering the ramekins with foil, baking them in a low oven, and swapping the whole eggs for yolks kept the pudding from curdling. We added cinnamon, sugar, and butter toward the end of baking to form a crispy, golden crust. Six ounces of French bread can be substituted for the rolls. You will need two 12-ounce ramekins for this recipe, but a 4-cup baking dish (measuring approximately 8½ by 5½ inches) will also work.

BREAD PUDDING

- 2 rustic French rolls (3 ounces each), torn into 1-inch pieces (3 cups)
- ¼ cup golden raisins
- 3 tablespoons bourbon
- ¾ cup heavy cream
- ⅓ cup packed (2⅓ ounces) light brown sugar
- ¼ cup whole milk
- 2 large egg yolks, room temperature
- 1 teaspoon vanilla extract
- ½ teaspoon ground cinnamon
  Pinch ground nutmeg
  Pinch salt
- 1 tablespoon granulated sugar
- 2 tablespoons unsalted butter, cut into ¼-inch pieces and chilled

BOURBON SAUCE

- 1 tablespoon bourbon
- ½ teaspoon cornstarch
- 3 tablespoons heavy cream
- 2 teaspoons granulated sugar
  Pinch salt

1. FOR THE BREAD PUDDING: Adjust oven rack to middle position and heat oven to 450 degrees. Grease two 12-ounce ramekins. Spread bread in single layer on rimmed baking sheet and bake until crisp and browned, tossing occasionally, 10 to 12 minutes. Let bread cool completely. Reduce oven temperature to 300 degrees.

2. Bring raisins and 2 tablespoons bourbon to simmer in small saucepan over medium-high heat and cook for 1 minute. Drain raisins, reserving liquid.

3. Whisk reserved raisin soaking liquid, remaining 1 tablespoon bourbon, cream, brown sugar, milk, egg yolks, vanilla, ¼ teaspoon cinnamon, nutmeg, and salt together in large bowl. Add toasted bread and toss until evenly coated. Let mixture sit, tossing occasionally, until bread begins to absorb custard and is softened, 20 to 25 minutes.

4. Stir reserved raisins into bread mixture until combined. Divide bread mixture evenly between prepared ramekins and cover each ramekin with foil. Place bread puddings on rimmed baking sheet and bake for 30 minutes.

5. Meanwhile, in small bowl, combine granulated sugar and remaining ¼ teaspoon cinnamon. Using your fingers, work butter into sugar mixture until small pea-size pieces form. Remove foil from bread puddings and sprinkle with butter mixture. Rotate sheet and continue to bake, uncovered, until custard is just set, about 15 minutes. Increase oven temperature to 450 degrees and bake until top is crisp and golden brown, about 10 minutes. Let bread puddings cool for 30 minutes.

6. FOR THE BOURBON SAUCE: Whisk 1½ teaspoons bourbon and cornstarch together in bowl until well combined. Heat cream and sugar in small saucepan over medium heat, stirring occasionally, until sugar dissolves. Whisk in cornstarch mixture and bring to boil. Reduce heat to low and cook until sauce thickens, 30 to 60 seconds. Off heat, stir in remaining 1½ teaspoons bourbon and salt. Drizzle warm sauce over each bread pudding and serve.

VARIATION

Bourbon Bread Pudding with Chocolate
We like the flavor of bittersweet chips here, but semisweet chips can be substituted.

Substitute ⅓ cup bittersweet chocolate chips for raisins, and omit step 2. Add all bourbon in step 3, and proceed with recipe.

Nutritional Information for Light Recipes

Analyzing recipes for their nutritional values is a tricky business, and we did our best to be as realistic and accurate as possible throughout this book. We were absolutely strict about measuring when cooking and never resorted to guessing or estimating. And we never made the portion sizes unreasonably small to make the nutritional numbers appear lower. We also didn't play games when analyzing the recipes in the nutritional program to make the numbers look better; we just tell it like it is.

To calculate the nutritional values of our recipes per serving, we used The Food Processor SQL by ESHA Research. When using this program, we entered all the ingredients in their raw form and used weights for important ingredients such as meat, cheese, and most vegetables. We also used all of our preferred brands in these analyses. Yet there are two tricky ingredients to be mindful of when analyzing a recipe—salt and fat—and they require some special rules of their own. Salt is tricky when analyzing a recipe because it is often used in unspecified amounts, or is added to cooking water that is then drained away. Here are the rules we used in order to be as accurate as possible. When the recipe called for seasoning food with an unspecified amount of salt and pepper (often for raw meat), we added ¼ teaspoon salt and ⅛ teaspoon pepper to the analysis. For food that was boiled in salted water then drained (as with pasta or blanched vegetables), we added ¼ teaspoon salt to the analysis to account for any that was absorbed during the boiling time. We did not, however, include additional salt or pepper in our analysis when the food was "seasoned to taste" at the end of cooking, or if the reserved salted cooking water was "added as needed."

As for fat, it can add up from some unexpected sources. For instance, take vegetable oil spray, which we often use for greasing baking dishes. To account for its use, we added three seconds of vegetable oil spray to the analysis whenever it was used. Meat is another variable source of fat, because how you trim it has a big impact on the numbers; for our light recipes, we trimmed away all visible fat. Salmon is also a problematic ingredient because farm-raised salmon is significantly fattier than wild salmon. To account for this, for each light salmon recipe we give nutritional information for both wild and farmed salmon.

So if you follow our ingredient lists and recipes carefully and accurately, we feel confident that our nutritional analyses will give you an accurate measurement of what you are consuming.

	Cal	Fat	Sat Fat	Chol	Carb	Protein	Fiber	Sodium
PUTTING LEFTOVER INGREDIENTS TO WORK								
Very Berry Smoothie	200	2 g	1 g	10 mg	40 g	8 g	4 g	280 mg
Quick Kimchi	60	0 g	0 g	0 mg	11 g	3 g	3 g	370 mg
Kidney Bean Salad	140	7 g	1 g	0 mg	15 g	5 g	4 g	520 mg
Quick Tomato Salsa*	15	0 g	0 g	0 mg	4 g	1 g	1 g	160 mg
Easy Tomato Chutney*	70	0 g	0 g	0 mg	16 g	1 g	1 g	260 mg
Watermelon and Feta Salad with Mint	120	6 g	4 g	25 mg	15 g	5 g	1 g	320 mg

*Per ¼ cup

	Cal	Fat	Sat Fat	Chol	Carb	Protein	Fiber	Sodium
SOUPS AND CHOWDERS								
Mushroom-Miso Soup with Shrimp and Udon	440	10 g	1 g	80 mg	65 g	22 g	5 g	2030 mg
Provençal Vegetable Soup with Pistou	270	11 g	2 g	5 mg	34 g	11 g	8 g	1090 mg
Farmhouse Vegetable and Barley Soup	370	12 g	7 g	30 mg	56 g	7 g	9 g	1240 mg
Creamy Curried Cauliflower Soup	190	10 g	3.5 g	0 mg	19 g	9 g	6 g	900 mg
Chilled Fresh Tomato Soup	180	9 g	1.5 g	0 mg	22 g	5 g	6 g	610 mg
Gazpacho	120	5 g	0.5 g	0 mg	16 g	4 g	3 g	380 mg
Gazpacho with Shrimp	250	7 g	1 g	240 mg	18 g	29 g	3 g	1450 mg
U.S. Senate Navy Bean Soup	360	12 g	4 g	45 mg	37 g	27 g	9 g	1400 mg
Moroccan-Style Chickpea Soup	230	8 g	3.5 g	15 mg	34 g	7 g	7 g	1180 mg

	Cal	Fat	Sat Fat	Chol	Carb	Protein	Fiber	Sodium
STEWS, CURRIES, AND CHILIS								
Chicken Tagine	480	12 g	1.5 g	75 mg	56 g	37 g	10 g	1910 mg
Quinoa and Vegetable Stew	310	10 g	1 g	0 mg	50 g	7 g	6 g	610 mg
White Chicken Chili	440	13 g	2 g	110 mg	35 g	45 g	7 g	1530 mg
Vegetarian Chili	530	12 g	1.5 g	0 mg	77 g	32 g	19 g	1690 mg
SIDE SALADS AND DINNER SALADS								
Cucumber Salad with Olives, Oregano, and Almonds	120	8 g	1 g	0 mg	9 g	2 g	2 g	820 mg
Cucumber Salad with Chile, Mint, and Peanuts	110	7 g	1 g	0 mg	9 g	4 g	2 g	780 mg
Cucumber Salad with Jalapeño, Cilantro, and Pepitas	110	8 g	1 g	0 mg	8 g	4 g	2 g	610 mg
Cucumber Salad with Ginger, Sesame, and Scallions	120	8 g	0.5 g	0 mg	10 g	3 g	2 g	590 mg
Fennel, Apple, and Chicken Chopped Salad	350	13 g	3.5 g	80 mg	28 g	30 g	7 g	830 mg
Chinese Chicken Salad	330	13 g	2 g	75 mg	26 g	29 g	4 g	1750 mg
Poached Shrimp Salad with Avocado and Grapefruit	280	14 g	2 g	160 mg	21 g	21 g	8 g	1200 mg
Poached Shrimp Salad with Avocado, Orange, and Arugula	270	14 g	2 g	160 mg	19 g	21 g	6 g	1200 mg
Pasta Salad with Arugula and Sun-Dried Tomatoes	350	13 g	4 g	10 mg	47 g	12 g	3 g	650 mg
Sweet and Tangy Coleslaw	170	7 g	1 g	0 mg	25 g	2 g	5 g	640 mg
Sweet and Tangy Coleslaw with Bell Pepper and Jalapeño	180	7 g	1 g	0 mg	26 g	3 g	5 g	650 mg
Sweet and Tangy Coleslaw with Apple and Tarragon	210	7 g	1 g	0 mg	36 g	2 g	6 g	640 mg
BURGERS, SANDWICHES, PIZZA, AND MORE								
Shrimp Burgers	340	14 g	2 g	165 mg	28 g	23 g	2 g	1160 mg
CHICKEN								
Sautéed Chicken Breasts with Oranges and Feta	390	13 g	3 g	115 mg	28 g	40 g	4 g	570 mg
Spa Chicken	190	4.5 g	1 g	110 mg	0 g	36 g	0 g	490 mg
Spa Chicken with Apricot-Orange Chipotle Sauce	290	7 g	1 g	110 mg	17 g	37 g	2 g	490 mg
Spa Chicken with Caramelized Onion and Whole-Grain Mustard Sauce	280	10 g	1.5 g	110 mg	7 g	38 g	1 g	830 mg
Moroccan Chicken with Green Olives	270	13 g	2 g	80 mg	19 g	21 g	3 g	460 mg
Thai Chicken with Basil	240	10 g	1.5 g	75 mg	9 g	27 g	0 g	640 mg
Sweet-and-Sour Chicken with Pineapple and Red Onion	430	9 g	1.5 g	110 mg	47 g	40 g	4 g	1010 mg
Sichuan Orange Chicken with Broccoli	350	10 g	1.5 g	110 mg	27 g	41 g	5 g	1580 mg
Chicken en Papillote with Zucchini and Tomatoes	290	12 g	2 g	110 mg	6 g	38 g	2 g	640 mg
Chicken en Papillote with Artichokes, Lemon, and Tomatoes	340	13 g	2 g	110 mg	17 g	40 g	9 g	720 mg
BEEF, PORK, AND LAMB								
Skillet-Glazed Pork Chops	320	8 g	2.5 g	110 mg	21 g	38 g	0 g	470 mg
Sautéed Boneless Pork Chops with Quick Apple-Ginger Chutney	390	11 g	2.5 g	110 mg	35 g	39 g	2 g	390 mg

	Cal	Fat	Sat Fat	Chol	Carb	Protein	Fiber	Sodium
BEEF, PORK, AND LAMB (*CONT.*)								
Maple-Glazed Pork Tenderloin	470	10 g	1.5 g	110 mg	48 g	36 g	0 g	980 mg
Maple-Glazed Pork Tenderloin with Orange and Chipotle	470	8 g	1.5 g	110 mg	56 g	36 g	0 g	740 mg
Maple-Glazed Pork Tenderloin with Smoked Paprika and Ginger	430	8 g	1.5 g	110 mg	49 g	36 g	0 g	740 mg
Spice-Rubbed Pork Tenderloin with Mango Relish	280	9 g	2 g	110 mg	12 g	36 g	2 g	570 mg
FISH AND SHELLFISH								
Lemon-Steamed Sole with Green Pea Sauce	190	6 g	1 g	75 mg	7 g	24 g	2 g	880 mg
Steamed Sole and Vegetable Bundles with Tarragon	230	9 g	4.5 g	90 mg	12 g	24 g	4 g	960 mg
Skillet-Braised Cod Provençal	320	10 g	1.5 g	75 mg	19 g	34 g	5 g	970 mg
Braised Cod Peperonata	260	6 g	1 g	75 mg	13 g	32 g	3 g	840 mg
Poached Cod with Miso, Shiitakes, and Edamame	330	11 g	1 g	75 mg	13 g	43 g	4 g	790 mg
Baked Sole Fillets with Herbs and Bread Crumbs	250	14 g	8 g	95 mg	12 g	19 g	1 g	790 mg
Baked Cod with Cherry Tomatoes and Artichokes	300	11 g	1.5 g	75 mg	15 g	34 g	6 g	810 mg
Miso-Glazed Salmon Fillets (Wild)	380	12 g	1.5 g	95 mg	25 g	37 g	0 g	1020 mg
Miso-Glazed Salmon Fillets (Farmed)	490	24 g	5 g	95 mg	25 g	38 g	0 g	1040 mg
Broiled Salmon with Pineapple Salsa (Wild)	320	12 g	2 g	95 mg	17 g	35 g	1 g	250 mg
Broiled Salmon with Pineapple Salsa (Farmed)	430	24 g	5 g	95 mg	17 g	36 g	1 g	270 mg
Broiled Salmon with Mango Salsa (Wild)	320	12 g	2 g	95 mg	18 g	34 g	1 g	250 mg
Broiled Salmon with Mango Salsa (Farmed)	440	24 g	5 g	95 mg	18 g	35 g	1 g	270 mg
Broiled Salmon with Honeydew and Radish Salsa (Wild)	310	12 g	2 g	95 mg	15 g	35 g	1 g	240 mg
Broiled Salmon with Honeydew and Radish Salsa (Farmed)	420	24 g	5 g	95 mg	15 g	36 g	1 g	260 mg
Pan-Seared Shrimp with Spicy Orange Glaze	150	6 g	0.5 g	160 mg	6 g	18 g	0 g	1050 mg
Pan-Seared Shrimp with Ginger-Hoisin Glaze	150	6 g	0.5 g	160 mg	7 g	18 g	0 g	1450 mg
Stir-Fried Shrimp with Lemon-Ginger Sauce	210	6 g	1 g	160 mg	15 g	22 g	4 g	1470 mg
Kung Pao Shrimp	290	15 g	2 g	160 mg	15 g	24 g	3 g	1120 mg
VEGETARIAN MAINS								
Skillet Brown Rice and Beans with Corn and Tomatoes	440	13 g	1.5 g	0 mg	73 g	12 g	9 g	900 mg
Spanish-Style Skillet Brown Rice and Chickpeas	440	13 g	1.5 g	0 mg	71 g	11 g	9 g	890 mg
Mushroom and Farro Ragout	410	13 g	7 g	30 mg	62 g	12 g	7 g	1160 mg
Chickpea Cakes with Cucumber-Yogurt Sauce	310	14 g	3 g	95 mg	31 g	15 g	5 g	730 mg
PASTA AND ASIAN NOODLE DISHES								
Linguine with Quick Tomato Sauce	480	13 g	2 g	0 mg	76 g	14 g	5 g	960 mg
Linguine with Quick Fire-Roasted Tomato Sauce	480	13 g	2 g	0 mg	76 g	14 g	5 g	1110 mg
Pasta with Roasted Cherry Tomatoes, Garlic, and Basil	490	15 g	2.5 g	0 mg	77 g	14 g	6 g	740 mg
Skillet Pasta with Fresh Tomato Sauce	230	4.5 g	0.5 g	0 mg	39 g	7 g	3 g	300 mg
Skillet Mussels Marinara with Spaghetti	140	3 g	0.5 g	15 mg	19 g	9 g	1 g	310 mg
Singapore Noodles with Shrimp	220	5 g	0.5 g	55 mg	34 g	9 g	1 g	1310 mg

	Cal	Fat	Sat Fat	Chol	Carb	Protein	Fiber	Sodium
GRILLING								
Grill-Smoked Pork Chops	400	10 g	3.5 g	115 mg	30 g	45 g	0 g	1070 mg
Grilled Blackened Red Snapper	290	14 g	7 g	95 mg	4 g	36 g	2 g	700 mg
Grilled Scallops with Fennel and Orange Salad	320	15 g	2 g	40 mg	23 g	23 g	6 g	1020 mg
SLOW-COOKER FAVORITES								
Slow-Cooker Curried Chicken Breasts	350	13 g	2.5 g	145 mg	8 g	49 g	1 g	620 mg
Slow-Cooker Gingery Chicken Breasts	350	13 g	2 g	140 mg	9 g	49 g	0 g	1270 mg
Slow-Cooker Balsamic-Braised Chicken with Swiss Chard	340	14 g	2.5 g	135 mg	18 g	38 g	5 g	1060 mg
VEGETABLE SIDE DISHES								
Braised Brussels Sprouts	110	6 g	3.5 g	15 mg	11 g	6 g	4 g	430 mg
Braised Brussels Sprouts with Curry and Currants	130	6 g	3.5 g	15 mg	15 g	6 g	5 g	430 mg
Sautéed Snow Peas with Lemon and Parsley	80	5 g	0.5 g	0 mg	8 g	3 g	2 g	300 mg
Sautéed Snow Peas with Ginger and Scallion	80	5 g	0.5 g	0 mg	8 g	3 g	3 g	300 mg
Sautéed Snow Peas with Cumin and Cilantro	80	5 g	0.5 g	0 mg	7 g	2 g	2 g	290 mg
Perfect Baked Potatoes	220	5 g	0.5 g	0 mg	41 g	5 g	3 g	10 mg
30-Minute Baked Potatoes	180	0 g	0 g	0 mg	41 g	5 g	3 g	10 mg
Spinach with Garlic Chips and Red Pepper Flakes	100	7 g	1 g	0 mg	6 g	4 g	3 g	115 mg
Roasted Sweet Potatoes	230	7 g	1 g	0 mg	40 g	3 g	7 g	120 mg
RICE, GRAINS, AND BEANS								
Simple White Rice	250	2.5 g	0 g	0 mg	52 g	5 g	0 g	300 mg
Toasted Orzo with Chives and Lemon	300	6 g	3.5 g	15 mg	47 g	12 g	3 g	520 mg
Toasted Orzo with Tomatoes and Basil	340	8 g	5 g	20 mg	48 g	15 g	3 g	640 mg
EGGS AND BREAKFAST								
Hard-Cooked Eggs	140	10 g	3 g	370 mg	1 g	13 g	0 g	140 mg
Ten-Minute Steel-Cut Oatmeal	140	2.5 g	0.5 g	0 mg	27 g	6 g	4 g	200 mg
Apple-Cinnamon Steel-Cut Oatmeal	480	8 g	1.5 g	5 mg	99 g	8 g	5 g	360 mg
Carrot-Spice Steel-Cut Oatmeal	310	8 g	1.5 g	5 mg	56 g	8 g	6 g	340 mg
Cranberry-Orange Steel-Cut Oatmeal	290	7 g	1.5 g	5 mg	56 g	8 g	6 g	310 mg
Breakfast Smoothies with Strawberries and Banana	230	2.5 g	2 g	15 mg	43 g	10 g	4 g	200 mg
Breakfast Smoothies with Pineapple and Mango	260	2.5 g	2 g	15 mg	51 g	9 g	3 g	200 mg
Breakfast Smoothies with Blueberries and Pomegranate	220	3 g	2 g	15 mg	40 g	9 g	3 g	210 mg
FRUIT DESSERTS, PIES, AND TARTS								
Berry Gratins	170	8 g	4.5 g	115 mg	22 g	2 g	2 g	85 mg
COOKIES, CAKES, AND CUSTARDS								
Angel Food Cakes	300	0 g	0 g	0 mg	67 g	7 g	0 g	160 mg
Chocolate-Almond Angel Food Cakes	330	2.5 g	1 g	0 mg	71 g	7 g	1 g	160 mg
Café au Lait Angel Food Cakes	300	0 g	0 g	0 mg	68 g	7 g	0 g	160 mg
Easy Lemon Soufflé	320	11 g	4.5 g	290 mg	47 g	10 g	0 g	250 mg

Conversions and Equivalencies

Some say cooking is a science and an art. We would say that geography has a hand in it, too. Flour milled in the United Kingdom and elsewhere will feel and taste different from flour milled in the United States. So we cannot promise that the loaf of bread you bake in Canada or England will taste the same as a loaf baked in the States, but we can offer guidelines for converting weights and measures. We also recommend that you rely on your instincts when making our recipes. Refer to the visual cues provided. If the bread dough hasn't "come together in a ball," as described, you may need to add more flour—even if the recipe doesn't tell you to. You be the judge.

The recipes in this book were developed using standard U.S. measures following U.S. government guidelines. The charts below offer equivalents for U.S., metric, and imperial (U.K.) measures. All conversions are approximate and have been rounded up or down to the nearest whole number.

EXAMPLE:

| 1 teaspoon | = | 4.9292 milliliters, rounded up to 5 milliliters |
| 1 ounce | = | 28.3495 grams, rounded down to 28 grams |

VOLUME CONVERSIONS

U.S.	METRIC
1 teaspoon	5 milliliters
2 teaspoons	10 milliliters
1 tablespoon	15 milliliters
2 tablespoons	30 milliliters
¼ cup	59 milliliters
⅓ cup	79 milliliters
½ cup	118 milliliters
¾ cup	177 milliliters
1 cup	237 milliliters
1¼ cups	296 milliliters
1½ cups	355 milliliters
2 cups (1 pint)	473 milliliters
2½ cups	591 milliliters
3 cups	710 milliliters
4 cups (1 quart)	0.946 liter
1.06 quarts	1 liter
4 quarts (1 gallon)	3.8 liters

WEIGHT CONVERSIONS

OUNCES	GRAMS
½	14
¾	21
1	28
1½	43
2	57
2½	71
3	85
3½	99
4	113
4½	128
5	142
6	170
7	198
8	227
9	255
10	283
12	340
16 (1 pound)	454

CONVERSIONS FOR COMMON BAKING INGREDIENTS

Baking is an exacting science. Because measuring by weight is far more accurate than measuring by volume, and thus more likely to achieve reliable results, in our recipes we provide ounce measures in addition to cup measures for many ingredients. Refer to the chart below to convert these measures into grams.

INGREDIENT	OUNCES	GRAMS
1 cup all-purpose flour*	5	142
1 cup cake flour	4	113
1 cup whole-wheat flour	5½	156
1 cup granulated (white) sugar	7	198
1 cup packed brown sugar (light or dark)	7	198
1 cup confectioners' sugar	4	113
1 cup cocoa powder	3	85
4 tablespoons butter[†] (½ stick, or ¼ cup)	2	57
8 tablespoons butter[†] (1 stick, or ½ cup)	4	113

* U.S. all-purpose flour, the most frequently used flour in this book, does not contain leaveners, as some European flours do. These leavened flours are called self-rising or self-raising. If you are using self-rising flour, take this into consideration before adding leavening to a recipe.

[†] In the United States, butter is sold both salted and unsalted. We generally recommend unsalted butter. If you are using salted butter, take this into consideration before adding salt to a recipe.

CONVERTING OVEN TEMPERATURES

FAHRENHEIT	CELSIUS	GAS MARK (IMPERIAL)
225	105	¼
250	120	½
275	135	1
300	150	2
325	165	3
350	180	4
375	190	5
400	200	6
425	220	7
450	230	8
475	245	9

CONVERTING FAHRENHEIT TO CELSIUS

We include doneness temperatures in many of the recipes in this book. We recommend an instant-read thermometer for the job. Refer to the above table to convert Fahrenheit degrees to Celsius. Or, for temperatures not represented in the chart, use this simple formula:

Subtract 32 degrees from the Fahrenheit reading, then divide the result by 1.8 to find the Celsius reading.

EXAMPLE:

"Roast chicken until thighs register 175 degrees."
To convert:

175°F − 32 = 143°
143° ÷ 1.8 = 79.44°C, rounded down to 79°C

Index

Note: Page references in *italics* indicate recipe photographs.

■ FAST (Start to finish in about 30 minutes)

■ LIGHT (See pages 412–415 for nutritional information)

A

All-American Mini Meatloaves, *141,* 141–42

All-American Potato Salad, 81–82

All-Butter Tart Shells, 378

Almond(s)

Cakes, 395–96

and Currants, Glazed Carrots with, ■ 298

Granola with Dried Fruit, *342,* 342–43

Toasted

and Honey, Crêpes with, 361

Lemony Green Beans with, ■ 295

Saffron, and Raisins, Couscous with, 321

and Saffron, Classic Rice Pilaf with, 317

and Tomato Pesto, Pasta with, ■ 217

Always-Fresh Herb Ice Cubes, 13

Angel Food Cakes, ■ *391,* 391

Apple(s)

-Cinnamon Steel-Cut Oatmeal, ■ 341–42

Crisp, Skillet, 366, *366*

Crisp, Skillet, with Raspberries and Almonds, 367

Fennel, and Chicken Chopped Salad, ■ *71,* 71–72

Galette, Easy, *375,* 375

-Ginger Chutney, Quick, Sautéed Boneless Pork Chops with, ■ 147–48

Morning Glory Muffins, 351, *351*

removing core from, 367

Strudel, Quick, 364–65

and Tarragon, Sweet and Tangy Coleslaw with, ■ ■ 83

Apricot(s)

Chutney, Pan-Roasted Lamb Chops with, 162

-Orange Chipotle Sauce, Spa Chicken with, ■ 107

-Orange Corn Muffins, 348

Artichoke(s)

and Cherry Tomatoes, Baked Cod with, ■ ■ 173

and Fennel, Herb-Rubbed Pork Tenderloin with, 157, *157*

Garlic, and Olive Oil, Spaghetti with, 216

Hearts, Roasted

with Fennel, Mustard, and Tarragon, 292

Artichoke(s), Hearts, Roasted *(cont.)*

with Lemon and Basil, 292, *292*

with Olives, Bell Pepper, and Lemon, 292

Lemon, and Tomatoes, Chicken en Papillote with, ■ 127

and Shrimp Lavash Pizza, ■ 96–97, *97*

Arugula

Avocado, and Orange, Poached Shrimp Salad with, ■ 78

Cherry Tomatoes, and Lemon, Farro Risotto with, *204,* 204–5

Chicken, Pine Nuts, and Lemon, Skillet Penne with, 234

Fontina, and Prosciutto, Easy Skillet Pizza with, 94

and Sun-Dried Tomatoes, Pasta Salad with, ■ ■ 79

Asian Braised Tofu with Butternut Squash and Eggplant, 211–12

Asparagus

grilling, at a glance, 273

and Herb Dressing, Salmon with, 178, *178*

Pan-Roasted, with Toasted Garlic and Parmesan, ■ 293

Pan-Roasted, ■ 292–93

Parmesan-Crusted, *293,* 293–94

Potatoes, Carrots, and Dill, Braised Chicken Thighs with, 126

Risotto Primavera, 203, *203*

Shrimp, and Carrots, Thai-Style Red Curry with, ■ 56

Steamed, Soft-Cooked Eggs with, ■ 331–32

Steamed Sole and Vegetable Bundles with Tarragon, ■ 167–68

trimming, 293

Avocado(s)

about, 73

and Grapefruit, Poached Shrimp Salad with, ■ 77–78, *78*

-Grapefruit Salsa, Spiced Swordfish with, ■ 176–77, *177*

Orange, and Arugula, Poached Shrimp Salad with, ■ 78

B

Bacon

freezing, 5

Onion, and Scallion Omelet Filling, ■ 334

-Wrapped Pork Chops with Roasted Potatoes, 153–54

Baked Cod with Cherry Tomatoes and Artichokes, ■ ■ 173

Baked Fish with Crisp Bread Crumbs, ■ 171, *171*

Baked Manicotti, 231–32

Baked Snapper with Roasted Ratatouille, *173,* 173–74

Baked Sole Fillets with Herbs and Bread Crumbs, ■ 170–71

Baking powder, 6, 8, 352

Baking soda, 6, 352

Balsamic-Mustard Foolproof Vinaigrette, ■ 64

Banana(s)

about, 354

Bread, *344,* 354

-Chocolate Bread, 354

Cream Pie, *373,* 373–74

freezing, 7

and Nutella, Crêpes with, 361

and Strawberries, Breakfast Smoothies with, ■ ■ 343

Barbecued Dry-Rubbed Chicken, 249–50

Barley

about, 206

and Beef Soup, *29,* 29–30

Stuffed Acorn Squash with, 196, *196*

and Vegetable Soup, Farmhouse, ■ 32–33

Basic Pizza Dough, 93

Basil

and Fresh Mozzarella, Cherry Tomato Salad with, 69

and Lemon, Roasted Artichoke Hearts with, 292, *292*

and Parmesan–Stuffed Chicken with Roasted Carrots, *100,* 128

shredding, 220

Thai Chicken with, ■ *119,* 119

and Tomatoes, Garlicky Potato Salad with, 82

and Tomatoes, Toasted Orzo with, ■ 320

C

K

Kale

Braised Hearty Greens, 301–2

with Pancetta and Pine Nuts, 302

with White Beans, 302

and Quinoa, Moroccan-Style, with Raisins and Pine Nuts, *206,* 206–7

and Sunflower Seed Pesto, Cheese Ravioli with, 230, *230*

White Bean and Rosemary Gratin with Parmesan Croutons, 209

Key Lime Pie, *358,* **374**

Kidney Bean Salad, ■ **10**

Kimchi

and Beef Stir-Fry, ■ 142–43

Quick, ■ ■ 10

Knives, holding, 22

Kung Pao Shrimp, ■ ■ **187–88**

L

Lamb

Chops

Grilled, with Shaved Zucchini Salad, ■ *261,* 261–62

Mediterranean-Style Braised, 161

Pan-Roasted, with Apricot Chutney, 162

Pan-Roasted, with Mint Relish, 162, *162*

domestic vs. imported, 162

Pita Sandwiches, Greek-Style, 91–92, *92*

rack of, preparing, 163

Rack of, Roast, with Whiskey Sauce, *130,* 163

resting, after cooking, 155

taking temperature of, 155

Lasagna

Classic, *214,* 231

Meaty Skillet, 237

noodles, breaking, 237

Skillet, with Italian Sausage and Bell Pepper, 237

Leek(s)

and Potato Soup with Kielbasa, 30–31

preparing, 25, 31

storing, 5, 7

Lemon grass, bruising, 212

Lemon(s)

Bundt Cakes, Glazed, 392–93

-Garlic Sauce, Spicy, 267

-Herb Cod with Crispy Garlic Potatoes, 172, *172*

and Herb Compound Butter, 13

-Herb Ricotta Fritters, ■ 13

juicing, 379

Lemony Green Beans with Toasted Almonds, ■ 295

making zest strips from, 106

–Poppy Seed Pound Cake, 392, *392*

Pudding Cake, 403

Soufflé, Easy, ■ 410

-Steamed Sole with Green Pea Sauce, ■ *164,* 166–67

Tarts, 379, *379*

Vinaigrette, Foolproof, ■ 64

Lentil(s)

about, 327

Braised, and Swiss Chard, Pan-Seared Salmon with, *164,* 178–79

Red, Spiced (Dal), 327

Red, Stew, Slow-Cooker, 276

Salad with Goat Cheese, 327

Salad with Olives, Mint, and Feta, *314,* 326–27

Soup, 39–40, *40*

Soup, Curried, 40

Lettuce

Chopped Cobb Salad, 73–74

Classic Caesar Salad, *62,* 64–65

Fennel, Apple, and Chicken Chopped Salad, ■ *71,* 71–72

Greek Chopped Salad, ■ 65–66, *66*

Grilled Pizza with Charred Romaine and Red Onion Salad, *271,* 271–72

Italian Chef's Salad, ■ 76–77

Poached Shrimp Salad with Avocado and Grapefruit, ■ 77–78, *78*

Thai-Style Beef Salad, 75

Turkey Taco Salad, 75–76, *76*

Lime, Key, Pie, *358,* **374**

Linguine

with Fresh Clam Sauce, 229, *229*

with Quick Fire-Roasted Tomato Sauce, ■ 218

with Quick Tomato Sauce, ■ 218

M

Mango(s)

cutting, 161

Dried, Tropical Granola with, 343

and Pineapple, Breakfast Smoothies with, ■ ■ 343

Relish, Spice-Rubbed Pork Tenderloin with, ■ 156, *156*

Salsa, Broiled Salmon with, ■ ■ 183

Salsa, Pork Tacos with, ■ *160,* 160–61

Maple (syrup)

about, 340

-Glazed Acorn Squash, *310,* 310–11

-Glazed Pork Tenderloin, ■ 154–55, *155*

with Orange and Chipotle, ■ 155

with Smoked Paprika and Ginger, ■ 155

-Pecan Cream Scones, Simple, 347

storing, 7

Maryland Crab Cakes, 193, *193*

Maryland-Style Corn Chowder with Crabmeat, 41–42

Mashed Potatoes, 307, *307*

Mashed Sweet Potatoes, 312

Mayonnaise, Garlic, 307

Meat

freezing, 6

resting, after cooking, 155

shopping tips, 4

storing, 6, 140

taking temperature of, 155

thawing, 140

see also Beef; Lamb; Pork

Meatballs, Turkey-Pesto, Spaghetti with, 225

Meatloaf mix

All-American Mini Meatloaves, *141,* 141–42

Classic Lasagna, *214,* 231

Skillet Weeknight Bolognese with Linguine, 234–35

Meatloaves, All-American Mini, *141,* **141–42**

Meat Lover's Calzone, 98–99

Meaty Skillet Lasagna, 237

Mediterranean-Style Braised Lamb Chops, 161

Mediterranean-Style Fish Stew, 50–51, *51*

Mediterranean Tuna Salad, ■ **80–81**

Mediterranean Tuna Salad with Carrot, Radishes, and Cilantro, ■ **81**

Mexican Beer and Tomato Cocktail (Chavela), ■ **11**